Silhouette of Elias Hicks

This profile of Elias Hicks was cut by Richard Field of New York City on 4th month 1829 from a shadow taken from life.

THE JOURNAL OF ELIAS HICKS

Edited by
Paul Buckley

Inner Light Books
San Francisco, California
2009

The Journal of Elias Hicks
© Paul Buckley, 2009
All Rights Reserved.

Except for brief quotations, no part of this publication may be reproduced, stored in a retrieval system, or transmitted, in any form or by any means, electronic, mechanical, photocopy, recorded, or otherwise, without prior written permission.

Cover and book design: Paul Buckley

Published by Inner Light Books, San Francisco, California
www.innerlightbooks.com
editor@innerlightbooks.com

Library of Congress Control Number: 2009934073

ISBN 978-0-9797110-4-6 (hardcover)
ISBN 978-0-9797110-5-3 (paperback)

Table of Contents

List of Illustrations x

Foreword: A Traditional Kind of Quaker xii

Introduction xv
  The Lightning Rod xvi
  The Abolitionist xvii
  The Writer xvii
  The Essential Biography xix

Some Notes on the Text xxi
  The Sources xxi
  Editorial Guidelines xxii
  Illustrations xxiii

Acknowledgments i

Some Account of The Life, Exercises, and Experience of Elias Hicks 1

1748-1770 2
  Birth 2
  Early Visitations of Divine Grace 3
  Childhood 4
  Early Trials & Temptations 5
  Apprenticeship 7
  Renewed Trials & Temptations 7
  Slow Progress in Religious Improvement 12

1771-1790 15
  Marriage 15
  Renewed Visitations of Divine Love 17
  First Appearance in the Ministry 18
  The Situation of Friends During the American Revolution 19
  A Visit to the Yearly Meeting at Philadelphia in 1779 21
    New Jersey 22
    Pennsylvania 22
    Back in New Jersey 23
    New York 23
  A Visit to Friends on the Mainland in 1781 24
  Visions & Afflictions 26
  A Visit on Long Island in 1782 28
  A Visit to the Meetings on the Mainland in 1782 29
  A Visit to Nine Partners in 1783 30
  A Visit to Some Inhabitants of Long Island in 1784 30
  A Visit to New York & Staten Island in 1790 33

A Visit to Vermont & New York in 1790 34
    Vermont 34
    New York 35

1791-1795 36
    A Visit with Some Inhabitants of Long Island in 1791 36
    General Visit to Friends in the Yearly Meeting of New York in 1791 & 1792 37
        New Jersey 38
        New York 39
        Connecticut 39
        Massachusetts 40
        New Hampshire & Vermont 40
        New York 42
    A Visit to the Subordinate Meetings of Ministers and Elders of the New York Yearly Meeting in 1792 44
    A Visit to Friends in New England & Vermont in 1793 44
        Connecticut 44
        Rhode Island 45
        Massachusetts 47
        New Hampshire 51
        Maine 53
        Back to New Hampshire 55
        Back in Massachusetts 56
        Back to Rhode Island 56
        Through Massachusetts to New Hampshire & Vermont 57
        New York 58
    A Visit to the Subordinate Meetings of Ministers and Elders of the New York Yearly Meeting in 1795 59

1796-1800 63
    A Visit to Friends in Pennsylvania, New Jersey, Delaware, Maryland, & Virginia in 1797 & 1798 63
        New Jersey 63
        Pennsylvania 65
        Delaware 66
        Maryland 67
        Through Lower Pennsylvania to Maryland 71
        Virginia 74
        Crossing the Potomac to Maryland 78
        Back in Pennsylvania 80
        Back in New Jersey 86
    A Visit to Friends & Other Inhabitants of Connecticut in 1799 89
    A Visit to Friends at Oblong & Nine Partners in 1800 93

Table of Contents

A Visit to Inhabitants of Long Island in 1800 93

1801-1805 .... **95**
   A Visit to New Jersey, Pennsylvania, & Some Adjacent Places 95
      New Jersey 95
      Pennsylvania 96
      Virginia 107
      Back in Pennsylvania 108
      Back in New Jersey 110
   A Visit to Friends in Canada & Some of the Northern Parts of
      the Yearly Meeting of New York in 1803 111
      New York 115

1806-1810 .... **122**
   A Visit on Long Island, Staten Island, & New York in 1806.... 122
   A Visit to the Quarterly Meetings of Purchase, Nine Partners,
      & Stanford, with some adjacent places in 1806 & 1807... 122
   A Visit to Nine Partners, Stanford, & Purchase Quarterly
      Meetings in 1807 131
   A Visit to the Subordinate Meetings of the Yearly Meeting of
      New York in 1808 133
   A Visit in Purchase & Nine Partners Quarterly Meetings in
      1809 135
   Brief Visits in 1810 & 1811 136

1811-1813 .... **137**
   Visits on Long Island in 1812 & 1813 137
   A Visit to Purchase Quarter in 1813 137
   Engagements at & about home 139
   Waiting for Way to Open 142
   A Visit to Friends in the Yearly Meetings of Philadelphia,
      Baltimore, & the adjacent parts of Virginia in 1813 145
      New Jersey 146
      Pennsylvania & Delaware 150
      Maryland 154
      Back in Pennsylvania 155
   At Home 157
      Butchering a Steer 169

1814 .... **171**
      War Taxes 175
      Thoughts on Horse Racing 180
   A Visit to Purchase Quarterly Meeting in 1814 193
      The Din of War 196
      Conscription Taxes 197
      War Taxes 202

A Visit to Scattered Families in Westbury Quarterly Meeting. 203

1815 ....**207**
   A Visit in New York & Long Island *210*
   A Visit to Families of Friends in the New York Monthly
      Meeting *215*
      Encounter with a Presbyterian Minister 218
   Engagements at & about home *223*
      Compliance with War Taxes 225
   At New York Yearly Meeting *228*
   Back Home *229*
      Thoughts on Horse Racing 241
   A Visit to the Monthly Meetings within the Circuit of Nine
      Partners Quarterly Meeting in 1815 .... *244*
   With Our Friends at Home *248*

1816 ....**254**
   General Visit to Friends in New England *254*
      Connecticut 254
      Massachusetts 254
      New Hampshire 255
      Maine 256
      Back Through New Hampshire 258
      Massachusetts 258
      Rhode Island 262
      Back in Connecticut 265
      Back in New York 266
   Engagements at & about Home *268*
   A Visit to the Bordering Inhabitants of our Quarterly Meeting *279*
   Visits with the Committee on the Subject of Schools *280*
   Endeavors at & about Home *287*

1817 ....**291**
      The True State & Condition of the Messiah 292
   A Visit to Some Parts of the Yearly Meetings of Philadelphia
      & Baltimore *308*
      New Jersey 309
      Pennsylvania 311
      Maryland & Virginia 314
      Through Delaware to Pennsylvania 315
      Back in New Jersey 318
   Back Home *320*

1818 ....**322**
   A Visit to Some of the Neighboring Inhabitants *325*
      The Justice Due the Africans & their Descendants 336

Table of Contents *vii*

A Visit to Friends in the Compass of Our Yearly Meeting in
    1818 & 1819... 342
        Connecticut 346
        Back in New York..347
The Requisites to the Being and Well-Being of a Christian 349

1819...**351**
    Continuing the Visits in the Yearly Meeting of New York 351
        Vermont 354
        Back in New York..357
    In & About Home... 363
    A Visit to the Yearly Meeting of Friends in Ohio 367
        Through New Jersey to Pennsylvania..........................367
        Ohio...369
        Back in Pennsylvania...372
        Through Virginia to Maryland 373
        Through Delaware to Pennsylvania 375
        Through New Jersey to Home................................375
    At Home 377
    A Visit to the Neighboring Inhabitants in 1819 & 1820........... 378

1820-1821 ....**380**
    Labors near & about Home... 380

1822...**384**
    A Visit to some parts of Pennsylvania & Baltimore 384
        Through New Jersey to Pennsylvania..........................385
        Maryland 386
        Delaware 390
        Pennsylvania 391

1823...**393**
        New Jersey 393
    A Visit to Some of the Lower Quarterly Meetings 395

1824-1827 ....**397**
    A Visit to the Quarterly Meetings of Cornwall & Stanford 397
    A Visit to Baltimore to Attend the Yearly Meeting................... 397
    A Visit to the Inhabitants of the Eastern Part of Long Island.. 397
    A Visit to Scipio Quarterly Meeting... 397
    A Visit to the Southern & Concord Quarterly Meetings.......... 398
    Visits to Friends in Jericho & Westbury Monthly Meetings.... 398

1828...**399**
    Visits to Friends in the Yearly Meetings of New York,
        Philadelphia, Baltimore, Ohio, Indiana, & Virginia in
        1828 & 1829.. 399

New Jersey 400
In & About Philadelphia..402
West through Pennsylvania...404
Encounters with Thomas Shillitoe 407
Into Ohio 410
Encounters with Elisha Bates 417
The Separation in Ohio Yearly Meeting 421
At Indiana Yearly Meeting..425
Indiana...426
Back in Ohio..427
Virginia & Southwestern Pennsylvania 428
Washington & Maryland 430
Back in Pennsylvania & Delaware 431
Back in New Jersey 434

1829..435
The Death of Jemima Hicks *437*
Finishing the Journey *438*
Vermont...445
Back in New York..446

1830..450

Quaker Structure & Terminology 454
Structure... *454*
Selected Terms *456*

Annotated Word & Phrase List 460

Selected People Mentioned 470

Places Mentioned 478
Connecticut *478*
Delaware... *478*
Indiana.. *478*
Maine *478*
Maryland... *479*
Massachusetts *479*
New Hampshire... *480*
New Jersey *480*
New York.. *481*
Ohio *485*
Pennsylvania... *485*
Rhode Island *487*
Vermont... *488*
Virginia *488*

Table of Contents

Bibliography **489**
On-line Resources..**490**
Index of People Mentioned **491**
Index of Places **496**
Key Word Index **506**

List of Illustrations

Silhouette of Elias Hicks .... frontispiece
First Page of the Original Manuscript xxvi
Map of Western Long Island & New York City 6
Seaman-Hicks Home 15
Saratoga (New York) Meetinghouse 25
Newport (Rhode Island) Meetinghouse 45
Conanicut Meetinghouse, Jamestown, Rhode Island 46
Sandwich Meetinghouse in East Sandwich, Massachusetts 50
Weare Meetinghouse in Henniker, New Hampshire 55
Friends Meeting-House, Haddonfield 65
Third Haven Meetinghouse in Easton, Maryland 69
East Nottingham Meetinghouse in Calvert, Maryland 72
Kennett (Pennsylvania) Meetinghouse 82
Upper Evesham (New Jersey) Meetinghouse 87
Mansfield (New Jersey) Meetinghouse 88
Centre (Delaware) Meetinghouse 105
Path of the 1803 Journey to Canada 116-17
Duanesburg (New York) Meetinghouse 125
Plainfield (New Jersey) Meetinghouse 147
New Garden (Pennsylvania) Meetinghouse 153
Flushing (New York) Meetinghouse 178
Cow Neck Meetinghouse in Manhasset, New York 206
Matinecock (New York) Meetinghouse 231
Oblong (New York) Meetinghouse 246
Amesbury (Massachusetts) Meetinghouse 259
Apponagansett Meetinghouse in Dartmouth, Massachusetts 262
Westport (Rhode Island) Meetinghouse 263
Jericho (New York) Meetinghouse 287

List of Illustrations

Randolph (New Jersey) Meetinghouse 310

Solebury (Pennsylvania) Meetinghouse 312

Wilmington (Delaware) Meetinghouse 316

Easton (New York) Meetinghouse 357

Fairfield (Ohio) Meetinghouse 371

Hopewell Meetinghouse in Clear Brook, Virginia 373

West Grove Meetinghouse, West Grove, Pennsylvania 387

Trenton (New Jersey) Meetinghouse 393

Path of 1828-29 Journey (eastern half of map) 400-01

Wrightstown (Pennsylvania) Meetinghouse 403

York Meetinghouse 406

Path of 1828-29 Journey (western half of map) 412-13

Mount Pleasant (Ohio) Meetinghouse 417

Concord Meetinghouse in Colerain, Ohio 420

Mount Pleasant (Ohio) Meetinghouse Interior 422

Newberry Meetinghouse in Martinsville, Ohio 427

Goose Creek (Virginia) Meetinghouse 429

Concord (Pennsylvania) Meetinghouse 433

Crosswicks (New Jersey) Meetinghouse 436

Smith's Clove (New York) Meetinghouse 449

Foreword: A Traditional Kind of Quaker

Larry Ingle

When doing research for my study of what I called the "Hicksite Reformation," I of course used the printed *Journal* of Elias Hicks, a — arguably *the* — major figure in that movement. I found it to be more than a little boring, containing little more than the dry facts surrounding the visits that marked so much of his ministry. I could nail him down certainly to a given place at a given time, but the excitement that he must have brought to the meetings he attended was strangely drained from the text. For a man with a reputation for having a strong charismatic appeal, one that could, to hear his opponents tell it, be quite divisive, he seemed almost devoid of life, so much so as to support an oft-heard criticism of Quakers — that they were mostly grey characters with little to recommend them to outsiders.

All of which makes this present volume a rewarding experience for those who want to understand history from the ground up. More than seventy years ago, a renowned historian, Carl L. Becker, wrote a book entitled *Every Man His Own Historian*. Becker meant much more about history than the point I am making here, but his title points up the value of this Paul Buckley edition of Hicks' *Journal* — the restoration of deleted material allows readers to get closer to the real Hicks, the Hicks who transcends and undercuts the myths that still, nearly 180 years later, surround him and his reputation. (More than 20 years ago, I visited a Conservative Friends meeting in North Carolina, one in which men and women still sat on opposite sides during meetings; when I told one Friend what I was doing in the Tar Heel State — research on the Hicksites — his mien instantly changed and he nearly visibly drew back as though risking some kind of contamination if he got too close. And he quickly changed the subject.) This volume allows us to see Hicks, not through the eyes of those who might refer to him as charismatic, but as one whose presence and words exuded a personal magnetism and could engender among his followers a willingness to struggle to achieve the things he preached about. He's never boring here.

Here is a Hicks who was neither a deist nor a Unitarian, was neither a rationalist nor some kind of what some in the 21st century might denominate a "secular humanist." He could not be called an orthodox Christian either, if by that phrase we mean a Trinitarian or some variety of scriptural literalist. As far as doctrines were concerned, Hicks comes across here as a rather traditional member of the Religious Society of Friends, one whose views correspond rather closely with the tradition that he represented and was a part of. He certainly could not embrace the relatively new evangelical doctrines relating to the final authority of the

Bible or the substitutionary theory of Christ's atonement for all humanity's sins. This rejection of the final authority of the Bible did not prevent him from studying and knowing the scriptures, something that Paul Buckley's careful notes help make startlingly clear. Hicks was, in short, a traditional kind of Quaker.

But Hicks was also a reformer who held that social change should grow out of a commitment to the right kind of religious education for youth. So he could not fairly be labeled a social activist, even though he clearly opposed slavery and the use of products made with slave labor. (In fact, the only work he published in his lifetime was a lengthy pamphlet calling for Quakers and others also opposed to slavery to eschew such products.) Social change, he firmly held, had to originate with individuals whose conscience or Inward Guide prodded them into a principled stand against an unjust system. As the *Journal* demonstrates, he rejected interfaith cooperation even against horrendous social evils, even war, holding that they were most effectively attacked by concerned and committed individuals acting as such. One's stand on something like paying taxes for war, for example, exemplified how the faith of the personal Christian might lead the person taxed, say, simply to refuse to pay taxes; Hicks would certainly not advocate starting a political movement that would seek to elevate that witness to a principle that others, outside the faith, would be expected to embrace.

There is also very little here about the reformation, as I called it, that he sought to achieve. (Actually it was a group of his followers in Wilmington, Delaware, who were more comfortable using the word "reform" than Hicks was; that's a story I've already told in that previous book I mentioned above.) For one thing, he did not see any sort of division coming, assuming that Friends would go along pretty much as they had. In some ways he was too close to the events to fully understand what was happening. He assumed that the audiences who came to hear him would take from his messages the guidance that spoke to their spirit and experiences. Naturally he thought that Friends would respond positively and support the kind of goals he suggested, and, ergo, the reformation of Quakerism would proceed apace.

Too, like most Quakers Hicks wanted to avoid conflict, even about things that to him were vitally important. So the things we now see as laying the groundwork for separation and feeding into it he simply ignored or overlooked. One looks in vain for the landmarks involved in the lead-up to the split of Philadelphia Yearly Meeting. Even when he was on the site of a division, such as the acrimonious one involving Ohio Yearly Meeting in 1828, his account of the conflict covers only a bit over one page so that the reader gets only a miserly taste of the problems underlying the division.

These memoirs about the momentous events of the 1820s within Quakerdom are from the pen of a partisan, no doubt, and they present one side, but their value as an eye witness to dramatic happenings cannot be gainsaid. We are indebted to Paul Buckley for making them available to us so that we can have an insight into a history that every person can see for him or her self.

Larry Ingle is the author of *Quakers in Conflict: The Hicksite Reformation*. Knoxville: The University of Tennessee Press, 1986.

Introduction

Elias Hicks (1748-1830) lived his entire life on Long Island. At least, his family, his heart, and his home remained there, but for much of his life, he could be found traveling in the ministry among the Religious Society of Friends in North America.

At its heart, this is a travel book. But unlike most travel books, it doesn't tell the story of a journey to a physical destination. This is an account of a man called by God – compelled repeatedly to undertake long and arduous travels in the ministry – beseeching people to turn to God.

Along the way, Hicks encountered primitive roads, storms and floods, bandits and religious opponents, blizzards and muck. Even the "city streets" were frequently deep with a paste-like mixture of mud and excrement. Whether on horseback, by buggy, or on a snow-sled, forty miles was a hard day's ride. He was hot, cold, hungry, frequently tired, and sometimes sick, but it was the people to whom he was sent that were his greatest exercise. Speaking only as led by the Holy Spirit or Inward Light, he delivered ministry of consolation and encouragement, prayers for hope and salvation, and at times, harsh censure. Or, when the Spirit so led him, he served merely as an example of faithful silence in the awful presence of his Creator. Release from duty came only when every responsibility had been fully discharged. He served only the Shepherd of Israel, pleading for and with the lost sheep of North America.

Elias Hicks was recognized as a minister in 1778, just one year before he began the first of his journeys among Friends. Over the next half century, he was to make numerous short trips and fifty-nine major ones, the last ending less than three months before his death. These journeys took him throughout the expanding frontiers of the young United States – as far west as Indiana in his eighty-first year – and north into Canada.

Most of those he visited lived isolated on farms. In 1800, no city in the nation had more than fifty thousand inhabitants – only five contained as many as ten thousand. Outside of these few eastern cities, there was little to do after dark. Books were scarce and most of the few, small newspapers only published once a week. When a traveler came to town, it was an event. When someone was willing to speak in public – no matter the topic – it was worth going. Meeting this need was a steady stream of itinerant preachers from a variety of denominations and Elias Hicks was a star on this circuit.

Unlike many other Quaker ministers of the time, Hicks appointed public meetings as well as those for Friends. He filled meetinghouses, taverns, temporary sheds, churches, courthouses, and even legislative chambers to overflowing. For many, he was the face of the Religious Society of Friends – probably seen by and preaching to more people than any other Quaker of his day. This popularity made his outspoken advocacy of religious tolerance, and his somewhat unorthodox religious views, particularly troubling to many in the Quaker leadership, especially in Philadelphia Yearly Meeting, and produced an escalating series of confrontations that ultimately resulted in the first serious and most defining separation among Friends. It's for this that he is best remembered today.

The Lightning Rod

The essential shape of the Religious Society of Friends today was formed by the separations of the 1820s. Two factions had emerged within the society. One (who called themselves Orthodox Friends[1]) advocated more involvement with the outside world and, in particular, more engagement with other Protestants. Theologically, they were more likely to see themselves as one Christian sect within a larger Christian Church and, consequently, adopted positions that were more consistent with those of mainstream Christianity than had their Quaker ancestors. They supported Bible Societies and missionary activities – behavior for which Hicks excoriated them. He was deeply distressed by what he saw as the religious innovations of the Orthodox. Because they held most of the leadership positions in the society – notably in Philadelphia Yearly Meeting – he feared they would pull it off its foundation and first principle: the divine guidance each person received by the inshining Light of Christ in his or her soul.

Opposed to the Orthodox was a fragile alliance of rural, theologically conservative Friends with others who, as children of the Enlightenment, entertained rationalist approaches to religion. These Friends were more open to commercial and political participation in the wider world. For their time, many of them would be considered liberals. In opposition to the Orthodox, both halves of this coalition cherished Friends' non-creedal heritage and resisted attempts to require particular beliefs as a standard for membership. Likewise, while Orthodox Friends placed increasing reliance on the authority of scripture, they insisted that ultimate religious authority rested in the direct inspiration of the Holy Spirit.

---

[1] It has often been assumed that the term "Orthodox" was assigned to them by their opponents following the separations – both sides claimed the titles "Friend" and "Quaker" for themselves. This is almost certainly true of the use of "Orthodox" as a stand-alone noun, but Hicks makes reference to "those who style themselves Orthodox" in a letter to William Poole dated December 4, 1824. My guess is that the word was self-applied as a descriptive adjective (with a lower-case 'o') to illustrate their claim to being true or mainstream Friends and was later converted into a title.

Introduction xvii

This diverse collection found its champion in Elias Hicks. Hicks came out of the first group. He was a deeply conservative man, both socially and religiously, and would have inclined to the idea that Friends were primitive Christianity revived, that is, the only true Christians. But an important element of his Quaker conservatism was a belief in religious toleration. He found repellent the idea of disowning other Quakers for holding "unsound" beliefs.

The Abolitionist

An implacable opponent of slavery, Hicks became a strong voice for uncompensated abolition. In his travels, he spoke out forcefully, directly confronting slaveholders and describing their behavior as evil. He appointed meetings for "the colored people" – African-American and Native American – and called for recognition of their full rights as citizens. In 1811, he published *Observations on the Slavery of the Africans and their Descendants, and on the use of the Produce of their Labour*, one of the few things he put into print.

Throughout his adult life, he refused to use goods that were the product of slavery. His uncompromising stand against the use of any item tainted with the least drop of sweat from slave labor was characteristic of the man. When he heard God's call, he followed faithfully, despite any and all opposition. This led inevitably to conflict with wealthier and more conventional members of his religious society, whose business activities ensnared them in an increasingly integrated economy – one in which it was ever more difficult to distinguish slave from non-slave goods.

But despite his opposition to slavery, Hicks never joined an abolition society. To him, such mixing with "the world's people" was impossible for a conscientious Quaker. He frequently preached against entanglement with the wider society, but it was too late. Economic opportunities generated by the budding industrial revolution were luring Friends into greater contact with non-Friends. Among other things, Quakers were becoming more and more involved in emerging industries such as railroads and canals, and interested in the benefits of higher education. Hicks believed such "creaturely activities" were inherently corrupting – distracting Friends from their proper role as a people chosen and drawn out of the world by God for God's own purposes. Ironically, those called Hicksites, who emerged from the separations, were to turn their backs on such views.

The Writer

Elias Hicks was reluctant to publish a record of his life. In 1823, his close friend William Poole wrote to him, asking if he intended to leave a journal of his life and experiences for future generations. Hicks' initial response was negative. As a Quietest, he distrusted any and all prepared ministry. He felt that everything he did must be under the direct inspiration of the Inward Light, so as to address the immediate needs of the people he was with. What he said to people in Philadelphia one day was what God called him to do then and there. However well suited it was for that audience, he did not feel at liberty to repeat it to other people at another time.

In response to Poole, he wrote, "although I have made some notes of my journeys and of some things that have transpired in the course of my pilgrimage, yet I have doubts of latter times – whether there is a propriety and any real utility in so much written testimony, whether it does not tend to clog and shut up the avenue to better instruction, and whether what is revealed to one generation is as likely to be as profitable to a succeeding generation as to that to which it was particularly directed and opened. And therefore, to intrude that upon a succeeding generation that was particularly adapted and suited to the state of a previous one, may it not have a tendency to cause the succeeding generation to look back to the letter instead of keeping a single eye to the Spirit, which can only furnish us with knowledge and ability to make progress in reformation."

Prodded again by Poole, he expanded on this theme in a later letter: "Could I pen down something that might be useful to the present and succeeding generation, and then be obliterated, it might not be amiss. But as I am looking forward in the faith that greater and brighter things will be opened to a succeeding generation than I and the people in this generation can bear, this makes me unwilling to leave anything of my experience that might tend to hinder the reception of those new and advanced revelations."

In the end, however, his friends' pleadings won him over. In the last year of his life, he compiled a manuscript, titled *Some Account of the Life, Exercises, and Experience of Elias Hicks*, from various travel and home journals, and from copies of letters he had saved.

At that time, the Society of Friends required that all such manuscripts be reviewed and approved by the yearly meeting's Meeting for Sufferings before publication. Although I have found no specific documentation that Hicks submitted his manuscript for their inspection and oversight, it seems unlikely that he would fail to observe "the good order of Friends." As a result, following his death, control of Elias Hicks' public image would have passed to the leadership of the Hicksite Yearly Meeting in New York.

The book published as the *Journal of the Life and Religious Labors of Elias Hicks* in 1832 differs greatly from what Hicks himself had written. Thousands of changes were made, ranging from individual words to the elimination of an entire trip through the eastern shore of Maryland and

Introduction xix

Delaware. Some of these edits seem to have been motivated by the ongoing conflicts between Hicksite and Orthodox Quakers. The wounds of separation were still raw. Numerous meetings at all levels were contending with wholesale disownments and disputes over ownership of records and property. Mindful of this situation, the committee charged with oversight of the manuscript seems to have carefully expunged material they judged would prove embarrassing or provide their Orthodox opponents with ammunition in the ongoing skirmishes. In particular, dreams and visions, most personal reflections and statements of religious belief, and even positive references to former companions who were now in the Orthodox camp were removed.

Other passages were removed or modified in the interest of shortening the work to a more manageable length, but the committee seems to have felt that some words or phrases were inappropriate. For example, "tarry" is frequently changed to "remain," and where Hicks had written, "we arrived in the edge of the evening," they substituted, "we arrived in the evening." The result was a book that is, for the most part, a dull compendium of travel notes. It conveys in detail where Hicks went, who he stayed with, and the lengths of his journeys, but only hints at what he thought or said, and fails to give voice to the spirit of the man.

Several volumes of sermons (taken down in shorthand and edited by others) and a collection of his letters were also published at this time. There is, of course, no way to judge the accuracy of the sermon transcripts, but the original manuscripts of most of the letters selected for publication are available in the Friends Historical Library at Swarthmore College. Comparison of the originals to the published versions shows that they have been subject to similar emendation.

None of these volumes remained in print for long and the myth of Elias Hicks has overgrown the reality of the man. In the nearly two centuries since his death, there have been two major biographies. The first, *The Life and Labors of Elias Hicks* by Henry W. Wilbur, was published in 1910. Depending almost entirely on printed sources, to a great degree it reflects the views of the Hicksite editors of the 1830s. The second, by Bliss Forbush, was published in 1955. Forbush had access to many of the original manuscripts for the letters and the memoirs, and the result is a better representation of the man, but an underlying bias is revealed in the title, *Elias Hicks: Quaker Liberal*. As you will see below, characterizing Hicks as a liberal fails to do justice to this complex man. All of these books are now out-of-print.

The Essential Biography

Elias Hicks' mother died when he was about eleven years old. His father seems to have been overwhelmed by the burden of raising six sons alone and soon afterward sent young Elias to live with an older brother. Growing up with inadequate adult supervision and minimal formal education, Hicks ran with a rough crowd of older boys, but a religious crisis in his late teens turned his life around. In 1771, he married Jemima Seaman, and through that marriage, claimed his membership among Friends. It is difficult to imagine that he could have engaged in his life of ministry without her love and support. They had eleven children together, but only four would survive them. Of their daughters, one died as an infant, one at about two years of age, and a third at twenty, while giving birth to their first grandchild. All four sons were to die as teens from a devastating, wasting disease. There are few outward signs of the grief Jemima and Elias bore from these deaths. Jemima died on March 17, 1829 and was buried on her husband's eighty-first birthday. Elias survived for just less than a year, following her on February 27, 1830.

Some Notes on the Text

The Sources

This work depends on several manuscripts from the Friends Historical Library at Swarthmore College. The primary text is an original manuscript in Elias Hicks' own handwriting. There are numerous edits and changes in that document. Some were made by Hicks, but many more appear to have been made by others, as evidenced by the variety of handwriting styles in which they appear. To the extent possible, changes made by Hicks have been retained, but edits by others have been removed and the original text restored. Where it is unclear who has made a change and the edit is not a grammatical or spelling correction, I have tended to use the original text. This is not, however, always possible. While much of the deleted text is simply crossed out and can easily be read, in some places pains were taken to completely obliterate the original. Where this occurs, it is noted in a footnote.

There are rips and tears, and smudging of old ink, resulting in some places where the manuscript is illegible. Some can be filled in from other sources. Where I can, I have included my best guesses of the missing material in square brackets. In two places – one covering a critical period in his late teens and the other extending from 1822 to 1828 – pages are missing from the original manuscript. When possible, these gaps are filled in from three other sources.

The second primary source is a travel journal in Hicks' hand detailing a trip to Philadelphia and Baltimore Yearly Meetings in 1822 and 1823. It seems likely these pages were written during those journeys. This is a very sparse text – for the most part reporting only dates, places visited, the names of people with whom he stayed, and the distances traveled. However, it provides details that are not available elsewhere and, in some cases, disagrees with material in other manuscripts. For the duration of that journey, it is treated as the primary source.

The FHL collection contains many original copies of letters in Hicks' hand. These have been drawn on to fill in gaps. Most significantly, the section of the original manuscript describing the death of Jemima Hicks is missing. A letter from Hicks to Jesse Townsend, dated 5th month 25th 1829, provides a detailed and especially personal account. This was copied into the text below. Likewise, the original of his final letter to Hugh Judge has been included at the close of the account.

Finally, Friends Historical Library has a manuscript – in distinctly different handwriting – which is very similar to the 1832 printed *Journal*. I believe it was prepared by the editorial committee for the typesetter and refer to it as the editorial committee manuscript. Once again, it contains a number of edits and changes. I assumed that the first draft of this document (i.e., prior to the edits) was closer to Hicks' original. Whenever possible, these edits have been removed. Where no other source is available, this document is used.

The number of individual words changed or deleted is overwhelming, but where a substantial amount of material has been removed, this will be noted in a footnote.

Editorial Guidelines

Hicks was an orator, not a writer, and it shows – he values words, but has little consideration for how they will present in written form. In the original manuscript, paragraphs run on for pages. Sentences twist and turn – crammed with subordinate clauses and interjections. Punctuation seems used chiefly to mark when a breath would be taken or a meaningful glance thrown at an audience.

To the greatest extent possible, I have preserved Hicks' words. Spelling (especially of place names) and punctuation have been corrected, but only as needed to help you follow his message. Hicks used only commas, periods, dashes, and occasional parentheses. To retain the characteristics of his voice, I have followed that convention, but with more of each – especially more dashes, parentheses, and periods to divide the text into digestible portions without losing the underlying sound of his voice. I have broken his sentences into pieces and introduced paragraphs. You will notice that this results in quite a large number of sentences that begin with "And …" These are all compromises that I hope give you a sense of the pace, rhythm, and cadence of his voice without becoming lost in his discourse.

The original manuscript was not divided into chapters and had no headings. These have been inserted to allow easier navigation of the document. Top level headings set off chronological periods – for the most part, one per year. Secondary headings delineate activities and tertiary headings are generally used to indicate when he has passed from one state to another while traveling.

Elias Hicks was an eighteenth-century Quaker. His vocabulary included some terms that were unique to that religious society as well as a variety of archaic words (e.g., "drave" as the past tense of "drive"). Some of these had been supplanted even in his lifetime. Rather than trying to make him sound like a twenty-first-century man, these have been retained with a definition in a footnote on its first use. These annotations have also been gathered together at the back of the book in separate sections on Quaker terms and structures. There, you will also find a dictionary of unfamiliar words and phrases, an annotated gazetteer of some of the places to which he traveled, and brief biographies of some of the more prominent people he mentions.

In a very few cases, corrections have made where it is apparent that what was written is something other than what was intended. These changes are likewise documented. Where it is obvious, purely grammatical errors (e.g., "was" instead of "were") have been corrected without annotation.

Hicks' use of scripture is important in understanding his message. Like many early Friends, Hicks knew his Bible intimately and quoted it instinctively. His language is riddled with biblical references and allusions, and he would have expected his listeners – Quaker and non-Quaker alike – to recognize them. It provided a common spiritual language and a set of shared stories that added richness both to his sermons and to his everyday speech. Since many of these will not be obvious to modern readers (and to allow you to look up the "back story" he presupposed), references have been noted the first time a verse is referenced.

Illustrations

Finally, a note on the illustrations. There were, of course, none in the original manuscript. Like other Quietist Friends, Hicks would have seen pictures as distractions that draw our attention away from the things of God to things of this world. The 1832 *Journal* was published without any illustrations and my first inclination was to follow that practice. But we live in different times.

This is a travel book. As Elias Hicks journeyed among Friends, he was most at ease when in a Friends Meetinghouse. Pictures of meetinghouses he visited have been included to give you a feeling for the diversity of places in which he spoke – from tiny buildings like those in Conanicut Island, Rhode Island and Concord, Ohio to the multi-story structures of Philadelphia and New York – and to provide context. Maps have been included to help you follow a few of his longer journeys and provide a sense of how arduous an undertaking these trips were. Dashes, such as the one below, mark the end of major sections. These have been taken directly from the original manuscript.

Acknowledgments

This project owes much to so many people and institutions.

First, I want to thank my wife, Peggy Spohr, for her patience and gentle chiding. Without her repeated reminder, "That book will never be done if you keep adding more things to it," I would still be adding and editing. Similarly, without the prodding of John Punshon, the project would never have been started.

Nearly as important were the resources of the Friends Historical Library of Swarthmore College. The unpublished manuscripts of Elias Hicks' memoirs and letters in their collections are the foundation of the whole book. Likewise, the silhouette of Elias Hicks that faces the title page and sets the tone for the text comes from their collection. These are used with the library's permission. Over the last nine years, the staff, especially Christopher Densmore, Patricia O'Donnell, Susanna W. Morikawa, and Mary Ellen Chijioke, has been exceptionally helpful and gracious. An equally valuable resource was Thomas Hill's Quaker meetings website.

For the maps and the drawing of the Seaman-Hicks home, Lawrence Sexton deserves special notice. All are the meticulous products of his pen. Every reader will feel a debt to Larry.

The meetinghouses pictures were selected from dozens offered by a variety of sources. Rita Varley of Philadelphia Yearly Meeting, Helen Garay Toppins of New York Yearly Meeting, and Jonathan Vogel-Borne of New England Yearly Meeting each supplied items from meeting archives. Credit is due to Meredith Cornell and Gordon Bugbee for sketches in those collections. Anne Thomason of Earlham College, Patti Kinsinger and Ruth Dobyns of Wilmington College, and Karen Campbell of the Mary L. Cook Public Library in Waynesville, Ohio searched their collections and forwarded possibilities, as did Christine Snyder.

Three people read and commented on earlier drafts, H. Larry Ingle (who also contributed an insightful foreword), Lloyd Lee Wilson (whose concise and thoughtful evaluation is on the back cover), and Charles Martin, my publisher. Each pointed out errors that repeated reviews had rendered invisible and asked questions that improved the supporting materials. Thomas Hamm and Ken Stockbridge supplied additional pieces of valuable information.

Finally, grants from the Sara Bowers Fund of Kennett Friends Meeting and the Lyman Fund, and unexpected checks from Ohio Valley Yearly Meeting and Ron Haldeman appeared at critical times.

To all these, and so many others, I am most grateful.

Some account of the life, exercises and experiences of Elias Hicks — from the beginning up to 131 of Journal

A prospect having often opened on my mind of leaving some account of my life, together with some of the many mercies and preservations, both spiritual and temporal, that has been graciously vouchsafed to me, by an all wise, and emerciful Creator and preserver, in passing through this vale of tears and world of probation, and feeling my mind, at this time, renewedly and weightily impressed therewith, in a sense of humble gratitude. I now begin this work.

I was born agreeable to the record of my birth the 19th day of the 3rd mo. 1748, in the Township of Hampstead in Queens County, Long Island, and Province of New York in North America. — My parents John and Martha Hicks, were descended from reputable families, and sustained a good character, among their friends, and those who knew them. My father was a grand-son of Thomas Hicks, of whom our worthy friend Samuel Bownas makes honourable mention, and by whom he was much comforted and strengthened, when a prisoner, through the envy of Keith at Jamaca on Long Island. — Neither of my parents were members in strict fellowship with any religious society, untill some little time before my birth, when my father was joined in society with friends, but as his residence was mostly some distance from meetings, and in neighbourhoods were very few friends dwelt, my company and conversation when young, and before I entered into a maried state, was mostly among those of other persuasions, or those still worse for me, who made no profession of religion at all, but lived in a state of much licentiousness, this exposed me to much temptation, and tho' I early felt the operation of divine grace, checking and reproving me for my lightness and vanity, and those evils incident to young minds, thus exposed. yet being of a lively active spirit, and very ambitious of excelling in my play and diversions, I often exceeded therein the bounds of true moderation, for which I often on my pillow felt close conviction, and fears therefor attended my mind in the night season, when very young. And here it may not be amiss, to mention a prospect I had in a night vision, when about the seventh year of my age, as I believe it was of considerable benefit to me afterwards. — I apprehended I was passing from school in my usual manner, and passing by a certain hedge on the way, in which there was a copse tree, with a hollow in it, wherein a little bird called the wren sometimes had eggs, and turning into the hedge in quest thereof, as I looked into the hole in the tree, and was about to put in my hand to feel for eggs, I thought I beheld the face of an Angel, as I had seen them represented

Some Account of The Life, Exercises, and Experience of Elias Hicks

A prospect often opened on my mind of leaving some account of my life, together with some of the many mercies and preservations, both spiritual and temporal, that have been graciously vouchsafed[1] to me by an all-wise and merciful Creator and Preserver in passing through this vale of tears and world of probation. Feeling my mind, at this time, renewedly and weightily[2] impressed therewith, in a sense of humble gratitude, I now begin this work.[3]

---

[1] Vouchsafe: bestow
[2] Weight, weighty: seriousness
[3] This entire page was deleted from the printed *Journal* and replaced with a new opening paragraph.

1748-1770

Birth

I was born, agreeable to the record of my birth, the 19th day of the 3rd[1] month 1748,[2] in the township of Hempstead in Queens County, Long Island, and Province of New York in North America.

My parents, John and Martha Hicks, were descended from reputable families, and sustained a good character among their friends and those who knew them. My father was a grandson of Thomas Hicks, of whom our worthy friend Samuel Bownas* makes honorable mention and by whom he was much comforted and strengthened, when a prisoner through the envy of Keith* at Jamaica on Long Island.[3]

Neither of my parents were members in strict fellowship with any religious society until some little time before my birth, when my father was joined in society with Friends. But as his residence was mostly some distance from meetings and in neighborhoods where very few Friends dwelt, my company and conversation[4] when young and before I entered into a married state, was mostly among those of other persuasions or those (still worse for me) who made no profession[5] of religion at all, but lived in a state of much licentiousness. This exposed me to much temptation. Though I early felt the operation of divine grace, checking and reproving me for my lightness[6] and vanity and those evils incident to young minds thus exposed, yet being of a lively active spirit and very ambitious of excelling in my play and diversions, I often exceeded therein the bounds of true moderation. For which, I often on my pillow felt close conviction[7]

---

[1] Friends traditionally did not use the common names for the days of the week and months of the year, since some of these names originally honored pagan deities. These were, instead, referred to by only by number (e.g., Thursday or Thor's Day was called Fifth Day and March, which was named for Mars, the Roman god of war, was called Third Month.).

[2] This is most likely an Old Calendar date, since Great Britain and its colonies did not adopt the Gregorian calendar until September 1752. In a letter to William Poole, dated 9th Month 12th 1823, Hicks states that this date was written in an old Bible in his father's possession.

[3] Brief biographies on some of the people mentioned in the text can be found in an appendix (below). Names included in the appendix are marked with an asterisk the first time they appear.

[4] Conversation: manner of conducting oneself in the world

[5] Profession: to claim membership

[6] Light, lightness: lack of seriousness

[7] Conviction: guilt

and fears therefore attended my mind in the night season,[1] when very young.

Early Visitations of Divine Grace[2]

Here, it may not be amiss to mention a prospect I had in a night vision, when about seven years of age, as I believe it was of considerable benefit to me afterwards.

I apprehended I was passing from school in my usual manner. Passing by a certain hedge on the way, there was a lopped[3] tree with a hollow in it, wherein, a little bird called the wren sometimes had eggs. Turning into the hedge in quest thereof, as I looked into the hole in the tree and was about to put in my hand to feel for eggs, I thought I beheld the face of an angel as I had seen them described by pictures in a book – the first prospect whereof struck me with terror as one guilty – and immediately thereupon, I thought there issued a flame out of the hollow of the tree and it enclosed me about, as a round ball or blaze of pure fire of about eight feet diameter, which struck me with great amazement and horror. Turning around to look for some relief, I apprehended I saw my father, standing just without[4] the flame, to whom I thought I cried with vehemence, but he appeared to be entirely calm and looked upon me without any show of concern. He very gently requested me to be still, which tended gradually to center my mind and compose it. In this situation I awoke, feeling a very agreeable and comfortable warmth, which together with finding myself safe in my bed, was cause of great gladness.

Nevertheless, the vision continued with me at times for years and was an excellent memento[5] and I believe had a tendency to preserve me from many temptations in my childhood and youth, for when after I was tempted to evil, this vision would often come up fresh[6] in view and strengthen [me] to resist, for fear of the fatal consequence, which I had in this vision such a feeling sense of (according to my then-childish idea of the place of judgment). And I have cause to believe that this prospect or secret intimation was a visitation[7] from my most merciful Redeemer – it being so adapted to my tender years. Therefore, I have accounted it as one of the many mercies that he has graciously vouchsafed to me for the redemption of my poor soul from the bondage of sin and death, and for all

---

[1] Season: this term can be used to refer to a variety of periods of time
[2] The next three paragraphs were deleted from the printed *Journal*.
[3] Lopped: pruned
[4] Without: outside, i.e., the opposite of "within"
[5] Memento: a reminder, warning, or hint as to future events
[6] Fresh: unaffected by the passage of time
[7] Visitation: a visit by God

which, with his righteous judgments, I bless and magnify his most holy name.

Childhood

When I was about eight years old, my father removed his habitation in order to settle on the farm his father had left him on the south side of the island near the seashore. This introduced a new scene of diversion to my active mind, that was prone to pleasure and self-gratification, as the shore abounded[1] with fish and wild fowl in abundance. I soon became a considerable artist at angling for the former and, as soon as my age was such that my father would entrust me with a gun, I early became a pretty good marksman at the latter and could, with a degree of certainty, shoot the wild fowl, ducks, or any other kind – singly flying in any direction – provided they came within reasonable reach of my shot. This kind of amusement soon got the ascendancy in my mind, insomuch that I could leave every other diversion for it, and here I may note that I believe it was, for a time, profitable to me in my exposed condition, as it had a tendency to keep me more at and about home and often prevented my joining with loose company, which I had frequent opportunity to do without my father's knowledge.

My mother, dying when I was about eleven years of age, left my father with the care of six children, three older and two younger than myself.[2] And he having for several years no housekeeper but a niece of his, a young woman who was likewise of a lively, cheerful temper. She was always ready in his absence to join us in mirth and vain amusements. Yet I did not give way to that, that was accounted disreputable, having always a regard to strict honestly and such a line of conduct as would comport with politeness and was agreeable to good breeding. Nevertheless, I was led very wide from the salutary path of Truth and true religion, and early learned to sing vain songs and to dance, when out of reach of my father's knowledge. For although he was careful to keep us, his children, as much as might be within the limits of truth, yet frequent opportunities offered for my joining young company of this description as I grew towards the state of a man.

I have oft thought, had it not been for the delight I took in my gun and in angling for fish, that occupied most of my leisure hours, I might have run out with my vain companions – with which I was surrounded – into many excesses to my utter ruin. For although the Lord was graciously near

---

[1] Abound: to have to overflowing
[2] The next four sentences were deleted from the printed *Journal*. The following six paragraphs were condensed to a few innocuous lines.

to my poor soul, and followed me with his reproofs,[1] and often set my sins in order before me, and brought me under judgment, and his dread made me afraid, yet through the proneness[2] of my natural desires after self-gratification, by giving way thereto, I was often led to exceed the bounds of reason and truth, and thereby commit sin.

Early Trials & Temptations

When I was about thirteen years of age, I was put one summer to live with one of my elder brothers who was married and settled some considerable distance from my father's. And being now at liberty (almost without any restraint), I took my swing in every diversion that offered through the medium of my companions and soon learned to delight in running horses. And being forward[3] for one of my years – both as to understanding and bodily ability – I thought myself suitable to accompany with young men, and by attending on horse races, card playing, and other vain amusements that frequently offered, I lost much of my youthful innocence and became considerably hardened in sin and vanity in the course of this season.

And here I may notice not only from sorrowful experience, but from observations that I have made since arrived to mature years, the great hurt many children receive by being too soon removed from under the watchful notice of their concerned parents and placed with such whose minds are not limited by the truth. For what ought parents be more engaged for (next to their own souls) than the right education and preservation of their tender offspring – that so they may be kept in innocence and, as much as may be, out of harms way? But if parents, from sinister motives or for want of due consideration, place their children when young from under their care – by which means their tender minds become wounded and so overcome with evil as to prove their ruin – will not the blood of their children fall upon their heads?[4] And in the day of solemn inquisition, it may be queried of them, what have you done with those lambs committed to your charge? – when a wounded conscience and confusion of face[5] may be their only answer.

I have oft thought when looking back on my conduct in the course of the season before mentioned, that had it not been for the providential care of my Heavenly Father, my life might have fallen a sacrifice to my folly and indiscretion, as I often rode races wherein I have since thought my life

---

[1] Reproof: disgrace or reproach
[2] Proneness: tendency
[3] Forward: mature
[4] Blood on their heads: hold accountable for (Ezekiel 33:4 & Acts 18:6)
[5] Confusion of face: shame, from Daniel 9:8

Western Long Island & New York City

was several times exposed to great dangers – in one instance more especially, when a large company was riding out to an adjacent plain in order for running horses.

I (with one or two others) set our horses to running – being some distance behind most of the company, who were riding but slowly on. As we came up with them, we supposed they would have given us the path, but they paying no attention to us, did not observe us till we had got just upon them. And I observing the man before me did not give way, I reined my horse to turn out of the path. And at the same instant, he turning his head and seeing me just upon him, suddenly turned the same way. And my horse, in order to avoid a thrust[1] and contrary to my motion, dodged the other way, by which means I flew from him nearly the distance of a rod.[2] And when I struck the ground, I was so stunned that I had neither sense nor feeling for a few moments, in which time my horse had got a considerable distance from me. But when I recovered my senses, I felt little or no hurt which I have since considered as a most merciful and unmerited preservation.

O my soul! What wilt or canst thou render unto the Lord for all his benefits? For his mercies are new every morning.[3]

---

[1] Thrust: collision
[2] Rod: 16.5 feet
[3] Lamentations 3:22-23

Apprenticeship

About the seventeenth year of my age, I was put an apprentice to learn the trade of a house carpenter and joiner – and this by no means placed me in a more favorable situation than before, for my master, although accounted an orderly man and frequently attended Friends meetings, yet being in an eager pursuit after temporal riches, was of but little use to me in my religious improvement. And being greatly engaged, we working from place to place wherever our business offered, I often had opportunity of falling into hurtful company.

Renewed Trials & Temptations[1]

And now arriving to a state of manhood, I was much exposed – more especially in consequence of a very pernicious and hurtful custom that prevailed through the unwarrantable indulgence of parents in this and some other parts of our country, *viz*,[2] that of young people getting together in companies, more especially on the evenings of the First Days of the week. And after passing the evening until late in foolish and vain conversation and some other vain amusements, then to couple out, as the young men and young women could agree and retire in secret,[3] where they spent the rest of the night, frequently in beds together.

O shameful custom and irreligious practice! How could parents ever indulge their children in such sinful, indecent, and immodest conduct? And it more especially commanded my admiration[4] – even in these, my young years – in finding Friends' children likewise indulged in this practice. For I then thought that if I lived to have children to bring up and educate, I could by no means indulge them in such improper conduct, for I have cause to believe that many families of young people (the females especially) have suffered great hurt and loss though this medium[5] – both as to their spiritual and temporal condition – and have pierced themselves through with many sorrows and some with incurable wounds as to their honor and reputation. For hereby, I have no doubt, the marriage bed has oft been defiled and a foundation laid for great uneasiness and disunity in many families – even sometimes to a breach of the conjugal band.

From the time of my going an apprentice till some little time before I entered into engagement of marriage, I passed through many trials and great exposure and I have oft thought, had it not been for the interposition of divine mercy and goodness, I was like to have fallen a prey to the many

---

[1] The next two paragraphs were deleted from the printed *Journal*.
[2] *Viz.*: that is
[3] Secret: private, unseen
[4] Admiration: astonishment
[5] Medium: course of action

and varied temptations to evil that surrounded me. For although I was taken in divers[1] snares, wherein my poor soul was deeply wounded and for which I afterwards felt the just indignation of an offended God, yet when I have looked back on this scene of my life and recounted the many great temptations and snares that I have escaped, and how I have been preserved from a bottomless gulf that opened wide to receive me, all that is truly sensible[2] within me has been bowed in humble admiration of the Lord's mercies and deliverance. And in humble gratitude, I was made to praise and magnify his great and adorable name, who is over all, God blessed forever.[3]

For in the midst of all my vanity and exposure to temptation, the Lord as a gracious Father was often near, and when I was alone, would incline my mind to solid[4] meditations. And being early learned to read, I took considerable delight in reading the Scriptures, in which I occupied some of my leisure hours to my real profit and religious improvement. And although my youthful companions would often endeavor to persuade me (and one another) that those amusements in which we spent so much of our precious time were innocent – even such as above mentioned, as also playing at cards (if only done for amusement) and singing vain songs with music and dancing. Yet being very early by the Divine Light convinced that its teachings were truth, it had the ascendancy in my mind above all the reasonings and persuasions of men, although my natural desires would gladly have received their reasonings for truth, that I might have taken my swing in pleasure with them without remorse and inward condemnation. But this, I found by experience, I could not do unless I first became hardened in sin – to a state of reprobation.[5] And this, I feared at times, would be my case for I had such a pronery[6] to levity and self-gratification that I often ran counter to clear convictions and went on for a considerable time, sinning and repenting, sinning and repenting. For the Lord in great mercy had regard to me in my tried condition and often opened a door of reconciliation to my poor soul. But I was too weak to keep my covenants in the midst of so great temptation until, by his righteous judgments mixed with adorable mercy, he opened to my mind in a very clear manner the danger I was in of falling into eternal ruin, insomuch that at times, in the midst of my ... merriment, my heart was

---

[1] Divers: various
[2] Sensible: aware
[3] Psalms 69:30 & Romans 9:5
[4] Solid: sober-minded
[5] Reprobation: shame or censure; the opposite of election; rejected by God and condemned to eternal damnation
[6] Pronery: disposition

> *Beginning with the word "merriment" (last line of the previous page), two pages of the original manuscript are missing. The four hundred and sixty-five words between the ellipses (up to the words "gathered me" at the middle of the next page) are taken from the editorial committee manuscript. Since an average page in the original manuscript contains nearly four hundred words, I estimate that between one-third and one-half of the original content (perhaps another vision) has been omitted by the editorial committee. That there may be more to this story is hinted at in the memorial Jericho Meeting wrote following his death. There, this scene is given a few additional details:*
>
> "On one occasion, when preparing to join in the dance, and surrounded by his jovial companions, the pure witness rose so powerfully in his mind, and so clearly set before him the evil tendency of the course he was pursuing, that he reasoned not with flesh and blood, but gave up to the heavenly vision, and in deep contrition and prostration of soul, entered into covenant with the God of his life, that if he would be pleased to furnish him with strength, he would endeavor not to be again found in the like disobedience; which covenant, through mercy, he was favored to keep inviolate."

often made very sad and while engaged in the dance, my soul was deeply sensible of its evil and folly. Even my reasoning powers, when thus enlightened by the clear evidence of Divine Light, were made to loathe it as a senseless and insipid pursuit, and utterly unworthy of a rational being. But although I formed resolutions to refrain from this evil and others of a like nature, yet it was difficult to resist the importunities[1] of my companions and I found by experience that, if I would altogether cease from them, I must wholly withdraw from the company of those who were inclined to such pursuits.

On the last occasion that I was present at a dance, and in which I was pressed to take a part, I was brought under great concern of mind and was struck with a belief that if I now gave way after forming so many resolutions and should again rebel against the Light, I might be left in an obdurate situation and never have another offer of pardon. I also clearly saw that this would be just and that my blood would be upon my own head. And feeling the dread of the Almighty to cover me and a cry raised in my soul towards him, when I was called to participate in the dance, it

---

[1] Importunity: inappropriate suggestion

seemed as though all my limbs were fettered and I sat down and informed the company that I was now resolved to go no further.

I was deeply tried,[1] but the Lord was graciously near, and as my cry was secretly to him for strength, he enabled me to covenant with him, that if he would be pleased in mercy to empower me, I would forever cease from this vain and sinful amusement. And he instructed me that if I would escape the danger of another trial, I must keep myself separate from such companions. And blessed forever be his right worthy name, in that he hath enabled me to keep this my covenant with him from that time inviolate.

In looking back to this season of deep probation, my soul has been deeply humbled. For I had cause to believe that if I had withstood at this time the merciful interposition of divine love and had rebelled against this clear manifestation of the Lord's will, he would have withdrawn his Light from me and my portion would have been among the wicked – cast out forever from the favorable presence of my judge. I should also forever have been obliged to acknowledge his mercy and justice and acquit[2] the Lord my redeemer, who had done so much for me. For with long-suffering and much abused mercy, he had waited patiently for my return and would have gathered me ... even before that time (as I well knew) as a hen gathereth her chickens under her wings, but I would not.[3]

Therefore, it is the earnest, breathing desire of my spirit, that all the youth, and others whom it may concern, may wisely ponder their ways, and not think that such vain and frivolous excuses, that all make who endeavor to justify themselves in such vain and wicked diversions, as that my parents judge it innocent or my teachers have instructed me to believe or that under the law it was accounted admissible will stand them in any stead in the day of solemn inquisition. For what are all those carnal[4] reasonings worth when put in the balance of the sanctuary against one single impression[5] or conviction of the Divine Light or Spiritual Lawgiver in the secret of our own hearts? This is clear and self-evident and therefore undeniable, but the other is at best but mere vague suppositions, without any solid foundations.

And I have oft thought of the conduct of those parents with admiration, who are spending their substance on idle dancing masters to teach their children this unnatural and unchristian practice – how much better it might be employed in relieving the poor and needy or

---

[1] Try: test
[2] Acquit: surrender any claim on
[3] Matthew 23:37 & Luke 13:34
[4] Carnal: worldly
[5] Impression: attack or assault

ameliorating the condition of the helpless orphans – and who, for excuse, plead the example of righteous David. But how unlike is their dancing to his, who did it only in worship and honor to his God and no doubt in the cross[1] to his natural will. And that is the reason it so displeased Michel, his lofty spouse, for his dancing was nothing but that overflowing of divine love inspired, when bringing back the ark or at seasons in his worship before God,[2] which well comported with that outward dispensation.

But we have a better and higher example than David – the Lord Jesus Christ, who is the mediator of a better covenant and established[3] on better promises. And this covenant is inward, even the law written upon the heart,[4] which no outward example of others can ever abrogate[5] or disannul.[6] Neither does his self-denying example or doctrines in anywise approbate or justify this foolish and idle practice, but in all parts thereof, condemn and disapprove it. For if none can be his disciples except they deny themselves and take up their cross daily[7] – as besure[8] none can – how can those be acceptable to him who are living in the daily gratification of their own licentious minds and wills? And in spending their precious time and talents, that he has blessed them with to occupy to his honor, to please themselves and vain companions in such fruitless and vain sports.

Neither have his self-denying apostles left us either example or precept whereby to justify such wanton and evil amusements. But we are by them exhorted to redeem the time, because the days are evil,[9] and to use diligence to make our calling and election[10] sure,[11] and to walk as we have them for example, and to follow them as they follow Christ, and no further.[12] Not a word of learning to dance or of dancing masters or of playing at cards, but to abstain from all idle and vain sports, foolish talking, and jesting – which are not convenient because contrary to Christian gravity and the self-denying example of our dear Lord, who

---

[1] Cross: opposed or contrary to
[2] 2 Samuel 6:16
[3] Establish: found or base
[4] Jeremiah 31:33, 2 Corinthians 3:3, & Hebrews 8:10 & 10:16
[5] Abrogate: formally abolish
[6] Disannul: cancel or make null and void
[7] Matthew 16:24, Mark 8:34, & Luke 9:23
[8] Besure: surely
[9] Ephesians 5:3
[10] Election: salvation – however, for Friends, election does not imply that one is predestined for salvation. This doctrine, also referred to as "predestination" or "foreordination," was vigorously rejected.
[11] 2 Peter 1:10
[12] John 13:15 & 1 Peter 2:21

when personally on earth, was a man of sorrows and acquainted with grief.[1] And therefore, the house of mourning is recommended to all that are wise in heart, for it is the fool's heart only that is captivated in the house of mirth.[2]

Slow Progress in Religious Improvement

My apprenticeship being now expired and I entered a little into the twenty-first year of my age. And my mind, through the Lord's mercy and judgments, somewhat awakened to see the folly and wickedness of those vain amusements before mentioned. I endeavored to leave them and gradually withdrew from the company of my former companions and more frequently attended meetings and became more acquainted with Friends. And although this was in some degree profitable to me, yet I made but slow progress in my religious improvement until several years after I had entered into a married state.

I have already observed that the delight I took in fishing and fowling had a tendency frequently to preserve me from falling into unlawful and sinful amusements and which, through the assistance and interposition of divine grace, I had now mostly forsook and withdrawn from. And now, I began to feel through the rising intimations and reproofs of the precious gift in my own heart that the manner in which I sometimes amused myself with my gun was not without sin. For although I mostly preferred going alone, whereby while waiting in stillness for the coming of the fowl, my mind hath been at times so taken up in divine meditations that they have been to me seasons of great instruction and comfort and wherein my gracious redeemer was striving gradually to turn my mind from such low[3] and perishing amusement. Nevertheless, at divers other times, when in company with others on a party of pleasure, and no fowls presented that were good and useful when taken, we have merely for sport and to try which could excel in shooting, fell upon the small, though innocent, birds that we could decoy and cause to fly over us that were of no use when dead, and destroyed many of them from wantonness or for mere diversion and for which cruel procedure my heart is sorrowfully affected whilst penning these lines. But this conduct, from the conviction I felt and the result of such reflection, soon appeared to be a great breach of trust and an infringement of the divine prerogative.

Therefore, it soon became a principle with me not to take the life of any creature, but such as were esteemed really useful when dead or very obnoxious and hurtful when living. And it also appeared to be a duty,

---

[1] Isaiah 53:3
[2] Ecclesiastes 7:4
[3] Low: vulgar, weak, or degenerate

when we apprehend it right to take the life of any of these, that we endeavor to do it in the most mild and tender manner in our power. For from due consideration, it must appear to every candid mind that the liberty we have for taking the lives of the creatures, and using their bodies to support ours, is certainly an unmerited favor and ought to be used as the mere bounty of our great Benefactor and to be received by us with great humility and gratitude.

I have likewise, from reflections founded on observation and from the nature and reason of things, been led to believe that we frequently err by the liberty we take in destroying what we esteem noxious creatures and not only abuse the power and rule given us over them by our great common Creator,[1] but likewise act very contrary to and subversive of our own true interest.[2] For no doubt, as all in the beginning was pronounced good that the good God had made,[3] there was a right proportion and a true medium and balance among the creatures that were to inhabit this lower world. And man being made as a crown to the whole, no doubt his true interest lay in preserving, as much as might be, this true medium or balance.

But man fell from the state of rectitude in which he was created – and wherein he only was capable of governing the creatures agreeable to the will of the Creator. Hence, by exerting his power over them under the influence of his fallen wisdom, and not understanding their true natures nor end[4] of their creation, he has wantonly fallen upon and destroyed such kinds as (to his limited understanding) appeared noxious because, at some times, they were observed to feed upon some of the fruits of the field that were the product of his industry – when a little care in frightening them away would have been sufficiently effectual and their lives preserved to fill up the place assigned them in creation. Hereby, the true balance has been so materially affected that the tribes of lesser creatures, such as reptiles and insects (which were to feed and support those creatures man had wantonly destroyed and which come not so obviously under man's comprehension, nor so generally within the limits of his power to destroy) have increased to a proportion sufficient to spread destruction and devastation over the fields and left the face of the earth, at times, as a scorched or barren desert.

For such has been the wisdom and goodness of the Supreme Being in the creation of man that he has so intimately connected his duty with his

---

[1] Genesis 1:26-28
[2] The remainder of this paragraph was substantially re-written and the next four were deleted from the printed *Journal*.
[3] Genesis 1:31
[4] End: purpose

truest interest – both in regard to temporals[1] as well as spirituals – that if he falls short in the first, he will likewise feel himself affected in the latter and, for every shortcoming or act of sin, feel the consequent reward[2] of punishment and disappointment.

Therefore, it is our indispensable duty, as reasonable, accountable beings, wisely to ponder our ways and previously consider the consequent effect of all our conduct. For if we are to give an account for every idle word (which we are to do[3]), it must appear clear to every rational mind (for the very idea of rationality secludes from the understanding everything that is irrational – which most certain every idle word must be) therefore, every idle or presumptuous act must be still more criminal. How presumptuous must it then appear from rational reflection for limited, borrowed[4] beings to sport themselves with the lives of other beings? However little they may appear in the view of proud man (who vainly supposes all made for his use), yet they may be as necessary a link in the great chain of nature[5] and creation as his own existence.

For although in the course of divine providence, we may be permitted to take the lives of such of the creatures (in a reasonable way) as are suitably adapted to the accommodation of our bodies in a line of real usefulness, yet that by no means carries any warrant for us wantonly, or in a sportive way, to destroy the lives of those that are not useful when dead. Neither is this privilege given to man, any partial[6] act of the deity, for we see he has given the same privilege to almost every other creature and also furnished them with means whereby they are enabled to take such of the creatures as he has intended for their use and by which the true balance might be maintained. And had man kept his station as well as the other creatures, I have no doubt but the true balance would have been at least much better preserved than it now is – if not inviolably kept.

---

[1] Temporals: temporal matters
[2] Reward: what one deserves, either good or bad
[3] From Matthew 12:36 ("But I say unto you, That every idle word that men shall speak, they shall give account thereof in the day of judgment.")
[4] Borrowed: not our own, i.e., belonging to God
[5] Great chain of nature: an ordered sequence of all beings, starting with God and extending to the "lowest creature." It was a way of understanding and explaining the order of the natural world that dates back at least to the classical Greek philosophers.
[6] Partial: biased or favoring one over another, i.e., not impartial – in this case, favoring humans over other creatures

Seaman-Hicks Home

1771-1790

Marriage

In the 22nd year of my age, I apprehended it right to change my situation from a single to a married state, and having previously gained an intimate acquaintance with Jemima Seaman, daughter of Jonathan and

Elisabeth Seaman of Jericho in the township of Oyster Bay. And my affection being drawn towards her in that relation, in a convenient opportunity I opened my mind to her and received from her a mutual return of affection and good will therein.

And after divers opportunities together, and duly weighing the subject as a matter of great importance and feeling a continual increase of mutual love, we were prompted to believe that our proceeding therein was consistent with truth. And having the full unity and concurrence of our parents and Friends concerned, we accomplished our marriage (after proceeding in due order preparatory thereto) in a solemn meeting of Friends at Westbury, the 2nd of 1st month in the year 1771. In which, we not only felt the consoling evidence of Divine Truth accompanying in this solemn season, but which remained as a seal upon our spirits – strengthening us together to bear with becoming[1] fortitude the vicissitudes, trials, and probations that fell to our lot and of which we had a large share in passing through this vale of tears and world of trouble.

My wife (though not of a very strong constitution) lived to be the mother of eleven children – four sons and seven daughters. Our second daughter died young with the smallpox – a very lovely, promising child – and the youngest was stillborn. The rest all arrived to years of discretion and afforded us considerable comfort, as they proved in a good degree dutiful children, though not without much bodily toil and exercise as all four of our sons were weakly and never able to take care of themselves, being all taken off their legs so as not to be able to walk after the ninth or tenth year of their age. The two eldest deceased in the fifteenth year of their age, the third about the seventeenth, and the youngest was near nineteen years when he deceased.[2] And although thus helpless, yet the innocency of their lives and the resigned cheerfulness of their dispositions to their allotments made the great labor and toil of taking care of them mostly agreeable and pleasant. And I trust we were preserved from murmuring[3] or repining[4] thereat, as believing it to be dispensed in wisdom agreeable to the will and gracious disposing of an All-wise Providence for purposes best known to himself.

When I have observed the great trouble and affliction that many parents have with undutiful children – especially their sons – when

---

[1] Becoming: admirable

[2] It is likely that all four sons died from a sex-linked recessive type of muscular dystrophy inherited from their mother. In this respect, it is notable that Jemima had no living brothers and that their first grandson, Elias Willets, suffered from the same disease.

[3] Murmuring: inarticulate, muttered complaints

[4] Repine: to feel discontented or dissatisfied

favored with health and strength to run at large, I could find very few parents but whose troubles and exercises in regard to their children far exceeded ours. And as their weakness and infirmity of body tended to preserve them in innocency and much out of the way of the troubles and temptations of the world, so we believe that in their deaths, they were happy and admitted into the realms of peace and joy – a reflection the most comfortable and joyous to parents of any in regard to their tender offspring.

The spring following our marriage, my wife's parents gave me an invitation to come and live with them and carry on the business of their farm. And they having no other child but my wife, I agreed thereto and continued with them during their lives and it became afterwards my settled residence. And entering pretty closely into business, I was thereby much diverted from my religious improvement for several years, although my advantages in that respect were greater than before, for I was now not only settled about three miles from meeting, but had the benefit of the company of divers, worthy, concerned Friends, who were now my neighbors and by whose conversation and example I was frequently excited[1] to my religious duty.

Renewed Visitations of Divine Love

In that respect, and being about the twenty-sixth year of my age, being again brought under some renewed exercise through the operative influence of divine grace, wherein I was led through adorable mercy to see that although I had ceased from many sins and vanities of my youth, yet there were many remaining that I was still guilty of, that had not as yet been atoned for, and for which I now felt the judgments of God to rest upon me. And a sense whereof caused me to cry mightily to the Lord for pardon and redemption, and he graciously condescended to hear my cry and to open my way[2] before me wherein I must walk in order to experience reconciliation with him. As I abode in watchfulness and deep humiliation before him, light brake forth out of obscurity, and my darkness became as the noonday, and I had many deep openings in the visions of light – greatly strengthening and establishing[3] to my exercised[4] mind. And my spirit was brought under a weighty travail[5] and labor in

---

[1] Excite: stir up or set in motion
[2] Open the way (also, "way opening" or "way opened"): something becomes possible (e.g., offering ministry in a meeting for worship or undertaking a journey in the ministry) by God's removal of a spiritual impediment or "stop."
[3] Establish: sustain and support
[4] Exercised: troubled
[5] Travail: toil, hardship, suffering

meetings for discipline[1] and my understanding much enlarged therein, wherein I felt a weight upon my spirit to speak to subjects as occasion offered, which often brought unspeakable comfort to my mind.

First Appearance in the Ministry

And now I began to have openings, leading to the ministry, and this brought on close exercise and deep travail of spirit. For although I had for some time spoken to business in monthly[2] and preparative meetings,[3] yet the prospect of opening my mouth in public meetings[4] brought me a renewed and close trial. Yet I endeavored to keep my mind quiet and resigned to the heavenly call – if it should be made clear to me to be my duty. Nevertheless, when soon after as I sitting in a meeting in much weightiness of spirit, a prospect opened and a secret, though clear, intimation attended to speak a few words that were then given to me to utter. Fear so prevailed that I did not yield[5] to the motion,[6] for which I felt close rebuke, and judgment seemed for some time to cover my mind. But as I humbled myself under his mighty hand, he again lifted up the light of his countenance upon me and enabled me to renew covenant with him, that if he would pass by this my offense, I would in future be faithful if he should again open the way therefor.

And it was not long after when I was again moved to express a few words, which I yielded to in great fear and dread. But O, the joy and sweet consolation that my soul experienced as a reward for this act of faithfulness. And as I continued persevering in duty and in watchfulness, I witnessed an increase in divine knowledge and an enlargement in my gift. I was also deeply engaged for the right administration of discipline[7] and order in the Church and that all might be kept sweet and clean – consistent with the nature and purity of the holy profession we were making – that so all stumbling-blocks might be removed out of the way of honest

---

[1] Meeting for Discipline: a business meeting (Also referred to as a "meeting of discipline").

[2] Monthly Meeting: A regional collection of preparative and indulged meetings that came together once a month (hence the name) for worship, business, and mutual support.

[3] Preparative Meeting: A local congregation, subordinate to a Monthly Meeting, that met weekly for worship and once a month to prepare (hence the name) business to be placed before the monthly meeting. Sometimes referred to simply as a "preparative."

[4] Public Meeting: A meeting for worship that is open to all

[5] Yield: surrender

[6] Motion: a prompting from God (Also, "leading")

[7] Discipline: the accepted manner of conduct among Friends; a synonym for "discipleship."

inquirers and that Truth's testimony might be exalted, the Lord's name magnified, who is over all, God blessed forever.

The Situation of Friends During the American Revolution

A civil war having raged, with all its cruel and destructive effects, for several years between the British Colonies in North America and the mother country, Friends, as well as others, were many of them exposed to many severe trials and sufferings. Yet in the colony of New York, Friends that stood faithful and did not meddle in the controversy (after a short season at first) had considerable favor allowed them, insomuch that although the yearly meeting[1] was held steadily through the war on Long Island – where the king's party had the rule – yet Friends from the main[2] – where the American army ruled – had free passage through both armies to attend the yearly meeting and any other meetings where they were led to attending, except in some few instances – a favor which they would not grant to their best friends that were of a warlike disposition – which shows what great advantage would redound[3] to mankind, were they all of this pacific and peaceable disposition. I passed myself through the lines of both armies six times during the war without molestation – both parties generally receiving me with openness and civility.

And although we had to pass a tract of country between the lines of the two armies of near, if not upwards at some times of thirty miles distance – which tract was much frequented by rapparees or robbers issuing out from both parties and who were in general a set of cruel unprincipled banditti – yet I met no interruption from them, saving at one time on my return from a visit to Friends of the Northern Quarter[4] of our yearly meeting in the year 1781.

I, with my companion from Long Island and some other Friends in company, was met by two of them in our way from Mamaroneck to Westchester Meeting and I, being a little ahead of the company, was first met and accosted by them in a very rough manner – I not seeing them until they spake and one of them demanded very roughly where we were going. I looked upon him in a very mild manner and informed where we

---

[1] Yearly Meeting: A regional group of quarterly meetings that met together annually (hence, the name) for worship, business, and mutual support. The name was used interchangeably to refer to the collection of subordinate meetings and the annual sessions. Each yearly meeting was independent of the others, although London and Philadelphia enjoyed an extra degree of prestige.

[2] Main: mainland

[3] Redound: to cast honor or blame

[4] Quarter or Quarterly Meeting: A regional grouping of monthly meetings that met together once each three months or quarter of the year (hence, the name) for worship, business, and mutual support.

intended – without the least interruption of mind. He then interrogated me further as to where we had been, what was our business, and where we were from, etc. To all which, I gave true and suitable answers in a mild and pleasant tone, by which they seemed entirely disarmed of their rage and violence, although they had just before robbed and beat a man. And the one that had hitherto stood silent, being the most overcome, said to his fellow, "Come, let's go. The Quakers go where they please." And they, turning away, left us to pursue our journey without further interruption, which I considered as a merciful preservation through the interference of Divine Providence, who by his power, not only sets bounds to the sea, and saith, "Hitherto shalt thou come and hither shall thy proud waves be stayed,"[1] but also limits the rage and will of wicked men and turns them from their purpose. And thereby delivers from their power and cruelty those that put their trust in him.

And although Friends in general experienced many favors and deliverances, yet those scenes of war and confusion occasioned many trials and provings[2] of various ways to the faithful. One circumstance in particular I am willing to mention as it caused me considerable exercise both in body and mind. It was in this manner. The new meetinghouse[3] belonging to Friends in New York had under it a large cellar that was generally let as a store.[4] Being taken by the king's troops for that purpose on their entering into that city, and finding what Friends had the care of renting it, their commissary[5] came forward and offered to pay the rent thereof – which said Friends, for want of due consideration, accepted – which caused great uneasiness to the exercised[6] part of Friends who apprehended it not consistent with our peaceable principles to receive pay for the depositing of warlike stores – in any of our houses especially.

And the subject being brought forward, became a weighty care to the yearly meeting in 1779. And Friends who had been active in the reception of the money, with some few others, not being willing to acknowledge what they had done to be inconsistent, nor to return the money to those from whence it came and, in order to justify themselves therein, referred to the conduct of Friends in Philadelphia in similar cases. And matters

---

[1] Job 38:11
[2] Proving: test
[3] Meetinghouse: Friends considered "church" to properly refer only to the people of God, not to any physical structure, so their buildings were called by this name. Other denominations buildings also might be called meetinghouses.
[4] Store: storage space
[5] Commissary: An officer in charge of the supply of food, stores, and transport, for a body of soldiers
[6] Exercised: active or involved

appearing difficult and very embarrassing, it was therefore agreed to refer the final determination thereof to the Yearly Meeting of Pennsylvania[1] and it was unitedly concluded that their judgment should be decisive in the case. Accordingly, it was referred to said meeting and a number of Friends appointed to attend that meeting therewith – among whom I was one of the number.

A Visit to the Yearly Meeting at Philadelphia in 1779

Accordingly, on the 9th day of the 9th month 1779, we set forward – my beloved friend John Willis being my company from home, he being likewise on the appointment. We took a solemn leave our families, they feeling much anxiety at parting with us in consideration of the many dangers we were liable to be exposed to in our journey, having to pass not only the lines of the two armies, but the desolate and greatly uninhabited tract that lay between them – insomuch that in many places the grass was grown up in the streets and many houses desolate and empty. However, believing it my duty to proceed in the appointment, my mind was so settled and trust fixed in the divine arm of power, that faith seemed to banish all fear insomuch that cheerfulness and quiet resignation was, I believe, my constant companion during the journey.

With little difficulty, we got permission to pass the out-guards of the king's army at Kingsbridge and proceeded on to Westchester and from thence passing on, took meetings at Harrison's Purchase and Oblong (the latter a monthly meeting) – we having the concurrence of our monthly meetings to take some meetings in our way, a prospect leading thereto having attended my mind for some time before I left home. We passed from thence to Nine Partners and attended their monthly meeting.

---

[1] Although the yearly meetings were independent bodies, London and Philadelphia Yearly Meetings were recognized as "first among equals."

New Jersey

We then turned our faces towards Philadelphia (having joined several others of the committee).[1] We had three reasons for passing this way – in order to fall in company of Friends of the committee who resided in those parts, and also to visit some meetings that lay on this route, and also by it we missed the armies of the contended parties and the suit[2] of war which was mostly carried on, on the seacoast and near it.[3] We likewise attended meetings at New Marlborough, Hardwick, and Kingwood and then to Philadelphia, where we arrived the Seventh Day of the week and 25th of 9th month, and attended the Yearly Meeting of Ministers[4] and Elders[5] which began at the 11th hour.

Pennsylvania

I also attended all the sittings[6] of the yearly meeting until the Fourth Day of the next week and was then so indisposed with a fever that had been increasing on me for several days that I was not able to attend any more during the sittings thereof and therefore, was not present when the subject was discussed and settled that came from our yearly meeting, but was informed by my companion that it was a very solemn, weighty season and resulted agreeable to the mind of the concerned part of our meeting – advising that the money be returned into the office from whence it was paid with our reasons for so doing – which was accordingly directed by our yearly meeting the next year.

---

[1] The next sentence was deleted from the printed *Journal*.
[2] Suit: prosecution
[3] At this time, the American army was in New Jersey between Hicks and the normal route from New York City to Philadelphia, which is closer to the seashore.
[4] Minister: This was an unpaid position among Friends, but one that required formal acknowledgment. When a local meeting recognized that a man or woman had a gift in vocal ministry and the quarterly meeting concurred, it was formally acknowledged by a monthly meeting.
[5] Elder: a man or woman appointed by a monthly meeting with the concurrence of the quarterly meeting to take responsibility for the spiritual condition of the meeting. This included overseeing the ministry offered during meeting for worship, nurturing the spiritual growth of members (especially the youth), and caring for the ministers. As a general practice, elders did not speak in meetings for worship. (Note: A person could not serve as both a minister and an elder.) Meeting of Ministers and Elders: all ministers and elders from a quarterly or yearly meeting met together just before the corresponding meeting for discipline. These were select meetings, but ministers and elders traveling with a minute from their home meeting were welcome.
[6] Sittings: sessions

On the Second Day following, the yearly meeting ended and I, being a little recovered and feeling the want of fresh air, left the city immediately and rode home with my kind Friend, John Shoemaker, to his house in a carriage – being very weak in body. And the next morning, John Willis, my companion, came to me, but I being still weak, it was thought best I should rest here another day – especially as the weather was some wet. But John proceeded on to attend the monthly meeting at the Falls which came the day following and I went the next day to Byberry Meeting, after which I rode with our valuable Friend, James Thornton, to John Watson's at Middletown, where my companion again met me. The day following being the time of their monthly meeting, we attended and found things in but poor order and discipline at a low ebb for want of faithful standard-bearers. From thence, we passed on through Wrightstown, Plumstead, and Buckingham, taking a meeting at each place to some satisfaction.

Back in New Jersey

From thence, passing on through Hardwick, where we stayed their monthly meeting wherein things appeared very low as to the right exercise of discipline. But feeling our minds engaged, we labored in the ability received for their assistance and encouragement. After which, we passed on to the Drowned Lands and attended a meeting with the few Friends of that place and some others who came in. But things as to religion appeared at a very low ebb, which makes hard work for the poor traveler.

New York

We passed from thence pretty directly to Nine Partners and, taking two meetings there, we passed on through Oswego[1] and Poughquaig and then Oblong Monthly Meeting – in all which several meetings, Truth favored insomuch that I left them with peace of mind.

From Oblong, we then turned our faces homeward and after passing a few miles on our way were overtaken by a constable with a warrant from a magistrate to bring my companion before him, who after examination, committed him to a board of commissioners as a dangerous person to travel at such a time. We were led to believe, after some inquiry, that our interruption was merely the fruits of envy and occasioned by two of my companion's acquaintance, who had fled from the Island for refuge. However, after a short time of detention (which gave opportunity for me to attend a small meeting in that part that I had passed from in some

---

[1] Note that Oswego does not refer to the city of that name on Lake Ontario in New York, but to the Quaker meeting now known as Bulls Head-Oswego about 200 miles south-east of there in Clinton Corners, NY.

heaviness, and a few families of my relations) he was set at liberty timely to attend the quarterly meeting at Oblong. After which, we passed on, taking meetings at Peach Pond, Amawalk, and the Monthly Meeting at Purchase and from thence, proceeded home and found my family well, which together with the preservations and favors experienced in our journey, impressed my mind with thankfulness and gratitude to the Great and Blessed Author of all our mercies.

I was from home in this journey about nine weeks, and rode about eight hundred and sixty miles.

A Visit to Friends on the Mainland in 1781

Having felt drawings on my mind from the close of the aforesaid journey, to make a general visit to Friends on the Main belonging to our yearly meeting, therefore with the concurrence of Friends and in company with William Valentine who, under a like concern had agreed to be my companion in this journey, I left home the first of the week and 4th of 3rd month 1781 in order to accomplish the same. We sat with Friends in our own meeting and then proceeded to Flushing and lodged.

The next day, the commanding officer of the king's guards at this place permitting us, we crossed the Sound to Frog's Neck and lodged with our Friend, Joseph Caustin, on said neck and the following day, attended an appointed meeting[1] at Westchester and then went forward, taking meetings as they came in course for fifteen days successively – the latter at the Little Nine Partners. And although in many places meetings appeared in a low state as to the life of religion, yet through divine favor help was afforded insomuch that I generally left them with the satisfactory evidence that my way had been rightly directed among them.

After the last mentioned meeting, we set forward towards Saratoga and lodged that night at an inn. At this place, the innkeeper's wife in the course of some conversation discovered that my companion and I were from Long Island, where the king's party bore[2] rule. And she being a friend to their cause, seemed much to admire[3] that we should leave there and come out among the Americans – signifying that if she was there, she should not be willing to come away. But when I informed her that I expected we should shortly return thither again, her admiration was still more excited and [she] seemed surprised how we should dare to do that.

---

[1] Appointed meeting: not a regularly scheduled meeting, often scheduled for a traveling minister. These may be held at a Friends Meetinghouse, a private house, or in a public building. (Also, a meeting by appointment)

[2] Bore: past tense of bear, in this case meaning the British army controlled Long Island

[3] Admire: surprise or amaze

Saratoga (New York) Meetinghouse

Whereupon I took occasion to show her how we stood in regard to the contending parties, informing her that we took no part in the controversy, but were friends to them and to all mankind and were principled against all wars and fightings. Therefore, the contending powers had such confidence in us and favor towards us that they let us pass freely on religious accounts – out and in through both their armies without interruption – a privilege they would not grant to their own people.

This account made her marvel greatly, having never heard the like before – however, she acknowledged it was very good and wished for herself that she could come into the same situation, but said she could not unless she first obtained retaliation for the wrongs she had received. After which, she said, she should be willing to forgive them – not considering that there was nothing to forgive where full pay or satisfaction had been received.

Nevertheless, this is the natural condition and disposition of all worldly-minded men and women who have not known through the powerful influence of the gospel of Christ the work of regeneration and the new birth, whereby they might have known redemption from such a malicious and revengeful spirit.

The next day, we passed on to Coeyman's Patent, on the west side of Hudson River (which we crossed at a place called Claverack Landing). A few Friends had lately settled at this place – it lay about twenty miles below Albany. We got here on Seventh Day evening and the next day had a meeting with the few Friends and some of their neighbors, who were mostly Baptists. It was the first Friends meeting ever held there. It was a satisfactory season, after which we then rode that afternoon about twelve miles towards Albany and lodged at an inn. And the next day, we reached Saratoga (since called Easton) and lodged with our Friend, Daniel Cornell.

It was late in the night before we got in and the evening snowy. And the country being new, Friends' houses were generally but poor, insomuch that at divers times whilst in these parts, I felt the snow fall on my face when in bed, by reason of which, I took a great cold when I first came here, but afterwards, I was much favored during our stay in the country – having got in good measure inured to the hardships we had to go through.

We attended the meetings belonging to this monthly meeting, being four in all, *viz*, Saratoga (alias Easton), Danby (about forty miles further to the north east), White Creek, and East Hoosac, where the monthly meeting at this time was held – it being held alternately at this place and Saratoga. We also visited nearly all the families belonging to this monthly meeting and had good satisfaction and a peaceful reward of our labors. From thence, we went to New Britain and visited three families, in each of which there was but one member of our Society. There is since a large meeting there.

From thence, we then returned to Nine Partners and attended their monthly meeting, as also several other meetings thereaway[1] that we were not at in our way up. After which, we took Oblong Quarterly Meeting and next, the Monthly Meeting of Chappaqua and thence, taking meetings at Purchase, Mamaroneck, and Westchester and from there, we passed the Sound again and got safe home the 15th of 5th month and was gladly received by my family and Friends, having been out in this journey about ten weeks and rode about eight hundred and forty-seven miles, attended thirty-two meetings (six were monthly meetings), and attended one quarterly meeting, and visited about ninety families.

In the latter part of this journey, between Mamaroneck and Westchester, we were met and insulted by the two robbers or rapparees as mentioned before.

Visions & Afflictions

In the fall of this year, 1781, I was taken with a fever which held me for several months, in the course of which, my natural strength became very much exhausted and some of my Friends were ready to conclude I should not stay long with them. And although the prospect as to outward appearance seemed at times to look very doubtful, yet I all along through the times of my indisposition had to believe that I should recover. Nevertheless, through the exercise and distress – both of body and mind –

---

[1] Thereaway: in those parts

that I experienced in this season of affliction, it proved a very humbling dispensation to me.

One circumstance in particular made it peculiarly exercising to my mind – although on that I principally grounded my belief of recovery – for when I was reduced nearly to the lowest state of bodily weakness during my complaint, a prospect opened on my mind to pay a religious visit to some parts of our island where no Friends lived and among a people who, from the acquaintance I had with them, appeared more likely to make a ridicule of me than to receive me or my doctrine – seeing I considered myself but a child as to such a service. But when the prospect first opened, it was very impressive[1] on my mind and an injunction seemed to attend, requiring my present assent thereto. Although I pleaded as an excuse my present weakness and inability of body – as well as unfitness, even if I was well, for such a service. But with all my reasoning and pleading, I could feel no excuse granted me, but the requisition[2] both day and night lay heavy upon me until by my standing out,[3] I was brought very low both in body and mind. And finding that I could get no peace nor rest to my mind in this state of refusal and that, if I did not yield, my life must go for my stubbornness – without any prospect of peace hereafter. After long struggling and pleading to be released without any the least prospect of obtaining my desire, I at length yielded to the heavenly call – which brought immediate peace and comfort to my afflicted soul.[4]

But after a little time of quiet, in which at times I had again to view the prospect and look at the difficulties that appeared many ways likely to attend the putting it in practice – not knowing any person in the parts I had in prospect that was likely to be willing to receive me or open their house for a meeting. These considerations brought renewed exercise and caused me several times during the time of my recovery to recant and draw back. And then, nothing but distress and anxiety of spirit was my portion until I again resigned thereto. And the Lord was very gracious – opening many things for my encouragement.

And one night, as I was musing on the subject in some distress of mind and getting a little quiet, I fell asleep, but seemed in vision to be in a great ecstasy[5] in regard to performing the visit and thought I was in the east side of the town where I was to have the first meeting. I thought, in the anguish of my spirit, I cried out aloud, "Where should I go to find a

---

[1] Impressive: inspiring deep feelings
[2] Requisition: A demand, usually made by a creditor that a debt be paid, or an obligation fulfilled
[3] Standing out: continued resistance
[4] The next two paragraphs were deleted from the printed *Journal*.
[5] Ecstasy: anxiety and fear

house for a meeting?" And I apprehended I saw a black man standing a little from me who had heard my cry and calling to me says, "Here, I will show thee the house." And stretching out his hand, pointed across to the south at part of the town and seemed to direct my sight to a particular spot. Although I knew not at that time anything of the place or whether there was a house there or not, but it quite eased my mind and I awoke, and felt comfortable, and ever after felt resigned to the prospect.

A Visit on Long Island in 1782

Accordingly, in the forepart of the next summer, after I had fully recovered my health, it opened as the right time to perform this service. And opening it to my Friends at a monthly meeting, obtained their unity and concurrence, and two Friends agreed to bear me company.[1] Accordingly, about the middle of the 8th month 1782, we set out on the visit.[2]

The first place that opened for a meeting was the town of Jamaica and when we came into the east part of the town, where (as expressed before) I thought I saw a black man directing me where to go, my dream came fresh in my mind and the prospect seemed as plain to me now as it did in the vision – but I had not opened it to my Friends and they proposed to go to a different part of the town. And I assayed[3] to go with them, but when I passed the street that led to the place pointed to by the black man, I felt a stop[4] in my mind and told Friends it felt most right to me to go down thither, to which they readily consented. And when I came in sight of the spot where my mind seemed directed in the vision, there stood a house thereon, but not knowing who lived in it, it was proposed to go on some distance further to a house of our acquaintance. But when I attempted to pass the aforesaid house, I felt again a full stop in my mind and told Friends I believed we must go to that house. Accordingly, we went and when we came in, the man (though a stranger) received us courteously, and when we informed him our business and that we had a desire to have a religious opportunity[5] with the neighbors, he freely offered us his house, which at this juncture was rendered convenient for a meeting by a new

---

[1] If a minister wished to travel in the ministry outside the territory of his or her home quarterly meeting, he or she would ask for permission from the monthly meeting before proceeding. One or more elders would be appointed to accompany him or her.
[2] The next three paragraphs were deleted from the printed *Journal*.
[3] Assay: attempt
[4] Stop: a spiritual obstacle to undertaking an action
[5] Opportunity: a chance to worship God in the manner of Friends. These frequently occurred in a home when Quaker ministers or elders visited.

addition which he had built to a shop adjoining – he being a trader – and in which the next day, he had expected to have deposited his goods, but would put it off one day longer to make way for the meeting.

And while we were conversing on the subject of the meeting, in stepped a religious black man and when he found there was a prospect of a meeting, he seemed to leap for joy and spake out and says, "I will go and give notice," and spake very encouragingly to the subject – the consideration whereof, and things turning so very agreeable to my prospect, made deep impressions of thankfulness and gratitude on my mind. After which, I opened to my Friends the prospect I before had seen of this place and how everything had turned out agreeable thereto, which had likewise a very strengthening and encouraging effect on their minds.

Accordingly the next day, we had a very favored meeting with a considerable number of the inhabitants who came in and behaved soberly.

After this, we took a meeting at Samuel Doughty's on the south side of the island to good satisfaction and then passed on to a Dutch settlement called the Flatlands, where we had some difficulty to obtain a meeting by reason the priest of the place was opposed thereto and the people seemed generally afraid to offend him, but said if he would consent, they should be very willing to attend. However, his assent could not be obtained, for he appeared very jealous lest his interest in the people might be affected and therefore would not give us his approbation. However, there was one man who seemed so much master of his own house that he said we were welcome to have a meeting in it – let others say what they might respecting it. Accordingly, a meeting was appointed. Although but small (the people we supposed were afraid to come, lest it should offend their priest), however we had a satisfactory opportunity with those who attended. The man of the house and his wife, in an especial manner, seemed considerably affected therewith and opened their house freely – pressing us to come and see them again.

From thence, we passed on and took meetings at Gravesend, New Utrecht, and then turning homeward, took one at Springfield – all to good satisfaction. From the latter, we rode home.

I was out about a week and felt the comfortable reward of peace for this tour of duty and very thankful to the Lord, my Gracious Helper, for his countenance and support in this arduous service. May his name be praised forever.

A Visit to the Meetings on the Mainland in 1782

In the fall of this year, 1782, I attended with a committee of the yearly meeting the quarterly meeting on the main with the monthly meetings thereto belonging, on a motion from said quarterly meeting for a division thereof.

We were out about seven weeks in this service and rode about six hundred and sixty miles.

A Visit to Nine Partners in 1783

In the fall of the year 1783, I attended the Meeting for Sufferings[1] at Nine Partners – it being held there at this time, as also that quarterly meeting – and took meetings held at Oswego and Poughquaig on my return. Was from home about eleven days and rode about one hundred and seventy miles. The reward of peace that I felt for this little tour of duty, together with finding my family well on my return, excited gratitude and thankfulness of heart to the Blessed Author of all our mercies and blessings, who in his faithfulness, richly rewardeth every labor of his dependent and devoted children.

A Visit to Some Inhabitants of Long Island in 1784

A concern having for some time impressed my mind to pay a religious visit to the inhabitants of some of the adjacent towns that were not in profession with us, and having obtained the unity and concurrence of my Friends therein, on the First Day of the week and 13th of 6th month 1784, I left home in order to perform that service. I attended our own meeting in the forenoon and, in the afternoon, one appointed at Hempstead Harbor to good satisfaction. Our next appointment was on Second Day at a village called Herricks, where dwelt a people of but little profession as to religion. Nevertheless, we had a refreshing season among them – the power and presence of the Lord being witnessed to preside amongst us in an eminent manner to the tendering[2] many hearts, and the exaltation of the peaceable kingdom and government of the Messiah. To Zion's King may all the praise be ascribed, who only is worthy forever.

From thence we went to the Widow Cornell's at Success, where we lodged and had a meeting there the next day to good satisfaction – many present being affected with Truth's testimony that ran freely over all, to the comfort and refreshment of the sincere-hearted. From there, we rode to Benjamin Doughty's and lodged. And the next day, had a meeting at the Little Plains (about a mile from our lodgings) among a loose, airy people. And the Lord's power was manifest for our help, setting things close home to their several conditions.

---

[1] Meeting for Sufferings: originally, a committee of London Yearly Meeting, established to address the costs of persecution (monetary or otherwise), that is, to assist Friends who suffered on account of their faith. Over time, it evolved into an executive committee for the yearly meeting. The name was adopted by other yearly meetings for their executive committees.

[2] Tender: become gentle, contrite, and compassionate

The day following, we attended two meetings – one at Jamaica and the other at a place called the Fresh Meadows, near Flushing. And although the people were too generally at ease and in an unconcerned state in regard to their religious improvement, yet through the interposition of divine goodness and mercy, some hearts were tendered through the convicting power of Truth and we comforted in the faithful discharge of duty. After these opportunities, we rode to our Friend, Isaac Underhill's, at Flushing and lodged and the next day, attended a meeting appointed in Friends Meetinghouse in that town, wherein the Master's presence was witnessed – to the comfort and satisfaction of the sincere-hearted.

From thence, we went to Newtown and lodged with a man not in profession with us, had a meeting at his house the following day wherein Truth favored in gospel communication suited to the states of those present, and relieving to my own mind. The four following days, we attended meetings at the Kills in Newtown, Bushwick, Brooklyn Ferry, Flatbush, Flatlands, and Gravesend. After the latter, we turned our faces homeward, taking meetings at Samuel Doughty's and one at a wigwam among the black people and Indians – both satisfactory seasons.

The next meeting was at Springfield, among a people who appeared to be in a state of great darkness – like a confused chaos – but the Lord was pleased, by his own power, to command the Light to shine in many hearts, insomuch that the meeting ended under divine favor. To him alone may all the praise be ascribed, who is worthy forever.

The day following, attended two meetings – one at Foster's Meadow, the other at the widow Keziah Mott's, after which we rode to my father's at Rockaway on the south side of the island and the next day attended a meeting there. And the day following, we attended two meetings at South Hempstead – the latter at the house of our Friend, John Smith – all I trust in a good degree, profitable and instructive seasons.

Our next and last appointment at this time was in the town of Hempstead the following day. It was a large,[1] satisfactory opportunity wherein divine help was afforded to minister suitably to the states of those present and to the comfort and edification of many minds. To the Master of our Assemblies[2] be the praise – nothing due to man.

From hence, I rode home and found my family well, having ridden, whilst out, about one hundred miles.

A few weeks after my return from the aforesaid visit to the inhabitants on the western part of the island, not feeling my mind released from the service, I again left home on the 4th of the 8th month following in order to finish the visit to the more southern and eastern parts.

---

[1] Large: lengthy and comprehensive
[2] Ecclesiastes 12:11

The first meeting I attended was again at Hempstead. From thence, I proceeded along the south side of the island, taking meetings at Thomas Seaman's near Jerusalem, Thomas Sands' at Huntington South, the next at Islip on Seventh Day, but not feeling clear,[1] appointed another the following day – being the first of the week. This proved a satisfactory season and that afternoon, I attended another meeting about thirteen miles farther east at a place called Blue Point, thence passing on along the south side of the island, took meetings at Patchogue, the Fire Place, Speonk, Quogue, Southampton, North Sea, Amagansett, and Montauk (at the east end of the island among the Indian natives). In all which, strength was afforded to preach the gospel in a good degree of divine authority, and general satisfaction of those assembled, and the solid peace of my own mind.[2]

In one meeting, a Presbyterian deacon being present made some objection to that part of the doctrine delivered that opposed unconditional and personal election and reprobation and, getting his Bible, raised some dispute, but was soon confounded and willing to let the subject drop.

After the meeting at Montauk among the natives, we returned that afternoon to a meeting at East Hampton, which we had appointed on our way down – it was held at the 5th hour. The priest of the town and a considerable number of his hearers attended and all passed away quiet. We passed from thence to the north part of the island, taking meetings at Sag Harbor, Shelter Island, Southold, Oyster Pond Point, Stephen Vail's (a little back from the Point), thence back, by Riverhead to Saint George's Manor, where we had a meeting – also all satisfactory seasons – from thence by Wading River, to Setauket and Stony Brook – taking meetings at the two last places to good satisfaction.

Especially the meeting at Setauket was an especially solemn time – the Lord's presence being witnessed to the tendering many hearts. After which, we took meetings at Jonah Wood's, and James Oakley's, and so home and found my family well. For which favor, with the peace and satisfaction I felt in the performance of this tour of duty, inspired my mind with gratitude and humble acknowledgments to the Lord, my Gracious Helper, for those enriching blessings.

In the 12th month following, feeling my mind drawn to a few places eastward on the north part of the island, I again left home on the 2nd of said month and took meetings at Huntington, Great Cow Harbor, Crab Meadow, Smithtown, Setauket, old man Miller's place, Wading River, Coram, Joshua Smith's (near the Branch), and from thence home. In all which meetings, Truth favored me with ability to discharge myself

---

[1] Clear: free of a spiritual obligation
[2] The next paragraph was deleted from the printed *Journal*.

faithfully,[1] to the peace of my own mind and I trust to the edification and instruction of the honest minded in the several meetings.

A Visit to New York & Staten Island in 1790

Having felt drawing on my mind to pay a religious visit to some not in profession with us on the western part of our island, New York, and Staten Island, after obtaining the concurrence of our monthly meeting, I proceeded therein the 28th of 3rd month 1790 - Fry Willis kindly bearing me company. Our first appointment was at Newtown, at the Widow Smith's, who received us and opened her house for a meeting which was held to good satisfaction. The next day, we had two meetings - the first at Friends Meetinghouse at the Kills, the other in the evening at a neighboring village called Juniper Swamp - both favored seasons, many hearts being tendered by the prevalence of Truth's testimony which, through heavenly help, was exalted over all.

The day following, way opening therefor, we had a meeting at Hurlgate in the afternoon to the general satisfaction of those present and to my own comfort - having been enabled to discharge myself faithfully in a plain way among them, after which we proceeded to New York. And the evening of the next day, we had a large and I trust profitable meeting in a public building called the City Tavern. Our next appointment was in Friends Meetinghouse, the evening following. It was a very large collection and, through the gracious extendings of divine mercy, Truth's testimony was exalted over all - to the comfort and strength of my own mind and the solid satisfaction and rejoicing of many present.

The day following we passed to Staten Island, and the next, being the first of the week, we had two meetings, the first at a friendly[2] man's house, by the name of Peter Prawl. It was a favored season wherein the Master's presence was witnessed eminently to preside - in the precious influence whereof, the gospel was preached in demonstration of the Spirit[3] and with power, to the awakening[4] and tendering the hearts of many present. To the Lord only wise, be the praise and glory of his own work, for he only is worthy forever.

The meeting in the afternoon, held at the house of the widow of our Friend, Thomas Ridgway, proved a laborous season, but I trust ended well. We had two more meetings on the island the next day and the solemnity attending gave encouragement to hope they were of some use

---

[1] Discharge myself faithfully: to offer appropriate vocal ministry
[2] Hicks uses the word "friendly" to refer to people who were not members of the Society of Friends, but in his opinion, were sympathetic to its beliefs
[3] 1 Corinthians 2:4
[4] Awakening: arousing

to those assembled. After which, we returned to New York with peace of mind, accompanied with the good wishes of many of those we had visited.

The day after our arrival in the city, was held Friends monthly meeting, which we attended, and the evening of the next day, had a large, satisfactory meeting in the suburbs of the town in a large building called the Hospital.

The next day at the 10th hour, we visited the poor in the poor house – the season was comfortable and satisfactory. At the 3rd hour, we had a pretty full meeting in a house belonging to the Methodists, which they offered us for that purpose, and at evening, had another large meeting in Friends Meetinghouse – both satisfactory seasons and I trust comfortable and edifying to many who attended. The next day, we spent in visiting a few families of Friends, as way opened. This closed our visit for this time to the city.

The next day being the first of the week and 11th of 4th month, we had a satisfactory meeting at Brooklyn on Long Island.

The two following days, we attended two meetings in our way home – the first at Samuel Doughty's at Jamaica South, the latter in Jamaica town – both favored seasons, for although many who attended were light and airy, yet through the prevalence of Truth's testimony, a comfortable solemnity was spread over the assemblies – insomuch that I left them in the feeling enjoyment of true peace of mind and returned to my family the evening following and found all well. For which, with other unmerited favors witnessed in the course of this small tour of duty, filled my mind with thankful acknowledgments to the Shepherd of Israel, who is over all, worthy forever.

A Visit to Vermont & New York in 1790

In the latter part of the summer of this year, I performed a visit in company with James Parsons of New York to some friendly people who resided in the towns of Strafford and Sharon in the State of Vermont, about fifteen miles west of Connecticut River.

I left home the 28th of 7th month, took the Quarterly Meeting of Purchase, and a meeting on First Day at Cornwall in Connecticut in our way, and passed on to Northampton [Massachusetts] on Connecticut River, from thence, up the east side of the river, through Massachusetts and part of New Hampshire as far as Hanover.

Vermont

Thence crossing the river, we rode about fifteen miles westerly to the town of Strafford, to the house of Timothy Blake, who was principal in collecting those friendly people – their first meeting was at his house. He appeared convinced of the principle of the Inward Light, as held by us, and had gathered a number into the same belief in a good degree, insomuch that they held two meetings when we came among them – one at his house and the other at the adjacent town of Sharon. But for want of keeping inward enough to the principle of Divine Light and Grace, they became weak and those who apprehended it their duty to teach had got too much out into words and speculative preaching and doctrine – which soon produced discord and a schism among them. Although they appeared to have been at times under divine favor and several of them had their understandings considerably illumined – insomuch that they requested and were joined in membership with Friends and their meetings came under Friends' notice, but being far distant from any other meeting of Friends and not keeping low and little[1] enough, they mostly ran out and got scattered[2] and their meetings dropped. Yet a few kept (or regained) their first love – several of whom afterwards removed nearer to Friends.

New York

We spent several days among them and then taking leave, returned homeward by Danby, Saratoga (alias Easton), and Hudson to Nine Partners – taking meetings as they fell in our way – and got timely to Nine Partners to attend their quarterly meeting. After which, we passed pretty directly home, taking a meeting at Chappaqua on First Day.

I was from home on this journey about three weeks and five days, attended two quarterly meetings and seven particular meetings,[3] and traveled about five hundred and ninety-one miles.

---

[1] Low and little: humble
[2] Ran out and got scattered: a flock is not following its shepherd's lead – an allusion to Christ as our shepherd
[3] Particular Meeting: a local congregation, whether an indulged meeting or a preparative meeting

1791-1795

A Visit with Some Inhabitants of Long Island in 1791

In the latter part of the winter and the spring of the ensuing year, in the drawings of gospel love and with the unity of my Friends, I performed a visit to a number of the adjacent towns and villages on our island among those not in profession with us. I was from home about two weeks and attended fifteen meetings and rode about one hundred and fifteen miles.[1]

In one opportunity, while out on this visit, as I was speaking under the lively[2] impression and power of Truth to the arousing and affecting the minds of many of the auditory,[3] it opened to me in an instantaneous and clear manner to say to the people that were present that some would never have such another opportunity and pressed the necessity of rightly improving the present. For it appeared to me that the time, at least of an individual, was limited to a very short space. Accordingly after the meeting, a youngerly man, then in health, returned home and his mind much effected with the declaration and was taken ill in about two days after and lived but a short time – being, from the time he was first taken, fully convinced that he was the person alluded to in the meeting.

And although my mind is established in the unerring faith of divine revelation, and that the Lord in his unbounded wisdom and power does still see meet[4] at times to reveal his secrets to his faithful, devoted servants, yet such is the prevalence of unbelief among the people in general in regard to the continuance thereof in this day, that it requires great fortitude and strength of faith to make public declaration of the most clear discovery of any subject opened on the mind by divine inspiration. And even when, through strength of faith resulting from the powerful influence and energy of Divine Truth on the mind, we are made willing to give ourselves wholly up as a trumpet in the Lord's hand – to speak through us what he pleases – yet (when something as related above is spoken through us) when the divine influence is a little withdrawn, we are very apt like Jonah of old to draw back for fear it should not be made manifest to the people. This was my lot in the present case. For although I was fully confirmed that at the time of my making this declaration I was so swallowed up in the divine influence that self was entirely reduced[5] and that there was nothing of the creature or man's part active therein, yet in viewing the force and fixedness of the expressions, I was let – through

---

[1] The next three paragraphs were deleted from the printed *Journal*.
[2] Lively: convincing
[3] Auditory: audience
[4] Meet: appropriate, suitable, or proper
[5] Reduce: subjugate to the will of God

fear – to make an abatement thereon, as a thing possible. In doing which, I believe the creature had a great share and which might very powerfully operate to prevent the good intended by this divine opening by leaving the mind in suspense, but which, in its certain and positive declaration, had struck the mind of the individual alluded to with great force – designed no doubt by his Merciful Creator to stir him up to use all diligence to redeem the few remaining moments allotted him on this stage of trial and be thereby prepared for his eternal state – so that in those failures, we very justly incur the censure of our dear Lord.

O thou of little faith! Wherefore didst thou doubt?[1]

General Visit to Friends in the Yearly Meeting of New York in 1791 & 1792

A prospect having for some time impressed my mind to make a general visit to Friends of our yearly meeting, and to take some meetings among those not in profession with us in parts adjacent, with the concurrence of my brethren at home, I set out on this service the 23rd of 10th month this year, and took meetings at Flushing, Newtown and Brooklyn, on my way to New York where our quarterly meeting was held at this time – it ended on the Sixth Day of the week. It was a solemn season and graciously owned by the Master's presence and many weighty subjects were opened through well qualified instruments to the satisfaction and encouragement of the living – being favored with the company of our beloved Friend, Mary Ridgway, and her companion from Ireland.

The 29th and seventh of the week, I proceeded on my journey with Andrew Underhill, who had kindly given up to bear me company. We went by water to Staten Island and, the next day being the first of the week, we attended two appointed meetings – the first at a friendly man's house (whose wife was convinced[2]), the latter at the house of a professor[3] among the Methodists – both favored seasons – many hearts being tendered through gospel communication, which flowed freely to the people.

31st and second of the week, had another meeting on the island, at the house of the Widow Ridgway, after which, in the evening we had a tendering season with the widow's family.

---

[1] Matthew 14:31
[2] Convinced or Member by Convincement: a person who becomes a member of the Religious Society of Friends by their own application
[3] Professor: one who claims membership in a religious body

New Jersey

The next day, we passed over to Rahway in East Jersey and on Fourth Day, 2nd of 11th month, we attended Friends meeting at Plainfield and an appointed meeting in the evening at Elijah Pound's, near Brunswick - both, I trust, profitable seasons to some present. We returned next morning to Rahway, and attended Friends meeting in that place and one in the evening at Woodbridge and returned to Rahway to lodge.

The next day, we passed over again to Staten Island and had two meetings in the southwestern part thereof, wherein help was afforded to discharge myself faithfully in a plain way, suited (as I believe) to the states of those who attended - being of different professions, such as Episcopalians, Presbyterians, Baptists, and Methodists. Returned again on Seventh Day evening to our lodgings at Rahway, to the house of our kind Friend, Joseph Shotwell.

And the next day being the first of the week and 6th of the 11th month, we attended their fore and after noon meetings - both, I trust, instructive, edifying seasons, worthy of remembrance. To the Lord only-wise, be the praise and glory of his own work, for to him it is due.

The following day, we attended an appointed meeting at the house of our Friend, Joseph Stackhouse, at the 11th hour in Elizabethtown and although small, yet it proved a satisfactory season, and one in the evening at Newark, held in their courthouse. The meeting was large and much crowded. I was drawn forth among them in a large doctrinal testimony - I believe to general satisfaction, and greatly to the peace and relief of my own mind.

Our next appointment was at a place called the English Neighborhood (the evening following) situated on the east side of Hackensack River, at the house of Thomas Frost, a doctor of physic.[1] And although it was the first meeting of Friends' appointment ever held at that place and the people mostly unacquainted with us and our principles, yet they came freely together and generally conducted[2] in an orderly, commendable manner. The meeting was much favored - being evidently owned by the Head of the Church - and ability received to communicate divers things relative to the true ground of real religion and spiritual worship, which appeared to obtain the general assent of those present.

---

[1] Doctor of physic: physician
[2] Conduct: behave

New York

The next day at evening, we had a meeting at the house of our Friend, Daniel Lawrence, at Tappan, and although small, was in the main a satisfactory season.

The three following days, we took two meetings by appointment in our way to Cornwall – one at Kakiat at the house of the Widow Seaman, the other at William Thorne's at Smith's Clove. In going to the latter place, we rode over the western part of the mountains, called the Highlands – I think it the most rough, disagreeable way I ever traveled. We got to the house of our Friend, William Titus, at Cornwall on Seventh Day evening.

The next day attended Friends meeting there, and one by appointment in the evening at New Windsor and lodged with our Friend, James Thorne.

The next day, we crossed Hudson River and took a meeting at the Fishkill in our way to Nine Partners, where we arrived on Third Day and attended the Quarterly Meeting of Ministers and Elders that opened at the 11th hour.

The two following days, the meeting for discipline and a parting meeting for public worship were held – they were all favored seasons in which the faithful had cause to bless the name of the Lord for his mercy in manifesting his gracious presence for the strength and help of his people and servants in the several sittings thereof. In a sense whereof, we parted from each other with mutual rejoicing.

Connecticut

On Sixth Day, we rode to Sharon in Connecticut, and the day following, held a meeting for the townspeople in a large upper room in their schoolhouse. A considerable number attended, and through heavenly goodness, it proved a memorable time. The testimony of Truth went freely forth among them, powerfully reaching[1] and tendering many hearts. To the Lord alone be the praise.

After this meeting, we rode to the house of Simeon Prague, about three miles north of the town, and attended a meeting that evening.

And next day being the first of the week, we rode to Goshen and attended the meeting held there at the house of Charles Richards, and notice having gone before of our coming, it was a pretty full meeting and ended to satisfaction.

---

[1] Reaching: mentally or spiritually stretching

Massachusetts

We passed from thence to Tyringham in the state of Massachusetts and on Third Day, attended a meeting in that neighborhood and passing on that afternoon and the next day, we got to Westfield, and lodged at an inn, and the following day held a meeting at our lodging for the neighborhood. After which, we rode to Norwich and attended a meeting that evening at the house of Phineas Mixer, which proved through heavenly help a comfortable edifying season – although the general part of those who attended were strangers to us and our principles.

New Hampshire & Vermont

The three following days, we passed on through the towns of Northampton, Hadley, Sunderland, Montague, Northfield, and Walpole [New Hampshire] to John Cook's in Claremont where we appointed a meeting to be held the next day. Our landlord took upon him the care to give the notice to his neighbors and having heard so much concerning Friends – that they sometimes sit their meetings in silence – he was afraid (as he after informed me when I passed that way again) to inform any of the meeting except two or three of his particular friends, lest, if it should prove silent, they might laugh him to scorn. In consequence whereof, the meeting was very small, but such was the kindness of Divine Providence that he did not fail to manifest his presence powerfully among (as it were) the two or three[1] – to the conviction and reproof of our unfaithful landlord – insomuch (as he informed me when I came that way again), his folly and blindness had given him much trouble and distress, insomuch that he was now very pressing and desirous I would appoint another meeting, that he might give all the neighborhood general notice. But we let him know that we were not at our own disposal and therefore, as no way appeared open in our minds for such an appointment at present, we could not comply with his present desire and so left him to reflect on his former omission.

But to return to our journey, after the last mentioned meeting, we passed the next day to Windsor, the southeasterly town of the state of Vermont, situated on the west side of Connecticut River. Here, we had a meeting in their courthouse, which was very commodiously fitted[2] for the purpose – it proved a solid, satisfactory opportunity – after which we rode to James Willard's in the town of Hartland. This was a person, although brought up without any particular knowledge of Friends, yet was so far one in principle with us that he had maintained by himself alone a testimony against a hireling ministry, against fighting, and oaths, and the

---

[1] Matthew 18:20
[2] Fit: make suitable or proper

superstitious observance of days and had, by sound reasoning, so far defeated all his opponents that he was permitted to remain quiet[1] – although his residence had mostly been among those rigid in the profession of the Presbyterians. We had a meeting in his house, which appeared always to be open to Friends (after gaining an acquaintance with them), but it being on the day set apart by those in authority as a day of thanksgiving, the meeting was small.

After which, taking leave of our kind landlord, we journeyed forward and got to the town of Sharon the next day – to the house of Jared Bassett, a friendly requester[2] who, with some of his neighbors who were likewise measurably convinced of our principles, held meetings together after our manner. Here, we continued some days visiting those friendly people and attended their meeting on First Day, 4th of 12th month, which through favor was, I trust, a profitable, edifying season.

On Third Day, we rode over to Hanover, a town on the east side of Connecticut River and the day following had a meeting in the east part of said town among a people mostly of the Baptist profession. It was, I trust, a profitable season – things relating to true religion and spiritual worship being largely[3] opened in testimony to the Truth we profess – as also after the meeting, in a time of free conversation on several material points (to wit) election, falling from grace, water baptism, and the right use of the scriptures. All which were opened apparently to the satisfaction of most present – at least so far as to suppress all opposition.[4]

The evening of the next day, we had an appointed meeting near Dartmouth College (so called). It proved a very disturbed opportunity by reason of the attendance of the young students, whose behavior was very rude and unbecoming—the most immoral characters abroad in the world – which shows the hurtful tendency of such places, being some of them mere seminaries of vice and licentiousness. Nevertheless, I hope the season may be profitable to some present.

We returned the next day to Sharon, to Jared Bassett's, and the following day, attended two meetings – one at Strafford and the other in the evening at a place called the Hollow – after which, we returned again to Jared Bassett's.

And the next day being the first of the week and 11th of 12th month, we attended the meeting at his house, which with the two last, were (to myself at least) satisfactory seasons.

---

[1] Remain quiet: be left alone
[2] Requester: a person who makes a request
[3] Largely: at length and in detail
[4] The next paragraph was heavily edited in the printed *Journal* to make it less censorious.

New York

Feeling conscious in myself of having discharged my duty faithfully among them and felt the answer of peace therein, the next day, we set out for Danby, the nearest meeting of Friends to this place, but by reason of a great fall of snow and the way very mountainous, we did not arrive there until the third day after we set out.

On the next day after our arrival, began their monthly meeting, which held two days. It was a low time, wherein I felt my mind much oppressed by reason of the apparent careless, indifferent[1] way Friends there were in of conducting the weighty affairs of the church – many of them appearing to act in their own spirit, in as light a manner as they would in their own trivial outward business. Much labor was bestowed in a plain way in order to impress their minds with the necessity of being more weighty in their spirits when they presumed to be active in the affairs of Truth – I hope to the encouragement of the honest-hearted. We stayed their First Day Meeting, which was large and proved a laborous season. I was favored to ease my mind among them, although they appeared too generally insensible of the operation of Truth.

After meeting, we rode that afternoon on our way towards Lake Champlain (about twelve miles) and attended a meeting at the house of our Friend, Joseph Button, that evening among a people mostly of the Baptist profession. It was a favored season and ability received to open many things in a plain way relating to the Christian religion and the strange, absurd doctrine of absolute personal election and reprobation exposed and confuted – as also that of the impossibility of falling from grace, and the true baptism[2] explained, in opposition to that of water.

After which, the next day, we pursued our journey towards Lake Champlain, where we arrived on the Second Day. We were in and about the neighborhood of the lake in different towns for about fifteen days and attended eleven meetings among Friends and others, to general satisfaction and the peace of my mind.

After which, we returned to Danby and from thence we passed on through Queensbury to Saratoga and Easton, in and about which place we had divers, comfortable, and edifying meetings among Friends and others, and then, passing on through Pittstown, Williamstown, East Hoosac, New Britain, Klinakill, and Coeyman's Patent, crossing Hudson River on the ice to the last mentioned place, and from thence to Hudson – most of the way on the river, on the ice. We had a meeting at each of those places to good satisfaction, as also one at Hudson the next day after our arrival there.

---

[1] Indifferent: not good or having no particular value
[2] Baptism: a spiritual trial

After which, we passed on, taking meetings at the Little Nine Partners and one at the house of our Friend, Tideman Hull, thence to the Creek, where we had a precious opportunity on the First Day of the week in a large meeting of Friends and others. And then taking meetings at Crum Elbow and Oswego, we got timely to Nine Partners to attend their preparative meeting the Fifth Day following, which proved a comfortable season, and the next day, attended a profitable meeting appointed at a place called Chestnut Ridge.

The two following days, we attended two meetings – one at the Branch and the other on the hill at Oblong (and the following day, their monthly meeting) – and returned to Nine Partners timely to attend the quarterly meeting, which began the next day.

The quiet and comfort of this meeting seemed much retarded by the forwardness[1] and inexperience of some in the ministry, which was cause of much affliction to my mind.

O what great need there is for those who apprehend themselves called to that great and solemn office to know self wholly reduced! For otherwise, there is danger of their endeavoring to clothe themselves with the Lord's jewels, which nevertheless will turn to their own shame and confusion. I had some close exercise in the Meeting of Ministers and Elders on that account.

On Sixth Day, we attended the monthly meeting at the Creek, which was attended with a degree of divine power, but not without suffering some hurt by the forward, unskillful workmen before mentioned.

After this meeting, we passed the River Hudson again and took meetings at Little Esopus, Marlborough, and Newburgh Valley,[2] and then returned to Nine Partners and attended their monthly meeting.

After which, taking leave of Friends there, we turned our faces homewards – taking meetings at Poughquaig, Amawalk, and one at Joseph Weeks' near Salem, at Purchase, Mamaroneck, and Westchester – all favored seasons, especially the last which was mostly composed of those not in membership with Friends. I was enabled, through divine aid, to open much doctrine to them – suitable to the occasion and to the states of those present – to their general satisfaction, and felt great peace in my labor, not only for the service of this meeting, but for all my past labor in this journey, wherein I had been graciously favored to my humbling admiration. To the Lord Only-wise be all the glory.

The next day, we rode to New York, where I lodged with my kind companion and was very cordially received by his beloved wife and many other near and dear Friends. We had been from the city four months and

---

[1] Forwardness: presumptuousness
[2] I cannot identify this place name. Most likely, Hicks meant Pleasant Valley

three days, and the next day being the first of the week, I attended their fore and after noon meetings, which were large, and the day following rode to my own home and (with a mind full of peace and solid satisfaction – the sure reward of obedience) found my dear wife and children all well. And with open, cordial, and sympathetic affection, embraced each other in endeared and mutual love. For which favor, as also for the manifold, unmerited mercies and preservations I have from time to time received, my spirit bows in humble adoration before thee, O Lord God of our health and salvation, and desires to ascribe unto thee greatness with glory, thanksgiving, and high renown, for thou art worthy to receive it throughout all ages and generations, world without end. Amen.

I was from home on this journey four months and eleven days, rode by computation fifteen hundred and eleven miles and attended forty-nine particular meetings among Friends, three quarterly meetings, six monthly meetings, and forty meetings among other people.

A Visit to the Subordinate Meetings of Ministers and Elders of the New York Yearly Meeting in 1792

The latter end of the 7th month 1792, I left home in company with some other Friends by appointment from the Yearly Meeting of Ministers and Elders to visit the subordinate meetings through the yearly meeting. I was from home near a month, in which time we visited most of the meetings of ministers and elders and attended many other meetings. And I believe the visit was truly useful as we had many seasonable and comfortable opportunities among Friends, and I trust the labor was blessed to some, and I felt peace of mind for this little tour of duty, and on my return found my dear wife and family well.

A Visit to Friends in New England & Vermont in 1793

A concern having for some time rested on my mind in the feelings of gospel love to pay a religious visit to Friends in New England, in the spring of 1793, I opened it to my Friends and obtained their certificate for that purpose – but did not proceed therein till after our yearly meeting.

Connecticut

I left home the 2nd of 6th month, being the first of the week, after attending our own meeting, and crossed the Sound that afternoon, and got to the house of our Friends, Daniel and Samuel Titus, at Horse Neck that evening. Here, I met my companion James Mott from Mamaroneck, who had kindly given up to be my companion in this journey.

Newport (Rhode Island) Meetinghouse

Rhode Island

We set forward next morning through the state of Connecticut, which took near three days, and arrived on Fourth Day at evening at the house of our Friend, Amos Collins, in Stonington. And the next day, we attended Friends meeting at Hopkinton in the state of Rhode Island. From thence, we proceeded on towards Newport – taking meetings in our way at Westerly, Richmond, South Kingston (upper and lower house), and Conanicut Island (all satisfactory opportunities). After which, we crossed the ferry to Newport and lodged with our kind and very hospitable Friend, the widow Mary Rodman, who, with her two very worthy daughters, Sarah and Hannah, treated us with great kindness and affection – and where we continued to lodge during our stay in that town.

The Meeting of Ministers and Elders opened the next day at Portsmouth, after which we lodged that night at our Friend, Jacob Mott's, and the next day, attended a meeting for worship[1] at that place, which was very large, and although things appeared very low as to the life and virtue of Truth (both among Friends and others) and lukewarmness[2] and indifferency seemed to prevail (which made it a laborous time for the

---

[1] Meeting for Worship (also, "meeting of worship"): A gathering for worship in the manner of Friends. At this time, all Friends meetings were unprogrammed. The congregation gathered at the designated time in silence. If one or more members felt called by God to offer ministry, he or she would do so. There were normally three meetings for worship in a week, two on Sunday – a forenoon meeting in the morning and an afternoon meeting in the late afternoon or early evening – and a midweek meeting usually on Wednesday or Thursday evening.
[2] Revelation 3:16

Conanicut Meetinghouse, Jamestown, Rhode Island

honest travelers), yet ability was afforded to discharge myself among them to a good degree of satisfaction and peace to my own mind. We returned that evening to Newport to the house of our kind Friend, Mary Rodman.

The yearly meeting closed on the Third Day following and although strength was afforded to discharge myself in the several sittings thereof – both for worship and discipline – in a manner productive of that true peace, which is the sure reward of a faithful discharge of duty. Yet it was but a dull time in the general and the Spring of Life seemed very low, occasioned in part, as I apprehended, by a very small number taking upon them the whole management of the business, and thereby shutting up the way to others and prevented the free circulation and spreading of the concern in a proper manner on the minds of Friends which, I have oft found to be of very hurtful tendency.

On Fourth Day morning, we left Newport and rode to Portsmouth and attended their preparative meeting. The meeting for worship was a laborous season in the forepart, in which it was my lot to be baptized[1] for the dead.[2] But as I patiently abode under suffering with the pure seed, the Lord was pleased to arise and give ability to come forth and sound an alarm to the dead, whereby his power and presence were experienced in good measure to cover the meeting – to the comfort and encouragement of

---

[1] Baptize: severely tested or tried
[2] 1 Corinthians 15:29

the living travelers. To the Lord alone be the praise, who is worthy forever.

The next day, we passed the ferry and rode to Tiverton on the main, and attended a meeting by appointment, which was chiefly made up of people not of our society. And through the prevalence of divine love after a season of close labor, strength was afforded largely to open the truths of the gospel in a clear manner – greatly to my own satisfaction and apparently so to most or all present, for which, my spirit was truly thankful.

The next day, we attended a meeting at Little Compton, which was large and mostly composed of people of other persuasions. It was a comfortable, edifying season – the Lord being graciously pleased to be near and afford wisdom and utterance – many things being opened in a doctrinal way suitable to the states of those present, in the clear demonstration of the Spirit and of power, in a sense whereof, the living were made to rejoice and return thankful acknowledgments for the vouchsafement of such unmerited mercy.

Massachusetts

The next day, we attended the monthly meeting of Friends at Westport for Acoaxet. The meeting for worship was large, being (like the former) mostly made up by people of other persuasions, wherein ability was afforded largely to open the nature of true worship and to show the fruitlessness of mere bodily exercise in our religious performances without the animating, quickening[1] virtue of the Word of Eternal Life influencing and assisting the soul in that solemn act. The meeting of discipline was small and very few of those present appeared to be under any right qualification be active in the affairs of the Church. Consequently, their business was conducted in great weakness, and in a way far short of maintaining the proper dignity of a monthly meeting, and no way seemed to open to afford relief as the disorder and weakness appeared to be much in those who assumed the place of leaders and heads in the meeting. And there was great and uncommon rawness in most of the youth, under the consideration whereof, my mind was deeply affected with concern for their own and the testimony's sake.

Our next appointment was at Centre on First Day and, previous notice being given of our coming, the meeting was very large – supposed to be near two hundred more than the house could hold. It was a precious, edifying season. After which, taking some refreshment in our way thither, we rode to Newtown and attended a meeting at the 4th hour after noon,

---

[1] Quicken: to give or restore life

which proved a large, satisfactory meeting and I felt sweet peace in this day's labor.

The next day, we attended the monthly meeting of Apponagansett (alias Dartmouth), which proved a hard, laborous season – things being much out of order with Friends there. And the young people mostly – and some of those that were older – were very raw and ungoverned, insomuch that the meeting was much interrupted by an almost continual running in and out (although frequently reproved for it) which made the prospect very afflicting – to see the professors of Truth so regardless of their own reputation and real good, as well as of the good and reputation of society. I left this place with a degree of sadness, on account of the prevailing darkness and ignorance, yet felt peace to attend my mind, having faithfully discharged myself among them.

We rode after meeting to New Bedford in company with our beloved Friend, Thomas Rotch,* who met us at this place, and lodged at his house, where we found a cordial reception and kind entertainment from him and his beloved wife, who appeared to be a loving pair of hopeful young Friends.

The next day, we attended their monthly meeting, which proved a very comfortable, edifying season. This monthly meeting was but newly settled and Friends appeared desirous of improvement – there being a number of hopeful young Friends in this place to whom my spirit was nearly united and a sympathetic travail experienced for their growth and preservation. My mind was covered with much sweetness in the course of this meeting and it proved a time of revival to my spirit – having experienced much depression and discouragement in the two foregoing monthly meetings.

The next day, we rode to Long Plain, and attended a meeting at the 11th hour, which proved through heavenly help a comfortable, edifying season. After which, we rode back to Acushnet, and attended a meeting at the 4th hour that afternoon, in which I found it my business to example the people to silence.[1] We returned that evening to our lodgings at New Bedford.

The next day, we embarked for Nantucket and arrived there before night, having sailed about sixty miles in our way thither. We took our lodgings at the house of our kind Friend, Samuel Rodman.* We stayed on island several days, in which time we attended their monthly meeting and Meeting of Ministers and Elders belonging thereto, and two meetings on the First Day of the week, after which on Second and Third Day was held

---

[1] Example the people to silence: remain silent in meeting for worship

their quarterly meeting, and on Fourth Day was at their middle week meeting in the north meetinghouse.

And although things in general were much out of order with many of the professors of Truth in this island, insomuch that the pure seed of the kingdom was much oppressed and gloominess seemed to spread over the camp, yet the Lord Almighty, in the riches of his love, was pleased to furnish ability to sound an alarm[1] to the dead and to press upon the lukewarm and careless professors the necessity of using all diligence to make their calling and election sure, while time and opportunity were yet graciously afforded – as also to administer of Gilead's Balm,[2] for the binding up the brokenhearted[3] and to encourage the faithful laborers in the family to a perseverance in faith and patience – to a remnant of whom my spirit was nearly united in the real bond of Christian fellowship. And our hearts were filled with gratitude to the God and Father of all our sure mercies, in that he was graciously pleased to distill the heavenly dew[4] to the refreshing the weary travelers and crowning[5] the several meetings with the glorious diadem[6] of his holy presence. To him alone be the praise, for he is worthy forever.

On Fifth Day, 4th of 7th month, we left the island and crossed over to Falmouth – about forty miles by water. After landing, we traveled about four miles to the house of our Friend, Richard Lake, and lodged, and the next day, attended their monthly meeting, which proved a time of deep exercise to my spirit – occasioned, as I believed, by the dead and lifeless state of the professors of Truth in that meeting. I sat through the meeting of worship in silence, under a great weight of death and sufferings and saw no way of relief until near the close of the meeting of discipline, when a prospect opened in my mind, with a degree of light to propose to Friends an opportunity of the men and women sitting together again at the close of their business – which was agreed to by Friends – and wherein, way was made to clear my mind in a good degree amongst them of the burden I had sat under, in a close searching communication of my prospects respecting their state as it opened in the view of my mind, which appeared to have considerable effect on the minds of some, although some others appeared too much in that state – of all others the most to be dreaded – of self-justification and of being righteous in their own eyes, which rendered them incapable of improvement.

---

[1] Joel 2:1
[2] Jeremiah 8:22 & 46:11
[3] Isaiah 61:1
[4] Deuteronomy 32:2
[5] Crowning: concluding
[6] Diadem: crown or symbol of honor

Sandwich Meetinghouse in East Sandwich, Massachusetts

I left that place the day following with some weight on my spirit, under a sense of the low state of things among them, and rode to Yarmouth and attended a meeting there the next day, which proved a satisfactory season.

And the three following days, we passed on through Sandwich, Pembroke, and Boston to Salem – taking meetings at Sandwich and Pembroke, both I trust profitable, edifying seasons to some present.

We got to Salem on Fifth Day, 11th of 7th month, just timely to attend their monthly meeting – having rode hard the morning and afternoon before to accomplish it. We had a pretty satisfactory time with Friends at this meeting, after which we rode back to Lynn and the next day, attended an appointed meeting there, which proved a large, favored and I trust, profitable meeting to many – not soon to be forgotten.

There being a considerable number of hopeful young people in this place, we had, in the afternoon, a precious opportunity at a Friend's house where there were a number of young people and others collected. It was a heart tendering season, for which, with other favors conferred from time to time, my heart was made truly thankful to the Father of mercies and God of all comfort,[1] who is over all, blessed forever,

---

[1] 2 Corinthians 1:3

We proceeded the next day to Amesbury and lodged with our Friend, Ezekiel Jones, and the next morning rode back to Newbury and attended Friends meeting at the 11th hour. And although small (Friends being much reduced in that place) yet some of the townspeople coming in, we had a precious opportunity together, to our mutual comfort – the way of life and salvation being clearly opened to them in the demonstration of the Spirit and with power, for which my spirit was reverently thankful. We rode back and attended a meeting at Amesbury that afternoon at the 4th hour. A large number of the townspeople (not members of our society) assembled with the few Friends of that place, insomuch that the house could not contain them. It proved a laborous season by reason of the prevailing death and darkness that seemed to spread – not only over Friends, but the assembly in general – which reduced my spirit into a state of deep suffering and baptism. But as I patiently endured the conflict, way was made and ability afforded to open to them their states and conditions, with the necessity of being redeemed therefrom, and the way whereby it must be effected. The people were generally solid and I trust it was a profitable season to many minds present. We returned that evening to the house of our Friend, Ezekiel Jones.

New Hampshire

The next day proceeded to Newton, where we had a meeting, which proved, I trust, an instructive, edifying season to some present, although the life of religion appeared very low in that place. We lodged here and, the day following, we went to Halestown (alias Weare) and took our lodging at the house of our Friend, Ebenezer Breed.

Their monthly meeting came on the next day, which we attended. Things in general appeared in a low state with Friends here – much of which weakness I apprehended arose from these two causes: the first of which was a froward[1] spirit that appeared very predominant in some members who were not under a right qualification to be active in meetings of discipline – not having their spirits sanctified and therefore, by their unseasoned offering and froward activity, were a great burden to the living concerned members – being often opposed to the right exercise of discipline, which caused divisions and parties in the meeting. And secondly, those Friends who seemed to have the cause of Truth at heart, for want of dwelling enough in the root and in that perfect love that casts out all fear, were led from an apprehension of necessity (in order to keep down those froward spirits) to make use of some undue methods in the exercise of discipline which, originating in fear and being the result of human contrivance, instead of subjecting had a tendency to strengthen

---

[1] Froward: perverse, difficult, hard to please

them in their opposition – as nothing can promote the Lord's work but his own peaceable Spirit and Wisdom, and which stands out of all human consultation and contrivance which, when given way to (although never so well intended) always mars his work. I was much exercised, both in the meeting for worship and that for discipline, and was helped to administer much counsel and advice for Friends' improvement in general and (in particular) that those before-cited difficulties might be removed. And [I] felt much peace in my labor.

The next day being the fifth of the week and 19th of 7th month, we rode to Epping, about forty-two miles, and lodged with our Friend, Joshua Fulsome, an approved minister, and attended Friends meeting there the following day, in the forepart of which, my mind was reduced into such a state of great weakness and depression that my faith was almost ready to fail, which produced great searchings of heart, wherein I was led to call in question all that I had ever before experienced. And in this state of doubting, I was ready to wish myself at home from an apprehension that I should only expose myself to reproach and wound the cause I was embarked in – for the heavens seemed like brass and the earth as iron.[1] Such coldness and hardness I thought could scarcely have ever been experienced before by any creature – such was the depth of my baptism at this time. Nevertheless, as I endeavored to quiet my mind in this conflicting dispensation and resign to my allotment, however distressing.

Towards the latter part of the meeting a ray of light broke through the surrounding darkness, in which the Shepherd of Israel was pleased to arise and by the light of his glorious countenance to scatter those clouds of opposition. And therein, ability was received and utterance given to speak of his marvelous works in the redemption of souls and to open the way of life and salvation and the mysteries of his glorious kingdom that are hid from the wise and prudent of this world and revealed only unto those who are reduced into the state of little children and babes in Christ.[2] It proved a time of renewed strengthening and consolation to myself and I trust so to many present. Renowned forever be the name of the Lord, who hath his way in the cloud and in the thick darkness[3] and who can cause the light to shine out of darkness[4] when he pleaseth, for the comfort and help of his devoted children, and cause their darkness to become as the noonday.[5]

---

[1] Deuteronomy 28:23
[2] Matthew 11:25 & Luke 10:21
[3] Deuteronomy 5:22
[4] 2 Corinthians 4:6
[5] Isaiah 58:10

Maine

We passed on from thence through Dover to Berwick, where the Monthly Meeting for Dover was held the next day. It proved a very exercising season, great weakness attending the meeting by reason of the same rending, dividing spirit getting in among Friends here as mentioned at the foregoing monthly meeting at Weare, which appeared to make great havoc among them, insomuch that a great number of members had been separated[1] and still were separating by denials from the monthly meeting. I had some close labor with them, not only by endeavors to stir up and warn the careless and refractory members, but also found it necessary to caution and warn those that had the chief management of discipline – believing they had too much departed from the meek Spirit of Jesus in ordering the affairs of Truth and, instead of giving the right portion of meat in due season to their fellow servants,[2] they had given way to a spirit of impatience and therefore, did not stand wholly clear of beating and abusing their fellow servants.

O how necessary it is for all those who think themselves called to be active in the discipline of the Church to know their own spirits fully subjected! That nothing of the unmortified will of the creature be found acting in the work of the Lord or mixing its own froward, unsanctified zeal with that true and holy fervor of soul that animates, quickens, and constrains[3] by the mere force and influence of the pure love of Christ, our holy head and heavenly high priest, and from whence it derives all its power and authority in putting right discipline in practice and laying true judgment on the head of transgressors and refractory members.

We tarried here the next day, it being the first of the week. The meeting was pretty large – of Friends and others – and favored with the reachings forth of heavenly regard to the consoling many hearts and refreshing the weary travelers, of which there appeared to be a small remnant preserved in almost every place. The meeting ended with humble supplication and praise to the Great Author of every blessing, who is over all, worthy forever.

The next day being the second of the week and 22nd of 7th month, we proceeded on towards Falmouth at Casco Bay, taking a meeting at Portland in our way thither.

On Fourth Day, we attended the monthly meeting of Falmouth and, on Sixth Day, the monthly meeting of Durham. They were, in the general, satisfactory seasons.

---

[1] Separate: disown
[2] Luke 12:42
[3] Constrain: compel

And the next day, we rode to Georgetown and attended a meeting appointed there at the 11th hour, after which, we proceeded on to the Widow Gardner's in a town called Bowdoinham – in getting to which place, we had to cross the great River Kennebec twice.

The next day being the first of the week and 28th of 7th month, there was a large meeting there – held by our appointment, there being no meeting in that place. It was a time of hard labor for a season, by reason of the indifference and ignorance of many present. Nevertheless, ability was afforded to discharge myself among them to pretty good satisfaction and, I believe, generally so to those present. And I trust with some, the season will not soon be forgotten.

We went by boat that afternoon up the aforesaid river about seven miles to the house of our Friend, George Ramsdale – having sent our horses there the night before – and the next day, we passed on to Vassalboro, and the day following, rode up the river to Fairfield and attended a meeting, and returned to Vassalboro that afternoon.

The next day, attended Friends meeting there, which proved a heavy, dull season till near the close, when ability was afforded me to clear myself among them in a close, searching communication that appeared to have a good effect and the meeting ended well.

We passed on that afternoon to Winthrop (twenty miles) and the next day, had a meeting there, after which we rode to Greene and from thence to Lewiston, taking a meeting at each place – both precious heart-tendering seasons, especially the latter, which was attended by a large number of young people, many of whom were greatly affected with the testimony of Truth, and we left them in a tender, loving frame of mind and rode that afternoon to Durham.

The next day being the first of the week and 4th of 8th month, we attended Friends meeting there, in which Truth favored to open many things in a doctrinal way – there being many present who were not in membership with Friends. I was likewise led to speak largely of the good effect of pure love.

We passed on from thence through Falmouth to Portland, where we had a meeting appointed for the townspeople. It was held in their courthouse and was, through heavenly help, an instructive season – many doctrines of the gospel being clearly opened and the absurd doctrines of original sin, predestination, as also the schemes of the universalists, atheists, and deists confuted from scripture and reason – accompanied with a pressing exhortation to all present, so to attend to the leadings[1] of the Spirit of Christ in their own hearts as to be sensible of their fallen

---

[1] Leading: a prompting from God – also, a "motion"

Weare Meetinghouse in Henniker, New Hampshire

conditions, and to so become acquainted with the necessity, means, and manner of their salvation. Truth was over all and I had great peace in my labor. We returned that evening to Falmouth, and the next day went to Windham and attended a meeting, wherein I was led to be an example of silence.

Back to New Hampshire

After which, we rode to the house of our Friend, John Robinson, and lodged, and a prospect opening towards paying another visit to Friends at Weare, we accordingly proceeded, taking meetings in our way at Gorham, Limington, North Sandwich [New Hampshire], and Gilmanton – all satisfactory seasons – and got timely Weare to attend their monthly meeting. And although the same dividing spirit was still discoverable among them, which produced much weakness, yet we had pretty good satisfaction in our visit.

We proceeded from thence through Pittsfield and Lee in our way to Dover, taking a meeting at each place, and got to Dover timely to attend their monthly meeting, held on Seventh Day, 17th of 8th month. And although discipline is at a low ebb with Friends here, yet, through divine condescension,[1] I hope the season was profitable and instructive to many present.

We tarried here their First Day Meeting in the forenoon and in the afternoon, had a satisfactory meeting at Kittery [Maine].

On Second Day, we attended meetings at Madbury and Rochester – both, I trust, profitable seasons.

On Third Day, we rode to Hampton and the next day, had a comfortable meeting with Friends of that place.

Back in Massachusetts

From thence, we returned to Salem and attended a meeting. From thence, we proceeded to Lynn, where we stayed over First Day and attended their fore and after noon meetings.

On Second Day, we rode to Boston and attended a meeting at the 11th hour. And although the meeting was but small – there being but very few Friends in that place and but a small number of the townspeople came in (and those mostly behaved very raw and strange) – yet we had pretty good satisfaction in giving them an opportunity, and way opened to clear ourselves among them. After which, we passed on, taking a meeting at Taunton, and so to the monthly meeting at Smithfield [Rhode Island] – held for Providence.

Things appeared but low with Friends of this monthly meeting by reason of their attention being too much turned to worldly concerns. We next attended the monthly meeting in the upper part of Smithfield (for Smithfield), being about nine miles from the latter. This was in the general a satisfactory season, and the following day, we attended the monthly meeting of Uxbridge, to good satisfaction.

Our next appointment was at Freetown, the first of the week and 1st of 9th month – a seasonable opportunity.

On Second Day, attended the monthly meeting at Swansea. Here, things appeared much out of order and in a low state, but through divine favor, I was abilitated to clear my mind among them in a way that I hope will tend to their profit.

Back to Rhode Island

From hence, we passed on to Providence, where we had a satisfactory meeting, and the four following days, we had meetings at Cranston, East Greenwich, Foster, and Scituate – all satisfactory meetings, particularly the last was an open, edifying season – many hearts being comforted through the favor of Truth, which prevailed over all, and was cause of deep thankfulness to my mind.

---

[1] Condescension: graciousness and consideration

Our next meeting was at Wankeg, on First Day and 8th of 9th month. It was a profitable, edifying season.

Thence passing on, we took meetings as they were laid out for us – on Second Day at Glocester, on Third Day at Douglas [Massachusetts], and Smithfield on Fourth Day. The latter was a large meeting and many things were opened in a clear manner – confuting that dark principle of election and reprobation, and the impossibility of falling from grace, and showing the necessity of regeneration through the operation of the one essential baptism of the Holy Ghost, and that all were the objects of universal and saving grace, and how all might be saved by it, if they did not reject it to their own destruction.

Through Massachusetts to New Hampshire & Vermont

The next day, we attended a meeting at South Mendon. It was a comfortable season to myself and, I believe, to most or all present and was cause of thankful remembrance.

From thence, we passed on taking meetings at Northbridge, Bolton, and Leicester, at which place we also attended a burial and had a favored opportunity with the people. From thence, we went to Richmond [New Hampshire] and attended their monthly meeting. Things were much out of order here and the meeting, being small, was in a weak situation. I cleared my mind in a plain way among them and found peace therein.

This was the last meeting we attended in the compass of the Yearly Meeting of Friends in New England. From thence, we passed on into the state of Vermont in order to visit Friends of our own yearly meeting who were resident in that state. We got to Sharon seasonably to attend their meeting on First Day, being the 22nd of 9th month, and the next day attended a meeting at Strafford. This was a dull, heavy time wherein I was led to example the people to silence.

The next day, we crossed Connecticut River into the town of Hanover and attended a meeting in a schoolhouse – no Friends living in those parts. It was a satisfactory season. We lodged with a friendly man by the name of John Williams who, with his wife, was convinced of the principles of Truth, yet found it a great trial, faithfully to take up the cross, as they lived among a people much opposed to them in that respect.

We left them the next day in a tender frame of mind and I have a hope they will make an improvement. We returned over the river and attended a meeting in the town of Norwich at the 4th hour after noon – a small, but favored, meeting. We lodged that night with friendly requester by the name of Zebulon Huntington.

The next morning, we returned to Sharon and attended a meeting at the 11th hour – it being their usual meeting day. It was a favored season.

The next day, we attended a meeting in the northeast part of the town of Strafford among those not of our society, after which we set forward for Lake Champlain. We got to Ferrisburg just timely to attend their meeting on First Day, 29th of the 9th month (which I sat in silence), and returned after meeting to the house of our Friend, Nicholas Holmes, and lodged.

The next day, we rode to our Friend, Cornelius Halbert's, and attended a meeting at the 4th hour. It proved a comfortable season – mostly composed of those not in membership with us.

From thence we proceeded to the Grand Isle, which is situated nearly in the middle of Lake Champlain, taking a meeting at Williston in our way thither. We had a comfortable meeting at our lodgings at this place, and then crossed over by water to the west side of the lake, to the River Au Sable and walked on foot about six miles up said river to the house of our Friend, Richard Keese, where we had a satisfactory opportunity in a meeting appointed in his house. It was a new-settled place and no meeting of Friends within forty miles.

We returned then to the Grand Isle, and the next day being the first of the week and 6th of 10th month, we attended another meeting there and the next day, returned to Monkton, to the house of our kind Friend, Nicholas Holmes, who had accompanied us in this little tour to the northward.

We rested the next day, and the day following had an appointed meeting at the house of my kinsman, Stephen Haight.*

On Fifth Day, we had a comfortable opportunity with Friends here at their preparative meeting, after which, we took leave of our Friends of this place and rode to Vergennes and lodged with our Friend, Thomas Robinson.*

New York

And the next day, proceeded on our way to Queensbury, where we arrived on Seventh Day evening.

The next day, the first of the week and 13th of 10th month, we attended two meetings – the first, at Friends Meetinghouse at the usual time and the latter at a Friend's house, where a considerable number of people that were not in profession with us assembled and behaved disorderly.

On Second Day, we rode to Easton and lodged with our Friend, William Coffin.

On Third Day, it being rainy weather, we rested.

On Fourth Day, we attended the Preparative Meeting of Ministers and Elders for Friends of Easton Monthly Meeting.

On Fifth Day, began their monthly meeting – which held three days – and in the general, conducted to good satisfaction.

I felt a near sympathy with Friends of this place, for as their monthly meeting was bordering on an extensive new-settling country, into which Friends were moving from various parts, that made the bounds of their meeting very wide and the members much scattered wide from one another. It caused much labor and exercise to the concerned part of the meeting in looking after and conducting the affairs of Truth and which likewise occasioned them to have almost continually a great load of business before the monthly meeting.

The day after the monthly meeting, being the first of the week, we attended a meeting at Saratoga. It was a large, comfortable, edifying meeting and very refreshing to my spirit, which had been much exhausted by the exercise and labor of the three foregoing days.

In the course of this week, we attended meetings at Greenfield, Ballston, Troy, Albany, and Coeyman's Patent and got into Hudson on Seventh Day evening.

The next day being the first of the week and 27th of 10th month, we tarried their morning meeting and then proceeded on, being desirous of reaching the quarterly meeting at Oblong that began on Third Day. We arrived there on Second Day evening, where we met with several beloved Friends from near our own homes to our mutual comfort.

After the close of this meeting, we proceeded directly home, where I arrived the 2nd of 11th month and found my dear wife and family in a pretty good state of health to our mutual rejoicing, and had renewed cause to bless the name of the Lord for his preserving providence and mercy, who is over all, worthy forever.

I was from home in this journey about five months, and traveled by land and water about two thousand, two hundred and eighty-three miles, having visited all the meetings of Friends in the New England states and many meetings among those of other professions, as also visited many meetings among Friends and others in the upper part of our own yearly meeting and found real peace in my labors.

A Visit to the Subordinate Meetings of Ministers and Elders of the New York Yearly Meeting in 1795

Left home the 26th of 7th month 1795 in order to join a committee of Friends appointed by the Yearly Meeting of Ministers and Elders this year to visit the quarterly and preparative meetings and Friends at large in those stations throughout the yearly meeting. From a concern that arose in that meeting occasioned by the many obvious deficiencies and departures amongst us as a people from the purity and simplicity of our holy profession, a minute[1] having been formed in said meeting and recommended to the inferior meetings, importing[2] the ground of this concern and for the purpose of stirring up and encouraging Friends to a diligent search and labor in order that the many weaknesses and hurtful disorders might be removed and a right reformation from the many prevailing weaknesses effectually take place.

This being the First Day of the week, I sat with Friends in their meeting at Westbury, and although it was a laborous time in the forepart, yet through the comforting assistance of heavenly help, it was made, I believe, an edifying season to many minds. I crossed the Sound that afternoon to New Rochelle, and the next morning met some of the committee at the house of our Friend, Hugh Judge. We had an opportunity with his family, which proved a refreshing season – it being evident that he and his wife joined heartily with the concern. We visited several other families that day and had the satisfaction to believe that the concern and labor were owned by the Head of the Church and, we believe, will be blessed to many.

The next day began the quarterly meeting at Purchase, which through the several sittings was made, I trust, a profitable season. It ended on Fifth Day.

The next day, we took opportunities with two families hereaway, which through the fresh extendings of holy help proved very instructive and encouraging. After which, we set out for Nine Partners – their quarterly meeting coming on the ensuing week.

I got thither on First Day morning, the 2nd of 8th month, and attended their meeting, which proved a heart-searching season – it being too manifest that many professors had suffered[3] their minds to be captivated by a worldly spirit, which had introduced great death and darkness into our meetings to the grief and trouble of the honest in heart. But help was graciously afforded to set forth in a plain manner the danger attending such a departure from the life and power of religion and for the stirring up the lukewarm from their supineness and ease, and the necessity of a more full dedication of their hearts and their all to the Lord's service.

The next day, we attended the Preparative Meeting of Ministers and Elders at the Creek, in which much weakness was apparent.

The three following days, we attended the quarterly meeting at Nine Partners – in the latter of which I was favored to ease my mind among them in a season of close searching labor by way of communication.

---

[1] Minute: A formal decision made by a business meeting. These were written during the business meeting in a bound, handwritten minute book.
[2] Import: communicate
[3] Suffer: allow

After which, the next day, we proceeded towards Easton in order to attend the quarterly meeting there and to visit the families of ministers and elders in the compass thereof, which we performed in about a week. And although weakness seemed to abound with Friends there, yet we were comforted in believing that the visit had some profitable effect and afforded encouragement and a renewal of strength to the sincere-hearted.

On Seventh Day, 15th of 8th month, we rode to East Hoosac [Massachusetts] and the next day attended Friends meeting there, which was large – many people of other societies attending. It proved an open, satisfactory time and ended under a renewed sense of the merciful extendings of holy condescending love, for which I trust many minds were made humbly thankful. The afternoon and next morning were spent in visiting the families of ministers and elders, and although things were not all well among them, yet we had satisfaction and peace in our own minds in a faithful discharge of the trust committed to us

The next day, we rode to New Britain and visited a Ministering Friend there – he being the only select[1] member in that meeting. From thence we passed on to Klinakill, where there was likewise but one member of the select meeting[2] – an Elder whom we visited – and then passed on to Coeyman's Patent, crossing the River Hudson in our way thither. Here were three select members to whom we paid a satisfactory visit and then proceeded on to the city of Hudson (crossing the aforesaid river again in the way).

The evening after our arrival and the next day, we took opportunities with the ministers and elders of that place. They proved seasons of heart-searching labor, things appearing much out of order with some of them. And among these, there was not wanting an apparent disposition to lay waste good order in the church.

O the great want of honest, faithful laborers in the vineyard![3]

After our services were finished here, we left them with the answer of peace[4] and rode that afternoon to Nine Partners, and the next day, attended Friends meeting at Stanford. It proved a season of hard labor by reason of the great want of solid weight and a living travail. In order to experience the renewals of strength, the testimony of Truth went forth freely for the stirring up and arousing the careless and supine from their

---

[1] Select: when applied to an individual, a minister or elder
[2] Select Meeting: A meeting that is not open to all. Most often, this term is used to refer to Meetings of Ministers and Elders, but it could also be used to describe a business meeting, since these were not open to non-members, or to a meeting for worship that was specially called for members only.
[3] Matthew 20:1-16 combined with Matthew 9:37
[4] Genesis 41:16

beds of ease,[1] after which, we visited two families of Friends and the two following days, finished our visit to the rest of the families of ministers and elders in the Creek Monthly Meeting.

And the rest of the week was taken up in visiting those under the notice of our appointment in the Monthly Meeting of Nine Partners. And I may truly say, it was, in the general, a sorrowful, affecting time in beholding the great departure of many of the ministers and elders in their families from that faithful discharge of duty that their stations require – for want of which, their children had almost all gone out of plainness.[2] We endeavored to lay before them, in sincerity and simplicity of heart, the great danger attending such a conduct and the necessity of a reform in those things and felt peace of mind in our labor.

On Seventh Day afternoon, we rode to Marlborough and attended Friends meeting there the next day. It was an exercising season by reason of the great rawness and inexperience of the members of the meeting too generally and the great lightness manifest in most of those of other societies – a number of whom were present. My mind, after a time of hard labor and suffering with the seed, opened to some service addressed to the latter class. After which, the way opened to have Friends selected, to whom my mind was led to communicate some things in a plain way in order for the stirring up to more diligence and circumspection in their families – to the better ordering and disciplining their children and households, for keeping things sweet and clean, agreeable to the simplicity of our holy profession, and had peace in my labor.

That afternoon and the two following days, we visited all the families of ministers and elders in that monthly meeting, except one. After which, I returned home, and found my family as well as usual – which I esteemed as a favor from my great and good Master and for which, with all his other mercies and preservations dispensed from time to time, I felt a return of thankfulness and grateful acknowledgment to him who is the Author and Giver of every good and perfect gift and who is over all, God blessed forever.

---

[1] Beds of ease: a phrase Hicks uses often in describing complacent and self-indulgent people such as those condemned in Amos 6:1&4:
Woe to them *that are* at ease in Zion, and trust in the mountain of Samaria, *which are* named chief of the nations, to whom the house of Israel came! ... That lie upon beds of ivory, and stretch themselves upon their couches.

[2] Plainness: the traditional Quaker set of clothes, also called plain clothes

1796-1800

A Visit to Friends in Pennsylvania, New Jersey, Delaware, Maryland, & Virginia in 1797 & 1798

Having for several years felt my mind drawn at times in gospel love to visit Friends of the Yearly Meeting of Pennsylvania and New Jersey, Delaware, and Maryland, with some of the hither parts of Virginia, and in the fall of the year 1797, apprehending the time drew nigh for the performance of said visit, I laid my concern before Friends and received certificates of their unity and concurrence from the monthly and quarterly meetings of which I was a member.

I left home the 12th of 12th month. Joseph Cooper, a member of our meeting in the station of Elder accompanied me in this journey. Taking leave of my family and friends in near sympathy and affection, we rode to New York and, our Meeting for Sufferings sitting there the next day, I attended. And the day following being the fourth of the week and, of course, the meeting day for Friends of the city, I felt most easy to stay the meeting, which proved a comfortable, strengthening season.

After which, I took leave of my Fiends there, parting from them in near unity and brotherly affection, and passed the next morning by water to Staten Island and the day following had two meetings there which, though small by reason of rain, were nevertheless both attended with a comfortable degree of divine favor.

New Jersey

The next day, we left the island and rode to Shrewsbury and the following day being the first of the week, we sat with Friends there and I trust it was a profitable season to some present and relieving to my own mind – strength and utterance being furnished to open divers truths of the gospel in the demonstration of the Spirit, accompanied with a good degree of the divine power. To God only wise be the praise, who is over all, worthy forever.

On Second Day, we attended a meeting at a Friend's house about seven miles on our way to Squan.

On Third and Fourth Days, we were at Squan and Squancome, both small meetings as there are but few of our society in those parts, yet they were in the main, satisfactory seasons. We also sat with Friends in their preparative meeting in the latter place, which appeared in a state of great weakness, but as way opened, I was led to make some remarks in order for the stirring Friends up to more diligence and circumspection, and the necessity of an inward travail for the arising of Truth, which can only qualify for the right ordering of the affairs of society.

The next day, we rode to Barnegat and, after an opportunity with Friends there, the following day, we passed on to Little Egg Harbor, where we tarried till First Day and 24th of the month. And notice being spread of our intention of attending Friends meeting there, many of the neighboring inhabitants came in and sat with Friends and were very attentive – divers truths of the gospel being opened in the clear demonstration of the Spirit, insomuch that I was helped to leave them with a peaceful mind.

25th: We rode to Great Egg Harbor and the three following days attended meetings at the upper and lower meetings of Friends there, as also an appointed meeting at or near the head of Great Egg Harbor River at a place called Stephen's Creek. They were generally small, yet attended with a good degree of openness and favor, for which my spirit was made humbly thankful.

On Sixth Day, 29th, we attended a meeting at Cape May, which through the gracious condescension of the Shepherd of Israel, was made a truly comfortable season, and the great name over all magnified and praised, who is worthy forever.

From thence, we rode to Maurice River and attended a meeting appointed at a friendly man's house by the name of Isaac Buzby. Truth favored with wisdom and utterance in dividing the word suitable to the states of those present – apparently to theirs and to my own satisfaction and comfort. We rode that afternoon to, and put up at, the house of a Friend by the name of Henry Rulon, where we had an appointed meeting the next day. After which, we passed on to Greenwich and the two following days, attended a meeting there and one at the head of Cohansey Creek, after which we rode to the house of our kind Friend, Mark Miller, at Salem and rested the next day.

And the day following, being the first of the week and 7th of 1st month, attended the meeting there, which was very large – many coming in that were not members – and the testimony of Truth was exalted over all, to the comfort of many hearts, and the praise and glory of his Grace,[1] who is the strength and helper of his dependent children.

Second Day, we attended a meeting at Woodstown (alias Pilesgrove). I was closely engaged among them in a searching testimony, pointing out the great danger and hurtful tendency of the want of unity, and a joining in with the spirit of the world, and neglecting a right conformity to the wholesome order established among us as a religious society – whereby many disorders had crept in, to the wounding of many. Strength was afforded and utterance given and Truth exalted over all opposition and disorderly spirits.

---

[1] Ephesians 1:6

FRIENDS' MEETING-HOUSE, HADDONFIELD

The four following days, we attended meetings at Penn's Neck, Mullica Hill, Upper Greenwich, and Woodbury. They were all seasons of favor, especially the last, where Truth was eminently exalted, and the doctrine of the gospel held forth in the demonstration of the Spirit, and the hearts of the faithful made to rejoice in a sense of the Lord's goodness – to whom belongs the praise of his own work forever.

On Seventh Day, we rested with our esteemed Friend, Joshua Evans.

First Day, attended Newton Meeting and the day following, that at Haddonfield – both of which were profitable, edifying meetings.

Pennsylvania

In the afternoon, after the latter, we crossed the River Delaware to Philadelphia and the three following days, attended the meetings in that city as they came in course. There being three meetings in this city, each consisting of a large number of Friends, they were all opportunities of favor, and I had much satisfaction in this short visit to Friends of this city – being comforted in the experience of an open door among them, both in meetings and in families where my lot was cast – and felt my spirit nearly united to a living remnant, especially a number of beloved youth, who are under the forming hand, preparing for service. Some of whom, I trust and believe, will be as valiants in their day for the promotion of the cause of

Truth and Righteousness in the earth. May the Lord bless and preserve them faithful to himself and cover their heads in the day of battle.[1]

On Sixth Day, 19th of 1st month, we left the city in order to attend a meeting at Darby. Notice having gone before of our intention, it proved an open time, but the meeting was hurt by an indiscrete appearance[2] towards the end, for which my spirit was clothed with sorrow – not only on the Friend's account, but especially on account of the people, for whose information and religious instruction my mind had been closely engaged. We rode that afternoon to Chester and lodged. The next day, we attended a meeting there, which was owned with manifestations of divine favor through the prevailing of Truth by way of testimony – being instructed to hand out doctrine suitable to the states of the people present.

Delaware

After which, we rode to Wilmington and the next day, being the first of the week and 21st of 1st month, we attended their fore and after noon meetings. I was silent in the first as to ministry, but through the merciful assistance of the Shepherd of Israel, the latter proved a comfortable, strengthening season. After a time of close exercise in silent labor and deep baptism into death and suffering with the seed, the testimony of Truth went forth with authority and as a holy flame against many things that opened to view as the cause of that deep oppression of the seed of life among them. The meeting ended under a sense of the Lord's goodness and many hearts were made to rejoice.

The six following days, we attended meetings at White Clay Creek, Appoquinimink, Duck Creek, Little Creek, Motherkiln, and Camden – the latter is a village where no meeting of Friends is held. Things appeared low in most of them as to the life of religion, yet through the condescending goodness of the Shepherd of Israel, I had an open door among them, and many gospel truths were held forth in the clear demonstration of the Spirit and with power. Especially the last was a time thankfully to be remembered by me and, I believe, by many others present. Thanks be to God for his unspeakable gift,[3] in that he is not leaving himself, nor his truly dependent children, without a witness in the hearts of the people.

The next day being the first of the week, we attended Milford Meeting. Things appeared very low, being but few of our society in that part, and those appeared very indifferent, and several of those few were absent.

---

[1] Psalm 140:7
[2] Indiscrete appearance: offer inappropriate vocal ministry
[3] 2 Corinthians 9:15

Second Day: We attended a meeting at Cool Spring and the next day attended an appointed meeting on our way towards Third Haven. It was held in a Friend's house, who had lately been received a member and who before was a professor with the people called Nicholites[1] – he appeared to be a pretty solid man. The meeting was in a good degree favored. The way of preparation (as held forth in John's dispensation) for the more full manifestation of the gospel state was set forth, with the nature of true Christian or spiritual baptism, and that John's baptism was only a figure[2] thereof and, therefore, was no part of Christ's baptism,[3] and consequently had no place in, nor could be of any use, under the dispensation of the gospel. There was a Baptist teacher present (and several of their members) but passed away without any opposition. And the people appeared generally satisfied and I parted with them in peace of mind.

Maryland

The six following days, we attended meetings at Northwest Fork, Marshy Creek, Centre, Greensboro, Tuckahoe Neck, and Tuckahoe. And although these meetings were small as to those who were joined in fellowship with us, yet they were mostly crowded-full meetings by the coming in of the neighboring inhabitants – divers of whom were holders of slaves and others very raw and ignorant. My spirit was much exercised in travail among them, being baptized into their low and uncultivated states. Nevertheless, through the merciful interference of the Shepherd of Israel, their lost and undone conditions without a Savior were clearly laid open before them, and the way of return, reconciliation, and salvation. Many present were aroused and reached to by the power of Truth that was graciously prevalent in most of these meetings, and their spirits greatly tendered, and the few faithful among them made to rejoice. And my spirit made humbly thankful in a sense of the Lord's goodness. To him alone be the praise – nothing due to man.

Three of the above meetings were held in meetinghouses belonging to a people under the denomination of Nicholites – being the followers of one Joseph Nichols. Many of them were led into great self-denial, particularly in regard to dress and household furniture. Indeed, their

---

[1] Nicholites: a sect founded in the 1760s by Joseph Nichols (ca. 1730-ca. 1775) in Delaware and Maryland. He appears to have been influenced to some extent by John Woolman. Many Nicholites affiliated with Friends in the early 19th century and the sect disappeared as an independent body.

[2] Figure: an imperfect prefiguration of a corresponding perfect thing that is still to come. To Hicks, it is an act, ceremony, or person in the Old Testament that prefigures an event, object, or person revealed in the New Testament. (See also, Type and Shadow)

[3] John 1 – especially verse 33

houses and all about the most strict of them appeared very simple and plain. They appeared one in principle with us – their faith and doctrine being founded on the manifestation and influence of the Divine Light, inwardly revealed. Most of them, of late, have requested to be joined in membership with Friends and have been received. Many of them appear to be a worthy people, yet I fear some were a little hurt by being too tenacious in their dress – particularly in making it a point to have all parts of their clothing white. Yet in general, they appeared to be a plain, innocent, upright-hearted people and I felt a concern lest they should be hurt by the great and prevailing deficiencies manifest amongst us, by many turning away from the purity and simplicity of our holy self-denying profession. This, I believe is a subject worthy the deep consideration of those delinquent brethren, for if it be a truth (as most certainly it is) that whosoever offendeth one of the least of those who believe in Christ, it were better for him that a millstone were hanged about his neck and he cast into the sea,[1] what will become of those who live in the daily practice of those things that give continual offense to their brethren and are stumbling-blocks in the way of honest inquirers?

After attending the aforesaid meetings, we passed on, taking meetings at Choptank, Third Haven, and Bayside on the eastern shore of Maryland. The two first were attended by many of other societies – a number of whom were Methodists – and at each, one of their Ministers, both of whom were very solid and gave great attention. One of them was much affected and wept freely for a considerable time and with divers others manifested their full satisfaction. My spirit was much humbled and made to rejoice in the Lord in that he was graciously near, and made bare his arm for our help,[2] and carried us through the exercise of those meetings – to the honor of his own name, who is over all, worthy forever.

After leaving Bayside, the next day, we attended a meeting which we had appointed the day before, on our way thither, at a village called Saint Michaels – among the Methodists (the people being nearly all of that profession in this place). It was held in their meetinghouse – there having never been a meeting appointed by any Friend in the place before, except a small opportunity by some women Friends some years before. There was at this time a general collection and, considering their ignorance of us and our manner of sitting in silence, they conducted pretty well.[3] The greatest disturbance and that which most effected my mind was the loud groanings of a particular individual, a man of that society who continually almost – while our Friend, Mary Berry, who was with us, was

---

[1] Mark 9:42, Matthew 18:6, & Luke 17:2
[2] Isaiah 52:1
[3] The next three sentences were deleted from the printed *Journal*.

Third Haven Meetinghouse in Easton, Maryland

communicating to the people – kept up a noise in that way, much to the disturbance of the meeting and greatly hindering the service thereof. After our said Friend had cleared herself and set down, way opening after a short time of silence, I stood up and, previous to my going on with the prospect before me, I opened to the people the hurtful tendency of such inconsistent conduct and how much like it was to the state of the Pharisees reprehended by our Lord. And so, as way opened in the Light, I turned the attention of the people to the necessity of inward and outward stillness as preparatory to the right performance of the great and solemn act of worship. Truth prevailed and silenced all noises, insomuch that a comfortable degree of the Divine Presence was witnessed, and many minds tendered and comforted, and divers gospel truths clearly opened to the apparent satisfaction of most present, and we left them with peace of mind.

And the next day, attended a meeting at Easton (alias Third Haven) among the black people, which we had given out some days before. It proved a favored opportunity to the edification, comfort, and encouragement of this poor, injured, and too much despised people – many of whom I believe have good desires begotten in their minds after the knowledge of the truth.

The next day being the first of the week and 11th of 2nd month, we attended Friends meeting at this place. The knowledge of our intention of being here being spread, the neighboring inhabitants generally came in, so that the house was much crowded. The gospel was largely and freely preached among them to the apparent satisfaction of all present. How marvelous is thy loving-kindness, O Lord, to the workmanship of thy holy hand.[1] How art thou graciously holding out from season to season offers of reconciliation to thy revolting and rebellious children and art calling to them by thy servants, now as formerly, "Return, return, repent and live for why will ye die, O house of Israel?"[2] saith your God.

We continued about this place until their monthly meeting, which was held on the following Fifth Day and attended their Meeting of Ministers and Elders for the same which came in the intermediate time. The monthly meeting was in some degree favored – divers things were opened for the improvement and encouragement of Friends in the well-ordering the affairs of truth.

The day following, we rode to Chester River and the next day attended Friends Monthly Meeting at Cecil. It was small, but Truth favored and ability received to labor for the stirring Friends up to more vigilance in a careful waiting for the arising of the Spring of Life, as nothing short of the divine power and renewed quickenings of the Holy Spirit can qualify for the promotion of good order and discipline in the Church.

The next day being the first of the week, we attended the meeting here and, notice being given to the neighboring inhabitants, many came in – most of whom appeared very raw and light. Nevertheless, as Friends kept down[3] to their exercise, towards the close of the meeting Truth came up into dominion and all that opposed it was made to bow and acknowledge its power. For which, my spirit was made thankful to the Author of Every Blessing.

Second and Third Days following, we attended two meetings – the first in Friends Meetinghouse at Chester River and the latter at Chestertown, in their courthouse – both pretty large meetings and overshadowed[4] with the same wing of divine power as the former (although we had to arrive at it through deep baptism and suffering with the seed, for those that reign with him must be willing likewise to suffer[5]). At that held in the courthouse, the people in the forepart were very light, often whispering to one another – a spirit of licentiousness appearing to be prevalent with many of them – but as Truth arose, they were gradually subjected until a becoming solemnity appeared in almost every countenance. And I trust some good was effected in some minds. But we

---

[1] Psalm 36:7 & Ephesians 2:10
[2] Ezekiel 33:11
[3] Keep down: humbly attend to
[4] Overshadow: shelter and protect
[5] 2 Titus 2:12

must leave the event to the Lord, to whom alone belongs all the praise, nothing due to man but blushing and confusion of face.

The next day, we attended a meeting at the Head of Chester. It was somewhat hurt in the forepart for want of room – the house not being sufficient to contain all who came and the weather too cold to stand without. Yet as it settled into a quiet, it proved a precious baptizing season. Many hearts were melted into deep contrition[1] – especially a portly, well-countenanced woman, who appeared for some time to withstand or endeavored to keep above what was communicated, but as Truth arose into dominion, she gradually yielded and finally not being able longer to hold out, bowed down her head and wept so as to be heard through the meeting, and continued in the same state of contrition to the close of the meeting, after which, I gave her my hand, which she received with tokens of sincere regard and with the stamp of deep humiliation in her countenance. Divers others appeared well affected and I had cause to hope that if the few Friends in that place show forth a good example, there will be some gathered.

Through Lower Pennsylvania to Maryland

The day following we attended the meeting at Sassafras to pretty good satisfaction and the next day, we rode to East Nottingham and attended their monthly meeting the day after. It proved a very exercising meeting, things being much out of order among them. I was led forth in a line of close searching labor, both in testimony in the first part of the meeting and likewise in discipline, but got little relief – saving from a consciousness in myself of having discharged my duty faithfully among them.

The next day being the first of the week and 25th of 2nd month, we attended their particular meeting, in which I had to expose in a large, arousing testimony, that spirit among Friends that pleads for joining with those actuated[2] in civil government and taking part therewith, and freely joining with the maxims[3] and spirit of the world. And Truth reigned triumphantly in this meeting over all opposition and disorderly spirits.

26th: We rested.

27th: Attended West Nottingham Meeting to good satisfaction, being made to rejoice in Truth's victory over death and darkness, for which the honest-hearted were made thankful.

28th: Attended a meeting, lately established about five miles distant from the former, which I sat mostly in silence, feeling no clear commission for preaching the gospel among them.

---

[1] The rest of the paragraph was deleted from the printed *Journal*.
[2] Actuated: active
[3] Maxim: a guiding principle for personal conduct

East Nottingham Meetinghouse in Calvert, Maryland

1st of 3rd month: Attended Little Britain Meeting, wherein I was opened and led into a large doctrinal communication, suited to the states of many present. The meeting was large and solid and I trust edifying and instructive to many present, but too many who have ears to hear[1] and are led to acknowledge to Truth delivered, nevertheless neglect the practical part, which is the most essential. They are, therefore, in a situation like those who, seeing their natural face in a glass, turn away and forget what manners of persons they were.[2]

2nd: Passed over the River Susquehanna and lodged at Richard Webb's at Fawn. Attended their meeting next day – it was a solid and, I believe to many, a profitable season.

4th and first of the week: Attended Deer Creek Meeting. It was large and favored with the overshadowing wing of heavenly regard, wherein was marvelously displayed the condescending goodness and mercy of a gracious God to his sinful creatures. The meeting being composed, in part, of a considerable number of dark, undisciplined spirits – many of whom (it was thought) had not been at any meeting for several years and some of them never at any of our meetings before – the meeting appeared to be

---

[1] Mark 4:9 (and several others)
[2] James 1:22-24

generally brought under a becoming solemnity and concluded to our solid comfort.

5th: Attended Bush River Meeting and, although it was made up generally by a loose, careless-minded people, yet Truth favored and through divine help the gospel was preached in the demonstration of the Spirit and with power – many present being made sensible of its baptizing influence and all contrary spirits appeared subjected and brought down[1] and Truth reigned triumphant.

6th and 7th: Attended the meetings of Little Falls, and Gunpowder – both seasons of favor.

8th: Attended Friends Monthly Meeting at Baltimore. It was I trust a profitable season, both in the meeting for worship and that for the discipline of the church. In the former, I was led in a large, searching testimony to set forth the great danger and hurtful effects of Friends joining in with the spirit of the world, in taking any part in the fluctuating governments, customs, and manners thereof – things opening clearly to set forth how the apostasy[2] took place through that medium, both among the primitive Christians and also in our own society in days past. And that the only way for us as a people to regain the primitive state was to return back into ancient simplicity by a separation from the world – its spirit, governments, manners, and maxims – and to make no league with those actuated thereby. Truth came into dominion and the faithful among them were strengthened. Praises forever be ascribed to the Shepherd of Israel, who is indeed a God near at hand and a Present Helper in every needful time.

9th: Rested and wrote to my family and Friends at home.

10th: Visited several families in the morning and, in the afternoon at the 3rd hour, attended a meeting among the poor at the almshouse belonging to this city. It proved a comfortable season and I was glad I gave up to the service.

11th being the first of the week, we attended Friends meeting in the forenoon and, some notice being given among the townspeople of our being there, it was large. And after sitting a considerable time in silent labor, wherein my mind was baptized into the states of those present, I stood up with a prospect of the hurtful tendency of pride, both in religious and civil society. Truth opened the way and gradually arose into a good degree of dominion and I trust it was a profitable, edifying season to many present.

---

[1] Bring down: humbled

[2] Apostasy: falling away from true religion. The theory of apostasy was central to early Friends understanding of the history of Christianity and of their place in it.

In the afternoon at the 3rd hour, we had a meeting with the black people and, except the hurt received by their long and untimely gathering, I think it was in the general a comfortable season and many among them appeared to be brought into a becoming solemnity. And we parted under the savor of Truth.

12th: Attended a meeting at Elkridge. It proved in the general a hard, laborous season, yet I trust a time of profit and favor to some. We rode that afternoon thirteen miles towards Indian Spring Meeting, which we attended the next day, wherein I was led in a plain, full, and clear manner to expose the enormous sin of oppression and of holding our fellow creatures in bondage, with the pernicious fruits and effects of it to those who are guilty thereof – and especially to their children who, being supported by the labor and toil of those held in slavery and thereby brought up in idleness, were led into pride and a very false and dark idea respecting God and his superintending providence, and many other evils fatal to their present and eternal well being., and tending to disqualify them from being useful in almost any respect, either to themselves or society, and thereby rendered unworthy of the respect of wise and good men, and therefore, are pests in society until reformed from those practices. Truth arose into dominion, and some present who were slave holders were made sensible of their conditions, and were much affected, and a hope was felt to arise that the opportunity would prove profitable to some and I left them with peace of mind.

Since which, I have been informed that a woman present at that season, who possessed a number of slaves, was so fully convinced[1] as to set them free, and joined in membership with Friends not long after, which is indeed cause of thankfulness and heartfelt gratitude to the great and Blessed Author of every mercy he vouchsafed to the children of men.

14th: Was at Sandy Spring meeting to satisfaction.

Virginia

15th: Attended Friends preparative meeting at Alexandria. It was a small weak meeting, a very few manifesting any real concern for the support of our Christian testimonies – being gathered there mostly from different parts of the country for the advancement of their temporal interest (and this being uppermost), it disqualifies for improvement in religious experience.

O that we as a people were more weaned from the world and its fading enjoyments, and our affections placed on celestial treasure. Then would the light of the church break forth out of obscurity and her darkness become as the noonday. Thousands would then be gathered

---

[1] Convince: convict or prove guilty

from the highways and hedges[1] and flock to the brightness of her arising, with everlasting joy upon their heads.[2]

16th: Rode to Fairfax – about forty-six miles.

17th: Attended their select quarterly meeting.[3]

18th: Being the first of the week, we attended the meeting at this place, which was large with Friends and others. I was led to open the great advantages attendant on a life of righteousness, from that scripture passage that righteousness exalteth a nation, but sin is a reproach to any people[4] – setting forth the difference between a righteousness founded on the laws, maxims, and precepts of men and the righteousness that is witnessed by faith in the Son of God as revealed to the hearts and souls of the children of men through the Holy Spirit. And although there were many raw and uncultivated spirits present, yet Truth came into a good degree of dominion and victory over all and I trust it was a profitable season to some.

19th: Attended the quarterly meeting for discipline, in which I had some service in opening the nature and end of discipline, and encouraging Friends to an improvement therein, to the solid satisfaction of the honest in heart.

The next day was the youths' meeting for the last time – the quarterly meeting, the day before, having concluded to discontinue the same after this time from a belief that its use was over and that it had become more hurtful than beneficial by reason of the great concourse of idle people coming together at that time – not so much for the sake of the meeting, as to see and be seen, and making it a place of diversion. I had considerable to say among them, but got but little relief by reason (as I apprehended) of the infidelity and prevailing of a licentious spirit too generally among the people, insomuch that I was satisfied the quarterly meeting had done right in discontinuing that meeting – believing, if continued, it would have been very prejudicial to the youth, for whose good in the first institution thereof, it was intended.

21st: Attended the preparative meeting of South Fork, which is a branch of Goose Creek Monthly Meeting. I was silent in the meeting for worship, but had some close labor with Friends in their preparative meeting – feeling my spirit much oppressed with a sense of the great lukewarmness and love of the world, which appeared to prevail in such a manner as that the business of the preparative meeting was conducted in a

---

[1] Luke 14:23
[2] Isaiah 35:10
[3] Select Quarterly Meeting: the Meeting of Ministers and Elders from all monthly meetings in a quarterly meeting
[4] Proverbs 14:34

very weak, vague manner – void of a right sense of the dignity of such a meeting, or any due concern for the preservation of right order. However, I felt peace of mind in a faithful discharge of myself among them.

22nd: Was at Goose Creek Preparative Meeting – it was large in the first sitting by the coming in of many of other societies – in which, after a considerable time of silent labor in deep baptism with the Suffering Seed, my mouth was opened in a clear, full testimony, directed to the states of those present. And many were brought under the influence of that power that smote Rahab and wounded the dragon.[1] Truth came up into dominion and a good degree of victory over all.

Nevertheless, such is the deadness and indifferency of some who go under our name that at the close of this very solemn meeting for worship, they withdrew with those who were not members and continued outdoors until the preparative meeting had proceeded considerably in its business, and then dropped in – one after another, in a very careless, unthinking manner – which grieved my mind. And I have often been affected with similar conduct in many places in this country, as also in some other parts – a conduct which appears to me to carry in it great indignity to our high and holy profession, and I believe is greatly offensive to the great Head of the Church, for the promotion of whose righteous cause these meetings of discipline are established. I believe one great cause of this sorrowful weakness and declension[2] is owing to a want of due administration of discipline by those who are called thereunto. For by overlooking one little thing after another, custom establishes those bad habits and great loss is sustained by the Church in general and by some of its members in particular. And it is very observable that meetings where those things are apparent are generally in a declining state.

I was exercised in a plain way of dealing with those delinquents, setting forth to them the hurtful tendency of such conduct. Truth prevailed, and many hearts were much tendered, and the hands of the faithful strengthened. To the Lord only wise be the praise of his own work, who is over all, worthy forever.

23rd: Attended a meeting at a place called the Gap, where there was a small meeting of Friends. It was a large collection by the coming in of others – many more than the house would hold. Many of them appeared to be a raw insensible people, void of any right idea or knowledge of true religion, which made the meeting very hard and laborous, yet not without

---

[1] Isaiah 51:9
[2] Declension: decline or degeneration

some degree of favor towards the conclusion by Truth's obtaining the victory over death and darkness.[1]

It may not be altogether improper in this place to make some mention of a prospect I had in a night vision whilst in this neighborhood, the night following the youths' meeting (before mentioned). As I lay in bed in a Friend's house about the middle of the night, I awoke and my sleep went from me, and my mind was brought into a state of deep exercise and travail from a sense of the great turning away of many among us from the law and testimony, and the prevailing of a spirit of great infidelity and deism[2] among the people, and darkness spreading over the minds of many as a thick veil – it being a time in which Thomas Paine's* *Age of Reason* (falsely so-called) was much attended to in those parts, and some who were members in our society (as I was informed) were captivated by his dark insinuating address and were ready almost to make shipwreck of faith and a good conscience.[3] Under a sense thereof, my spirit was deeply humbled before the Majesty of Heaven and, in the anguish of my spirit, I said, "Lord, spare thy people and give not thy heritage to reproach[4] and suffer not thy truth to fall in the streets."[5] And after having spread my supplication before him after this manner, and acknowledged with gratitude his multiplied mercies, my mind was made easy and I fell into a sweet sleep.

And in vision, there opened before me the appearance of a bright rainbow that extended from one side of the horizon to the other, through the zenith from the northwest to the southeast, and in a seeming soft language, it revived on my mind, this is the token of the covenant that God made with his people, that he would not again destroy the world with a flood.[6] Great Babylon was now brought into remembrance before God and her cup was full[7] and her fall was near at hand, and that the Lord is now arising and will give her, her due.

And I awoke and my mind was much comforted in the prospect, believing that the vision was true, and the interpretation thereof sure – that the Kingdom of Antichrist had now got near to its height. That Satan

---

[1] The next four paragraphs were severely edited in the printed *Journal* to remove mention of Hicks' "night vision."
[2] Deism: a belief in the existence of God combined with a rejection of revealed religion. It should be noted that Hicks' opponents frequently accused him of deism and he always rejected the claim.
[3] 1 Timothy 1:19
[4] Joel 2:17
[5] Isaiah 59:14
[6] Genesis 9:12&15
[7] Revelation 16:19 & 17:4

(or the man of sin[1]) had laid his top-stone by leading his votaries to an open acknowledgement of their disbelief, which has been his aim and design[2] through the many ages of the world, but which he has never been able to effect in so full and public a manner as in those latter days, and whereby his dark cunning is exposed, insomuch that he, the man of sin and son of perdition, is now fully revealed to all the faithful followers of the Lamb of God who taketh away the sin of the world[3] from all his sincere-hearted children, who love him above all. From a sense whereof, my spirit was bowed in humble acknowledgement before God.

Therefore rejoice, O heaven and be glad, O earth! For the Lord is arising in the greatness of his power and will rule and reign,[4] whose right it is both now and forever.

24th: Attended the monthly meeting at Fairfax. It was an exercising season, things being much out of order for want of more faithfulness among the members and a due attention to discipline. I labored among them in the ability received, for their encouragement and stirring up to their respective duties, but alas for us, most men mind their own things and not the things that are Jesus Christ's.[5] A worldly spirit too much prevails among the professors of Truth – to their great hurt and reproach of that right worthy name by which we are called, to the great grief of the honest in heart, who are in travail for Zion's prosperity, and Jerusalem's peace.

25th: Attended their First Day Meeting. It was large and in it strength was graciously afforded to minister to the people in Truth's authority, and which came into dominion over all.

Crossing the Potomac to Maryland

This afternoon, we passed over the great River Potomac in our way to Bush Creek in Maryland which, by reason of rain, was very full and made the passage difficult, especially in crossing a creek (after we had crossed the river) which had a bridge over it, but the waters were so high that it was nearly to our horses backs in getting to the bridge – and that so afloat that the horses could scarcely get on it. We got to the bridge by going on the top of a high fence that led to the end thereof, leading our horses by our sides to the foot of the bridge, and then turned them loose and drave them over. The last fell through with its hinder parts and appeared to be in danger of being ruined, but recovered itself without hurt. My horse fell off

---

[1] 2 Thessalonians 2:3
[2] Design: purpose or intention
[3] John 1:29
[4] 1 Chronicles 16:31
[5] Romans 8:5

into the creek and plunged all over in the water, but soon came up and swam to the shore. There was a Friend in company with a one-horse wheel-carriage and there appeared no probability of getting him over with the carriage, but by swimming him through the creek. And this appeared a considerable risk, but it was a place where there was no other way of getting over, and no inhabitant on this neck of land anywhere near, and night coming on. So, we drave the horse with the carriage into the creek, which was quite deep in the middle, and the carriage, with the weight of the iron that was on it, soon sank and drew down the horse. But as he went under, it appeared to give him a fright and he sprang to it and swam with such violence that the motion seemed to raise the carriage again and he took it safe over. And having all got through this imminent danger without any hurt to ourselves or our horses (except the Friends' clothes in the box of the carriage got wet), it was cause of thankfulness and gratitude to the Great Author of every mercy and blessing.

We then passed on to a Friend's house by the name of Richard Richardson, where we had a meeting the next day with his family and a number of the neighboring people who were not Friends. It proved a favored season and I trust will not soon be forgotten by some present. May it fasten as a nail in a sure place,[1] and to some (I have a hope) it may be as bread cast upon the waters to return after many days.[2]

The day following we attended Bush Creek Meeting. Notice having gone forward some days before of our intention of being there at this time, it was large and greatly favored with the prevalence of Truth by way of testimony, in which many things relative to true gospel worship were clearly opened, and the fallacy and fruitlessness of all will-worship[3] and mere bodily exercise in matters of religion manifested to the view of all present that had ears to hear and hearts to understand[4] what the Spirit saith to the churches. It was a very solemn time, worthy of grateful remembrance.

28th: Attended Pipe Creek Meeting, wherein I was greatly afflicted with evil thoughts that would keep arising in my mind, insomuch that I was almost at times taken off from my proper exercise, which very much grieved my spirit. But as I endeavored to keep up the warfare, I was led to believe it was the case of too many present and that by giving way to such thoughts, some had become captivated by their own lusts – to the

---

[1] Isaiah 22:23
[2] Ecclesiastes 11:1
[3] Will-worship: Will-worship: putting one's own will or desires ahead of God's. In this instance, adopting forms of worship that are determined by one's own preferences, rather than worshiping according to the divine will
[4] Matthew 13:15 & Acts 28:27 – both quoting Isaiah 6:10

wounding one another and divers disorders – and a want of unity had got in among them, and many hurt thereby. I was led into the necessity of bearing testimony against these things as way opened, and calling the attention of all present to the Light, Spirit, Grace, and Truth of our Lord Jesus Christ, our holy pattern, as the only place of refuge and preservation from these and all other hurtful things. After which meeting, the Friend (where we lodged) informed me the next morning, that himself and wife were uneasy (seeing no Friends had come in to see us after the meeting) and was afraid that they would judge them of having informed me of their conditions – seeing the states of many had been so exactly told them in the meeting. But I told him they need not be troubled, as they knew themselves to be clear.

Back in Pennsylvania

The two following days, we attended meetings at Menallen and Huntington – they were both exercising seasons. Nevertheless, Truth favored with ability and understanding to hand forth in a close searching manner things suitable to the states of those present and not without a crumb of consolation to the few honest-hearted, who were in travail for Zion's arising, and who went mourning on their way, being bowed in spirit from a sense of the great turning-away from the law and testimony, and the prevalence of a spirit of ease and great indifferency, whereby many wrong things had entered.

From thence we passed on to Warrington and Newberry, in each of which meetings Truth favored with victory, and the hid things of Esau or the first nature (which are earthly) were brought to light, searched out, detected, and condemned[1] and the new or second birth[2] (which is spiritual and to which is the promise[3]) and the manner and way in which it is brought forth and effected clearly shown and pointed out with the blessing attendant thereon – to the comfort of the faithful and the few willing-minded among them, and for the stirring up and arousing the lukewarm, careless, and indifferent professors from their beds of ease and carnal security.

The latter meeting especially was a time to be remembered. Many hearts were greatly affected and I trust the season will not soon be forgotten by some. I was very thankful for the relief I felt to my own mind after many days of deep baptism with the Suffering Seed. Religion appeared to be at a very low ebb in those parts, through the prevalence of a worldly spirit, which makes hard work for the poor travelers who have

---

[1] Jeremiah 49:10 & Obadiah 1:6
[2] 1 Peter 1:23
[3] Romans 4:16

to go up and down among them, as with their hands upon their loins for very pain.¹ Did those lukewarm, careless professors rightly consider the great distress and exercise they bring upon their concerned brethren, who are in travail for their redemption and salvation, and who are going up and down as with their lives in their hands, through difficulties and danger, being in jeopardy by sea and by land, and among false brethren?² One might reasonably suppose it would be a means to stir them up to more diligence and circumspection – that so they might thereby comfort them in their exercises and relieve them in their tribulations. Then, they that sow and they that reap might rejoice together, and joy in the God of their salvation.

Our next meeting was at York, where we tarried two days and were at their monthly meeting, wherein things appeared distressingly low as to the right conducting of discipline in Truth's authority. Indeed, the meeting seemed sunk so below any right sight and sense of right order that no way opened to administer much or any help, so that we left them without obtaining much relief of mind and passed on, taking a meeting near Wright's Ferry. After which, we crossed the great River Susquehanna and took meetings at Lancaster, Lampeter, and then to Sadsbury on the First Day of the week and 8th of the 4th month. This latter, through hard labor, proved a season of enlargement in a line of close doctrine suited to the varied states of those present and some minds appeared to be much humbled. May it not be in vain, but as seed sown on good ground.³

10th: Attended at West Caln Meeting.

11th: At Fallowfield – both favored meetings.

12th: Attended London Grove Meeting, wherein I was led to open the duty and obligation incumbent on ministers, elders, overseers,⁴ and heads of families, which was introduced with this query of the prophet Ezekiel, "Watchman, what of the night?"⁵ – showing how that for want of keeping up a strict watch, with an eye single⁶ to that inward Holy Monitor or Spirit

---

¹ Jeremiah 30:6
² 2 Corinthians 11:26
³ Matthew 13:23
⁴ Overseer: A person appointed by the monthly meeting to "exercise a vigilant and tender care over their fellow members; that if anything repugnant to the harmony and good order of the society appears among them, it may be timely attended to and not neglected" (from the 1806 *Rules of Discipline of the Yearly Meeting of Friends held in Philadelphia*). While the Elders were responsible for the spiritual condition of the meeting, the overseers were concerned with ordinary behavior.
⁵ Although the image of a watchman is used several times in Ezekiel, the quote is from Isaiah 21:11
⁶ Matthew 6:22 & Luke 11:34

Kennett (Pennsylvania) Meetinghouse

of Pure Unerring Wisdom, many hurtful and destructive things had got in among us. And especially for want of a right, godly care in parents and heads of families over their children and those under their charge, many pollutions had got in and spread among them – especially the youth – not only in regard to a departure from the simplicity and purity of our holy, self-denying profession in dress and address, but also in many other unseemly and reproachful practices, which is but the natural consequence of parents indulging undue liberties in their children. It was a solemn time – worthy of grateful remembrance.

13th: Was at West Grove Meeting, in which I had to go through a similar exercise from a sense of the great want of faithfulness among the members, whereby many deficiencies were apparent to the wounding of the faithful. Truth favored with ability to clear myself among them with plainness of speech, which was cause of thankfulness to the honest-hearted.

14th: Attended New Garden Meeting mostly in silence, in which I had peace.

15th and first of the week: Attended Hockessin Meeting and, at the 4th hour after noon, were at Centre.

16th: At Kennett. These were for the most part suffering seasons, for although there is a small remnant preserved, who are in travail for Truth's arising, yet the greater part are too much captivated by a worldly spirit which leads into a neglect of attending meetings and great carelessness in respect to the right ordering their families. By reason whereof, many undue liberties have got in among them, wounding the faithful.

17th: Attended Chichester Meeting. It was a time thankfully to be remembered. The everlasting gospel of peace and salvation was preached in Truth's authority, and all contrary spirits were subjected and brought down, and Truth reigned triumphantly over all.

Magnified forever be the name of the Lord,[1] who made bare his arm[2] for our help and the strengthening and refreshing of my poor soul, which had been at times – for days and nights past – ready to sink into discouragement and dismay, by reason of the deep baptisms I had to pass through, unknown to man, but in fellowship with the Suffering Seed that lies smothered and pressed down in the hearts of many careless, lukewarm professors, as a cart under sheaves.[3]

O how does darkness and death spread itself as a curtain in this once highly favored land? Alas for the people! For the professors of Truth! What will become of them, unless they repent and turn to the Lord? For parents and children in some places are so estranged from the law and testimony that many seem plunged into the condition of Jerusalem formerly, when this pathetic[4] lamentation was taken up by the dear Master, "O Jerusalem, Jerusalem, thou that killest the prophets, and stonest them that are sent unto thee. How oft would I have gathered thee as a hen gathereth her chickens under her wings, and ye would not! Therefore, your houses are left unto you desolate."[5]

O how is this verified! What great desolations, in a religious sense, are apparent with many professors. And how are the poor servants that are sent forth among them for their recovery as with their lives in their hands? Like killed and stoned and are often so plunged into death and sufferings as almost to despair of life.

O the pangs that my poor soul has endured of late in many places so that I had oft to say (in secret) with the holy apostle, "Surely, we are in jeopardy every hour."[6] No tongue can tell nor is it in the power of language to communicate the distress and anguish that is sometimes endured by the poor travelers in filling up their measure of the afflictions

---

[1] 2 Samuel 7:26
[2] Isaiah 52:10
[3] Amos 2:13
[4] Pathetic: pitiable or causing deep sadness
[5] Matthew 23:37-38
[6] 1 Corinthians 15:30

of Christ for his body's sake, even the church.[1] But in this also, we are sometimes strengthened to rejoice that we are accounted worthy to suffer with him – that so, when he is pleased to arise in his own strength as the light of the morning,[2] we may be permitted to reign with him and rejoice with joy unspeakable and full of glory.[3]

The three following days, we were at Concord, Birmingham, and Bradford – all favored meetings through fervent labor and the prevalence of Truth by way of testimony. May the Lord make it effectual and fasten it as a nail in a sure place.

21st: Was at East Caln – mostly silent.

22nd and first of the week: We were at Uwchlan. The meeting was large, wherein I had to expose the danger of self-righteousness, or a trust in natural religion, or mere morality – showing that, that was no more than the religion of atheists and was generally the product of pride and self-will. And however good it may appear to the natural unregenerate man, is as offensive in the divine sight as those more open pollutions that appear so very reproachful to the eyes of men. Truth favored in a large, searching testimony, to the convicting and humbling many hearts, and comfort of the faithful.

23rd: Attended the meeting at Nantmeal – mostly in silence.

The three following days, we were at Pikeland, Valley, and Willistown meetings – all in a good degree favored.

27th: Was at Goshen. The meeting was large, wherein I had to caution Friends against mixing with the people in their human policies and outward forms of government – showing how in all ages those that were called to be the Lord's people had been ruined and destroyed by such associations, manifesting clearly by scripture testimonies and other records that our strength and preservation consisted in standing alone and not to be counted among the people or nations who were setting up partial and party interests – one against another – which is the true ground of all war and bloodshed, being actuated[4] by the spirit of pride and wrath which is always opposed to the true Christian Spirit that breathes peace on earth and good will to all men.[5] And therefore, we cannot use any coercive force or compulsion by any means whatever – not being overcome with evil, but overcoming evil with good.[6] And although there were many opposite spirits present who, in their creaturely wisdom and human policy, are

---

[1] Colossians 1:24
[2] 2 Samuel 23:4
[3] 1 Peter 1:8
[4] Actuate: spur to action
[5] Luke 2:14
[6] Romans 12:21

pleading for those kinds of associations and taking part with those political governments, yet Truth favored and came into a good degree of dominion over all – to the strengthening and encouraging the true travailers for Zion's prosperity.

29th and first of the week: Attended Middletown Meeting and, at the 4th hour after noon, were at Providence – both large, crowded meetings, there being more than the houses were sufficient to contain. Truth favored in an eminent manner, especially in the former, where many hearts were deeply bowed from the sensible[1] evidence of the prevailing of the divine power that was in dominion over all, to the tendering of the hearts of most present. It was a precious season, worthy of thankful remembrance and humble gratitude to the Blessed Author of all our rich mercies and blessings, who is over all, God blessed forever.

30th: Attended the Monthly Meeting at Providence (consisting of the Particular Meetings of Providence, Middletown, Springfield, and Chester). Things in this meeting appeared in a low state, as to the right ordering of the affairs of the church by reason whereof, many and great were the apparent deviations among them. Many of their youth were gone out into the foolish fashions and vain customs of the world to that degree, as not to retain any marks of true primitive plainness.

O how is the gold become dim, how is the most fine gold changed![2] And many parents, that retain a good degree of outward plainness themselves, have nevertheless (for want of dwelling enough in the pure Spring of Divine Life) suffered the eye of their minds to be so far blinded by the god of this world as not only to suffer these improper indulgences in their families, and among their children, but in some instances, are ready to plead for them. The sense whereof much affected my mind – under which exercise I was led forth in a line of close searching labor among them, in order for the stirring up Friends to more diligence and honest care in those respects which I trust afforded a degree of comfort and strength to the honest-hearted and procured peace to my own mind, which is a treasure I prefer to all this world's glory and honor.

1st of 5th month: Attended the meetings of Springfield and Haverford – both favored, profitable seasons.

2nd: Was at Newtown. This was a thorough season, in which, in a line of close searching labor, I was led to set forth the danger of trusting the salvation of our souls on anything short of a full surrender of our wills, and an entire dedication of our hearts, to the Lord in a humble circumspect walking before him by separating ourselves from the world – its spirit, manners, maxims, governments, honors, and customs – all which

---

[1] Sensible: obvious or recognizable
[2] Lamentations 4:1

are polluted, as arising from the lusts of the flesh, the lusts of the eye, and the pride of this life.[1] Truth rose into victory, to the tendering many hearts and to the comfort and strength of the faithful. Surely, God is good to Israel, although in a state of great revolting, but he delighteth in showing himself merciful. Praised and magnified be his great and adorable name, over all forever.

3rd and 4th: Attended meetings at Radnor and Merion, and then passed on to Philadelphia in order to attend their quarterly meeting, which opened there on the 5th and seventh of the week, with a Meeting of Ministers and Elders, and closed on Third Day of the following week and 8th of the month, with a meeting for the youth and one for the black people in the afternoon. I think in the general, it was a time of favor through much hard labor in the several sittings. And indeed, we have no reason to expect to come at the spring any other way, but by faithfully digging, as with our staves, while there remains so much rubbish on the well's mouth.[2]

9th: Attended the Select Quarterly Meeting at Abington, and the day following, the quarterly meeting of discipline. I was engaged among them in each meeting and the favor extended was cause of thankfulness to the honest in heart.

11th: Returned to Philadelphia and in the afternoon passed over the River Delaware to Haddonfield in West Jersey.

Back in New Jersey

12th: Attended a monthly meeting at Upper Evesham. It was a low time – not much of that divine life and power that only can qualify for the right conducting of discipline to be felt among them and left them without much relief of mind.

13th and first of the week: Attended meetings at Lower Evesham and Cropwell. In the former, I was helped to labor pretty largely in testimony, to the comfort of a few honest-hearted and a number of tender-minded youth, but the greater part of the meeting appeared to be in a state of great insensibility and ease – a situation which is generally callous to all the tender invitations and entreaty of their Friends, who are in travail for their redemption and salvation, and are too much like the deaf adder that will not listen to the voice of the charmer, although he charm ever so wisely.[3] In the latter meeting, I was silent as to ministry.

14th: Attended the monthly meeting at Haddonfield, in which I labored in the ability received for their help and improvement, but alas,

---

[1] 1 John 2:16
[2] Numbers 21:18, perhaps combined with Nehemiah 4:10
[3] Psalm 58:4-5

FRIENDS' MEETING-HOUSE, MEDFORD, NEW JERSEY.

Upper Evesham (New Jersey) Meetinghouse

some meetings are so lost to the life of true religion and so many, who go under our profession, sunk into such a state of indifferency and lukewarmness, that the affairs of the church are too much conducted in a kind of rotation[1] and creaturely wisdom, void of that true weight and feeling sensibility that only gives right qualification for service in the church. Hence, great weakness ensues, and the way of right reformation closed, and Truth prevented from arising in its primitive splendor and beauty.

15th: We were at Moorestown and Rancocas. In the former, the power that smites Rahab and wounds the dragon was prevalently manifest to the tendering many hearts, and Truth came into victory over all. Praised forever be the right worthy name of Israel's King, who in holy condescending love was pleased to make bare his arm for our help, and once more redeemed my poor soul of adversity and the deep depressing baptisms that for some days past it had been plunged into – suffering with the seed that lies pressed down in the hearts of many lukewarm, worldly-minded professors, as a cart with sheaves.

---

[1] Rotation: recurring succession of duties. In this case, it likely refers to a practice of people in the meeting taking turns at holding various positions of responsibility.

Mansfield (New Jersey) Meetinghouse

From thence we passed on, taking meetings at Mansfield Neck, Burlington, Mansfield, and Bordentown. They were all favored meetings, Truth being near for our help.

20th and first of the week, we were at Trenton. The meeting was large – many of the townspeople came in of other professions – and strength was made manifest (in the midst of weakness) and, as Truth arose, the gospel was preached in the dear demonstration of the Spirit. Many hearts were tendered and comforted, and the few faithful made to rejoice, in a grateful sense of the Lord's mercies.

22nd: Was at Stony Brook Meeting, wherein my heart was made glad through holy help, being enabled to labor among them in Truth's authority to the comfort of the willing-hearted and the solid peace of my own mind.

The two following days, we were at Plainfield and Rahway – in the latter, wholly silent, but the former was a time of close labor in a clear plain way for the stirring up the minds of the people to more diligence and an inward humble walking with the Lord,[1] which appeared to be too much wanting among them.

25th: Attended an appointed meeting at Newark, a town wherein no Friend resides. The meeting was small and those gathered appeared mostly in a loose uncultivated state of mind. Nevertheless, I believe there were some thoughtful persons present, and I trust the meeting was in some degree profitable, and I left them with peace of mind, and passed

---

[1] Micah 6:8

over that evening to New York in order to attend our yearly meeting that opened there the next day with a Meeting of Ministers and Elders. After the first sitting of which, I rode home, not only to see my dear wife and family from whom I had been absent more than five months, but also to assist them in getting out to the yearly meeting. They were all glad to see me, and I them, and indeed our rejoicing was precious and mutual – in and under a sense of the Lord's mercy and goodness, for whose gracious preservation and help in this arduous journey, my spirit was made to bow in humble adoration and praise beyond the expression of language.

O my soul! What canst thou render unto the Lord for all his benefits? Nothing can be more acceptable, than an entire surrender of thine all to his holy disposing and to endeavor, as at the present time, to continue humbly to worship at the footstool[1] of his holy throne of grace. Amen.

I was from home in this journey about five months and two weeks, and rode by computation about sixteen hundred miles, and attended about one hundred and forty-three meetings.

A Visit to Friends & Other Inhabitants of Connecticut in 1799

Having felt a concern for some time to pay a religious visit to some towns and places in Connecticut and to be with the few Friends at West Hartford in the way, I laid the same before my Friends in the fall of the year 1799 and received a minute of concurrence and unity from our monthly meeting for that purpose.

I left home the 26th of 10th month and proceeded to Oblong in order to meet a committee of our yearly meeting, appointed this year to visit the Quarterly Meetings of Nine Partners and Oblong, and the monthly meetings belonging thereto, on a prospect of a new arrangement of those meetings, so as to establish another quarterly.

I accompanied the committee in the attendance of both quarterly meetings, after which I proceeded into Connecticut, taking meetings in our way to West Hartford in the following manner (to wit): three in the town of Sharon, one at Cornwall, one at Goshen, and one at Litchfield – they were all favored meetings. Four of them were held in meetinghouses belonging to the Presbyterians. The latter was but small, considering the largeness of the town and the great openness manifested by their leading members – there being three of their ministers and some other leading characters present. Truth was prevalently manifest in this meeting, tendering and comforting the honest-hearted – a number of whom, I believe were present, whose words and gestures clearly manifested a hearty thankfulness for, and satisfaction with, the meeting. And although the great opposition those meet with in coming out of their old traditions

---

[1] Psalm 99:5 & 132:7

may prevent any open and manifest effects for the present, yet I believe it will be as bread cast upon the waters that will return after many days so that his word that goeth forth may not return void, but will accomplish the thing whereto it was sent,[1] to the praise and glory of his own worthy name, who is over all, God blessed forever.

After this meeting, we passed directly to West Hartford and lodged with our Friend, Ebenezer Crosby, whose daughter Abigail had come in company with us from Nine Partners. She was a discreet religious young woman whose mind, I apprehended, was under the operation of the forming hand for her good. May she be preserved in faith and patience under the varied turnings thereof upon her, and then, I make no doubt, she will become a useful member in the church.

The next day, we rode to Springfield, about twenty-six miles north of this place, and attended a meeting there the next day. And although the people appeared generally raw and ignorant as to the internal work of true religion on the heart, being mostly Baptists and Presbyterians, whose doctrines lead them to place too much trust and dependence on the external works of a Savior without them and an imputative righteousness[2] without experiencing the internal work of sanctification wrought[3] by the Spirit and Power of a Savior within them – which is a very dangerous error. Nevertheless, Truth favored insomuch that divers appeared to be tenderly affected and manifested much satisfaction with the opportunity – as did the auditory in general.

We rode back that afternoon to West Hartford, and the day following being first of the week and 17th of 11th month, we attended Friends meeting and another at the house of our Friend, Ebenezer Crosby, in the evening. They were full meetings by the attendance of many of other societies – mostly Presbyterians. Truth favored in an eminent degree in both opportunities, but especially in the latter, wherein it rose into great dominion, breaking down and apparently reducing every contrary spirit, whereby a remarkable calm and general solemnity was felt to spread over the assembly to the solid rejoicing and comfort of many hearts, and the exaltation of the cause and testimony of our God, who for this and his multiplied favors and blessings, vouchsafed from time to time, is worthy of all honor, dominion, and glory, both now and forever.

The next day, feeling my mind drawn to some other of the adjacent towns, we rode about ten miles to a place called Poquonock, a thickly

---

[1] Isaiah 55:11

[2] Imputed righteousness: the doctrine (rejected by Friends) that people are considered to be righteous (i.e., righteousness is imputed to them) due to Christ's atoning death, while remaining sinners.

[3] Wrought: formed or fashioned

settled village in the west part of the township of West Windsor, where we had a precious opportunity that evening in a large schoolhouse. And although the notice was very short, it being late in the afternoon when we came there, yet when we came to the meeting, which began at the 6th hour, the house was nearly full and soon after taking our seats, was crowded with as many as it could well contain. And a commendable silence maintained during the silent part of the meeting, which we thought a little uncommon inasmuch as the people were generally strangers to us and our ways. And after a time of solemn waiting, my mouth was opened in a clear full testimony, wherein the doctrines of the gospel were largely and plainly held forth in the demonstration of the Spirit and with power – to the tendering of many hearts and the apparent satisfaction of the people in general – many expressing their thankfulness for the favor received, and we left them with the answer of peace in our own minds, and in a full persuasion that the Lord is secretly at work in the minds of many of the people in these parts, in order to deliver them from the power of their dark and blind leaders (who, for a long time, through their carnal and lifeless teachings and doctrines and many vain traditions have formed almost a total eclipse between God and their souls). May the Lord hasten this good work in his own time, that so those merchants of Babylon[1] that are trafficking in the souls of the people – those blind guides[2] – may be so discovered, that no man may buy their merchandise any more.

The day after, we attended a meeting in Windsor. The people here seemed to be more under the dark power of their teachers – being much blinded with the prejudice of education, so that the meeting was but small. Nevertheless, Truth favored with ability to preach the gospel with a good degree of divine authority, to the comfort and edification of some seeking minds present.

The two following days, we attended Friends meeting at Hartford, the latter of which was appointed by our Friend, Jervis Johnson from Ireland – both comfortable seasons.

The sixth of the week and 22nd of the month, we rode into the city of Hartford and, way opening for an opportunity with the people, a meeting was accordingly appointed at the 6th hour in the evening, to be held in a large meetinghouse belonging to the Presbyterians. A large number of the citizens assembled – supposed to be near a thousand – among whom were most of the principal inhabitants. The Lord, in whom was our trust, was graciously near and furnished with ability to conduct the meeting to the satisfaction and peace of our own minds, the edification of many present, and general satisfaction of the assembly.

---

[1] Revelation 18
[2] Matthew 23:16-24

We rested on Seventh Day and on First Day, we were again at Friends meeting at West Hartford. And notice of our being there having spread, a considerable number of the neighboring inhabitants and some from the city came in. It was a season of high favor – many weighty truths of the gospel were clearly opened, and the way of life and salvation set home[1] to the minds of the people in an affecting manner, and a general solemnity appeared to reign in almost every countenance, to the silencing every opposite spirit. The hearts of Friends, with my own spirit, were bowed in humble acknowledgment and gratitude to the Lord our Helper, for the vouchsafement of so great a mercy. Under a solemn sense thereof, we parted and took leave of each other in great nearness of spirit.

On Second Day, we turned our faces homeward, taking meetings in our way at New Cambridge, Woodbury (at which place we had two meetings), Middlesex, Stamford, and again at Middlesex on First Day. These were generally seasons of divine favor – edifying and instructive.

After which, we passed on into the state of New York and took meetings the six following days at Rye, White Plains, North Castle, Chappaqua, Amawalk, and Croton. And as my mind was led in faith and patience to close in with the baptismal influence of the Spirit of Truth, it was thereby reduced into a state of suffering with the precious seed in the hearts of the people, and wherein, their divers states were felt and way made to divide the word aright[2] to those assembled – those meetings being a mixed number of Friends and others. Truth was exalted and set over every contrary spirit and the honest-hearted comforted and encouraged to persevere in the way of righteousness, the work whereof is peace, and the effect thereof, quietness and assurance forever.

The following First Day, we attended Friends Meeting at Westchester and in the afternoon we had an appointed meeting at Eastchester – principally among those not in society. And we had cause in both these meetings to magnify and adore the name of the Lord, who deigned to be near with his saving help and furnished with ability to preach the gospel of life and salvation in the clear demonstration of the Spirit – the power attending, convicting and tendering many hearts. And the few Friends who dwell in that place were strengthened and encouraged, and my spirit refreshed and made to rejoice in those closing opportunities. After which, I returned home, and found my dear wife and tender children all well, to our mutual rejoicing.

I was out about six weeks, and attended about thirty meetings, and two quarterly meetings.

---

[1] Set home: made clear and irrefutable
[2] 2 Timothy 2:15

A Visit to Friends at Oblong & Nine Partners in 1800

On my return from my late visit in Connecticut and some other places on the main, I felt my mind not fully clear of a prospect I then had of a few other places. And the way opening with greater clearness, and feeling a motion of love to draw toward again attending the ensuing Quarterly Meetings of Oblong and Nine Partners, I set out after attending our quarterly meeting at Westbury in 1st month 1800 – took Purchase Meeting on First Day in our way to Oblong, which I sat through in silence. I had Amos Whitson as a companion. We passed from thence to Oblong – attended their quarterly meeting, after which we took a meeting at Kent in our way to Nine Partners. The people of this place are mostly of the Presbyterian society. A considerable number collected and conducted in an orderly manner, and I trust the opportunity was a season of profit, and I hope the labor therein bestowed may be to some of those present as bread cast upon the waters.

After attending the Quarterly Meeting of Nine Partners, we took meetings in our way to Cornwall and Goshen among those not of our society, though nothing very remarkable turned up in either. We had a comfortable meeting at Cornwall, after visiting some Friends, Charles Richards and the Thomsons, who appeared to be going into a separation from Friends (having already set up a separate meeting, for which they were not long after disowned) having given way to some very inconsistent notions in which they became hardened so as not to take the tender counsel and advice of their Friends, who labored much with them for their recovery.

From thence, we returned homeward – took a few meetings in our way, mostly among people of other persuasions – and got well home on First Day evening, the 16th of 2nd month, after attending the morning meeting at New York. As I took this little journey in part to fill up what seemed lacking in the other, I now felt clear, and my mind was accompanied with true peace, which raised in me humble acknowledgments and gratitude to the Great and Blessed Author of all our mercies.

A Visit to Inhabitants of Long Island in 1800

Soon after my return from the above little journey, I felt my mind drawn in the renewed feelings of gospel love to pay a religious visit to some of the inhabitants of our island, not of our profession. And after having opened my prospect to Friends and obtained the unity and concurrence of our monthly meeting, I performed that service in the latter part of the fall and beginning of the winter following.

I was out from home twenty-seven days, and rode about one hundred and ninety miles, and attended thirty-five meetings – only two of which were held in our meetinghouses. They were generally seasons of great favor, in which my mind was deeply bowed under a humiliating sense of the Lord's mercy, extended from day to day, not only in opening the hearts of the people to receive us and our testimony with manifestation of much love and good will, but also in furnishing matter suitably adapted to the states of those assembled, insomuch that Truth was raised into victory in a remarkable manner in almost every meeting, and in several to a very eminent degree, even beyond (as I thought) what I had ever before experienced at any time. It ran atop of all like oil[1] and seemed as much as human nature could bear. All appeared broken down by its precious and embalming[2] influence, in which the Lord was worshipped, and his great and glorious name praised and exalted over all, who is worthy forever.

---

[1] The imagery of oil running over all is one that Hicks will employ frequently. Although there is no exact match in the Bible, it may be that he was inspired by Psalm 133:
Behold, how good and how pleasant it is for brethren to dwell together in unity! It is like the precious ointment upon the head, that ran down upon the beard, even Aaron's beard: that went down to the skirts of his garments.

[2] Embalm: preserve in sweet and honored memory

1801-1805

A Visit to New Jersey, Pennsylvania, & Some Adjacent Places

In the spring of 1801, feeling my mind engaged in the love of the gospel to proceed in a visit to Friends in some parts of Jersey and Pennsylvania, and some places adjacent thereto, I left home the 11th of 4th month, with the concurrence and unity of my Friends.

On the Seventh Day of the week, I rode to New York and attended Friends meetings there on First Day, both fore and after noon. And although the life of religion appeared at a low ebb with Friends of that city in too general a manner, yet a number of the younger class and some more advanced in life give some hope of improvement. My mind was deeply engaged among them and through the condescending goodness of the Shepherd of Israel, strength was witnessed to preach the gospel in the demonstration of the Spirit and with power, insomuch that a fresh visitation was extended to many present. May it rest and be fastened by the Master of Assemblies as a nail in a sure place, to the honor of his great and glorious name, who is the Blessed Author and Finisher[1] of every good word and work.[2]

New Jersey

Second Day, we left the city – Edmund Willis kindly giving up to accompany me and be my companion in this journey – and passed by water directly to Elizabethtown Point, and from there rode to Woodbridge and lodged and, the next day, rode to Upper Freehold, and the day following being the fourth of the week, we attended Friends meeting there, in the neighborhood called Robins Meeting at the usual time, and at the 4th hour after noon attended Upper Freehold Meeting. The former was but a small, weak meeting, but information being generally spread, many came in who were not members, and it proved a profitable, edifying season – worthy of grateful remembrance. The latter was rather a season of suffering with the seed – I being mostly shut up as to any ministerial communication, yet was content, being willing to let patience have its perfect work.[3]

The next day, we attended the meetings of Crosswicks and Upper Springfield – at both of which meetings strength was afforded to communicate what opened in the line of duty in such a manner as to find relief of mind, which I account a great favor.

---

[1] Hebrews 12:2
[2] 2 Thessalonians 2:17
[3] James 1:4

Pennsylvania

Sixth Day, we rode to Philadelphia and the next day the Yearly Meeting of Ministers and Elders opened and, on the ensuing Second Day, the Yearly Meeting of Discipline. It was very large and continued by adjournments through the week and closed on Seventh Day. Many weighty subjects were opened for deliberation, but through the prevalence and mixture[1] of unsubjected spirits, who were too froward and active in their own unmortified wills, much weakness was apparent, which greatly increased the burden of the living and truly baptized members – of which class there was a very considerable number who were deeply engaged for the promotion of the cause of Truth and that the family-at-large might be kept in decent and commendable order, consistent with the gospel of Christ, and become established on the ancient foundation of our holy profession. These were nearly united in spirit and in travail for Zion's arising, and the Lord was graciously pleased to water these together at seasons with the descendings of heavenly dew, by which encouragement was witnessed to persevere in patience, and in thankful acknowledgment for his continued mercy, and were favored to return from their annual solemnity with rejoicing for all the good the Lord had been pleased to favor them with.

We tarried in the city over First Day and attended the forenoon meeting at Market Street. It was very large, wherein my spirit was set at liberty and ability afforded to divide the word among them according to their varied conditions in a large, searching, and effectual testimony, whereby a holy solemnity was witnessed to spread over the meeting to the great rejoicing of the honest-hearted.

But alas, how oft are those seasons of comfort interrupted and hurt by the indiscreet forwardness of some who have been called to publish the gospel, but for want of dwelling enough in the root have branched out in the fertility of their own natural abilities, and become too active in their own spirits, and are thereby not only in danger of losing their gifts and falling into a bewildered state, but these often hurt the service, and take off the savor of many of our most favored solemnities. This was affectingly the case at this time by the addition of a long, but very lifeless testimony. And although delivered in sound words, yet being destitute of the life and power, tended greatly to burden the living and grieve the upright in heart.

Great advantage would redound to the church in general (and to this class of its members in particular), if those who stand in the station of Elders were more deeply centered in their minds to the Well-Spring of Eternal Life – waiting and feeling after a Spirit of right discerning – that so

---

[1] Mixture: mixing in incompatible elements

they might be enabled to judge righteous judgment[1] and distinguish rightly between the living and the dead. Then would the hand be seasonably laid upon the head of this transforming Spirit and those in danger of being deceived thereby witness preservation.

We left the city on Second Day, 27th of 4th month, and passed over into the Jerseys in order to take some meetings that I had not been at. We were at five in the course of the week and although the life and virtue of true religion appeared to be at a low ebb among those professing with us in too general a manner in those meetings, yet as public notice was given of our attendance, many of the neighboring inhabitants came in – among whom, I believe, there were some seeking minds. These generally add life to meetings and draw down the compassion and tender regard of the Heavenly Parent who, in his condescending goodness, made way for the gospel to be preached among them in these several meetings in a good degree of the divine authority – insomuch that many minds were tenderly affected and the assemblies solemnized, the lukewarm aroused and the hypocritical, worldly-minded professors forewarned of the danger their situations exposed them to. And my spirit was made thankful for the relief I obtained, although through a line of deep, inward travail and baptism with the oppressed seed. But the Lord's power arose in victory over all, to the honor of his right worthy name, who will be glorified in his saints,[2] and sanctified in all those who come near him.

We returned to the city on Seventh Day and attended the Quarterly Meeting of Ministers and Elders, in which I was led in a short, but relieving testimony to call Friends' attention back to primitive simplicity and integrity and the great need there is of being more separated from the world – its spirit, manners, maxims, and customs – and to live daily under an exercise and travail for the arising of that life and power that can only enable us to separate from those things that have a tendency to hurt and defile, and through which life and power, ministers and elders can only be rightly qualified to lead and feed the flock over whom the Holy Ghost hath made them overseers, consistent with divine appointment. For want of which fervent labor and travail, great weakness is apparent amongst us as a people in many places, and the great and worthy name by which we are called oft times dishonored – to the grief of the upright in heart, who are exercised for Israel's prosperity and Jerusalem's peace and who go almost daily, as with their hands on their loins for very pain.

First Day: Attended the Northern District Meeting in the morning and that at Market Street in the afternoon. They were both instructive, edifying seasons, wherein I had full opportunity to relieve my mind, being –

---

[1] John 7:24
[2] 2 Thessalonians 1:10

through gracious assistance – led in the clear openings of the Divine Light to set forth the great danger of mixing in with the spirit of the world that leads to strife and contention, and the promotion of parties and party animosities in civil governments. All which, have a direct tendency to engender war and bloodshed, and therefore inconsistent for us as a people to touch or take part with or to suffer our minds to be agitated thereby – as it always has and always will lead those that are leavened therewith out of the meek Spirit of the Gospel that breathes peace on earth and goodwill to all men.[1]

I was likewise led, especially in the latter, to set forth the ground of unbelief, and the medium through which deism and infidelity entered and darkened the mind, and to open the way in a very clear manner how all might come to the knowledge of and firm belief in the outward manifestation of Christ as set forth in the scriptures. And that, although it was not to be comprehended or truly believed in through the mere natural force or effects of our rational powers, yet when opened to us through the right medium (the revelation of the Spirit), it could easily be accounted for as a process purely rational and wherein the soul might become established in the full belief thereof, beyond the least shadow of doubting. This was the Lord's doing and marvelous in our eyes.[2] And Friends were much comforted and united in this day's exercise, and my spirit made joyful in the saving help and continued mercy of Israel's true Shepherd, who is over all, worthy, and blessed forever.

Second Day: The quarterly meeting was held. It was likewise a time of favor in which divers communications opened, tending to unite Friends in an exercise for the advancement of the testimony, and that the many causes of weakness that brought pain and many deep baptisms on the living part of the body might be done away, and the camp cleansed.

Third Day morning: I left the city on with a peaceful mind and rode to Frankford. Attended a meeting there in the forenoon and one at Germantown in the afternoon, in both of which I labored in the ability received. The first was a very searching season – things were laid open in such a manner that the dead in some instances seemed to be raised, and that power felt that opened the graves formerly. And some of those who were settled down in their polluted rests – their heavens were shaken and their rocks made to melt by the fervent heat of the Divine Word, which was as a fire and a hammer. Truth prevailed, and was eminently in dominion over all.

---

[1] The first two sentences in the next paragraph were deleted from the printed *Journal*.

[2] Psalm 118:23, Mark 12:11, & Matthew 21:42

Fourth and Fifth Days: We attended the Quarterly Meeting of Abington, in which I was exercised in a line of close fervent labor – both in the Meeting of Ministers and Elders and the quarterly at large. It was a season that gave hope of some improvement in many, but others appeared too much in a state of self-sufficiency – a most deplorable condition, sickly and wounded, that refuses to be healed. For these, my mind felt pained.

O that they might, ere the day of their visitation[1] passeth over, witness their eyes anointed with the eye-salve of the gospel,[2] that so they might be brought to see the precipice on which they stand, and be thereby reduced into the valley of humiliation, where alone true honor and right exaltation are known and where they might experience a being washed from all their pollutions and healed of all their wounds.

Sixth Day, attended a meeting at Byberry and, through the Lord's presiding presence, it proved a day of signal[3] favor, wherein the doctrines of full and complete redemption from sin and death were clearly opened, and Truth exalted over all the dark tenets and carnal reasonings of men, that gender[4] to unbelief and infidelity. Seventh Day, returned to Abington, where we had another large, favored meeting, wherein many things were opened in a plain way, tending to gather the minds of the people out of the spirit of the world that leads to strife and contention and from whence party animosities arise (a sure prelude to war) and calling their attention home to the great gospel privilege (the holy unction and anointing within) so that they need not that any man teach them, but as the same anointing teacheth.[5] And which, as they come to believe in and obey, would qualify them to judge all ministry and from whence it had its rise and spring, and thereby be delivered from all false glosses[6] and mixtures in religion, and become established in that, that never fell, the immoveable rock, Christ Jesus, against which the gates of hell would never be able to prevail.[7]

First Day and 10th of 5th month: We attended Horsham Meeting and in the afternoon, the meeting at North Wales. It was a day of high favor – the Lord's arm being graciously made bare for our help. The meetings were very large – many not of our society attended. The gospel was freely

---

[1] Day of Visitation: According to early Friends, each person faced choice between spiritual life and death at a single, particular point in his or her life. The outcome was to choose either God and salvation or eternal damnation. Later Friends (including Hicks) believed that God offered this chance repeatedly throughout each person's life.
[2] Revelation 3:18
[3] Signal: remarkable, significant
[4] Gender: engender, produce
[5] 1 John 2:20-27
[6] Gloss: An interpretation or explanation of a text
[7] Matthew 16:18

preached among them in the clear demonstration of the Spirit. These were truly humbling seasons, especially the former, wherein a great number were much contrited and wept freely. And the rocks seemed to melt at the presence of the mighty God of Jacob,[1] whose power was prevalently witnessed in that large assembly, to the praise and exaltation of his great and glorious name.

Second Day: Attended the meeting at Plymouth and although an evident want of that primitive zeal and integrity that distinguished our worthy predecessors was affectingly manifest with too many of those who fill up their places in outward profession, yet it was comforting to find that the Shepherd of Israel was still graciously pleased to continue his merciful visitation and renew his gracious calls to these to return and renew covenant with him, which was the substance of this day's testimony and labor. May the Master of Assemblies make it effectual to all that were present of this description is my sincere prayer.

Third Day: Was at Providence Meeting, which was small. Nevertheless, through gracious regard it proved an edifying, heart-tendering season – the states of the people being opened and spoken to in the authority of Truth, to their great humiliation – many hearts being much broken and reduced, and the Lord's name and power over all exalted.[2]

After this meeting, my mind was turned towards the Quarterly Meeting of Caln to be held this time at Sadsbury, a new-established quarterly meeting in the county of Chester. And finding it necessary to comply with the motion, as believing that my peace consisted in it, we set out immediately after dinner – having thirty miles or upwards to ride to it and it opening the next day, being the fourth of the week and 13th of the month. The journey proved very wearisome to my infirm body, being much troubled at this time with the gravel[3] or something of that nature, which by hard or constant riding produced much pain, with which I was greatly afflicted during the time of this quarterly meeting – especially in the forepart of the public meeting that preceded the meeting for discipline. My pain was great, insomuch that I was under necessity of withdrawing twice in a short time and was near concluding I should be obliged to wholly leave the meeting – my distress of body being very great. But feeling my mind drawn to the people – there being a large congregation present – accompanied with a small opening, I returned into the meeting and after a short time, way opening to stand up – though in great

---

[1] Psalm 114:6-7

[2] The next paragraph was edited in the printed *Journal* to minimize Hicks' physical distress.

[3] Gravel: kidney stones – Hicks seems to have frequently suffered from these

weakness of body and mind. But as I attended to the opening (though small in the beginning) and kept down in the gift – moving forward by gentle gradations as way was made – I was enlarged in clear, pertinent doctrine. And Truth arose into dominion in an eminent manner and ran over all as oil, to the comforting and breaking many hearts, and reducing and silencing every opposite spirit, so that a very precious solemnity was spread over the meeting – to the rejoicing of the upright in heart, the relief to my own mind, and alleviation of my bodily affliction.

These are high favors. May a humbling and grateful sense thereof rest continually upon thee, O my soul, and may thou never forget how much thou owest to thy Lord![1] How deep and solemn are thy obligations to the God of thy salvation![2] How hath he often taken thee out of the horrible pit and out of the miry clay, and set thee upon a rock and put a new song into thy mouth – even praises, high praises to him![3]

From this meeting, we returned to Caln, and attended their monthly meeting, held the sixth of the week. I was enabled to labor among them in much plainness – both in the meeting for worship and in the discipline – and left them with a peaceful mind.

The three following days, we attended meetings at Robeson, Exeter, and Reading. The number of members which constituted these meetings was small, but a considerable number of the neighboring inhabitants attended. Ability was graciously afforded to preach the gospel freely in each and the power attending broke and tendered many hearts. And an excellent savor and solemnity was felt to spread over the meetings in a very eminent manner. For this, I was made humbly thankful to the bountiful Author of all our Blessings. These favors were more than an adequate reward for all my toil and exercise. Although I had been for some days past under the pressure of much bodily infirmity, accompanied with seasons of great uneasiness and pain, but the Lord's power was over all and kept my mind in patience and sweet peace from day to day. Blessed forever be his right worthy name.

Fourth of the week and the 20th of the 5th month: We attended the meeting at Maidencreek, after which that afternoon and the next day we crossed the Blue Mountains to Roaring Creek. And the next day being the sixth of the week, we attended a meeting there. Both of these meetings were crowned with the Lord's presence and were tendering seasons, edifying and instructive.

The morning following we rode to Catawissa and attended their monthly meeting and we continued there over First Day. I was enabled

---

[1] Luke 16:5
[2] Isaiah 17:10
[3] Psalm 40:2-3

through the Lord's good presence attending, to labor among them – both in the meeting for discipline and those for worship – in much plainness. Divers matters relative to the well-ordering of the affairs of Truth were opened, which proved instructive and edifying.

After the latter meeting, we passed on that afternoon fifteen miles to Berwick, crossing the River Susquehanna in our way. Although my bodily indisposition still continued, the day following being the second of the week and 25th of 5th month, we had a meeting there among the townspeople and the few Friends of that place. It was a comfortable season, edifying and strengthening to Friends and confirming to a number who were looking towards us with desires for further information.

After this meeting, we rode to Fishing Creek – about eighteen miles. And the day following, had a very satisfactory meeting at that place. For although in this journey for a considerable time past, I have been mostly attended with much bodily infirmity, yet the Lord in his abundant mercy hath been graciously pleased to keep my mind stayed[1] upon him, insomuch that my trust and confidence hath not at any time failed – not even when I have been reduced into a state of great distress and suffering and my poor soul plunged into the mighty abyss of surrounding darkness and sunk, as it were, to the bottom of the mountains.[2] But as I patiently abode under those trying baptisms, in which I witnessed a fellowship with the sufferings of Christ and was made willing to endure my portion thereof – which he had left behind for his servants and ministers to fill up for his body's sake (the church), he did not fail to raise my spirit out of this horrible pit. Therein I had been a partaker with the Suffering Seed in the hearts of those who – through supineness, ease, forgetfulness, unbelief and a worldly spirit – had become like a bottomless abyss of corruption, darkness and error. I was enabled, through a real feeling of their deplorable states, to administer to their several needs and open to them their conditions, insomuch that many were pricked in heart and convinced of the error of their ways and were led to give God the glory of his own work.

O, saith my soul! May all those who are sent out on this solemn embassy[3] and most important service dwell low in their minds and keep a single eye to the Lord's honor, that so self may be thoroughly abased.[4] Otherwise, there is great danger in those trying and most afflictive dispensations of the mind's getting into a state of impatience, and therein be led to judge the people of hardness and a spirit of opposition. This will

---

[1] Stay: focus
[2] Jonah 2:3-6
[3] Embassy: the mission of a person sent to represent a sovereign
[4] Abase: lower in rank or honor

not fail, as given way to, of centering the minds of such either into a state of silent sadness and discouragement – so that like the disciples formerly, they will be for sending the people away fasting and empty[1] – or else raise in them a hot fiery zeal, in which they will throw out some hard censures or harsh reproof, untempered with that charity requisite and necessary always to attend every gospel communication. For want thereof, both speaker and hearers will be wounded and much a hurt done. Many opportunities, I believe, that might have been crowned with the Lord's presence and truth in them exalted over all have been entirely lost through these means.

Nay, I have no doubt but some meetings have been held to the dishonor of Truth and wounding many tender minds. And I have sometimes been afraid that some, who are rightly called and sent on this greatest of errands, have so far missed their way by letting up[2] under some of those excruciating baptisms which they have been led into in order to qualify them rightly to administer to the states of the people. The impatient spirit brought a gloom of darkness over their minds, and which has continued with them from day to day – greatly to their distress. Although they have continued to attend meetings, they have been so shut up in total darkness as not to see any way of relief except in uttering their complaints – similar to the murmurings of Israel in the wilderness.[3]

Where I have found such things left on record, I have thought they always tended to discouragement and dismay when coming from the leaders of the people. For although the Lord was graciously pleased to condescend to the weakness of that people and delivered them out of the distress that their impatience had brought upon them, yet he very clearly manifested his displeasure thereat. And if only one instance of impatience and improper zeal in Moses drew upon him such severe censure (as we read it did[4]), how ought all those who are now called forth as leaders of the people to stand always on their guard against every motion of impatience and impure zeal, lest they also fall under the displeasure of the Captain of their Salvation.

For although after those gloomy dispensations we may be again favored, in renewed mercy, and helped out of this horrible pit and witness the lifting up of his glorious countenance upon us, yet this is no proof of the rectitude of our conduct – any more than his showing mercy to Israel after their murmurings was a justification thereof. Yet I have been afraid that some have considered those renewed favors as a consequence of their

---

[1] Matthew 15:32 & Mark 8:3
[2] Let up: give up
[3] Exodus 16:7-8, Numbers 14:27 & 36
[4] Numbers 20:1-12

own sufferings. This, to me, carries too much of selfishness and savors of a desire of clothing ourselves with the Lord's jewels instead of rendering to him with heart-felt gratitude the glory of all his works and receiving this act of unmerited redemption from the gloom that our own impatience and the want of a thorough reduction of self had cast us into. This flows purely from his forbearing mercy, condescending goodness, and free love.

After the aforesaid meeting, we rode to Muncy, and lodged with our kind Friend, William Ellis.

The next day being the fourth of the week and 27th of 5th month, was held their middle week meeting. And notice being spread of our being there, it was large. And although I had to sit some time in the forepart of the meeting in much weakness and depression, both of body and mind, yet as I abode in patience and resignation to my present allotment – willing to be anything or nothing and to do or to suffer according to the Master's will – after a time of solemn waiting, a little opening presented, attended with some glimmering of light. As my eye was kept steadily to it, I felt a necessity to stand up with it and which, as I proceeded in guarded care, opened to a large field of doctrine, suitably adapted I believe to the states of those present, insomuch that a very comfortable solemnity was felt to spread over the meeting to the rejoicing of the hearts of the faithful.

After this meeting, feeling myself very unwell with a hard cold which had attended me for some time, we rested a day or two with our aforesaid Friend in order to recruit[1] – I being much worn down by constant traveling under such bodily infirmities.

The 30th and seventh of the week, we attended a meeting at a place called Pine Grove, a small meeting of Friends being in that place.

On First Day, we had a large meeting by appointment at a town called Williamsport. It was held in their courthouse, but the room was not large enough to contain the people. And although very much crowded and many standing, they behaved soberly and a blessed meeting we had. I was led forth among them in a large, affecting testimony wherein the truths of the gospel were clearly opened and explained to the weakest capacities. The Lord's power was in dominion in a very eminent manner.[2] My mind was so swallowed up in this day's exercise, that while on my feet, I was scarcely sensible whether I was in or out of the body. When I sat down, my strength was much exhausted and I in such a state of perspiration that I was thoroughly wet from head to foot with excessive sweating. It was a season thankfully to be remembered and greatly refreshing to my drooping spirit – making up every deficiency for the want of bodily

---

[1] Recruit: regain one's health
[2] The next two sentences were deleted from the printed *Journal*.

Centre (Delaware) Meetinghouse

health, insomuch that I could with heartfelt gratitude cheerfully acknowledge it was the Lord's doing.

After this meeting we set forward on our journey towards Redstone, taking meetings in our way at Job Packer's, Milesburg, Halfmoon, and Dunnings Creek, after which we passed directly over the Alleghany Mountains into the compass of Redstone Quarter.

The first meeting we fell in with on the western side of the mountains was Sewickley, a branch of Redstone monthly meeting, which we attended on Fourth Day, 10th of 6th month.

After this, we took Providence on Fifth Day, Centre on Sixth Day, and Fallowfield on Seventh Day. And although these were seasons of close exercise, accompanied with some painful labor and deep baptisms in suffering with the seed, yet my mind was favored in the openings of gospel light to discharge myself in those meetings, so as to leave them with solid peace of mind. I believe they were seasons of renewed visitation to many that attended, that will not soon be forgotten by them.

On First Day, we attended the meeting at Pike Run, and the two following days, were at Westland and Redstone Meetings. My mind was under a very great pressure of distress in passing along through those six last mentioned meetings – both from an inward sense and an outward discovery of great weakness prevailing among a number of their leading members. This was occasioned by an unwarrantable credulity and letting out their minds to listen to and believe in the vulgar and shamefully ridiculous notion of witchcraft, insomuch that some of their leading members openly acknowledged that they believed that a family of their near kindred – several of whom were troubled with a kind of periodical fits – were actually bewitched by one of their neighbors, which was (as they thought) the sole occasion of their complaint. My spirit was exceedingly grieved by their asserting their belief of those abominable reports and by discovering how their minds were led away thereby to believe a lie.

And this delusion was greatly added to by a certain boy or lad in the neighborhood who pretended[1] to tell secrets and that he could see any person whom any should inquire after, although in a very distant part of the world, and would pretend to tell persons who came to see him, although they lived on the other side of the Atlantic, that he could see the very place of their residence and of what materials their houses were made – as though he was present at the place – and could tell the conditions and dispositions of persons whom he had never before seen, and what they were guilty of – as to their private sins – and who was a witch and who not. He had so got the ascendancy in the minds of those who had foolishly given way to the absurd notion of witchcraft, that whatever he said in those respects was to them as oracles. So that if he impeached the most unblemished character of being a witch or guilty of any baneful sin, they were ready to believe it – by which great hurt was done.

I was exceedingly burdened therewith, and had conversation with divers on the subject, but they were so carried away with these fanatical notions that the most sound reasoning seemed to have no weight with them. Though they all pretended to bring forward support of their vain and ideal[2] notions, it was simply the say and report of others. Indeed, they appeared to have a much firmer belief in those ideal or imaginary spirits than in the God whom they professed to worship, for it is a gospel truth, that we cannot pay homage to two masters. And while any man or woman can give way to believe in such things, so as to go to dark, undisciplined, and irreligious men to be healed of those infirmities that they are told are the effect of witchcraft, it is certainly denying the God that made them, who only hath all power in heaven and in earth, and can wound and heal, kill and make alive at his pleasure.[3]

---

[1] Pretend: claim or assert
[2] Ideal: arising from one's own ideas
[3] At this point, there are four manuscript lines that have been crossed out. Only a few words are legible: "And it is astonishing to consider how any member of our

God forbid, saith my soul, that any professing the name of a Quaker should ever thus desert the God of his salvation. For if he doth, it will no doubt tend to his confusion[1] and in which state, he will be given over to strange delusions, even to believe a lie – a most wretched state for any poor soul to be in. I was enabled through condescending goodness to clear my mind among them by divers, large, full testimonies to the Truth and the excellency of its power to deliver from everything that tends to hurt or defile, insomuch that I left them with peace of mind.

We proceeded to Connellsville, where we had a very comfortable, heart-tendering season, among a few Friends and the town's people. Next, we attended Sandy Hill Meeting.

Virginia

And the day following, were at Sandy Creek Glades – both comfortable seasons. These closed our visit to Redstone Quarter.

After this, we returned across the Alleghany Mountains, intending to take the meetings at Hopewell, in compass of Fairfax Quarterly Meeting.

We got to Bear Garden Particular Meeting on First Day, having rode hard the day before in order to reach it – not having much prospect thereof when we left Sandy Creek, the distance between the two places was about ninety-two miles and the way very mountainous and having but little more than a day and a half to ride it. This meeting, in the forepart, was very laborous, but ended well and we left them with solid satisfaction and passed on to Back Creek Meeting that afternoon, held near a small town or village called Penn's Town. Many of the neighboring people came in, so that the meeting was pretty large and I had considerable to communicate among them, but without obtaining much relief of mind.

In the course of this week, we attended meetings at a place called the Ridge, Centre, Crooked Run, Mount Pleasant, Hopewell, and Lower Ridge. On the First and Second Days of the following week, we were at Middle Creek and Berkeley Meetings. These were (most of them) favored seasons – particularly that at Middle Creek, wherein the Lord's presence was powerfully manifest. Truth rose into great dominion and ran over all as oil, preciously uniting and edifying the honest-hearted and breaking down all opposition, affecting and mollifying the hearts of almost the whole assembly. It was indeed a precious solemnity not soon to be forgotten, but to be held in grateful remembrance.

---

society that…in whom are hid all the treasures of wisdom and knowledge [Colossians 2:3] could go to Beelzebub … " Not much more can be read with any certainty.

[1] Confusion: ruin or perdition

Back in Pennsylvania

After these meetings, we turned our faces homewards, taking meetings in our way at Little York, Columbia, Pottstown, and the Great Swamp (alias Richland). These were, through divine favor, instructive seasons.

The next meeting was at Plumstead (in the compass of Bucks Quarterly Meeting), which we attended on Third Day, 7th of 7th month.

On the two following days, we were at Buckingham and Wrightstown Meetings. My mind in those meetings was brought under a close exercise from a prospect of Friends being too much leavened into the spirit of the world – its customs and maxims – by which many appeared to be greatly wounded and had become as dwarfs in our Israel.[1] And I believe nothing contributed more to this than their becoming parties in the civil government and taking offices therein, for here, the spirit of contention gets in and a striving to be uppermost and fill the principal seats. Then party animosities take place, from whence are derived envying and grudging one against another, and then to reviling and neighbors speaking evil one of another. Hence wars and fightings arise – as from their proper and natural ground.

As any Friend or Friends give way to these things, it leads and leavens their minds into the spirit of the world, which is a spirit of darkness that blinds the understanding and hardens the heart and draws into many hurtful and pernicious practices, such as distillation and dealing in ardent spirits,[2] drinking strong drink, and handing it out in their fields to their workmen to stimulate them to an excess of labor. Hence, an excess of drinking strong drink is gradually introduced among the poor laborers – by which many families are ruined.

My spirit was deeply exercised on those accounts and as I patiently endured the baptisms I had to go through and submitted to communicate what appeared to open in the clearness, I was enlarged in setting forth the dangerous and hurtful tendency of such conduct, and its great inconsistency with our holy profession, and to exhort Friends to withdraw therefrom as the means (together with a more frequent recurrence to the first principle of our profession, the Light Within) whereby deliverance and preservation could only be experienced. The Lord was graciously with us in those meetings, and the faithful were encouraged and edified, and many hearts greatly tendered, under a sense of the Lord's mercy and goodness extended to us in these seasons.

---

[1] Dwarfs were forbidden to be priests (Leviticus 21:20).
[2] Although Hicks has written "arduous," he clearly intended "ardent" or distilled liquors.

On Sixth Day, we attended a meeting at Makefield and in the afternoon, had a large meeting at Newtown. It was held in their courthouse and mostly made up of those not professing with us. I felt in this meeting the pressure and prevalence of a spirit of darkness and unbelief, and was led to open the ground thereof, and to show its inconsistency with the self-evident experience of every rational mind. Although men in the ignorance and darkness of their own hearts may strive to settle themselves in unbelief in order to live quietly in the gratification of their own wills and creaturely appetites, without any control – and take their swing in all kinds of evil which would be the natural tendency thereof, could they become established therein, but that they never can fully come to this. For that just witness placed in every bosom as a Reprover for sin will continue to disturb all those false rests and shake every heaven of man's making.

Although men through the hardness of their hearts may not submit to the guidance of this just principle, so as to have a saving belief therein, yet they will thereby be compelled into a belief similar to that of the devils. This, they never will be able fully to divest themselves of by all their carnal reasonings and fleshly wisdom. It will continue, at times, to make them fear and tremble and by its tremendous power, will cause the very top of their Sinai to shake and blast all their false hopes. For it is the determinate counsel of unerring wisdom that the hope of the hypocrite shall perish.[1] Therefore let all prize the day of their visitation while the Lord is graciously striving with them by the clear, self-evident touches of his Light in their hearts, in order that the wicked may turn from his wicked way and the unrighteous from his unrighteous thoughts and turn unto the Lord who will have mercy upon him, and unto our God who will abundantly pardon him.

The meeting at Makefield was likewise a precious opportunity – the Lord being mightily with us in our passing along from season to season – to our humbling admiration, furnishing with strength for every service, so that we indeed found him to be strength in weakness and riches in poverty.[2] For I never felt greater weakness and nothingness (as to self), than in this journey and could truly say that our sufficiency was not of ourselves, but of God, and that the Lord was our strength from day to day, who is over all, blessed forever.

The three following days, we attended meetings at Middletown, Bristol, and the Falls. I was led forth in these meetings thoroughly to show wherein real Christianity consists, and that although the people of Christendom had the name of Christians, yet so long as they lived in the

---

[1] Job 8:13
[2] 2 Corinthians 8:9, 12:9

gratification of their own wills and carnal lusts – from whence discord, animosities, envyings, strife, and every evil work originated – they were only heathens in disguise. For true Christianity is nothing else but a real and complete mortification of our own will, and a full and final annihilation of all self-exaltation. And the contrary is the true antichrist that sitteth in the seat of God, who opposeth and exalteth himself above all that is called God or that is worshipped.[1] Therefore, no man or woman is any further Christians than as they come to experience the self-denial, meekness, humility and gentleness of Christ as the lamb of God who taketh away the sin of the world, ruling and reigning in them, so as to become their real life – in and by which, they become partakers of the divine nature and know the life of God raised up in the immortal soul. This is the new birth, or Christ formed in us, and without which, as our Lord told Nicodemus, no man can see the kingdom of God.[2]

Back in New Jersey

After these meetings, we crossed the River Delaware into the Jerseys, taking meetings on our way at Kingwood, Hardwick, Mendham, and one near Paulingskiln, and from thence, to Cornwall in New York state. We came here Seventh Day evening, the 18th of 7th month, and the next day was at their First Day Meeting.

I was much worn down by constant traveling and hard labor, and felt much fatigue when we came here. In going to this meeting, I felt a desire to rise in my mind that I might have a good silent meeting and the prayer of my spirit was answered, for I had not sat long before a perfect, sweet calm ensued wherein my whole man was swallowed up in divine seraphic enjoyment, insomuch that not only my mind, but also my wearied body forgot all its toil. My soul was so inflamed with gratitude to the all bountiful Author of all our Rich Mercies and blessings that praises and thanksgiving ascended as incense from the altar of my heart to his great and glorious name, who remains to be God over all, blessed in himself and in his son, Christ Jesus, throughout all ages, world without end. Amen.

In the course of this week, we took meetings at Newburgh Valley, the Paltz, and Marlborough, and on Fifth Day were at Cornwall Monthly Meeting. The meeting for worship that preceded the business was large. I was led among them in a line of close searching labor, which for some time seemed to have but little entrance[3] among them – people being too generally disposed while in a state of unsoundness to shut themselves against that which they know (if they lay open to receive) would find out

---

[1] 2 Thessalonians 2:4
[2] John 3:3
[3] Entrance: permission or allowance to enter one's mind

all their secret, lurking places. There self-love and self-will lie shrouded under a mask of doing good, while it is gratified in the full enjoyment of all its beloveds, and with whom it is daily committing adultery and fornication. But as I continued to persevere in faithfulness to the opening (although the prospect for a time seemed discouraging) Truth began to make way by its own power and gradually spread over the meeting, breaking down all opposition, and tendering and mollifying many hearts.

The meeting for discipline appeared to be pretty well conducted, there being a remnant, I believe, honestly engaged for the promotion of the cause of Truth and these the Lord delights to favor and furnish with strength to carry on his own work of Truth and Righteousness in the earth. He will continue to reward these with the real enjoyment of his life-giving presence, while those who sit as mere idle spectators will be sent empty away.[1]

On Sixth Day, we had an appointed meeting at the house of our Friend, Thomas Jones, at Wallkill and on Seventh Day, one at Goshen, and on First Day, was at Smith's Clove – all satisfactory seasons, especially the latter, wherein Truth was powerfully manifest to the tendering and mollifying the hearts of the people in a remarkable manner, so that a very precious solemnity was witnessed spread over the meeting.

After these meetings, we turned homewards, taking meetings at Kakiat, Tappan, and New York, in our way, and got well home on Fourth Day evening, the 29th of 7th month. I found my family in usual health, which, together with an endeared and cordial reception in the feelings of mutual love and flowings of that peace of mind attendant a faithful discharge of manifested duty, filled my heart with thankful acknowledgments to the great and bountiful Author of Every Blessing.

I was from home in this journey three months and eighteen days and traveled by computation about sixteen hundred and thirty miles.

A Visit to Friends in Canada & Some of the Northern Parts of the Yearly Meeting of New York in 1803

In the fall of the year 1803, I performed a visit to Friends of Upper Canada in the compass of our yearly meeting and some other of the northwestern parts thereof. Daniel Titus was my companion in this journey. We left home the 20th of 9th month and proceeded directly to Canada in company with two other Friends, who, with us, were appointed to attend the Monthly Meeting of Adolphustown on a particular concern relative to that meeting.

---

[1] Luke 1:53

We were at but three meetings in our way thither – two at Hudson on First Day and one at the Black River. We got well to Adolphustown on Third Day evening, the 3rd of 10th month, having rode to get there about four hundred and ten miles and crossed the great River Saint Lawrence in our way, which appeared to be a dangerous passage.

We crossed it in two branches – an island lying in the middle. Each branch was near five miles over. We crossed the latter in the dead of the night by the light of the moon in two small flat-bottomed boats – one of them so small as to carry only one horse, and three in the other. This latter passage lay open to the great Lake Ontario and the wind being from that quarter caused the swell frequently to wash into our boats, insomuch that we had considerable labor to throw out the water as fast it came in. But my confidence was in him who hath the winds and the waves at his command,[1] and this kept out fear, and we got safe over about the 1st hour of the night.

On Fourth Day, we attended Friends meeting at Adolphustown as it came in course. It proved an instructive, favored season.

Fifth Day, rode to Green Point in the township of Sophiasburgh to the house of our Friend, Daniel Way, and had an appointed meeting there at the 3rd hour that afternoon wherein Truth favored and through the prevalence of its power attending the communication, many minds were much bowed and their hearts tendered by its secret, mollifying influence. Our next appointment was in the neighborhood of our Friend, Robert Hubbs, on Seventh Day. Composed mostly of people not of our society, it was a comfortable, edifying season, after which we proceeded to the township of Hallowell, to the house of our Friend, Thomas Boorman, near the West Lake[2] and on First Day, attended Friends meeting there, and on Second Day, had an opportunity with the people at the east end of said lake. The meeting was held at the house of a professor among the Methodists.

Those two last meetings were eminently favored – Truth rose into dominion and ran as oil over all opposition, to the instruction and comfort of many minds, and the Lord was praised for his goodness and for his merciful, loving-kindness to the children of men. We returned that evening to the west end of said lake, to the house of our Friend, Jacob Cronk, and lodged.

---

[1] Psalm 107:25, Mark 4:35-41

[2] There is some confusion here. The preparative meeting in Bloomfield, Ontario was renamed West Lake in 1829. In addition, one of the quarterly meetings in Canada Half Yearly Meeting was named West Lake – i.e., the western part of Lake Ontario. East Lake was a preparative meeting in this quarter.

Third Day, 11th of 10th month, we returned to the house of Cornelius Blount, where the meeting for Friends of the West Lake was held. It was the time of their preparative meeting and many of the neighboring inhabitants came in and sat with Friends during the time of worship – the forepart of which was rather low and depressing. But as patience was abode in and right attention given to a small opening that presented, and as I moved therein with care, Truth gradually arose into dominion, powerfully breaking down all that stood in its way. Whereby, many hearts were comforted and refreshed, and a general solemnity spread over the meeting, insomuch that we could truly say, "Hitherto hath the Lord helped us."[1]

After Friends' preparative meeting was over (which was held in an orderly manner), we returned that evening to the house of our Friend, John Dorland, in Adolphustown – he having kindly accompanied us since we left that place.

Fourth Day, attended the preparative meeting there. The meeting for worship was large by the coming in of many of those who were not members. They manifested great willingness to hear the truths of the gospel declared, yet too many appeared careless and unconcerned in regard to the practical part, that in them was fulfilled the saying of the apostle, "They being as men beholding their natural face in a glass and turning away forget what manner of persons they were." And this, it is to be feared, is too much the case with many amongst us as a people, who are pleasing themselves with hearing the Truth declared and rejoice in the privilege of sitting under a free, living gospel ministry (through the labor and exercise of the faithful), but suffer the cumbering[2] cares and pleasures of this life so to divert them from a right improvement of their own gifts that they, in a religious sense, may justly be compared to idle drones,[3] who live on the labor of the industrious bee and are contenting themselves in a situation like the foolish virgins that, although they have lamps, yet are without oil in their vessels. But alas, what will these do when the awful midnight cry is heard, "Behold the bridegroom cometh"?[4] Then fear and dismay, with an utter exclusion from the marriage chamber, will be the woeful doom of all careless and lifeless professors.

---

[1] 1 Samuel 7:12
[2] Cumber: distress or encumber
[3] Drone: a male honeybee, which does not work, but only serves to impregnate the queen
[4] Matthew 25:1

O that all might lay these things to heart and endeavor in awful fear to have their day's work done in the day time. For behold, the night cometh, wherein none can work.[1]

On Sixth Day, we attended Friends Preparative Meeting at Kingston. And on Seventh Day, had a meeting in the town of Kingston in the courthouse – the first Friends meeting ever held in that place. The people appeared much unacquainted with the order of our meetings. Some of the principal men seemed at a loss how to behave themselves in the time of silence, but during the communication, they were generally quiet and solemn. And Truth arose into victory, furnishing doctrine clothed with the divine power, carrying full conviction to the minds of most present.

The next day being the first of the week, we attended again with Friends at their meeting held at the house of the Widow Brewer – they not having any meetinghouse in this place – and in the afternoon, had an appointed meeting in the west part of this township on the bay – held at the house of John Everitt, a man not in strict profession with any religious society. These were both seasons of heavenly refreshment – the life ran as oil over all. Many hearts were much broken and contrited under the precious, mollifying influence thereof. Praised and magnified forever be the name of the Lord, for his mercy and loving-kindness to the children of men.

The 17th, we returned on our way towards Adolphustown and attended a meeting appointed at an inn in the town of Ernest. This also proved, through the condescending mercy and goodness of the Lord our gracious Helper, a blessed season and, through the efficacious power attending the word preached, many hearts were pierced and the whole assembly solemnized. And we parted from each other with thankful hearts, and rode to Adolphustown and lodged with our Friend, Daniel Haight.

The day following we had an appointed meeting at his house for the neighboring inhabitants, who were (many of them) professors among the Methodists. And through divine goodness, it was to me a season of great refreshment and the assembly were generally broken and contrited through the convicting power of divine love, which was mercifully vouchsafed to us at this season.

We then proceeded again to our Friend, John Dorland's, and rested the next day – being some unwell and considerably wearied by such constant traveling.

Fifth Day and 20th of the month, we attended the Monthly Meeting for Friends of the lower part of the Province of Upper Canada held in this

---

[1] John 9:4

1801-1805 *115*

place. This closed our visit in these parts, after which we took leave of our Friends in much brotherly affection – their hearts being contrited and cheeks bedewed with tears whilst closing our farewell addresses. After which, we rode directly to Kingston (about thirty-five miles) and there took boat immediately and crossed one branch of the River Saint Lawrence that evening, and likewise crossed the island that lies between before dark – it being about five miles over. But the wind being unfavorable, we did not cross the other branch till next morn. We lodged in a small house – being the only one on that side of the island. Our accommodations were very poor, having to lie on the floor and benches, but having the best of company, peace of mind and a firm trust in the divine blessing, it kept us comfortable and pleasant.

New York

The next day being the 22nd of the month, we crossed early in the morning and rode that day to our Friend, Samuel Brown's, at Black River. And the next day being first of the week, we tarried there and had two meetings with his family and the neighbors – divers of whom were sober, religious Baptists. They were both favored seasons. May the Lord bless his own work and seal it to the lasting advantage of those who attended.

24th and 25th: We rode to Utica on the upper part of the Mohawk River (eighty-five miles).

26th, 27th and 28th: We rode about one hundred and eighteen miles to Palmyra in the Genesee country to the house of our Friend, Abraham Lapham.

29th: We rested.

30th: Being first of the week, we attended Friends meeting in that neighborhood and one in the evening, appointed at a friendly man's house whose wife was a member, about six miles distant from the former. They were both, I believe, profitable and edifying seasons.

31st: We attended a meeting in the town of Palmyra, appointed principally for those not of our society. It was a large, solemn meeting wherein the truths of the gospel were largely opened to the affecting, solemnizing, and comforting many hearts.

1st of 11th month: Rode to Bristol (about eighteen miles) and attended a meeting at the 3rd hour after noon. It was held in a Baptist meetinghouse. It was a hard, exercising season. Those who attended appeared to be mostly very insensible of any right religious concern and exercise, being most of them Baptist professors. Nevertheless, through ability received after a considerable time of hard, silent labor, Truth's testimony was exalted among them, and some hearts were reached and tendered thereby. And I left them with peace of mind.

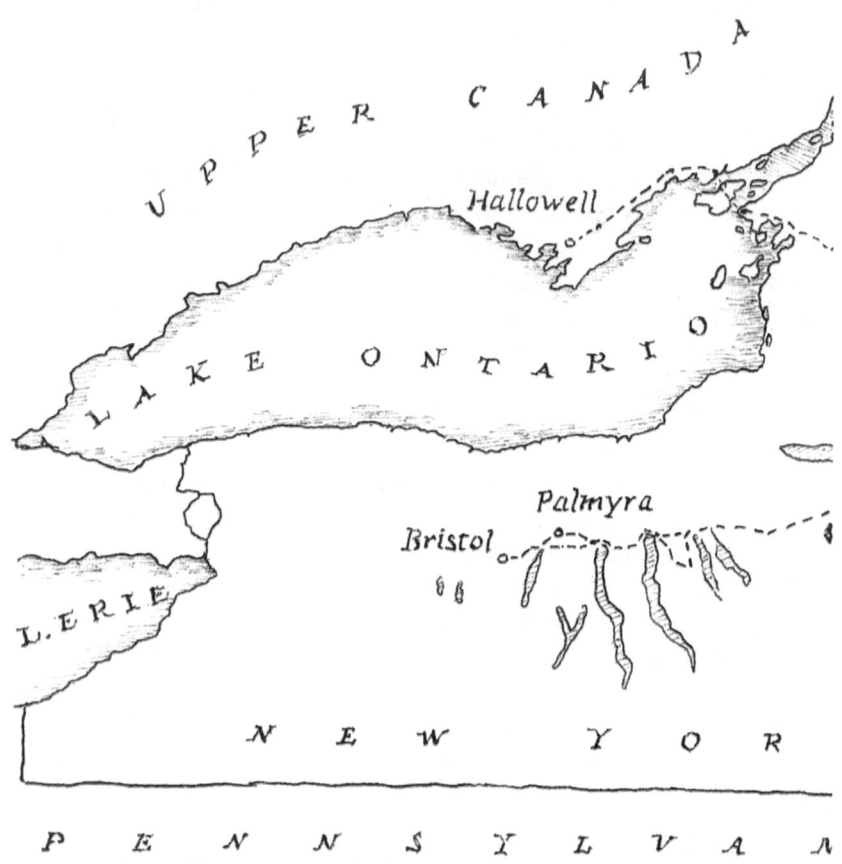

The next day, we then rode back to Cayuga Lake (thirty-seven miles) and lodged at an inn.

3rd: We rode to a town called Scipio where a few Friends resided and who were indulged with holding a meeting[1] by direction and under the care of the Monthly Meeting of Farmington. Here, we had a meeting at the 11th hour – it being their meeting day, of course. It was very small and laborous in the silent part thereof, but as a right exercise in waiting was patiently maintained, Truth gradually arose into dominion in a very instructive manner, and to the refreshing and comforting our minds in the sweet enjoyment of the Divine Presence, who manifested himself to be graciously near for our help in the needful time.

---

[1] Indulged Meeting: a meeting, subordinate to a monthly meeting, that differs from a preparative meeting in that it meets for worship only and does not prepare agenda items for the monthly business meeting.

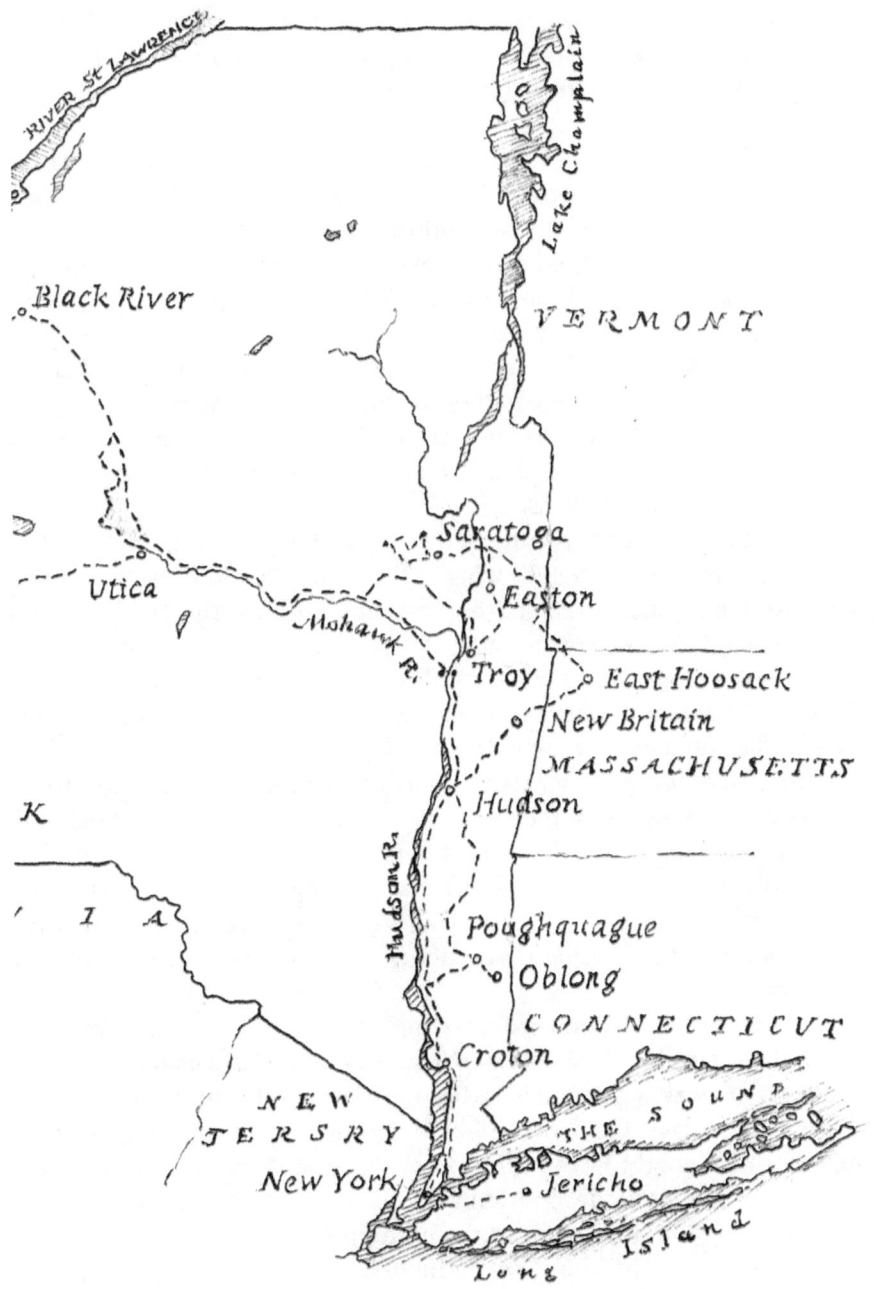

Path of the 1803 Journey

After dining with our friends, we took leave, turning our faces homeward and in four days got to Galway, to the house of our Friend,

Philip Macomber. And the next day, we rested, and the three following days, we attended the meetings of Galway, Ballston, and Newtown – they were all comfortable, edifying seasons.

12th: We rode to Troy.

13th and first of the week: We attended two meetings – the first at the 11th hour at the house of Zachariah Garnrick (about four miles from Troy), where the few Friends of that place and the adjacent neighborhoods hold a little meeting. It was enlarged at this time by the coming in of others who were not of our society and the Lord rewarded us bountifully and gave us a heavenly season together, wherein his name was gloriously exalted over all. And we parted with thankful hearts. The latter was held at Troy in their courthouse. It was a large gathering, but hard and laborous.

14th: We rode to Pittstown and attended a meeting at the 2nd hour. It was a satisfactory season and I hope profitable to some – the others appeared to be too much at ease.

15th: We rode to Easton, attended the Quarterly Meeting of Ministers and Elders, and the two following days, we attended the Quarterly Meeting for Discipline and the parting meeting for worship. The latter was a heavenly, baptizing season, wherein Truth was raised into dominion in a very eminent manner, and the hearts of many much broken and contrited, and a general solemnity spread over the meeting, and the Lord's name praised and exalted over all, who is worthy forever.

After which, we rode that afternoon to Saratoga, crossing the River Hudson in our way, and the next day rode to South Greenfield and attended a meeting at the 2nd hour after noon.

19th: Rode to Providence and after a meeting there, rode back again that afternoon to North Greenfield. And the next day being the first of the week, we attended a meeting there. It was large and favored, as were the two former.

21st: We had an appointed meeting at Saratoga Springs among a people not very unlike those whom the scribes of the Jews called publicans and sinners. It was a profitable, edifying season – those present mostly appearing to receive the word with readiness and apparent good will, insomuch that it might have been said of some of them, as our Lord said concerning some of this description in his day, that they were more likely to enter the kingdom than some of the high professors of religion and who make a great outward show of godliness, but are void of the power thereof.

23rd and 24th: We attended the Monthly Meetings of Saratoga and Easton, and the day following, had an appointed meeting at White Creek. The next day, we rode to East Hoosac.

The 27th and first of the week: We attended Friends meeting here. It was a very comfortable season. The Lord was with us and by his power made way in the hearts of the people for the reception of the testimony given us to bear among them. And we left them with thankful hearts and rode that evening to our Friend, David Lapham's, in the township of Hancock.

The next day, we had a meeting at his house for the neighboring inhabitants at the 2nd hour. They were mostly professors among the Baptists, who conducted very orderly. And the Lord in his never failing mercy, favored us together with a solemn, instructive season.

The next day, we passed on to New Britain and rested the following day.

Fifth of the week and 1st of 12th month: We attended the meeting there, as it came in course. It was very large, occasioned partly by our being there, and a marriage likewise accomplished thereat. And I think in the main, it was a favored, comfortable season.

Sixth Day: We attended a meeting at Klinakill and on First Day were at Hudson, where we had – with Friends and others at their meeting – a refreshing opportunity. The Lord was graciously near, furnishing with strength and utterance, evidencing of the divine power attending, to the rejoicing of the faithful, confirming to the weak and wavering, and convicting the indolent, the disobedient, and gainsayers.

Second Day: We rode to the Little Nine Partners and the four following days, we attended meetings at this place, Pine Plains, Stanford, and Creek. These were comfortable meetings, wherein through the prevalence of Truth, many were convicted, their hearts tendered, and the faithful few encouraged and made to rejoice, and the Lord's name praised and exalted over all.

On Seventh Day evening, we had an appointed meeting at the house of Thomas Wilbur (about four miles from the latter) and although hard and laborous, yet I trust in a good degree profitable and instructive.

On First Day, we went to Crum Elbow Meeting. It was very much crowded and the house not sufficient to hold the people. The season appeared somewhat to represent the time when the miracle of the loaves and fishes was performed, for the people's attention appeared to be generally outward – many having come together out of curiosity to see and hear with their outward senses. This makes hard work for the travelers who are faithfully engaged in Zion's cause. I sat long in silence – in great poverty and want – for the people appeared to be void of any spiritual food and no offering prepared. But as I abode in patience and in the faith, the query ran through my mind, is there not a lad present that may have a few barley loaves and fishes?[1] A young man soon after stood up who I believed for some time had something on his mind to offer and by a short, but pertinent communication opened my way. And soon after he sat down, I stood up and the Lord made way among the people while I was led to open in a very enlarged manner what the young Friend had dropped and which was extended in a marvelous manner over the whole assembly, so that it might be said indeed, that, "All did eat and were filled and many fragments remained to be gathered up." It was the Lord's doings and marvelous in our eyes.

Our two next appointments were at Pleasant Valley and the Branch on Second and Third days. These were comfortable and I trust profitable seasons.

The four successive days, we attended the Monthly Meetings of Oswego, Nine Partners, Creek, and Stanford – all seasons of great favor, wherein I was largely opened in the line of gospel ministry in four, several,[2] searching testimonies, greatly to the comfort of the honest, faithful travelers, and to the rebuke and warning of the careless, hypocritical, and worldly-minded professors.

On First Day, we attended the meeting at Nine Partners and notice having been previously given of our intention of being there, the meeting was very large. And the Lord's power was present with us, enabling [me] to discharge myself faithfully among them and instructing [me] to divide the word to their several conditions. And the season concluded with prayer and thanksgiving to his great and adorable name, who is overall, God blessed forever.

After this, apprehending I felt liberty to turn my face homeward, and having for the two successive days meetings appointed at Chestnut Ridge and Poughquaig, we proceeded accordingly. And although I was under considerable infirmity of body and traveled in much pain, yet through gracious aid, furnished from the Adorable Fountain of All Wisdom and Strength, I was enabled to attend them to my own comfort, and the comfort and encouragement of my friends – being led forth in both of them in large, affecting testimonies to the baptizing and humbling the minds of many present and refreshing the faithful few, whom the Lord delights to honor.

On Fourth Day, we crossed the Highlands and rode down to the mouth of Croton River (about forty-two miles). It was wearisome to my afflicted body, but through faith in the divine sufficiency (believing it right for us so to proceed), I was sustained even beyond rational expectation.

---

[1] John 6:9
[2] Several: separate and distinct

The day following being Friends meeting day in that place, we had a comfortable opportunity with them – together with some of their neighbors. It was, I believe, an instructive, edifying season to many. May it fasten as a nail in a sure place.

After this, we passed on to New York, where we tarried over First Day and attended their fore and after noon meetings, as also an appointed meeting in the evening at their new meetinghouse. They were large and very laborous, yet I trust in the main, profitable meetings.

On Second Day, 26th of 12th month, we rode home and I found my family well, which, together with the Lord's mercies and preservations vouchsafed to me in this arduous journey, filled my heart with gratitude and thanksgiving to his great and worthy name, to whom belongs all praise, adoration, and worship from the rising of the sun to the going down of the same, throughout all ages, world without end. Amen.[1]

I was out in this journey about three months and six days, and rode by computation fifteen hundred and seventy-five miles.

---

[1] Psalm 113:3, Ephesians 3:21

1806-1810

A Visit on Long Island, Staten Island, & New York in 1806

In the spring of the year 1806, feeling my mind drawn in gospel love to pay a religious visit to some of the neighboring towns and villages on our island, Staten Island and New York among those not in profession with us, and opening my concern to our monthly meeting, I received the concurrence and unity of my Friends therein. I was from home in this service about twenty days and had about thirty meetings among those not of our society – generally to good satisfaction and the peace of my own mind. Many in most places appeared convinced of the truth and propriety of our doctrine and principles as communicated. And divers feelingly expressed their satisfaction therewith and the heart-felt comfort they witnessed in those opportunities. And I had cause to hope that Light was breaking forth in some places that had long been under the power of great darkness through the undue force of wrong customs and a false education – principally propagated by a lucrative, antichristian ministry.

My mind was often affected in considering the emptiness and fruitless state of many of those professors under different names, who had a form of godliness (and were very zealous in attending to the outside[1] ceremonials of what they called religion and worship), but in their lives and conduct denied the power thereof[2] – being persuaded by their blind guides to believe that they might be saints while they were sinners and stand in a state of justification without sanctification, which is a false and very dangerous doctrine.

O saith my spirit! May the Light of Israel arise and come forth, and by the brightness of his arising, dispel all those mists and fogs – those works of darkness that those blind guides have raised up between God and the souls of the people – and deliver the nations out of the hands of all oppressors, that so none (at the awful closing period) may witness verified in themselves that solemn truth that, if the blind lead the blind, both shall fall into the ditch.[3]

A Visit to the Quarterly Meetings of Purchase, Nine Partners, & Stanford, with some adjacent places in 1806 & 1807

In the fall of the year 1806, feeling my mind drawn to visit to some parts of the Quarterly Meetings of Purchase, Nine Partners, and Stanford with some adjacent places not among Friends, after obtaining the unity

---

[1] Outside: outward
[2] 2 Timothy 3:5
[3] Matthew 15:14

and concurrence of our monthly meeting therein, I set forward the 8th of 12th month (Thomas Willis* kindly joining me as a companion in this journey) and proceeded directly to New York, where I met my companion who had gone on the day before.

On Third Day, we attended our Meeting for Sufferings and in the evening, we had an appointed meeting at Brooklyn. It was a solemn, comfortable season.

Fourth Day being Friends meeting in the city and notice being given of our intention of being there, it was a pretty large meeting and in a good degree favored with the spreading of the divine canopy,[1] wherein strength was afforded to communicate to the various situations of those present – to the honest-hearted and truly exercised travelers (of which number, I trust there are a few preserved in this city of great stir and commotion), comfort and encouragement – and to the careless, the unguarded, and refractory, caution and rebuke.

After which, we passed on to Mamaroneck and lodged with our kind Friend, Richard Mott. The three following days of this week, we attended the Monthly Meetings of Purchase, Chappaqua, and Amawalk, and stayed over their First Day Meeting at Amawalk – which was large by the coming in of others – and had an appointed meeting in the evening at Peekskill. These were all seasons of favor – comforting and refreshing to my mind.

On Second Day and 15th of the month, we proceeded on our journey and got in seasonably to the house of our kind Friend, Enoch Dorland, at evening, at or near Oswego.

Third Day, rode to Nine Partners.

Fourth Day, we attended the Monthly Meeting of Oswego. Both the meeting for worship and that for discipline were well conducted and Truth reigned, which made them comfortable and instructive.

On Fifth, Sixth, and Seventh Days, we attended the Monthly Meetings of Nine Partners, Creek, and Stanford. Nothing transpired in either of these unusual.

First Day, we attended Friends meeting at North East and also a meeting in the evening at Little Nine Partners – both seasons of favor.

On Second Day, we rode to Hudson and the next day being their monthly meeting, we attended and likewise had a large public meeting in

---

[1] The image of God's canopy, spreading over and protecting, shows up several times. Although the word, canopy, does not occur in the King James Version, the sense in which Hicks uses it is consistent with a pavilion, as in Psalm 27:5, Psalm 31:20, and Jeremiah 43:10 and may depend to some degree on these passages. In his letters, Hicks also quotes from Alexander Pope, whose *Essay on Man* contains the line, "My footstool earth, my canopy the skies," which echoes Isaiah 66:1 and Acts 7:49.

the evening with Friends and others, and have cause to acknowledge the goodness and mercy of the Shepherd of Israel, in that he hath been pleased graciously to manifest his presence and power for our help and encouragement from season to season, enabling us to labor to the comfort and refreshment of the honest-hearted and faithful among the brethren and sisters, and to impart counsel and caution to the varied states of those among whom our lots were cast – to the stirring up the pure mind in many, insomuch that in many places it appeared to be a renewed visitation of divine love to the people. For which, many hearts, with our own, were made thankful.

On Fourth and Fifth Days, we had meetings with Friends at Klinakill and New Britain and on Sixth Day, had an opportunity with those not in profession with us at a place called Philipstown. The meeting was held in a meetinghouse belonging to the Presbyterians and a precious season it proved – to the tendering of the hearts of most present, Truth prevailing over all, to the praise and glory of his Grace, who hath called us to labor in his vineyard.

We went from this place to Troy and attended Friends meeting on First Day and had a large, public meeting in the evening with the townspeople.

On Second and Third Day evenings, we had meetings in the towns of Waterford and Lansingburgh – the former held in a meetinghouse belonging to the Methodist Society and the latter in the Episcopal meetinghouse, by their voluntary permission. These were all seasons of favor, especially the latter, in which Truth was powerfully manifest, solemnizing the assembly, and tendering and melting many hearts into contrition and an acknowledgment to its divine power.

Fourth Day: Attended Friends midweek meeting and preparative at Troy and attended another appointed meeting for the townspeople in the evening. And the next morning, previous to our leaving the town, we had a precious opportunity with three or four families of Friends, the heads of which were all brethren and sisters of each other by blood or marriage. It was a season wherein the Lord was pleased to magnify his power and cause every heart to bow and acknowledge to its blessed and mollifying influence, which was prevalently over all to our mutual rejoicing.

The season being over, we took leave of our friends (in the sweet sense thereof) and rode that afternoon to Albany and attended a pretty large meeting held that evening in their courthouse. It was, I believe, to many a profitable, edifying season.

Sixth Day morning: Feeling my mind drawn to have a select opportunity with the few members of our society resident in this city, and they being notified thereof, came together early in the forenoon. And we

Duanesburg (New York) Meetinghouse

had a satisfactory season together, in which I was favored to clear myself of a burden I felt on their accounts in a plain, tender manner, to the comfort of the sincere-hearted and to the stirring up the careless and lukewarm.

After which, we took our leave in brotherly affection with a quiet and peaceful mind, and with an evidence of having faithfully discharged our duty, which made our journeying forward pleasant as we passed on to Duanesburg, where we arrived that evening.

Seventh Day, we rested.

First Day, 4th of 1st month 1807: We attended the meeting here and notice being spread of our attendance, it was a very large meeting, wherein Truth reigned. Many doctrinal truths were opened to the people and the gospel preached in the clear demonstration of the Spirit. To the Lord only wise, gracious and merciful be the praise, who is the Blessed Author thereof – nothing due to man.

The next day, we had a meeting in our way to Otego appointed in a friendly man's house near a village called Charleston, in which gospel communication was prevalent to the tendering and contriting many hearts.

We reached Otego on Fourth Day a little before meeting time, it being Friends meeting day there, which afforded but little opportunity of notifying their neighbors, but some got knowledge thereof and attended. It was a glorious meeting, which richly paid us for all our toil in getting there – yea, a hundred fold! Magnified forever be the name of the Lord, who graciously manifested his power for our help – to the wounding and comforting many hearts and causing the faithful to rejoice together in the sweet incomes[1] of his love and life.

Fifth Day: Attended the middle week meeting at Burlington. The neighboring inhabitants having notice of our coming, generally attended and although the life did not appear to rise so high as in the foregoing season, yet in the main I believe it was a profitable, edifying season.

Sixth Day, we rode to Deruyter.

On Seventh Day, we rested and mended our carriage that was exceedingly racked[2] and some broken by our journey to this place, which was through the roughest piece of traveling I ever rode with a sled.

On First Day, we attended Friends meeting here. It was much crowded – the house being but small – and the Lord was with us and magnified his power to the reaching and tendering many hearts. The gospel was freely preached and appeared to be freely received by the auditory in general.

Second Day, we had a meeting at a town called [New] Woodstock at the 11th hour and one in the evening at Cazenovia. There were no Friends living in either of these places and the people in general appeared dark and ignorant, yet they were attentive to what was communicated, and many of them appeared thankful for the opportunities and desired our longer continuance among them. But we took our leave and left them with our minds clothed with peace and turned our faces homeward, being desirous of getting back timely to attend the ensuing Quarterly Meeting of Nine Partners to be held the forepart of 2nd month.

We took meetings in our way to Burlington (feeling our minds drawn to return by that place) at Hamilton, Brookfield, Bridgewater, and one in the evening between Bridgewater and Burlington – held in a schoolhouse at a village in the township of Brookfield. These were all favored meetings, comfortable and instructive – many hearts being reached and affected with the power of Truth, which was prevalently manifest for our help.

First Day, we were at Burlington and notice being generally spread of our being there, it proved the largest meeting ever before held in that place. And through the Lord's goodness and mercy to us, it was made a season gratefully to be remembered by, I believe, the greater part of the meeting.

---

[1] Income: coming in of a divine influence
[2] Rack: pull out of shape

This season being over, we had another meeting in the evening in a neighboring town called Pittsfield. It was held in a large schoolhouse, there being no member of our society there. This was likewise an edifying opportunity.

The next day, we proceeded to Otego and attended a meeting there at the 11th hour by a previous appointment at our request. It was a large meeting and graciously favored with the overshadowing wing of divine kindness to the tendering many hearts.

Third Day, we had an appointed meeting in the township of Hartwick[1] held at a friendly man's house by the name of Stephen Holden. His wife was a member of our society and accounted a worthy Friend, but some months before had given way to temptation and fell into a degree of mental derangement and made way with herself,[2] which was a very great trial and loss to the family.

From this place, we returned to Duanesburg and attended their monthly meeting held on Sixth Day. This meeting was composed of the preparative meetings of Duanesburg, Otego, Burlington, and Deruyter. The latter meeting was near ninety miles from the place where the monthly meeting was held at this time. Friends are much scattered in this new country, by reason whereof but few in some meetings have much opportunity of attending their monthly meetings, which is a great loss to many families – especially the children, many of whom have very little opportunity of the improving company of experienced Friends in meetings of discipline or otherwise. I have often thought it a very weighty matter for a Friend to move with a family of children so far from meetings – and especially meetings of discipline, which I have oft considered as schools of very profitable instruction to well-minded youth.

This is a new monthly meeting, made up of Friends of but small experience – many of them newly received members, of course. The business of the meeting was but weakly conducted. We labored among them in the ability received for their instruction and help, and there appeared a readiness in some to receive – who, I trust, will become useful members as they abide[3] in humility and are faithful to the measure of grace received.

Seventh Day: Rode to Oakhill and on First Day attended Friends meeting there. It was a very full meeting and proved satisfactory and instructive.

The four following days, we were at meetings at Scott's Patent, Bern, Rensselaerville, one in a Friend's house between the last mentioned place

---

[1] The rest of this paragraph was deleted from the printed *Journal*.
[2] Make way with self: commit suicide
[3] Abide: wait patiently

and Coeyman's Patent, and one at the latter place. They were seasons of general satisfaction – especially the last, which was a very large precious meeting in which the truths of the gospel were largely declared in the demonstration of the Spirit. Many hearts were tendered and contrited, and the Lord's name praised and magnified, who is over all, worthy forever.

The 6th: We rode to Hudson and passed most of the way on the river on the ice, the weather having been for some days past extremely cold and frosty.

Seventh Day evening: We had an appointed meeting at Looneburg, which lies on the west side of the River Hudson and opposite to that city.

First Day: Attended Friends meeting at Hudson. Both these latter meetings were held, I believe, to general satisfaction and I trust were profitable and instructive to many who attended.

From hence we passed on to Nine Partners and got there seasonably to attend with the committee of the boarding school held there by and under the direction of our yearly meeting – we being members of the committee that had the oversight of that institution – and by accounts now rendered, the school appeared in a prosperous state, but a considerable difficulty attended in procuring suitable tutors and caretakers in the family.

On Third Day, the select quarterly meeting of this place was held and on Fourth Day, that for discipline. And although there was a degree of favor experienced, yet in the general, it was a trying, laborous season. This is a large quarterly meeting and many who attend are mere birthright members[1] and (having never known the baptizing power of Truth to sanctify and prepare for right and useful membership) are but as dead weights in our religious meetings. And some others who have joined the society by convincement, for want of faithfully attending to that which first convinced them, have lost their first love and suffered their minds too much to center back again into the world and the love of it, and have thereby become stumbling-blocks in the way of others. These bring much exercise and concern to the living, who are daily engaged for Zion's cause and that Truth may prosper and prevail in the earth.

On Fifth Day, we had an appointed meeting at Pleasant Valley – it was a comfortable, instructive season – and another seasonable opportunity in the evening at Poughkeepsie, mostly made up of those not in membership with us.

On Sixth Day, was at West Branch Meeting. It was pretty full, wherein I had to go down into deep baptism with the dead, being plunged into the feeling of a state of great stupidity, ignorance, and unbelief. But as I

---

[1] Birthright member: a person whose parents were members of the Religious Society of Friends when he or she was born and who is therefore automatically also a member

patiently sat under the burden, light sprang up and life came into dominion, wherein I was led in a very clear manner to show the ground from whence all this darkness and unbelief proceeded, and that it was from a want of due attention to and right belief in the inward manifestation of Divine Light that reveals itself in the heart of man against sin and uncleanness, and at the same time, shows what is right and justifies for right doing.[1] And that it is only owing to this want of attention and belief in this divine principle by the children of men that makes the atheist, the deist, the predestinarian, and universalian – with every other profession or denomination of Christians which do not believe in the sufficiency of that divine principle to procure for us a state of freedom from sin in this life. And without which, no salvation can be witnessed either here or hereafter by any accountable being. And the reason of this ignorance and unbelief is founded in their unwillingness and refusal of making use of the means appointed by our gracious Creator as the only medium by which that knowledge is to be obtained – on which the belief of this necessary and very essential doctrine of perfection from sin is founded.

Therefore, while men disregard this inward divine principle of Grace and Truth, and do not believe in it as essential and sufficient to salvation, they must remain to be either atheists, deists, predestinarians, Arminians, universalians, or some other of the unbelieving sects in that necessary and very essential doctrine of perfection, as contained in that clear, rational, and positive injunction of our dear Lord in Matthew 5th and 48th verse, "Be ye therefore perfect, as your Father which is in heaven is perfect."

And we cannot rationally suppose they can ever be otherwise while they continue in this situation, as nothing else is sufficient – but this Light – to produce that knowledge on which this belief is founded.[2]

For as the knowledge and belief of the possibility of a man's communicating his thoughts (with his situation and place of residence) to his friend or acquaintance in a distant country through the medium or power of twenty-six letters or characters (while they remain thus widely situated) by penning those letters on paper (arranged by natural or rational science) and sending them by post, depends on our acquaintance and knowledge of those letters and their powers – which we can only obtain by learning them under the guidance and direction of a tutor qualified for that purpose and without which we should remain in a state of ignorance and unbelief therein – so certain it is, respecting the former proposition.

---

[1] The rest of this paragraph was deleted from the printed *Journal*.
[2] The next four paragraphs were deleted from the printed *Journal*.

Likewise, a man with ten simple numbers or figures (and being rightly instructed in the use of them) can demonstrate with rational certainty that the three angles of every triangle are precisely equal to two right angles – which nevertheless, he that is ignorant of those things cannot possibly believe and will ever remain in a state of ignorance and unbelief in the premises – unless he pursues the means by which this knowledge and belief is attainable.

My mind was likewise largely opened to communicate with clear, rational demonstration, how we all might by faithful attention and adherence to the aforesaid divine principle (the Light Within) come to know and believe the certainty of those excellent scripture doctrines of the coming, life, righteous works, sufferings, death, and resurrection of our Lord and Savior, Jesus Christ, our Blessed Pattern and that by this Inward Light only, we are prepared for an admittance into the heavenly kingdom when done with time.

In this manner, and much more largely and clearly than I can now remember or recapitulate, was my mind led forth to unfold[1] the mysteries of the gospel – apparently to the comfort, satisfaction, and instruction of most present.

It was a day of high favor, wherein the Lord's arm was made bare for our help and the exaltation of his own glorious and holy name, who is over all, blessed forever.

This favored opportunity being over, we rode that afternoon to Samuel Dorland's, where a meeting was appointed for us that evening, which we attended, and lodged with our worthy Friend, Enoch Dorland.

Seventh Day: We crossed the mountains called the Highlands in our way homeward and got well to our Friend, Abraham Underhill's, at Croton River at evening.

The next day being first of the week, we attended Friends meeting there. And notice being given of our attendance, the meeting was pretty full and graciously attended with the Divine Presence, in which strength was received to preach the gospel in the demonstration of the Spirit. It was a season thankfully to be remembered.

Second Day and 9th of 2nd month 1807: We rode to New York where I was gladly received by my beloved daughter Abigail and her kind companion – we being mutually glad to see each other.

The next day, we attended our Meeting for Sufferings, after which I rode home that evening and found my dear wife and children well to our mutual rejoicing. And we greeted each other with thankful hearts.

---

[1] Unfold: explain

I was from home in this journey about two months and attended forty-five particular meetings, nine monthly meetings, one quarterly, and our Meeting for Sufferings twice, and traveled by computation, upwards of seven hundred miles.

A Visit to Nine Partners, Stanford, & Purchase Quarterly Meetings in 1807

After returning from the aforesaid journey, I continued mostly at and about home for several months, attending our several meetings as they came in course, as also at different times, appointed some meetings among those not in profession with us in some adjacent neighborhoods to which I could go and return in a few days. In all which seasons, I have thankfully to acknowledge the Lord was near and graciously manifested himself to be a Present Helper in every needful time, furnishing with ability to labor in the work of the gospel, to the convincing and comforting many hearts, and to the solid relief and peace of my own mind.

In the ensuing fall, having felt my mind renewedly engaged in gospel love to visit a few of the meetings of Friends in the three lower quarters on the main belonging to our yearly meeting and to take some meetings in divers places in those parts among those of other professions, I left home, with the unity of my friends, the 31st of 10th month 1807 and Seventh Day of the week and went to New York – having my beloved wife (who proposed to be my companion in part of this journey) with me. We also took our two youngest daughters with us, in order to place them in the boarding school at Nine Partners. We tarried in New York over First Day and attended Friends meetings – that at Pearl Street in the morning and at Liberty Street in the afternoon. They were both, I trust, profitable meetings – more especially the former, in which Truth prevailed and came up into dominion in a very prevalent manner to the solemnizing and comforting many hearts and was very strengthening to my mind in the prospect before me.

On Second Day, we set out for Nine Partners and got there seasonably to attend the quarterly meeting for discipline the ensuing Fourth Day. And the latter part of the week, we spent in attending the Quarterly Meeting of Stanford, after which we returned to the boarding school. And as we had placed our daughters there, and I being one of the committee having the superintendence thereof, I felt my mind led to spend some time in the family and among the children. I accordingly tarried with them about ten days, after which (way opening to proceed) I went as far as Hartford in Connecticut, accompanied by two Friends of Nine Partners. The weather being cold and unsettled, my wife remained in the school assisting the caretakers until I returned.

We took several meetings in our way thither and one as we returned and were at several in and about Hartford – mostly among those of other professions. And the Lord, magnified forever be his right worthy name, was graciously pleased to be with us and manifested his power for our help, giving wisdom and strength, tongue and utterance, teaching to divide the word aright to the states of the people, whereby his righteous cause was exalted in many minds and his glorious, Holy Truth raised into dominion over all in divers of those favored opportunities – to the praise of his Grace, who is over all, God blessed forever.

On my return to the school, I again spent some days with the family and caretakers in the oversight thereof. After which, my wife and I took leave of our children and friends in much mutual affection, and set our faces homeward. We took Oswego Monthly Meeting in our way on Fourth Day, 16th of 12th month and the next day, had an appointed meeting at Poughquaig.

On Sixth Day, we rode through the mountains to Peekskill and lodged with our kind Friend, Nathaniel Brown. We stayed their First Day Meeting and on the second of the week, we had an appointed meeting at a place called Crompond. It was held in a meetinghouse belonging to the Presbyterians by their proposal.

On Fourth Day, was at Amawalk, on Fifth Day at Chappaqua, and on Sixth Day, had an appointed meeting at a place called Sing-Sing. This was likewise held in worship house belonging to the Presbyterians by their consent.

On Seventh Day, rode to New York and on First Day, attended Friends meeting there.

We left the city the third day following in our way home, but a storm coming on soon after we left town increased to that degree, that when we came to the ferry at Hurlgate – where we intended to cross – we found it impassable. We then turned our course and rode up to our Friend, Joseph Byrd's, at Harlem and lodged and I, having felt my mind drawn towards having a meeting at that place (when passing down to the city), but admitting some doubts to arise in regard to the clearness of the prospect, I omitted it. But now, way opening with more clearness, we had one appointed the next day, which proved a favored season. After which, we crossed the ferry that afternoon and rode to Flushing.

And the next day being the fifth of the week and 31st of 12th month, we attended Friends meeting there, after which we rode home that afternoon and were gladly received of our Friends.

And my spirit was made humblingly joyful in believing that the Lord Almighty had graciously condescended to be with us, to lead us in the way, manifesting his loving-kindness and mercy in a greater or lesser degree in every of those opportunities, to the convicting, convincing, edifying, and comforting many hearts, and to the encouragement of the honest travelers Zionward. May his right worthy name be praised and exalted above all forever.

As our return home at this time was hastened by the inclemency of the season – we being out with a carriage and likely to be shut up from traveling by the snow – my mind was not relieved of the prospect before me. Therefore, after tarrying at and about home a few weeks, I again left home with the unity of my Friends, in order to finish what was left behind of my former concern. Charles Willets, a Friend and neighbor, accompanied me.

We set out the 24th of 1st month 1808 and took the three Quarterly Meetings of Purchase, Nine Partners, and Stanford as they came in course, and likewise five particular meetings in the intermediate space between Purchase and Nine Partners Quarters.

We were from home at this time about five weeks and attended three quarterly meetings, one monthly, and twenty-three particular meetings.

And I have abundant cause, with humble gratitude, to admire the adorable loving-kindness and condescending goodness of a gracious God to me, a poor creature, in enabling me to surrender all up to his heavenly disposal – to be anything or nothing, as he would have me to be – leading me from place to place as a weaned child by the guiding of his power and the influence of his precious love, and teaching me not only how to suffer want, but likewise how to abound, and in every situation and dispensation that he is pleased to lead into, to be therewith content. Under a renewed sense whereof, my spirit is led to acknowledge that great and marvelous are thy works, Lord God Almighty. Just and true are thy ways, thou King of Saints.[1] Even so. Amen.

A Visit to the Subordinate Meetings of the Yearly Meeting of New York in 1808

In the spring of the year 1808, our yearly meeting from an exercise in observing the many deficiencies as brought up in the reports from the several quarterly meetings constituting it, issued an epistle[2] or minute of advice and caution to its subordinate meetings. And in order to strengthen and enforce the same, and to make it the more effectual to promote a reformation, appointed a committee to attend therewith. And being one

---

[1] Revelation 15:3
[2] Epistle: a letter sent by a yearly meeting. Annually, each yearly meeting sent general greetings to the other yearly meetings and to its subordinate meetings. Sometimes, it also sent a separate letter to subordinate meetings containing queries or giving direction.

appointed with divers other brethren and sisters (as a concern of a similar nature had for some time previous thereto attended my mind), I willingly engaged therein.

Accordingly, at the close of the yearly meeting we agreed to enter upon the service at the succeeding Quarterly Meeting at Nine Partners and to attend in succession the Quarterly Meetings of Stanford and Easton as they came in course. Two men and three women Friends joined me in this northern tour (and divers other of the committee attended at the quarters). After taking those quarters, we proceeded to attend with the minute all the monthly meetings constituting them (except the three distant ones of Adolphustown in Upper Canada, and Farmington and Scipio in the Genesee) – also a considerable number of the preparative meetings, as way opened therefor.

And although great and many were the apparent deviations and departures of many of our members in the varied classes of society from that ancient simplicity and integrity that marked the conduct of our worthy predecessors in the dawn of this latter gospel day – by which declension many of those noble testimonies given us to bear for the Prince of Peace and the promotion of the cause of Truth and Righteousness in the earth were but weakly supported by many and by others almost wholly neglected and let to fall to the grief and wounding of the hearts of the faithful, and reproach of our Christian profession. Nevertheless, we had abundant cause gratefully to acknowledge the condescending goodness and mercy of the great Head of the Church in uniting us together in the work and in owning the concern from place to place – giving full evidence thereto in a general manner by the attendant manifestations of his love and power – thereby enabling and qualifying his weak and unworthy (though devoted) servants (who were very sensible they had no might nor ability of their own to perform the service they were engaged in to his honor or the promotion of his righteous cause) to communicate counsel and encouragement, reproof and caution, as occasion required and opportunity offered. By which, the faithful were strengthened and made at times to rejoice together and to the opening of the hearts of Friends in a very general manner, cordially to receive us and the concern with much unanimity.

We had many precious opportunities as we passed along – both in public meetings (many of which were much crowded by the coming in of those not in membership with us) as also in meetings for discipline – Truth being often raised powerfully into dominion over all, insomuch that in many of those favored seasons, we were strengthened to set up our

Ebenezer[1] and to say, in the heart-felt language of filial and grateful acknowledgments, "Hitherto hath the Lord helped us."

And I believe it was a season of renewed powerful visitation and manifestation of the Lord's mercy to many (not only to the members of our society, but also to others that are without) who were favored with the privilege of attending the public meetings.

After getting through this part of the service (which took us between nine and ten weeks, in which time we traveled one thousand miles and upward, and attended three quarterly meetings, seventeen monthly meetings, sixteen preparative meetings, and forty public meetings for worship – including those that preceded the monthly and preparative meetings), we returned home until the time of the next quarters coming on, when I again joined some of the committee and attended the quarterly meetings of Westbury and Purchase and all the monthly meetings constituting them (except Purchase Monthly Meeting). And I may say with gratitude of heart that the same divine power that attended in the foregoing part of the visit was again manifested for our help in going through and finishing the service – to the humble admiration and solid peace of my own mind, and the praise of his own right worthy name, who is over all, God blessed forever.

How great and wonderful[2] is his goodness and loving-kindness to the children of men! His mercies are present every moment and as saith the prophet, "They are new every morning." Therefore, saith my soul, "Let all praise and exalt him above all, from the rising of the sum, even to the west, for his mercy endureth forever."[3]

A Visit in Purchase & Nine Partners Quarterly Meetings in 1809

The latter part of the winter and spring of the year 1809, with the concurrence of our monthly meeting, I made a pretty general visit to the meetings of Friends within the Quarterly Meeting of Purchase, and some in Nine Partners Quarter, and appointed a considerable number of meetings among others in the parts adjacent, and found great openness generally among the people to hear Truth's testimony. And a number I believe received it with openness and sincerity of heart. And my heart was made glad in believing that the Lord was graciously near and accompanied the word preached with his heart-tendering power – to the comforting and refreshing of the broken-hearted and to the reviving the spirit of the contrite ones, and stopping the mouths of gainsayers. For which favors, my soul was often bowed in deep humility and contrition of

---

[1] Ebenezer: a memorial stone set up by the prophet Samuel (1 Samuel 7:12)
[2] Wonderful: something that caused wonder or astonishment
[3] Isaiah 45:6

spirit, accompanied with grateful acknowledgments and thanksgivings for his wonderful works to the children of men.

Brief Visits in 1810 & 1811

The year 1810, I spent mostly at home, except performing a visit to some of the neighboring inhabitants not in membership with us, in which service I was from home a few weeks in the spring, and in the summer, performed a visit to the Half Year Meeting at Canada by appointment from our yearly meeting.

1811-1813

The year 1811, I likewise spent at and near home in attending our own and some adjacent meetings, as also some meetings in divers neighborhoods among others. And [I] had frequent cause to rejoice in a living hope that Truth was gradually arising, and the true light shining more and more in the hearts of the people, and that in the Lord's time, it would be exalted and become a great mountain and fill the whole earth.[1]

Visits on Long Island in 1812 & 1813

In the winter and spring of the year 1812, with the concurrence of my Friends, I spent about four weeks in visiting the neighboring inhabitants not of our society. I had eight and twenty meetings, all held in private houses. Many of them were very large, crowded meetings and the Lord was graciously near – comforting and refreshing the sincere-hearted, and opening counsel to those who wanted information, and sealing his testimony to the minds of the people – to the exaltation of his own righteous cause and the glory of his excellent name, who is over all, God blessed forever.

In the forepart of the winter, 1813, feeling a renewed concern toward the neighboring inhabitants of our island and New York not in profession with us – many of whom, as sheep without a shepherd, appeared to be under exercise and concern to be rightly instructed in the way of peace[2] and salvation. In gospel love and with the unity of my friends, I paid them a visit – had upwards of twenty meetings in the different parts, much to my own satisfaction and I trust to the edification and comfort of many who attended. The Lord, our Gracious Helper, being near, covered the assemblies with his solemnizing presence and power, instructed to divide the word to the several states in the demonstration of the Spirit. For which unmerited favors, I was made at seasons to rejoice and in deep humiliation and thankfulness of heart, to joy in the God of my salvation, who does wondrous things in mercy for the children of men, in order to hide pride from man and turn him from his unrighteous purposes, and save his soul from the pit, that so he may know and seek after God.

A Visit to Purchase Quarter in 1813

Before I had got fully through this little tour of duty, a further prospect opened toward a visit to Friends and others in the compass of

---

[1] Proverbs 4:18, 2 Peter 1:19, & Daniel 2:35
[2] The War of 1812 interferred with shipping, a major industry in New York and New England, and was therefore not popular in those areas. Hicks may be confusing these anti-war sentiments with an openness to pacifism.

Purchase Quarterly Meeting and some of the neighboring parts of the state of Connecticut where none of our society reside. And under the impression of duty, I laid the concern before our monthly meeting held 1st month 1813 and received its concurrence in a short minute for that purpose.

I left home the 6th of 2nd month following, my kind Friend, Gideon Seaman,* an elder and member of Westbury Monthly Meeting, accompanied me in this visit.

I took New York in my way and attended the forenoon meeting at Pearl Street and afternoon meeting at Liberty Street on First Day and had an appointed meeting on Second Day evening in the northeast part of the town in a large room in a public house. It was a large and favored season, many came – more than the house could contain. The two foregoing meetings were also favored, strengthening opportunities, affording encouragement in my first setting out in the weighty and solemn service before me as I always esteem that, when appointing meetings and more especially those among strangers – many of whom know little of us or of the manner in which we hold our meetings and therefore are apt to get restless and sometimes much disquieted at our sitting so long in silence (as we often have to do) – that it requires in Friends, at such seasons, a very deep indwelling with the seed of life to prevent being jostled[1] or interrupted in our inward travail and waiting for the pure motion of life, lest by their eagerness to hear words, Friends on those occasions might be led to venture on too small a motion and without sufficiently turning the fleece again and again, and to feel clearly that the dew[2] is in it. For want of this care, there is danger sometimes of our running in vain[3] and so not profit the people at all nor procure peace to our own minds.

I was from home in this journey about four weeks, and rode upwards of three hundred miles, and attended twenty-five meetings, and our Meeting for Sufferings twice. Twelve of those meetings were among people not of our society (and where there are no meetings of Friends) among whom, I found great openness to receive us and our testimony – many expressing their satisfaction with the opportunities, and manifested a desire in most places that we would stay longer with them and have more meetings. And indeed, Truth was so prevalent in those meetings as not only to silence (at least for the present) all opposition, but in many of

---

[1] Jostle: disturb or upset
[2] Hicks has written "the woe is in it." This is almost certainly not what he meant. He seems to be referring to the story in Judges 6 of Gideon testing whether he correctly understands God's command by repeatedly feeling for dew on fleece that has been left on the ground overnight.
[3] Galatians 2:2 & Philippians 2:16

them to reign triumphantly over all, whereby many minds were comforted and instructed, and the power of Truth exalted, and our hearts made glad in believing that the Shepherd of Israel is still availingly stretching forth the crook[1] of his love, and will gather many from the highways and hedges, whom, as they attend to his call and abide faithful to the end, he will clothe with the wedding garment and admit into the marriage chamber of the Lamb[2] – while many of those who have been long and often invited, but are nevertheless making excuses in order to attend to their farms, their merchandise, their oxen, etc., will not be able to enter.[3]

Engagements at & about home

[4]Sixth Day [26th of 3rd month 1813]: My worldly concerns engrossed most of my time. How true is that saying, "Ye cannot serve two masters."[5] O how hard a master the world is and from whose servitude I often feel strong desires to be fully redeemed, that all my time may be more fully dedicated to the service of my Heavenly Master, whom I oft feel I sincerely love.

Seventh Day: This day, I spent mostly in repairing a vehicle in which I have ridden several thousand miles in my religious engagements. Most of the evening was spent in reading the excellent doctrine of our Lord relative to the Comforter,[6] and the union and communion between himself and his faithful followers as recorded by John the Evangelist. If it is sweet and pleasant to read, how much more precious and excellent to know and witness it in our own experience.

First Day: Our meeting this day passed in silent labor. The cloud rested on the tabernacle[7] and although it was a day of much rain outwardly, yet very little of the dew of Hermon[8] appeared to distill among us. Nevertheless, a comfortable calm was witnessed toward the close, which we must render to the account of unmerited mercy and love.

Second Day: This day mostly spent on a visit to a sick friend who appeared comforted in the visit. Spent part of the evening in reading part of Paul's Epistle to the Romans.[9] What a pity it is he did not explain himself better, and then Peter would not have accused him for writing

---

[1] Crook: a shepherd's staff
[2] Revelation 19:9
[3] Luke 14:15-24 & Matthew 22:1-12
[4] At this point, a page has been torn out of the manuscript.
[5] Matthew 6:24 & Luke 16:13
[6] John 14:15-16:4
[7] Numbers 9:15-23
[8] Psalm 133:3
[9] 2 Peter 3:15-16

things hard to be understood. But what a mercy it is that we have the son himself [to turn] to in all cases – more especially in those that [require] explanation, wherein [all] may receive a full inter[pretation,] if they believe [in him] and love his cross.[1]

Third Day: I was busied most of this day in my common vocations. Spent the evening mostly in reading Paul. Found considerable satisfaction in his first Epistle to the Corinthians, wherein he shows the danger of setting too high a value on those who were instrumental in bringing to the knowledge of the truth, without looking through and beyond them to the great First Cause and Author of Every Blessing, to whom all the praise and honor is due.[2]

Fourth Day: It is trying to nature to bear one's own poverty and want, and this is often greatly added to by the wickedness and carelessness of others, with whom in our commerce in the things of this world, we seem to be under the necessity to be at times conversant with, and which at times brings to view just Lot's situation in Sodom.[3]

Fifth Day, 1st of 4th month: At our meeting today, found it (as usual) a very close, steady exercise to keep the mind centered where it ought. What a multitude of intruding thoughts imperceptibly (as it were) steal into the mind and turn it from its proper object whenever it relaxes its vigilance in watching against them. Felt a little strength just at the close to remind Friends of the necessity of a steady perseverance by a recapitulation of the parable of the unjust judge[4] – showing how men ought always to pray and not to faint.

Sixth Day: Nothing material occurred, but a fear, lest the cares of the world should engross too much of my time.

Seventh Day: Had an agreeable visit from two ancient friends, whom I have long loved. The rest or the day, I employed in manual labor, mostly in gardening.

First Day: …[5] felt my mind drawn to attend today [a meeting a few miles from home – held for the present by indulgence of Friends.][6] It being

---

[1] The last two sentences were deleted from the printed *Journal* and the manuscript page has been badly damaged, resulting in about seven words being missing from the last sentence. The words in square brackets are a best guess of its contents.

[2] The next paragraph was deleted from the printed *Journal*.

[3] Genesis 19

[4] Luke 18:1-8

[5] This is the back of the damaged page. Two or three lines were damaged and missing. The remaining text is almost completely illegible. Words in square brackets are from the editor's copy of the *Journal*.

[6] The rest of this paragraph and the next one were deleted from the printed *Journal*.

the second meeting in which was brought to my remembrance a prospect I had about thirty-five years ago of many being gathered in that quarter and the adjacent parts in some future time, and a hope revived at this solemn season that the time was now not very far distant when it would be accomplished.

May the Lord hasten it in his own time that the people (many of whom are wandering up and down as sheep without a shepherd) may be gathered to the fold of rest, and come truly to know and hear the voice of the true Shepherd and Bishop of Souls,[1] and be led by him into the green pastures of life, where they may lay down in safety and none make them afraid.[2]

I was led forth in a line of encouragement and caution to a seeking, travailing remnant and in warning to the indolent, the whole,[3] and the self-righteous – endeavoring to show them the danger of resting in such a polluted state. Many hearts were contrited and broken into tears, and a comfortable solemnity clothed the meeting, for which our hearts were made thankful to the Gracious Author of all our Blessings.

Second Day: This day spent in manual labor – a less proportion of which would suffice for me were every other man disposed to do their part – but the poor and the indolent must and will be helped.

Third and Fourth Days: Mostly occupied in my temporal concerns, with attendant poverty of spirit, and a sense of want, and a hanking[4] after spiritual food, free from condemnation.

Fifth Day: Attended our preparative meeting at which our queries[5] were read and answers prepared to go to the yearly meeting – but too much, I fear, in a formal way and may, if not well guarded against, become a snare to us, as the brazen serpent was to Israel.[6]

Sixth Day: I can say little more than that I wearied myself with hard labor in assisting my workmen in laying up stone wall for fence. At evening, read Paul's Epistle to the Galatians, wherein I think he has fully

---

[1] 1 Peter 2:25
[2] Psalm 23
[3] The meaning of "whole" is obscure.
[4] Hank: hanker or desire
[5] Queries: Each yearly meeting had a set of questions that were answered by its subordinate meetings annually. Each preparative meeting sent its answers to the monthly meeting. The monthly meeting, in turn wrote summary answers that were forwarded to the quarterly meeting. The answers from each quarter were read at the annual sessions of the yearly meeting. Originally, these were used to collect practical information (births, deaths, etc.), but over time began to inquire into the spiritual state of the meeting as well. The wording of the queries changed rarely and the answers in many cases were repeated word-for-word.
[6] Numbers 21:9 & 2 Kings 18:4

shown the final end and abolishment of all outward ordinances and observations in matters of religion.

Seventh Day: This day, I spent mostly in manual labor – some little interruption of mind by the improper conduct of one of my laborers. Oh, how hard a thing it is to find in such, honesty, industry, and a suitable deportment united in the same person. And yet, it is no more than ought to be in every man, and it is always their duty and interest to be so.

First Day: At our meeting today, the fire seemed very low on the altar. Dullness and a spirit of heaviness were too predominant with many – occasioned, no doubt, by a too near attachment to the world and the things of it, and too much lightness and vanity with others.

Alas, how much good seed is lost by the wayside, in stony places, and on the thorny ground![1]

Just at the close, I was engaged to call the attention of the people to the necessity of always having a proper point or object to aim at – a right center to all their hopes and desires – and that God was the alone proper object for man to set his heart upon, as the doing his will is the whole sum and substance[2] of all true religion and worship.

Second Day: Nothing material to remark

Third and Fourth Days: Spent in usual labor, with a peaceful mind.

Waiting for Way to Open

Fifth Day: Attended our monthly meeting today, at which I received a certificate of the unity and concurrence from the monthly of my Friends with a prospect I had previously opened to them of performing a religious visit to Friends and others in parts of the Yearly Meetings of Pennsylvania, Baltimore, and the adjacent parts of Virginia.

How mortifying are those prospects to the natural man – to be called to the performance of a duty that it feels itself destitute of every right means and capacity to effect and is, therefore, brought under the entire necessity of trusting in and depending upon that invisible arm of power that is beyond the reach of all mortals to command or control.

Sixth Day: Felt much poverty of spirit at our Preparative Meeting of Ministers and Elders. How necessary it is for such as fill those stations in society, to dig faithfully with their staves (like the elders, princes, and nobles of Israel formerly, by the direction of the lawgiver, saying, "Spring up, O well, sing ye unto it."[3]) that so they may be favored both with the upper and the nether spring.[4] For how otherwise can they be good way-

---

[1] Mark 4 – The Parable of the Sower
[2] Substance: a spiritual reality. The opposite of a shadow
[3] Numbers 21:17-18
[4] Joshua 15:18 & Judges 1:15

marks[1] and ensamples[2] to the flock over whom the Holy Ghost has made all the rightly qualified of this description overseers, and who will have to give an account for the flock under their charge.

Seventh Day: Spent in my usual vocation as a farmer or husbandman, in which I need incessantly to watch against the intrusions of worldly cares.

First Day: Had close exercise, through the greatest part of our meeting today in opposing a dull, drowsy spirit, which, through unmerited mercy and help, I vanquished towards the close. Soon after which, I was unexpectedly called upon to sound an alarm to the youth and to show them the danger of suffering the intruding vanities and follies of the world to steal away their affections from their supreme, good, and Blessed Author of their being and well-being – in and on whom they ought to fix their only best hope and trust, who is the true and only source of all felicity[3] and blessedness in time and in eternity.

Second Day: My temporal concerns necessarily engaged my attention today, in pursuing of which, nothing transpired to interrupt or turn the mind from its proper center.

The four following days were principally devoted in attending our quarterly meeting – held at this time in New York. I think on the whole, it was a favored season. The canopy of the Heavenly Father's love was sensibly felt to overshadow the meeting in its several sittings. I spread before the meeting of discipline my prospect of a religious visit to Friends and others in some of the southern states, with the certificate of concurrence from our last monthly meeting. The meeting fully united therewith and endorsed the same on the back of my certificate, by which I was fully left at liberty by my Friends to pursue the journey as way should open therefor.

What deep obligations devolve upon us when thus liberated by our Friends and separated to travel in the service of the gospel, that we are careful in no case to make the gospel chargeable[4] to any, nor abuse our power in the gospel, but in deep humility and reverential fear, wait for the putting forth of the Shepherd of Israel and know him to go before. Then will the Lord's cause prosper in our hands, and his people be edified and instructed – and we comforted in our labors of love – to the glory and praise of his right excellent name, who is over all, God blessed forever.

Seventh Day: Was busied today in my farming business, endeavoring to get all my temporal concerns properly arranged – expecting shortly to

---

[1] Way-mark: a guide to travelers
[2] Ensample: example
[3] Felicity: state of happiness
[4] Chargeable: for a charge, i.e., for pay

leave home and proceed on the visit previously alluded to in the foregoing note – as I consider it my especial duty (as much as in me lies) to leave all in a state of peace and quiet, that nothing may go with me from home that may tend to interrupt or disquiet the mind while traveling in this weighty service, nor leave cause for any to complain that I leave behind.

First Day: Having felt my mind inclined to see Friends in their meeting at Bethpage before I left home, I went there today, accompanied by my wife and two youngest daughters and a sober young woman of our neighborhood. Their company was pleasant and I trust the season was profitable and edifying to a number present, after a time of deep inward travail and suffering. How oft are the living baptized for the dead, in order for their arising? For if the dead are not raised, preaching is vain.[1]

Second and Third Days: Spent in my preparative business, looking for the time of setting out on my intended journey, expecting the way will shortly open. May I be ready and willing when the time comes, without murmuring or complaining. For, as I trust and believe a dispensation of the gospel is committed to me, woe is me if I preach not the gospel.[2]

Fourth Day: Alas, how the cares of the world intrude on the mind and engross its attention, if they are not carefully watched against with fervent prayer!

Fifth Day: Attended our Fifth Day Meeting. Found it necessary to engage in a close warfare against a dull, heavy spirit that seemed very prevalent in the meeting. But as I kept up the struggle and divers times renewed the attack with fresh vigor, I was favored with a good degree of victory towards the close, when a ray of light broke forth, attended with peace and quietude of mind – an ample reward for all my toil.

Sixth Day: I endeavored to spend this day as I ought. Met with some interruption from a careless neighbor by the trespass of his unruly creatures. How much more comfort and satisfaction would neighborhoods enjoy, did all honestly endeavor to walk uprightly, agreeable to that excellent rule left us by Jesus Christ, "All things whatsoever ye would that men should do to you, do you even so to them, for this is the law and the prophets."[3]

Seventh Day, 1st of 5th month: Still pressing after a more full release from the world and its cares. Endeavoring to redeem the time, because the days are still evil[4] or attended in many respects with much evil. The alarm of war[5] is heard in the land and much contention among the people.

---

[1] 1 Corinthians 15:13-14
[2] 1 Corinthians 9:16-17
[3] Matthew 7:12
[4] Ephesians 5:16
[5] Jeremiah 4:19 & 49:2

1811-1813 145

Flee, O my soul, to thy rock, the name of the Lord![1] For in it is safety and a sure refuge from all the storms[2] and tempests that assail poor mortals in passing through this vale of tears and state of trial and probation.

First Day: Had to suffer through the meeting today.

Alas, how oft have the poor ministers to be baptized for and with the dead?

Second Day: Still pressing after a release from my worldly cares, as the time is near at hand when I shall proceed on my proposed journey to the south and west on my good Master's business. I hope in the way he is pleased to lead.

Third Day: Felt much poverty of spirit today, although nothing particular has occurred, either on the right hand or left. Therefore, I feel, in a good degree, a peaceful mind, which is worthy of thanksgiving.

Fourth Day: Still pressing after a full settlement of my temporal concerns that I may be in a state of readiness to pursue my journey as soon as the way opens.

Fifth Day: Was favored towards the close of our meeting today to discharge another debt of love and care to my Friends as it was likely to be the last opportunity I should have with them before I proceeded on my intended journey. And through the prevalence of gospel love, it was made a tendering, baptizing season to some. And we parted under a degree of the uniting influence of it.

Sixth Day: Still aiming at the same mark of readiness and preparation for my journey – expecting to leave home tomorrow and proceed therein, if the cloud is removed from the tabernacle and the light should lead the way.

A Visit to Friends in the Yearly Meetings of Philadelphia, Baltimore, & the adjacent parts of Virginia in 1813

8th of 5th month 1813 and seventh of the week: Having for some time past felt an engagement of mind to make a visit in gospel love to Friends and others in some parts of the Yearly Meetings of Philadelphia, Baltimore, and the adjacent parts of Virginia, with the concurrence of my Friends, I commenced the journey on this day, after a precious, solemn season with my family, in which I was favored in fervent supplication, to recommend them to the divine protection and preserving care of the Shepherd of Israel. And under a thankful sense of his loving-kindness, [we] took leave of each other in much affectionate sympathy and

---

[1] Deuteronomy 32:3-4
[2] Isaiah 25:4

brokenness of spirit, and rode to New York with a peaceful and quiet mind. My kinsman, Isaac Hicks* of Westbury, kindly accompanied me in this journey.

First Day: Attended Friends meetings there – in the morning at Pearl Street House and in the afternoon, at Liberty Street. They were both laborous seasons through the medium of communication and I hope profitable to some (as in all right labor we are encouraged to believe there is profit). After these opportunities, together with a favored season in a family of Friends (the heads of which were Elders), I felt a pretty full release from the city at present.

New Jersey

Second Day: Proceeded on our journey to Newark, where we attended a meeting appointed for us at the 3rd hour. It was on the whole, I think, a favored season. Many truths of the gospel were opened to the people and appeared to have a good degree of entrance[1] on the minds of some present, though others appeared to be too much fettered by the prejudice of education to be profited unless some dispensation is meted out to them to break those bonds asunder. The meeting closed in solemn quiet and I left them with a peaceful mind. After which, we rode to Rahway and lodged.

Third Day: This afternoon at the 3rd hour, we attended a meeting previously appointed at Elizabethtown. Many of the most respectable inhabitants attended, among whom were the governor of the state of New Jersey and his wife and a very considerable number of young people. The Lord, who is a Never-failing Helper to those that trust in him, was near, furnishing with ability to preach the gospel of life and salvation to the people in the clear demonstration of the Spirit and with a power attending that produced great brokenness of heart and contrition of spirit among them, and the power of his divine love was felt to spread over the meeting as a precious canopy. We parted with them rejoicing in his loving-kindness – still extended to his backsliding and offending creature, man, in humiliation and deep thankfulness of heart for such unmerited favors.

Fourth and Fifth Days: We attended Friends meetings at Plainfield and Rahway and on Sixth Day, we had a favored meeting at New Brunswick among the townspeople. Many truths of the gospel were opened to their consideration and a comfortable solemnity was witnessed to spread over the meeting.

Seventh Day: We rode to Upper Freehold, intending to be at Friends meeting at the East Branch in that township on First Day. We lodged at the house of our Friend, George Frost, where I had lodged before in my way

---

[1] Entrance: positive influence

Plainfield (New Jersey) Meetinghouse

through the Jerseys about twelve years prior to this time. We met a very kind reception from our said Friend and his family, and it seemed like a fresh renewal of friendship and affection between us. How consoling it is for the weary traveler to meet with kind friends. It is as a brook by the way[1] in a time of drought.

First Day: We attended East Branch Meeting as above proposed. The forepart was exercising through the want of a lively exercise among the members – too many of whom seemed in a dead, lifeless state as to a right, religious concern. This makes hard labor for the living, exercised members and is very trying to those who visit them in the service of Truth. Yet as we kept up the travail for Truth's arising, and patiently abode under suffering, a degree of light broke forth and led to a seasonable and, I trust, instructive communication, in which I found relief and peace in the labor, which I consider a great favor.

Second Day: Was at Upper Freehold Meeting. It was a season of deep suffering in the forepart, in which my spirit was deeply baptized with and for the dead. But as I patiently submitted to the crucifying operation of the present dispensation, a degree of light sprang up, and in it, I was led to view the declaration of the apostle Paul, how that death reigned from Adam to Moses,[2] and to show to the people that all the unregenerate were under the influence and power of the same death. For in Adam all die (that is, in the transgressing state). And that it is only by and through our attention being turned to the inward divine law (which the apostle calls

---

[1] Psalm 110:7
[2] Romans 5:14

the law of the Spirit of Life in Christ Jesus[1]) and our yielding full obedience thereunto, that we can be set free and delivered from this law of sin and death that was typed out[2] by Israel's deliverance from the bondage of Pharaoh by a full and implicit obedience to the outward commands of God through his servant Moses. And as I attended carefully to the opening, Truth arose into victory and administered cause of thanksgiving under a grateful sense of the continued mercy and loving-kindness of our gracious Creator to his backsliding creature, man.

The three following days, we attended meetings at Crosswicks (alias Chesterfield), Upper Springfield, and a meeting called the Mount. These were all favored meetings, wherein the Lord's presence and power were manifested, to the tendering and contriting many hearts, giving tongue and utterance, and through which the gospel was preached in the demonstration of the Spirit and with a power attending that carried sharp reproof to the disobedient and unfaithful, and strength to the weak and feebleminded, and encouragement to the honest-hearted, humble travelers – to the mutual rejoicing the sincere-hearted. And for all which favors, my spirit was made humbly thankful to the Shepherd of Israel, to whom all the glory and praise is due, for his mercy endureth forever.

Sixth Day: Attended Friends meeting at Old Springfield. It was a precious, baptizing season. The Lord's presence and power were felt to spread over the meeting to the tendering and contriting many hearts and to the comfort and encouragement of the honest-hearted travelers Zionward. And the meeting closed under a thankful sense of divine favor, with prayer and praise.

Seventh Day: We were at Mansfield and on First Day, was at Bordentown in the morning and at Lower Mansfield in the afternoon. These meetings were well attended and very solemn – the two latter (by Friends account) unusually large.

O how good is the Lord, and greatly to be praised for his marvelous works, and his never-failing loving-kindness to the children of men!

Second Day: We were at Burlington. In this meeting, my mind was opened largely to set forth the nature and design of the gospel dispensation. And that as none had ever been perfect in it but the man, Jesus Christ, we had not a right (as his professed followers) to take the example of any – save his – as our real, perfect rule of life, as all who have gone before us have (in a greater or less degree) through the undue force and prejudice of education, fallen short of his perfect rule – left us in his example and precepts – the apostles themselves not excepted.

---

[1] Romans 8:2

[2] Type out: prefigure or foreshadow as a type, i.e., an imperfect symbol of a perfect anti-type. (See also, Figure and Shadow)

And that the Christian professors in the varied ages of the Church had very much marred and obstructed the work of reformation by suffering themselves to be too closely attached to their several, particular leaders, and have therefore justly thrown themselves open to the censure of the apostle's reprehension,[1] wherein he blames some of the primitive Christians for setting themselves one against another by the partial respect each had for the minister by whom he had been brought over to the Christian faith – one crying, "I am of Paul," and "I of Apollos," and "I of Cephas," and (some more wise), "I of Christ"[2] – and to whose example all ought to have looked, and not turned their attention so much to the instruments through whom only they were brought to believe in him, and who pointed them to him as the only means and way to obtain salvation and eternal life.

And that, although many of our worthy predecessors (according to their measure of light) endeavored faithfully to do the work of their day, yet none of them had been so entirely emancipated from the undue force of education, as to see clearly through the cloud of prejudice and, therefore, were in the practice of divers things not consistent with that perfect justice that the example and precepts of our Lord call for, and which are in full unison with the perfect righteousness of the gospel. The word was preached in a large searching testimony, I trust through divine assistance, in the demonstration of the Spirit, to the comfort and encouragement of the sincere in heart, and the peace of my own mind.

Third Day: Was at Rancocas. The meeting was solemn and the Lord's presence was felt to preside to the humbling many minds. And many truths of the gospel were, I trust in an instructive manner, spread before the people.

Fourth and Fifth Days: We attended meetings at Mount Holly, Upper Evesham, and at Easton (on Fifth Day afternoon). They were all favored meetings. In the two former, my mind was largely opened in two doctrinal testimonies, wherein the design and end of all the shadows[3] of the law were clearly opened, and the necessity of their entire abolishment by the death and resurrection of Christ – showing how, that by the primitive Christians retaining many of the shadows of the law, the apostasy broke in upon the Church (to its utter ruin) and, that by the retention of some of the same shadows, the reformation had been and is still greatly retarded, and will never progress on its right foundation until those shadows are all

---

[1] Reprehension: rebuke
[2] 1 Corinthians 1:12
[3] Shadow: an imperfect or insubstantial thing that foreshadows a corresponding reality or "substance." (See also, Figure and Type)

discarded and done away. My mind was deeply humbled under a sense of the Lord's mercy.

The three following days, we were at Lower Evesham, Cropwell, Chester, Westfield, Haddonfield, and at Newton - taking two meetings each day.

Pennsylvania & Delaware

After the latter, it being First Day evening, we crossed the River Delaware to Philadelphia. In those meetings, my mind was deeply humbled under a grateful sense of the Lord's continued mercy to an unworthy people - rendered so by the continued disobedience and revolting of great numbers who go under our name, not only among the youth, but with many of riper age, whose experience and daily observation (we might reasonably suppose), had they endeavored to improve by it, would ere now have taught them better. But how true is that saying of the great Master, "If the light in thee become darkness, how great is that darkness."[1] And this has fallen to the lot of these by turning their backs upon the true light and adhering to their own carnal reasonings and fleshly consultations, whereby they have been left (like Balaam through his covetousness[2]) to justify themselves in many things that the true light in them - had they been obedient to its first manifestations - would not have approved. Therefore, these are left, as a reward of their disobedience, to believe a lie to their own confusion.

My mind was largely opened in these meetings, not only to commemorate the Lord's gracious dealings with the children of men, but likewise to set forth and open to the several auditories the subtle workings and varied transformations of that diabolical spirit, wherein he lies in wait to deceive and counteract the gracious designs of heaven among the children of men. And under a renewed sense of the Lord's continued mercy, my spirit was led to exclaim, as uttered formerly, "Great and marvelous are thy works, Lord God Almighty. Just and true are all thy ways, thou King of Saints."

The following week, we spent in the city - except Seventh Day, on which we rode out and attended two meetings - in the morning at Frankford, and at five in the afternoon, at Germantown. These were both favored seasons. After which, we then returned at evening to the city.

And the next day being first of the week and the 6th of 6th month, we were at Friends meeting at Arch Street in the morning and at the Northern District in the afternoon. And some previous notice being given of my intention of being at them, they were unusually large - more so, it was

---

[1] Matthew 6:23
[2] Numbers 22

thought, than had been known before and many had to go away for want of room, as the crowd was so great out and about the doors that many could not get within hearing. It was supposed there were three thousand people at the first and, at the last, many more than the rooms could contain. And through the marvelous condescension and loving-kindness of our gracious God, my mind was strengthened and qualified to preach the gospel of peace and salvation to the people in the demonstration of the Spirit and with a power attending that set home the doctrine – to the humbling conviction and contrition of any minds – in a large testimony at the first to the excellency of a life of strict and impartial justice and righteousness as the only right foundation of every real religious and moral[1] virtue and without which, no true virtue could possibly exist.

The communication comprehended much salutary caution, reproof, and encouragement suited to the varied states present – under a sense of which my mind was deeply humbled and had gratefully to acknowledge, this is the Lord's doings, and marvelous in mine eyes.

The latter was likewise a favored season, wherein many truths of the gospel were opened to the people, tending to lead the minds of people from all dependence on traditional religion and worship, and to gather them home to the eternal substance in themselves – Christ, the Hope of Glory[2] and Light of the World,[3] by the influence of whose Light and Spirit, we only can be enabled to obtain victory over the world and its spirit, and become qualified to worship the Father in spirit and in truth.

The 7th, we left the city and previous notice having gone forward, in the course of the week and the next First Day, we attended eleven meetings in the following order.

On Second Day, at Darby.

On Third Day in the morning at Haverford and at the 5th hour after noon, at Merion.

Fourth at the Valley.

Fifth at Radnor (which was their monthly meeting).

Sixth at Newtown in the morning and in the afternoon at Springfield.

Seventh at Middletown in the morning and in the afternoon at Providence.

First Day, at Chester in the morning and in the afternoon at Chichester.

And to my humbling admiration, that although I was taken very unwell on Third Day afternoon (before the third meeting as above arranged) and continued so through the week and until the last meeting –

---

[1] Moral: based on natural religion or social principles
[2] Colossians 1:27
[3] John 8:12

insomuch so that for several days, I could take scarcely any nourishment at all (as my stomach loathed all food), yet I was strengthened to go through the service of these meetings (which was very large and laborous generally in each) so that at the close of some of them, my strength was so exhausted, being wet from head to foot with extreme sweating (the weather being warm) and my body all in a tremor through great bodily weakness and indisposition – that to look forward, it seemed to me after divers of those exercising seasons nearly impossible for me to reach the next. But that which is impossible to man, we often find easy to the Great Helper of his people and as my care was wholly cast upon him, he graciously accompanied by his holy presence from meeting to meeting. And although when I first sat down in many of those meetings, the force of my complaint seemed to absorb all my strength – both of body and mind – yet, as I endeavored to center in quiet, I seldom sat long ere the light sprang up and dispelled all the darkness and opened doctrine new and old, and strengthened to communicate in a way of clear demonstration – to the comfort and instruction of the honest-hearted, and setting home conviction and reproof to the delinquent, and extending a visitation of entreaty and love to the beloved young people whose minds were not yet hardened in vice – showing them what great and everlasting benefits and blessings would redound to them by an early dedication of their hearts to the Lord.

My mind at the close of these large, solemn meetings (for many were very large – more than the houses could contain) was generally centered in perfect peace, wherein I was led to contemplate his marvelous loving-kindness to me, a poor unworthy creature, and his wonderful works in mercy to the children of men – waiting in long forbearance for their return and continuing his call to them by his Spirit through his servants and messengers, rising up early and sending them that no means should be left untried for their recovery and reconciliation.

O what shall we render to the Lord for all his benefits?[1]

Having been very unwell – as before observed – most of the last week, I found it necessary to lay by a day or two, which we did at the house of our Friend, John Talbot, and with a little rest, soon found myself better and, being desirous to improve the time, we again proceeded.

Took Concord Meeting on Fourth Day and 16th of the month, Wilmington on Fifth Day, Centre on the Sixth, Hockessin on the Seventh, and on First Day was at Kennett. I was helped to get through the service of these meetings to my own satisfaction and peace of mind – although some of them were very laborous and exercising through a want of faithfulness

---

[1] Psalm 116:12

New Garden (Pennsylvania) Meetinghouse

and a great lack of a right concern and zeal for the support and maintenance of our Christian testimonies, which in some families were very much neglected and let fall.

I was led forth generally in those meetings in close, searching testimonies, tending to arouse Friends from their beds of ease and carnal security – brought upon them by an inordinate love of the world and an increase of temporal blessings, in which their principal enjoyments were too much centered – loving the gifts and forgetting the giver. I labored fervently among them, and especially so in the latter meeting, wherein my mind was largely opened to unfold to the audience many of the deep mysteries of the gospel state – making them plain and easy to be understood by the most ignorant whose minds were in any degree turned to inquire the way to Zion. It was a high day,[1] in which the Lord's power was manifested in an eminent degree, breaking down and contriting many hearts, and Truth appeared to reign triumphantly over all – to the praise of his Grace, who is over all, God blessed forever.

The following week, we attended meetings at Birmingham, Willistown, Goshen, West Chester, Bradford, and Marlborough – mostly, pretty full meetings, and generally favored and satisfactory, and in some of them (as in many foregoing opportunities), the Lord's power was eminently exalted and set above and over all error and untruth.

On First Day, 27th, we attended two very large meetings – in the morning at London Grove and in the afternoon at New Garden – in both

---

[1] High day: a day of special solemnity (see John 19:31)

of which my mind, I trust, was opened by that divine key that when it opens, none can shut, and when it shuts, none can open,[1] and strengthened to declare largely of the things of God and the way to eternal life - to the satisfaction and peace of my own mind and I trust to the edification and instruction, as well as conviction and reproof, of many present - the Spirit assisting to divide the word severally to everyone according to the necessity of their several states. It was a day thankfully to be remembered.

In the course of this week, we attended meetings at West Grove, at East and West Nottingham, Eastland, and Little Britain. These were all satisfactory seasons, and particularly that at East Nottingham was a heart-searching opportunity, wherein Truth was raised powerfully into dominion over all. Many were broken and contrited, and a number wept freely for a considerable time. Surely it was the Lord's doing and it was marvelous in our eyes.

Maryland

On Seventh Day, we crossed the River Susquehanna and rode into the neighborhood of Deer Creek, intending to be at the meeting there on First Day. This also proved a very precious meeting, wherein the Lord's power was eminently manifested, and every mind appeared to be humbled through its blessed influence, and the meeting ended with solemn supplication.

The two following days, we attended meetings at the Little Falls and Gunpowder. And after the latter, we rode into Baltimore and the two following days, attended Friends meetings there as they came in course, at the close of which was held their Monthly Meetings for the Western and Eastern Districts. They were very laborous seasons, but ended to pretty good satisfaction. There appeared to be a concerned remnant in each meeting, through whose care the discipline appeared to be pretty well supported.

After the latter meeting, we left the city and rode to Elkridge in order to attend a meeting appointed for us there the next day, being the sixth of the week. This was a satisfactory opportunity.

The next day, we attended Indian Spring Meeting. It was a solemn and I trust profitable season to some. May it remain with them as bread cast upon the water that may return after many days.

After this meeting, we rode to the city of Washington, and the next day being the first of the week and 11th of 7th month, we attended a meeting there in the morning and in the afternoon, one at Alexandria in Virginia. These were both very hard, laborous meetings. The people

---

[1] Isaiah 22:22 & Revelation 3:7

appeared very destitute of any real religious engagement – their minds being so swallowed up in their political controversies and other worldly engagements that there seemed to be very little room in their thoughts for anything else – that I felt but little satisfaction in those meetings, except a consciousness of having done my duty in laying before them in a plain manner divers truths necessary for them to be in the practice of – and without which, they could not be real Christians nor obtain an inheritance in the kingdom of heaven.

The three following days, we attended meetings at Georgetown, Sandy Spring, and Elkridge. We had been at the latter place the week before on Sixth Day: These were seasons of favor – many truths of the gospel were, I trust, clearly opened to the people, accompanied with right authority, to the humbling many minds, and Truth reigned over all.

After the latter, we rode back to Baltimore that afternoon and attended a meeting previously appointed for us at the 5th hour and the next day being Friends Meeting in the Eastern District. And public notice given of our intention to be there, these were both large meetings in which I was led forth in two, large, doctrinal testimonies – I trust to the edification and comfort of many minds. After which I felt easy and clear to leave the city.

Back in Pennsylvania

We therefore proceeded that afternoon about fourteen miles on our way towards Little York in Pennsylvania, where we arrived the next day a little before evening. And on Seventh Day, had a comfortable, instructive meeting there. After which, we rode to Columbia, crossing the River Susquehanna in our way thither. And the next day being the first of the week, we attended Friends meeting there. It was large for that place – more came than the house could contain, some going away for want of room. It was a favored season – the Lord's power was manifest and Truth reigned over all. And I was made to rejoice under a humbling sense of his continued mercy and gracious assistance from day to day, wherein we had cause often to set up our Ebenezer and say, in the language of one formerly, "Hitherto hath the Lord helped us."[1]

The three following days, we attended meetings at Lampeter, Sadsbury, and Doe Run, wherein our Gracious Helper, whom we waited upon and trusted in, manifested himself to be a God near at hand and a Present Helper in every needful time and was not only mouth and wisdom, tongue and utterance, but likewise sealed the truths communicated by the attendant evidence of his own power – humbling and contriting many hearts, bringing all under subjection to the authority

---

[1] 1 Samuel 7:12

of Truth, insomuch that I had often in deep thankfulness of heart to query like David, "What shall we render unto the Lord for all his benefits?"

We proceeded thence, taking meetings at Fallowfield, East Caln, Downingtown, and on First Day, 25th of 7th month, was at Uwchlan Meeting. It was, I trust, a profitable, instructive meeting, as were also the three foregoing. And I found peace in my labors, which is the sum of the whole matter.

On Second Day, we crossed the River Schuylkill in our way to Plymouth, where by previous notice being sent forward, we had a meeting appointed at the 4th hour after noon, which we accordingly attended. And the next day, had an appointed meeting at Abington. These were both large meetings in which the Lord's power was felt to preside. The latter especially was a very comfortable, satisfactory meeting, wherein many truths of the gospel were opened to the people's consideration, and they pressed to an engagement of mind to realize them in their own experience – setting forth the great and singular advantage and benefits that would most certainly result to them and to society, in their so doing. The Lord's power was felt to preside and Truth reigned over all opposition.

The four following days, we were at Byberry, Middletown, Bristol, and the Falls. As these were large meetings, wherein through gracious assistance, my mind was strengthened to labor largely in the gospel – endeavoring by plain and conclusive arguments drawn from scripture testimony and their own experience to gather the minds and attention of the people, from every nonessential and false trust, home to the sure foundation, the elect,[1] precious cornerstone, which is Christ in them by his Spirit, the hope of glory. These were solemn seasons, wherein the people's minds were generally humbled, the honest-hearted comforted, the youth encouraged and instructed, and the lukewarm and refractory cautioned and reproved. And the Lord's power exalted over all, to the rejoicing of the sincere-hearted, and the peace of my own mind.

The next day being first of the week and 1st of 8th month, we attended Trenton Meeting in the morning and were at Stony Brook at five in the afternoon. The meeting at Trenton was thought to be the largest that had been held in that place. It was a favored, precious meeting, wherein the Lord's power was eminently manifest. And my spirit was made to rejoice and joy in the God of my salvation, who had made bare his arm of divine sufficiency and, as I trusted in him, carried me through and over every trial and tribulation that attended in the course of this journey – enabling me to labor faithfully in the work of the gospel (I trust) to the exaltation of

---

[1] Elect: selected for its excellence

his own righteous cause of power and Truth and Righteousness – and the peace and comfort of my own mind.

These meetings closed my visit in those parts. We then proceeded directly to New York, where we arrived on Third Day before noon. And as Friends monthly meeting for the city was to be held the next day, we concluded to stay and attend it. After which, I rode home and found my family all well, for which favor – together with his other multiplied mercies and blessings conferred in the course of my pilgrimage through this vale of tears – inspires my heart with gratitude and thanksgiving to the great and Blessed Author of my being and well-being, who is over all, God blessed forever.

At Home

Fifth, Sixth and Seventh Days: Made preparations for again entering into the necessary cares of my family.

First Day: After a pretty close exercise in silence in our meeting, I was led to call Friends' attention to more strict watchfulness and circumspection, and to show the necessity of progressing in the work of righteousness, and not to continue any longer at ease in a formal, customary way, which is sure (if continued in) to produce dwarfishness[1] and death, not only to individuals, but also produceth languor and dullness in meetings – greatly distressing to the living, exercised members.

The following week was spent in my common vocation as a farmer except that on Seventh [Day], the 15th of 8th month, I went to Setauket to see a sick Friend who had lately been received a member, but was so weak in a declining state as not likely ever to be able to attend a monthly meeting. We had a meeting with her and some of her neighbors the next day, after which I returned home that evening (about thirty miles).

Second, Third, and Fourth Days: Passed as usual in a peaceful attention to my ordinary vocations.

Fifth Day: At meeting, my mind was solemnly humbled in a fresh commemoration of the gracious dealings of our Heavenly Father towards the workmanship of his holy hand – especially to his revolting and backsliding creature, man, whom in great mercy, he is visiting and revisiting in the midst of his iniquities, inviting him in long-suffering loving-kindness to repent and return, that he may bring back his soul from the pit, to be enlightened with the light of the living.[2]

Sixth and Seventh Days: Spent in attending on my temporal concerns, which was trying to the creature, through indisposition of body and much poverty of spirit.

---

[1] Dwarfishness: stunted development
[2] Job 33:30

First Day: At our meeting today – which I attended more from a sense of real duty than from any expectation of comfort, as my bodily indisposition and poverty of spirit still continued – nevertheless, my mind, soon after I took my seat, was opened into a view of the great hurt man sustained by suffering himself to be led and governed by his external senses, as it is the external sense that man is endued[1] with (as an animal creature) that constitutes his probationary state and through the medium thereof, he only is exposed to temptations. For had he watchfully attended to the internal sense and voice of God to his soul (which his dependent state justly required of him), the tempter would have found no more place in him, than he did in the blessed Jesus.

Hence, the way of our return lies open before us through the Grace of God (or Comforter) by whom the internal sense of the soul is again arrested[2] and strict obedience to its dictates required. And if yielded up to in uprightness and faithful submission, the external senses are thereby subjected and regulated, and every undue desire and passion subordinated, and the creature returns a willing subject to the Creator, and primitive harmony is restored.

I had largely to communicate on this subject and to show to the auditory how wonderfully gracious and merciful the Lord is, who in long-suffering loving-kindness is dispensing to every state according to their several necessities, not suffering even a sparrow to fall without his heavenly notice.[3]

The rest of this week was spent in my ordinary vocations. And my farming business being very pressing and it being difficult to procure suitable help, my mind was over-burdened with care and my body with labor, which seldom fails of producing leanness of spirit (in a lesser or greater degree) in proportion to the excess of worldly cares.

First Day, 29th of 8th month: Attended our meeting in silence.

O what a precious enjoyment to know both soul and body in humble silence, prostrate at the throne of grace.[4]

Second Day: Had invitations to attend the funerals of two deceased women Friends on the day following, one of whom in a declining state had been lately, at her request, received into membership by our monthly meeting, but was never able to attend – she living in the town of Setauket, far distant from her Friends. We had a solemn meeting at her funeral, agreeable to her request before her decease, at which a large number of the

---

[1] Endue: endow with qualities
[2] Arrest: remain fixed in consideration of a subject
[3] Matthew 10:29
[4] Hebrews 4:16

townspeople attended and many, although generally strangers to us, were glad of the opportunity and appeared well affected therewith.

The rest of this week spent about home in usual avocations.

First Day, 5th of 9th month: Attended the indulged meeting at Jerusalem, which in the main, I think was a favored season, although somewhat hurt in the forepart by an unsavory appearance in the ministry.

Second, Third, and Fourth Days: Occupied in attending to my farming business, which (for want of suitable, faithful laborers) is often attended with much care and too much bodily labor for my time of life – not well to be avoided without too much suffering.

Fifth Day: Attended our preparative meetings, at which one of our overseers brought forward information of one of our members having, through unwatchfulness and want of faithful attention to the witness of Truth in his own mind, given way repeatedly to use strong drink to excess. This information affected my mind in degree both with joy and sorrow. I was glad because from my knowledge of the case, I was fully in the belief it had been too long procrastinated – not only to the hurt and loss of the individual, but also had brought reproach upon the society and wounding the noble cause we are engaged to espouse. And it was cause of real sorrow when brought, to reflect on the distressed state of the individual and the great affliction it must necessarily produce to his wife and children and near connections.[1]

O how necessary to keep up a steady watch and warfare against this sore evil that destroys so many tens of thousands of the children of men both in soul and body!

Sixth and Seventh Days: Spent in much bodily pain from a supposed rheumatic complaint in one of my limbs.

O how needful a virtue is patience in seasons of affliction to keep us from ungrateful murmurings by which men and women often greatly offend their gracious and beneficent Creator, who designs nothing but good to his creature, man, in all the varied dispensations of his divine providence.

First Day: At our meeting today, I was led to show to the people the great harm and loss neighborhoods, as well as the community at large, sustain for want of a careful submission to the law of the land – where it did not interfere with conscience. And that those, who from their licentious and immoral pursuits were often transgressing against the moral precepts of the law, were not worthy of living in a free country, while making breaches against the civil policy thereof merely to satisfy their own creaturely and selfish gratifications – as an honest and faithful

---

[1] Connections: family and close friends

attention to the moral law of the country we live in will, in a certain degree (as the apostle expressed), be as a schoolmaster to lead to Christ,[1] as he only who is faithful in the unrighteous mammon, is likely to make any proficiency in obtaining the true riches.[2]

Second, Third, and Fourth Days: Spent in my ordinary vocations – attended with frequent, internal requests for continual preservation.

Fifth Day: Attended our monthly meeting, at the first sitting of which my mind was opened into a clear view of the necessity of our coming to experience the resurrection from a state of spiritual death to a renewal of spiritual life through the resurrection of Christ by his life and power in us, as nothing short of that can give full and satisfactory evidence of his (and our) resurrection from the dead. And on this internal testimony, our whole salvation depends. And because we now know and feel that because he lives, we live also, and the life that we now live is by faith in the Son of God. Hence, we come to know (agreeable to Paul's declaration) Christ formed in us[3] – both as the Son of God and son of man, which is the sum and substance of the gospel state.

Sixth and Seventh Days: Spent in manual labor – a reasonable portion of which I consider my duty and delight. And the more my delight because I esteem it my reasonable and Christian duty and as I also abhor idleness and sloth.

First Day: Sat our meeting in silence under a pretty lengthy testimony of a ministering Friend from abroad, who introduced his communication with the following saying of Christ, "Except ye eat my flesh and drink my blood, ye have no life in you. For my flesh is meat indeed, and my blood is drink indeed."[4] And to show that it was to be spiritually understood and internally received, he further added, "The words that I say unto you, they are Spirit and they are Life."[5] An excellent subject indeed, and while he kept to his text and the subject, it seemed lively. But he after a time departed from it and the life, I thought, very much departed with it. How very necessary it is for ministers to keep a steady eye to the openings of Truth and not suffer any premature birth to rise up and get in and scatter their attention. For want of this care, I have often thought many good openings have been much lost and the work thereby marred.

First Day, 10th of 10th month: Alas, how fleeting is time! Three weeks have elapsed since my last note, in the course of which I have attended two funerals. Take care, O my soul! And do not grow careless and

---

[1] Galatians 3:24
[2] Luke 16:11
[3] Galatians 4:19
[4] John 6:53-54
[5] John 6:63

forgetful when drawing near to the eve of life, lest the world and its cares get in and choke the bubblings of the celestial spring, through the abundant cumber that seems necessarily attendant on my present state in striving to help and comfort others.

First Day, 17th of 10th month: Spent the week past principally in attending on my outward avocations, except the attendance of the funeral of a young man on Fourth Day, at which we had a solemn opportunity, wherein I was exercised publicly to set forth the necessity and great propriety of an early and timely preparation for death and to show to the people the way and means by which it only can be effected – founded an the declaration of the apostle Paul where he asserts that, "Not by works of righteousness that we have done, but by his own mercy he saveth us, by the washing of regeneration, and renewings of the Holy Ghost."[1] The opportunity closed with comfort and peace of mind, which is the true crowning period.

I sat our meeting today in silence, feeling nothing to exercise my mind in a communicative way.

Seventh Day: Spent this week mostly in the busy round of outward care in my temporal concerns, saving the attendance of our monthly meeting on Fifth Day and Select Ministers and Elders Meeting on Sixth Day. In both of which, my mind was exercised on account of the apparent languor respecting the right management, and want of firmness in the execution of our discipline – even in Ministers and Elders – by reason whereof, the society was very much enveloped in a state of weakness.

First Day: Felt my mind clothed with great weakness and a feeling sense of my own insufficiency, while sitting in our meeting today. Nevertheless, I was led to view in prospect and contemplation, the great and essential advantages that result to individuals and society in general by a strict and steady attendance on religious meetings from a real sense of duty, as there is nothing in the outward conduct of men and women that more fully denotes a mind fixed on God – its Maker – for support and countenance[2] while passing through the changes and vicissitudes of this mortal life. The subject spread and led to communication and opened to a large field of doctrine, in which the gospel was preached in the authority of Truth. And a very comfortable solemnity covered the meeting.

Third Day: Attended the funeral of an acquaintance, a convinced person – it being his request on his death-bed and also that a meeting might be held at his funeral. It was accordingly so ordered and proved a very solemn, affecting season – particularly so to the near connections of the deceased. The Lord was graciously near, furnishing ability to bear

---

[1] Titus 3:5
[2] Countenance: favor or patronage

ample testimony to many truths of the gospel. The people were very attentive and many hearts were broken and contrited, and the Lord's name and power exalted over all.

Seventh Day: The three preceding days, I attended our quarterly meeting. It was held at this time at Flushing. The Meeting of Ministers and Elders and the meeting for discipline were very laborous, heart-searching seasons. The meeting for worship was a quiet, favored meeting under the ministry of our Friend, Henry Hull, from Stanford in Nine Partners. We had great cause to acknowledge the goodness and continued mercy of Israel's Shepherd, who not only furnished wisdom and ability to search out the hidden things of Esau (or the first nature) and to set judgment upon the head of the transgressing nature in those meetings set apart for the well-ordering of the affairs of the church, but also graciously condescended in the closing meeting held for worship to gladden our hearts by the effusions of his love – causing the light of his countenance to shine upon us.[1] Whereby the minds of the faithful were influenced to return thanksgiving and praise to his ever adorable name, who remains to be God over all, blessed forever and ever.

First Day: Sat our meeting in silence and was much interrupted by the intrusion of unprofitable thoughts, against which I had to struggle through most part of the meeting.

Second and Third Days: Spent in my necessary avocations, but not without considerable fear attending my mind, lest my temporal concerns too much intrude and indispose the mind in regard to heavenly meditations. Nothing material occurred the rest of the week.

First Day: Silence as to words sealed my lips through the meeting again today and may they remain shut in all our solemn meetings, unless opened by the Key of David.[2]

For the course of this week, I attended the funerals of two Friends – at both of which, meetings were held. In the first, my mind was largely opened on the subject of religion, wherein I was led to show to the auditory how that a right consideration and frequent remembrance of our latter end tended to lead into the realities thereof, which consisted in nothing but acts of real obedience and humble submission to the manifested will of our Heavenly Father, through the inspiration of his Grace and Light in our own hearts. And that as we were careful to have this in our daily experience, it qualified to answer the great end for which we were created, which is to glorify God and enjoy him, and be thereby prepared to meet death with an even and tranquil mind – having known

---

[1] Psalm 4:6 & 89:15
[2] Isaiah 22:22 & Revelation 3:7

its sting, which is sin, taken away by the death of the cross.[1] I was also led to expose the doctrine of personal and unconditional predestination and election and to show the fallacy and inconsistency thereof with the divine character.

In the latter, I was concerned to show the dangerous and hurtful tendency of our submitting to be led and governed by the customs and manners of others without a strict and careful examination thereof, and bringing them to the test of the Light in our own conscience. For although the frequency of a thing, and an habitual conformity to that which is not right, often blunts the edge of conviction and reconciles us to that, that is contrary to Truth and derogatory to[2] our true interest, yet the use of[3] sinning will not lessen the guilt. But in the awful day of final decision, all our fig-leaf coverings will be ripped off and things will then appear as they really are. Then shall we all stand in need of that substantial covering, represented by the coats of skins that the Lord made for our first parents[4] (and gave them in lieu of their fig leaves, that is, something of their own inventing), that so their nakedness might no longer be exposed.

My mind was also opened to set forth the design and end of the shadowy or law dispensation and how, by its consistency and harmony in all its parts, it was a just figure and representation of the gospel state and dispensation. Yet many of its precepts were not good nor consistent with the justice and mercy of the all-beneficent and gracious Jehovah, but only so as they stood in relation to the very low, degraded, and wicked state of mankind at that time and, therefore, justly suited to Israel's state and the states and conditions of the surrounding nations concerned therein. As saith Ezekiel, "Wherefore I gave them also statutes that were not good, and judgments whereby they should not live."[5]

First Day, 14th of 11th month: Attended Cow Neck Meeting to satisfaction.

The rest of this week, I spent at home, being closely engaged in business and in making preparation for the more comfortable accommodation of my stock[6] through the inclemency of the approaching winter – considering that a merciful man is merciful to his beast[7] – as I consider it not right to keep in my possession, and under my immediate

---

[1] 1 Corinthians 15:55-57
[2] Derogatory to: takes away from
[3] Use of: being used to
[4] Genesis 3:7&21
[5] Ezekiel 20:25
[6] Stock: farm animals
[7] Proverbs 12:10

notice, any more of the animal creation than I can render reasonably comfortable.

On Fifth Day was our monthly meeting, in which my mind was engaged to show the great benefit that would result to society, and to its members as individuals, by right exercise and faithful execution of our discipline – without fear or favor – and that some cases of disorder in an individual might turn up, which (with its attendant circumstances) might render it not only necessary to disown the person, but would also prove more to his true interest, and the advancement of the cause and testimonies that we as a people are engaged in, than the reception of any untimely or unseasonable acknowledgment could possibly be, as I have always considered it required not only deep and solid consideration, but suitable time of waiting, in order rightly to qualify a person to make an acknowledgment for an offense committed against a religious society.

First Day, 21st of 11th month: My mind was closely engaged and largely opened in our meeting today to show the inconsistency and unrighteousness of a conformity to the vain and foolish customs of the world – demonstrating from the scriptures that in all ages of the world since the fall of our first parents, the customs of men and women in their natural estate were vain and that there was a certain degree of wickedness attached to every vanity. Hence, the necessity of our carefully guarding against the conformity to any custom or tradition until we have first brought it to the test of the Light in our own consciences and the reason of things, and also to its consistency with the precepts and example of our Savior Jesus Christ. And if relating to our duty towards our fellow creatures, examine whether it comports with that most excellent, pure rule given by him as a criterion of conduct, "All things whatsoever ye would that men should do unto you, do you even so to them. For this is the law and the prophets."

Second, Third, and Fourth Days: Passed over without any particular occurrence

On Fifth Day, I was invited to the funeral of a Friend who was a member of Bethpage Particular Meeting, which I attended. And after the internment, a solemn meeting was held in which my mind was largely opened to set forth to the people the great necessity, as well as wisdom and propriety, of an early preparation for death – showing them the way whereby it could only be rightly effected. It was a season of renewed visitation to a remnant and many hearts were broken and contrited.

First Day, 28th of 11th month: Feeling my mind drawn last evening and this morning to attend Friends meeting at Matinecock, I submitted thereto – going alone. In the forepart of the meeting, I had to combat a spirit of ease and stupefaction, which is generally prevalent among the worldly-minded. Although they may be pretty steady in attending meetings, yet it is to be feared with little or no profit, if it be true what the beloved apostle has affirmed that, "If any man love the world, the love of the Father is not in him."[1]

In the latter part, I was led to view the excellency of the pacific principles of the gospel as promulgated by Jesus Christ and his apostles, and to show to the people the very great and essential benefit and blessing that would result to the professors of Christianity by a strict adherence and submission thereunto – as they stand in direct opposition and contrariety to the spirit of violence and war, and breathe forth nothing but peace on earth and good will to men. It proved through mercy a season of favor. Many hearts were contrited, and the faithful and poor in spirit comforted and strengthened, and my own mind inspired with gratitude and thankfulness for such unmerited mercy.

First Day, 5th of 12th month: The six working days of last week were principally spent in my worldly concerns, except attending our Fifth Day Meeting and the Charity Society[2] meeting yesterday – an institution of Friends for the schooling of the children of the poor, black people. Our funds, agreeable to the last report of a settlement with the Treasurer, amount to thirteen hundred and odd dollars, the interest of which is yearly expended for the above purpose by a committee of the society, who superintend the schooling of said children. The directors of the society are limited at thirty members, who meet quarterly for the promotion and oversight of the institution.

I sat our Fifth Day Meeting in silence and was favored in like manner today, in poverty of spirit, which terminated in a peaceful close.

Nothing transpired in the course of last week worthy of particular notice.

First Day, 12th of 12th Month: At our meeting today, my mind was largely opened to set forth before the people the difference between the law state and that of the gospel.[3] And how that the former being weak through the flesh, God sending his son in the likeness of sinful flesh, and for sin, condemned sin in the flesh that the righteousness of the law might be fulfilled in us, who walk not after the flesh, but after the Spirit[4] – showing that nothing short of a full submission to the law of the Spirit of

---

[1] 1 John 2:15
[2] The Charity Society of Jericho and Westbury Monthly Meetings was formed in 1794 "for the use and benefit of the poor among the Black people and more especially for the education of their children."
[3] The next sentence was deleted from the printed *Journal*.
[4] Romans 8:3-4

Life in Christ Jesus can set free from the law of sin and death. It was, I trust, an instructive, edifying season – worthy of grateful remembrance.

Second Day afternoon: I rode to New York in order to attend the Meeting for Sufferings to be held the next day. It opened at the 9th hour. We got through the business at two sittings and closed in the evening.

Fourth Day afternoon: I rode home.

On Fifth Day was our monthly meeting at which we had the company of our Friend, Henry Hull, from Stanford. The meeting for worship was, I think, a favored, comfortable season and the testimonies communicated, instructive and edifying. Such repeated favored seasons make it evident beyond controversy that we are still a highly favored people and shall be accountable according to the manifold mercies and blessings bestowed upon us. For we have great cause often to query (like the psalmist formerly), "What shall we render unto the Lord for all his benefits? For his mercies are new every morning and his faithfulness every night."[1]

Sixth and Seventh Days: Spent in my ordinary concerns, yet I trust my mind was preserved in a state of watchfulness and care, that what I do – even in my temporal business – may all be done to the glory of God, and be useful to myself and to my fellow creatures.

First Day, 19th of 12th month: While silently musing in our meeting towards the latter part, a subject opened that led to the necessity of communication, wherein that petition that in the prayer our Lord taught his disciples (to wit), "Thy kingdom come, thy will be done, on earth as it is in heaven"[2] was opened to the audience. And the necessity of our individually witnessing it fulfilled in us – as the only medium through which we can obtain salvation and a preparation for the kingdom of heaven – pressed upon the people, showing from the analogy of things that, as there is nothing but the Lord's will done in heaven, that a soul that is not reconciled thereto, so as to become its chiefest delight, cannot enter therein nor partake of its celestial enjoyments.

The rest of the week was carefully employed in my household concerns, with the attendance of our Fifth Day Meeting, agreeable to my invariable practice when at home, if not prevented by indisposition. It was a quiet, comfortable meeting under the ministry of our Friend, Henry Hull, who was again with us.

Sixth Day: Attended the funeral of our honest Friend, Richard Townsend. There was a large collection of Friends and neighbors – he being generally esteemed. A meeting was held on the occasion, which proved a very solemn season. The people's attention was called to the necessity of a timely preparation for death, in a large, arousing testimony,

---

[1] Lamentations 3:22-23 & Psalm 92:2
[2] Matthew 6:10

setting forth to the assembly the great and singular advantages which would redound to the children of men by their obtaining right ideas and apprehensions of God, the want of which left them to be led away into a belief of many strange and ideal notions concerning him, and particularly that of foreordination[1] – the inconsistency of which, my mind was led to unfold to the auditory by this undeniable argument (and others not recited). That, as God's ordination and God's creation, as also God's will, are always in perfect unison, and cannot be diverse one from the other, and as all that he wills and all that he creates is immutably good, agreeable to his own declaration when he finished the work of creation, hence, whatever he ordains must likewise be immutably good. Therefore, if there is any such thing as sin and iniquity in the world, then God has neither willed it nor ordained it as it is impossible for him to will contradictories. And secondly, if he has previous to man's creation willed and determined all his actions, then certainly every man stands in the same state of acceptance with him. Hence, a universal salvation will certainly take place in the universe, which, I conceive, the favorers of foreordination would be as unwilling as myself to allow.[2] And moreover, if man was not vested with the power of free agency and a liberty of determining his own will in relation to a choice of good or evil, he could not be an accountable creature. Neither would it be in his power to commit sin.

It was a time of favor, and the Lord's blessing on the labors of the day was reverently supplicated. O, saith my soul! May they have the desired effect.

First Day, 26th of 12th month: Sat the greater part of our meeting in much weakness and poverty of spirit – to which I felt perfectly resigned, believing it to be agreeable to the Lord's will. But towards the close an honest, elderly Friend (though young and small in such service) expressed a sentence or two accompanied with a degree of life, which seemed to give spring to a concern on my mind that led to communication. The subject that opened was to show how plainness and simplicity were the true marks and badges of the Lord's people and children in every age of the world – witnessed to by the true nature and analogy of all things in the universe, and confirmed by the testimony of the Grace and good Spirit of God through his servants in all the generations of mankind.

The youth were exhorted and tenderly invited to submit to the cross of Christ, with the assurance vouched[3] by the experience of all the faithful that if they bowed willingly to his yoke, it would become not only easy

---

[1] Foreordination: predestination
[2] Allow: believe
[3] Vouch: testify to

but delightful.[1] But alas, how true is that declaration of the prophet, "Who hath believed our report? And to whom hath the arm of the Lord been revealed?"[2] Certainly to none but the obedient, which number, if we are to judge by their fruits, is doubtless very small.

Second, Third, and Fourth Days: Spent mostly in my temporal business, but not without a watchful care lest it should engage too much of my attention. The evenings were partly spent in reading the scriptures, in which I greatly delight. How excellent are those records. Although old, yet seem ever new.

The prophecy of Micah was a part of my present reading. What a dignified[3] sense and clear view he had of the gospel state and worship. And how exceedingly it lessened the service and worship of the law in his view, when he had such a clear sense given him of its full and complete abolishment – with all its shadowy rituals – when he was led to set forth its insufficiency[4] (although carried to its greatest extent, as also the most exalted worship of the Gentiles in causing their children to pass through the fire to Molech[5]) which he sets forth by this exalted language, "Wherewith shall I come before the Lord and bow myself before the high God? Shall I come before him with burnt-offerings, with calves of a year old? Will the Lord be pleased with thousands of rams, or with ten thousands of rivers of oil? Shall I give my first-born for my transgression, the fruit of my body for the sin of my soul?"[6]

No, none, nor all of these were sufficient to give access to the Divine Presence nor to the divine law – they being only shadows and therefore could only give access to the outward law and outward lawgiver, which were only shadows of the true (to wit) Moses and the law and ordinances given by him. For Moses and his outward law and ordinances stood in the same relation to outward Israel (under the shadowy dispensation) as Christ, the spiritual Moses, with his spiritual law written in the heart, does to his spiritual Israel under the gospel, which is a dispensation not of shadow, but of substance – as is clearly shown by the sequel of the testimony of Micah above alluded to, where he goes on as follows, "He hath showed thee, O man, what is good" (then certainly not shadow nor sign,[7] but real substance) "and what doth the Lord require of thee?" (not by an outward, but by his inward, divine law) "but to do justly, to love

---

[1] Matthew 11:29-30
[2] Isaiah 53:1 & John 12:38
[3] Dignified: stately, noble, majestic
[4] The next phrase was deleted from the printed *Journal*.
[5] Leviticus 18:21, 2 Kings 23:10, & Jeremiah 32:35
[6] Micah 6:6-7
[7] Sign: an outward representation that symbolizes an inward, spiritual reality

mercy, and to walk humbly with thy God" – which is the sum and substance of all true religion and worship, and needs not the continuance of any outward elementary[1] washings nor eatings or drinkings,[2] but opens to the necessity of our drinking at that spiritual river, the streams whereof make glad the whole heritage of God.[3] And those that drink thereof will never thirst again[4] – at least for the water of any other stream.

Fifth Day: Sat our meeting today in silence. It is not unpleasant to feel ourselves sometimes circumstanced[5] as Mordecai formerly at the king's gate and in its season is as grateful to the truly humble and submissive mind, as riding on the king's horse and all bowing before us.[6,7]

Butchering a Steer

Sixth Day: Spent part of this day and the evening in assisting my workmen in slaying a fat beef and laying it away for part of our winter's provision. After which, my mind was seriously impressed with the subject and led to take a view of the whole process and the extraordinary change that had taken place in so short a space with a strong, well-favored, living animal, that in the morning was in a state of health, vigor, and comely proportion, and at the close of the evening, all its parts were decomposed, and its flesh and bones cut into pieces and packed away in a cask with salt to be devoured by the animal-man – its entrails already devoured by the swine, and its skin deposited with the tanner to be converted into leather for man's use.

What a wonderful wreck[8] in nature, affected in so short a period by two or three individuals, but which cannot be restored to its former state by all the combined power and wisdom of all the men in the universe, through all the ages and generations of men.

My meditation hereon produced this query: Is it right, and consistent with divine wisdom, that such cruel force should be employed and such a mighty sacrifice be made necessary for the nourishment and support of these bodies of clay?[9] Or is there not a more innocent and more consistent

---

[1] Elementary: composed of elements or matter
[2] Hebrews 9:10
[3] Psalm 46:4
[4] John 4:14
[5] Circumstanced: in the condition of
[6] The reference is to the story of Mordecai, the hero of the book of Esther. Briefly, when the Jews are threatened, Mordecai sits at the king's gate in protest. Later, the king honors Mordecai by ordering his enemy lead him through the streets on the king's own horse.
[7] The next four paragraphs were deleted from the printed *Journal*.
[8] Wreck: act of destruction
[9] Job 13:12

medium to be found, amply to effect the same end of man's support? And if so, will it not become a duty? If not for the present generation, for those in future to seek it and employ it.

1814

Seventh Day: Nothing transpired today either on the right hand or the left[1] worthy of particular notice.

First Day, 2nd of the 1st month 1814: Another year is ended.

Query: O my soul, how hast thou improved it? And what progress hast thou made in thy heavenly journey?

As I sat in our meeting today, my mind was led to contrast the law and gospel or shadow and substance. And as I sat musing, the fire burned and my heart became warmed within me, then spake I with my tongue[2] and endeavored in a zeal for the Lord's cause to open to the people the superior excellency of the gospel – above and beyond that of the law – as set forth by the precepts, doctrines, example, and commands of our great and gracious lawgiver, Jesus Christ.[3] And that the former stood and was only and alone known in the fulfillment and final abolishment of the latter, wherein the atonement was witnessed by a complete sacrifice of self and a crucifixion of the old man with his deeds[4] in unison with the sacrifice of our Lord in his own body on the tree.[5]

The life arose towards the close of the meeting in a good degree of dominion, through hard labor and toil. For many professors lie so securely in their graves, that nothing short of the powerful voice that raised Lazarus formerly,[6] is sufficient to quicken and raise them from their beds of ease.

Second Day: This day principally spent in making provision – the more favorably to meet the inclemency of the increasing winter.

Third Day: Spent as yesterday. In the evening, read Thomas Ellwood's relation of his suffering and cruel usage from his father, because for conscience sake he could not pull off his hat and stand bare before him, and for using the plain language of thou and thee, instead of the plural you.[7]

Alas, what a spirit of pride, arrogance, and cruelty governs the children of men while living in the lusts of their fallen nature – estranged from God, and from his true nature and image.

And it's to be feared that many in this day, who profess to be the successors of those primitive sufferers – our worthy predecessors, who

---

[1] Ezekiel 21:16
[2] Psalm 39:3
[3] The rest of the paragraph was deleted from the printed *Journal*.
[4] Romans 6:6 & Colossians 3:9
[5] Acts 5:30 & 10:39 & Galatians 3:13
[6] John 11:38-44
[7] *The History of the Life of Thomas Ellwood*

stood faithful and patiently bore the burden and heat of the day[1] through many years of cruel persecution – are now turning back like a broken bow[2] and through the fear or favor of men are balking[3] their testimony, which their forefathers in the Truth purchased at so dear a rate, and are ready to account many of them but small[4] or as indifferent things, that may or may not be attended to at their own pleasure.

But alas for these! It's to be feared they will never have a view, much less be permitted to enter the Promised Land, the heavenly Canaan, but will fall in the wilderness as did the unbelieving and rebellious in former ages.[5] For these, I often mourn and take up a lamentation when I behold the children of believing parents turning aside, disobedient to their parents, and disregarding the travail and exercise of their concerned Friends, who are laboring for their return. But these who are faithful to give the watchword in season[6] will be clear of their blood. And the Lord will be clear and he will have a people, for he, as formerly, will send his servants into the highways and hedges and gather from thence, that his house may be filled. But those children of the kingdom, who are making excuses and will not come when they are bidden, will be cast out into outer darkness, where will be weeping and gnashing of teeth.[7]

Fourth Day: This day, I was employed as a carpenter in making some conveniences for my stock and felt wearied at evening with the labor of the day, but was comforted with a peaceful mind – feeling myself at peace with all men, a blessed privilege, is it not? Yea, it is the Lord's doings, and marvelous in mine eyes.

Seventh Day: Attended the funeral of an ancient Friend. A meeting was held on the occasion, wherein I was exercised in a large, arousing testimony suited to the occasion. May it be to the honest inquirers as a nail fastened in a sure place, and to those who yet remain unwilling to surrender, as bread cast upon the waters, found after many days.

First Day, 9th of 1st month: At our meeting today, I was led to reflect on my frequent appearances in the ministry at home, and ready to admire that the source was not exhausted, or why I was led so often to communicate to almost the same assembly. But these meditations were soon superseded by a renewed living concern, which opened again to communication in a deep searching testimony, wherein I was led to show

---

[1] Matthew 20:12
[2] Psalm 78:57
[3] Balk: shirk or evade
[4] Small: insignificant
[5] Numbers 14:26-32
[6] Proverbs 15:23-24
[7] Matthew 8:12 & 22:13

the fallacy and weakness of all man's creaturely and carnal reasoning, and that it was all estranged from God, and stood in the ignorance and corruption of his fallen nature. That man never had nor could have (consistent with his true nature as a dependent being[1]) a right to assume a power to use his reason at his own discretion and will, but only in submission and subservience to the dictates of the Light and Spirit of his Creator, as paramount both to his reason and animal senses. That his reason is given him to govern as an agent under his Creator, to govern and keep in due order the animal senses – not according to his own discretion and will, but agreeable to the notices and manifestations of the Divine Spirit or Inward Law and known will of his Heavenly Father. It was a humbling season, and many hearts (with mine own) were bowed in reverence under the sensible[2] impress[3] of the divine power.

The rest of the week, I spent in my usual engagements and in visiting some of my friends.

First Day, 16th of 1st month: Sat our meeting in silence today.

The three following days, I spent in attending on my usual avocations and in visiting two of my sick neighbors, one of whom was a young man who was convinced of the truth as held by us in his young years. He spake very sensibly of the work of Truth on his mind in the early part of his convincement, and of the awe that covered his spirit through the sensible impressions of the divine power, and recapitulated the precious seasons he had witnessed in the fields sitting on rocks and stumps of trees. And that he now felt his love to reach forth and embrace the whole human family. He appeared to be in a sweet and quiet frame of mind, though so weak as not to be able to speak louder than a whisper.

What a brave[4] thing it is when the youth submit willingly to the visitations of divine love in their tender years. How amiable they appear and how peaceful their close – a pearl to be valued above all temporal enjoyments.[5]

Fifth Day: This being the time of our monthly meeting, we had the company of two Friends from abroad, one of whom appeared largely in the line of the ministry.[6] But a fear attended my mind, lest he had not sufficiently attended to that command, which forbids sowing our ground

---

[1] Dependent being: one that is subordinate to and dependent on God
[2] Sensible: palpable, something that can be felt
[3] Impress: impression
[4] Brave: praiseworthy
[5] Matthew 13:45-46
[6] Appeared largely in the line of the ministry: spoke at length and in depth in meeting for worship

with mingled seed, and that we do not suffer a garment of linen and woolen to come upon us.[1]

O how necessary it is for all those who apprehend they are called to the work of the ministry to know self fully reduced! Otherwise, they may be in danger of endeavoring to cover the harlot with the Lord's jewels[2] – and with fair words and fine speeches deceive the hearts of the simple.[3]

Sixth Day: Attended our Preparative Meeting of Ministers and Elders. Had to drop a caution, founded on the failure of Moses and Aaron at the rock in Horeb, when instead of speaking to the rock as commanded, he smote it with his rod, with the addition of "Hear now, ye rebels! Must we fetch you water out of this rock?" Which act, being the effect of mere creaturely zeal and warmth of his natural passions, lost them much, as it prevented their entering into the Promised Land.[4]

O how needful it is for those who are called to stand as a medium[5] between God and the people to be deeply attentive to the word of command, and not add thereto nor diminish therefrom[6] under the penalty of his displeasure. For if he spared not Moses, who was only guilty of this one fault in his administration, how much less can we expect that he will spare us, if we should add to or diminish from the word of prophecy?[7]

Seventh Day: Assisted a sick neighbor to settle his outward business by writing his will and seeing it executed. After which, I endeavored to stimulate his mind with a concern rightly to improve the few remaining moments that might be permitted him on this side the grave, that so he might be prepared to meet death with a peaceful and tranquil mind.

First Day, 23rd of 1st month 1814: Attended Westbury Meeting, at which there was a funeral of a deceased Friend, an ancient woman. It was a large meeting by reason of many Friends and neighbors coming from a distance to attend the funeral. I had good service among them in the line of the ministry by way of caution, encouragement, and reproof. In all which, I was led to press upon the auditory the necessity of a submission of our wills to the divine will, as the only medium through which we could become qualified to answer the great end of our creation, which is to glorify God and enjoy him.

Second Day: Attended the funeral of a pious young Friend of our meeting who departed this life with a consumption after lingering a few

---

[1] Leviticus 19:19
[2] Ezekiel 16:16-17 & Hosea 2:5&13
[3] Romans 16:18
[4] Exodus 17:6-7 & Numbers 20:7-13
[5] Medium: intermediary
[6] Deuteronomy 4:2 & 12:32
[7] Revelation 22:18-19

months. His corpse was carried into our meetinghouse at Jericho. There was a large meeting on the occasion, and through the prevalence of the divine power that presided over the assembly, it proved a very solemn time. Many hearts were broken and contrited by the force of the testimony that went forth, powerfully clothed with the demonstration of the Spirit, and the Lord's name was exalted over all opposition.

War Taxes

Third Day: This being the time of our quarterly meeting, I was mostly employed through the week in attention thereto. It was, I think, through the several sittings a solemn searching time. My mind was closely engaged on several subjects appertaining to our Christian testimonies and particularly in respect to that against war – war being now in the land and Friends (with others) called upon for supplies to carry it on by way of taxes which were levied varied ways on the inhabitants. I felt my mind deeply engaged to lay before Friends the inconsistency of our actively complying with any such military requisitions – believing that if we did, we should not only become accessories in the war, but should have to bear a part of the guilt of shedding the blood of our fellow creatures.

The Lord's power was felt to preside, and the testimonies borne on the occasion were evidently clothed with divine authority, to the keeping down all opposition. And the minds of the faithful were inspired with humble gratitude and thanksgiving to the Lord, our Gracious Helper, under a renewed sense of his continued mercy to us as a people, and to all the workmanship of his holy hand in general.

First Day, 30th of 1st month 1814: As I was sitting in our meeting, my mind became exercised in contemplating on the danger that some of my fellow professors of the Christian name are exposed to by placing their chief dependence for justification and salvation on the imputative righteousness of Christ performed without them – without coming to know a complete remission of their sins, and living a life of righteousness through faith in the operation of God, and a submission to the work of his Spirit in their minds – by which (according to the apostle's exhortation) they can only be enabled to work out their own salvation with fear and trembling, as it is God that worketh in the willing and obedient soul – both to will and to do of his own good pleasure.[1] But this can only be witnessed by such as experience their own wills to be mortified and slain by the power of the cross inwardly revealed, whereby the true spiritual atonement is made[2] and the man of sin in us sacrificed – and which is the substance of that sacrifice and atonement made by Jesus Christ in his

---

[1] Philippians 2:12-13
[2] The rest of the paragraph was deleted from the printed *Journal*.

outward body on the tree, in which he abolished the law of carnal commandments that stood in meats and drinks, and divers washings, and carnal ordinances that could not make the comers thereto perfect as pertaining to the conscience,[1] taking it out of the way, nailing it to his cross,[2] thereby finishing transgression and putting an end to sin.[3] That is, all transgression and sin that accrued to the Israelites by and through their omission of a compliance with those carnal commandments and ordinances. And he, having by the sacrifice of his body on the tree, put an end to this law of commandments that stood in carnal ordinances. Hence, all sin and transgression that was manifest by this law was put an end to – the law being fulfilled and done away that made their observance binding, as it is only by the law that we have the knowledge of sin. For where no law is, there is no transgression.[4] Therefore, as there is no law now requiring those meats and drinks, and divers washing baptisms, and carnal ordinances that were appendages and attached to the law of carnal commandments – which, no doubt, John's baptism and the Passover supper (that our Lord partook of with the disciples as the last Jewish rite he would ever conform to) were part of. Therefore, there can be no sin in the omission of all these under the gospel dispensation, as the law that made them binding is done away and abolished. Of the like nature also was their Seventh-Day Sabbath and all their other legally instituted holy days, as the law that enforced them is at an end. The omission of their observation can be no crime for (as before observed), where no law is, there is no transgression.

I was largely opened to communicate on some of those subjects, and to show to the people wherein the true harmony between the law dispensation and that of the gospel consisted. It was a season worthy of grateful remembrance. The meeting closed with thanksgiving and prayer, under a renewed sense of the continued mercy of our gracious God, who is over all, blessed forever.

Second Day: Being unwell with a cold I kept house and read.

Third Day: Having the evening before received an invitation to attend the funeral of a deceased neighbor, about four miles distant from my dwelling, and although I was still considerably unwell, yet understanding it was the desire of the deceased on her deathbed that I would attend, I felt my mind drawn and inclined to go. And I was glad I gave up thereto, as it proved, through heavenly help, a solemn, instructive season, wherein my heart and mouth were opened by him, who when he opens, none but

---

[1] Hebrews 9:9
[2] Colossians 2:14
[3] Daniel 9:24
[4] Romans 3:20 & 4:15

himself can shut, to declare largely of the way of life and salvation to the people in the clear demonstration of truth, to the bowing of the assembly in general, and to the humbling and contriting many hearts. To the Lord alone be the praise, for to him it is only due.

Fourth Day: Still unwell. Kept house mostly.

Fifth Day: Ventured out to our meeting. Was considerably afflicted with my cold and cough. The meeting was held in silence.

The two following days and the forepart of the next week, I was mostly employed in preparing for the press a small treatise on slavery and on the use of the produce of the labor of slaves,[1] having laid it before our Meeting for Sufferings that sat this week. I obtained their concurrence for printing it, and being in the city, I attended Friends meetings as they came in course on Fourth and Fifth Days, and returned home on Sixth Day.

Nothing particular transpired on Seventh Day:

First Day, 13th of 2nd month: Was largely opened in communication on divers subjects in a very searching testimony that brought a covering of great solemnity over the meeting – to the comforting of the honest-hearted, but was a season of sharp reproof to the unfaithful and lukewarm.

Fifth Day: Attended our monthly meeting, at which nothing opened worthy of particular notice.

Seventh Day: I attended the funeral of the wife of John Wine, a Friend of Flushing.[2] There were a promising young couple and bid fair[3] to become useful in society. They both came among Friends by convincement and were nearly united in principle and affection. This made their separation very trying to the survivor, which nevertheless he bore with a good degree of Christian patience in full assurance that his loss – which was very great – was her still greater and eternal gain.[4]

We had a very solemn meeting on the occasion, in which I was exercised in a large, affecting testimony – to the tendering and contriting the hearts of the assembly in general. The Truth was raised into dominion, breaking down all before its influential, searching power, and was cause of deep gratitude and thanksgiving to the Lord, our Gracious Helper, for his unmerited mercy still dispensed in his long-suffering loving-kindness to the children of men.

Feeling my mind inclined to sit with Friends here (the next day being the first of the week) the people were notified thereof at the close of the

---

[1] *Observations on the Slavery of the Africans and their Descendents, and on the Use of the Produce of their Labor*
[2] The rest of the paragraph was deleted from the printed *Journal*.
[3] Bid fair: seem likely
[4] Philippians 1:21

Flushing (New York) Meetinghouse

foregoing opportunity. It was a full meeting, in which Truth favored and furnished with matter suited to the states of those present, which made it an instructive, edifying season. And the canopy of love was felt to spread sweetly and very comfortably over the assembly. And I parted with them in the fresh feelings thereof, and with a peaceful mind, and a thankful sense of the Lord's mercy.

Nothing particular occurred in the course of the week, but the precious savor that was witnessed in the two aforementioned opportunities, remained as a canopy over my mind, and was cause of humble gratitude and thankfulness to the Blessed Author of all our rich mercies and blessings.

First Day, 27th of 2nd month: My mind in our meeting today, after a considerable time of humble, quiet waiting and seeking to be gathered to Shiloh,[1] was led in prospect to view the great and singular advantages that would redound to the children of men by an early acquaintance with the Lord, and by continually looking to him and relying on him as the primary and alone object of their faith and hope. The prospect enlarged and opened to a communication through which Truth was raised to a

---

[1] Genesis 49:10

comfortable degree of dominion and spread a solemn covering over the assembly. And many hearts were contrited and made glad from a feeling sense of the Lord's mercy vouchsafed to us at this season.

O how good is the Lord, and how greatly to be praised! For his mercy endureth forever.

The rest of this week, I was occupied in my temporal concerns.

Sat our Fifth Day Meeting in silence, in which I had to maintain a steady warfare against the intrusion of unprofitable thoughts.

O how precious it is to be favored to gain a complete victory over these and the mind brought to witness a profound stillness where nothing reigns but Jesus, in his inward, spiritual government.

First Day, 6th of 3rd month: In our meeting today, I had again to enter the lists[1] against the prevailing evils of the day, some of which I had to expose, and to show how we must enter the church militant,[2] if ever we enter right, so as to become a useful member thereof, and be truly comforted and profited thereby.

The communication was introduced by our Lord's parable of the supper,[3] which shows how those, who have something of the pleasures and treasures of this world to gratify and comfort themselves with, will not come in, although invited. But those who are brought to a full sense of their wretched and forlorn condition without God and without a Savior – compared by the parable to those who are poor and destitute of every comfort, and scattered in the highways and hedges – necessity compels these to seek a place of refuge. And having tried every means they had in their power, and every invention[4] that man has sought out in the way of salvation – and after all, finding themselves still left in a state of disappointment – are made willing to surrender all up, and sell all[5] (these being the terms of the invitation), and which only are enabled then to purchase the field wherein the pearl of great price lies. The word went forth with power and struck home to many minds, and a very solemn weight appeared to cover the assembly in general.

Second, Third, and Fourth Days: Spent in a quiet attention to my temporal concerns, with the attendant blessing of peace of mind, yet not without some intervals of interruption from the loose and the vain with which this neighborhood is too much infested.

---

[1] Lists: a place of combat
[2] Church militant: the Church on earth considered as warring against the powers of evil
[3] Luke 14:15-24
[4] Invention: something contrived by the human mind
[5] Matthew 19:21, Mark 10:21, & Luke 18:22

Alas, what black demon can so gain the ascendancy in and over the mind of the amiable creature, man, as to cause him to delight and take pleasure in wickedness and villainy? Can it be anything less than some hellish fiend that should thus induce him to err and persevere in mischief?

Thoughts on Horse Racing

Fifth Day: Was our preparative meeting, in which the overseers brought forward an information against one of our members, a young man, for deviations from plainness, and being guilty of attending on horse races, and suffering his horse to run for a wager – all which manifest a very worthless disposition and much vanity of mind, very unworthy the least member in our community.[1] And what should induce any of our young men to stoop so low and thus degrade themselves is not easily to be accounted for. The meeting felt tenderly for him as he had not had a guarded education,[2] he being left an orphan when small by the death of his father. In considering his condition (he being a relative), I was induced to enlist myself voluntarily in the meeting's service to pay him a visit, and the meeting added another Friend to join me therein.

I was likewise engaged in the meeting for worship to call Friends' attention to the necessity of greater purification – both in body, soul, and spirit – as the only medium through which we could gain an inheritance in the kingdom of heaven – showing by the analogy of reason, that a purified soul could not be content to inhabit in a polluted body, and that if the inside was made clean, the outside would be clean also,[3] and that true and genuine Christianity will lead to cleanliness in our persons, in our houses, and in all our concerns – and all this from real love and duty to our Creator, and not from any germ[4] of pride or vainly to make a show, but from a real desire of effecting holiness in the fear of the Lord.

First Day, 13th: A comfortable meeting today, mostly in silence, but closed with solemn supplication, wherein my mind was led to set forth how our gracious and beneficent Creator – that although he sees all our wants and stands always disposed (before we ask him) to redress all our real grievances and dispense good to us whenever he finds us in a condition fit to receive, yet as he is a God of justice and truth, he delights to see his people and children grateful and humbly sensible of their dependence on him for every blessing. Therefore, he permits them, at

---

[1] Hicks' reaction to the charges is particularly interesting in light of the description above of his own involvement in horse racing when he was a youth. Interestingly, the next sentence was deleted from the printed *Journal*.

[2] Guarded education: education in Friends Schools

[3] Matthew 23:25-26 & Luke 11:39-40

[4] Germ: that from which a thing will emerge

times – when he sees meet to influence their minds thereto – to approach his sacred presence in humble and devout prayer, and which also affords to these who are thus devoted, sweet and heavenly consolation and joy.

I spent this week mostly at home overseeing my temporal concerns.

Attended our monthly meeting on Fifth Day, at which we received information from the women's meeting of the departure of one of our members, a young woman who had gone out in her marriage[1] with one not a member, whom they concluded ought to be disowned – with which the men's meeting concurred. This is a weakness among our young members that is, in the general, very pernicious in its consequences. And it too often happens through the neglect of care and right concern in parents and guardians, who for want of living near the Truth and under right religious engagements themselves, are too often led away to seek after riches for their children, and are more desirous that their children get companions that are wealthy and rich in this world's treasure than such as are truly religious and virtuous – by which, a foundation is often laid by such indiscreet parents for very many, very unhappy connections, by which the religious improvement and advancement of their tender offspring is often entirely intercepted and prevented – and all their prospects of temporal comfort and joy rendered abortive.[2] And they have to drag out a miserable existence until death dissolves their obligations.

First Day, 20th: As I sat in our meeting, my mind was brought under exercise from an enlightened view of the life of Solomon, that wise king of Israel, as delineated by his own pen,[3] and from which we learn the insignificancy of all consolation and joy that hath its source in temporal and mortal things, as they will and must end in vanity and vexation of spirit. And that to fear God and keep his commandments is not only the whole duty of man, but likewise the only blessed and eternal source of all true joy and never-ending felicity.

The subject spread on my mind and led to communication, in which I endeavored, in the ability afforded, by persuasive arguments to engage the minds of the auditory – both old and young – in the pursuit of that invaluable treasure that waxeth not old, but endureth forever,[4] that will bring true joy to the immortal soul, and that adds no sorrow.

Nothing particular occurred in the course of this week, except that a care and fear attended my mind, lest the cares of this world and the increase of temporal things might too much interrupt and intrude upon

---

[1] Go out in marriage: marry someone who was not a Quaker and, consequently, lose membership among Friends
[2] Abortive: doomed to fail
[3] The books of Proverbs and Ecclesiastes are attributed by some to Solomon
[4] Luke 12:33

my spiritual concerns. For riches are ever deceitful,[1] and always promise more than they have in their power to perform.

First Day, 27th: Feeling my mind inclined to sit with Friends at Bethpage today, I yielded to the motion and attended their meeting. And although I had not a great deal to communicate, yet what I had appeared to reach home to many minds and rendered it a comfortable meeting – not only to myself, but to the assembly in general. The subject which opened for communication was the necessity and excellency of integrity. And that although we were so wise and knowing as to comprehend all knowledge, yet if we were destitute of integrity and sincerity of heart, we should but share the fate of fools at last, and be not a whit better for all our wisdom and knowledge.

Second, Third, and Fourth Days: Spent in close attention to my temporal concerns, the care for which, and for their right ordering, is constantly necessary, insomuch as I often admire how it is that I sometimes hear people say they seem at a loss how to spend their time, when not only my temporal, but in a special manner, my spiritual concerns are always urgent and pressing, insomuch that I find not a moment to be idle.

So true is that declaration of the Most High verified, "In the sweat of thy face shalt thou eat bread, till thou return unto the ground. For out of it wast thou taken. For dust thou art and unto dust shalt thou return."[2] And as the wise man saith, "All things are full of labor."[3] Therefore, we ought not to repine or murmur at our lot, but receive all as at the hand of the Lord with thanksgiving.

Fifth, Sixth, and Seventh Days: I attended three funerals, one on each day successively.

The first was a very ancient female, upwards of ninety years of age, belonging to Westbury Meeting. We had a solemn meeting on the occasion, in which Truth favored, opening suitable doctrine and setting it home to the states of those present, who were mostly Friends. The hid things of Esau (or the first nature) and the secret lurking places of self were searched out and exposed – for which my mind (with the honest-hearted present) was made glad in the Lord and in the apparent workings of his power and wisdom.

The two latter were not members of our society, but were friendly-disposed. They were seasons of favor – a meeting being held at each and both largely attended by the neighboring inhabitants. The doctrines delivered were well adapted to the conditions of the auditories and were

---

[1] Matthew 13:22 & Mark 4:19
[2] Genesis 3:19
[3] Ecclesiastes 1:8

set home to many minds in the demonstration of Truth – to the breaking and contriting many hearts. And thanksgiving and praises were returned to the Shepherd of Israel as a tribute of gratitude for such unmerited mercies.

First Day, 3rd of 4th month: Our meeting today was favored with the overshadowing wing of Divine Truth. And its testimony was exalted over all – to the contriting and comforting many minds. But alas, what small advancements are made by those who are often dug about and watered[1] by the compassionate Shepherd of Israel, whose mercy is still eminently dispensed to man, the workmanship of his holy hand.

I attended two funerals in the course of this week, one on Fifth Day after the sitting of our preparative meeting, and the other on Sixth Day. Both were young men in the prime of life, the latter unmarried, who was the son of a cousin of my wife. They had a healthful family of children and had never met with the like trial before. It was therefore a very affecting scene to both parents and children – they having been before favored with almost an unbroken scene of worldly prosperity, this made the wound sink deeper. We had a very solemn meeting on the occasion, wherein I was largely opened to preach the gospel in the demonstration of Truth and, among other doctrines, to show to the people the necessity and sure felicity of an early preparation for death, and that God was the alone proper object for man to set his heart and affections upon. The auditory were mostly such as were not in membership with Friends, many of whom were much broken and contrited. And a general and very precious solemnity was spread over the meeting to the gladdening of many minds from a sense of the Lord's continued and unmerited goodness and mercy to the children of men – still showing his unwillingness that any should die in their sins, and that all might repent, turn to him, and live.

First Day, 10th of 4th month: I had a hard, suffering meeting today, in which I witnessed not only deep inward poverty, but had to struggle with unprofitable thoughts, with very little ability to maintain the warfare. But under the consideration that it was altogether equal, if not better than my deserts could justly require, I was preserved from murmuring or complaining at my lot, being willing to receive evil as well as good at the hand of my gracious and compassionate Lord, when he sees meet to permit or dispense it.[2]

The rest of this week was principally occupied in a close application to my temporal concerns (saving the attendance of our monthly and select preparative meetings, which came at this time), believing with the apostle

---

[1] Luke 13:8
[2] Job 2:10

that he that is not carefully industrious to labor for his own[1] and household's comfortable support may be considered to have denied the faith and is worse than an infidel[2] – as they are generally careful on those accounts.

First Day, 17th of 4th month: The meeting today was pretty open and comfortable.

The rest of the week was mostly taken up in attending our quarterly meeting, held at New York at this time.

First Day, 24th: Sat our meeting mostly in silence.

Second, Third, and Fourth Days: Taken up principally in caring for my temporal concerns.

Alas, what a deal of precious time is taken up for the accommodation of those houses of clay[3] that must shortly return to the dust from whence they were taken, and which often burden and too much indispose the mind for heavenly and spiritual meditations, unless carefully watched and strongly guarded against.

Fifth Day: I was wholly silent in our meeting today, in the course of which I had full evidence of the truth of that saying of the great Master that of ourselves, without him, we can do nothing.[4]

Sixth and Seventh Days were accompanied with heart-searchings, discouragement, and dismay, in which I witnessed the truth of that saying that, "Vain is the help of man,"[5] whose best efforts often tend more to sully and weaken, than to brighten and strengthen the minds of those they strive to help. And this is principally owing to their dwelling on the surface and judging from the outward appearance, instead of digging deep in search of the real mind of Truth, that only can enable to judge with righteous judgment.

First Day, 1st of 5th month: Sat our meeting in silence and in much poverty of spirit. And when the season for closing the meeting seemed near at hand, I looked over the assembly (which was pretty large) with a degree of sympathy and compassion, and which brought to my remembrance the compassionate saying of our Lord to his disciples on (as I apprehended) a similar occasion (to wit), "If I send them away fasting, they may faint by the way." This put a stop to my mind in regard to closing the meeting. And as I knew I had nothing to give, I looked around to see what was to be done, when a friend stood up with something representing the five loaves and the fishes that were found formerly in the

---

[1] Acts 20:33-35, 1 Thessalonians 2:9, & 2 Thessalonians 3:7-8
[2] 1 Timothy 5:8
[3] Job 4:19
[4] John 15:5
[5] Psalm 60:11 & 108:12

lad's basket, and as they were broken, she handed them to the company until all appeared satisfied – for which I was thankful.

Seventh Day: The week hath passed away.

O time, precious time! How swift thou passes on by us, almost unenjoyed and unimproved. How soon thou wilt land thy traveling pilgrim in the house appointed for all living,[1] where, O my soul, thou knows there is no repentance nor amendment known. Prepare then. O prepare for thy bed of clay.

First Day, 8th of 5th month: A poor, silent meeting until near the close, when a little light sprang up and dispelled the darkness and sweetened all the bitter.[2] By such things as these we are instructed, and learn to know our dependent state, and that it's the Lord's doings and marvelous in our eyes.

Nothing uncommon transpired in the course of this week, save as usual, bonds and afflictions[3] for the gospel's sake (spiritually and inwardly experienced) await me – from a view and sense of the spread of evil, and the great want of faithful testimony-bearers in society, and the languor and weakness that abound – that I am sometimes led almost involuntarily to cry, "Alas for the day!"[4]

First Day, 15th: My mind was deeply exercised in our meeting today on divers, important subjects, and largely led forth in communication. But for want of a more full openness and preparation in the auditory to receive, made the labor arduous and exercising, but I trust profitable to some.

The rest of the week was employed in my usual attention to my necessary temporal concerns and unfailing attention to those of a religious nature – our monthly meeting coming this week and our yearly meeting near at hand, the Meeting for Ministers and Elders commencing on Seventh Day, which my wife and I attended at the 10th hour. It was, I think, in a good degree a favored time, as were the public meetings on First Day – both fore and after noon.

On Second Day, the yearly meeting for discipline opened at the 10th hour, and continued by adjournments until the evening of the Fifth [Day], and was, in the main, a comfortable, profitable season – evidencing in the several sittings that the Lord had not forsaken his people, but was still graciously manifesting his presence and power for our comfort and help in ordering the affairs of the Church.

---

[1] Job 30:23 (The whole of this paragraph seems to be a meditation on Job)
[2] Exodus 15:22-25
[3] Acts 20:23
[4] Joel 1:15

On Sixth Day, Friends turned their faces towards home, where I arrived with my wife and two younger daughters (that constitute my present family, except servants) at evening.

The next day, felt myself in a cheerful readiness to put my hands to whatever they found to do, as right to be done.

First Day, 29th: Felt myself so much indisposed with a cold and considerable pain of body as to be prevented from attending our meeting today. In reflecting thereon, and how very seldom I had been thus prevented for many years past, it was cause of thankfulness and gratitude to our Gracious Helper and Preserver for the portion of bodily health allotted me in the course of his divine providence. Whereby I have been almost invariably of ability of body for a number of years to attend all our religious meetings, which I consider and number among our chiefest blessings and benefits.

The latter end of this week, I joined our Friend, William Flanner, who was here on a religious visit from Ohio and attended a number of meetings in divers places where no meetings of our society were held – I, having had a prospect thereof some time before. We were out three days and attended five meetings. The first was with Friends at Bethpage, the rest among friendly people and those of other professions. They were, I think, all favored seasons – the Lord's presence and power being manifested for our help, furnishing ability to minister suitably to the different states of the people in the demonstration of the Spirit. Whereby many hearts were humbled and contrited, and the assemblies solemnized, and Truth raised into dominion over all. And our hearts were made glad under a humbling sense of the continuation of the Lord's mercy and compassion still extended to the children of men.

We returned home on First Day evening, the 5th of 6th month:

The three following days, I was about home, mostly employed in my temporal concerns.[1]

On 5th Day, attended the funeral of a Friend – a member of Flushing Monthly Meeting. He had been for several years in a low, disconsolate state of mind and finally gave way so far to temptation as to cut his own throat, by which he put an immediate end to his existence – a very uncountable[2] procedure, especially as he had (to outward appearance) everything about him that could be thought necessary to make his life comfortable – having a competency of this world's goods, an amicable wife, and a number of agreeable children. But when we give way to a murmuring disposition, it makes room for the tempter and he leads us to a distrust in the divine providence and disannuls all his blessings.

---

[1] The next paragraph was deleted from the printed *Journal*.
[2] Uncountable: unaccountable or inexplicable

The next day attended the funeral of a friend of Westbury Meeting. A solemn meeting was held on the occasion, in which I found it my place to be an example of silence.

Seventh Day: Spent at home.

On First Day, 12th of 6th month, I attended two meetings by appointment among those not of our society – in the morning at Cold Spring Harbor, and at four in the afternoon, at Huntington. They were both seasons of extensive labor, and I hope profitable to some, and productive of peace to my own mind.

On Second Day, went to New York in order to attend the Meeting for Sufferings, which I attended the next day, and returned home at evening.

Fourth Day: Attended my temporal concerns with usual industry. Nothing transpired worthy of particular notice.

Fifth Day: Attended our monthly meeting, at which several matters occurred producing exercise to my mind, which led to a communication of prospects. And although some diversity of sentiments was expressed, yet I was favored so to unfold the subjects that they were concluded in a general unity.

Sixth and Seventh Days: Spent in my usual affairs.

First Day, 19th of 6th month: I was led in our meeting today to set forth the excellency of true and real poverty of spirit, as it is that only that can produce that true humiliated[1] state to which the blessing is annexed.

Second, Third, and Fourth Days: Were spent as nearly agreeable to the allotment of providence as I well could in the cares of my family concerns.

Fifth Day: As I was sitting in our meeting, enjoying the especial advantages which are attached to silent meetings when the mind is silently prostrated at the throne of grace, and helped to be sequestered from all intruding thoughts, and wholly centered in and upon Jehovah, the alone object of worship and adoration – the subject opened and spread in a way which led to communication, in which I had to show that there were but two proper motives or inducements for the right attending religious meetings.

The first related to such as were unbelievers or those who were ignorant of the right way of worshipping God in and under the dispensation of the gospel (which according to our Lord's declaration to the woman of Samaria is only to be performed in spirit and in truth[2]). Therefore, the principal motive with these is to be informed and instructed – and for which cause, more especially, the Lord hath ordained a ministry in his Church by means of instruments rightly qualified thereunto by the baptismal influence of the Holy Ghost.

---

[1] Humiliated: humble
[2] John 4:23-24

The second relates to such as are already instructed and informed, and their judgments are convinced – whose motive (to be proper and right) can be no other than solely to meet together, to wait upon and worship God in spirit and in truth without any regard or consideration as relates to any external ministry or means whatever. As it is only in a state of entire sequestration from everything of an outward or external nature that the soul is permitted to enter into the holy place not made with hands,[1] when the veil (that is, all externals) is drawn away by the entire crucifixion of the old man and the soul admitted into the immediate presence of Jehovah,[2] by which it can only be rendered capable of worshipping him, in spirit and in truth, as the gospel requires.

Sixth and Seventh Days: Spent in my usual vocation as a farmer.

First Day, 26th of 6th month: Attended two meetings by appointment among those principally not of our society. The first was held in a Friend's house at a place called the Half Way Hollow Hills, the latter at the 4th hour after noon, at a village called North Babylon, in the township of Huntington. It was held in a schoolhouse – a pretty large room. It was a pretty large meeting, mostly of the Presbyterian order. The people conducted very soberly, becoming[3] the occasion. It was a very solemn, favored season, many hearts were contrited and made thankful for the opportunity. And my heart was much enlarged in love to the assembly, and I trust I felt a mutual return thereof from most present, for which I was made thankful to the Shepherd of Israel for the continuation of his gracious regard in manifesting his presence and making bare his arm for the help of his devoted servants – showing himself indeed to be a God near at hand, and a Present Helper in the needful time, worthy to be praised and adored by the children of men from the rising of the sun even to the west, throughout all ages, world without end.

The rest of this week I spent mostly about home, being closely engaged in getting of hay, which for want of suitable help, made it necessary to labor myself beyond what seemed suitable for one of my age. But I felt peace of mind in so doing, although I suffered some pain of body as the result of my labor.

First Day, 3rd of 7th month: Sat our meeting in silence. At the 3rd hour after noon, attended the funeral of a deceased neighbor. And although my mind was brought under some exercise that led to communication, yet I found very little relief, owing (as I apprehended) to the prevalence of an opposite, libertine spirit in many present, who are generally disposed to make a mock at and ridicule everything serious, or that has the

---

[1] Acts 7:48 & 17:24
[2] Hebrews 10:19-20
[3] Becoming: suitable or fitting

appearance of religion and godliness – rebellious children who hate the Light because their deeds are evil, who take more delight in reveling and drunkenness than in the fear of the Lord. For these, I often feel sad and my mind goes clothed (as it were) underneath with sackcloth unseen by the world.

O when will these be awakened to a right sense of their miserable condition? I often fear that some of them have nearly sinned out their day – to whom the scripture declaration will apply, as to such as have been often reproved, but still harden their necks. They shall suddenly be cut off and destroyed, and that without remedy.[1]

Second, Third and Fourth Days: Busily employed in my husbandry concerns with my mind clothed with peace towards all men and with hope towards God my Savior. And comforted at times in the remembrance of that apostolic declaration, where he asserted, "We know we have passed from death unto life, because we love the brethren."[2]

Fifth Day: Attended our meeting in silence, the fire being low on the altar.

Sixth and Seventh Days: Closely engaged in making and securing hay for the accommodation of my stock the ensuing winter, as I consider it a duty to provide a plenty of good provender[3] for them, so as to render their lives as comfortable as may be, whilst under my care.

First Day, 10th of 7th month: As I sat in our meeting today, my mind was led into a consideration and prospect of the excellency and amiableness of justice, and of the vast advantage which would derive[4] to the children of men by a strict adherence thereto, as it would mightily tend to regulate our conduct – both as it relates to our duty to God, our Creator, and also to man, our fellow creature – and therefore ought to be the governing principle and main spring of all our conduct, as well in temporals, as our spiritual concerns. The subject spread and enlarged and opened to communication, and I trust proved an instructive, comfortable season to some present. And I felt a reward of peace in my labor.

Second Day: Attended the funeral of a deceased neighbor. And although not a member of our society, yet being convinced of our principles and friendly-inclined, the family desired a meeting might be held at the funeral, which was accordingly agreed to. It was a large collection of people of various denominations, and a considerable number of the looser sort. I had an open, favored time among them, in which Truth's testimony arose into dominion over all – to the humbling and

---

[1] Proverbs 29:1
[2] 1 John 3:14
[3] Provender: feed or fodder
[4] Derive: come

contriting many hearts. And a general solemnity was felt to cover the meeting, to the praise of his Grace, who is over all, God blessed forever.

Third and Fourth Days: Occupied in my usual concerns, but did not feel that full peace of mind with my Fourth Day's exercise as is generally my experience, owing (as I apprehended) to the want of a more full attention to a small intimation respecting that day's employment.

Remember, O my soul, that all thy success in temporals, as well as all thy sweet, inward, heavenly consolations, depend upon thy faithfulness and ready submission to those inward divine intimations! And although sometimes small, yet ought to be considered by thee binding and obligatory, as the only source from whence all thy true peace and joy is derived.

Fifth Day: Was our preparative meeting, and as it was the one preceding the quarterly, the queries were read and answered, but I apprehended in a way not tending to much profit – either by reason of one or two improper questions being added to the queries of late, which (to many Friends) appeared inconsistent to be answered, or from the want of a more lively exercise spiritually with the members – or both might have had a share in producing a dull distressing season. And no way seemed to open for any relief, so we had patiently to bear it. And for my part, I thought it required a large share of Job's patience to sit the meeting through without murmuring. The chariot wheels seemed to go exceedingly heavily on,[1] as though almost sunk in the slough of despond,[2] but we did what we could, and so left the matter, and I returned home with a heavy heart and was preserved, I trust, from murmuring at my lot.

Sixth Day: Spent in gathering in my harvest and some other small exercises, and the day closed with a quiet and peaceful mind.

What a paradise it is when this is our lot!

Seventh Day: Visited two Friends who were under some bodily infirmity. The visits were mutually comfortable – such opportunities, when rightly conducted, tend to the increase of friendship and mutual love.

First Day, 17th of 7th month: Feeling my mind drawn to sit with Friends in their meeting at Westbury today, I yielded to the motion, but it proved an exercising, laborous meeting – but little life to be felt. Nevertheless, way opened for a short communication pointing particularly to the state of the meeting, which I hope was profitable to some.

---

[1] Exodus 14:25

[2] The slough of despond is a bog in Bunyan's *Pilgrim's Progress* into which Christian falls under the weight of his sins and his guilt.

At the 3rd hour after noon, I attended the funeral of a very ancient woman of the neighborhood of Westbury – not a member in society, but the family desiring the company of Friends, a number collected with others, and it proved a pretty solemn time. My mind was led to open to the assembly, the especial advantages that would result to us as rational, accountable beings by a timely preparation for death, and that it was our especial duty, as well as best interest, to make it at all times the primary object of our concern.

Second, Third, and Fourth Days: Spent principally in family cares and my husbandry concerns.

What a favor it is for such an active creature as man, possessed of such powers of body and mind, always to have something to do and for those powers to act upon. For otherwise, they would be useless and dormant, and afford neither profit nor delight.

Fifth Day: Attended our monthly meeting. It was an exercising season – especially the meeting for worship that I think was much hurt by the communication of a ministering Friend from abroad. It was attended with so much mere creaturely warmth and animation as to render it unacceptable, and as I apprehended, hurtful to the meeting and the cause it was intended to advance. What a pity it is that any who apprehend themselves called to this very important work should make such grievous mistakes – to the wounding the minds of the living, sensible members.

Sixth Day: Attended our Select Preparative Meeting of Ministers and Elders. It was, I think, a season of profitable exercise, in which some of the hidden things of Esau (or the first nature) were searched out and exposed.

Seventh Day: Labored hard in my harvest field. And although sixty-six years of age, I found I could wield the scythe and cradle[1] nearly as in the days of my youth. And it was a day of thankful and delightful contemplation – my heart was filled with thankfulness and gratitude to the Blessed Author of my existence in a consideration of his providential care over me in preserving me in health and in the possession of my bodily powers – the exercise of which was still affording me both profit and delight. And I was doubly thankful for the continuance and united exercise of my mental faculties, not only in instructing me how to exert and rightly employ my bodily powers in the most useful and advantageous manner, but also in contemplating the works of nature and providence, in the blessings and beauties of the field – a volume containing more delightful and profitable instruction than all the volumes of latter learning and science in the world.

---

[1] Scythe and cradle: a tool used to cut hay by hand

What a vast portion of the joys and comforts of life do the idle and slothful deprive themselves of by running into cities and towns to avoid laboring in the field – not considering that that is the only true source that the gracious Creator of the universe has appointed to his creature, man – from whence to derive his greatest temporal happiness and delight, and which also opens the largest and best field of exercise to the contemplative mind, by which it may be prepared to meet (when this mortal puts on immortality) those immortal joys that will ever be the lot of the faithful and industrious.

First Day, 24th of 7th month: I went to our meeting today in much poverty of spirit and in full expectation of passing it in silence. But I had not sat long before my mind was led into a view of the singular benefit derived to the children of men by the denial of self, and a daily and faithfully taking up and bearing the cross, as it is the only way by which we can come to experience real sanctification and justification. The subject spread and opened to communication, in which things were laid home to the states of many present in a clear manner, and the danger of their situations exposed. It brought a solemn covering over the meeting, for which I was thankful.

Second and Third Days: I spent in securing my harvest.

This week being the time of our quarterly meeting, the Meeting of Ministers and Elders opened on Fourth Day at the 10th hour. It was a season of close searching. The deficiencies of ministers and elders were laid open, and the hurtful tendency thereof exposed. A number appeared deeply concerned on account of the prevailing weakness with some in those exalted stations in society.

On Fifth Day was the meeting for discipline. It was also a very searching time – a season of deep exercise to my mind, in which the hurtful tendency of many apparent deficiencies was laid open and exposed, and Friends exhorted to greater faithfulness and diligence in the right support of those noble testimonies given us to bear for the promotion of righteousness and peace on the earth.

On Sixth Day was a general public meeting in which my mind was enlarged in gospel communication, wherein Truth was exalted and raised into dominion, to the comfort and edification of many minds, and sweet peace to my own. After which, Friends separated to their several homes in much nearness of affection and mutual love.

Seventh Day: Spent in my temporal concerns.

First Day, 31st of 7th month: A silent meeting today, for which I was thankful. And although faithfully laboring in the Lord's vineyard produceth peace and joy to the willing mind (although it may have to bear the burden and heat of the day), yet when permitted a season of rest, it is also sweet and grateful.

A Visit to Purchase Quarterly Meeting in 1814

Having for some days past felt my mind inclined to attend the ensuing Quarterly Meeting at Purchase, I spent most of this week in that service. Left home on Second Day and returned on the following Sixth Day at evening. I felt but little satisfaction in this short tour of duty, except in one or two visits in Friends' families. Most of the sittings of the quarterly meeting seemed to be clothed with great weakness, and some parts distressing.

Seventh Day: Exercised in my husbandry business and the evening closed with a peaceful mind.

First Day, 7th of 8th month: Felt so much bodily indisposition as to prevent attending meeting. And even this induced thankfulness and gratitude on recollecting how very seldom this had been my lot for many years.

O what shall I, a poor worm,[1] render unto the Lord for all his benefits?

Second, Third, and Fourth Days: Spent principally in looking to and overseeing my temporal business. Still feeling some slight touches of bodily indisposition, which seemed to announce this language (in unison with everything that is mortal), remember to die.[2]

Fifth Day: Attended our preparative meeting. What a privilege! The very name points to care, as saying, "Be ye therefore ready."[3]

Sixth Day: Did as Peter and some of his fellow disciples, when not directly employed by their Master, but waiting and watching for his coming – went fishing. In which, I succeeded to satisfaction.

Seventh Day: Labored in the field and the day closed with a quiet and peaceful mind, which I esteem the greatest treasure.

First Day, 14th of 8th month: As I sat in our meeting today, my mind was impressed with the remembrance of the declaration of the Prophet Isaiah when reproving the house of Israel under the similitude of a vineyard for their backsliding and breach of covenant and great wickedness, which he closes with this notable saying, "Therefore hell hath enlarged herself, and opened her mouth without measure – and their glory and multitude, and their pomp, and he that rejoiceth shall descend into it."[4] Setting forth thereby, the natural tendency of evil, and certain

---

[1] Psalm 22:6
[2] This reminder of mortality is reported to have been whispered in the ear of Roman generals (in Latin, *memento mori*) while riding in a victory parade.
[3] Luke 12:40 & Matthew 24:44
[4] Isaiah 5:14

destruction of evil doers, who harden themselves in sin. The subject opened and led to a large exhortatory and cautionary communication, also setting forth the great obligations parents and guardians are under to their tender offspring and children under their charge, and the incalculable loss that children sustain where parents and guardians neglect their duty in timely care for their right instruction. It was a solemn time and I hope profitable to some by stirring them up to more diligence.

The rest of this week, except attending our monthly meeting on Fifth Day, was spent in close attention to my temporal concerns. And the urgent necessity attending my present business induced me to labor beyond what my judgment approved, which, though somewhat painful to the body, was nevertheless, I trust, free from sin.

First Day, 21st of 8th month: A silent meeting today, which closed with a peaceful mind.

Second, Third, and Fourth Days: Passed without anything transpiring worthy of particular notice.

Fifth Day: A silent meeting, as it respects myself.

Sixth and Seventh Days: Spent in my south meadows (about ten miles from home) assisting my hands[1] in making and securing hay. And on my return visited a pauper, a poor widow, with the surplus of our provisions, for which she was very thankful.

First Day, 28th: My lips, at our meeting today, were closed in solemn silence.

Second, Third, and Fourth Days: Diligently employed in what my hands found to do, for I see no time when it would be right to indulge in idleness. Nay, I very much doubt Methuselah's finding any such time, even in the nine hundred and sixty-nine years of his age.[2]

Fifth Day: Sat our meeting in much weakness and poverty of spirit, but felt peace at the close.

Sixth and Seventh Days: Closely engaged in my temporal business, but did not forget my accountability to my great Lord and Master for the right use of every portion of precious time he is pleased to dispense to me.

First Day, 4th of 9th month: My mind, while sitting in our meeting today, was led into a contemplation of the great and excellent advantages resulting to those, who had placed their supreme trust in the arm of divine sufficiency. And while musing thereon, and the manifold blessings attendant on such a state, there was brought to my remembrance the exhortation of Solomon, Proverbs 5th & 3rd, "Trust in the Lord with all thy heart and lean not to thine own understanding."

---

[1] Hand: a hired laborer
[2] Genesis 5:27 – Methuselah is the oldest person mentioned in the Bible

The subject spread and opened to a communication, in which the audience were pressingly invited and encouraged to lay hold and make choice of this only sure rock of refuge[1] – an entire trust and confidence in God and in the arm of his salvation – as those who trust in the name of the Lord have never been confounded.

The rest of this week was spent in my usual vocations. Except attending our preparative meeting on Fifth Day, nothing transpired worthy particular notice.

First Day, 11th of 9th month: As I was sitting in our meeting today, my mind was led into a train of solemn reflection from the revival of these expressions of Christ to his disciples, "In the world ye shall have tribulation, but be of good cheer, I have overcome the world."[2] And which opened into an enlightened view of the especial advantages and deep consolation derived to the true Christian by a firm belief therein, as the expressions evidently carry in them an earnest[3] to the true believer of his being likewise enabled to overcome, as he is faithful in treading in the path of self-denial, agreeable to his Heavenly Pattern.

The subject opened to communication, in which the audience was pressingly invited and encouraged to enter earnestly into this most necessary and interesting warfare – as nothing short of overcoming the world, the flesh, and the devil can restore to us an uninterrupted peace and entitle us to the white stone in which the new name is written, which none can read, but he who hath it.[4]

The succeeding days of this week were attended to as they passed, but nothing transpired unusual or that required any particular mark or note.

Our monthly meeting was on Fifth Day. And although we had a pretty trying case before us, yet we got through without interruption or any breach of Christian harmony.

First Day, 18th of 9th month: A satisfactory meeting today – more so than for several weeks past. The testimony of Truth went forth freely, and I think clothed with a good degree of power and demonstration of the Spirit, which produced a peaceful and thankful mind.

The rest of this week, I was closely engaged in preparing my fallow ground and sowing my wheat and rye – being willing to do my part carefully and industriously. And then I can with more confidence place my trust and dependence on a gracious and beneficent Providence for a

---

[1] Psalm 94:22
[2] John 16:33
[3] Earnest: a foretaste or promise of something to be received in abundance in the future
[4] Revelation 2:17

blessing on my labor. For where care and industry are wanting, there is none for him to bless.

The Din of War

First Day, 25th of 9th month: A silent meeting today, as to any vocal communication, but my mind too much intruded upon by unprofitable thoughts – being interrupted by the unchristian commotions and din of war that are at present mightily prevailing in our land and the frequent reports of blood and slaughter witnessed among professed human rational beings.[1] But alas, how inhuman and irrational do they prove and proclaim themselves to be, who can deliberately imbrue[2] their hands in each other's blood for this world's honors and profits and dare at the same time to call themselves Christians, although so utterly estranged to the real Christian spirit and life.

The remaining part of this week spent in my usual vocations.

First Day, 2nd of 10th month: I was led in my communication today to show the unreasonableness of most people in looking for and depending to be made Christians by the ministration of men and information derived from books and writings, when alas, the ministration of angels would be entirely insufficient for that purpose, as the ministration of the son and sent of God – even the Divine Word that was in the beginning with God, and was God[3] – is only sufficient to effect that great and blessed end. And that not by anything which he has spoken, commanded, or done without us, but by what he speaks, commands, and does within us – we yielding and submitting thereto by faithful obedience. And there is not another way by which any have or can be made a real Christian – a true, sincere, sensible follower of Christ in spirit and life.

Nothing unusual transpired in the course of the six working days of this week.

First Day, 9th of 10th month: While sitting in our meeting today, there was brought to my remembrance the following portion of Paul's exhortation to his son Timothy (as recorded in his first epistle, chapter 4th, verses 8th, 9th, & 10th). "For bodily exercise profiteth little, but godliness is profitable unto all things, having promise of the life that now is, and of that which is to come. This is a faithful saying and worthy of all acceptation. For therefore we both labor and suffer reproach, because we

---

[1] The War of 1812 was ongoing. It was one month since a British army had burned Washington, DC, and only two weeks since the Battle of Plattsburgh was fought in northern New York.
[2] Imbrue: stain or defile
[3] John 1:1

trust in the living God, who is the Savior of all men – especially of those that believe."

The subject spread and my mind was opened to take an enlightened and enlarged view thereof, insomuch as to be induced to believe that a necessity was laid upon me to communicate it to the assembly. And as I yielded thereto, it still enlarged and led to an open field of doctrine, clothed with gospel authority, which produced a most precious solemnity and calm over the meeting. It was evidently the Lord's doing and it was marvelous in my eyes, and my spirit was made thankful for the renewed and unmerited mercy and favor.

Conscription Taxes

Second and Third Days of this week: Spent in attending our Meeting for Sufferings, at which information was received through one of its corresponding members that the legislature of our state, now sitting in special sessions, were about forming a bill to lay a heavy tax on the members of our society – to be paid in lieu of personal military service – which if passed into a law, would be likely to expose many of our members to severe sufferings. The subject brought considerable exercise over the meeting, which led into a discussion of our testimony against war, in which it appeared manifest that the deficiency of many of our members, in regard to a right support thereof, tended to obstruct in a very considerable degree our stepping forward (consistent with the nature of our appointment) to seek redress therein. Nevertheless, after a considerable time spent thereon, and many different prospects advanced, the meeting so far agreed as to separate a committee of six Friends to pay especial attention to the subject, who were directed to proceed therein as the necessity of the case might require and way should open for.

Fourth Day: Spent in assisting two of my neighbors to settle their business, and wrote a will for each of them. This is a business that every man ought to attend to and complete in time of health.

Fifth Day: Attended our preparative meeting and it being the one preceding our quarterly meeting, the queries were to be answered. And as one of the overseers was likely to be necessarily absent from the preparative, they met a day or two previous thereto and prepared essays[1] of answers. And the one that attended produced them to the meeting at the time of entering upon reading and answering the queries. And as I had long believed from observation and experience that the method was inconsistent with the nature of our profession and right order of our discipline – as well as in its tendency, very hurtful and weakening to the meeting. My mind was very much exercised on the occasion, and the more

---

[1] Essay: first draft

so in finding several Friends giving in to adopt the practice. But after the matter had been pretty fully spoken to under a weight of concern, Friends agreed to lay the essays aside and not notice them, which was a considerable relief to my mind.

Sixth and Seventh Days: Passed without any particular to notice.

First Day, 16th: My mind was brought under a renewed exercise in our meeting from a view and consideration of the very small improvement and progress made by a great portion of our society in religious experience when compared with the opportunities they were so abundantly favored with from time to time. It led to a communication on the subject, which was introduced by a revival of Paul's reprehension of the Hebrews (5th 12th), "For when for the time ye ought to be teachers, ye have need that one teach you again, which be the first principles of the oracles of God, and are become such as have need of milk and not of strong meat."

The subject spread and brought a solemn weight over the meeting. And Friends were pressingly excited to greater diligence in the right improvement of their precious time, that so when the day of solemn inquisition comes, they may be prepared to give in their account with joy and receive the desired and peaceful answer of, "Well done good and faithful servant. Thou hast been faithful over a few things, I will make thee ruler over many things. Enter thou into the joy of thy Lord."[1]

On Fifth Day was monthly meeting, the business of which was, I think, well and harmoniously conducted.

The rest of the week, I was busily employed in my usual vocations. In the course of which, divers things occurred that induced gratitude and thankfulness of heart to the Blessed Author of all our mercies.

First Day, 23rd: A silent meeting today. What a precious thing it is to be taught to know when to speak and when to be silent.

This week was held our quarterly meeting, this time at Flushing. It was, I think, through the several sittings, a searching, instructive, favored season. In the Meeting of Ministers and Elders and meeting of discipline, many of the hid things of Esau (or the first nature) were searched out and made manifest, and their inconsistency with the gospel dispensation and hurtful tendency exposed – particularly, that of coveting and grasping after riches. To obtain which, many of the members of our society had launched into extensive business – more particularly, in the line of commerce. And in order for the carrying it on, had involved themselves in debt beyond their ability to pay. And in order to keep up a false credit, had through a show of friendship and a deceptive appearance of having

---

[1] Matthew 25:21 & 23

great possession, drawn in others to lend them money and become their sureties for large sums, until both the borrowers and lenders were involved in utter ruin – to the great scandal of themselves, the distress of their families, and reproach of our holy profession.

And others there were that for want of keeping close to the foundation principle of our profession – the inward Divine Light and faithful testimony-bearer in the heart and conscience – had given way to busy themselves in and take a part in the political disputes and controversies among the people relative to the governments of this world, which at this time ran high and had produced war and distress in the land. By which, they not only grieved their concerned Friends, but brought much reproach upon themselves and their profession. My mind was deeply exercised on account of these things, and I was constrained to bear a full and faithful testimony against all such inconsistent and unchristian conduct, and to call Friends' attention to the necessity of a more close adherence to the internal principle of Divine Light and Truth, as the only sure Director and Preserver in times of trial.

The closing meeting held for worship was eminently favored with the Divine Presence. And the concurring testimonies borne gave evidence of his presiding power. And the great name was supplicated. And gratitude and thanksgiving were rendered to him for his continued mercy.

First Day, 30th of 10th month: In the forepart of our meeting today, my mind seemed clothed with great weakness and much interrupted by the continued succession of unnecessary and unprofitable thoughts. But as I continued to endeavor to draw my attention from them (although to little effect), towards the close of the meeting my mind was unexpectedly arrested with a subject very interesting to every immortal soul – that of coming to believe in and become settled on the eternal and unchangeable rock of salvation, Christ the Divine Light, as prophesied of, not only as a light to enlighten the Gentiles, but to be God's salvation to the ends of the earth.[1]

The subject spread, accompanied with life, which, as I communicated under the influence thereof, it spread over the meeting and became a comfortable, refreshing season. It was evidently the Lord's doing and worthy of thankful acknowledgment for the unmerited mercy.

Second, Third, and Fourth Days: Busily employed with my workmen, assisting them in securing our corn, etc. It was a bountiful crop, which made the labor pleasant and the heart thankful.

Fifth Day: At our meeting today (which was larger than usual, occasioned by the marriage of one of my daughters[2]), I was led to set forth

---

[1] Acts 13:47
[2] The youngest daughter, Sarah, married Robert Seaman.

by public testimony the excellency of the divine fear and its blessed and salutary effects on the minds of those who live daily under a humbling sense thereof – and by the persuasive language of entreaty, endeavored to arrest the minds of the tender and beloved youth present with a sense of the necessity of having it to dwell richly in their hearts as the only sure means of preservation from the many evils and temptations that abound in the world. It brought a comfortable calm over the meeting and a fit preparative for the quiet and orderly accomplishment of the intended marriage. It was cause of thankfulness to my mind – having been favored to have four daughters out of five agreeably married in the comely order of Friends. The other, yet single, a tender precious young woman, observing with pious submission her parents' counsel. But this is a blessing that few parents enjoy – except those who live under a daily concern (with timely and continued care) to watch over and nurture their tender offspring in the fear of the Lord.

Sixth Day: Accompanied our daughter with her husband to his father's house and returned in the evening.

Seventh Day: Spent in my family cares and ended the week with a peaceful mind.

First Day, 6th of 11th month: My lot was silence today – a pleasant lot indeed, when the Master wills it so.

Second, Third, and Fourth Days: Employed diligently in my ordinary affairs.

The rest of the week was devoted to religious concerns. Had the company of a ministering Friend from West Jersey on Fifth Day at our meeting, through whose fervent labor the life was raised into dominion, which made it a comfortable and instructive season. Accompanied him the two following days to Bethpage and Jerusalem, having a meeting at each place – both of which were seasons of favor.

First Day, 13th: Passed our meeting again in silence, under the comfortable auspices of a mind resigned either to speak or be silent.

Second, Third, and Fourth Days: Spent in my usual concerns.

Fifth Day: Was our monthly meeting, at which we had the company of the same Friend as attended our meeting the Fifth Day preceding. I had near unity with him in his exercise and had to bear a corresponding testimony – both in the men's and women's meeting. It was a season of favor – much suitable counsel was administered, tending to excite Friends to greater faithfulness and circumspection in the right ordering of their families and in the bringing up and educating their children in the nurture and admonition of the Lord, consistent with our holy profession.

Sixth and Seventh Days: Returned (as respects the mind) like Mordecai to the king's gate, while my hands were busily employed in my family affairs.

First Day, 20th: Having felt my mind for some time increasingly inclined to sit with Friends in their meeting at Matinecock, I thought it right at this time to attend thereto. But when I came there, my mind felt so vacant and void of concern that for some time I was ready to conclude that (if my coming was of any use) it would all be included in my personal presence as an example of silence. But after a time of quiet waiting, a subject presented, and the life arose with it and opened to a large communication in which the gospel was preached in the demonstration of the Spirit and with such power attending as produced a very solemn covering over the meeting. And many hearts present were broken and contrited, for which favor my heart was clothed with gratitude and thanksgiving to the Bountiful Author of all our mercies and blessings, and who is over all, God blessed forever.

The rest of this week, I spent about home, mostly employed in my temporal concerns.

Passed our Fifth Day Meeting in silence, and the week ended with a peaceful mind, which I account as an unmerited favor.

First Day, 27th: Feeling my mind drawn to sit with Friends at Westbury, I accordingly attended their meeting, in which I was led to set forth the excellency of the state (described by the apostle Paul) that is freed from condemnation and is effected by a full submission and obedience to the law of the Spirit of Life in Christ Jesus that sets free from the law of sin and death.[1] It was an open and, I trust, a profitable opportunity to some present and I felt peace in my labor.

Second Day: Attended the funeral of a neighbor whose wife was a member of our society. And although he had been a very intemperate man, yet towards his close, he signified a desire to be laid in Friends' burial ground, which was allowed. His widow being very desirous I should attend the funeral, I went accordingly with several other Friends. The neighborhood being chiefly Dutch people, a considerable number attended – among whom we had a solemn opportunity. The testimony borne had a very reaching effect on many, especially among the youth, and I was made thankful for the opportunity.

Third and Fourth Days: Occupied in laying in my winter's store of provisions.

Fifth Day: Attended our meeting. It was a quiet, encouraging season. Towards the latter part, I was concerned to show to Friends the hurtful

---

[1] Romans 8:1-2

tendency of evil thinking, which I introduced by that ancient, short saying, "Evil be to him, that evil thinks."[1] The subject enlarged and spread increased weight over the meeting, and many minds were humbled and contrited. And we parted under the solemn covering.

Sixth and Seventh Days: Occupied in my usual concerns, with attendant peace of mind.

First Day, 4th of 12th month: A quiet silent meeting today.

Second, Third, and Fourth Days: Diversely engaged. Some of the time occupied in rendering some assistance to the poor in the city of New York with many other Friends – the present tumultuous state of public affairs having reduced many of the laboring part of the citizens to a suffering state for want of the necessaries of life.[2]

War Taxes

Fifth Day: In the meeting for worship that preceded our preparative meeting, I felt my mind renewedly engaged to call Friends' attention to a faithful support of our Christian testimonies – particularly, those against war and injustice – and that all might, with firmness, maintain our Christian liberties without fear, favor, or affection against every encroachment of the secular powers – as in the present disturbed state of public affairs. Laws had recently been enacted levying taxes and other requisitions for the support of war that was now spreading and making its destructive ravages in our once peaceful land. A solemn weight covered the meeting during the communication and I was favored to relieve my mind for the present from the weight of concern and exercise it lay under on those accounts.

Sixth and Seventh Days: Busily engaged in my family concerns, believing with the apostle that he that doth not take the necessary care for his own and family's comfortable support may be considered to have denied the faith and is worse than an infidel, as they are generally careful on those accounts.

First Day, 11th: Being invited to attend the funeral of a friendly woman, a widow of my acquaintance in our neighboring town of Hempstead and feeling an inclination thereto, I attended accordingly. There was a considerable collection, mostly made up with Episcopalians, Presbyterians, and Methodists, among whom my mind was enlarged in gospel love and led to sound forth the glad tidings[3] of life and salvation through Jesus Christ – the second Adam, the Lord from Heaven, a

---

[1] This quote is from Edward III and is the motto of the Order of the Garter.
[2] The War of 1812 had severe economic effects on the American shipping industry.
[3] Tidings: news

Quickening Spirit – opening to the people how that by a full submission to the inward operation of this Spirit (a manifestation of which is given to every man to profit withal[1]), we experience the truth of that remarkable saying of the apostle Paul that, "As in Adam" (or the first fallen nature) "all die, so in Christ" (the second Adam or the second, renewed, and re-quickened state[2]) "all are made alive."[3] And therefore, "Born again, not of corruptible seed, but of the incorruptible seed and Word of God that liveth and abideth forever."[4]

It was a highly favored season in which the Lord's power was exalted and Truth reigned over all to the bowing the assembly in general. And many hearts were broken and contrited. It was evidently the Lord's doing and marvelous in mine eyes, which engaged renewed gratitude and thankfulness of heart for the unmerited mercy.

Second and Third Days: Spent in attending our Meeting for Sufferings in New York, in which an opportunity opened to relieve my mind of a concern I had been for some time exercised under, on account of some recent laws enacted by the general government of this country and the legislature of the state of New York, which, in their tendency, were opposite to our testimony against war and injustice, and were likely to produce much suffering to the faithful in our society, who saw they could not yield to the requisition of those laws without balking their Christian testimonies in these respects. I was led to excite Friends to unity in this concern, as the want of uniformity would very much tend to lay waste those precious testimonies and increase the sufferings of the society.

Fourth Day: Attended our neighboring Monthly Meeting of Westbury. My mind was engaged to call Friends' attention to a more close adherence to right discipline – the right management whereof could not be rightly and profitably effected without keeping to a right and sound form. I felt satisfaction in my labor, in a belief that the honest-hearted were strengthened and encouraged.

A Visit to Scattered Families in Westbury Quarterly Meeting

Fifth Day: Attended our own monthly meeting, at which we had the company of our Friend, John Winslow, from the district of Maine in New England. His gospel labors in the line of the ministry were acceptable and edifying. At this meeting, I opened to my Friends a prospect that had for some time attended my mind to make a visit to some scattered families of our society that resided in the outskirts of our quarterly meeting – some of

---

[1] 1 Corinthians 12:7
[2] 1 Corinthians 15:45
[3] 1 Corinthians 15:22
[4] 1 Peter 1:23

whom, being some distance from meeting, but seldom attended. I had also a view of visiting some families of friendly people that were not members and appointing some meetings among some of the neighboring inhabitants of other societies. The meeting united with the prospect and left me at liberty to pursue it, as way might open.

On Sixth and Seventh Days, I accompanied our Friend, John Winslow, to Bethpage and Jerusalem – attending a meeting in each place. And the Lord our Gracious Helper was near, strengthening and qualifying to preach the gospel of life and salvation in the clear demonstration of the Spirit and with power, to the humbling and contriting many present, and rejoicing the minds of the honest-hearted.

First Day, 18th: I attended our own meeting and was favored therein with a lively, impressive testimony which produced a very comfortable solemnity over the meeting and rendered it an instructive, edifying season.

On Second Day, by appointment, I met our Friend, John Winslow, at a meeting in the town of Oyster Bay, where we again witnessed the Shepherd of Israel to be near, enabling us to discharge ourselves faithfully to the people, setting the truth above error – and left it upon them whether they will hear or forbear.

On Third Day evening, had an appointed meeting for the black people in our meetinghouse at Jericho. It appeared to be owned in a very especial manner by the Master of our Assemblies – furnishing doctrine suited to their states and conditions. And Truth reigned over all, powerfully evidencing that the Lord our God is no respecter of persons,[1] but is gracious and merciful unto all, and that in every nation, kindred, tongue, and people, those that fear him and work righteousness are accepted of him.

Fourth Day: Attended an appointed meeting at a friendly man's house by the name of Amos Cheshire, about four miles easterly from Jericho. It was a highly favored season. Most present were affected by the prevalence of Truth that ran as oil over all. Surely it was the Lord's doing and worthy of grateful acknowledgments and thanksgiving for the unmerited favor.

In the evening, we attended another meeting at Cold Spring Harbor at the house of Divine Hewlett. And although not so open as the former, yet we were favored to clear ourselves among them and left them with the reward of peace in our labor.

Fifth Day: Attended a meeting in the morning at the house of a friendly man on Huntington West Neck and in the evening, one at the west end of the town of Huntington at Peleg Woods. The first was a very

---

[1] No respecter of persons: shows no partiality between people – from Acts 10:34

precious season to the visitors and, I trust also to most or all of the visited. The latter was a stripping[1] time in the forepart, but I trust, ended well.

Sixth Day: Visited some families on our way home, which visits I believe were mutually comfortable.

Seventh Day: Spent in repairing the traveling vehicle of our friend aforenamed, who had accompanied me in the above tour, and attending a little to my temporal concerns.

First Day, 25th: My mind, while sitting in our meeting today, was opened on the subject of faith, in the revival of that scripture passage *viz*, "All men have not faith."[2] I was led in a clear full testimony to show to the auditory why all men have not faith, although the means of obtaining it were freely offered to the acceptance of all – yet not to be obtained by man's natural wisdom or acquirements, but only by and through the operation and inspiration of the Grace and Spirit of God, as man yields in obedience and submission thereunto. Hence, he comes to know God by the inward experimental[3] touches of his own life and power in his soul, and hence springs up in him – as he patiently submits thereunto – that living, operative faith that works by love to the purifying of the heart. But such as are exercising themselves in their own speculative wisdom and refuse submission to the manifestations of divine grace, these have not faith, because they reject the only means by which it can be obtained. The Truth was raised into dominion and ran freely over all as oil, to the praise of his Grace, who is over all, God blessed forever.

Second and Third Days: Busily employed in my husbandry and family affairs, each day closing with a peaceful mind.

Fourth and Fifth Days: I attended the midweek meetings at Westbury and Cow Neck. And previous notice being given of my intention of attending them, they were larger than usual at that time in the week. And through the gracious condescension of Israel's Never-failing Helper, my mind was opened to declare to the people of the things concerning the kingdom of God[4] in two, large, doctrinal testimonies (one at each place) suited to the states of the auditories. The doctrines delivered distilled as the dew on the minds of many who were present, causing tears of contrition to trickle down their cheeks. Surely, such seasons are as a brook by the way to the honest-exercised traveler Zionward, as they tend to an increase of faith and inspire with fresh courage to persevere in the heavenly journey.

---

[1] Strip: expose one's true character or condition
[2] 2 Thessalonians 3:2
[3] Experimental: based on direct, personal experience rather than mere testimony or conjecture
[4] Acts 1:3, 8:12, & 19:8

Cow Neck Meetinghouse in Manhasset, New York

I also attended an appointed meeting in the intermediate evening at Hempstead Harbor. And although I was led in my communication to treat in a full, clear manner on divers particular doctrines of the gospel, yet it seemed to have but little entrance in the minds of those present, which made the exercise arduous and afforded but little satisfaction in the end. This I have found mostly to be the case in neighborhoods where the minds of the people are led to adhere to outward, formal, and ceremonial performances in religion – and especially where much self-activity and bodily exercise is superadded,[1] which is very much the case with the principal part of this neighborhood. And those not of this description are (except a few) in a state of lukewarmness and almost entire indifferency respecting those things that belong to their soul's salvation.

On Sixth Day, I attended a funeral of a person who had deceased in a Friend's family, and wherein he had been a laborer for many years in the neighborhood last mentioned. And although but a few collected, yet the opportunity was solemn and the testimony borne had a reaching effect on the minds of divers present – especially on several of the youth. May it be fastened by the Master of Assemblies as a nail in a sure place.

Seventh Day: Occupied in my temporal concerns, and the week and the year ended with a peaceful mind.

---

[1] Superadd: add on top of what has already been added

1815

First Day, 1st of the 1st month 1815: My mind, while silently waiting in our meeting, was opened to view in prospect the beauty and excellency of order. And as it spread on my mind, I felt constrained to communicate on the subject, and to show how all things that continued in full subjection to the divine will were preserved in the same beautiful order they were arranged in from the beginning. And that all disorder sprung from and was the effect of a will separate and distinct from the divine will. And as God is a God of order, and is also the Creator of all things, of course there can be no order and right harmony in his creation, but what he is the sole author of. Hence, the necessity of every created being becoming wholly subject to his heavenly and divine will, as nothing else can possibly restore the creation to its primitive order and harmony. And when this is effected, there will be a perfect annihilation to every distinct and separate will in the whole creation, from the will of our Heavenly Father. Then all creation will stand in a state of subservience to the divine will. Then will the morning stars again resume their song, and all the sons of God shout for joy.[1]

O happy day! May the Lord hasten it in his own time.

Second Day: I attended the funeral of a young man, who was killed by the falling of his horse. He was in company with a number of loose young men at a tavern, where they had been running horses. And he being one who rode in a race, his horse flung him off in a fearful manner. Nevertheless, he escaped unhurt. But shortly after, as he was riding from the tavern, his horse fell with him and he died with the hurt he received by the fall in about a week after.

The accident had considerable effect on his young companions and impressed their minds with sadness and alarm. They were generally present at his funeral, as also were most of the youth in the neighborhood for a considerable distance round – who, with others of riper years, made a large collection. And the Lord, who is always graciously near and ready to help in every needful time, opened my mouth among them in a large, affecting testimony suiting to the several states of the auditory. It was a very humbling, solemn season, not soon to be forgotten by many present. And my spirit was made thankful for the unmerited favor.

After the funeral, I went with my wife and daughter Elisabeth to Islip to see our grandson,[2] who is in a weakly, declining state, and returned home the next evening.

---

[1] Job 38:7
[2] Elias Willets (1800-1818), son of Phebe and Joshua Willets, suffered from the same degenerative disease that killed all four of Elias Hicks' sons in their teens.

Fourth Day: Attended on my family concerns.

Fifth Day: Attended our midweek meeting in silence. Had the company of our Friend, Phebe Merritt, from New York, who also sat most of the meeting in silence, but appeared towards the close in a short testimony, which spread a good degree of life over the meeting, which was truly gladdening.

Sixth and Seventh Days: Occupied in temporal concerns. Part of the time employed in assisting an ancient Friend (upward of ninety years of age) in settling his business and writing his will – and he appeared competent to the purpose, both as to memory and understanding.

First Day, 8th of 1st month: My mind was in unison with the exercise and testimony of our Friend, Phebe Merritt, who was again with us at our meeting today. And I found it my duty towards the close of the meeting, to set my seal thereto in a short, impressive testimony. And I trust the meeting closed under a sensible degree of divine favor, worthy of our thankfulness and gratitude.

Second and Third Days: While my hands were busily employed in my temporal business, my mind was often led to soar above all these temporal enjoyments and to contemplate on things of an eternal nature. And in the course of my meditations, [I] was led to contrast those who are led and influenced by the wisdom and will of man, with those who are led and influenced by the wisdom and will of God, and was let to see how of necessity the former must be ruled and governed by the wisdom and power of man – hence the necessity of coercion, and hence the necessity of war, as every government of coercion must of necessity be set up and maintained by the force and fear of the sword or other armor[1] efficient to take life, as that is the last alternative in every government set up in the wisdom and will of man.

But those who are led and influenced by the wisdom and will of God have no necessity of being governed by anything else than the divine wisdom and will, through the power of persuasive love. And no other coercion can ever be necessary in the kingdom of heaven, where nothing reigns but love, peace, and joy undefiled and without intermission.

And O that every rational inhabitant of this terraqueous globe were so inspired with a real, soul-craving desire after the enjoyment of this heavenly and peaceful kingdom, as not to rest until they had gained a satisfactory assurance that their names were enrolled in that city that hath foundations, whose builder and maker the Lord is.[2]

Fourth Day: I rode to New York in order to attend the funeral of our beloved Friend, Matthew Franklin, the next day. He was taken (as

---

[1] Armor: weapons
[2] Hebrews 11:10

supposed) with an apoplectic fit,[1] while speaking in the morning meeting in Pearl Street on the preceding First Day – and appeared lively in testimony, but was suddenly stopped by the feeling of indisposition and sat quietly down, but soon arose and withdrew, and was followed by some of his friends, and would have fallen as soon as he got out had he not been upheld by them, and in a few minutes, fell into an almost senseless state as to the body and was not able to speak afterwards, and quietly expired at about half past seven in the evening of the following day. And we trust, has safely landed in that celestial port, where the wicked cease from troubling, and the weary soul is at rest.[2]

He appeared innocent and amiable in his life and conversation, and generally beloved by his friends and acquaintance – especially the youth for whose improvement and preservation he often appeared very solicitous. The unusually large attendance at his funeral, and the solemnity that appeared in the countenances of the multitude assembled (the meetinghouse, although large, was thought not sufficient to contain more than two-thirds of those that gathered) carried full evidence of the foregoing representation, as did also the testimonies borne on that solemn occasion.

I attended (beside the funeral on Fifth Day) two other meetings. One at Liberty Street in the morning – it being Friends midweek meeting for that place – and a meeting for the people of color in Pearl Street. The latter was very large. My mouth was opened in each assembly to speak of those things that relate to the kingdom of God, especially at the funeral and in the meeting for the people of color. My mind was largely opened to preach the gospel in the demonstration of the Spirit. And the Lord's power attended, to the humbling and solemnizing the assemblies. It was evidently the Lord's doing, and marvelous in mine eyes, and may all the honor and praise be ascribed to him, for he only is worthy, both now and forever.

Lie low, O my soul, and be humbled in the dust from a due sense of such unmerited mercy.

On Sixth Day, I rode to Manhattanville and attended a meeting there in the evening. It was in the main, I think, a favored season. The Truth was largely declared and appeared to have a reaching effect upon most present.

Seventh Day: Returned to the city and attended a meeting in the evening in the Bowery, which I had appointed before I left town the day before. It was a very solemn, quiet meeting. The testimony of Truth flowed

---

[1] Apoplectic fit: probably a cerebral hemorrhage
[2] Job 3:17

freely and I hope had a profitable entrance with some. May it prove as a nail fastened in a sure place.

A Visit in New York & Long Island

First Day, 15th of 1st month: I attended Friends Meetings in New York – was at Pearl Street in the morning and the other in the afternoon – and was largely opened in both meetings, and was led in the course of the testimonies clearly to open divers particular doctrines of the gospel, and fully to distinguish between the law state and that of the gospel, and to show to the people how, that as all the shadows of the law stood in and consisted of outward and elementary things, they must end in the gospel – which is the substance of all shadows and of course supersedes them all[1] – so that no believer in him (although a Jew, one brought up in all the shadows of that dispensation, such as circumcision, the Passover supper, every kind of sacrifice by fire, and every ablution or purification by elementary water – even John the Baptist not excepted), would lie under any necessity to comply any longer with any of those rituals or outward ordinances – being all abolished by the sufferings and death of Jesus Christ. And that, therefore, no guilt would attach to any believer – even though he had been brought up a Jew – by the complete omission of all the ordinances, baptisms, suppers, and other rituals of that dispensation that stood and consisted in outward and elementary things. It was indeed a day of favor, in which the Lord's power was exalted, and his name and Truth set above all error and untruth.

On Second Day evening, attended the Meeting for Sufferings, which stood adjourned to that time on a particular occasion. And we sat again the next day, when we finished the business before us. And in the evening I attended a meeting I had appointed for the laboring class of the community and for those in low circumstances. The weather was very inclement – it being a snow storm that prevented most of the women from attending – but there was a considerable, large number of men, who conducted with great order and solemnity, and received with much attention the truths delivered, which inspired a hope that the opportunity would be blessed – to the encouragement and real benefit of many of them.

Fourth Day: I attended Friends Meeting in Pearl Street, which proved a comfortable and, I believe, instructive season to some – especially among the youth – after which, I returned home with peace of mind and a thankful sense of the continued mercy of a gracious God to his creature, man, amidst all his backslidings and transgressions.

---

[1] The rest of the sentence and the following one were deleted from the printed *Journal*.

Fifth Day: Attended our own monthly meeting, in which I had to lay before Friends the great advantage that would result – not only to us as individuals, but also to society – through individual faithfulness, and a full belief and trust in the divine providence, and a strict and undeviating adherence to the order and discipline of the Church. And had peace in my labor.

Sixth Day: I attended the funeral of Charles Valentine, son of David, at Moscheto Cove. It was very largely attended by Friends and others. I had an open time among them, which was introduced with this scripture exhortation (Galatians 5th & 1st). "Stand fast therefore in the liberty wherewith Christ hath made us free, and be not entangled again with the yoke of bondage."

The subject was largely opened, showing how that all the works of the flesh did in a lesser or greater degree bring the mind under a yoke of bondage. And that the fear of death was a principal one, out of which many others originated, such as every means of self-defense that consisted in war and warlike preparations – as also every ceremonial performance in matters of a religious nature, such as water baptism and what is called the ordinance of the supper (in the use of outward bread and wine) – all which not being essential, brings a yoke and burden on the believer in Christ, as he came purposely to set his followers free from all signs and shadows, and bring them into the possession and enjoyment of the substance. And thereby, to know all the shadows to flee away and come to an end – as Christ-manifested is the substance and end of all shadows. It was a highly favored season. The Truth was raised into dominion and ran freely, to the humbling and contriting many hearts. And may the praise, the honor, and the glory be all ascribed to him, who opens and none can shut, and when he shuts, none can open, and who remains to be God over all, blessed forever.

Seventh Day: Attended to some necessary repairs about my farm and tenements.[1] As being much from home attending to my religious engagements in Truth's service, when I feel a liberty to be at home, I find it needful to be industriously employed to keep my temporal concerns in order, so that when I leave home on Truth's account, my mind may be at liberty without caring for or thinking much about them.

First Day: Attended our own meeting, mostly in silence.

The rest of this week was principally taken up in preparing for and attending our quarterly meeting, which was held at Westbury. It was pretty largely attended – both the meeting for discipline and that for public worship. The latter was somewhat hurt by an unskillful

---

[1] Tenement: building

appearance[1] in the forepart, but ended well. In the Meeting of Ministers and Elders, as also in that for discipline, a living exercise and concern was prevalent with divers Friends – not only in searching out the causes of the numerous weaknesses and deficiencies that were manifest in society, but also in endeavoring their removal by much tender and pressing advice and counsel suited to the states of those who were delinquent. Many minds were brought under a humbling exercise and travail of spirit in those solemn opportunities. And divers young Friends, who were under the forming hand, preparing for usefulness in the Church, came forth at this time and publicly espoused the cause of Truth and Righteousness – uniting with their elder brethren in the exercise and travail that were felt to be prevalent in those favored opportunities. My spirit was led into near sympathy with these, and fervent was the desire and prayer of my mind for their preservation in the right path of duty, that so they might grow up and become useful in society, and faithful laborers and pillars in the Lord's house, that should go no more out.[2]

First Day, 29th: We had a comfortable meeting today – mostly in quiet, silent retirement, saving towards the close. My mind was quickened and opened to a short communication in the remembrance of the case of Joseph and his brethren,[3] wherein I was led to recapitulate their envy and hatred towards him, and to show how their wicked intentions in selling him to prevent his rising to the power and dignity that his dreams appeared to forebode, were the very means (in the ordering of Divine Providence) of accomplishing their fulfillment – and, of course, made their bowing and making their obeisance to him much more humiliating than it would have been had they conducted themselves towards him in the line of true brotherhood, and he had been raised to the dignity and power he was by some other way. But herein was the true proverb verified, "Let envy alone and it will punish itself." I was led further to open the malignity[4] and baneful effects of those hateful and very evil propensities. A solemn weight covered the meeting. And we parted under a thankful sense of the present favor.

The rest of this week, I spent in my ordinary vocations and in visiting some friends under bodily affliction.

First Day, 5th of 2nd month: I left home in order to proceed again in the concern I had engaged in – to visit some of the inhabitants in some of our neighboring towns, and some scattered families of Friends and friendly people. I spent the week in this service.

---

[1] Appearance: presentation of vocal ministry
[2] Revelation 3:12
[3] Genesis 37:12-36
[4] Malignity: wicked hatred

I attended nine meetings, all by my appointment in places where no meetings are held (except one) and visited eleven families of Friends and friendly people. And although I left home under much depression of spirit attended with great discouragement, insomuch that I was brought near to a conclusion it would be safest to tarry at home and wait for a more full manifestation. But as I brought the subject to the test in my own mind and patiently waited for an answer in much abasedness[1] and humiliation, a small degree of light sprang up, in which the voice said, "Go and trust in the Lord to open the way" – which centered my mind in a state of perfect acquiescence. And I proceeded accordingly, seeing nothing further when I left home than to attend the Meeting of Friends at Bethpage, which was the first I attended. But before the close of that meeting, Light sprang up and the way in which I should advance clearly opened. And as my trust and dependence were fixed in the arm of divine sufficiency, strength and ability were furnished from season to season faithfully to espouse the cause of Truth and Righteousness, and to preach the gospel in the clear demonstration of the Spirit and with power – to the convincing and contriting many minds, and to the relief and comfort my own – inspiring continual thankfulness and gratitude to the Blessed Author of all our mercies.

I returned home on Seventh Day evening, accompanied with true peace of mind.

First Day, 12th: Attended our own meeting and after a pretty long season of solemn silence, my mind was opened to communication in the revival of the following declaration of the apostle James, "For as the body without the spirit is dead, so faith without works is dead also."[2]

The subject was largely and impressively opened, which brought a solemn covering over the meeting and made it a season of comfort and edification. Surely such seasons administer cause for all the humble and contrite in heart to thank God and take courage,[3] and press forward in the holy and heavenly way.

Second Day: I found liberty to occupy this day in my temporal concerns.

Third Day: I attended the funeral of a friendly man at Jerusalem. There was a very large collection of people, composed of the different classes of civil society. And although it was a time of extreme frost and cold, and the means for rendering the rooms wherein the people assembled comfortable [were] very inadequate for that end, yet they were generally very quiet and orderly, and appeared to pay great attention to the doctrines

---

[1] Abasedness: being in a low, humble or downcast state
[2] James 2:26
[3] Acts 28:15

delivered – my heart and mouth being opened among them to speak of the things concerning the kingdom of heaven, and to set forth in a clear and forcible manner the way and means of man's salvation, and that nothing short of a freedom from sin and the experience of a real righteousness would be sufficient to effect that great and happy end.

Fourth Day: I attended the Monthly Meeting at Westbury. Had some close, searching exercise – both in the meeting for worship and that for discipline – tending to quicken Friends' minds to a more lively concern for the arising of the divine life in their meetings, that so their faith might be productive of good works, and they qualified to serve the Lord in newness of life and not in the oldness of the letter.

Fifth Day: I attended our own monthly meeting. We had but little business to attend to at this time. I found it incumbent before the meeting closed to submit a prospect that attended my mind – to visit the families of Friends of the Monthly Meeting of New York – to the consideration of the meeting, and received Friends' united concurrence therein.

Sixth Day: I spent with my family and in my family concerns. And in the evening, attended a meeting I had appointed at Wolver Hollow, a neighborhood consisting mostly of Dutch people. It was a very solemn, quiet meeting and I had good service among them to the mutual comfort and edification of most present.

Seventh Day: I left home again on my former concern in visiting some more of the scattered families of Friends and friendly people in the suburbs of our quarterly meeting – having not fully accomplished that service. Our first meeting was the next day at Rockaway among my relatives and acquaintance, that having been the place of my former residence. And although the meeting at this time was small – partly occasioned by the inclemency of the weather – yet through the gracious extendings of divine love, it proved a favored season.

After this, we proceeded eastward on the southern part of the island and had five more meetings among those not in membership with us – except here and there, a scattered family or part of a family. Yet numbers of them appear to be convinced of the truth of the doctrines and principles of Friends, many of whom, I believe, if they continue faithful to their convincement, will in time become members with us.

We also had some edifying seasons in the few scattered families of Friends in this quarter, and in a number of families of friendly people, and returned home on the Fifth Day evening following, and found sweet peace in thus dedicating myself to the promotion of the cause of Truth and Righteousness in the earth.

Sixth and Seventh Days: Devoted to the care of my family and household concerns, which I find to be my incumbent duty when at liberty from my religious engagements and gospel services – believing with the apostle, that he that is not industriously careful for his own and family's good accommodation in temporal things has denied the faith. And in that respect, is worse than an infidel.

First Day, 26th of 4th month: Attended our own meeting today.

Second Day: Attended the funeral of a friendly woman. And the family being friendly-inclined, a meeting was held on the occasion, which proved a profitable, edifying opportunity.

A Visit to Families of Friends in the New York Monthly Meeting

Third Day: I proceeded to New York in order to attend the monthly meeting the next day, in which I opened my prospect of visiting the families belonging thereto, with which the meeting united. But feeling a draft[1] to attend the monthly meeting to be held at Flushing the next day before entering on the family visit, I accordingly went.

The meeting for worship that preceded that of discipline was a favored season in which Truth reigned. I likewise had a large, favored meeting with the townspeople in general in the evening, and the next day returned to New York.

Seventh Day, 4th of 3rd month 1815: I began the family visit. Sat with twelve families, in some of which I felt the renewed visitation of the Heavenly Father's love, in which the visited and visitors were united in the bond of Christian fellowship, which tended to inspire with strength to persevere and trust in the Lord, who hath graciously promised that they who trust in him shall not be confounded.[2] But in others, things were much out of order, and darkness spread over us, at times as a curtain, when we found it needful to be clothed with faith and patience. And as these were abode[3] in, after a time of suffering with the seed, way was mostly made to set the testimony of Truth over darkness and error – to the conviction and instruction of many, and to the peace of my own mind.

Samuel Parsons kindly accompanied me in the greater part of the visit, and cordially united and sympathized with me therein.

First Day: I attended the meetings at Liberty Street, both fore and after noon, and sat with four families, and in the course of the week, seventy more, in which we met with a variety of states and conditions – which renders such services truly arduous and exercising, requiring great inward attention to the divine gift, as nothing else can open to the diverse states of the people and qualify to speak suitably to their several conditions – to

---

[1] Draft: a sense of duty
[2] Psalm 22:5
[3] Abode: past tense of abide

their improvement and help – and give the answer of peace to those under such exercises.

I also attended Friends midweek meetings at Pearl and Liberty Streets. At the former, was a marriage. It was a time of unusual favor, in which the descendings of the Heavenly Father's love were felt to cover the very large assembly in a very eminent manner – my mouth being opened in a large, impressive testimony, in which in a clear, instructive manner, I had to set forth the great difference between a believer and an unbeliever. Showing how the former was, by faithfulness and obedience to the inward divine gift of grace, daily improving and advancing in divine wisdom and knowledge, and in the enjoyments and consolations always attendant thereon, while the latter is sinking deeper and deeper into a state of darkness and error – and the distresses and vexations that naturally result from unbelief. It was a high day, in which Truth was exalted over all opposition and error, to the rejoicing of many minds, and to the bowing of mine into deep thankfulness and gratitude to the Author of every blessing. Surely it was the Lord's doing and marvelous in our eyes. Therefore, let all the praise be ascribed to him who is over all, blessed forever.

First Day, 12th: Attended Pearl Street Meeting fore and after noon. Both meetings were much hurt by a long, tedious, and lifeless communication in each by a Friend from abroad. It very much shut up my way and was, I apprehend, a great loss to the meetings, as it very much hurt the solemnity.

In the course of this week, I sat with twenty-nine families, attended Pearl Street Meeting on Fourth Day, after which I rode home in order to attend our own monthly meeting, and returned on Seventh Day to the city.

First Day: Attended Pearl Street Meeting in the forenoon and Liberty Street in the afternoon, both comfortable seasons, and in the course of this week, sat with seventy-seven families.

First Day, 26th: Attended Pearl Street Meeting, both fore and after noon, and an appointed meeting at Liberty Street in the evening. They were large, full meetings, and through the condescending goodness of Israel's Shepherd, they were eminently favored – my mouth being opened in each to preach the gospel in the demonstration of Truth – to the comfort, edification and instruction of many (or most) who attended, as appeared by their solemn and satisfactory deportment. And I was truly thankful that I had been enabled to get through this day's exercise to the peace of my own mind, which I esteem the best treasure.

Second Day: Sat with five families in the city and in the afternoon, crossed the ferry to Brooklyn and visited three families of Friends in that neighborhood – they being members belonging to Liberty Street Meeting. I also had an appointed meeting in the evening for the inhabitants of Brooklyn. It was well attended and proved an instructive, favored season – gratefully to be remembered.

Third Day: Rode to Manhattanville and visited the families of Friends in that place – and three families on the way – and returned to the city next morning and attended Friends Preparative Meeting in Pearl Street. And it being the time of answering the queries, it proved an exercising time – Friends having too generally got in the habit of making use of words which rendered their answers evasive, and not giving a direct answer to the question, and by which the deficient members were very much covered, and which tended rather to set them at ease than to stir them up to more diligence and care. My mind was deeply exercised – things appearing very much out of order with many in this city and the number of the faithful very small. I endeavored to discharge myself faithfully among them, and found peace in my labor.

In the afternoon, I had a select opportunity with the ministers and elders and overseers, in which opportunity, I in good measure relieved my mind from a burden I had been under for some time respecting Friends in those stations. And in the evening, I had an appointed meeting in the east part of the town, principally among those not in membership with us. It was held in a large, commodious building erected for the purpose of schooling the children of such poor people that did not belong to any society of professed Christians.[1] There was at this time a school held in it, consisting of nearly four hundred such children, the charges of which were defrayed by the charitable donations of the citizens at large. It is a very benevolent institution, and the school well conducted. The meeting was large, consisting (as was supposed) of a thousand people, to whom the truths of the gospel were largely opened – to the comforting and instructing many minds, and administering reproof to the lukewarm, the licentious, and immoral. A general solemnity spread over the meeting. And we parted under a deep and humbling sense of the unmerited favor.

Fifth Day: Attended the Preparative Meeting at Liberty Street, which was a comfortable meeting. The queries appeared to be answered with much more consistency than at the other meeting. The afternoon and evening, spent in the family visit, as also the two following days.

First Day, 2nd of 4th month: I attended Pearl Street Meeting in the morning and that at Liberty Street in the afternoon. And public notice being given of my intention of being at the latter, it was large. I also had an appointed meeting in the evening at Pearl Street – it was also very large. They were all seasons of favor, especially those at Pearl Street, wherein

---

[1] Nearly all educational institutions at this time were run by churches

Truth reigned and the people's minds were solemnized, and the faithful comforted and made glad together under a grateful sense of the continued mercy and long-suffering loving-kindness of Israel's Shepherd to the workmanship of his holy hand.

Second Day: Sat with four families in the forenoon. And in the afternoon, had an appointed meeting at Flatbush near the west end of Long Island, where no Friends live – the inhabitants being mostly Dutch people, the descendants of the ancient Hollanders. They had but little acquaintance with us or our principles. The meeting was held in their courthouse. A respectable number collected and behaved quietly, becoming the occasion. And our Gracious Helper was near, furnishing doctrine suited to their states and conditions, which had a reaching and salutary effect upon many minds. And through the prevalence of the power of Truth that arose into dominion, divers hearts were broken and contrited. And we parted from them with thankful hearts, and returned to the city that evening.

Third Day: Attended the Meeting of Ministers and Elders, composed of the select members of the Monthly Meetings of New York and Flushing. It was a solemn and, I hope, profitable time.

The next day was the Monthly Meeting of New York, in which I was favored to close my visit to Friends there in an opportunity with the members generally together – both male and female, select from others – wherein I discharged myself fully, to the peace of my own mind and, I trust, to the comfort and encouragement of the faithful, and at the same time, administering reproof and correction to the lukewarm and unsound members, and strength to the weak and feebleminded. And the great name was supplicated in behalf of his people, that he would still strive with them, both in mercy and judgment, as he should see meet in his matchless wisdom and loving-kindness, and not give his heritage to reproach, lest the people without[1] be led to inquire, where is their God.[2]

Encounter with a Presbyterian Minister

Fifth Day: I turned my face homeward, having a meeting at Newtown Kills at the 11th hour and another in the town at evening. They were favored seasons, although the latter was somewhat interrupted at the close by a hireling minister of the Presbyterian order, who took some exceptions to the doctrines delivered respecting water baptism, imputative righteousness, and the hire of ministers. The latter, I conclude, touched him in the most tender part. But the arguments he advanced in support of these appeared very weak, being unfounded and fallacious. And the

---

[1] People without: people not within the Society of Friends
[2] Joel 2:17

scripture passages that he quoted to prove his positions were in direct opposition thereto. For the proof of water baptism, he made use of the doctrine of the apostle Paul – and especially that part wherein he thanks God that he had baptized but a very small number, positively asserting that Christ sent him not to baptize.[1] And if so great a minister as Paul had no commission nor authority to baptize (that is, with water), who had converted so many to the Christian faith, and set up and established many churches in parts where no other of the primitive ministers had yet traveled, surely he could not think it needful. For otherwise, he must have fallen very short of fulfilling his ministry if water baptism is as needful as many professed Christians make it in the present day. But if we conclude, as I apprehend we are all bound to do, that Paul (as he himself asserts) was not a whit behind the chiefest of the primitive apostles,[2] then we may then safely conclude that water baptism hath no part in the commission of a gospel minister. And consequently, is no part of the gospel dispensation, but was only made use of in condescension to the weak state of the Jewish believers, in the same way as circumcision was made use of by Paul.[3] And indeed, it is abundantly evident that all the rituals of the law were continued for many years, if not through the whole of the first century, by most of the Jewish Christians. But it is evident that it was all in condescension to the weak state that the believers were in through the force of tradition and custom – having been long in the use of outward shadows and types, the way did not open to shake them all off[4] at once. But as the Light of the glorious gospel should arise, they would gradually recede and give place to the substance, just as when the sun – that celestial orb of light – rises above the horizon, all the shadows of the night flee away.

And in regard to imputative righteousness, some Christians affirm that the righteousness of Christ (wrought without us) being imputed to believers, they are thereby justified without any works of righteousness carried on in us, by and through the operation of the Grace of God – we yielding thereunto and cooperating therewith. But according to that great testimony of the apostle Paul, where he asserts that, "The Grace of God that bringeth salvation hath appeared unto all men, teaching us that denying ungodliness and worldly lusts, we should live soberly, righteously, and godly in this present world" (Titus 2nd 11th & 12th).

Now will any be so inconsistent with Truth and Righteousness as to assert that a man is justified merely by the imputative righteousness that

---

[1] 1 Corinthians 1:14-17
[2] 2 Corinthians 11:5
[3] 1 Corinthians 7:17-19
[4] Shake off: give up the use of

Christ wrought in the outward manifestation – without his coming to know in his own experience, those works of righteousness wrought in him, as above expressed by the apostle? And which he must be a party in or they cannot be wrought, as mere grace (or a mere belief in grace) does not do the work of righteousness. But faith in the sufficiency of the grace is the first previous work of the mind of man. But if that belief is not carried into effect, that faith cannot save him – for faith without works is dead, being alone, just as the body without the spirit.

And I think the conclusive arguments of the apostle James are quite sufficient to prove these things to every judicious mind. For although the harlot Rahab had (from what appears) a full belief that Israel's armies would conquer the land of Canaan – and it is likely many thousands more of the Canaanites had the same belief – but as none others of them added good works to their faith but she, consequently none others were saved.[1]

Likewise, Abraham believed he was required to sacrifice his son, as the scripture assures us. But had he not went forward to put it in execution, his faith, instead of being imputed to him for righteousness,[2] would have greatly administered to his condemnation. And instead of becoming the friend of God, he would have been cast out of his favor, so that by his works only was his faith made perfect.

But the great error of the generality[3] of professed Christians lies in not making a right distinction between the works that men do in their own will and by the leadings of their own carnal wisdom, and those works that the true believer does in the will and wisdom of God. For although the former – let them consist in what they will, whether in prayers, or preaching, or any other devotional exercises – are altogether evil. So on the contrary, those of the latter – let them consist in what they may, whether in plowing, in reaping, or in any handicraft labor, or in any other service, temporal or spiritual, as they will in all be accompanied with the peace and presiding of their Heavenly Father – so all they do will be righteous and will be imputed to them as such. And these, and these only, will witness the blessing pronounced by the royal psalmist, where he saith, "Blessed is he whose transgression is forgiven, whose sin is covered. Blessed is the man unto whom the Lord imputeth not iniquity, and in whose spirit there is no guile."[4] And who are those whom the royal prophet here designates? Why none but such who have carefully and strictly adhered to the teaching of the Grace of God, and who by its teaching and aid, have denied themselves of all ungodliness and worldly

---

[1] James 2:25
[2] James 2:23, Romans 4:3 & 9, & Galatians 3:6
[3] Generality: people in general
[4] Psalm 32:1-2

lusts, and have come to live soberly, righteously, and godly in this present world, "Looking for the blessed hope and the glorious appearing of the great God and our Savior, Jesus Christ, who gave himself for us, that he might redeem us from all iniquity and purify unto himself a peculiar people, zealous of good works."[1]

And in order to prove the consistency of Christian ministers taking pay, and making contracts with the people for their preaching, and letting themselves out to the highest bidders, he brought forward quotations from the same Paul, who is so very shrewd[2] against hirelings – showing both by his example and precepts, that it is more blessed to give than to receive,[3] and that parents or leaders ought to care for the children, and not the children for the parents.[4]

The quotations he brought forward were founded principally on these two, 1 Corinthians 9th 13th & 14th. "Do ye not know that they which minister about holy things live of the things of the temple, and they which wait at the altar are partakers with the altar? Even so hath the Lord ordained that they that preach the gospel should live of the gospel."

In order to understand correctly how far proof will arise from these passages of scripture, it will be necessary to consider the ground upon which the priesthood was established under the law – and likewise the reason and ground upon which their maintenance was instituted – because it was all a work of Perfect Wisdom. And first, the dispensation of the law was outward and local, so likewise was the priesthood – none being eligible to that office but the family of Levi. And in consequence of their being appointed to that office, they were deprived of having their portion or allotment in the land, but the Lord was to be their portion – except that they were to have room for residence and some suburbs about their dwellings for their convenience.[5] And their office was to kill and prepare the sacrifices that the people brought of their holy things as offerings to the Lord, so that they were under the necessity of doing a great deal of manual labor for the people. And therefore, in order that they might have a livelihood among their brethren, the Lord had let one-twelfth (that is, Levi's lot) to farm among his brethren. And they were bound to return to their brethren (the Levites) one-tenth of their increase to reward them – not only for the abundant manual labor they were bound to do for them, but also in consideration of their having the improvement and profits arising from Levi's portion of the promised land.

---

[1] Titus 2:12-14
[2] Shrewd: severe, harsh, or stern
[3] Acts 20:35
[4] 2 Corinthians 12:14
[5] Joshua 14:4

Now to make a right bearing between the shadow and substance, and render it eligible under the gospel for its ministers to take pay, they must be such as are immediately called (as was the house of Levi). And in consequence, they must be deprived of any allotment in the land – saving room for residence and some small suburbs. They must likewise be under the unavoidable obligation of doing a great deal of manual labor in outward things – or otherwise they are not entitled to any outward pay. And all this only as their duty to him who hath called and appointed them without making any contract with the people at all for their service – for this was not admissible under that dispensation, for all that did that were reproached by the Lord's prophets as hirelings. An instance to the point is the case of Micah (Judges 17th 5th), who had a house of idol gods. And he hired a Levite to be his priest, and gave him for his service ten shekels of silver by the year, and a suit of apparel and his victuals. And indeed, we have in this Levite a true specimen of a hireling, for when the Danites proposed to his consideration, which would be best for him – whether to be a priest to the house of one man or to a tribe and family in Israel – he soon solved the question, and it made his heart glad. And he took Micah's ephod, teraphim, and graven image – and added theft to covetousness – and went with the Danites, and became their idol priest.[1]

Secondly, we are next to consider the perfect analogy between the service of the priesthood under the law and their wages agreeable to Paul's expressions, "They that minister about holy things, live of the things of the temple, and they that wait at the altar are partakers with the altar."[2] Now the things of the temple and of the altar were all the Lord's things. And as the priests and ministers were also the Lord's, he rewarded them out of his own holy things – and justice required that it should be so. And the priests under the law had no right to call on the people for any pay, because there was no contract between them. So likewise under the gospel, the Lord's true ministers must be such as are immediately called of God – as was Aaron. But as there is no outward holy land under the gospel, so neither is there any outward holy offerings or sacrifices, nor any outward holy temple or altar of man's building – so likewise, no outward victims to be slain or consecrated, hence no outward reward. But the Lord's ministers under the gospel are all called and commissioned by his Spirit, and clothed with his power and authority[3] to preach the gospel – not with wisdom of words, lest the cross of Christ should be made of none effect.[4] For the preaching of the cross is to them that perish, foolishness.

---

[1] Judges 17 & 18
[2] 1 Corinthians 9:13
[3] Luke 9:1
[4] 1 Corinthians 1:17

But unto such as are saved, it is the power of God.[1] Hence those who preach the gospel, live of the gospel.[2] That is, as the gospel is the power of God,[3] which is communicated to the people by gospel ministry, by which they are fed and comforted spiritually – as the Israelites were outwardly, by their outward sacrifices, of which the priests who ministered took their share with the people. So likewise, the ministers of the gospel, who minister to the people spiritually in holy things, they also take their share and are made to rejoice together,[4] spiritually and mutually.

And herein consists the true analogy between the shadow and substance – the first being the type (which consisted in outward things) and the latter the anti-type (consisting in spiritual things). For if the reward of the Lord's ministers under the gospel for their gospel labors is to consist in outward temporal things, and likewise the reward of the Lord's ministers under the law was of the same kind, then it will no longer hold (as is generally agreed by Christians) that the first is type and the latter its anti-type – but it will be only type for type and shadow for shadow. Of course, we must look for another dispensation in order to do away the shadow and make way for the substance. But thanks be to God, who giveth us the victory through our Lord Jesus Christ,[5] who is the end of the law to all those that believe[6] and are witnesses of his spiritual appearance in their hearts to take away sin and finish transgression and fulfill all righteousness[7] in those who willingly deny themselves and take up their cross daily and follow him in the way of regeneration. Even so, let it be, saith my spirit, with the spirits of the faithful. Amen forever.

Sixth Day: I had an appointed meeting in the town of Jamaica at the 3rd hour after noon. It was in the main a favored meeting, although long in gathering. The truths delivered had an affecting reach on many minds, and I was made thankful for the precious solemnity that prevailed over the meeting. And we parted under a comfortable sense thereof. After which, I returned home, and found my family well, and my mind clothed with peace – which favor inspires grateful acknowledgments to the Bountiful Author of every blessing.

Engagements at & about home

Seventh Day: Rested with my family.

---

[1] 1 Corinthians 1:18
[2] 1 Corinthians 9:14
[3] Romans 1:16
[4] John 4:36
[5] 1 Corinthians 15:57
[6] Romans 10:4
[7] Matthew 3:15

First Day: Attended our meeting to good satisfaction. And the three following days, spent with my family and in my family concerns.

Fifth Day: Attended our preparative meeting – previous to the sitting of which, I attended a funeral of one of our neighbors. The corpse was laid[1] in our meetinghouse yard and the people (after the funeral) came into the meeting. It was a large collection, in which the truths of the gospel were largely opened to the people, and the humbling power of Truth spread over the assembly, to the contriting many hearts.

Sixth and Seventh Days: Spent in my family concerns.

First Day, 16th: Attended our own meeting – sat it through in silence. It was laborous and exercising in the forepart, in which I felt reduced into a state of baptism with and for the dead. But as I abode in the patience, toward the close Light sprang up and relieved from the burden.

Second Day: Spent in my temporal concerns. What a strict and continual guard and watch it requires, when engaged in any worldly business, to keep the mind free and loose from everything of a terrestrial nature, so that at the first beck[2] or motion of the Divine Intelligencer,[3] we may be ready to obey and submit willingly to its holy requiring without consulting with flesh and blood.

Third Day: I attended the funeral of a deceased Friend. A meeting was held on the occasion at the place of her residence. The neighborhood was mostly of the Presbyterian order, many of whom attended. I had an open time among them to declare of the things pertaining to the kingdom of heaven. Many gospel truths were plainly set forth and exalted over all untruth and error. It was indeed a season thankfully to be remembered and my heart was bowed in grateful acknowledgments to the great and Blessed Author of all our mercies.

Fourth Day: At the funeral yesterday, I was requested by several of my Friends to attend the funeral of a deceased friendly man, who had been a professor among the Methodists, but whom I had for some time believed was pretty fully convinced of the principles of our profession, but the trial of parting with his fellow professors and making a full surrender had kept him back. But being brought on a bed of languishing,[4] he yielded and acknowledged to the truth, and desired that in future that his family would attend Friends Meetings. And towards his close, in order to give full testimony to his belief, requested in a solemn manner that after his decease, his body might be taken into Friends Meetinghouse at Bethpage (which was not far from his dwelling) and a meeting held there at his

---

[1] Lay: place in a grave or bury
[2] Beck: the slightest indication of a command, e.g., a nod
[3] Intelligencer: one who conveys information
[4] Psalm 41:3

funeral, and desired that I might be requested to attend. On consideration of the subject, Friends were easy to comply with his request and a meeting was held accordingly. It proved a very solemn, affecting time. Many hearts were tendered, and much brokenness and contrition were manifest in the meeting, through the prevalence of the divine power that accompanied the word preached. Surely it was the Lord's doing, and truly marvelous in the eyes of his people.

And O, saith my spirit! What shall we render unto the Lord for all his benefits? For his mercies are new every morning.

Fifth Day: Attended our monthly meeting, and on Sixth Day, our Preparative Meeting of Ministers and Elders – in both of which, my mind was engaged to stir up Friends to more watchfulness and circumspection for the right ordering of the concerns of the society and maintenance of our Christian discipline.

Seventh Day: Spent in my family concerns and ended the week with a quiet mind.

First Day, 23rd of 4th month: Attended our meeting in silence. It was rather an exercising, dull time, but we ought not to murmur, for if we had had our deserts, it might have been more so.

Compliance with War Taxes

The rest of this week principally taken up in attending our Quarterly Meeting in New York. It was rather an exercising time in the general, for not only the answers to the queries from the several monthly meetings manifested many deficiencies as to the right support of our Christian testimonies and discipline, but the diversity of sentiment among the active members respecting the full support of our testimony against war also produced much exercise to the faithful – especially in regard to the active compliance in the payment of a tax levied by the general government of the United States for carrying on war and other purposes of the government, which many Friends believed could not be actively complied with consistently with our testimony on that head. And for refusing the payment of thereof, a number of Friends had suffered in their property by distrain[1] to a considerable amount more than the tax demanded – some even three or four-fold – whilst some others actively complied and paid the tax, and justified themselves in so doing, which caused considerable altercation in the meeting. Nevertheless, I believe Friends were generally preserved in a good degree of harmony with each other.

My mind was deeply baptized into the weak state of society, and I labored in the ability received to stimulate and encourage Friends to

---

[1] Distrain: the seizure of goods or money by the state in recompense for unpaid taxes

faithfulness and perseverance, that so all our precious testimonies for the Prince of Peace might be held up and exalted as a standard to the nations.[1]

First Day, 30th: A silent meeting.

The rest of this week spent in my family cares, except attending our Fifth Day Meeting, which I sat in silence.

First Day, 7th of 5th month: I sat our meeting again in silence. The repeated seasons of rest that I have witnessed since returning from my arduous labor in New York have brought to my remembrance the saying of the dear Master to his disciples, when returned from the service they had been sent about in visiting and preaching repentance to the Israelites and healing their sick, etc. "Come ye yourselves apart into a desert place, and rest awhile."[2] I accounted it a favor, for which I was thankful to the Bountiful Author of all our blessings.

No particular call to any religious service during this week, except in attention to our preparative meeting. Silent in the meeting for worship.

First Day, 14th: Indisposition of body prevented my attending meeting. Therefore, spent the day quietly at home and in reading a portion of Mosheim's *Ecclesiastical History*[3] of the Fifth Century, and which is indeed enough to astonish any sensible, considerate man. To think how the professors of that day could be hardy[4] enough to call themselves Christians, while the conduct of the very best of them seemed rather to resemble demons than Christians – using every artifice that their human wisdom could invent to raise themselves to power and opulence, and crush down their opposers by almost every cruelty that power, envy, and malice could inflict – to the entire scandal of the Christian name, and changing the pure, meek, merciful, suffering, and undefiled religion of Jesus into an impure, unmerciful, cruel, bloody, and persecuting religion. For each of those many varied sects of professed Christians (in their turn), as they got the power of the civil magistrates on their side, would endeavor – by the sword, by severe edicts, and banishment – to reduce and destroy all those who dissented from them, although their opinions

---

[1] Jeremiah 50:2 & 51:27

[2] Mark 6:31

[3] Johann Lorenz von Mosheim was a German Lutheran divine and Church historian. His *Ecclesiastical History* (full title: *An ecclesiastical history, ancient and modern, from the birth of Christ to the beginning of the present century: In which the rise, progress, and variations of Church power are considered in their connexion with the state of learning and philosophy, and the political history of Europe during that period*) was first published in 1726 in Latin. An American edition was printed in 1797-99. It was considered objective in its day, but the American edition included an eight-page addition, titled "Vindication of the Quakers," disputing Mosheim's characterisation of the sect.

[4] Hardy: bold or audacious

were not a whit more friendly to real, genuine Christianity than the tenets of their opposers. For all were – in great measure, if not entirely – adulterated and apostatized from the true spirit of Christianity that breathes peace on earth and good will to man.

The rest of the week, I spent in my family cares, except Fifth Day, which was the time of our monthly meeting, in which the women's meeting brought forward for our consideration and concurrence requests to be joined in membership for eight individuals. Six of these were children, at the request of their father. Another, a minor of about ten years, who appeared very desirous of membership – she sent forward her request, joined by her parents. The other, an adult of a promising aspect, the mother of several children – she had been brought up and educated in the Episcopal profession, but being favored with opportunity of attending Friends Meetings, was convinced of the Truth as held by us and cheerfully submitted to the cross, accounting the reproaches of Christ a greater treasure than all the comfort and delights that could be found among her former associates in an outside, pompous[1] profession. Their requests were all admitted by the meeting. It was, I think, a comfortable instructive season.

First Day, 21st of 5th month: While sitting in our meeting, my mind was led into a consideration of the testimony of the apostle John where he assures us, agreeable to Truth and right reason[2] that, "God is love, and that they who dwell in love, dwell in God, and God in them."[3]

My mind was opened to set forth to the people the excellency of this state and the certainty of its possible attainments by all such as sincerely desire salvation. And in order to its attainment, [they] are willing, through and by the leading and teaching of divine grace – which the apostle Paul assures us (agreeable to our own sensible experience) has appeared to all men[4] – to forego all our selfish and creaturely inclination, and to deny self, and by bearing our cross daily to a full crucifixion of the old man with all his corrupt and ungodly deeds, and thereby come to know a putting on the new man[5] – even Christ or a salvation state – agreeable to another declaration of the same apostle, where he asserts that, "He that is in Christ

---

[1] Pompous: characterized by pomp or a stately show

[2] Right reason: this is a term that figures prominently in the writings of some early Friends. In the seventeenth century, the mind was understood to be a property of the soul and right reason referred to thinking under divine guidance, as opposed to ordinary reasoning. Although Hicks seems to use the term in the same way, it is not clear that he recognizes the distinction. He may mean only "correct or accurate reasoning" rather than "divinely guided reasoning."

[3] 1 John 4:16

[4] Titus 2:11

[5] Ephesians 4:24 & Colossians 3:10

is a new creature, all old things are done away, and all things become new, and all things of God."[1]

I was likewise led to show the good fruits that would be the natural result of such a state – as certain as good fruit from a good tree[2] – for we should no longer love as man loved in his fallen state, from any selfish motive – self being slain – but we should love as God, with a disinterested[3] love. And then, not our friends and neighbors only, but our greatest enemies also, and become qualified sincerely to pray to God for them.[4] Hence, we should then be brought to discover that all such among Christians who pray for the downfall or overcoming of their enemies by force of war – or by any other means than pure disinterested love – pray not in a Christian spirit, nor by the leading and influence of the Spirit of God, but in their own spirit, and by the leading and influence of the spirit of antichrist. Therefore, such prayers are not heard, but are an abomination in the sight of a pure and holy God,[5] who cannot behold iniquity with approbation. My mind was largely and impressively opened on the subject, and with solemn weight left it upon the auditory, which was larger than usual. May it have its desired effect is the sincere desire of my spirit.

Second Day: I attended the funerals of two elderly men of Bethpage Meeting – they were neighbors. They were both interred in the meeting's ground at the same time – the one a member, the other educated among Friends, but had lost his right.[6] A meeting was held on the occasion. There was a very large collection of people, and it proved a solemn and, I trust, an instructive time to some present. May it fasten as a nail in a sure place.

At New York Yearly Meeting

The rest of this week (except the usual weekly attendance of our meeting) was spent in family cares and in preparation for the attendance of our approaching yearly meeting, which opened with the Meeting for Ministers and Elders on Seventh Day. But through indisposition in a branch of my family, I was prevented attending at the first opening, but got to the city seasonably to attend the First Day Meetings. Was in the morning at Pearl Street, which I think was a favored, edifying season. In the afternoon, I was at Liberty Street. And although the meeting was

---

[1] 2 Corinthians 5:17-18
[2] Matthew 7:17
[3] Disinterested: unbiased by self-interest, free of self-seeking
[4] Matthew 5:44
[5] Luke 16:15
[6] Lost his right: had lost his membership in the Society of Friends or been disowned

pretty large, and in a good degree solemn, yet it was an exercising season to the living sensible members.

In those large meetings, where Friends are collected from various parts – the weak and the strong together – and especially in those for worship, it is very essentially necessary that Friends get inward and wait in their proper gifts – keeping in view their place and standing in society, especially those in the ministry. For otherwise, there is danger from a desire to do good – of being caught with the enemy's transformations, particularly with those that are young and of small experience. For we seldom sit in meetings but some prospect or another presents that has a likeness (in its first impression) to the right thing. And as these feel a natural timidity of speaking in large meetings, and in the presence of their elderly Friends, they – apprehending they are likely to have something to offer – are suddenly struck with the fear of man,[1] and thereby are prevented from centering down into their gifts, so as to discover whether it is a right motion or not. And the old accuser of the brethren,[2] who is always ready with his transformations to deceive, charges with unfaithfulness and disobedience – by which they are driven to act without any clear prospect, and find little to say, except making an apology for their thus standing – by which they often disturb the meeting, and prevent others who are rightly called to the work, and thereby wound the minds of the living, baptized members.

On Second Day, the meeting for discipline opened and continued by adjournments until Sixth Day. And although divers weaknesses were manifest in transacting of the business – for want of a deep indwelling with the pure Spring of Life and each patiently abiding in his own proper gifts without envying others – yet I think in the main, it was a favored meeting. Divers brethren were largely opened to speak to subjects of concern that came before us in the life and in the clear demonstration of the Spirit, as scribes well instructed, bringing out of the heavenly treasury things new and old.[3]

We returned home on Seventh Day:

Back Home

First Day, 4th of 6th month: Being invited to the funeral of a young woman in the compass of Westbury Meeting, I attended that meeting, which was very large – much more so that usual – occasioned in part by the funeral. And although the forepart of the meeting was dull and exercising, yet as my mind centered under a patient exercise and travail,

---

[1] Proverbs 29:25
[2] Revelation 12:10
[3] Matthew 13:52

way gradually opened to communication, in which I was enabled, through adorable condescension, largely and livingly to declare to the people of the things concerning the kingdom of heaven, and their own present and everlasting peace. It was a season of great favor, thankfully to be remembered.

The rest of this week, I spent at home, in usual peace of mind – nothing transpiring worthy of particular notice.

First Day, 11th: My mind was brought under exercise as I sat in our meeting, in remembrance of Paul's declaration how that most men mind their own things, and not the things that are Jesus Christ's.[1] And as I continued under the exercise, way opened to communication, which brought a comfortable solemnity over the meeting.

Second and Third Days: I spent in attending our Meeting for Sufferings in New York – a service that I have been under appointment to for near forty years.

Fourth Day: Most of this day spent in some necessary repairs about my house. How much is saved by timely and prudent care.

Fifth Day: Being our monthly meeting, at which we had the acceptable company of our Friend, John Comly,* a fellow-laborer in the gospel with whom I felt near sympathy and unity in travail. I accompanied him the next day to a meeting he had appointed at Matinecock, in which he was favored with a pretty large testimony in the plainness and simplicity of the gospel. I took my leave of him and his companion, Stephen Comfort, that afternoon and returned home.

Seventh Day: Spent in my common avocations and the week closed with a peaceful mind.

First Day, 18th: My mind, towards the close of our meeting, was opened into a view of the excellency and advantage of having our minds actuated[2] invariably by a principle of strict and impartial justice, and of having just ideas and apprehensions of the divine character – as nothing short of it is able to establish our faith in God on its right basis, and to give us an unshaken hope and trust in his divine sufficiency, and bring us to experience in possession that love of our benevolent Creator and of our fellow creatures that casteth out all fear.[3] As I communicated, the prospect enlarged and brought a solemn weight over the meeting. And we parted under a sense of the favor.

The rest of the week was spent in close attention to my temporal concerns, except attending our Fifth Day Meeting as usual.[4] And should

---

[1] Philippians 2:21
[2] Actuate: inspire or enliven
[3] 1 John 4:18
[4] The rest of the paragraph was deleted from the printed *Journal*.

Matinecock (New York) Meetinghouse

have closed the week as usual with a peaceful and tranquil mind, had not one of my Friends improperly interfered in business of concern between one of my neighbors and myself, respecting laying out ground for a turnpike, and in which his injudicious conduct very much interrupted my mind. How very necessary it is, even for men of good intentions, to be very careful that they do not officiously meddle with that which is not their proper business, lest they expose themselves to the censure of being busybodies in other men's matters.

First Day, 25th: Sat our meeting today in solemn silence, being much depressed in mind on account of the improper conduct of some of my Friends – fellow members in society – by which I apprehended the noble cause we had espoused was in danger of being hurt and the unity of the Church broken, which to me was a cause of real sorrow of heart.

Except attending our Fifth Day Meeting, which I sat in silence, the rest of this week was occupied in my common vocations and ended with a peaceful mind, which is a hidden treasure of more value than the golden wedge of Ophir.[1]

First Day, 2nd of 7th month: As I sat in our meeting, my mind was early impressed with that important scripture passage of the psalmist –

---

[1] Isaiah 13:12

"Let God arise, let his enemies be scattered."[1] It led to communication, in which my mind was largely opened to set forth the very necessary truths it comprehended – especially as it regards man's salvation, for it shows clearly that man may prevent his thus arising and thereby hinder his own salvation. And secondly, it shows, that unless we know him to arise, and become supreme and chief ruler in our hearts agreeable to his own good will and pleasure, we cannot be saved nor come to know his enemies to be scattered. Therefore, it becomes us, as poor helpless creatures, patiently to wait and quietly to hope for his arising, with penitent hearts and willing minds – ready to receive him in the way of his coming, although it may be as a refiner with fire or as a fuller with soap.[2] And it is also necessary for us to know this arising to be within us and not without us, and to be with power – binding the man of sin and son of perdition (which is self), or the strong man armed, who while he rules, his goods are at peace. But when we permit a stronger than he (who only is God) to come in or arise with power, he will bind the strong man armed, and cast him out, and then he will spoil his goods,[3] that is, cleanse the heart from all the old rubbage[4] of sin and uncleanness, and purify his temple, and make it a fit receptacle for his holiness to dwell in. It was a season of favor. Many gospel truths were clearly opened to the auditory who gave solid attention. May they fix as a nail in a sure place.

I was under considerable bodily indisposition most of this week – on Fifth Day, so much so as almost to give up the prospect of getting to meeting. But put on my usual resolution and went, and was glad in so doing, as there I met with that peace of God that passeth all understanding,[5] which is only known by being felt. And [I] had to declare to my Friends how good it is to trust in the Lord with all the heart, and lean not to our own understandings,[6] lest they fail us.

Sixth Day: I attended the funeral of a kinsman – a neighbor who had spent most of his life in a careless, irreligious manner – very seldom attending any religious meetings. Of course, he was very ignorant as it respected the things of God and his own salvation. But for a year or more before his death, he was greatly afflicted with the cancer in his face – from which he suffered long and very deeply – which brought him to a solemn consideration respecting his latter end. And I had a hope it worked for his good, as it brought him into a state of resignation, insomuch that he bore

---

[1] Psalm 68:1
[2] Malachi 3:2
[3] Luke 11:21-22
[4] Rubbage: rubbish
[5] Philippians 4:7
[6] Proverbs 3:5

his affliction with much patience and quietude of mind. My heart and my mouth were opened on the occasion to warn the people and to call their attention to the necessity of an early preparation for death – showing them how it bordered even on presumption for such poor, impotent,[1] helpless creatures as we are, whose time is dealt to us by moments,[2] that we should even to dare to close our eyes to sleep without first being well-assured that our peace was made with our great and gracious Creator. Many minds were considerably humbled, and I hope the labor will not be lost, but be as bread cast upon the waters, that some may gather after many days.

First Day, 9th of 7th month: We had a comfortable, favored meeting today. My mind was also set at liberty to preach the gospel in the clear demonstration of the Spirit, and to show unto the people that the reason why they were not healed of their many infirmities was not because there was not balm in Gilead and a physician there,[3] but because they were not willing to seek him in the right way and receive him in the way of his coming, which is inwardly, as a refiner with fire or a fuller with soap to purify from all the old leaven[4] of self, and to cleanse the heart[5] from all self-righteousness and self-sufficiency – that a thorough crucifixion of the old man with all his unrighteous deeds may be witnessed, and the creature set at liberty to serve the Lord in newness of life.[6] The meeting closed with solemn supplication and thanksgiving for the Lord's continued mercy.

Second, Third, and Fourth Days: Spent in my family affairs – mostly attended with sweet peace of mind, although accompanied with much bodily pain, which is more or less my common lot. But what a great portion of severe bodily pain may be endured without a murmuring thought, while accompanied with true peace of mind and a conscience void of offense toward God and man. A rich consoling treasure!

Fifth Day: This being the time of our preparative meeting at which our queries were answered, I had to admonish Friends to feel deeply after their own states. For as it is by individuals that meetings are composed, so every individual ought to know how far their particular state corresponds with what is queried after – that so by a united labor and an inward investigation of our own particular states, we may be enabled to form true and righteous answers to the superior meetings. For if they are false, it will

---

[1] Impotent: physically weak or disabled
[2] This is a near quote from *A New-Year's Thought and Prayer*, a hymn by John Newton, who also wrote *Amazing Grace*.
[3] Jeremiah 8:22
[4] 1 Corinthians 5:7-8
[5] James 4:8
[6] Romans 6:4

be accounted lying – and that not unto men, but unto God[1] – and thereby our queries be rendered very hurtful to us, instead of being helpful.

Sixth and Seventh Days: I occupied myself in my usual business, not feeling any particular religious draft – saving the necessity of keeping up the daily watch, that no intruding thoughts lead into temptation or prevent my daily converse[2] with the God of my salvation, whose presiding fear I have long experienced to be the only sure antidote against all evil.

First Day, 16th: My mind was led forth in our meeting today in a large, clear testimony clothed with gospel authority, which was introduced with the following apostolic exhortation (Romans 12th 9th & 10th), "Let love be without dissimulation. Abhor that which is evil. Cleave to that which is good. Be kindly affectioned one to another with brotherly love, in honor preferring one another." I was led to show that this undissembling love was not to be known by man in his fallen nature, but only by the regenerated soul – the new man in Christ, who had come to know in degree of the partaking of the divine nature,[3] as no other nature is congenial with this love – a love which the beloved apostle tells us casteth out all fear. It was a season of favor, thankfully to be remembered.

The remaining part of this week was mainly employed in helping to gather in our harvest, except attending our monthly meeting on Fifth Day and Preparative Meeting of Ministers and Elders on Sixth Day – both of which were rather dull, poor meetings.

Alas, how the cares and cumbers of this world, like thorns and briars choke the good seed and prevent it bringing forth fruit.[4] Be watchful, O my soul, that so thou mayest know thy seed time and harvest not to fail.

First Day, 23rd: My present allotment is a state of depression and poverty of spirit, but considering myself worthy thereof, I do not complain. In this condition, I accompanied my family to meeting as the best thing I could do – not feeling the least qualification to be in any degree useful to myself or to others, except in a voluntary surrender of myself to be anything or nothing, as he, who has a right to dispose of his own workmanship at his own pleasure, should see meet. But I had not sat long in this submissive state, ere a prospect presented to my mind that opened to a field of labor, in which I had to espouse the Master's cause and demonstrate to the people present the just and indubitable[5] right he had to them and all their labor without the promise of any reward. And

---

[1] Acts 5:4
[2] Converse: conversation
[3] 2 Peter 1:4
[4] Matthew 13:7, Mark 4:7, & Luke 8:7
[5] Indubitable: impossible to doubt

that our true and real felicity – in time and in a future state – solely depended on this complete and willing surrender of ourselves and all we have to his holy and gracious will, as nothing short thereof can produce our real sanctification and adoption.

Second and Third Days: Produced nothing worthy of particular notice.

Fourth Day: Our Quarterly Meeting of Ministers and Elders was held at Westbury. I attended under great depression and poverty of spirit by which my lips were sealed as to any communication. The greatest part of the meeting, I sat resigned to my lot and heard my Friends (or some of them) express their exercise,[1] which was principally directed to ministers and elders – especially in regard to an honest, careful exercise of their gifts as such – and also alluding to the dullness and want of life that too generally attended those meetings. I felt very little effect wrought in the meeting from their labor and could take no part in it. But as I sat patiently waiting and endeavored quietly to endure the cloud that spread itself, or was spread as a veil over the meeting, it clearly opened on my mind that it was not brought over us in consequence of a lack in ministers, as it respects their ministerial gifts, nor from a lack of care in elders in watching over them, but from a much more deep and melancholy cause (to wit) the love and cares of this world and the deceitfulness of riches, which – springing up and gaining the ascendancy in the mind – choke the good seed like the briars and thorns, and render it fruitless.[2] And this produceth such great death and barrenness in our meetings. And as the matter spread with a degree of animation on my mind, I found it my place near the close of the meeting to open the prospect and sound an alarm to Friends, which appeared to have a quickening effect on many minds, and enabled us at parting to renew our trust in the almighty arm of divine sufficiency, and still to believe that the Lord had not altogether forsaken his people,[3] but was still mindful of the seeking remnant of his heritage,[4] and still continued his gracious calls to his backsliding children.[5]

Fifth Day: Was the meeting for discipline. It was likewise rather an exercising season, but I hope attended with some profit.

Sixth Day: Was the parting meeting held for public worship. It was a large, crowded meeting, but was somewhat hurt in the forepart by the appearance of one young in the ministry – by standing too long and manifesting too much animation. And although, I believed he was under the preparing hand, fitting for service in the Church as he keeps low and

---

[1] Express their exercise: offer ministry
[2] Matthew 13:22 & Mark 4:19
[3] Psalm 9:10
[4] Micah 7:18
[5] Jeremiah 3:14 & 22

humble, and does not aspire above his gift into the creaturely animation. For there is great danger (if such are not deeply watchful) of the transformer getting in and raising the mind into too much creaturely zeal and warmth of the animal spirit, whereby they may be deceived and attribute that to the divine power, that only arises from a heated imagination and the natural warmth of their own spirits, and so mar the work of the Divine Spirit on their minds, run before their gift[1] and lose it – or have it taken away from them. Whereby they fall into the condition of some formerly (as mentioned by the prophet), who in their creaturely zeal kindle a fire of their own and walk in the sparks of their own kindling. But these, in the end, have to lie down in sorrow.[2]

Towards the close of the meeting, as Friends kept quiet and solid, way opened for further communication, which brought a comfortable solemnity over the meeting. And we parted from each other with gladdened hearts, under a grateful sense of the Lord's mercy to his unworthy creatures.

Seventh Day: I turned my hand again to my usual industry in my family affairs with a peaceful mind.

First Day, 30th: Devoted this day as usual to the attendance of our own meeting, in which I had not sat long, silently musing, ere my mind was opened into a view of the divine attributes – especially that of God's unchangeableness – and which I had to contrast with the changeable and unstable state of man. And was led in the view thereof to show to the people how that all our infelicity[3] arose out of our unsettled state and the want of being established or fixed on some steadfast and invariable principle. And as there is none other but God, consequently all our true felicity and salvation depends on our being entirely settled and fixed in and upon him. By which, we are brought likewise to witness the same unchangeable state – having the feet of the mind[4] established on the immoveable rock, Christ, the Light of the World and the real spiritual life of all true believers. And that nothing short of this experience ought to satisfy or give rest to any seeking, panting soul[5] after God, its redeemer.

The rest of this week, I attended on my family avocations with a general peace of mind, taking our Fifth Day Meeting in course – nothing

---

[1] Run before their gift: get ahead of the leading of the Holy Spirit
[2] Isaiah 50:11
[3] Infelicity: a state of unhappiness and misfortune
[4] The expression, "feet of the mind" seems to originate in *Of True Resignation* by Jakob Boehme (1575-1624), a German mystic who may have influenced some early Friends, possibly including Isaac Penington (see next)
[5] *Some Directions to the Panting Soul* is one of the major works of Isaac Penington.

unusual occurring, but having daily and continual cause of thankfulness to the Bountiful Author of every blessing, both temporal and spiritual.

First Day, 6th of 8th month: My lot was to suffer the greatest part of our meeting today, until near the close, when I found it my place to unite in a short testimony with a female fellow-laborer in calling the attention of the people to an inward exercise and a faithful improvement of the gift or talent committed to them while time and opportunity offered – that so when called, they might be prepared to render up their accounts with joy.

Spent the six working days of this week as usual in and about home, feeling no call abroad to any religious service, but felt it my incumbent duty simply to wait and to watch at the King's gate.

First Day, 13th: Towards the close of our meeting, my mind was led to view the great and singular advantages that would result to mankind by a full surrender of their wills to the divine will – not only in our religious concerns, but also in things of a temporal nature, and indeed in everything we do and take in hand to do. The subject became very impressive, insomuch that I found it my place to spread it before Friends and the auditory, and to set forth the inconsistency of men and women in first acknowledging the entire supremacy of the Divine Being, and their own dependant state as tenants at will[1] of the sovereign Lord of the universe, and at the same time, presumptuously exercising an independent will and judgment in their temporal concerns – and mostly so even in their religious, insomuch, that without breach of charity, we may safely aver[2] that the generality (even of professed Christians) serve and worship the creature more than they do the Creator. And to which, we may refer the rise of all the misery and wretchedness of man. And that to rise out of his fallen state, he must come to know a complete sinking down into a state of nothingness of self and a full surrender of his will to the divine will, and not to move in anything without being conscientiously satisfied it is in correspondence therewith. Then should we move on safely, and peace of mind would be our daily attendant.

In the course of this week, I was indisposed – being afflicted with much bodily pain – but was enabled to attend our monthly meeting on Fifth Day, at which we received extracts[3] from our yearly and quarterly

---

[1] Tenant at will: one who holds or possesses property solely at the pleasure of the lessor

[2] Aver: declare to be true

[3] Extracts: prior to the publication of books of discipline or of annual minutes, the formal minutes adopted by superior meetings were copied and these extracts were sent to each subordinate meeting. These were collected into a "Book of Extracts" which was used for guidance by local congregations.

meetings, with the printed epistle from London.[1] They furnished suitable advice on several subjects, particularly relative to a right attendance of our religious meetings. The latter, I found my mind impressed with a concern to second[2] and call the careful attention of Friends thereto, as that upon which our religious advancement principally depends.

First Day, 20th: Feeling a draft on my mind to sit with Friends of Bethpage Meeting, I yielded thereto. I sat the meeting mostly in silence – it being rather a dull, low time and but little life discoverable in the meeting. Yet near the close, I felt a small motion leading to communication. And as I gave way thereto, a small stream of life arose and ran through the meeting. And we parted under a sense of its comforting influence, with thankful hearts.[3]

Through the week, I attended to my usual vocations as far as ability of body permitted. Attended our Fifth Day Meeting in silence – was somewhat interrupted by the improper conduct of some of my neighbors, which brought to my remembrance the case of just Lot while in Sodom, as rehearsed[4] by Peter, "For that righteous man dwelling among them, in seeing and hearing, vexed his righteous soul from day to day with their unlawful deeds."[5]

First Day, 27th: My mind was solemnly exercised during the greatest part of our meeting, and deeply impressed with the spirit of prayer and supplication.

O how awful is the prospect of approaching the majesty of heaven in solemn prayer! How it reduces the creature and shows him his entire unworthiness and helpless state. Well might the prophet thus exclaim, "When I heard, my belly trembled! My lips quivered at the voice. Rottenness entered into my bones and I trembled in myself that I might rest in the day of trouble."[6]

As I sat under the humbling prospect, I was strengthened towards the close of the meeting – with a bowed down mind and bended knees – to address my humble petition on behalf of myself and my Friends before the throne of grace, expressive of the desire of my soul that we might be kept

---

[1] At this time, the epistles from London Yearly Meeting were customarily forwarded by other yearly meetings to their subordinate meetings to be read. This practice was to become a point of contention as evangelical theology increasingly entered into the contents of those epistles.
[2] Second: support and encourage
[3] The next paragraph was deleted from the printed *Journal*.
[4] Rehearse: reiterate
[5] 2 Peter 2:8
[6] Habakkuk 3:16

– both old and young – at all times under a humbling sense of the divine fear, as that on which all our safety and preservation depended.

Second and Third Days: I spent with a family of my Friends some distance from home, my wife accompanying me. I, having been for some time under considerable exercise and concern on account of some uneasiness and disunity which subsisted among them – greatly to their hurt – I entered fully into the subject and was favored, through patient perseverance, to bring matters to a peaceful close. For which, I was thankful, as the harmony of the family had been for several years very much interrupted.

Fourth Day: We returned home.

Fifth Day: Attended our midweek meeting, in which I was silent.

Sixth Day: I spent principally in assisting a Friend, who was somewhat straitened[1] in getting along with his husbandry, having been indisposed.

Seventh Day: Attended the funeral of a very ancient woman Friend, an elder in society. She lived to the age of ninety-seven years – an example of prudence and plainness, of an innocent life and conversation, and generally beloved by her acquaintance. A large collection of Friends and others attended. A meeting was held on the occasion, in which I was led to set forth the great and singular advantages the true believer had over the unbeliever, and to show to the people the great necessity of care that we did not place any confidence in a mere traditional or historical belief, without coming to a real experimental knowledge of God and Christ. It was a solemn time – many hearts were tendered with the savor of Truth that spread over the meeting.

First Day, 3rd of 9th month: Feeling a small draft of love and concern to sit with Friends of Westbury at their meeting today, I yielded thereto. It proved rather a low, dull season – very little life felt to be stirring in the meeting – but a little before the close, I felt my mind quickened in the remembrance of the occurrence that took place with Jesus and his disciples a little before he was taken prisoner and carried before Pilate. But in a particular manner, my mind was impressed with the proceedings of Judas the traitor, who (as it opened on my mind) was a true figure of self in man, which is the true son of perdition and man of sin. And I was led in the opening to warn Friends to beware of him – each one in themselves – for otherwise, he would deceive and betray them, as Judas did his Master, and which will as certainly destroy the precious life in us, as that brought Christ to his crucifixion, and which tends to scatter and expose to trial and temptation. It spread with weight over the meeting and many minds were solemnly affected. Surely the Lord's mercy is still great towards his

---

[1] Straitened: constrained

backsliding people, as he continues striving to gather and preserve them from all evil.

The rest of the week, I spent as usual – nothing particular occurring.

First Day, 10th of 9th month: This day, I was pretty closely engaged – attended our own meeting in the morning and an appointed meeting at Jerusalem in the afternoon. Both were meetings of favor, and comforting seasons to the upright in heart.

Second Day: Visited a sick brother.[1] Found him very ill – his case being such as to render his recovery very doubtful. It caused much distress in the family.

O how wise it is for such dependant creatures as we are, and whose stay here is so uncertain, to be always in a state of readiness to meet every probable event. What consolation it affords in such trying seasons, when we can come to say, "Lord, thy servant is ready."[2]

I returned home on Third Day evening.

Fourth and Fifth Days: Employed as usual, and on Sixth Day paid him another visit. Found him much better and the family cheerful.

O how unstable a creature is man! Full and empty, joyful and sorrowful, as things go well or ill. And all this is for want of having the mind centered in and on God, its alone proper object and sure balance of the soul.

I tarried over First Day and had an appointed meeting in the neighborhood. And although not so large as I have sometimes had in that place, yet it was in the main an open, favored season – exciting thankfulness to the Blessed Author of all our mercies.

I returned home that evening, leaving my brother in a favorable way of recovery, attended with a hope that the visitation will be profitable to him and his family, if they rightly improve it.

The rest of the week, I spent at and about home. Attended our monthly meeting on Fifth Day and the funeral of a female relative on Sixth Day, who was taken off very suddenly with an apoplectic fit. Such instances speak a language to survivors very urgent and expressive, "Be ye therefore ready."

First Day, 24th: After a considerable time of silent waiting in our meeting, my mind was quickened in the remembrance of the following declaration of the apostle Paul, "By grace are ye saved through faith, and that not of yourselves. It is the gift of God, not of works, lest any man should boast."[3]

---

[1] Probably Stephen, who died in 1816
[2] 2 Samuel 15:15
[3] Ephesians 2:8-9

The subject opened to communication, wherein I had to unfold to the people the utter incapacity man lay under (in his fallen or natural state) of doing anything that would in the least degree further his salvation or be acceptable to God, as a part of his necessary duty or service to him. And that it would be very unwise and dangerous to presume or attempt any such thing – unwise, because it is impossible for him to effect, and dangerous, lest he should do something that might warm or stir up his own passions (or those of others) in such manner as to apprehend that a degree of the divine power attended – which would tend to lead to a very fatal error, a continuance in the presumption, which can produce no other than darkness and death to the soul. And in which state, they could not possibly avoid boasting and thereby counteract the apostle's doctrine. And indeed, it would be justifiable to boast if we could do the least thing of ourselves without the immediate aid of divine grace. For strict justice cannot deny the ascription[1] of merit to any cause that produces a real good work. But as no mere man can possibly ever be such a cause, so he can never merit any good from his own works, and therefore, never have a right to boast. All this, the truly humble are abundantly sensible of, and therefore dare not attempt anything in a religious way in their own time and will but wait patiently for the immediate inspiring of divine grace – to whose power only, as the procuring cause of our salvation, all merit is due.

The rest of the week, I spent in my usual avocations, not omitting my religious duties as they opened on my mind.

First Day, 1st of 10th month: My mind, while sitting in our meeting today, was led into the consideration of the real necessity there was of each individual coming to know God before they could worship him acceptably in spirit and in truth. For if we are ignorant of him, our worship would be no better than the worship of the Athenians to an unknown God.[2] The subject enlarged and opened to the communication of divers truths of the gospel, and gave cause gratefully to acknowledge the mercy and goodness of our Heavenly Father to his backsliding children.

Thoughts on Horse Racing

The six following days, I was occupied in and about home with a grieved mind most of the time on account of the conduct of some of my neighbors – particularly one of my tenants and one other, who spent the week principally attending on horseracing – a most pernicious practice, leading to more evil than almost any other wicked custom that the loose and the vain are so foolishly addicted to. For it's not only spending our

---

[1] Ascription: giving credit
[2] Acts 17:23

precious time in a vain and wanton manner, but likewise manifests great ingratitude to the Great Author of all our blessings – if not a total disbelief in him. For how can it be supposed that a rational mind, that has a real belief in God, could have hardiness[1] enough to drive a horse in a race to gratify a number of idle and vain spectators? And if for a bribe or a wager, it adds greatly to the sin, as it is then accompanied with covetousness and dishonesty.[2] For from the best observation that I have been able to make upon such men as practiced horseracing for wagers, I have not discovered one but what would make use of every undue method that was in their power to gain their point – provided they could do it in some secret or evasive way, so as to escape the law.

And when we consider that the horse is one of the chiefest of the temporal blessings conferred on man by a gracious and beneficent Providence, to abuse him without cause by driving in a race, where his life and the life of his rider are both at stake (as it sometimes happens that both are killed) is no doubt both cruel and wicked – especially when we consider (as agreeable to the universal observation of mankind) that not one, single, real good ever has or ever can be looked for from it to any man – for the truth of which, I dare appeal to any rational man that was ever in the practice – as a thing that has never produced one hour of real peace of mind.[3] Or not more than the highwayman has found by robbing on the highway, for as both practices arise from the same causes (to wit) self-will and self-gratification, so the effects will be the same to both. And "There is no peace to the wicked,"[4] as saith the Lord by his prophet.

First Day, 8th of 10th month: As I sat in our meeting, the declaration of Paul, introductory to his Epistle to the Hebrews, presented to my mind and opened to a very interesting communication, showing how that, "God, who at sundry times and in divers manners, spake in time past unto the fathers (in Israel) by the prophets, hath in these last days spoken unto us by his Son, whom he hath appointed heir of all things,"[5] which renders it necessary for every true follower of him to hear him in all things – as now, under the gospel dispensation, we have no other sufficient teacher but the Lord Jesus Christ – by his Spirit in our hearts. Therefore, they who do not hear and obey him cannot be saved, but (agreeable to the testimony of Moses), "The wrath of God abideth on them."[6]

---

[1] Hardiness: audacity
[2] The rest of the paragraph was deleted from the printed *Journal*.
[3] The rest of the paragraph was deleted from the printed *Journal*.
[4] Isaiah 48:22 & 57:21
[5] Hebrews 1:1-2
[6] Psalm 78:31

Second and Third Days: Were taken up in attending our Meeting for Sufferings.

The rest of the week, I was occupied in my temporal concerns, except attending our preparative meeting on Fifth Day.

First Day, 15th: Although in going to meeting today my mind was under the impression of poverty and spiritual want, yet I had not sat long ere light sprang up and opened to the communication of divers weighty gospel truths necessary for all to know and believe. In the unfolding whereof, I was led to open to the people how that every birth was clothed in its own proper nature and which must be congenial to the spring or source from whence the birth derived its existence. Hence (agreeable to the apostle Paul's declaration), "The first man is of the earth, earthy. The second man is the Lord from heaven, and as we have borne the image of the earthy, so also we must bear the image of the heavenly."[1] Therefore, as the earthy (or animal part) in man must draw all its succor and support from the earth, and cannot be comforted nor subsist without earthly food, so neither can the spiritual part (or the immortal soul) of man be comforted or subsist in its true life without spiritual food,[2] which I was led to explain in this supposition by way of a simile.

Admitting[3] the animal-man to be immortal, but still clothed in the same animal or earthly nature – in which state, he could derive no comfort nor support from anything but earthly or elementary food and water to nourish him and satisfy his hunger and thirst – and suppose him then deprived of all those earthly comforts, by which, he would be soon brought into the pangs of death (or as one expiring with hunger and thirst) and yet could not die, but his life continued in full vigor – susceptible of all the dying pains of a poor mortal just ready to perish with hunger and thirst in the extreme – and his body exposed to the pinching cold of winter without clothing.

Here, we have a complete view of the wretched state of every fallen man and woman that does not come to experience the new birth and thereby become a partaker of the divine nature – as no other nature can be happy and rejoice in the things of God. Therefore, every man and woman that dies in their fallen state – without witnessing the divine life and nature renewed in them or, as the apostle hath it, who do not witness a being created anew in Christ Jesus unto good works[4] – must inevitably (agreeable to the above simile) be eternally miserable, as in their natural

---

[1] 1 Corinthians 15:47 & 49

[2] The rest of the paragraph and the next two were deleted from the printed *Journal.*

[3] Admit: assume for the sake of argument

4 Ephesians 2:10

state, they have no relish for the things of God nor for the nourishing food of the Kingdom of Heaven, but must be ever under the excruciating pains of death—but yet not able to die, for death will flee from them[1] and leave them to endure their own torments in the furnace of their own preparing.

This and much more, I was led to open in the Light of Truth at this solemn time – for the Lord's power spread over the meeting in a very weighty and sensible manner. And we parted under the precious covering.

O that our hearts might be continually inflamed with gratitude for such unmerited mercy!

A Visit to the Monthly Meetings within the Circuit of Nine Partners Quarterly Meeting in 1815

Fifth Day: Since First Day, I have been busily employed in putting my family affairs in order, so as to leave home in order to fulfill my appointment from the yearly meeting to visit the Quarterly Meeting of Nine Partners with the monthly meetings constituting it in company with a committee for that purpose.

This being the time to set out, I also attended the funeral of a deceased neighbor on Fourth Day, where I had a favorable opportunity of expostulating[2] with a large assembly on the fallen and weak and helpless state of man and the necessity of his witnessing, through the aid of divine Grace or Spirit of his Creator, a redemption therefrom, as the only means whereby he can be saved, and be again renewed into his divine image, and become a partaker of his real nature – as no other nature can be happy in the enjoyment of him.

I accordingly left home on Sixth Day, 20th of 10th month 1815. My wife and daughter, Elisabeth, set out with me with a view of bearing me company in part of the visit. We rode through New York to Westchester and lodged with our kind Friends, Thomas and Elizabeth Underhill, in our way to West Hartford in Connecticut – that being the first monthly meeting to be taken in the arrangement made by the committee.

Seventh Day: We continued our journey to Middlesex and lodged with our Friends, Samuel and Phebe Bishop.

First Day: Attended Friends Meeting there. And some notice being given to the neighboring inhabitants of our coming, the meeting was large. And through the condescending goodness of the Shepherd of Israel, it proved a comfortable, edifying season. The doctrines of the gospel were

---

[1] Revelation 9:6
[2] Expostulate: to plainly demonstrate in a friendly manner

freely and largely communicated and Truth raised into dominion over all to the glory of his Grace, who is over all, God blessed forever.

Second Day: We proceeded on our journey, taking Bridgeport in the way, in order to visit a female Friend of our acquaintance who lived in that town – far separated from her Friends and relatives. Her husband, being a seafaring man, was from home on a voyage. She was comforted and glad in the visit, although short. After dining with her and staying as long as our time would admit, we proceeded that afternoon to Woodbury and lodged with Elijah Sherman, a friendly man of the Methodist persuasion and an old acquaintance, where we were hospitably entertained.

The next day, we rode to West Hartford and put up with our kind Friend, Ruth Gilbert, widow of Charles Gilbert.

Fourth Day: Being their usual middle week meeting, we attended. And although small, [it] was nevertheless a precious favored season. The states of those present were spoken to in the fresh flowings of gospel love, to the tendering and contriting the hearts of most present. Surely it was the Lord's doing, and worthy of deep thankfulness to him, as the Alone Author of every blessing.

Fifth Day: Was their monthly meeting – held at this time out of its usual course to accommodate the yearly meeting's committee. It proved a satisfactory season. The few Friends constituting it appeared to conduct the business which came before them in a good degree of propriety and harmony.

Sixth Day: We took leave of our Friends there and rode to Oblong – a long, tedious day's journey of about fifty-five miles – and the way rough and hilly. We lodged with our Friend, Azariah Howland, and the next day attended Oblong Monthly Meeting, which proved, through heavenly help (particularly the part for worship) a comfortable, edifying meeting. And near the close, feeling a draft on my mind to be there the next day at their First Day Meeting, I informed Friends thereof before we parted. And notice being given to the neighboring people of my intention, the meeting was large. And through the unmerited condescension of our Gracious Helper, ability was given to preach the gospel in the clear demonstration of the Spirit and with power, to the humbling and contriting the spirits of most present. And Truth raised into dominion, to the praise of his Grace, who calleth us to glory and virtue.[1] After this favored meeting, we parted with our Friends under a lively sense of the Lord's goodness, and rode that evening to Nine Partners and took quarters with our kind relations, Isaac and Anne Thorne.

---

[1] 2 Peter 1:3

Oblong (New York) Meetinghouse

The two following days, we attended the Monthly Meetings of Nine Partners and Oswego, which were in the main solemn, edifying seasons.

Fourth Day: We rode to Cornwall, leaving my wife and daughter with our relations at Nine Partners.

And the three following days, attended the Monthly Meetings of Cornwall, Marlborough, and Rosendale Plains. And with grateful hearts, we had abundant cause to acknowledge the goodness and never-failing loving-kindness of our Heavenly Father in condescending to be with us from day to day – making bare his arm for our help, furnishing with ability for the work we were engaged in – both in meetings for worship and those for the right ordering of the affairs of the Church – crowning the several opportunities with his gracious presence, to the solemnizing and tendering the hearts of the people, and comforting and gladdening the sincere in heart, who prefer the prosperity of Zion to their chiefest joy.

First Day: We attended Marlborough Meeting. And some notice being given to those of other societies of our being there, the meeting was large – the house much crowded. And through divine favor extended to us, it proved an awakening, precious season. The testimony of Truth went forth with power and reigned victoriously over all.

We tarried here until the next day, and then returned to Nine Partners in order to attend the quarterly meeting, which opened the next day with a Meeting of Ministers and Elders. Here, I again met my wife and daughter.

The quarterly meeting closed on Fourth Day afternoon and was in the main an instructive, favored season – although considerably interrupted by the imprudence of a Friend in his unwarrantable opposition to a concern that was opened to draw Friends off from the too free and unnecessary use of articles that were the produce of the labor of the poor, enslaved, black people, and which was wrest[1] from them by their hard-hearted taskmasters in a state of cruel bondage. For whose sufferings, my mind was deeply exercised.

Fifth Day: Rode to Stanford and attended the Quarterly Meeting of Ministers and Elders, which through condescending goodness proved a comfortable, edifying opportunity, as was that for discipline the following day.

The quarterly meeting closed with a meeting for worship on Seventh Day, and was a season thankfully to be remembered by every sensible mind present. For he that opens and none can shut, and shuts and none can open, was graciously near and condescended to open many deep and necessary doctrines of the gospel in a full and clear manner, in the demonstration of the Spirit attended with power, to the humbling and solemnizing the minds of most present, and exaltation of Truth, which was raised into dominion and ran sweetly over all.

We returned that evening to Nine Partners, intending to sit with Friends there the next day. And some public notice being given of our being there, the meeting was large. And although it proved rather an exercising season and the labor hard, yet I trust it was a season of profit and instruction to many.

After this meeting, feeling myself released from any further service (the committee having fulfilled their appointment) and my wife feeling anxious to return home, we took leave of our Friends on Second Day afternoon and rode to our Friend, Enoch Dorland's, at Oswego. And the next day, rode to Croton and lodged with our Friend, James Jordan.

Fourth Day: We proceeded on our journey to Manhattanville and lodged with our Friend, Joseph Byrd. And the next day, attended the little meeting of our Friends at that place, after which we rode down to New York and took up our quarters at the house of our Friend and kinsman, Whitehead Hicks.*

We tarried in town until Seventh Day morning, and then took leave of our Friends and rode home, where we arrived just before evening,[2] and

---

[1] Wrest: take by force

[2] The rest of the paragraph was deleted from the printed *Journal*.

found our children and family well, except our daughter Sarah (wife of Robert Seaman) who was quite unwell – being in travail and was delivered of a daughter about seven or eight hours after our arrival, which was cause of thankfulness, not only for her safe delivery, but also for our returning so seasonably as for her mother to be with her in the time of her exercise.

We were from home a little more than a day over four weeks, in which time I traveled four hundred and eighty-four miles, and attended two quarterly meetings (which held five days), seven monthly meetings, and five particular meetings. And we had especial cause of gratitude and thankfulness of heart to the Great and Beneficent Author of every blessing, in that our journey was prosperous and we preserved in a comfortable degree of bodily health during the time, although a season of very general indisposition with those among whom we traveled.

With Our Friends at Home

First Day, 19th of 11th month: I sat with our Friends again in our own meeting and found it my place to set them an example of silence – feeling my situation like Mordecai's when sitting at the king's gate, a state as grateful to a humble mind as riding the king's horse and more safe, as there is less danger of falling.

Fifth Day: Another silent meeting.

Seventh Day: Attended the funeral of a deceased neighbor who put an end to her own life by hanging herself.

Alas, what poor, helpless, unwise creatures we are, when left to our own disposal.

My mind was largely opened to set forth to a large auditory assembled on this solemn occasion, the great and blessed effects of a firm belief and faith in the living God, as it has proved an antidote to all evil in every age of the world, and to every individual who has had this true and living faith, as it is that by which the just live. And this (the apostle saith) is our victory, even our faith.[1] And without it, it is impossible to please God. The Lord's power accompanied the communication and many hearts were broken and contrited by its heavenly influence. May it not pass away as the morning dew,[2] but fasten as a nail in a sure place, driven by the Master of our Assemblies, is the fervent desire and prayer of my mind.

First Day, 26th: I passed our meeting today mostly in silence, except just before the close I found it my place to remind the meeting of the complaint of the apostle Paul in his second epistle to his beloved Timothy concerning some in that day, who were, "Ever learning, and never able to

---

[1] 1 John 5:4
[2] Hosea 13:3

come to the knowledge of the truth."[1] The occasion of which was, as it opened on my mind, their neglect of practical duty and unfaithfulness in what they styled little things and thereby rendered themselves unfit and unworthy of being made rulers over more. And yet [they] were continually seeking after knowledge in greater things through the medium of the outward ear and creaturely comprehension – loving to hear the Truth declared and doctrines communicated, but unwilling and neglectful of putting them in practice – and therefore, made no advancement in true learning. And I had to warn my Friends to be careful not to lay themselves liable[2] to the same reprehension. And found sweet peace in this small portion of duty.

The rest of the week, I spent about home, being somewhat indisposed.

Sat our Fifth Day Meeting in silence, quietly waiting, as at the king's gate, for renewed instruction.

First Day, 3rd of 12th month: My mind has been much shut up since I returned home. Sat our meeting again today in silence, but felt a daily exercise and concern relative to a religious visit in New England, which has for months past been ripening on my mind – but have a prospect of some services about home ere I engage therein.

Lay low, O my soul, that thou mayest be rightly and wisely directed therein! For thou well knowest the greatness and vast importance of the work thou art called to. And that, of thyself, thou art utterly destitute of any right ability to perform it to thy own good or to the glory and honor of thy chiefest good, who is the Lord alone, thy Gracious and Sufficient Helper.

Second and Third Days: Attended to some necessary concerns about home, preparatory to the approaching winter.

Fourth Day afternoon: Rode to Flushing in order to attend their monthly meeting the following day, with a further prospect of having two other meetings on Sixth and Seventh Days – one at Newtown and the other at the Kills – in my way to New York, where I felt drawings on my mind to be on First Day.

Accordingly, after attending the monthly meeting, having the company of my kind kinsman, Isaac Hicks from Westbury, with the assistance of some Friends of Flushing, we procured the appointment of a meeting the next evening at Newtown at the 6th hour – principally for those not in membership. And as there were no Friends residing in the village, the meeting was held in a large upper room at an inn, which was nearly filled with sober and orderly behaved people. And through heavenly help, it proved a comfortable, edifying season. The doctrines of

---

[1] 2 Timothy 3:7
[2] Liable: subject to the possibility of doing or undergoing something undesirable

the gospel were freely and largely opened, apparently to the general satisfaction of those present – many hearts being humbled and contrited.

The next day, we attended an appointed meeting in Friends Meetinghouse at the Kills. And although not large, yet it proved a precious, tendering opportunity to most present – worthy to be remembered with thankfulness and gratitude to the Blessed Author of all our multiplied favors and blessings. After which we dined with our kind Friend, Jane Betts, and then proceeded to the city.

First Day: We attended Pearl Street Meeting in the morning and that at Liberty Street in the afternoon. In the former, the testimony of Truth went forth with power, and its dignity and excellency exalted over all opposition to the praise of his Grace, who is calling and leading all his devoted and obedient children out of darkness into his marvelous light,[1] wherein they are brought to witness a full remission of their sins and an inheritance among all those that are sanctified in Christ Jesus, our Lord.[2]

The latter meeting I sat mostly in silence, but towards the close I was led forth in a short, searching testimony – which brought a solemnity over the meeting – under which covering, the meeting closed.

Second Day: I attended a committee of the Meeting for Sufferings, and in the afternoon, a funeral of one not a member, but whose parents were friendly-inclined and frequently attended Friends Meeting. And they, hearing of my being in town, requested my attendance on the funeral. And being disposed thereto, I attended accordingly, and had an open time to declare the Truth to those present – suited to the occasion of our meeting – and many minds were humbled.

Third Day: I attended the Meeting for Sufferings, and on Fourth Day, the weekly meeting at Pearl Street, at which there was a marriage, which occasioned the meeting to be quite large, and in which my mind was exercised in an unusual manner, as the subject that first presented after my mind had become silenced was the remembrance of the manner in which the temporal courts among men are called to order. And it became so impressive, as to apprehend it right to make use of it as a simile – much in the way the prophet was led to make use of some of the Rechabites to convict Israel of their disobedience and want of attention to their law and lawgiver.[3]

I accordingly was led to cry audibly three times, "Oyez! Oyez! Oyez! Silence all persons, under the pain and penalty of the displeasure of the judge and court!" Which unusual address had a powerful tendency to arrest the attention of all present, and from which I took occasion (as Truth

---

[1] 1 Peter 2:9
[2] 1 Corinthians 1:2
[3] Jeremiah 35

opened the way) to reason with the assembly that if such a confused mass of people as are generally collected together on such occasions – and from very different motives, and many from mere curiosity to hear and see the transactions of the court – should all in an instant so honor and respect the judge and court, as immediately to be still and silent at the simple call of the crier, how much more reasonable is it for a collection of people, promiscuously[1] gathered to the place appointed in a religious way, to wait upon and worship the Judge of heaven and earth – to be still, and strive to silence every selfish and creaturely thought and cogitation of the mind, as such thoughts and cogitations would as certainly prevent our hearing the inward divine voice of the king of heaven, and as effectually hinder our worshipping him in spirit and in truth, as the talking of the multitude at a court of moral law would entirely hinder the business thereof. And as I proceeded with this simile, the subject enlarged and spread, accompanied with gospel power and the evident demonstration of the Spirit, whereby Truth was raised into victory and ran as oil over all. And the meeting closed with solemn supplication and thanksgiving to the Lord, our Gracious Helper, to whom all the honor and glory belongs, both now and forever.

We left the city that afternoon under a grateful sense of the Lord's goodness and rode to Flushing, where we had a public meeting appointed for us that evening. It was a large collection, mostly of those not in membership. It was a solemn season, instructive and edifying.

I returned home the next day and found my family in a reasonable state of health. Surely may I not, with propriety and humility of heart, exclaim with one formerly, "What shall I render unto the Lord for all his benefits? Are not his mercies new every morning? And his faithfulness faileth not."

Sixth and Seventh Days: I was industriously occupied in my family affairs, and the week ended with peace of mind.

First Day, 17th of 12th month: I was led in our meeting today to call Friends attention to the cross, assuring them by plain reasoning that if we lived without the cross, we must expect to die without the crown.[2] For as the cross consisted only in doing right, and doing right only in a conformity to the will of our Heavenly Father and doing all our works agreeable to his good pleasure and not our own, therefore, doing right is always a cross to our fallen nature, as nothing can do right in the sight of God, but a birth or child of God. For although a man in his fallen state may

---

[1] Promiscuous: mixed, usually it means containing both men and women, but it can also mean people of various religious denominations

[2] Hicks' language here may be an intentional echo of William Penn's *No Cross, No Crown*. That title comes from Luke 9:23 and 2 Timothy 4:7-8.

do a moral act, that in itself is a right work, yet doing it for his own pleasure and will – and not because it is agreeable to the will and pleasure of his Creator – therefore, it cannot be accepted as a good act, because the motive and principle were evil, being selfish and not of God.

Second Day: Busily employed about home and in home affairs.

Third Day: Visited a sick Friend at his request. Assisted him in settling his business and wrote his will. Surely this is a work which requires sound judgment and discretion – therefore, ought always to be done in time of health with proper deliberation and not in haste.

Fourth Day: Attended Westbury Monthly Meeting to my own and, I trust, my Friends comfort and satisfaction. And I believe it was a season of instruction and profit to many who were present. May it fasten as a nail in a sure place.

Fifth Day: Attended our own monthly meeting. The meeting for worship, through close labor, proved a quickening, tendering season to many present. In the meeting for discipline, I found it my duty to spread before my Friends a concern that had for many months been (at times) very impressive on my mind, to pay a visit in gospel love to Friends and others in some parts of the Yearly Meeting of Rhode Island. Which, after due deliberation thereon, they united with and gave me their certificate, signed by the clerks[1] of the men's and women's meetings, declarative thereof – leaving me at liberty to pursue the prospect as Truth might open the way. This brought me under serious reflections in a view and consideration of the great responsibility that naturally attaches to those who thus go out on this solemn embassy with the concurrence of their Friends. As not only their own reputation as ministers of the gospel must rise or fall according to their good or ill conduct, but likewise that of their Friends and the society they profess to be ministers of – and also the Truth which they seem to espouse, instead of being advanced, may be retarded thereby.

Lay prostrate, O my soul, at the throne of grace! And seek that wisdom that only is profitable to direct,[2] that thou mayest be thereby strengthened to endure hardness as a good soldier[3] and servant of the Prince of Peace.

---

[1] Clerk: There was no paid staff in Friends meetings. The clerk was a member appointed for a term to preside at business meetings. In principle, this conferred no special status on the person asked to serve, but in practice, clerks exercised a great deal of influence in most meetings. Particularly skilled individuals would often continue in the position for many years.

[2] Ecclesiastes 10:10

[3] 2 Timothy 2:3

Sixth and Seventh Days: Busily employed, so to arrange matters at home as to part with it with a peaceful mind.

First Day, 24th: A profitable, edifying meeting with my Friends at home – being led to sound forth a gospel message among them in an arousing, searching testimony by which many minds were humbled and contrited.

Second and Third Days: Employed in making preparation for my proposed journey.

Fourth Day: Attended Friends Meeting at Westbury, at which there were two marriages consummated, which occasioned the meeting to be very large – many of other societies coming out of curiosity to see the manner of our marriages – among whom, I was largely opened in communication to set forth many gospel truths necessary to be believed in and witnessed in our own experience in order to our salvation. It was a season of favor – a very solemn time. May it be blessed and sanctified to the lasting benefit of all who were present, is the fervent desire and travail of my spirit.

Fifth Day: Attended our meeting in silence.

The two following days, busily engaged in arranging my temporal concerns and putting them in order, that I may leave home with a peaceful mind.

First Day, 31st: A solemn meeting today, in which my mind was led forth in humble supplication for support and preservation in my proposed journey. And that the Lord, our Gracious Helper, in his guardian care would be pleased to be near my dear family and Friends at home and be their comfort and strength in every needful time. And that all those who sit in darkness and the shadow of death,[1] like dry bones in the valley,[2] might be redeemed therefrom and translated into the kingdom of his dear Son,[3] that so his Truth might prosper and spread from sea to sea, and from the rivers to the ends of the earth,[4] that his great and excellent name might be praised and magnified by all the nations of the earth,[5] from the rising of the sun, to the going down thereof,[6] world without end. Amen.

---

[1] Psalm 107:10 & Luke 1:79
[2] Ezekiel 37
[3] Colossians 1:13
[4] Psalm 72:8
[5] Psalm 72:17 & 86:9
[6] Psalm 50:1

1816

Second and Third Days: Still busily engaged preparatory to leaving home, with a prospect of setting out on Fourth Day morning, if way should open, which I did accordingly.

General Visit to Friends in New England

Fourth Day of the week and 3rd of 1st month 1816: After taking a solemn and affecting opportunity with my dear wife and children, I took leave of them under a sense of the Lord's goodness and gracious regard, and proceeded on my intended journey, and called on my kind kinsman, Isaac Hicks of Westbury, who had previously concluded to go with me as a companion. And we proceeded that afternoon to New York, where we tarried over the next day.

Connecticut

And on Sixth Day morning, we left the city and arrived at Bridgeport in Connecticut on Seventh Day evening, where we had a small, though comfortable, meeting the next day at the house of Thomas Woodward, whose wife was a member of our society. After which, we proceeded to New Haven and lodged.

Second Day: We proceeded to Hartford and lodged.

Massachusetts

Third and Fourth Days: Rode to Leicester and lodged with our Friend, Pliny Earle.*

Fifth Day: Had an appointed meeting there at the 11th hour. A number of the neighboring people (not of our society) attended with Friends, among whom was their priest. It was, I think, a season of favor, in which my heart and mouth were opened under, I trust, the influence of gospel love to declare the way of life and salvation to the people – proving from the scriptures and clear rational demonstration that nothing short of the inspiring Spirit of Truth could enable any rational creature to make the least progress in a real Christian life or qualify to worship the Father of Spirits in spirit and in truth, and that a confession[1] to all or any creeds and forms of religion – however specious[2] in their appearance – without the immediate aid of this inspiring Spirit, would in the end leave the soul in utter disappointment. I was also led to show the unreasonableness and inconsistency of the doctrine of unconditional election and reprobation,

---

[1] Confession: a public affirmation of a statement of faith or a creed
[2] Specious: pleasing or beautiful

and that it was impossible to be drawn from a right and enlightened view of the divine character.

There occurred one circumstance in the meeting that, as it was in itself improper and gave some interruption to my mind, I am willing to mention as a caution. When the meeting had got pretty quietly settled and my mind opened with a prospect to stand up – just before I was about to arise – there came in a stranger (in appearance) and a Friend that sat near me spoke to him to come forward and called him "parson" (meaning a priest), which I was very sorry to be informed of. And I think that Friends ought to be exceedingly careful never to inform traveling ministers the state or condition of those who attend their meetings, as it not only has a tendency to close up the way very much of real gospel ministers, but when close and plain things are delivered, they often are judged of having outward information of the condition of those to whom it applies, which, if it be the case, it almost renders their doctrine useless. But if from inquiry, such find that the speaker was utterly ignorant of them from any outward discovery, it is then much more likely to fix on their minds and become useful.

After dining with our Friends, we proceeded on our journey about thirteen miles that evening with a view of endeavoring to get an opportunity with Friends at Bolton the next day. But the morning opened with a pretty severe snow storm, which rendered it inadmissible.[1] However, we proceeded in the morning through the snow and much difficulty to that place, where we tarried until First Day, when we had a very comfortable, edifying meeting with Friends. We continued there, at the house of our kind Friend, John Fry, until Second Day morning and then proceeded to Lynn.

New Hampshire

Third Day, 16th: We proceeded to Seabrook in order to attend the quarterly meeting, which opened the next day with a Meeting of Ministers and Elders. And on Fifth Day was the quarterly meeting of discipline, preceded by a meeting for worship. It was a season of favor, especially the meeting for worship, wherein my mind was largely opened to preach the gospel in the demonstration of the Spirit, to the comfort and edification of the upright in heart – many being reduced into a state of humble contrition and thankfulness for the unmerited mercy.

On Sixth Day, we proceeded to Epping, where by previous notice, we had a meeting in the evening in which the Lord's power and presence presided in a very eminent manner, and his Truth raised into victory over all and ran as oil – to the quieting and solemnizing everything that stood

---

[1] Inadmissible: not to be considered

in opposition to its pure, holy influence. I scarcely ever was at a meeting, wherein all were so swallowed up in a profound solemnity, that when the meeting closed, it was some time before any removed from their seats. Surely it was the Lord's doings and marvelous in mine eyes.

From thence we went the next day to Lee, and had a small comfortable meeting at the 11th hour, and then proceeded to Dover.

First Day: Attended Friends Meeting there at the 11th hour. At the close of which, feeling a draft of love towards the townspeople at large, with the unity of Friends, there was a meeting appointed in the evening, and general invitation given to the inhabitants, at which there was a very large collection of the various sects, amongst whom my mind was largely opened and my tongue unloosed[1] (I trust by him who opens and none can shut, and shuts and none can open) to declare of the things concerning the kingdom of God and to point out to the people in a very clear manner the way of life and salvation, unfolding many important doctrines of the gospel in the clear demonstration of the Spirit – to the bowing and humbling many minds present, and to the rejoicing of the hearts of the faithful. Under a sense whereof my mind was bowed in deep abasedness for the present favor.

Maine

Next morning, we proceeded to Berwick. Had an instructive, edifying meeting there in the evening, wherein many hearts (with mine own) were made thankful for the present mercy.

The next day, we proceeded to Portland, a town adjoining on Casco Bay, and the following day being the fourth of the week, we rode to Falmouth and attended their select meeting, constituted of the ministers and elders belonging to Falmouth Meeting. It was small and the business conducted in a very weak, and in my view, a very improper manner. For previous to the meeting, it appeared that the clerk had, at his leisure, entered the meeting as though at meeting,[2] and made answers to all the queries, so that when the meeting collected, they had nothing to do but to hear him read over what he had before written, and which without any alteration were approved, some representatives to the quarter appointed, and the meeting closed. On taking a view of the subject, I was led to believe that meetings held in such a way brought no honor to the cause nor strength nor profit to those who attend them.

---

[1] Luke 1:64

[2] Meetings in the nineteenth century had bound, handwritten minute books. When Hicks writes that the clerk had "entered the meeting as though at meeting," he is saying that the clerk had written minutes in the official minute book, as if the meeting had been held.

At the close of the meeting, we rode to our Friend, John Winslow's, and lodged.

The next day, attended their monthly meeting, and the two following days, we attended the select meeting at Windham and their monthly meeting.

First Day: Attended Windham Meeting.

Second Day: An appointed meeting at Gorham.

On Third Day, we rested and wrote.

Fourth Day: Their quarterly meeting opened at Windham, which closed on Fifth Day.

Sixth Day: Had an appointed meeting at Falmouth.

On Seventh Day, rode to Durham.

First Day: Attended their meeting, which was large – notice having been given to the neighboring inhabitants of our coming.

Second Day: Rode back to Portland and had an appointed meeting with Friends and friendly people that evening.

On Third Day, attended an appointed meeting at Cape Elizabeth, after which we returned to Portland and had a large public meeting in the evening.

Fourth Day: Was at Scarborough, after which I felt my mind released from any further service in this quarter. But before I proceed, was led in humble gratitude and thankfulness of heart to acknowledge the goodness and mercy of Israel's Shepherd, who in his never-failing love was graciously near from place to place and clothed the assemblies with his presence and power – opening my mind with his life-giving presence in every meeting of worship to preach the gospel, to the humbling and contriting many minds, and to the comfort and edification of the willing and upright in heart. Surely it is the Lord that worketh in us and for us. Magnified and adored be his right worthy name, both now and forever – to whom all the praise belongs, nothing due to man.

After the meeting at Scarborough, I went with my kind Friend, William Cobb, to his house at Gorham – he having taken me in his chaise[1] from Portland to Scarborough, as our way of traveling was with a sled, but the snow on the seacoast was so wasted[2] as to render it difficult getting along therewith. It was therefore concluded that my companion should go back into the country to Gorham, where the snow was more plenty, and William accompanied me as aforesaid, and we met again in the evening at his house, and the next day, returned to Berwick, and the day following, to Dover.

---

[1] Chaise: a light, horse-drawn carriage
[2] Waste: melt away

Back Through New Hampshire

On Seventh Day, I proceeded to Rochester, accompanied by Thomas Stackpole. My companion being unwell, it was thought best for him to rest until our return. We took the upper meeting in that town in the evening, and the next day at the 11th hour, were at the lower meeting. After which, we returned to Dover to attend a meeting in the evening, which had been concluded to be appointed previous to my going out. And general notice having been given, it was very large. They were all seasons of favor, in which the Lord's presence was felt to preside and Truth raised into dominion – particularly the latter, wherein my heart and mouth were largely opened and the gospel preached in the clear demonstration of the Spirit attended with power to the solemnizing of this large assembly. Truth reigned and the meeting closed with humble supplication and prayer to the Lord for the unmerited favor.

Second Day, 12th of 2nd month: We returned to Seabrook, to our kind Friend, Joseph Philbrick's, and had an appointed meeting there that evening.

Massachusetts

And the next day, proceeded to Amesbury and Newbury. Had a meeting at each place – the latter in the evening. They were open, favored seasons, particularly the meeting at Amesbury in which Truth prevailed and ran as oil over all. A ministering Friend observed after the meeting that he believed the witness was raised in every mind present. It was indeed a precious, strengthening opportunity to my own mind.

May the honor and praise be all ascribed to Israel's Shepherd, to whom it is altogether due. How deeply humiliating are such continued mercies, dispensed to us poor unworthy creatures. Lay low, O my soul! For thou well knowest that it is the Lord's power only, clothed in righteous judgment and never-failing mercy, that has raised thee from the dunghill[1] where thou hadst plunged thyself by thy own follies. Yea, it is he who has plucked thy feet out of the mire and clay of sin, and set them on a rock, and strengthened thee in faith to believe that – as thou dwells in deep humiliation before him, resting on his mercy until self is fully mortified and the old man with his deeds is utterly crucified – he will establish thy going and put a new song into thy mouth, even eternal praises to thy God.[2] Even so be it. Amen.

---

[1] 1 Samuel 2:8 & Psalm 113:7
[2] Psalm 40:2-3

Amesbury (Massachusetts) Meetinghouse

We left Newbury on Fourth Day morning, and returned to Salem. Attended their middle-week meeting the next day as it came in course, at which there was a marriage consummated between two worthy Friends – elders in society. It was a comfortable, edifying season, in which I was led to set forth the deep and solemn obligations that mutually attach to the parties entering into the marriage covenant – obligations that could never be rightly and harmoniously fulfilled, so as to render the parties truly happy together, unless they were (previous to their engagement) of one mind and one heart in all matters of importance, but more especially, in regard to their principles of religion and faith. If these are diverse, it will most certainly embitter their enjoyments, and produce discord in their family, and tend to wound and distract the minds of their children (should they be favored with any) that it bespeaks great presumption and folly in young people to risk the attempt, especially on such slender reasons as are commonly brought forward, as a plea that one of the parties may change their opinion and come to unite with the other. But this is very fallacious as, "What may be, may not be."[1] And no man of reason will trust thereto in the most trivial matters, for each generally supposes themselves in the right, and looks for the other to condescend and conform. And therefore, the breach often becomes greater.

On Sixth Day evening, we had an appointed meeting for the townspeople in general. It was very large, consisting of the various religious sects and some of almost every description of people that commonly reside in such populous towns. I was largely opened among them in the ministerial line, in which I was led to set forth the excellency of man's primitive state (before the fall) in which he was placed by the wisdom and goodness of his All-wise and Gracious Creator, and furnished with sufficient light and understanding to know that he was altogether the work of his almighty power, and that he derived his life and existence – with every other blessing he had or could have – from his bountiful hand. Under a just sense whereof, while he stood in this happy state, every desire of his soul flowed with a continual assent to him as his only Comforter and Preserver. And in which state, he realized the condition the apostle reminds us of in this exhortation, "Pray without ceasing, rejoice evermore, and in everything give thanks"[2] – this being the only true delineation of a faithful servant of God. But from this happy state, man fell. But his fall was not affected in any degree by any preordination of (nor foreknowledge of) his gracious Creator, but by a wrong use and abuse of those powers and capacities conferred on him as a free-agent creature and without which he neither could have known nor served his God. Therefore, man's fall was altogether an act of his own choice – contrary to known duty – and had it not been so, he could not possibly have felt guilt and condemnation for what he had done.

I was also led to open to the people that the great end of Christ's coming was to introduce the gospel, which is the last and most blessed dispensation of God to the children of men, as by it only can man be restored to this primitive state, and without which restoration he cannot effectually serve God in spirit. And this gospel, our Lord told his disciples, his Father would send them in his name, and which is the Holy Ghost,[3] or Power of God, sent down from heaven.[4] And which well agrees with the doctrine of the apostle Paul, where he tells us that the gospel is the power of God unto salvation to all that believe, which supposes that those who do not obey the Spirit of Truth (or Holy Ghost) that convinces them of sin,

---

[1] Scottish proverb
[2] 1 Thessalonians 5:16-18
[3] John 14:26
[4] 1 Peter 1:12

do not believe the gospel, and therefore are not benefited by it. And therefore, of course, they remain under the power and dominion of sin.

After this laborous, favored meeting, I felt myself much indisposed with a very severe cold and fever, and had to keep house until the next Third Day, when we proceeded to Lynn.

And the following day, we attended their middle-week meeting. And notice being given of our intention of being there, it was large. And the testimony of Truth went forth freely to the tendering many minds, and the comforting the faithful and upright in heart.

The next day, we proceeded on our way to Long Plain, where we arrived the day following about noon. Had a meeting there that evening, and the day following had a meeting at the 11th hour at Acushnet. They were both favored meetings.

We then proceeded to New Bedford, and the next day, the first of the week and 25th of 2nd month, we attended their fore and after noon meetings, wherein my mind was largely opened in gospel communication – tending to expose the man of sin and son of perdition, and that he was nothing but self in man. Showing how, that in his mysterious workings in leading man to endeavor to imitate God in doing good and performing acts under the show of religion and religious worship (but all done in his own will and time), the whole mystery of iniquity is comprehended.[1] And as this serpentine wisdom is the highest state of knowledge that man is endowed with under God (as declared in the beginning that the serpent was the most subtle of any beast of the field[2]), that is, the highest wisdom that the mind of man is endued with (independent of God) and in which consists the power of his free-agency. So of course, there is nothing that can detect it, but the wisdom and inspiring Spirit of God. And as this serpentine wisdom is the highest rational ability comprehended in the immortal soul of man, and the center of his free-agency, so likewise, the Tree of Knowledge of Good and Evil is likewise in the center of the soul – that is, an independent capacity in which man presumes to know good and evil for himself and so become as God,[3] that is a presumptive capacity of knowing and doing good without God.

And in man's thus turning away from his God and the inspirings of his Holy Spirit consists his fall – as he takes upon himself an independent state, and assumes the right of self-government, and becomes his own director. Therefore, his salvation wholly consists in surrendering up this self-ability – letting it die on the cross and returning into a state of full submission to the leading and sole guidance of the inspiring Spirit of God.

---

[1] The rest of the paragraph was deleted from the printed *Journal*.
[2] Genesis 3:1
[3] Genesis 3:22

Apponagansett Meetinghouse in Dartmouth, Massachusetts

My mind was largely opened in these and other truths of the gospel in those meetings, whereby Truth was raised into dominion over all, to the comfort and peace of my own mind, and to the apparent satisfaction, instruction, and edification of the rightly-exercised and seeking minds present.

The three following days, we attended meetings at Newtown, Centre, and the Monthly Meeting of Dartmouth or Apponagansett, in each of which, I was largely opened in gospel communication – particularly in the latter. The Truth was powerfully raised into dominion over all, to the reducing and humbling all present – spreading a precious solemnity over the meeting and much contrition of spirit was manifested. It was the Lord's doing, and to him belongs all the praise of his own work, nothing due to the creature but blushing and confusion of face from a full sense of the unmerited mercy.

Rhode Island

Fifth and Sixth Days: We had meetings at Acoaxet (alias Westport) and Little Compton. In both, the gospel was preached in Truth's authority – the latter especially was a powerful, melting season to most present,

Westport (Rhode Island) Meetinghouse

inspiring the mind with deep thankfulness and gratitude to the Bountiful Author of every blessing.

Seventh Day: We proceeded to Newport on Rhode Island and attended Friends fore and after noon meetings on First Day.

On Second Day, had an appointed meeting at Portsmouth, after which, with peace of mind, we left the island that afternoon and went to Tiverton, and lodged with our kind Friend, Joseph Barker. Had an appointed meeting there the next day and the day following, was at Swansea. Truth was eminently exalted in these meetings, especially the latter was a powerful, baptizing season, in which the Lord's presence was witnessed – bowing and reducing all under its calming and solemnizing influence. And much brokenness and contrition of spirit was manifested to spread over the meeting – not only with Friends, but by many others not in profession with us, to the encouragement and gladdening every sincere mind for the unmerited favor. After this solemn meeting, we took leave of our Friends and rode that afternoon to Providence.

The next day, we attended Friends Meeting there, as it came in course, in which my mind was led to exemplify and set forth the excellency and blessed effects of true and strict justice in all our dealings and commerce between man and man as rational, social beings, which was introduced into my mind by the remembrance of this saying of the wisest of men (to wit) Solomon, "Righteousness exalts a nation, but sin is a reproach to any people."

My mind was opened to show the great and essential difference there is between the righteousness of man – as comprehended and tolerated by the laws, customs, edicts, and traditions of men – and the righteousness of God – which is altogether comprehended in pure, equal, impartial, and unchangeable justice – showing that every act of man that is not in conformity to this pure and impartial justice is sin. And that whatever we do that has a tendency, either directly or indirectly, to counteract this pure, simple, impartial justice, cannot be considered as any part of that righteousness that exalts a nation, as it cannot bring glory to God. For no righteousness (but God's righteousness wrought in man by this pure principle of justice) can possibly glorify him, as this must be the foundation of every virtue in man.

It was a season of close searching labor by which the hidden things of Esau (or the first nature) in which the serpentine wisdom works to the deceiving [of] multitudes was brought to light and exposed – especially that cunning, sophistical[1] reasoning in the wisdom of this world that many people are making use of to justify themselves, and thereby stifle and put to silence the convictions of conscience, while acting in direct opposition to this pure principle of justice by continuing a traffic in and making themselves rich by a commerce in the produce of the labor of the poor, afflicted, and deeply oppressed Africans and their descendants held in a state of slavery by the mere force of war, and which is wrested from them by its cruel force without their consent. Truth was exalted over all, and unrighteousness exposed, and its evil effects on societies and individuals manifested.[2]

After this laborous meeting, not feeling myself clear of the town, I appointed another meeting in the evening. And public notice being given, it was large – not only of the white inhabitants, but a large number of the people of color also attended. It was a season of favor and much doctrine communicated suited to the states of those present – tending to the edification and instruction of the seeking minds of the varied sects (a variety of which were collected in this solemn assembly) which I closed with a peaceful mind.

And the next day, we proceeded to Scituate. Had a very edifying, tendering meeting there.

---

[1] Sophistical: using intentionally deceptive arguments
[2] Ships and merchants from Rhode Island (including some prominent Quakers) were deeply involved in the slave trade until it was abolished in 1807. At that point, the traffic in human cargo was replaced in large measure by shipping the products of slave labor.

The day following being the first of the week, we were at Friends Meeting at Foster – a small meeting of Friends, but a very considerable number of the neighboring people came in of different persuasions, among whom I was led to open and explain many essential doctrines of Christianity, which – crossing the carnal views of these outside professors and striking at their creaturely activity in their religious services – I felt as I proceeded a strong spirit of opposition in some of this description. But Truth favored, so that no outward opposition was manifested and the meeting closed under a covering of solemn quiet.

Back in Connecticut

On Second Day evening, we attended an appointed meeting in Friends Meetinghouse at Plainfield. There are but a few Friends belonging to this meeting, the whole consisting of but three families, but a considerable number of their neighbors came in and sat with us. We likewise appointed another meeting the next day at a Friend's house in the northern part of this town at the 2nd hour after noon, which was well attended by the neighboring people. These two latter meetings closed my visit to Friends and others in the compass of Rhode Island Yearly Meeting. They were opportunities of favor, in which much gospel instruction was communicated – to the general edification, comfort, and satisfaction of the people, and which was acknowledged by many of them by word and gesture. And in parting with them, I felt the incomes of sweet peace as a crown to all my deep exercises and arduous gospel labors in this visit to my Friends and others in the compass of that yearly meeting where my lot was cast – a sense of which humbles my mind in deep thankfulness and gratitude to the Bountiful Author of all our mercies and blessings, and who is over all, God blessed forever.

We proceeded from hence on Fourth Day, directly to the city of Hartford, and on Fifth Day evening had a large meeting there, held in a meetinghouse belonging to the Baptist Society. I was led forth among them in a large, doctrinal testimony, showing how that by Christ coming in the flesh, he had fulfilled the law of Moses relating to the religion and worship of that dispensation, which stood in mere legal righteousness, consisting of mere carnal ordinances, and relating only to the outward or animal body – made up of circumcision, a Seventh Day Sabbath or rest, outward sacrifices, elementary washings and cleansings, and the blood of slain beasts, etc. – all which were only applicable to mere animal bodies, and therefore could not effect the soul, nor make the comers thereunto perfect, as pertaining to the conscience.[1, 2] And that all these were ended

---

[1] Hebrews 10:1 & 9:9
[2] The rest of the paragraph was deleted from the printed *Journal*.

and abrogated by the sacrifice of Christ's body on the cross, and whereby he fulfilled all the righteousness of that dispensation (as he declared to John the Baptist), and finished transgression and put an end to all the legal sins of that covenant. Insomuch that after, he said that it was finished, and he gave up the ghost, and the veil of the temple was rent in twain[1] – that after this, everyone who was under this covenant might now forbear (if they believed in Christ) complying with any of these rituals of the law that consisted in outward and elementary things without being guilty of any transgression or sin, as Christ is the end of the law to all that believe.

I was likewise led to open the true Christian Sabbath, which is the antitype of that typical[2] one, which does not consist in a rest to bodies merely for a day, but in a perpetual rest to the soul[3] by its coming into Christ, and submitting to the government of his Spirit, and entirely ceasing from its own willings and runnings,[4] by which reconciliation is witnessed and peace made with our Heavenly Father. These things and much more I had to open to the people in the fresh feelings of the love and life of truth, which was exalted over all.

The next day, we rode to Woodbury with a prospect of getting a religious opportunity with the people. But way not opening for it, we proceeded the next day to New Milford.

Back in New York

And the next day being the first of the week, we had a comfortable, edifying meeting with Friends and a large collection of their neighbors with them. After which, we rode that afternoon to Oblong.

The next day attended the monthly meeting there. In the meeting for worship, the Lord's power was eminently exalted and Truth was raised into dominion – the season was deeply instructive and edifying.

The next day, we had an appointed meeting in the town of Patterson, where no Friend resides. It was held in a schoolhouse and proved, through divine favor, an instructive, baptizing season. From thence we proceeded to the Valley, and the following day had a precious, strengthening opportunity with Friends and others in Friends Meetinghouse there. After which we rode to North Salem.

And the next day being their middle-week meeting, we attended. And notice being given of our being there, it was considerably enlarged by the coming in of a number of the neighboring inhabitants. The forepart of the meeting was laborous – my mind, in silent waiting, was dipped into a

---

[1] John 19:30 & Mark 15:37-38
[2] Typical: characteristic of a type which will be fulfilled in an antitype
[3] Matthew 11:29
[4] Romans 9:15-18

deep sense of poverty and darkness. And as I sat patiently under the impression, I was led gradually into a view of the cause – which appeared to be too much creaturely activity and a froward will. And as Light began to arise and expel the darkness, there was brought to remembrance these expressions of Solomon, "Keep thy foot when thou goest to the house of God, and be more ready to hear than to offer the sacrifice of fools. For they consider not that they do evil,"[1] and also that, "the talk of the lip tendeth to penury."[2]

These were opened in a way that led to communication, in which I had to show the very hurtful tendency of creaturely activity in matters of religion and religious worship, and the absolute necessity of a complete redemption from self and all self motives in the great work of our salvation. And as I proceeded, the life arose and Truth prevailed and spread over the meeting in an eminent degree.

After this favored meeting (at a Friend's house, in converse with a Friend), I found there was sufficient cause for my exercise. And I was glad that I was altogether ignorant of it from any outward information.

The next day, we had an appointed meeting at Amawalk. It was favored with the Lord's presence and power, and many hearts were contrited and made thankful under a sense of his continued mercy.

We proceeded from thence to Peekskill, where by previous appointment, we had a meeting the following day, which was likewise crowned with his blessing. Surely the Lord is good and gracious and his mercy endureth forever. For did he deal with us according to our deserts, surely we might ere now all been consumed.[3] For as I passed along from place to place, I discovered great unfaithfulness and want of right submission to the divine will – both with many Friends, as well as those without. Under a feeling sense whereof, I was often led in a line of close, searching doctrines, by which the hidden things of Esau (or the works of the first birth or fallen nature) were brought to light and exposed in a way that showed it was the Lord's doings and marvelous in mine eyes. Under a sense whereof, my heart, with the hearts of the faithful few, was made glad in his power and his everlasting loving-kindness to the children of men.

The next day being the first of the week, we attended Croton Meeting. It was large for that place by the coming in of those of other societies – the number of Friends there being small. The doctrines of the gospel were freely and largely preached among them, to the instruction and

---

[1] Ecclesiastes 5:1
[2] Proverbs 14:23
[3] Lamentations 3:22

edification, I believe, of most present, and to the peace and comfort of my own mind.

Our next meeting was at Chappaqua, which was a large, favored season. And the two following days, we had meetings at Croton Valley and North Castle – in both of which I was helped to clear myself among the people in a line of plain doctrine.

The next day and the fifth of the week, had an appointed meeting at Purchase. It was a large, satisfactory meeting.

The two following days, we attended meetings at Mamaroneck and Westchester, in both of which, the Lord's power was manifested for our help, and the gospel preached in the demonstration thereof, and its divine influence tendered and contrited many hearts – especially in the latter, which being the last meeting I had in this journey, it proved a crowning season in which Truth was raised into victory over all, and the Lord's name praised and magnified for his goodness and marvelous loving-kindness to the children of men.

After this solemn meeting, I felt myself at liberty to return home, where I arrived safe that evening and found most of my family in usual health,[1] although divers had been much indisposed during my absence. And one of my daughters had been brought very low a few days before my return – insomuch that her life was despaired of – but was now on the recovery. And an infant grandchild had been taken away by death a few days after I left home on this journey. In all which trials, I was strengthened quietly and patiently to acquiesce in the divine disposing, who doth all things right,[2] and which settled my mind in a state of solid peace and thankfulness to the Lord, who is the Blessed Author of all our mercies, and who causes all his faithful servants to witness that he is indeed a God near at hand and a Present Helper[3] in every needful time.

I was from home nearly three months in this journey, traveled upwards of one thousand miles, and attended fifty-nine particular, three monthly, and two quarterly meetings.

Engagements at & about Home

First Day, 31st of 3rd month 1816: Having returned from my aforesaid journey last evening, sat with our Friends in our own meeting today. Felt things to be very low in a religious sense and my mind clothed with much poverty, which appeared to me, in the openings of Truth, to be occasioned by Friends suffering their minds to be too much overwhelmed with the

---

[1] The rest of the paragraph was deleted from the printed *Journal*.
[2] Nehemiah 9:33
[3] Psalm 46:1

surfeiting[1] cares of this life, which I was led to open to them in a plain, though tender manner – which had a reaching effect on the meeting, to the contriting many hearts. May it fasten as a nail in a sure place is the fervent desire of my mind.

Fifth Day: Since First Day, I have been somewhat circumstanced as Mordecai formerly at the king's gate – waiting and watching in much poverty of spirit against intervening[2] temptations while making some necessary arrangements respecting my temporal affairs – being desirous that they may all be so conducted under the ordering and limitation of Truth as to accord with the will of my Heavenly Father, and thereby bring glory to his excellent name. Sat our meeting today in silence.

Sixth and Seventh Days: Nothing transpired requiring particular notice.

First Day: I was led in our meeting today (under a sense of the great want among mankind in general of a right concern to become acquainted with their Creator) to set forth the great loss and suffering that must necessarily result to them from this state of ignorance, and want of the true knowledge of God, and of his will concerning them.

Seventh Day, 13th of 4th month: This week has passed since First Day without feeling sufficient to warrant the making a short note, but being at present musing on the past time and feeling no condemnation. Although I had passed the present week mostly in caring for my temporal concerns, yet not so much, I trust, from the love I have for the world or the things of it, but more especially from a sense of duty – that I may honestly provide for the outward welfare of myself and family and, through the blessing of a kind and benevolent Providence on my frugal industry, have a sufficiency, when called from my home and from every temporal enjoyment there for the gospel's sake – to keep the gospel free from charge and that I abuse not my power in the gospel – a care that I often fear is too much wanting by some who go out on that solemn embassy, which, if not guarded against, may not only tend to frustrate the end of their labors, but prove a stone of stumbling to many seeking minds. For how inconsistent it must appear in those who profess to have taken up their cross to self and the world to follow their self-denying Savior in the plain path of duty, to be anxious about what they shall eat or drink, or what they shall wear,[3] or manifest a hanking after praise or applause from their Friends or others,[4] or have their hands and hearts open to receive the gratuities of the rich – all which may be considered (when sought after) as bribes to the receivers,

---

[1] Surfeiting: indulged to excess
[2] Intervene: hinder
[3] Matthew 6:25 & 31
[4] Matthew 6:2, 5, & 16

and which places such under the appellation of hirelings. For although there may not have been any previous contract, yet the receiving benefits in that way, I conceive, will bring the receiver under obligations to the giver, and which places the individual in a situation not fit for a free minister of the gospel.

First Day: Sat our meeting today mostly in silence and in suffering with the seed that lies oppressed as a cart under sheaves in the minds of most of the professors of Christianity. But towards the close, a gleam of light brake forth in the remembrance of that saying of Christ, where he tells us that the kingdom of God is within, and that it doth not come through outward observation.[1] The subject spread and opened lively on my mind, which led to communication and brought a solemn weight over the meeting. And we parted under the favor.

The three following days, I kept much within – being under very considerable bodily affliction – although at intervals, so as to pay some necessary attention to my family affairs, not being willing to let any portion of precious time pass away unimproved, as I cannot suppose that any part of our time is dispensed to us for naught.

Fifth Day: This was the time of our monthly meeting, and at which the queries were answered and accounts prepared to go up to the yearly meeting. How deep and solemn our deliberations ought to be on such occasions. Not only that our answers may be consistent with Truth without any false coloring or evasion, but that all may be done under the influence of that divine power that humbles and abases the creature, and which only can qualify for the Lord's work and service – whether in ministry or discipline. At this meeting, I returned the minute[2] I had from the meeting to perform my late visit to Friends in New England with a short account of my journey.

Sixth Day: Attended our Meeting for Ministers and Elders, at which nothing unusual occurred.

Seventh Day: Quietly spent in my temporal concerns.

First Day, 21st: My mind, in our meeting today, was brought under a deep, feeling exercise in sympathy with backsliders and such as having been often reproved, continue still to revolt. The testimony of Truth went forth to these in a searching, arousing manner. May it prove effectual to produce in such more stability and faithfulness to the convictions of divine

---

[1] Luke 17:21
[2] The custom among Friends was for a traveling minister to carry the minute from his or her home meeting stating their approval of the undertaking. During the journey, those visited endorsed it, often in a note on the back of the page, expressing their approval or disapproval. On completing the journey, the minute was returned to the minister's home meeting and kept in the meeting records.

grace, which – as they become fully obedient unto – will work their salvation. Otherwise, these may share the fate described by one formerly, "He, that being often reproved, hardeneth his neck, shall suddenly be cut off, and that without remedy."

The rest of this week, I spent principally in attending our quarterly meeting held at this time in New York. It was in the main a favored season, but would have been more so had not some in the ministry quite overshot the mark by unnecessary communication.[1] For as we are limited creatures, we are in that sense as vessels that when full, we can hold no more – even of that, that is good, or may be esteemed so by the communicator. But it will pass away unregarded, and the attempt to enforce it becomes burdensome, and of course, taketh away the life from the meeting and brings over it a gloom of death and darkness that may be sensibly felt.[2] This is a very serious loss to a meeting. Therefore, very great care ought to rest on the minds of ministers – how they add, when things are left well before.

First Day, 28th: A silent meeting today.

Second Day: In the afternoon of this day, I accompanied our Friend, John Bailey from Pembroke in New England, to a meeting he had appointed at Jerusalem. There was a considerable collection, but the meeting proved trying and laborous – not only in the silent part, but when our Friend was communicating. There seemed to be a great weight of death over the meeting and the people appeared generally very dull and lifeless. And I was very much borne down under a feeling sense of it, insomuch that I had not the least prospect that I should have anything to communicate – as I saw nor felt nothing in myself to offer – nor did there appear any disposition or fitness in the people to receive. But just before the close, some time after my Friend had sat down, there was a small presentation opened on my mind attended with a degree of life, which, as I yielded thereto, it spread a comfortable degree of life over the meeting generally, insomuch that I thought that the fragments that were left after each had had their portion were much more than the whole stock in the beginning – like the fragments of the loaves and fishes, when the multitude was fed formerly.[3]

I accompanied the aforesaid Friend on Fourth Day to Bethpage, but sat the meeting in silence. John appeared in a pretty long testimony, but it was rather a dull, heavy season, and but little life to be felt – so true is that saying that, "Except the Lord build the house, they labor in vain who

---

[1] The next three sentences were deleted from the printed *Journal*.
[2] Exodus 10:21
[3] Matthew 14:20 and parallels

build it, and except the Lord keep the city, the watchman waketh but in vain."[1]

John returned with me and attended our meeting the next day. He had a pretty good time in the meeting and was led pretty clearly to open divers passages of scripture, which rendered the season instructive and satisfactory.

Sixth and Seventh Days: Passed without anything transpiring worthy of remark.

First Day, 5th of 5th month: Being invited to attend the funeral of one of my wife's cousins on Cow Neck, I accompanied her thereto. It was a large collection of people, but by their untimely and irregular gathering, the opportunity was much interrupted. Yet through the condescending goodness of Israel's Shepherd, the testimony of Truth went forth freely to the people – to the tendering and contriting many hearts, particularly among the youth. May it fix on their minds as a nail driven by the Master of Assemblies in a sure place.

The rest of this week, I spent about home, being somewhat unwell – yet not so much so, but that I attended our preparative meeting on Fifth Day.

First Day, 12th: Feeling considerably indisposed, I did not get out to meeting today, yet had to reflect how very seldom I had been prevented by indisposition for many years past, being generally preserved in health, a favor worthy of grateful acknowledgments.

Fifth Day: Attended our monthly meeting. It was a low, dull season through the greater part of the first meeting. But just before the close, a small gleam of light appeared, which, with a short communication from a female, brought the meeting to a pretty comfortable close.

Sixth and Seventh Days: Spent in my family avocations – clothed with poverty of spirit, yet not altogether cast down – being encouraged at times with the remembrance of the divine promise succeeding the flood, that, "While the earth remaineth, seedtime and harvest, cold and heat, summer and winter, and day and night, shall not cease."[2] And as in my past winter journey, I witnessed summer and harvest, so now I may rest patiently in the divine promise with the assurance that as winter in due course has succeeded summer, so likewise summer, by and by in its turn, will succeed winter. And the time of the singing of birds will come,[3] and the drooping spirit will again rejoice in the Lord, and joy in the God of its salvation.[4]

---

[1] Psalm 127:1
[2] Genesis 8:22
[3] Song of Solomon 2:12
[4] Habakkuk 3:17

Nothing requiring a note the following week, except that on Seventh Day, 25th of the month, I proceeded to New York in order to attend our approaching yearly meeting, which opened for ministers and elders at the 10th hour this morning. But the morning being rainy, we did not arrive in season to attend the first meeting, but were at the afternoon sitting. The meeting continued by adjournments until the following Sixth Day and was in the main, I think, a favored meeting – the Lord graciously manifesting himself to be near, suppressing froward spirits that would now and then start up to the hurt of the meeting, and uniting the living, baptized members in a joint travail for the promotion of right order and the increase of the Messiah's kingdom in the earth.

We returned home on Seventh Day:

First Day, 2nd of 6th month: Attended our meeting in the morning in silence, but in the afternoon meeting (appointed by a Friend from Pennsylvania), I had a pretty full opportunity (after the Friends who appointed the meeting had relieved their minds) to call the people's attention to the only sure guide, the Light of God's Spirit in their own hearts and minds, and which reveals to every man and woman all things that they had ever done – as Jesus did to the woman of Samaria[1] – reproving for the evil and justifying for the good. And were men and women all as faithful to themselves as this Divine Reprover is to them, they would all witness the blessing of peace. And if they held out in faithfulness and obedience to the end, the answer of, "Well done, good and faithful servant," would be the happy portion of all these.

Fifth Day: Attended our meeting in silence.

First Day, 9th: Had the company of two female ministering Friends from Philadelphia at our meeting, which proved a hard, laborous season. One of them was exercised in public testimony and although she appeared to labor fervently, yet but little life was felt to arise during the meeting. This makes the work hard for the poor, exercised ministers, who feel the necessity publicly to advocate the cause of Truth and Righteousness, and yet obtain but little relief by reason of the deadness and indifference of those to whom they are constrained to minister. I found it my place to sit silent and suffer with the seed.

Second Day: Went to New York, in order to attend our Meeting for Sufferings, which came the next day at the 9th hour in the morning. I accordingly attended and returned home that afternoon.

The rest of the week, I spent about home. Attended our preparative meeting on Fifth Day. The meeting for worship was held in silence – a hard, trying meeting[2] – and which is not unusual at this season of the year,

---

[1] John 4
[2] The rest of the paragraph was deleted from the printed *Journal*.

which I apprehend arises from these two causes in general – the spring being a time in which people in general enter afresh into the concerns of this life, and are often led into new schemes and, enter into them with too much avidity.¹ By which means, both body and mind are too much borne down and exhausted. And coming to meeting in this worn state, as soon as they become still, a dull stupor pervades their whole system and they have to labor hard through the meeting to keep from falling asleep. And divers are often overcome therewith. And the lengthening days and an increase of heat adds to their debility – that it requires the greatest possible care in Friends to avoid these things and keep in the true moderation. Otherwise, we may be in danger of falling under the censure of oppressing the creation and of abusing ourselves – both in body and mind – which may prove to us an irreparable loss, which no increase of earthly good will ever be sufficient to indemnify.

First Day, 16th: My wife being under an appointment to meet some women Friends at Bethpage meeting, I accompanied her thither. It proved an exercising meeting – especially in the forepart. But as I submitted cheerfully and patiently to endure the present baptism (which, indeed, as the experienced Paul well observes is a being baptized for the dead), towards the latter part of the meeting, that all-quickening and vivifying power that raises the dead to life was felt gradually to arise – by which my mind was quickened and led to minister to the states of many present. And life spread over the meeting to the tendering of many hearts. And we parted under a grateful sense of the Lord's mercies, that indeed the query of the Royal Psalmist is worthy to be had in continual remembrance, *viz*, "What shall we render unto the Lord for all his benefits?"

Spent the rest of this week about home, attending our monthly meeting on Fifth Day, but nothing unusual transpiring. Closed the week in silence.

First Day, 23rd: Had the company of our Friend, Mary Post from Westbury, she being engaged in a visit to the families of Friends in our monthly meeting – a very useful service when rightly entered into. My mind in this meeting was brought under exercise in the remembrance of the following exhortation of the wise king Solomon, *viz*, "Keep thy heart with all diligence, for out of it are the issues of life."² From a consideration of which, I was led to believe there was a very great lack of care among people generally in duly guarding³ the rising cogitations and thoughts, as

---

[1] Avidity: eagerness and greed
[2] Proverbs 4:23
[3] Guard: keep safe from. In this case, preventing against intrusive thoughts distracting people from their right relationship with God.

it is the avenue[1] by which all temptations enter and get place in the mind, and if suited to our natural propensities, too often overcome and lead to undue conduct. The subject spread on my mind and led to an impressive and, I trust to some, an instructive communication, for which my mind was made gratefully thankful to the Author of Every Blessing.

Fifth Day: Had the company of our aforesaid Friend at our meeting today, whose simple and plain communication tended to quicken. And a comfortable degree of life accompanied my mind during the meeting, which I accounted a favor, having for some time past witnessed much poverty of spirit in our meetings.

The rest of the week, I attended to my temporal concerns as much as my state of health permitted. But being much indisposed with pain in my right hip joint and which with a little exercise would extend down my thigh and leg, often with excruciating pains, that it was but little I could do, but take a little oversight of business.[2] This I consider one among many other such like mementos to remind me of the approach of my bodily dissolution.

Be attentive, O my soul, that so thou mayest be in a state of readiness when the midnight cry is heard, "Behold the bridegroom cometh."[3]

First Day, 30th: My mind was led into close exercise and travail in the prospect of the very great apparent want of truth and justice among the generality of the professors of Christianity – even of the foremost classes of the different sects. The subject spread and opened to communication, in which the attention of the auditory was impressively called to the subject as one of the greatest moment[4] – both in respect to our temporal, as also in a very especial manner, our spiritual good – as every other virtue must fail and prove abortive, where truth and justice are wanting.

The rest of this week passed away without any matter worthy of remark, except great poverty of spirit being almost continually my attendant companion.

First Day, 7th of 7th month: My mind was opened and enlarged in communication in our meeting today on the subject of the universal love of God to the children of men in not only extending his gracious call to all, but causing them to hear it, agreeable to that scripture testimony, "All have heard, but all have not obeyed."[5] And there are many other plain testimonies in the scriptures of the same import, clearly showing that

---

[1] Avenue: route for access
[2] Descriptions of Hicks' physical distress are played down here and on the next page in the printed *Journal*.
[3] Matthew 25:6
[4] Moment: importance
[5] Romans 10:18 & 16

man's destruction and misery is altogether the result of his own misconduct and disobedience to divine requisition without any necessity laid upon him by his gracious Creator to err or to swerve from the path of rectitude, insomuch that the Lord will be clear of the blood of all his rational creation. As saith the prophet, "O Israel, thou hast destroyed thyself, but thy help is in me"[1] – and many other passages express the same.

My mind was led to open those subjects in a clear manner to the people, and that the want of a right faith in God and Christ was one of the greatest obstacles to their living a just and righteous life in the sight of their Creator, as the just can only live by faith.[2] The meeting was large, and many hearts were convicted, comforted, and contrited. To the Lord only belongs all the praise, nothing due to man but blushing and confusion of face.

In the course of this week, I was much unwell – had a pretty hard turn with the gravel, a very distressing complaint. I have likewise been much afflicted of late with a hard pain in my right hip and down my thigh and leg to my ankle, which prevents my walking or stirring much about unless I ride, as walking or moving about on my feet exceedingly increases the pain – all forewarning me that my glass is almost run[3] and my day of labor – both in a religious and moral relation – drawing to a close.

My indisposition prevented my attending our preparative meeting on Fifth Day. These things all unitedly conspire to sound forth this language, "Remember to die." O that I might witness with the worthy Paul, more and more a daily death to everything that tends to hinder my steady walking in the path of duty[4] – that so my day's work may be finished in the day time.

First Day, 14th: Having so far recovered from my indisposition as to get to our meeting today, my mind was opened in a living, powerful testimony to the excellency of the gospel dispensation, in which Christ by his Light and Spirit was come to teach his people himself[5] – a teacher not to be removed into a corner,[6] a shepherd ever present to lead and feed all his sheep that hear his voice and follow him and do not follow the stranger,[7] nor listen to the voice of any outward, hireling teachers –

---

[1] Hosea 13:9
[2] Habakkuk 2:4, Romans 1:17, Galatians 3:11, & Hebrews 10:38
[3] The allusion is to sand running through an hour-glass, measuring the length of our lives
[4] 1 Corinthians 15:31
[5] Hicks is quoting George Fox.
[6] Isaiah 30:20
[7] John 10:4-5

although they charm never so wisely for gifts and rewards. It was a season of favor, and many hearts were warmed and contrited by the prevalence of Truth, and the Lord's name was praised, who is over all worthy forever.

Fifth Day: Attended our monthly meeting, at which the queries were read and answers made to go to the quarterly meeting. To judge from which, it would appear that we were generally a clean, upright people, but I fear our answers are becoming too much like too many of us – more in show and outside appearance than in spirit and substance. And by this formal way of answering, unless great care is taken, our queries may do us much more harm than good. This fear often attends my mind and induces me to call the attention of my Friends from the letter of discipline to the spirit and substance, without which all letter and outward order, however beautiful in the outward appearance, is but as sounding brass and tinkling cymbal,[1] and will in the end only deceive and disappoint us, and unveil our nakedness.[2]

Sixth Day: Was our Preparative Meeting of Ministers and Elders, in which our answers made the same good-like appearance – insomuch there was scarcely anything to find fault with. I hope it may stand the test in the day of trial – this we ought carefully to consider. Otherwise, in the end, we may fall short when it may be too late to retrieve the loss.

The rest of the week, I attended to my temporal business as far as my bodily infirmity would permit, although at times my exercise produced very acute pains. But I find it needful to keep up a continual watch – that I do nothing to promote or encourage idleness, that bane to every Christian virtue. And especially at such a time as this, when most of our capable, well-looking, young men are running into cities and populous towns to engage in merchandise or some other calling by which they may live by their wits – being unwilling to labor with their hands, although it is the most sure way marked out by divine wisdom for our truest comfort and peace here, and a right preparation for eternal joy hereafter. And although many fatal consequences have befallen many of those who have thus run out in trade and mercantile business – apparently to the ruin of both body and soul, and the great injury and distress of their families – yet because some few have made themselves rich in temporal things by those pursuits, it has so blinded the minds of many that they will not take warning, but go on in their willful way to their own utter ruin.

First Day, 21st of 7th month 1816: This day at our meeting, my mouth was opened in a full testimony introduced from this scripture passage, "Wherewith shall a young man cleanse his way? By taking heed thereto

---

[1] 1 Corinthians 13:1
[2] Isaiah 47:3

according to thy word."[1] I was led in my communication to show to the people that in this word was comprehended the great gospel privilege – the word nigh in the heart and in the mouth[2] – that it was not a literal or outward word, nor any created thing, but the uncreated Word, Christ, by whom all things were created,[3] or at first spoke into existence and order,[4] as nothing else could enable us to cleanse our way or live a righteous holy life. And that it was only by a living faith in this inward, operative, powerful Word, that any could please God or be acceptable to him. And that it was the only means by which we could be saved. And that it was offered to the acceptance of all, and therefore, all were encouraged to lay hold of the offered mercy and not slight the day of their visitation.

Second and Third Days: I was busied in overseeing my temporal business, attended at times by much bodily pain, and which, I trust and hope, I endured without improperly complaining or murmuring.

And the three following days, I attended our quarterly meeting held this time at Westbury. I think in the main, it was a favored season and the meeting, large and solemn – the Divine Presence and power evidently felt to preside, to the humbling of many minds and producing contrition of spirit – and the gospel labors, instructive and edifying.

Seventh Day: Spent in caring necessarily about many things, like Martha of old.[5]

First Day, 28th: A quiet day – sat our meeting in silence.

Fifth Day: A silent meeting – the rest of the week, as to bodily exercise, mostly occupied in my temporal affairs.

First Day, 4th of 8th month: My mind settled in quiet with the exercise of this day. Besides the usual care and industry necessary in my temporal concerns – that all things might be rightly arranged – I attended, in the course of this week, our preparative meeting on Fifth Day and the funeral of a deceased neighbor on Sixth Day. It was a large, promiscuous assembly, among whom my mouth was opened in a large, searching testimony suiting the occasion, whereby many hearts were tendered and much brokenness appeared in the meeting. The Truth delivered being set home to the consciences of many by the prevalence of the divine power that was eminently in dominion over all.

First Day, 11th: I trust the exercise and travail of our meeting today tended to profit.

---

[1] Psalm 119:9
[2] Deuteronomy 30:14 & Romans 10:8
[3] John 1:1-3
[4] Genesis 1:3, 6, 9, etc.
[5] Luke 10:41

Second Day: I attended the funeral of our Friend, Edmund Pearsall of Flushing. His corpse was carried into the meetinghouse there and a large, solid meeting was held on the occasion.

Third Day: I attended our Meeting for Sufferings in New York, which I think was an instructive season.

Fifth Day: Attended our monthly meeting, at which I opened to Friends a prospect that had for several months attended my mind to pay a religious visit to the bordering inhabitants of our quarterly meeting, and had their unity therein.

Sixth and Seventh Days: I spent in my usual avocations.

First Day, 18th: My mind, as I sat in our meeting, was opened into a view of the great benefits and supreme felicity that man derives and only can derive from the true knowledge and right fear of his Creator – and which knowledge and fear, no man can witness or have experience of but by the revelation of the Spirit of God or by the aid of that Light that Jesus Christ told the Jews was the condemnation of the world, or of all those who did not believe in and obey it,[1] and which is an inward and not an outward light, and all its manifestations are in the mind or heart of man. And I was led to show to the people that this doctrine was altogether the most rational and such as no man of right reason could rationally doubt or dispute. I hope the season was instructive to some, and might tend to remove doubts from some doubting minds – as from the sensations I had, I was led to believe there were some such present.

Second, Third, and Fourth Days: I attended to my temporal concerns clothed with much poverty of spirit, yet not altogether cast down nor discouraged respecting my spiritual welfare – although a fear attended, lest I went backwards, rather than forward.

Fifth Day: A quiet, silent meeting.

Sixth and Seventh Days: Paid some attention to my temporal business, although at times in much bodily pain, which (more or less) attends me daily and has for several months past.

A Visit to the Bordering Inhabitants of our Quarterly Meeting

First Day, 25th: According to the prospect opened at our last monthly meeting, I attended two appointed meetings in a neighboring town (to wit, Hempstead) – in the morning at the 11th hour at a friendly man's house by the name of Samuel Carman, and at the 4th hour after noon, at John Raynor's (about four miles distant from the former), he also being kind and well-disposed towards Friends, and I believe pretty fully convinced of the rectitude of our principles, but hath not as yet given up in faithfulness

---

[1] John 3:17-19

to them, so as to attend our religious meetings – except when held in his house or somewhere in the neighborhood not very far distant.

These were both pretty full meetings, there being as many people as the rooms would well accommodate. And through the gracious condescension of the Shepherd of Israel, the word went forth freely among them in a full, impressive testimony at each place – to the tendering and contriting many hearts, and to the promoting an increase of love to the Truth and to the promoters of it. And I took my leave of them (especially at the latter place) in the fresh feelings of mutual Christian affection, and returned home that evening with a quiet, peaceful mind – the assured reward of faithfulness.

The rest of the week, I spent in my usual avocations, not omitting the attendance of our meeting on Fifth Day, which I sat in silence.

First Day, 1st of 9th: I attended an appointed meeting among my relatives and acquaintance at Rockaway, the place of my former residence when young, while living in my father's house. The meeting was not large, but proved a precious, tendering season – many hearts being much broken and contrited by the prevalence of divine love and power that accompanied the testimony borne, and spread generally over the meeting, to the praise of his Grace, who is calling us to glory and virtue.

Visits with the Committee on the Subject of Schools

A concern for the guarded education of the youth among Friends having for many years past exercised our yearly meeting, and many advices and recommendations issued therefrom to the quarterly and other subordinate meetings in order to stir up Friends to vigilance and care therein – that proper schools might be established among them under the care of pious tutors, that so, Friends' children, while getting their necessary school-learning, might be religiously instructed, and preserved from ill-examples and the company of such children as are viciously inclined, by which their tender minds might be wounded and led from the simplicity of Truth. And in order further to stir up Friends to this concern, our last yearly meeting directed the quarterly meetings to appoint committees to visit the monthly and preparative meetings to encourage Friends therein. And I being one among other Friends appointed by our quarter for that purpose, we attended the monthly meetings of New York and Flushing in the course of this week. And I am thankful in believing that the service was owned by the Head of the Church, who was graciously near and furnished with matter, insomuch that I have cause to believe that the opportunities at each place were instructive and edifying, affording encouragement to the willing-minded.

First Day, 8th of 9th month: I found it my place to be at home today, and of course attended our own meeting. And although for the most of the forepart of the meeting, I apprehended I should be permitted to have sat the meeting in silence, yet about the middle thereof, my mind was quickened in the remembrance of the testimony of Solomon, where he tells us that, "Wisdom is the principal thing."[1] And as the subject spread on my mind, I was led to consider how all men speak highly of it, and yet at the same time, are not at all rightly acquainted with its beginning, and are therefore mostly living all their days without the right knowledge of and acquaintance with it – as it is not to be derived[2] to man through any other medium than the true fear of the Lord, which we are told is the beginning of wisdom.[3] And as it is only begun in man by this true fear, so likewise it is the middle and the end – as every advancement in true wisdom is only by the fear of the Lord. Surely then, it is the most precious of any to the children of men.

I spent the rest of the week about home. Attended our preparative meeting on Fifth Day – the meeting for worship was held in silence. Our yearly meeting's minute of advice on the subject of schools was at this time received, but as it was expected that the quarterly meeting's committee on that subject would shortly attend the preparative, the consideration thereof was deferred to the time of their attendance.

First Day, 15th: By appointment I attended two meetings – one at Cold Spring, at the home of Divine Hewlett at ten o'clock in the morning, and the other in Friends Meetinghouse at Oyster Bay at the 3rd hour after noon – both pretty well attended by the neighboring inhabitants, among whom I was helped to preach the gospel in the demonstration of the Spirit, accompanied with such a degree of the Lord's power and presence as to produce a precious solemnity over the assemblies – especially the latter, wherein many truths of the gospel were largely opened, to the humbling and contriting the hearts of a number present. Surely it was the Lord's doings, and to whom all the praise and glory are and ought to be ascribed, both now and forever.

In the course of this week, I attended our own and Westbury Monthly Meeting in company with the quarterly meeting's Committee on the Subject of Schools. These were both favored opportunities. The concern was opened in a very impressive manner and spread weightily over the meetings – the men and women sitting together while this subject was before them. And I have a hope that Friends will be strengthened and encouraged to persevere in the concern and keep it on its right base – that is a concern for the religious and moral instruction of our youth while at school by placing them under the care of pious tutors, who may cooperate

---

[1] Proverbs 4:7
[2] Derive: communicate
[3] Psalm 111:10

with the endeavors of religiously concerned parents, who are more desirous that their children may be brought up and educated in the fear of the Lord and in his nurture and admonition, than that they should make great advancements in scholastic science or in the riches and popularity of the world – all of which are of momentary duration and unworthy of much of the care of a rational, immortal being, especially when compared with the blessings attendant on a truly moral and religious life, walking in the fear of the Lord.

First Day, 22nd: In prosecution of the concern I had engaged in to visit the neighboring inhabitants, I forwarded notice to Friends of Matinecock that I proposed to attend their meeting at this time – desiring that public notice might be given to their neighbors that were not members, which was accordingly done. By which means, the meeting was very large – more so than I had ever seen it before – among whom I was helped to labor in the cause of the gospel, opening many important scripture passages, tending to elucidate and confirm many points of our doctrine and principles to my own and apparently to the general satisfaction of the assembly.

At three o'clock in the afternoon, I attended another meeting at Moscheto Cove held in the house of the widow Hannah Valentine. This was also a large, favored meeting in which many truths of the gospel were clearly and satisfactorily opened. And I returned home that evening with peace of mind from an inward sense that I had faithfully discharged myself among the people concerning the things that related to their salvation.

The rest of the week, I was occupied at and about home. Attended our Fifth Day Meeting in silence.

First Day, 29th: I attended Friends Meeting at Cow Neck. And previous notice being given of my being there, the meeting was large and favored in a good degree with the overshadowing of the Divine Presence – enabling [me] to preach the gospel in the demonstration of the Spirit and with power, to the breaking and contriting many hearts.

And at the 3rd hour after noon, by previous appointment, had a meeting at Hempstead Harbor, at the house of Daniel Robbins. This was rather a hard, exercising meeting, yet I trust in the main, a profitable season.

The following part of the week, I spent mostly in the oversight (and a little helping put forward) of my farming business.

Sat our Fifth Day Meeting again in silence, at which we had the company of our Friends, Isaac Martin* and Henry Shotwell from Jersey.

First Day, 6th of 10th month: Attended our meeting in silence. It was in the main, I think, a weighty, solemn season. At three in the afternoon, I had an appointed meeting in a neighborhood of the people of color – mostly made up of the black people and was held in one of their houses. It was a season of favor and I hope it may prove profitable to them, as it produced peace in my own mind for this portion of dedication to duty in the cause of righteousness.

Second Day: Our Friend, Joseph Bowne, being on a religious visit among us, had an appointed meeting at our place at the 11th hour today. It proved a comfortable, edifying season, after which I rode to New York in order to attend our Meeting for Sufferings, held the next day at the 9th hour. In the course of the business that came before us, the meeting was led into an exercise on behalf of that portion of the descendants of the Africans that are still held in bondage in our state, and a proposition was made for addressing our state legislature on their accounts, in order if possible, to obtain a law for their emancipation. Apprehending, that as the greater part of these long-oppressed people had now obtained their freedom, to those who were still held, their condition felt much more aggravating and their bondage much more intolerable – insomuch that it appeared to us altogether just and consistent with the duty of the legislature to restore to them the just right of freedom. After due consideration, the proposition was acceded to and a committee named to draft an essay of an address accordingly.

Fifth Day: This being our preparative meeting in which our queries were read and answers prepared to go to the quarter, I felt my mind exercised on account of the many deficiencies apparent – particularly in the non-attendance of our religious meetings, as a failure in that often leads to greater deficiencies in other respects.

First Day, 13th: My mind was pretty largely opened in testimony to the sufficiency of the Divine Light. The season was solemn and, I hope, instructive and profitable to many present.

At three o'clock in the afternoon, I attended an appointed meeting in Wolver Hollow, a neighborhood composed mostly of the descendants of the Dutch. The season was favored and instructive, tending to edification. And I parted with them under a humbling sense of the present favor.

Fifth Day: Our monthly meeting being held at this time, answers were received from our preparative meetings to the five queries usually answered, in which divers deficiencies were stated. But (this being frequently the case), it produced little or no concern to a greater portion of the members. And this having been long the case, I have been afraid at times that the queries would become a snare to us, and prove rather hurtful than helpful.[1]

---

[1] The next paragraph was deleted from the printed *Journal*.

Sixth Day: Attended our Preparative Meeting of Ministers and Elders at which a motion was made for the addition of members in the station of elders. But as our meeting was made up principally by members of that description, I felt doubts respecting such addition, as the number of elders was already more than three-fold to that of the minister. Also apprehending that by adding our youngerly, improving members to the station of elders as soon as they might appear ripe for that station, might in some instances tend to shut up their way to a higher and more valuable calling – that of the ministry. For I have often been led to admire why there should be such an abundant number of appointed elders and so few rightly called ministers in our society. And I believe it requires great care how we bring forward Friends to the station of elders, unless there appears real need for such additional appointments.

First Day, 20th: Had a conflicting season in the forepart of our meeting today with a worldly spirit and the benumbing consequences of a desire after riches. And while laboring under a feeling of these states, with their stupefying effects – which were even intolerable to bear – it often ran through my mind, "The cares of the world, the deceitfulness of riches, and the lusts of other things, like briars and thorns, choke the good seed and prevent its growth."[1] And as I continued patiently under the labor, towards the close of the meeting, light sprang up and dispelled the darkness – in which also strength and ability were dispensed to communicate in a lively and clear manner of the pernicious effects of those things, wheresoever they obtained the ascendancy in the minds of men and women, elucidating the subject by the parable of our Lord concerning the rich man and Lazarus the beggar.[2] And it was, I believe, a season of real instruction to some present, which I hope may not be soon forgotten.

At three in the afternoon, I attended a meeting I had previously appointed at a friendly man's house in a neighboring village. It proved a satisfactory season to my own mind, and generally so, I believe, to all who attended. These favors are not to be lightly esteemed, but held in grateful remembrance.

In the course of this week was our quarterly meeting, held at this time at Flushing. And although some of the sittings were exercising and laborous, yet in the main, I think, it was a favored, edifying season. And we parted at the close of the public meeting on Sixth Day under a thankful sense that the Shepherd of Israel had not forsaken his people, but was still graciously near, a Present Helper to all his faithful and devoted children.

In the course of this meeting, on the evening of Fifth Day, I had an appointed meeting in the town of Jamaica among those not in profession

---

[1] Mark 4:19 & Matthew 13:7&22
[2] Luke 16:19-31

with us, which proved a very solemn, satisfactory season. The people's minds appeared to be gathered into true stillness, a situation most suitable to be taught and instructed.

First Day, 27th: Sat our meeting mostly in silence, but towards the close, my mind was opened and led to communicate a short, but lively testimony, which was introduced by the greatest part of the First Psalm of David.[1] In the opening of which, the meeting appeared generally to be gathered into a sweet, comfortable solemnity. And we parted under a solemn sense of the unmerited favor.

In the course of this week, I attended (in company with most of the committee of the quarter on the concern relative to schools) the two preparative meetings in New York, and that at Flushing – also an appointed meeting at Brooklyn on Third Day evening and one at Newtown on Fifth Day evening. The latter was a very instructive favored meeting.[2]

The one at Brooklyn was so interrupted in its first gathering by a cry of fire in the street, and the unreasonable timidity of the people, that for a considerable time it appeared as though the opportunity must be put by – the meeting being principally made up of people of other societies. But as the few Friends present kept their seats after the alarm of fire began to cease, some who in the fright had run out, returned. But the unreasonable fear they had given way to had jostled their minds in so great a degree that they were not in a situation to be much benefited by the meeting. My mind was much affected on the occasion in considering what a poor, weak, unstable situation the minds of the people were in without any solid stay[3] or trust in the Lord, whom they profess to meet together to worship.

The opportunities in the preparative meetings were very instructive, edifying seasons.

---

[1] Psalm 1
Blessed is the man that walketh not in the counsel of the ungodly, nor standeth in the way of sinners, nor sitteth in the seat of the scornful.
But his delight is in the law of the LORD; and in his law doth he meditate day and night.
And he shall be like a tree planted by the rivers of water, that bringeth forth his fruit in his season; his leaf also shall not wither; and whatsoever he doeth shall prosper.
The ungodly are not so: but are like the chaff which the wind driveth away.
Therefore the ungodly shall not stand in the judgment, nor sinners in the congregation of the righteous.
For the LORD knoweth the way of the righteous: but the way of the ungodly shall perish.

[2] The next two paragraphs were deleted from the printed *Journal*.

[3] Stay: reliance

First Day, 3rd of 11th month: Sat our meeting today altogether in silence.

Spent the rest of the week principally in attention to my temporal concerns (which I believe to be a Christian's reasonable duty), except that I attended (in company with some of the quarter's committee) on Fifth Day, the Preparative Meeting at Cow Neck. I sat the meeting for worship in silent suffering, but was led in the preparative meeting pretty largely to open the nature and design of the concern of the yearly meeting in regard to the pious and guarded education of the youth of our society – particularly while young and at school – in getting their necessary school learning. That they might as much as possible be kept out of harm's way by being placed at schools under the care of pious, religiously-concerned persons – members in society who would be likely to cooperate with the religious concern of their parents, in endeavoring as much as might be, to bring them up agreeable to apostolic exhortation, "In the nurture and admonition of the Lord."[1] For there is nothing that can more nearly and necessarily engage the minds of rightly exercised parents (next to their own souls) than the religious welfare of their children. For parents who can live in the neglect of this great and incumbent duty, must be dead to every right exercise and concern for the preservation and everlasting welfare of their tender offspring.

First Day, 10th: Sat our meeting in silence. After which, I rode about sixteen miles to visit a sick brother and returned the next day.

Had to reflect on the great and serious loss sustained by a great share of mankind from the want of due attention and a right perseverance in the way of known duty while young in years – that when they are advanced in age, and bodily infirmities interfere and increase upon them, they are tossed up and down in their minds, and can find no sure place of refuge for their souls – like a ship in the midst of the ocean without a helm,[2] and which can find no safe anchoring ground.

On Fourth Day, attended the funeral of a young woman on Cow Neck, who was taken away very suddenly with about three hour's illness. I had an open time among the people that were assembled on this solemn occasion, and was led to call their attention to the propriety and necessity of an early preparation for death. And that it manifested great presumption in such a poor, impotent creature as man, who was so sensible of the uncertainty of time, to dare to lay his head down at night to take his natural rest without knowing his peace made with his God.

Fifth and Sixth Days: Attended, in company with some of the committee of the quarter on the subject of schools, the Preparative

---

[1] Ephesians 6:4
[2] Without a helm: lacking any means to steer or control, rudderless

Jericho (New York) Meetinghouse

Meetings of Matinecock and Bethpage – both of which were open, favored seasons while the subject of our appointment was under consideration.

On Seventh Day, I attended the funeral of a very aged man of my acquaintance, being upwards of ninety years old, who lived in the town of Hempstead. There was a pretty large collection of the neighboring inhabitants present, among whom I was led and strengthened to open divers necessary and important doctrines of the gospel in the clear demonstration of the Spirit and, I trust and hope, to the edification and religious instruction of many present. Surely it was the Lord's doing, and to him belongs all the praise and honor of his own works, and nothing due to man but blushing and confusion of face.

Endeavors at & about Home

First Day, 17th: Sat our meeting in silence. It was a quiet solid season.

The rest of the week, I was occupied in my husbandry business, except attending our monthly meeting on Fifth Day.

First Day, 24th: My mind, in our meeting today, was led into a humbling exercise under a sensible view of the great ascendancy of evil over the good among mankind in general – not excepting the best regulated society among men. I was also led, under the saddening prospect, to communicate to the meeting the sensible impressions of my mind thereon, together with the cause and causes of this great degeneracy from the simplicity of the gospel of Christ – that it was the effect of a spirit of ease and carnal security, and a being led and governed in our conduct and works by custom and tradition, without taking the pains to examine whether they were founded in Truth and Righteousness or not. And when at times, they are awakened by the convicting evidence of Truth on the mind, instead of willingly submitting thereto, they call to their aid all the powers of their reasoning faculties to drown the Reprover's voice, that so they may rest secure in their ceiled houses[1] – lathed and plastered by a round of carnal reasoning.

Alas for these in the trying hour of final decision. How dreadfully saddening will be their prospects in a dying hour.

Nothing else occurred in the course of the week of moment sufficient to put on record.

First Day, 1st of 12th month: I sat with Friends at Westbury. The meeting was for the most part a dull, exercising season, but towards the close I had a short testimony given me to communicate, in which the state of the meeting was so opened as to have a very reaching effect on most present – which spread life over the meeting, and much tenderness and contrition were apparent. Surely, have we not cause for these favors often to say with one formerly, "What shall we render unto the Lord for all his benefits?"

Second Day: I attended the funeral of a near kinsman at Far Rockaway, at which I had a very open time among the people collected on that solemn occasion.

I returned home on Third Day. And the weather being cold and inclement, I was indisposed for several days after, which prevented my attending our meeting on Fifth Day – a circumstance which very seldom happens, as I am generally preserved in the enjoyment of such a state of health as to attend meetings when at home without much omission, which I consider as one among many especial blessings and favors dispensed by a kind and beneficent Providence to me, a poor unworthy creature.

First Day, 8th: I left home this morning, and rode to New York, and attended Friends Meeting at Pearl Street that afternoon, in which I had to suffer being dipped into a state of death. I felt as though baptized for the dead, but as I patiently endured the exercise, I was helped towards the close to spread my exercise before the meeting. And a degree of life was felt to arise, and some were quickened. But with too many, there appeared to be a great want of a right, inward engagement and travail of spirit, and these were sent empty away.

---

[1] Haggai 1:4 – having a sealed house (i.e., one with a ceiling) was still something of a luxury in the early nineteenth century.

I tarried in town until Fourth Day, it being the time of our Meeting for Sufferings, in the course of which we prepared a memorial[1] to lay before the legislature of our state in behalf of the black people still held in bondage among us. A committee was separated to attend therewith, and we have a hope that it may prove effectual for their relief.

Fifth Day: Attended our preparative meeting and had to spread before my Friends the exercise of my mind on account of the neglect of too many among us in respect to the due observance of discipline – which is a source of great weakness to society, and especially so to those who are delinquent.

Sixth and Seventh Days: Spent in my usual vocations, accompanied with quietness and peace of mind.

First Day, 15th: Almost as soon as I had taken my seat in our meeting today, there was brought to my remembrance the following exhortation of the apostle, accompanied with a degree of life, "To do good and to communicate, forget not."[2]

And as I quietly attended to the impression, it led to communication and opened to a field of doctrine, tending to show the indispensable obligation every real Christian lies under – let his allotment in the Church or in the world at-large be what it may – to comply therewith. It being a divine requisition, it was therefore reasonable to suppose that by a life of steady and uniform industry (and from which man derives greatest felicity on earth), through the divine blessing, every individual would be enabled to fulfill the obligation – by which means all the misery and distress that arise from poverty and want would be done away from the Church of Christ. And agreeable to the prophecy of Isaiah, "No wasting nor destruction be found within her borders."[3] And each individual Christian would have it in his power to witness in his own experience that it is more blessed to give than to receive, as we should thereby approach nearer to our Divine Original, from whom we receive every blessing – both spiritual and temporal.

The following part of the week, I spent in my usual occupations, except attending our monthly meeting on Fifth Day.

First Day, 22nd: This day, I attended the funeral of my brother, Stephen Hicks, at Rockaway. There was a pretty large collection of people on the occasion, among whom I was led to labor fervently in the gospel and largely to declare of the things concerning the kingdom of God. The season was solemn and, by the prevalence of the divine power that attended, many hearts were contrited and a precious solemnity was

---

[1] Memorial: an aid to memory
[2] Hebrews 13:16
[3] Isaiah 60:18

spread over the assembly – worthy of our deepest gratitude and thankfulness of heart. And I returned home that evening with sweet peace of mind.

Having for some time felt a draft on my mind to appoint a few meetings in some adjacent neighborhoods to the south and east from us, I left home on the Seventh Day of this week accompanied by my neighbor Jacob Willits, Junior, and rode that afternoon to our Friend, James Rushmore's, at the Half Way Hollow Hills, where by previous notice, we had a comfortable, satisfactory meeting in the evening, mostly made up by those not in membership with us.

And the next day, first of the week, we had two meetings – in the town of Islip, in the morning, at the residence of my son-in-law, Joshua Willits, and at the 3rd hour after noon in the schoolhouse in the village of Babylon. These were very solemn, effective[1] meetings, wherein many truths of the gospel were largely and livingly opened in the demonstration of the Spirit attended with a power that humbled and contrited many hearts, and brought a general solemnity over the meetings.

The next day, we rode to our Friend, Thomas Whitson's on the south side of our township. Had an appointed meeting there that evening, which was also favored with attendant gospel power, whereby my mind was opened and led to sound forth an arousing testimony in order to the stirring up of many present, who, for want of faithfulness and obedience to manifested duty, were much behind in their day's work, and which, as it opened on my mind, was not only a cause of great loss and disadvantage in a religious sense to themselves, but also to their families and their tender offspring. Things were laid close home to these, and they excited to more faithfulness and religious engagement.

Here, I was informed of the death of our Friend and neighbor, Elizabeth Jones, wife of Samuel, whose funeral was to be the next day. This induced us to return home early in the morning in order to attend the same. And as she had many connections, there was a very large collection of people on the occasion – many of whom were of divers different persuasions – among whom, my heart and mouth were opened to preach the gospel and to open to the people the principles of the Christian religion in a full and clear manner, in the authority of Truth. It was a highly favored season, in which Truth reigned triumphant, and the Lord's name and power were praised and exalted over all.

---

[1] Effective: powerful in its effect on people.

1817

Fifth Day, 2nd of 1st month 1817: I attended our meeting as usual – it was quiet and comfortable. Near the close I had a short testimony to communicate, to the excellency and exalted privileges of the Christian state, which brought a precious covering over the meeting.

First Day, 5th: Very soon after I took my seat in meeting today, my mind was brought into a feeling sense and view of the superior excellency of the true Christian religion. And which can only be known and possessed by a full and entire subjugation of our wills to the divine will, and living in the practical part of that reasonable injunction of our blessed Lord to, "Seek first the kingdom of God and his righteousness," then every other blessing that is needful and comfortable for us will be added[1] in the openings of the divine counsel.

But alas, how few there are who pay any right attention to this excellent requisition! But contrariwise,[2] go on in their own wills and in the prosecution of their own schemes of profit and pleasure – most generally at least, until they marry and settle themselves in the care and concerns of a family. In all which time, scarcely one in ten thousand of the human family even think of seeking first the kingdom of God or its righteousness – or even asking counsel of him in the weighty concern of marriage, upon a right procedure in which, their present and future happiness greatly depends. And for want of this right, previous care, families are mostly unhappy by their going forward in their own wills, and according to their own natural lusts and affections. They are often very unequally yoked together.[3] And when these have a family of children about them without any right ability and qualification to instruct them, confusion and disorder ensued. And the poor children are left to grow up without right cultivation, as the bushes in the wilderness, a lamentable case indeed – a view of which has often clothed my mind with mourning on behalf of these. I was led largely to open these subjects to the meeting under the influence of gospel love, and found peace in my labor – the sure reward of faithfulness to manifested duty. Whether the people will hear or forbear,[4] it is not the business of the instrument to be careful about, as the word that goeth forth will not return void, but will accomplish the thing whereto it is sent – either to instruct and comfort or to reprove and condemn.

---

[1] Matthew 6:32-33
[2] Contrariwise: on the contrary
[3] 2 Corinthians 6:14
[4] Ezekiel 2:5&7, 3:11&27

The True State & Condition of the Messiah

The rest of the week, I was mostly employed in my temporal concerns, except attending our preparative meeting on Fifth Day. The meeting for worship was, I think, a favored season,[1] in which I was led to open to Friends the true state and condition of the Messiah in his outward advent.[2] And that he was a true and real man, possessed of the same nature as our first parent, Adam, and subject to the same trials and temptations as he was (while he stood in obedience to his Maker),[3] and lay exposed to the same possibility of falling. But by his faithfulness to divine requisition and the leadings of Holy Spirit, he overcame the wicked one.[4] And by persevering therein, he soon became established beyond the possibility of falling – thereby setting an example to all his followers and assuring them for their encouragement that would they come up in the same line of faithfulness and persevere under the leadings of the same Holy Spirit – a manifestation of which all have received to profit withal – they might all come to know the same establishment, and be strengthened through divine aid to rise superior to all temptations and the possibility of falling. For to effect this by his example, his precepts, doctrines, and commands was the great and glorious end of his coming as the second Adam,[5] to make up the deficiency of the first.[6]

First Day, 12th: A silent meeting today.

Fourth Day: Feeling my mind drawn to attend the Monthly Meeting of Westbury held today, I proceeded accordingly. In the meeting for worship, I was led to show to Friends, under the similitude of Israel's travels, that it was not enough to be delivered from our former sins, nor to be delivered from the Red Sea of trials and obstructing temptations, so as to rejoice on the banks of deliverance, and be fed with heavenly manna – even angels' food[7] – nor to journey on towards the promised Canaan, as far as Korah and his company,[8] and to see, like them, the wonder-working power of Jehovah in the wilderness to land them safe beyond Jordan's stream[9] – unless they also came to witness a complete death to their own

---

[1] The rest of the paragraph was deleted from the printed *Journal*.
[2] Advent: Jesus' coming into the world
[3] Hebrews 4:15
[4] Luke 4:13
[5] 2 Corinthians 15:45-47
[6] Hebrews 8:7
[7] Psalm 78:25
[8] The story of the revolt of Korah is told in Numbers 16
[9] The words, "to land them safe beyond Jordan's stream" were excised from the printed *Journal*. Other phrases in this sermon, e.g., "banks of deliverance" and "heavenly manna" are also not typical of Hicks' vocabulary and are not from

wills, so as to be entirely submissive to the will of our Heavenly Father. For otherwise, they would be left to encompass (as it were) a mountain in the wilderness,[1] until the old man (that is, self-will) is entirely worn out and dies there[2] – on this side Jordan. For nothing short of that will open Jordan's streams and enable us to go through dry shod.[3]

I had largely to open to Friends the mystery of our redemption in the demonstration of the Spirit, showing the necessity of continual perseverance and making progress in our heavenly journey. Otherwise, we shall be liable to fall into a state of ease[4] and carnal security, and thereby make shipwreck of faith and a good conscience, and our latter end be worse than the beginning[5] – like those of Israel, who fell in the wilderness and never obtained the promised land.[6]

Fifth Day: Attended our monthly meeting. Was engaged to stir up Friends (as it was the time of answering our queries) to more diligence by faithfully scrutinizing their own individual states through the medium of the queries – by which means, they would be truly useful to us. For otherwise, the reading and answering them would become a dead, lifeless form.

First Day, 19th: A silent meeting today, in which my spirit was grieved (as is too often the case in our meetings) from a sense of the great want of real spiritual life, and the apparent deadness and formality which too generally prevail, whereby it often happens that a number appear drowsy and nodding – and some falling asleep – to the great trouble and exercise of the living, concerned members, who are often led to mourn in secret on those accounts.[7]

In the course of this week, I attended our quarterly meeting being held at this time at Westbury. It was a season of close, solemn searching, wherein through the animating influence of the Divine Light and Life, the hid things of Esau (or the first nature) were brought to light and judged. And although some, who had long covered themselves as with thick clay[8] and were solacing themselves in their ceiled houses, kicked like Jeshurun

---

scripture. They would, on the other hand, fit nicely in a Methodist hymn. At that time, Quakers did not sing hymns, so their presence is curious.

[1] Deuteronomy 2:1-3
[2] Deuteronomy 1:3
[3] Dry shod: with dry shoes, i.e., just as the Israelites crossed the Jordan River on dry land (Joshua 3)
[4] Amos 6:1
[5] 2 Peter 2:20
[6] Numbers 14:26-38
[7] Jeremiah 13:17
[8] Habakkuk 2:6

of old[1] when they were made to feel the piercing edge of that sword that divides between soul and spirit, joints and marrow, and is a discerner of the thoughts and intents of the heart.[2] Yet Truth had its way over all their opposition, and in the closing meeting, reigned triumphant over all. Blessed be the Lord for his unspeakable gifts dispensed to his faithful children.

First Day, 26th: My mind, in our meeting today, was led to reflect on the excellency and powerful effect of true faith. And as the subject opened, I found it my place to spread the prospect before the meeting. In the communication whereof, life sprang up and Truth was raised into dominion over all, and my heart was made thankful for the unmerited favor.

The rest of the week I was busily employed in my domestic affairs, and in taking the oversight and care of my stock – the weather being very cold and frosty, and the earth covered with snow.

Attended our meeting on Fifth Day, at which there was a funeral of a deceased Friend, an ancient maiden. I sat the greater part of the meeting in silence, in which time there were two short testimonies delivered, but without much apparent effect, as the seed of immortal life was too much pressed down, as a cart with sheaves. And nothing is sufficient to raise a meeting from such a state of death and stupor, but the life-giving presence and powerful word of him who raised Lazarus from the grave.[3] And as I patiently endured the necessary baptism for the dead, towards the close of the meeting a little gleam of light appeared, in which there was brought to my remembrance that passage of the wise man that, "It is righteousness that exalts a nation." And as my inward eye was kept to the opening, it spread and life sprang up, in which I felt the woe,[4] and in which I felt the truth of that saying that, "The Lord's people are willing in the day of his power."[5] And as I yielded to communication, the life was raised into dominion and ran as oil over all. Surely it was the Lord's doing and marvelous in mine eyes.

First Day, 2nd of 2nd month: I was largely led forth in our meeting today on the different dispensations communicated to man by his gracious Creator in order for his recovery out of the fall – pointing out to the people the difference between the law state and that of the gospel, showing that the former was a mere figure or prelude to the latter, and that the first, with all its elementary rituals, ceased where the latter began. The first only

---

[1] Deuteronomy 32:15
[2] Hebrews 4:12
[3] John 11
[4] Woe: distress or misfortune
[5] Psalm 110:3

affecting the body, the latter principally the soul – the first only the shadow of good things, the latter the substance of all good to man – by which, he is altogether redeemed from sin and death, as he submits willingly and fully to the power of the gospel and is thereby prepared for an inheritance in eternal life.

In the course of this week, beside giving the necessary attention to my temporal affairs, I made several friendly visits to the families of some particular Friends, in company with my wife and daughter, Elisabeth. And although I met with some occurrences – one in particular, which produced considerable exercise to my mind – yet I had satisfaction in the visits, believing that when they are properly made, they often prove mutually comfortable and encouraging.

Sat our meeting on Fifth Day in silence.

First Day, 9th: Had a silent meeting today.

This week afforded occasion of deep inward exercise and seasons of heart-searching from a view of the manifest declension of many among us from that honest simplicity and faithfulness that so eminently characterized our worthy predecessors – as also the increase of vanity and immorality among the people without – and which I fear may have been increased through the want of faithfulness among us in the right and full support of our Christian testimonies.

First Day, 16th of 2nd month: Soon after I took my seat in our meeting today, my mind was quickened and led into a sympathetic feeling with the state of Elijah when he fled from the wrath and persecution of Ahab and Jezebel.[1] When under great discouragement and dismay, he bemoaned his condition – that they had pulled down the Lord's altars, slain his servants and he only was left, and they sought his life.[2] But the Lord told him for his encouragement, that there were seven thousand yet left in Israel that had not bowed their knee to the image of Baal.[3] But these, no doubt, were so scattered and dispersed among the people, that Elijah could scarcely find one to open his mind to, and therefore felt himself as one alone. And this, no doubt, is the lot of some of the Lord's most faithful servants in the present day. And was it not for the same divine help and succor that Elijah experienced, some of these at times would be altogether cast down and discouraged.

The subject spread and enlarged and opened to a field of doctrine, wherein I was led to show to the people how the mystery of iniquity[4] [Satan] had wrought in and under every dispensation of God to the

---

[1] 1 Kings 19:1-3
[2] 1 Kings 19:10
[3] 1 Kings 19:18
[4] 2 Thessalonians 2:7

Church through his varied transformations – always resembling as much as may be, an angel of light[1] – by which he lies in wait to deceive, and has generally deceived, and still deceives, the greater part of the people of all the nations under heaven – setting up his post by God's post,[2] and leading his votaries to perform their worship and works just like the Lord's servants, with only this difference – that it's done in a way and time of their own heart's devising. And there is no other distinguishing mark than that the Lord's children are all taught of the Lord. And they are made to know it, for in righteousness they are established, and great is the peace of these children.[3] But there is no peace to the wicked – to such as walk in their own wills and in the way of their own heart's devising.[4]

In the course of this week, on Fifth Day was our monthly meeting, at which we had the company of a ministering Friend from one of our upper quarters. He preached the Truth to us in a pretty correct manner. But I thought I never saw with greater clearness than at this time, how that ministers might preach the Truth and yet not preach the real gospel. And herein is witnessed the truth of that saying of the apostle, "The letter (however true) killeth, but the Spirit (and the Spirit only), giveth life."[5] And it's a brave thing when ministers keep in remembrance that necessary caution of the Divine Master not to premeditate what they shall say, but carefully to wait in the nothingness and emptiness of self, that what they speak may be only what the Holy Spirit speaketh in them.[6] These then, will they not only speak the truth, but the Truth accompanied with power, and thereby profit the hearers?

First Day, 23rd: A silent meeting today.

Nothing transpired in the course of this week that required particular notice.

Sat our meeting on Fifth Day in silence.

First Day, 2nd of 3rd month: Having felt my mind for several weeks past drawn to visit Bethpage meeting, I rode thither today, my wife accompanying me. It was rather a low, dull time, but as I continued in the patience, a small prospect opened on the excellency of justice and the right bringing up of children. It led to a communication, instructive and edifying, for which I was made thankful.

First Day, 9th: This day as I sat in our meeting, my mind was led to view the exalted and precious state those enjoyed, who were brought by

---

[1] 2 Corinthians 11:14
[2] Ezekiel 43:8
[3] Isaiah 54:13-14
[4] Jeremiah 18:12
[5] 2 Corinthians 3:6
[6] Matthew 10:19-20, Mark 13:11, & Luke 12:11-12 & 21:14-15

their faithfulness to witness in themselves the fulfillment of the first and great commandment – that of loving God above all – as they would thereby likewise know the fulfillment of the second – that of loving their neighbor as themselves.[1] And as the subject spread on my mind, I believed it right to spread it before the assembly, which brought a precious solemnity over the meeting. And I trust it was an instructive season to some present.

This week principally spent in the care of my temporal concerns and in lending assistance to the needy – in the course of which, my mind was often attended with a comforting ejaculation[2] after this manner, "The Lord is my strength and my song,[3] the lifter up of mine head[4] and my salvation. Therefore, I will not fear what man can do unto me.[5] He leadeth me about and instructeth me, and preserveth me from the snare of the fowler,[6] and from the strife of tongues.[7] Selah."[8]

First Day, 16th: Our meeting today was large and solemn and mostly silent. A little before the close, an exhortation of the apostle Peter was brought before the view of my mind as follows, "Be sober, be vigilant, because your adversary the devil, as a roaring lion, walketh about seeking whom he may devour."[9] And as the subject opened, I found it my duty to spread it before the meeting with some observations thereon, tending to excite the people to diligence, inasmuch as there could be no doubt of the truth of the apostle's testimony. Hence, it was necessary for each one to keep the watch, resisting of him, steadfast in the faith. The communication, though short, was so attended with the quickening power of the gospel, as to reach to and affect and tender many minds, and brought a solemn awe over the meeting. Such seasons are worthy of grateful acknowledgments to the Blessed Author of all our rich mercies.

Spent this week mostly at and about home, enjoying sweet peace of mind, and the solace of heart-felt thankfulness to the Shepherd of Israel for the unmerited favor.

Attended the funeral of a deceased neighbor on Fourth Day and our monthly meeting on Fifth Day. The funeral was largely attended by the neighboring inhabitants, among whom I was led forth vocally to espouse

---

[1] Matthew 22:37-39 & Mark 12:29-31
[2] Ejaculation: a short prayer
[3] Exodus 15:2, Psalm 118:14, & Isaiah 12:2
[4] Psalm 3:3
[5] Psalm 118:6
[6] Psalm 91:3
[7] Psalm 31:20
[8] Selah: A Hebrew word of uncertain meaning that occurs at the end of a line in some psalms
[9] 1 Peter 5:8

the cause of the gospel in a large, impressive testimony – to the humbling many hearts and solemnizing the assembly in general. May it be to many of these as bread cast upon the waters, gathered after many days.

First Day, 23rd: Our meeting today was a season thankfully to be remembered. The subject that arrested my mind and led to communication was a comparative view of man with the rest of the animal creation, showing that man – although endued with a rational understanding and blessed with a measure and manifestation of the Spirit of God to guide him infallibly in the way of his duty – had nevertheless swerved much further from the state of rectitude in which he was created than any other creature, and was much more changeable and unstable than they – this, a sure mark of his fall. And although continually liable and willing to change to gratify his own will and the humor[1] of others, and the changeable customs and manners of a vain world – yet ever averse to that necessary and laudable change, whereby he might regain paradise and renewed communion with his Maker.

This and much more, I was led to open to the auditory in the demonstration of the Spirit – showing the way of man's return, whereby many minds present were humbled and contrited, and to the solid satisfaction and comfort of my own.

On Fourth Day, I attended a marriage at Bethpage. It was, I think, a solid instructive season.

On Fifth Day, attended our own meeting – it was held in silence.

The rest of the week I was busily attentive to my usual avocations.

First Day, 30th: I attended Westbury Meeting, wherein my mind was opened into a view of man's primitive state, the manner and means of his fall, and the way whereby he only can be restored – all which I had largely to spread before the meeting. In addition to which, I had also to caution Friends, particularly the youth, against letting their minds out into a search and pursuit after forbidden knowledge – particularly that of the origin of evil, which in the present day is a subject of much conversation and inquiry. As man in the beginning was forbidden the knowledge of good and evil,[2] and that command is as binding and obligatory on man in the present day as it was in the primitive, therefore, all those who presume in their own wills and creaturely wisdom – independent of the teaching of the Spirit of God – to know good and evil, do thereby desert God, and so become dead to the divine life. And this is man's fall and is a most certain introduction to atheism and deism.

---

[1] Humor: whim
[2] Genesis 2:17

I was much engaged in the course of this week in endeavoring to arrange and settle some difficulties in the neighborhood, and in regulating some of my own temporal affairs.

Sat our meeting on Fifth Day in silence.

First Day, 6th of 4th [month]: Sat our meeting today in silence. And in the afternoon at the 4th hour, we had a meeting appointed by a Friend from abroad, who was accompanied by another ministering Friend. Both appeared in public testimony,[1] but neither appeared to be clothed with gospel authority. And such was the pain and travail of mind I experienced that I was ready to cry out for anguish of spirit and call its name Ichabod, for the glory was departed, as the ark of the testimony was in danger[2] (at least of falling into the hands of Philistines).

The most of the week, I was occupied about home. Attended our preparative on Fifth Day and this being the time of answering our queries to go forward to our yearly meeting, I was led to make several remarks to Friends to stir them up to more faithfulness – in order that we might profit by the queries and be prepared to answer them with more clearness and propriety, according to truth and justice.

First Day, 13th: Sat our meeting in silence.

This week was our monthly meeting, at which the state of society – as represented by the answers to the queries from our preparative meetings – was attended to and a summary thereof forwarded to the quarterly meeting to be held the following week. This order of reading and answering the queries quarterly – if rightly attended to, and Friends were generally kept lively in spirit, and were zealously engaged for the promotion of Truth – would, I believe, be productive of much good to the society. But alas, there are so many who seem lulled asleep in the lap of the world and their minds clothed with so much indifferency, that it is to them but a dead, lifeless form. Surely these reap little or no advantage from their right of membership among us.

Sixth Day: Was our Preparative Meeting of Ministers and Elders, in which nothing transpired worthy of notice.

First Day, 20th: Our meeting today, as well as at some former times, has been rather heavy and dull.

In the course of this week, I attended our quarterly meeting held at this time at New York. It was in the general, rather a low time, although not without some manifestations of divine favor. Therefore, we had no cause for murmuring, but rather of rejoicing, in that we were not cast off and forgotten – which might have been as consistent with our deserts.

---

[1] The rest of the paragraph was deleted from the printed *Journal*.

[2] 1 Samuel 4:21 – Ichabod, meaning "no glory," was the name given to Eli's grandson when the Ark of the Covenant was captured by the Philistines

First Day, 27th: Sat our meeting again in silence.

My present allotment is to be mostly at home – involved mostly in temporal concerns for myself and others. And I trust, instead of increasing my love to the world and the things of it, I am fast weaning from it, and my love continually increasing and strengthening to higher and better objects – as my attention to the world and its cares arises from necessity and duty, and not from love, except that I love to do my duty in all respects to God my Creator, and man my fellow creature – believing that there is no real Christianity without it.

Our Fifth Day Meeting was quiet and solemn, wherein I had to remind Friends that it was not enough to say with Peter – when queried of by his Master whether he loved him – to say, "Yea, Lord."[1] For this is no more than every professor is ready to say, although they may be quite void of any true sense thereof. But we must come to know him and love him in such manner as when brought to a full trial of our faith and love, we can say as Peter did in his third answer, "Yea, Lord! Thou knowest all things – thou knowest that I love thee!"[2] For this is the situation of mind that prepares to be at his disposal and to endure hardness for his sake in the Christian warfare.

First Day, 4th of 5th month: My mind was led into an interesting view and reflection on the following gracious invitation of our Lord, "Come unto me, all ye that labor and are heavy laden. Take my yoke upon you and learn of me, for I am meek and low in heart, and ye shall find rest to your souls."[3] And as the subject spread on my mind, attended with a degree of life, I was constrained to communicate the prospect – showing that Christ's yoke was nothing less, nor more, than the revealed will of his (and our) Heavenly Father, which, as it is faithfully submitted to, yokes down and keeps in subjection every desire and propensity of the human mind that stands in opposition thereto – insomuch that the creature hereby knows God's kingdom to be come, and his will to be done, in earth as it is done in heaven. And the reward of rest and peace, promised in the closing part of the invitation, is experienced.

The following part of this week spent principally in my usual vocations, except attending our preparative meeting on Fifth Day, and at the 3rd hour after noon, the funeral of our Friend, Joshua Powell of Westbury, who was taken from us after a short illness by a sudden inflammation and mortification[4] in one of his arms. How true is that

---

[1] John 21:15-16
[2] John 21:17
[3] Matthew 11:28-29
[4] Mortification: gangrene

saying of the prophet that all flesh is as grass that soon fadeth away[1] or by the scythe is suddenly cut down. Just such is man – alive today, tomorrow is dead.[2] This subject very sensibly impressed my mind at the funeral, and led to a very awakening[3] communication that had a very reaching effect on the assembly. I hope the word that went forth will not return void, but prove a blessing to some who were present.

First Day, 11th: Our meeting today was a trying season – but little felt of the real virtue and life of religion. It seemed as though we were in a worse condition than the multitude formerly. For there was a lad found among them with five barley loaves and a few fishes, which served for the blessing to operate upon and enlarge, so as to suffice the multitude – and fragments remaining.[4] But we were almost or altogether destitute of anything for the blessing of heaven to act upon. Therefore we ought not to murmur, although we were sent empty away.

Except attending our monthly meeting on Fifth Day and assisting some of my neighbors to settle their business in which a dispute had arisen, I was principally occupied in my temporal concerns through the week.

First Day, 18th: A silent meeting today.

The rest of this week busily employed preparatory for leaving home to attend our approaching yearly meeting. Left home early on Seventh Day morning and got into the city seasonably to attend the opening of the Yearly Meeting of Ministers and Elders at the 10th hour.

On Second Day at the same hour, the meeting of discipline opened and continued by adjournments until the Seventh Day following. In the forenoon about the 11th hour, it closed under a comfortable evidence of the presiding of the Divine Presence – and which, with thankfulness and gratitude we have humbly to acknowledge, has in gracious condescension been vouchsafed to us in the several sittings of our large, solemn assembly – in as great, if not greater, degree than has been witnessed in any previous season – tending to unite all the rightly concerned members in a living travail for the promotion of the cause of Truth and Righteousness, and the spreading and exaltation of those precious testimonies given us as a people to bear for the Prince of Peace.

First Day, 1st of 6th month: Attended our own meeting today in humbling silence.

Spent the week in and about home, except attending the funeral of our ancient Friend, Isaac Underhill of Flushing, on Sixth Day, on which

---

[1] Isaiah 40:6-8 & 1 Peter 1:24-25
[2] Matthew 6:30 & Luke 12:28
[3] Awakening: rousing
[4] John 6:9-13

occasion a meeting was held in Friends Meetinghouse at that place. It was a very solemn and, I trust, a profitable season to some present. My mouth was opened among them to testify of the things concerning the kingdom of God, in a large, affecting testimony, whereby many hearts were contrited and made humbly thankful for the present favor. And I was glad in believing that the Lord is still mindful of his people, and is graciously disposed to strengthen and support them in the needful time as their eye is kept single to him, looking to him only for help and salvation.

First Day, 8th: Had a comfortable meeting today. Truth's testimony went forth freely to the people, to the comforting and contriting many minds present. This is the Lord's doing and worthy of grateful acknowledgments from his people for such continued, yet unmerited mercy.

On Third Day, I attended the meeting at Bethpage, appointed by our Friends, Elizabeth Coggeshall* and Ann Shipley of New York, who were now among us on a religious visit. It was, I think, a season of great favor – not only the two women appeared in seasonable and appropriate testimonies, tending to gather the minds of the people into a very comfortable solemnity, but also my heart and mouth were opened in a large, affecting testimony, which found a ready entrance into the minds of most present – breaking down all opposition, contriting many hearts by the prevalence of Truth that ran as oil over all. After which, our Friend, Elizabeth, closed the service in solemn supplication. It was a day of favor, worthy of grateful remembrance.

On Fifth Day, I attended our preparative meeting, in which I had some service for the promotion of Truth's cause.

The four other days of this week, I spent in my usual, necessary avocations.

First Day, 15th: Nothing in particular to remark respecting the exercise of this day.

On the Fourth Day of this week was held our monthly meeting, in which I was led into some close searching exercise in order to stir up Friends to more diligence and circumspection, that so their light might shine forth to the help of others, and their conduct appear consonant with their profession. In this meeting, I found it expedient and consistent with my duty to open to Friends a prospect and concern that had for a considerable time rested on my mind to pay a visit in gospel love to Friends and others in some parts of the Yearly Meetings of Philadelphia and Baltimore. The subject obtained the solid attention of the meeting, and Friends appointed to confer with me on the subject, and, as way opened, prepare an essay of a certificate for that purpose and produce it to our next meeting.

First Day, 22nd: Sitting in our meeting today, my mind was led into a view of the great and singular advantages that would accrue to the children of men from their having right and just ideas of good and evil – as the want of which was the principal cause of all the distress and misery that fell to their lot, both here and hereafter. The subject spread (as I was led to communicate) and opened to a large field of doctrine, which had a very reaching effect upon the assembly. And a very precious solemnity was spread over the meeting, for which my heart was made truly glad with that gladness that hath no sorrow with it.

The rest of the week, I was busily employed in the care of my temporal concerns, which nevertheless has no tendency, if kept within right bounds, to prevent internal religious exercises and spiritual meditations and soliloquy.[1]

Sat our Fifth Day Meeting in silence.

First Day, 29th: I sat our meeting in a sense of great weakness, in which I realized the truth of David's testimony, "Verily, every man at his best state is altogether vanity."[2]

Except attending, in silent meditation, our Fifth Day Meeting and the funeral of the only daughter of my brother Samuel on Seventh Day, I was engaged as usual during the week in my family cares, which indeed is an arduous task if rightly performed and every department[3] duly cared for in its right season, consistent with our moral and religious duty.

The funeral mentioned above was a solemn one, in which I was largely led forth to testify of the things concerning the kingdom of God – opening the way of life and salvation to the people in the demonstration of the Spirit. And the assembly was generally solemnized by the efficacy of the power that attended, and Truth raised into victory over all. Such favors are truly worthy of deep, heart-felt gratitude and thanksgiving to the God and Father of all our sure mercies, who is over all, worthy forever.

First Day, 6th of 7th month: Soon after I took my seat in our meeting today, my mind was opened into a view of the great need man stands in of a Savior, and that nothing can give him so full and lively a sense thereof, as a true sight and sense of his own real condition – by which he is not only brought to see the real want of a Savior, but is also shown thereby, what kind of a Savior he needs. That it must not only be one who is continually present, but who is possessed of a prescience[4] sufficient to see at all times, all man's enemies and every temptation that may or can await him, and power sufficient to defend him from all and at all times. And

---

[1] Soliloquy: talking to oneself
[2] Psalm 39:5
[3] Department: a part of a whole
[4] Prescience: foreknowledge

therefore, such a Savior as man wants, cannot be one without him, but must be always present – just in the very place man's enemies assault him, which is within, in the very temple of the heart – as no other Savior but such a one, who takes his residence in the very center of the soul of man, can possibly produce salvation to him. Hence, for man to look for a Savior or salvation anywhere else than in the very center of his own soul is a fatal mistake and must consequently land him in disappointment and error.

I was led forth to communicate largely to the people on the subject, and on the blessed effects that do and will result to all those who find such a Savior, and who in humility and sincerity of heart follow him faithfully in the way of his leadings. It was a solemn season and a day thankfully to be remembered.

I was taken up principally the rest of this week (except attending our preparative meeting on Fifth Day) in my hay harvest. It's a laborous season and is made much more so by reason of there being so few faithful laborers among those who offer themselves as such – most of whom are more anxiously careful how they may obtain the highest wages than they are engaged honestly to strive justly to earn them, which makes the care and oversight of such business rather irksome and unpleasant, which if otherwise, would be very agreeable and often very delightsome.[1]

First Day, 13th: I sat our meeting in silence.

This week, I was mostly taken up in caring for and assisting in my hay harvest, as through the kindness of the season, our fields have brought forth plenteously.

On Fifth Day was our monthly meeting, at which Friends united with the concern which I had laid before them at the preceding monthly meeting – to pay a visit in gospel love to Friends and others in some parts of the Yearly Meetings of Philadelphia and Baltimore. A certificate was prepared for the purpose and signed by the clerks of the men's and women's meetings, leaving me at liberty to proceed therein as way should open.

First Day, 20th: A solemn and, I trust, profitable meeting today, in which the gospel was preached freely in the demonstration of Truth, and a precious covering was felt to spread over the assembly, and sweet peace clothed my mind at the conclusion. Surely the Lord is a bountiful and rich rewarder of all his faithful servants, who serve him not for reward, but for the sake of that love wherewith he loveth them, and which he so abundantly sheddeth[2] abroad in their hearts,[3] that they are thereby drawn to love him above all. And in and under the influence of this precious love,

---

[1] Delightsome: delightful
[2] Shed: scatter
[3] Romans 5:5

they are led and constrained to serve and worship him freely for his own sake, because he is worthy, and not for any reward to themselves, because they are altogether unworthy. And because that precious love wherewith he hath loved them,[1] and with which he hath filled their hearts, hath banished and dispelled out of their hearts every germ of self-love, and all kind of selfishness. Nevertheless, of his own rich bounty and free will, without any real merit on our part, he abundantly and plenteously bestoweth his blessings upon all his faithful servants and children, whereby their love to him is continually increased until he becomes their all in all,[2] their alpha and omega,[3] and are brought into the possession of that perfect love that casteth out all fear, and in which they are enabled continually to worship and adore him, who liveth forever[4] and who only is everlastingly worthy of all blessing and praise.

In the course of this week was our quarterly meeting held at this time at Westbury. It was a season of exercise to all who were concerned for the promotion of right order in the Church. And much counsel, reproof, and admonition were communicated under right influence for the stirring up the negligent and refractory members to more faithfulness and attention to their several duties and a more full submission to the manifestations of divine grace in their own minds, that they may be thereby strengthened to arise and shake themselves from the dust of the earth,[5] and separate themselves from those hindering and annoying things that divert and turn them aside from their Christian duty and those things in which their best interest consists. The meeting for worship was likewise a favored season. Many very important truths of the gospel were clearly opened in the demonstration of the Spirit. And the meeting closed under a thankful sense of the present, unmerited mercy. And the living among us separated to their several homes with grateful hearts.

I laid before this meeting my prospect of a religious visit as aforementioned and received the unity and concurrence of the men's and women's meetings, and an endorsement thereof was made on my certificate and signed by the clerks of both meetings. And being now left at liberty, and separated[6] to the work whereunto I believed myself called by the Holy Spirit, and knowing my own insufficiency, and that of myself, I can do nothing, all that remains for me is to cast my care wholly on him[7]

---

[1] John 17:26
[2] 1 Corinthians 15:28
[3] Revelation 1:8&11, 21:6 & 22:13
[4] Revelation 4:9 & 15:7
[5] Isaiah 52:2
[6] Separate: set apart for a particular purpose
[7] 1 Peter 5:7

who hath called – in the full faith that as I abide in the patience and in a full submission to his heavenly will, he that putteth his servants forth, will in his own right time go before them and make way for them[1] – where without, there is no way – and will make darkness light before them,[2] and will not forsake, but safely carry them through and over all the opposition and discouragements that either men or devils may or can cast in the way – to the exceeding praise of his grace, and to the glory and exaltation of his great and excellent name, who is over all, God blessed forever.

First Day, 27th: My mind, while sitting in our meeting today, was led into a view of the great necessity there was of more faithfulness and attention to the inward principle of Divine Truth or Inward Teacher in the mind, as professed by us as a people. For want of which, many were led into divers errors and deficiencies, which in their tendency not only led to great weakness, but to the encouragement of evil doers in their evil practices – a sight and sense of which had for some time been a cause of much exercise to my mind. The subject became very impressive on my mind, insomuch that I found it necessary to spread the subject before the meeting in a large, arousing testimony – laying before the auditory the great danger many were in for the want of a living concern to work out (through the assistance of divine grace) their salvation while the day of visitation was lengthened out[3] – as nothing short of a full submission to the operation of Divine Truth on their minds could fit and prepare them for the awful approaching season, when the pale-faced messenger[4] shall arraign us before the judgment seat of him, whom we can neither awe nor bribe,[5] to give an account of the deeds done in the body, whether good or evil.[6] A solemn weight spread over the meeting and many minds appeared to be deeply humbled. May the exhortation be fixed in their remembrance as a nail in a sure place that may not be moved, is the fervent desire of my mind.

The rest of this week, I was busily employed in endeavoring so to arrange my temporal matters that when I leave home on the prospect before me, I might feel my mind at full liberty therefrom. And that no occasion may be given through the medium of any of my temporal engagements for the enemies of Truth to gainsay or find fault to the disadvantage or reproach of the great and dignified cause I was about to embark in – as I have been led to believe some who have gone out on this

---

[1] Isaiah 45:2 & Luke 1:17
[2] Isaiah 42:16
[3] Lengthen out: extended, i.e., not over
[4] Pale-faced Messenger: Death's messenger
[5] This phrase comes from Chapter 8 of William Penn's *No Cross, No Crown*.
[6] 2 Corinthians 5:10 & Romans 14:10 & 12

solemn embassy, for want of this care have given too much occasion for censure, and have thereby wounded the cause they have proposed to promote, and brought much exercise on the minds of the faithful.

On Fifth Day at our meeting, my mind was deeply bowed in commemoration of the Lord's continued mercies, and that indeed it might be said of us (as it was of Israel formerly) that, "It was of the Lord's mercies we were not consumed." And I was made thankful in believing that there was a small remnant who were preserved faithful to his name and cause, and who were the salt of the society,[1] and for whose sake he would not utterly cast us off nor forsake us. Surely it is of his unmerited mercy that we are not swallowed up in the mass of the people and numbered among the unstable multitude who have no sure and solid foundation to rest their hopes upon, but are trusting in a ceremonial religion and man's invention – all which in the day of trial will fail them and afford no succor to the soul.

First Day, 3rd of 8th month: My mind was brought under exercise in our meeting today in a view of the great want of diligent attention to the Light Within, or that measure of the Spirit given to every one of God's rational creatures to profit withal – even those who were so far convinced as to acknowledge its excellence – and yet were almost daily neglecting its reproofs and turning aside from its teachings, by which their understandings became darkened and they were left in a dwarfish, unstable condition without any solid ground of hope. The subject spread, and my mind was led into a large, arousing testimony setting forth the danger of such a state and the fatal consequences that would naturally and certainly be the effect of such delinquency if continued in. Truth prevailed, and many minds were sensibly bowed and affected by its power. And a very general solemnity spread over the meeting to the praise of his Grace, who is calling all his faithful and obedient children out of darkness into his marvelous light.

The rest of the week spent as usual without occasion for any remark.

First Day, 10th: A peaceful, quiet meeting today in silent waiting.

The rest of the week, except attending our Meeting for Sufferings and preparative meeting on Fifth Day, was taken up in my outward business – with a steady view to my religious engagement, that with all readiness I might be prepared to embark therein when the full time arrived.

First Day, 17th: A silent meeting.

This week taken up preparatory to my journey. Attended our monthly meeting on Fifth Day. And feeling my mind drawn towards an opportunity with the people of color before I left home, I mentioned it to

---

[1] Matthew 5:13

the meeting. And with the unity of Friends, a meeting was appointed for them on the following First Day at the 4th hour after noon. I also gave Friends of Bethpage Meeting information that I felt my mind drawn to sit with them in their meeting the next First Day and left them at liberty to inform their neighbors thereof.

First Day, 24th: Agreeable to prospect, I attended Bethpage Meeting in the forenoon. It was large, and I think greatly favored with the overshadowing wing of divine kindness. Truth rose into dominion and bowed the assembly by the prevalence of its power – for which my spirit was made deeply thankful.

The meeting for the black people was held at the 4th hour. And I was enabled to clear my mind among them, although it was a season of hard labor. After which, I felt my mind clear to set forward on my intended journey, which I did on the 4th day following.

A Visit to Some Parts of the Yearly Meetings of Philadelphia & Baltimore

Fourth Day, 27th of 8th month 1817: I left home in the afternoon in order to accomplish my contemplated visit to Friends and others in some parts of the Yearly Meetings of Philadelphia and Baltimore, agreeably to the contents of a certificate granted me by our monthly meeting and endorsed by the quarterly meeting. And feeling my mind drawn to attend the Meeting of Friends at Flushing the next day, we rode there and lodged – my son-in-law, Valentine Hicks,* accompanying me in the journey.

And notice being given in the neighborhood of my intention in being there, the meeting was large. And the Lord graciously manifested himself to be near and enabled me to discharge myself faithfully among them under the feeling influence of gospel love, to the contriting of many hearts. And Truth appeared in dominion over all, for which favor I was made abundantly thankful, not only on my own account and the account of those present, but especially so on account of my dear family and Friends at home, who gave me up with great reluctance on account of my present bodily indisposition – being under the pressure of a heavy cold and very hard cough, which (in their apprehensions) rendered me unable to travel in so arduous a service until I might be recovered therefrom. But the time appearing to be come for my setting out, and the way appearing open, I considered it safest to cast my care wholly upon him who I believed had called me to the work, in the faith that as I continued to go forward as he was graciously pleased to open the way and make it clear before me, all would be well – whether it terminated in life or in death.

The next day being the sixth of the week, we had an appointed meeting in Friends Meetinghouse at the Kills in Newtown. The meeting there having been discontinued for a number of years and now there being but one member of our society left in the neighborhood, there was a considerable number of people of other persuasions collected. And the Lord graciously condescended to enable me to preach the gospel among them and to open divers doctrines of the Christian religion suited to their several conditions, in the demonstration of Truth for their consideration and instruction. And the people were very solemn and quiet, and I hope the labor will not prove in vain, but be to some of them as bread cast upon the waters, gathered after many days.

We rode after this meeting to New York and rested on Seventh Day.

First Day, 31st: We attended Pearl Street Meeting in the morning and that at Liberty Street in the afternoon. They were both full meetings. And although I was still under considerable bodily indisposition, yet through the condescending goodness, I was strengthened to discharge myself faithfully in both opportunities, and felt peace in my labors of love among them – being led in each meeting to declare largely of the things concerning the kingdom of God, and to point out to the people, in a clear manner, the way to peace and salvation.

New Jersey

On Second Day afternoon, we proceeded on our journey to Newark, a town in East Jersey where we attended a meeting at the fourth hour. Previous notice having been spread in the town of our coming, the meeting was larger than usual for the place – I having had several meetings there before. There is no member of our society residing in the town, the inhabitants being principally of the Presbyterian order.

All was quiet and a general solemnity spread over the meeting, and Truth and its testimony were raised into dominion. Surely it is the Lord's doing, and my spirit was made gratefully thankful for the unmerited favor.

The next day, we attended a meeting appointed for us in Elizabethtown. Here likewise, there is no member of our society. The meeting was small, yet through condescending goodness, it proved, I trust, a comfortable, instructive season to some present. And I parted with them with peace of mind – the sure reward of faithfulness. From this place, we rode home with our kind Friend, Henry Shotwell of Rahway, who met us here.

And the next day, we attended Friends Meeting at Plainfield. And notice being given of our coming, the meeting was large, in which the Lord's power was manifested, and his arm made bare for our help – through which, way was made and utterance given to preach the glad tidings of life and salvation to the people in the demonstration of the Spirit. And many hearts were broken and contrited by the prevalence of its

Randolph (New Jersey) Meetinghouse

power. May the glory and the praise be all ascribed to our Gracious Helper for such continued mercy. For he only is worthy thereof, as nothing is due to the creature, but blushing and confusion of face. After this favored meeting, we rode back, towards evening, to Rahway.

The next day being the fifth of the week, we attended Friends Meeting there. The meeting was much enlarged by the coming in of many of the neighboring inhabitants that were not members. Many gospel truths were opened to their consideration, and its power ran as oil over the assembly to the silencing all opposition. And a perfect calm was witnessed to spread over all – I have not often witnessed such a perfect quiet. Such seasons are truly encouraging, and worthy of thanksgiving and praise to the Blessed Author of such unmerited favors.

Sixth Day morning: We took leave of our kind Friends at Rahway, and rode to Mendham (alias Randolph). And the next day, we had an appointed meeting there at the 10th hour. It proved a solemn, instructive season. And I left them with peace of mind and proceeded that afternoon to Hardwick.

And the following day being the first of the week, we attended Friends Meeting there. It was large for the place, notice having spread of our being there. And through heavenly help, the gospel was preached in the demonstration of the Spirit. And by the influence of its power, a general solemnity was spread over the assembly and many hearts were broken and contrited.

Pennsylvania

Second Day: We proceeded to Stroudsburg in Pennsylvania, where we arrived about the 3rd hour after noon. Here, we had a meeting by appointment, the next day at the 3rd hour. It was well attended by the Friends of that place and many of the neighboring inhabitants. It was a very solid, instructive season. Surely such unmerited favors greatly enhance our obligations to our all-gracious Benefactor, and tend to inspire the minds of his humble, dependant children with gratitude and thanksgiving.

From this place we proceeded to Richland and attended Friends Meeting on Fifth Day. It was much enlarged by the coming in of many who were not members. From thence, we went to Plumstead, where by previous appointment we had a meeting the next day. Both these meetings were seasons of favor. Surely it is cause of deep humiliation when we consider the many sorrowful deviations which are obvious among us from the simplicity and purity of our holy profession, and the great want of faithfulness in the support of those noble testimonies given us to bear for the Prince of Peace. And yet nevertheless, in the midst of all our backslidings, the condescending goodness of our Heavenly Father is such as to break the bread and distill the water of life[1] often on our gathered assemblies, to the satisfying the hungry and thirsty soul, and causing his heavenly rain to descend on the thoughtless and worldly-minded professors, whose hearts are like the dry and barren ground, and in order that they may be softened and be rendered fit for the seed of his heavenly kingdom to take root and grow in – to the praise of his grace and the glory of his great and excellent name.

From Plumstead, we proceeded to Buckingham and rested on Seventh Day – I being still unwell with a cough, although much better than when I left home.

First Day: We attended Friends Meeting here. It was large and favored with the overshadowings of the Heavenly Father's regard, to the rejoicing of the faithful.

Second Day: We rested with our ancient and worthy Friend, Oliver Paxton, who was under deep bodily affliction and appeared drawing fast towards his close. He was lively in spirit, and cheerfully and patiently resigned to his Heavenly Master's will. It was comfortably instructive to be in his company.

On Third Day, we were at Solebury Meeting, of which our aforesaid Friend was a member. And although in much weakness and affliction of body, he accompanied us thereto, and a blessed meeting we had. After

---

[1] Revelation 21:6, 22:1&17

Solebury (Pennsylvania) Meetinghouse

which, I parted with him in near unity of spirit – and which was a final parting to us as to the body, for he lived but a short time after. He was an elder and judge in Israel and his memory will be precious to all the living who were acquainted with him and knew his worth.

The three following days, we attended meetings at Wrightstown, Makefield, and Newtown – all large, favored meetings, in which Truth's testimony was exalted over all opposition.

On Seventh Day, we rested and wrote to our families.

First Day, 21st of 9th month: We attended Horsham Meeting. It was very large, and strength was afforded to communicate to the people, and open many gospel truths in the clear demonstration of the Spirit, to the relief of my own mind and, I trust, to the general satisfaction, comfort, and instruction of the assembly in general, which was composed of various denominations of professed Christians, besides Friends.

Second and Third Days. We attended meetings at Upper Dublin and North Wales, in both of which, the Heavenly Father's power and presence were felt to preside in an eminent degree – breaking down and reducing by its blessed influence all opposing and contrary spirits, and covering the assemblies with a precious solemnity – especially the latter, in which Truth reigned triumphantly over all.

Fourth Day: We had an appointed meeting in a village called Norristown. It was held in their courthouse, there being only a few scattered members of our society living in the place. The meeting was pretty large – principally of people of other professions, among whom was the chief judge and several lawyers and priests. All were quiet, and through the condescending goodness of the Shepherd of Israel, it was, I trust and believe, to most present a very instructive and precious season.

Fifth and Sixth Days: We were at Friends Meetings as they came in course at Plymouth and Providence. And notice being given of our coming, they were much enlarged by the coming in of the neighbors who were not members. These were precious opportunities, in which help was afforded to preach the gospel of life and salvation to the people, accompanied with a power that broke down and subjected all to its blessed influence. For which unmerited favor, the hearts of the faithful were made to rejoice, and in deep humiliation to return thanksgiving and praise to the Benevolent and Gracious Author of all our blessings.

On Seventh Day, we rested at the house of our kind Friend, Enoch Walker, at Charlestown.

First Day: Attended the meeting at that place. It was large – many more attending than the house could contain.

And the three following days, we attended meetings at the Valley, Pikeland, and Nantmeal – all precious meetings, in which the Lord's presence and power were manifested for our help.

Fifth Day: We proceeded to Columbia, a town situated on the east side of the River Susquehanna. Had an appointed meeting there the next day, in which Truth prevailed. Nevertheless, a hireling priest, who attended the meeting, afterwards made some objection to the doctrine delivered, as it counteracted his traditional belief concerning the atonement, the carnal ordinances of water baptism and the outward bread and wine, preaching for hire, and the scriptures being the only rule of faith and practice – the fallacy and inutility[1] of all which had been laid open and exposed – which made him kick like the galled[2] horse when touched on the sore place. And indeed, it is not to be wondered at, as it goes to overthrow all their craft, by which they have their wealth.

We proceeded from thence to Little York, and rested on Seventh Day.

First Day: Attended Friends Meeting there. It was a pretty large, favored meeting, but not feeling my mind fully clear, I proposed another meeting in the evening. And notice being given accordingly, it was very large – more than the house could contain. It was a blessed meeting, in which the Lord's presence and power were manifested and Truth raised into dominion over all.

The four following days, we had meetings at Newberry, Warrington, Huntington, and Menallen. In these opportunities, my mind was much engaged to turn the attention of the people from man – and from all dependence on anything without them – to the inward principle of Divine

---

[1] Inutility: uselessness
[2] Galled: sore from chaffing

Light and Truth, the Great Gospel Minister that – as it is heeded and obeyed – leadeth into all truth and out of all error. And without whose teaching, the true and saving knowledge of God and Christ, which only brings eternal life to the soul, can never be obtained – although we may be favored to sit under the most powerful gospel ministry through the instrumentality of man, however divinely qualified to that end, from youth to old age – as all that the best outward instrumental help, either from reading the scriptures or hearing the gospel preached in the clear demonstration of the Spirit, can do for any man is only to point to and lead the minds of the children of men home to this divine inward principle, manifested in their own hearts and minds.[1] But unless they become subject to its teachings by believing in it as the only sufficient rule of faith and practice, and follow it as such in the way of its leadings, all will be in vain as it respects our eternal salvation. These were all favored, instructive seasons, worthy of grateful remembrance.

Maryland & Virginia

From Menallen, we rode to Baltimore in order to attend the yearly meeting at that place, where we arrived on Sixth Day evening, the 10th of 10th month.

The Yearly Meeting of Ministers and Elders opened the next day at the 10th hour, and the Yearly Meeting for Discipline at the 10th hour on the following Second Day, and continued by adjournments until the next Sixth Day at evening, when the meeting closed under an evident sense of divine favor – and which had been graciously extended through the several sittings of the meeting. I had much general and particular service in the course of the meeting – both in those for worship and those for discipline – tending to gather Friends' minds to an inward, faithful exercise for the support and promotion of those noble testimonies that we, as a people, are called to bear for the Prince of Peace, and for the exaltation of Truth and Righteousness in the earth. And the Lord, our Gracious Helper, by his presence and power manifested himself to be near – setting home the doctrines delivered to his witness in the hearts of most present. Whereby, Friends appeared generally to be united in spirit, and comforted together under a renewed sense of the Lord's goodness. And we parted from each other with thankful hearts.

The meeting being ended, we left the city the next morning in order to take a few meetings that lay westerly or southwesterly from this place. We were out from the city about two weeks and attended the following meetings (to wit), Pipe Creek, Bush Creek, Fairfax, Goose Creek, South Fork, Alexandria, Washington, Sandy Spring, Indian Spring, and Elkridge

---

[1] The next sentence was deleted from the printed *Journal*.

– all favored meetings, in which the Lord's power and presence were manifested for our help, enabling [me] to preach the gospel in the authority of Truth – to the comfort and instruction of the honest seekers, and to the rejoicing of the hearts of the faithful, and administering reproof and caution to the disobedient and ungodly, and to such as are living at ease without God in the world. And I felt sweet peace in my labors of love among them.

After the latter meeting, we returned again to Baltimore on Sixth Day afternoon, the 31st of 10th month. Here, we continued until the 11th of 11th month, not only attending Friends usual meetings as they came in course in the city, but likewise their monthly meetings and quarterly meeting were held during the time. In all of which, I was led into much exercise and religious labor – both in the ministry and in the discipline and order of the Church. We had likewise, during our stay in the city, three very large, satisfactory, evening meetings with the citizens at large – two for the white people and one for the people of color – among whom I was led forth and strengthened largely to declare of the things concerning the kingdom of God, and to open to their consideration divers important doctrines of the gospel in the authority and demonstration of Truth – apparently to their general satisfaction, and to the comfort and edification of my Friends, and the solid peace of my own mind. And I took leave of them, under the precious uniting influence of the Heavenly Father's love, and the covering of deep thankfulness and gratitude for the unmerited favor.

On Third Day, the 11th of the month, we left the city and proceeded to a place called Bush River, where there is a small meeting of Friends.

And the three following days, we attended meetings there, at Deer Creek, and East Nottingham – all favored seasons.

Through Delaware to Pennsylvania

After the latter on Seventh Day, we proceeded to Wilmington and attended Friends Meetings there the next day, both fore and after noon, in which Truth favored with ability to preach the gospel in the demonstration of the Spirit – suited I trust, to the states of many or most of the people that composed those large assemblies. And I left them with peace of mind.

On Second Day, I rode to London Grove accompanied by my kind Friend, William Poole* of Brandywine, my companion being disposed to tarry a day longer at Wilmington.

On Third Day, the quarterly meeting opened there with a Meeting of Ministers and Elders, in which I was led to open to Friends of that meeting the great obligations and accountability that attached to those who consented to take seats in such meetings, which placed us in the forefront

Wilmington (Delaware) Meetinghouse

of society and consequently were looked to as the leaders of the people. And therefore, if we should fall short in faithfully holding up those precious testimonies we are called to bear for the Prince of Peace, and in leading forward the flock by advancing the reformation as Truth opens the way, we shall become stumbling-blocks in the way of the honest travelers, and thereby shut up their way to improvement – by which they may be discouraged and fall back and be lost. In consequence whereof (it is to be feared), their blood might be required at the hands of such unfaithful and dilatory[1] shepherds. It was an instructive, searching opportunity, in which Truth prevailed in a humbling degree.

    The next day was the meeting of discipline. It was also a very favored, searching season, in which many of the hid things of Esau (or the first nature) were brought to light and exposed – to the reproof of the careless, worldly-minded professors, and to the comfort and encouragement of the honest-hearted. After which, feeling a draft of love to those not in membership with us, I proposed an opportunity for them the next day. And Friends uniting therewith, a meeting was accordingly appointed. It was a large gathering and mercifully owned by the Head of the Church by the gracious manifestation of his Divine Presence, under which blessed influence, the gospel was preached in the demonstration of the Spirit. And

---

[1] Dilatory: procrastinating

I parted with them under a thankful sense of the Lord's mercy, accompanied with a peaceful mind, and rode that afternoon to Concord.

On Sixth Day, we rode to Darby and lodged with our kind Friend, Edward Garrigues,* who accompanied us the next morning to Philadelphia. Here, we continued about a week – taking Friends Meetings in the city as they came in course. And as the rumor[1] of our coming had spread in the town, the meetings were greatly thronged[2] – and at some places many hundreds more than the houses could contain. People of varied professions, and even some of almost every description – high and low – appeared eager to attend. It seemed a renewed visitation to the people in general – Friends and others – and not only at meetings but in Friends' families where we visited. They so watched our movements that large numbers, especially of the younger classes, would soon collect at Friends' houses where we were – that those opportunities were made seasons of instruction and edification. For the Lord, I believe, beheld them with a gracious eye, and opened my heart and mouth in converse and communication, to the comfort and satisfaction of their inquiring minds, and enabled me in each meeting to communicate in the line of the gospel in large, affecting testimonies – to the instruction, comfort, and edification of the assemblies in general. And I felt a great power of love to flow freely towards them, which caused my heart to rejoice. And I was made glad in believing that it was the Lord's doing, and it was marvelous in mine eyes.

After I had gone through Friends Meetings, I felt my mind drawn to have a public opportunity for those not of our society. And Friends uniting therewith, it was concluded to be held on the evening of Sixth Day. And Friends apprehending that the numbers who would be desirous of attending would be very great, it was appointed at Arch Street, their largest house. And as the notice was given at the monthly meeting at that house, Friends likewise appointed a large committee of men and women Friends to have the oversight of its gathering, and to keep Friends out until their neighbors should first have seats. But the number that collected of other people was so great, that it was supposed as many went away after the house was filled – and the yard around the house as far as they could hear – as there were in the house. Every avenue[3] in the house was filled with people standing as close as they could crowd together. Such a collection of people I never saw together before on any such occasion. It was with great difficulty that I got into the meeting. And when I had taken my seat, in viewing the crowded state of the multitude, I was ready to fear that the pressure of the people upon one another would destroy the

---

[1] Rumor: talk of a distinguished person or of a laudatory nature
[2] Thronged: crowded
[3] Avenue: aisle

solemnity of the meeting. But as I centered down[1] to the gift, life and strength sprang up, and faith was increased, and the Lord made bare his arm for our help, and soon opened my mouth among them – which brought a precious calm over the assembly. Indeed, I scarcely could have thought it possible had I not seen it – that such a large, promiscuous multitude, made up almost of every description of people, should in a few moments be brought into such a perfect state of quiet and remain so for hours until the meeting closed – especially as in the midst of the meeting, while I was communicating, some ill-advised persons (in order to disturb the meeting) made a great cry of "Fire!" – rattling their engines along the street near the house. But it had no tendency to break the solemnity of the meeting, so that my heart and all that was alive within me, with the rest of the few Friends that were present, were bowed in humble thankfulness to the Lord, our Gracious Helper, for such a marvelous and unmerited favor. And as my whole man was filled with a flow of heavenly love to the multitude, it was likewise very comfortable to feel a mutual return from them, as all that could come near me manifested it – both by conduct and gesture[2] – all being eager to take me by the hand, as they could come near me. Such a time I never witnessed before. For when I reached out my hand to them, I oft had two of their hands in mine at once. Surely it was the Lord's doing and to him belongs all the praise and glory of his own work – nothing due to the creature, but blushing and confusion of face. So let it be, amen, saith my spirit.

Back in New Jersey

After having got thus favorably through my service in the city, the next morning I took an affectionate farewell of my Friends there in much unity of spirit, and passed over the Delaware to Newton in Jersey, where by previous appointment, I had a meeting at the 11th hour. A considerable number of Friends accompanied me thither from the city. Here, we had another precious, instructive meeting.

And the next day being first of the week, we attended Friends Meeting at Woodbury. And notice being spread of our intention to be there, it was unusually large. And through the condescending goodness of him who opens and none can shut, my heart and mouth were opened in a large, effective testimony, in which was opened to the people divers of the most essential doctrines of Christianity – I trust to the general instruction and edification of those present, and to the comfort and peace of my own mind.

---

[1] Center down: turn inward and focus spiritually

[2] The rest of the paragraph was edited in the printed *Journal* to eliminate references to people wishing to shake Hicks' hand.

The seven following days, we attended meetings at Mullica Hill, Upper Greenwich, Upper Penn's Neck, Pilesgrove, Salem, Alloways Creek, and Lower Greenwich. These were all large, favored meetings – particularly the one at Salem, at which place the county court was then sitting, which was adjourned by the judge in order to give the people generally an opportunity to attend the meeting, which they did. The judge and lawyers, with the rest of the court, also attended. The gospel was preached to them and the doctrines of Christianity largely opened, apparently to the satisfaction of all, as no opposition appeared – Truth being raised into dominion over all that was contrary to its blessed influence.

From the latter place, we proceeded on Second Day, the 8th of 12th, to Maurice River (alias Port Elizabeth), where we had a very instructive, edifying meeting the next day.

And the day following, we rode to Little Egg Harbor. And the next day being the fifth of the week, we attended Friends Monthly Meeting there. The meeting for worship was favored, and Truth prevailed by way of testimony, and many gospel truths were opened to the consideration of the people, whereby many hearts were humbled and contrited.

The meeting for discipline was very weakly conducted – the order of Truth being at a low ebb with Friends of this place, and but little hope of improvement unless the younger classes in society come forward in more faithfulness than their elder brethren had done – as many (of the few that are left) appeared to be settling on their lees,[1] without any thought or prospect of advancing the noble testimonies we are called to bear.

Our next meeting was at Barnegat. And the day being rainy, it was but small – yet a precious, favored season.

The next day being seventh of the week, we rode to Squan.

And the two following days, we attended the meeting at that place and at Squancome. But the weather being still rainy, these were also small meetings. But the Power of Truth being present for our help, rendered the opportunities instructive and edifying.

After the latter meeting we proceeded to Shrewsbury, and on Third Day, the 16th of 12th month, we had an appointed meeting there. It was large and satisfactory, many gospel truths were fully and clearly opened to the apparent satisfaction and, I trust, to the instruction and edification of the assembly in general. It was a very solemn meeting, in which Truth was raised into dominion, humbling and contriting many hearts, and which brought my religious labors in this journey to a peaceful close.

---

[1] Zephaniah 1:12

After which, I passed directly home the three following days, and found my dear wife, children, and grandchildren in usual health, to our mutual rejoicing. For which favor, together with the continued evidences of the divine favor that had accompanied me in this journey – strengthening and enabling me from day to day for the faithful performance of the work and service the Lord had appointed me – impressed my mind with deep thankfulness and gratitude for the unmerited mercy.

Praise the Lord, O my soul, and forget not any of his benefits![1] For he hath dealt bountifully with thee,[2] and set thee above all thine enemies,[3] to the exaltation of his own glorious name and power, and who is God over all, blessed forever.

Back Home

First Day, 21st of 12th month: I again met with my Friends at home in our own meeting and was glad to see them, having been absent near four months, in which time I traveled about eleven hundred miles, and attended eighty-five meetings for worship, and eleven for discipline.

And now at home, I find no time to be idle, for in this first meeting, my mind was brought under exercise and had to tell my Friends, that if we would be Christians, we must be united to Christ and learn by his example to do good for evil, as it is no certain mark of a real Christian to be in the practice of mutual returns of good offices to one another – as sinners give and lend to sinners, to receive as much again.[4] And I found afterwards that there was just occasion for my exercise, as some of my neighbors – members of society – had been disputing and differing about trivial matters of property.

Alas for such! What peace can they have on earth? And much less can they hope for any in heaven, when done with time? As such dispositions cannot possibly be happy in the presence of a just, holy, and merciful Being, who is love ineffable.[5]

I sat our meeting on Fifth Day in silence, and nothing unusual occurred the rest of the week.

First Day, 28th: I was led, while sitting in our meeting today, into a view of the great want, generally manifested by the people, of living in the fear of the Lord and of seeking to be initiated into his kingdom of peace and love – as nothing short of it can administer to any the joys of salvation

---

[1] Psalm 103:2
[2] Psalm 13:6 & 116:7
[3] Psalm 27:6
[4] Luke 6:34-35
[5] Ineffable: indescribable and inexpressible

or produce a real redemption from the power of evil. The subject spread on my mind and opened to a pretty full communication in the line of close caution and warning to the indolent and unconcerned respecting the necessary preparation for our final change. A solemn weight spread over the assembly, and I have a hope the labor will not be all lost, but sink deep and remain on some minds.

In the course of this week my case seemed to resemble Mordecai's of old. After riding the king's horse, he had to retire to the king's gate, and there wait for fresh direction. I also felt my mind brought into a waiting, quiet state, in poverty of spirit.

1818

Attended our Fifth Day Meeting mostly in silence, except just before the close, I had to remark to Friends the great advantage that derived to us by being embodied together in religious society under the influence of Truth, as our duties and religious obligations became more binding upon us – especially the diligent attendance of meetings for worship, which gave us frequent opportunity of inquiring into our own states – and how far we stood accepted in the divine sight, and at peace with him, and with all men. For this is a very requisite care that ought not to be neglected, but always be first in our minds.

First Day, 4th of 1st month 1818: Having felt my mind for several days drawn and inclined to sit with my Friends at Matinecock, on this day I went accordingly, accompanied by my wife and daughter, Elisabeth. And although the meeting was not altogether so large as at some other times on this day of the week – the weather being cold – yet the opportunity through the manifestation of divine regard, by which I was enabled to preach the gospel in the demonstration of truth, was rendered an instructive, edifying season. And we were comforted together under a renewed sense of the Lord's goodness.

Second Day: I attended the funeral of a neighbor. It was a promiscuous gathering of different societies of professed Christians – among whom, I was largely led forth to declare of the things concerning the kingdom of God, and to open to the people in a clear and impressive manner, the way and means by which we may come to have an inheritance therein. And that nothing short of our coming into a passive, will-less[1] state – as a little child, agreeable to the doctrine of our Lord (Mark the 10th, verse 15th) – will ever enable or qualify us for that blessed inheritance, where nothing that worketh an abomination or maketh a lie can ever enter.[2] It was a season of favor, in which Truth had the victory, and I felt peace in my labor of love among them.

Third Day: I went to New York, accompanied by my son-in-law, Valentine Hicks, in order to attend the monthly meeting of Friends there, which came the next day – I attended accordingly. It was a pretty full meeting, in which I was led in a close, searching line in my testimony, which made some of the worshippers in the outer court[3] to wince like the galled horse when rubbed in a raw place.

---

[1] Will-less: giving up one's own desires and surrendering one's will to God
[2] Revelation 21:27
[3] The temple in Jerusalem contained a number of separate courts. Gentiles were only allowed in the outermost one. "Worshippers in the outer court" are those who are least faithful to the will of God.

Alas for such professors! What will they do in the end, when the winds blow and the rains descend? Surely their sandy foundation will fail them.[1] Then will they be made to call to the rocks and mountains of their own exalted self-righteousness to cover them[2] from the prevailing indignation that they have brought upon themselves by their own neglect of a right improvement of the talent with which they had been entrusted, and which they had buried[3] in an earthly mind, but their cries will be in vain, as the hypocrite's hope will perish.

Fifth Day: I attended Friends midweek meeting at Flushing at which there was a marriage, by reason of which it was much enlarged by the coming in of many of the neighboring inhabitants that do not usually attend. It was a favored season, in which I was led to communicate divers, important doctrines of the Christian religion, and to open the true ground of the marriage covenant – whereby male and female may be rightly joined together, so as to become true helpmeets[4] and blessings to each other. After which, I returned home that evening with the blessing of peace, the sure reward of faithfulness, and retired willingly to the waiting gate[5] of inward trust and poverty of spirit.

First Day, 11th: My mind was led into a view of the incumbency[6] of doing all our works to please God, and not to please ourselves or one another. And that the only way to please our neighbors to edification was to do all to please the Lord, who hath promised that if our ways please him, he will make our enemies to be at peace with us.[7] The subject spread and led to communication, in which the people were invited to acquaint themselves with God, and be at peace with him by doing his will and not our own, whereby good would come unto us – hence we should please one another to our mutual edification and comfort.

On Fifth Day was our monthly meeting. It was a season of exercise, occasioned by a case of difficulty being improperly introduced into the meeting. This was done while I was absent from home, but as soon as I heard the subject opened, I saw clearly the meeting could not get along with it in its present form, as the meeting had taken ground which was not tenable. I therefore advised to dismiss the subject for the present and let it be taken up anew – unless by a further investigation by the overseers, it should be settled – which was agreed to by the meeting.

---

[1] Matthew 7:21-29
[2] Revelation 6:16
[3] The Parable of the Talents – Matthew 25:14-30
[4] Helpmeet: a suitable helper, usually applied to a spouse
[5] Proverbs 8:34
[6] Incumbency: duty or necessity
[7] Proverbs 16:7

How necessary it is for those who take an active part in the discipline of the Church to wait for a right qualification and not to put a hand to the work until they are rightly called and furnished with that wisdom that is profitable to direct. For otherwise, instead of advancing the cause of righteousness, they may retard its progress and do harm to themselves, like Uzza of old, when he put forth an unsanctified hand to steady the ark.[1]

I opened in this meeting to my Friends a prospect I had of paying a religious visit to some of the neighboring inhabitants not in membership with us in the borders of our quarterly meeting – with which the meeting united and left me at liberty to pursue the prospect as way might open for it.

The rest of this week was spent in the care of my necessary temporal concerns. And the week ended with peace of mind and a thankful heart for the continued blessings of a gracious Providence.

First Day, 18th: Our meeting today was favored, and Truth's testimony exalted, and the gospel preached in its own authority – and a precious solemnity spread over the meeting, and which ended in thanksgiving for the present mercy and solemn supplication for the continuance of divine regard.

In the course of this week was held our Quarterly Meeting at Westbury. It was a favored season – particularly the last day or closing meeting for public worship, in which the Lord's presence and power were manifested in an eminent degree, and Truth's testimony was exalted, and a precious solemnity spread over the assembly to the convicting, contriting, and comforting many hearts – to the praise of his Grace, who is calling us out of darkness into his marvelous light.

First Day, 25th: A silent meeting on my part today. How comfortable it is to sit silently under the shadow of our own vine and our own fig tree, where none makes afraid.[2]

Second Day: I attended the funeral of my eldest and last surviving brother[3] – I being the last and only survivor of six brethren, and am now arrived nearly to the age of three score and ten, and therefore cannot expect many more days, as I continually feel time making its ravages on the animal system, and which, as a faithful herald exclaims repeatedly to the inward ear, "Prepare to die."

There was a large, promiscuous collection of different societies of people attended the funeral, among whom I was largely led forth to declare of the way of life and salvation, and to open many, very important

---

[1] 2 Samuel 6:6-7 & 1 Chronicles 13:9-10
[2] Micah 4:4
[3] Samuel Hicks

doctrines of the Christian religion. And the assembly was generally very quiet and attentive. And I believe to many, it was a season of solid instruction and edification. And I left them with peace of mind and a thankful heart.

I attended our Fifth Day Meeting as usual, and mostly in silence.

On Sixth Day, I attended the funeral of a person not in membership at the request of his widow and family. It was principally made up of the poorer kind of people, who made little or no profession of religion – except a few Friends and some of the Methodist Society. I was deeply baptized into a feeling of their weak state, in which I was led to communicate according to their capacity to receive, which brought a comfortable solemnity over the assembly to their general satisfaction. And I felt peace in my labor of love among them.

First Day, 1st of 2nd month: As I sat musing in silence in our meeting, my mind was led into a view of the great mischief and harm that result to mankind by their giving way to harbor and indulge vain and evil thoughts. The subject spread and led to communication, in which I had to show to the assembly that our redemption and salvation principally depended on a right government of our thoughts. And that if men and women were as fearful of evil thinking as they are of evil doing, and as desirous of avoiding one as the other, they would soon find themselves empowered as fully to avoid evil thinking as to avoid evil doing. And this would be a suppression of sin in its first rise. And there is no other way for any man or woman to become righteous and holy in the sight of God – who as certainly at all times sees our evil thoughts – and more so than man can see our evil actions. And yet, nevertheless, poor, blind, forgetful man will please and entertain himself with abundance of evil thoughts in the open view of his Maker, while at the same time, he would dread to expose them by overt acts in the view of men. This shows how much more predominant the fear of man is (with the most of mankind) than the fear of God, their Creator. I hope the opportunity was profitable and instructive to some present.

A Visit to Some of the Neighboring Inhabitants

Second Day, 9th of 2nd month: I rode to New York in order to attend the Meeting for Sufferings, which came the next day – which I attended accordingly. After which, I spent several days in the city and neighborhood in prosecuting the concern I opened before our last monthly. And my kinsman Isaac Hicks accompanied me.

I attended Pearl Street Meeting as it came in course on Fourth Day, and had an appointed meeting in the same place in the evening for the townspeople at large. It was a very full meeting – many more collected than the house could contain.

The next day, I attended Friends Meeting at Manhattanville in Harlem town and in the evening had a public meeting in the city in Friends Meetinghouse in Liberty Street. These were all full, favored meetings in which Truth reigned and subjected (at least for the present) all contrary spirits – which was cause of humble thankfulness to my mind.

We left the city on Sixth Day and had an appointed meeting in Brooklyn in the evening.

On Seventh Day, we had two meetings in Newtown – the first at Friends Meetinghouse at the Kills and the latter in the center of the town in the evening. These three latter meetings were principally made up of people of other societies, who behaved very commendably and appeared well affected with the meetings. And Truth's testimonies were largely and satisfactorily opened in each meeting, to the comforting and contriting many hearts, and to the solid peace of my own mind.

On First Day, the 15th, I attended Friends Meeting at Flushing. And some notice having been spread of my coming, it was large – and was added to by a number from Newtown of other societies, who had attended the two meetings held there the day before. This was also an open, instructive meeting, in which divers doctrines of the gospel were communicated in the life, to the edification of the people.

The next day, I returned home and found my family well, which, with the peace of mind that accompanied, produced thankfulness of heart to the Blessed Author of all our mercies and blessings.

Fifth Day: I attended our monthly meeting. It was rather a dull, exercising season, in which I was led into some painful labor.

On Sixth Day, I proceeded again on the visit to some of the neighboring inhabitants. Had an appointed meeting in the evening at Hempstead Harbor, and the next evening at the lower part of Cow Neck – both full meetings. In the former, I was largely opened by way of testimony and many important doctrines of the gospel were communicated for the instruction and edification of the people. And I left them with peace of mind. In the latter, I was mostly silent.

On First Day, I attended Friends Meeting at Cow Neck, which was well attended – many of the neighboring inhabitants coming in that were not members, who behaved soberly. It was a favored, satisfactory season, in which Truth reigned.

In the evening, I had a pretty large, instructive meeting in the village of Herricks. It was a solemn time in which many truths of the gospel were clearly opened, apparently to the satisfaction and edification of the assembly in general. And I returned home next morning with peace of mind.

On Fourth Day, I attended Bethpage Meeting, at which there was a marriage, which occasioned the meeting to be very large – I think it was much the largest I had ever seen in that place. There were a large number of young people, and although many of them appeared raw and undisciplined, yet they generally conducted orderly during the meeting. And I had a pretty open time among them, being led to set forth the nature and dignity of the marriage covenant when rightly entered into – and the sad reverse when rashly and unadvisedly undertaken – and especially so when unequally yoked together and of different persuasions as to religion. For being disunited in the main point, it most certainly must tend to disturb their quiet and embitter their enjoyments. And the offspring of such connections are greatly to be pitied – attached by nature to both parents, how confused must be their ideas in regard to which they shall follow. And if, as it often happens, the boys go with their father and the daughters with their mother – hence, children that ought to be bound together in the strongest ties of natural affection and consanguinity[1] are in early life divided in principle and in conduct, by which they become alienated from each other. To avoid which, the youth were earnestly and affectionately invited and admonished to put in practice the exhortation of Jesus Christ to his immediate followers and the people which resorted to hear him, *viz*, to seek first the kingdom of God and his righteousness, in a full belief that as we comply therewith, all other things needful and consolatory[2] will be added.

I attended our own meeting the next day in silence. And feeling a stop in my mind at present as to the further attention to the visit before me, I turned my attention to my family concerns – not being willing to spend any of my precious time in idleness.

First Day: Sat our meeting in silence. It is a precious thing, and very consoling to all Zion's exercised travelers in the path of duty, to be instructed how and when to speak, and when to keep silence.

Fifth Day: A silent meeting.

Spent the rest of the week in attention to my civil concerns.

First Day, 8th of 3rd month: A favored, open time in our meeting today, in which the gospel was preached in its own authority, and in which the excellency and reality of the divine principle of Grace and Truth was opened and explained – showing it to be the same breath of life that was breathed into man on the day of his creation, and which constituted the divine image in man, and is the Lamb (or innocent life) of God, and which innocent life was slain in our first parents by their first transgression. Hence, it is called, "The Lamb slain from the foundation of

---

[1] Consanguinity: descended from a common ancestor
[2] Consolatory: bringing consolation

the world,"[1] agreeable to the scriptures, but not otherwise slain, than by man's rejecting of it, and turning away from it, into the serpentine wisdom by which man became dead to this divine life – and that dead to him. Hence, the denunciation was fulfilled on man, "In the day thou eatest thereof," (that is, in the day thou turnest away from this divine life and presumest to know good and evil for thyself), "thou shalt" (or wilt) "surely die."[2] Which was accordingly fulfilled on our first parents in the day of their transgression, and consequently on all their offspring who have followed their example. Hence it follows, agreeable to the apostle Paul's doctrine, that "As in Adam all die" – that is, as in our transgressing like Adam, we take upon us Adam's nature in the fall (which nature is a state of death), so on the contrary, as we turn inward to the Divine Light and Law, and repent us of our transgressions, and become sincerely obedient thereunto by denying ourselves and taking up our cross daily, hence we come into the obedience of Christ – not doing our own will, but the will of our Heavenly Father,[3] whereby, we put on Christ[4] and become partakers of his divine nature. And thereby, come to witness in our own experience (not only that in Adam, that is, in Adam's nature in the fall – that we have taken upon us by our own transgression, and not by Adam's), that we die or witness a state of death to the divine nature. So likewise in our coming into the obedience of Christ, we take upon us his divine nature and are thereby made alive,[5] and come to witness the Lamb (that was slain in us while we remained in Adam's nature) to rise from the dead and become Christ in us, the Hope of Glory, or the Lamb of God which taketh away the sin of the world. Therefore, all the varied names given in scripture to this Divine Light and Life, such as Emmanuel, Jesus, Sent of God, Great Prophet, Christ, our Lord, Grace, Unction, Anointing, etc. mean one and the same thing – and are nothing less nor more, than the Spirit and Power of God in the soul of man, as his Creator, Preserver, Condemner, Redeemer, Savior, Sanctifier, and Justifier.

Spent the rest of the week at and about home.

Attended our preparative meeting on Fifth Day – sat the meeting for worship mostly in silence.[6] Had some exercise in the preparative meeting in rectifying a mistake in the overseers in reporting a case of disorderly conduct of one of our members, but which finally settled in unity.

---

[1] Revelation 13:8
[2] Genesis 2:17
[3] Luke 22:42
[4] Galatians 3:27
[5] Ephesians 2:1
[6] The rest of the paragraph was deleted from the printed *Journal*.

First Day, 15th: In the course of our meeting, I felt constrained to communicate some plain truths in doctrine and in caution to the unguarded and refractory – but which seemed too much to rebound[1] for want of a disposition in such to receive, and who are apt to kick against the Truth when it is plainly told them. This causes hard labor to the messengers that, although they feel the woe and are constrained to labor, yet find little satisfaction therein, except in the consciousness of having faithfully done their duty to their careless and deficient brethren and fellow creatures.

In the afternoon, I proceeded in the concern before expressed in visiting some of the neighboring inhabitants. Had an appointed meeting at Jerusalem in the evening.

On Second Day, had a meeting at a friendly man's house about four miles westerly from thence, and on Third Day, at another friendly man's house further on in a southwesterly direction among a people in moderate circumstances as to this world, but whose minds seemed generally open to receive the doctrines of Truth. I also had a meeting in the evening of this day in the town of Hempstead. They were all large, favored meetings – especially the latter, which was unusually so, and in which the truths of the gospel were largely communicated – apparently to the general satisfaction and edification of the assembly, and to the peace of my own mind.

We returned home the next day, taking Westbury Monthly Meeting in our way.

Fifth Day: Attended our monthly meeting. In the meeting for worship, I was led to open to Friends the many precious advantages and privileges resulting from a firm faith and sincere trust in the Almighty Jehovah, as thereby we come to witness all those great and precious promises fulfilled that the scriptures mention, and know in our own experience that they who trust in the Lord are never confounded.[2]

The rest of the week, I was busily employed in a variety of mortal concerns, as I find no time to be idle – either in body or mind – as nothing affords so much true peace as a consciousness of the right improvement and employment of precious time.

First Day, 22nd: By previous appointment, I attended a meeting at the house of our Friend, James Rushmore, at the Half Way Hollow Hills at the 11th hour, and in the evening at a place called Babylon on the south side of the Island. But through the extreme inclemency of the weather, they were small – especially the first, where it was like the two or three as to number, yet I found a good degree of satisfaction in faithfully attending to the

---

[1] Rebound: be thrown back or rejected
[2] Psalm 22:4-5

appointment, although I had to ride a dozen miles or more through the storm that was so extreme as to prevent nearly all the neighbors from attending the meeting. And in our passing from one meeting to the other, the wind blew with such violence that our carriage seemed several times near blowing over. But we got along safe and had a comfortable meeting at the latter place in the evening. After which, I rode to my son-in-law's, Joshua Willits' at Islip, and lodged.

I spent most of the next day at his house, and on Third Day at the 11th hour had a pretty large, favored meeting at the house of our Friend, Thomas Whitson, at South Oyster Bay. After which, I returned home.

In our Fifth Day Meeting, I was made an example of silence.

First Day, 29th: In our meeting today, I was led into an enlightened view of the excellency of faith and its blessed effects on the minds of those who come to witness its lively operation. The subject opened to communication in a large, affecting testimony, recapitulating its wonder-working power in the holy ancients, and showing that its efficacy was the same now as in former days to those who become rightly initiated into it through faithful obedience to divine requiring – as nothing else will establish us in that living faith that works by love and gives victory over the world.

Fifth Day: Attended Friends Meeting at Matinecock, in which I was an example of silence. At the second hour after noon, I attended the funeral of Charles Thorne, a friendly man in the neighborhood of Moscheto Cove. There was a large collection of the neighbors, among whom I was led to communicate largely, and open divers essential doctrines of the gospel, and to show and set forth the design and end of the types and shadows of the law dispensation given to Israel – and to Israel only – and how they were finished and abolished by[1] the coming of Christ, through his sufferings, death, and resurrection, and which led to the introduction of the gospel state, or to the diffusion[2] of the Spirit of Truth[3] (or Holy Ghost) in the minds of the believers – by which only, we can come to have a living faith made perfect by good works, because faith without works is dead.[4]

First Day, 5th of 4th month 1818: A silent meeting today.

This week, busily employed in my temporal concerns – even so as to occasion wearisomeness at some times. What a comfortable state would even this world afford, if men and women were all honest enough to do

---

[1] This sentence has been edited in the printed *Journal* by removing the words, "the coming of Christ, through his sufferings, death, and resurrection, and which led to."
[2] Diffusion: outpouring or spreading widely
[3] John 14:17
[4] James 2:14-26

their right portion of labor. For want of which, thousands in every country are inventing pitiful and unrighteous schemes to obtain a livelihood from the labors of others. These – let them be high or low, learned or unlearned, rich or poor – make up that class of mankind who grievously oppress and grind the faces of the poor.[1]

First Day, 12th: I had a precious open time in our meeting today, in which I was led largely to open many truths of the gospel in a clear, instructive manner, which brought a precious solemnity over the meeting – and the meeting closed under the sensible covering of divine favor.

Fifth Day: Attended our monthly meeting – it being the time for preparing answers to the queries to go up to the yearly meeting. It was, I believe, a season of profitable exercise.

First Day, 19th: I had good service in our meeting today, and through the overshadowing wing of divine kindness, it proved a precious opportunity.

In the course of this week, I attended our quarterly meeting, held at this time in New York. It was a favored season in the several sittings of it – affording encouragement to the honest-hearted to persevere on in their heavenly way, without turning aside to the right hand or the left[2] through fear, favor, or affection. The labor, in the line of communication, fell mostly to my lot.

First Day, 26th: I was made an example of silence through our meeting today.

Nothing of particular notice occurred in the course of this week.

First Day, 3rd of 5th month: I attended the funeral of our ancient, worthy Friend, Jacob Underhill of Cedar Swamp. There was a very large collection of Friends and neighbors assembled on the occasion – he being very generally beloved and esteemed by his acquaintance and Friends. And a very solemn meeting was held at the meetinghouse at Matinecock on the occasion, in which I was largely led forth in ministry and doctrine to the contriting many hearts, and to the general satisfaction and edification of the assembly, and to the peace of my own mind.

In the afternoon, I had an appointed meeting at the house of Amos Cheshire, a friendly man of my acquaintance, about four miles easterly from our village, which through divine favor was made an instructive, profitable season, in which Truth was exalted over all opposition.

Fifth Day: I attended the funeral of my kinswoman, the widow Sarah Albertson. A solemn meeting was held on the occasion at Friends Meetinghouse at Westbury, in which I had good service, being led to open in a clear manner, the superior excellence of the divine principle of Light

---

[1] Isaiah 3:15
[2] Deuteronomy 5:32

and Truth – borne testimony to by the society ever since we have been a people – showing that, where that is wanting or is not given heed to, everything else will and must fail of effecting the great work of our salvation, as no other means are adequate to that end. It was a season of favor, in which I was largely opened to declare of the things concerning the kingdom of heaven, and to open to the people many truths of the gospel in the demonstration of the Spirit accompanied with power, to the solemnizing and tendering many minds. Surely it was the Lord's doing, and to him belongs all the praise, nothing due to man.

First Day, 10th: A hard, trying meeting – mostly silent.

Fifth Day: Had the acceptable company of our Friend, Mary Naftel* from Old England. She labored in the ability afforded for our help and encouragement – which honest travail does not fail of meeting its own reward, true peace of mind, which is the richest treasure.

First Day, 17th: Silent in our meeting today:

Fifth Day: Attended our monthly meeting. Had the company of our esteemed Friend, Phebe Field from Scipio. Her company – together with her lively, simple, plain testimony corresponding with our profession – were truly acceptable and refreshing.

Seventh Day, 23rd: I left home early in the morning in order to attend our yearly meeting, accompanied by my wife and daughter, Elisabeth. We arrived in New York timely to attend the first sitting of the Meeting of Ministers and Elders, which opened at the 10th hour.

The meeting of discipline opened the following Second Day at ten o'clock and closed on Fifth Day evening. It was shorter (as to time) than usual, but I think in the main, it was a favored meeting, and closed well under a humbling sense of divine condescension and regard. And Friends separated to their several homes under a feeling sense of brotherly love.

First Day, 31st: Attended our meeting in silence and in much poverty of spirit. And although we had the company of a ministering Friend[1] from abroad, who appeared pretty large in testimony, yet it seemed void of life to me, which I was willing to conclude was my own fault. We had another meeting appointed at the 4th hour after noon by two women Friends from West Jersey. This was also a meeting of exercise to me – without laying anything to the charge of my Friends.

Fifth Day: A silent meeting. The rest of the week laborously exercised in my temporal concerns.

O how killing too much bodily labor is to our best spiritual life! And although it may be no more than is our duty to do in order for the comfortable accommodation of our families, and timely payment of all our

---

[1] Ministering Friend: A man or woman traveling in the ministry

just debts, and punctual performance of all our contracts, yet even then, Divine Wisdom has so wisely ordered the events of things as to impress caution on our minds by not suffering us to reap much spiritual content or inward enjoyment from bodily exercise or worldly care, lest (as man is naturally prone to seek earthly things) he might become so swallowed up in his temporal enjoyments as to neglect the one thing needful – that of laying up treasure in heaven.[1]

First Day, 7th of 6th month: We had a large meeting today, and having been made an example of silence for a number of meeting days past, I also looked for the same at this time, till nearly half the time of our meeting was expired. All which time, I sat clothed in darkness – a darkness which could be felt. But after wrestling for about an hour, a gleam of light sprang up, and a prospect revived that presented at the opening of the meeting and enlarged with increasing weight until it led to communication. In the course of which, the original state of man was considered and presented to the view of the audience, and the state of rectitude in which he was placed by his gracious Creator. Also the way opened by and through which he fell, in a way clearly to discharge and exculpate[2] the All-equitable and Perfect Jehovah from any blame, as having any part or hand

in man's fall and ruin, and placing it wholly on his own turpitude,[3] by making a wrong use of his liberty and by making his election to evil instead of good – when both lay open before him – at his own choice. And therefore, if he would pursue evil instead of good, he had none to blame but himself – the Lord would be clear and his faithful servants would be clear – their blood will be upon their own heads.

Fifth Day: Attended our preparative meeting. My exercise and testimony led to show the excellency and necessity of silence to man in all his attempts to approach the Divine Being in solemn spiritual worship – not only as to the body, but also the mind must be silenced, according to that saying of the prophet, "Be still and know that I am God,"[4] with which our Savior's testimony well agrees, where he assures his disciples that he is the vine and they are the branches, and except the branch abide in the vine it withereth, and that without him, they can do nothing.[5] And as it is the sap from the vine that can only quicken and vivify the branch, so nothing short of the will, life and power of the Creator – spiritually dispensed to the creature – can enable him to perform worship in spirit and in truth. And as nothing but man's assuming an independent will in

---

[1] Matthew 6:20
[2] Exculpate: clear from guilt or blame
[3] Turpitude: wickedness
[4] Psalm 46:10
[5] John 15:5-6

opposition to the divine will, and becoming active therein, occasioned his fall and separation from his Maker, so likewise, nothing but a renunciation of that will, and a cessation from all self-activity as an independent creature, can unite and restore him again, or enable him to worship in spirit and in truth.

First Day, 14th: Having not fully performed my contemplated visit to our neighboring towns and villages, and way opening for a further procedure, I attended two appointed meetings today – in the morning at Cold Spring Harbor and at the 4th hour after noon at Huntington – both pretty full meetings, in which my exercise was laborous. But I had a hope they were profitable meetings to some present. I returned home in the evening.

Fifth Day: Attended our monthly meeting, at which we had the company of our valued Friend, William Jackson* from Pennsylvania. His plain, lively testimony – together with his company and solid deportment – did my heart good, as it brought to my remembrance some of our primitive worthies. But few such examples in this day, and more is the pity.

Sixth Day: I attended the funeral of our Friend, Jacob Smith of Westbury. His death was very sudden and unexpected, which made it the more trying to his family. A meeting was held on the occasion. It was largely attended by his friends and other neighboring inhabitants. The opportunity was solemn and instructive, wherein the gospel was preached in the liberty of Truth and demonstration of the Spirit, and many hearts were humbled and contrited. Thanks be to God for the unspeakable gift.

First Day, 21st: I proceeded again in order to accomplish my aforesaid visit to the neighboring towns and villages. By previous notice, a meeting was appointed at Great Cow Harbor (about twelve miles to the eastward) at the 4th hour after noon at the house of a friendly man by the name of Henry Scudder.* It was large and favored.

And the five following days, I attended meetings appointed at the following places. At Elias Smith's in the west part of Smithtown on Second Day at the 4th hour after noon.

At the Village of the Branch on Third Day at the 11th hour.

At Stony Brook on Fourth Day at eleven o'clock, and at the 4th hour after noon had a meeting at Setauket.

On Fifth Day at the 4th hour after noon, had one at a place called Hauppauge.

On Sixth Day at the 11th hour, near Commack at the house of our Friend, Jacob Harnad, and at the 4th hour, had our last meeting in this tour at the house of Jonah Wood at Dix Hills. He is a grandson of Jonah Wood (deceased), a friendly man who resided in the same place, where I often had meetings while he was living – he being a man convinced of the principles of Friends, but never came forward to join the society, which I apprehended was a loss to himself and family.

These meetings were all owned by the Master of our Assemblies. Although great weakness and ignorance were manifest in many that attended, nevertheless the Lord was graciously pleased to condescend to their low estates, and opened my mouth in doctrine suited to their states and conditions. And I returned home on Seventh Day with a thankful heart and a peaceful mind – the natural result of faithfulness in the Lord's work.

First Day, 28th: Attended our own meeting, which I sat the greater part in silence. But towards the close, had a short testimony to deliver which was introduced by the remembrance of the account given by the evangelist of the pool of Bethesda, and our Lord's healing the impotent man that had long waited there to be healed, but was not. Therefore, our Lord compassionated[1] his case and healed him,[2] which shows how good it is to have steady, persevering faith and hope in the means God appoints for our salvation.

Fifth Day: A silent meeting.

The rest of the week I was busily employed in the oversight of my hay harvest and in assisting in getting it into the barn – the fields having brought forth bountifully, which greatly enhances our obligations to the benevolent Giver.

First Day, 5th of 7th month: My mind, in our meeting today, was humbled under an awakened sense of my own imperfections and the impotency of our common nature. And in this humiliated state, my mind became clothed with the spirit of prayer and supplication, which gave utterance vocally to present our petition to our Heavenly Father for the continuance of his mercy and that he would increase our faith and confident dependence on him as our only source of help and salvation.

Fifth Day: Attended our preparative meeting. The meeting for worship was a lively meeting, although silent or nearly so. The diffusion of real friendship and brotherly love was felt to preside.

First Day, 12th: I sat our meeting in silence, endeavoring to be edified by a communication from a young minister from Cow Neck, which was sensible and in a good degree lively. How much more comfortable it is to sit under a testimony that comprehends good sense, and by which the understanding of the people is spoken to, than such as are delivered in a high sound of many words, and yet so unconnected as to be difficult to comprehend the subject matter the speaker really aims at – or such as are

---

[1] Compassionate: regard or treat with compassion
[2] John 5:2-9

delivered in a kind of prophetic tone without power,[1] which some speakers are too apt to fall into – insomuch, that we are sometimes ready to doubt their call to that highly important and dignified office. These often cause deep exercise and concern to the living baptized members.

Fifth Day: Attended our monthly meeting at which the queries were read and the usual number answered in order to represent our state to the quarterly meeting. And things appeared well with us, if the answers given in were a true representation of our state.[2] But a fear often attends my mind when answering queries, lest they become a snare to us by too easily sliding along[3] in the common or usual way without getting down into a heartfelt examination and deep, honest inquiry into the true and real state of things among us.

First Day, 19th: I again was made an example of silence.

In the course of this week our quarterly meeting was held. It was, I think in the main, a favored season, in which Divine Goodness manifested a renewed extension of unmerited mercy to us poor, helpless, and unworthy creatures. We had at this quarter the company of our esteemed Friend, Gerard T. Hopkins* from Baltimore. He appeared lively in his gift, to our mutual edification.

The Justice Due the Africans & their Descendants

It fell to my lot in the meeting for discipline to revive the concern for the melioration[4] of the condition of the Africans and their descendants – not only as it respected those who are still held in a state of abject bondage and oppression, but also on behalf of those who have been set free, but who, nevertheless continue (in a very general manner) in a degraded and helpless state for want of being placed – as strict justice would dictate, if rightly adhered to by the people and government – upon the ground of equality with the rest of the inhabitants. And I am fully in the belief that divine justice will not be satisfied, nor the black stain for the shedding of innocent blood and cruelly oppressing of this people will ever be taken from the inhabitants of this land until that strict justice is done them and they placed by the laws of our country in the same state of equality – in every respect – as the rest of its inhabitants, and in the enjoyment of the

---

[1] "High sound ... prophetic tone:" it isn't clear what Hicks means by these phrases. It is possible that he considers some ministers to be "high sounding" or pretentious, but it is more likely that he is referring to an artificial, sing-song manner of speaking that became common in the eighteenth century among Friends ministers when giving ministry.

[2] The rest of the paragraph was deleted from the printed *Journal*.

[3] Slide along: let slide or give insufficient attention to

[4] Melioration: amelioration or improvement

full right of civilized man, which is their just and righteous due. And which privileges, if duly and rightly administered to them, would bring them to be as good and useful citizens as those of any other nation.

I also was led to call upon my Friends to persevere in this noble and righteous concern – that nothing might be left undone on our parts in restoring strict justice and right to this deeply oppressed part of our fellow-creatures – not only on their account and for their relief, but that on our own accounts also, as believing we are in a very peculiar manner called upon, agreeably to our profession of being led and guided by an unerring principle of perfect righteousness, to exalt the standard of Truth and Righteousness in the earth. And believing, as I do, that it is not in the power and wisdom of man to effect this by all coercive laws that can be enacted, nor by all the force of the arm of flesh – as nothing can destroy and put an end to sin and wickedness, but a principle in man of perfect righteousness and justice, and this adhered to by man in so full and complete a manner as to have no fellowship or communion, either immediately or remotely, with any acts of injustice or oppression, either directly or indirectly. Hence, I believe that if we as a people were faithful and obedient to this first principle of our profession, we should be led thereby to abstain from all kinds of commerce or dealings in the produce of our country (or elsewhere) that we had good cause to believe originated out of or through the medium of the labor of slaves – wrested from them and sold by their tyrannical masters. And I am well assured that nothing short of such an exalted testimony to Truth and Righteousness will ever put a full end to oppression and injustice. And I believe he who called our worthy predecessors to exalt the testimony of Truth in the earth, and who is still calling us to advocate this noble cause, is looking for this testimony of strict justice and righteousness at our hands.

And O, saith my soul! That we as a people, called as we are to be a light to the world, might so persevere in faithfulness and obedience to the teachings and inspiring of Light and Truth in our hearts. By which, we should be enabled to unite together for the exaltation of this noble testimony, and the increase of the spiritual Messiah's kingdom of truth, righteousness, and peace in the earth. And which, in its progression, will break down and dissolve all the kingdoms of this world, until they become the kingdoms of our Lord and of his Christ, and he comes to reign, whose right it is.[1]

The subject spread with unusual weight over the meeting, and many brethren appeared deeply affected therewith, and divers came forward by expression to encourage its progress and to stimulate each other therein –

---

[1] Revelation 11:15

that my heart was truly gladdened under a sense of the prevalence of Truth that was felt to preside in the meeting, clearly manifesting that the concern was owned by the Head of the Church.

First Day, 26th: A silent meeting today.

Passed this week in much poverty of spirit accompanied with a peaceful mind.

Sat our Fifth Day Meeting in solemn silence.

First Day, 2nd of 8th month 1818: Feeling my mind disposed to sit with Friends in their meeting at Bethpage, I went thither today accompanied by my wife. And although my mind felt rather depressed from a sense of the low state of things among them, yet I was led to communicate some plain things – showing that true religion did not consist in going to meetings, and making a profession of it, but in works of real righteousness, and in a strict and daily conformity and submission to the cross, and a steady obedience to the law of the Spirit of Life in Christ Jesus, which only can set free from the law of sin and death.

Fifth Day: A silent meeting on my part.

The rest of the week, I was taken up in temporal matters, having workmen of various kinds to overlook and assist – even at times to a degree of wearisomeness, insomuch that were it not for the calls of necessity and duty, I should endeavor to quit them all – to be free from their cumber and interruption, as they do often interfere with better concerns and those of a higher and more excellent nature.

First Day, 9th: A silent meeting

Fifth Day: Was our preparative meeting. Silence was my lot in the meeting for worship.

First Day, 16th: Our meeting was larger than usual by the excess of strangers that did not usually attend. Very soon after taking my seat, my mind was impressed with a view of the baneful tendency of pride, and its hurtful effects on the children of men universally[1] as the primary evil, and the last we obtain victory over. For when that is thoroughly subdued and kept under, no evil can assail us. For self and selfishness – both of which are generated from pride and in which all evil is comprehended – will die when pride is altogether subdued. The prospect led to communication and opened into a pretty full and effective testimony – to the tendering and humbling many minds. May it fasten as a nail in a sure place, that so it may continue in remembrance for many days and bring forth fruit, is my fervent prayer.

Fifth Day: Attended our monthly meeting. In the meeting for worship, I renewed the example to silence.

---

[1] The rest of the sentence and the next two were deleted from the printed *Journal*.

First Day, 23rd: In the course of our meeting, my mind was led into a view of the necessity of the cross, consistent with that saying of the Lip of Truth:[1] "If any man will come after me, let him deny himself, and take up his cross and follow me." The subject spread and led to the necessity of communication, in which the way and work, and its effect upon the man of sin (or self) was opened. Showing how, when submitted to and borne, the transgressing nature in us is reduced and subjected by the operation of its power – through which the true liberty is known, and the captive soul set free[2] and made to rejoice on the banks of deliverance.

Fifth Day: Attended our meeting in silence. And in the afternoon, attended the funeral of a friendly man, at which there was a large collection of people of various professions – a promiscuous gathering among whom my mouth was opened to testify of the things concerning the kingdom of heaven, and to open the way of life and salvation to the people, and the only means by which it ever was or can be effected, *viz*, the Grace of God (or Light of Truth) revealed in the hearts and consciences of men and women as a Swift Witness[3] against all manner of sin and iniquity. Life sprang up and the gospel was preached in the demonstration of the Spirit, wherewith many were affected and edified.

First Day, 30th of 8th month: The consideration of the great advantages, which would result to the children of men were they possessed of right ideas and a right understanding of the divine character, opened to an exercise and concern, from an impressive belief that there was a great shortness in that respect – even among professing Christians – in a general way. And that for want of a right improvement of the talent or talents dispensed by our gracious Creator to his creature, man, or that manifestation of the Spirit given to every man to profit withal – which, if rightly improved, would bring us to know and witness the true and saving knowledge of God, and give us right ideas of the divine character, and by which (if rightly adhered to), our salvation would be effected. I was led to communicate on the subject, which brought a very comfortable solemnity over the meeting.

Fifth Day, 3rd of 9th month: A silent meeting today:

First Day, 6th: Having for some days past felt drawings on my mind to attend Friends Meeting at Westbury, and way opening for it today, I went thither accompanied by my wife. It was rather a trying, exercising season in the forepart, but towards the close my spirit was set at liberty, and an opening presented, attended with life, in which I was led to open and show to those present, the necessity of an entire renunciation of self in

---

[1] Proverbs 12:19
[2] Luke 4:18
[3] Malachi 3:5

order to come to a saving knowledge of God and a qualification to worship him in spirit and in truth by an entire cessation from all our own willings and runnings – both in body and spirit, and in thought. And although this is an attainment which man cannot arrive at by dint of[1] his own sufficiency, but which nevertheless, man may attain to by a right faith in God and in the sufficiency of his power – therefore, we ought not to let in discouragement from a sense of our own impotent state, but continue to strive to enter in at the strait gate[2] of self-abasement and renunciation, and persevere therein, and leave the rest to the Lord. And then, no doubt, we may be brought to experience and exclaim with one formerly, "Thou wilt ordain peace for us, for thou hast wrought all our works in us."[3]

Fifth Day: Attended our meeting as usual when at home. Was much cumbered in the forepart of the meeting with unprofitable thoughts, such as relate to our temporal concerns, which produce poverty of spirit in religious meetings and ought to be strove against in order to obtain a release from them. And although it is what we cannot do in our own time and strength, yet as we continue to strive and do not give over the struggle, but persevere in faith and patience to obtain the blessing – as Jacob did when he wrestled with the angel[4] – we shall witness an overcoming in the Lord's time and strength, and know our light to arise out of obscurity, and our darkness to be as noonday. Then are we qualified to worship the Father in spirit and in truth – in the beauty of holiness[5] – and nothing can hinder or let. Then can we do the Lord's work with a willing heart agreeably to his will, without the fear or favor of mortals. Then can we minister, if called thereto, in the demonstration of the Spirit accompanied with power, which causes it to be instructive and edifying to the hearers.

First Day, 13th: My mind, as I sat in our meeting today, was led under exercise from the remembrance of the 22nd verse of the 45th chapter of Isaiah, *viz*, "Look unto me and be ye saved, all the ends of the earth, for I am God, and there is none else."

I was largely opened on the subject as I communicated, and Truth was raised into dominion, whereby the minds of many were humbled and contrited, and the meeting generally solemnized and edified. And I felt sweet peace in the labor.

Fifth Day: This being the time of our monthly meeting, we had the company of our Friend, William Rickman* from old England – now on a

---

[1] By dint of: through persistence
[2] Matthew 7:13 & Luke 13:24
[3] Isaiah 26:12
[4] Genesis 32:22-32
[5] 1 Chronicles 16:29, Psalm 29:2, & Psalm 96:9

religious visit in this country. And as I had for some considerable time past felt my mind drawn to make a visit in the love of the gospel to Friends in the compass of our yearly meeting, with a view also to appoint some meetings among those of other persuasions, it appeared right to spread the concern before my Friends at this time, who (after due consideration) united with me therein and directed the clerk to furnish me with a minute of concurrence on the occasion, leaving me at liberty to pursue the prospect as Truth might open the way.[1]

This brought renewed exercise, as it placed the weight and burden of concern on my own shoulders, as I was only to move as Truth should open the way, so that not only my own reputation as a gospel minister was at stake, but likewise the society among whom I stood as a distinguished member. But what made it still more weighty and important was the honor of the cause of Truth and Righteousness, which I had now taken upon me to espouse and promote – which made the undertaking appear very weighty and solemn.

Fifth Day, 24th: A quiet silent meeting.

On Seventh Day, I attended the funeral of a young Friend, a kinsman who had been in a declining state for more than a year. There was a large collection of Friends and neighbors on the occasion. The corpse was taken into the meetinghouse and a meeting held before it was interred – which is mostly the case among Friends in this part of the society. It proved a very exercising season in the forepart. And although divers ministers were present, yet all seemed shut from any communication until the meeting seemed drawing to a conclusion, when my mind was set at liberty from its bonds, and a degree of light arose and dispelled the darkness, in which I was led to open the cause and ground of the prevailing darkness that had been so generally spread over us, and that it was owing to the people's living too much to self and serving self when they ought more faithfully to serve the Lord and live unto the Lord. I was led, in a brief way, in a close, searching testimony, which I had a hope would have its use, at least with some present.

First Day, 27th: In our meeting today, my mind was largely opened into the substance of things referred to by the shadows and symbols of the law or outward dispensation. And as the prospect spread and enlarged, I found it necessary to spread it before the assembly, and to show the difference between the law state and that of the gospel. And that as the shadows and symbols of the outward law dispensation stood and consisted in real, essential,[2] and substantial things suited to our outward nature and life – so likewise, the substance of those shadows (as they were

---

[1] The next paragraph was deleted from the printed *Journal*.
[2] Essential: existing, real, or actual

intended to point to spiritual things) must also consist in real, essential, and substantial things suited to our inward and spiritual nature and life. And therefore of course, all the shadows of the law are at an end where the gospel state is known and experienced. It was a season of favor, and renewedly strengthening to my mind and, I believe, instructive and edifying to many present. Thanks be given to Israel's Shepherd, for his continued mercy.

Fifth Day: Attended our preparative meeting, at which the queries were read and answers given in to the usual five to go to the quarterly meeting. And I thought from the tenor of the answers, if correct, we were a favored people.

First Day, 11th: Our meeting was large, in which the gospel axe was laid close to the root of the corrupt tree – showing how every tree that did not bring forth good fruit must be hewed down – let it have ever so specious an outward appearance – and burnt up by the fire of oblivion.[1]

Fifth Day: Attended our monthly meeting, at which answers to the queries were produced from the preparative meetings. And although I feared the answers made in our preparative made us appear more correct than we really were, yet those from the other branch of the monthly meeting were still more perfect. And although I felt some doubting, yet a degree of gladness attended in a hope that we were on the improving hand.

A Visit to Friends in the Compass of Our Yearly Meeting in 1818 & 1819

After this meeting, nothing in particular transpired until I proceeded on my intended journey, which was on the 21st of 10th month 1818 and fourth of the week in the morning. Samuel Willis, a member of our meeting and an elder, joined me as a companion. We proceeded to Flushing in order to attend our quarterly meeting, which opened with a Meeting of Ministers and Elders at the 10th hour.

The next day was the meeting for discipline and the day following, a public meeting for worship. And through the condescending goodness of the Shepherd of Israel, the several seasons were truly comfortable, instructive, and edifying, in which Truth's testimony was exalted over all opposition, to the praise of his Grace, who is calling us to glory and virtue.

From Flushing, we proceeded that afternoon to Newtown and attended a public meeting in the evening among those of other societies.

And the next day being the seventh of the week, we had an appointed meeting in Friends Meetinghouse at the Kills and another in the evening at

---

[1] Matthew 3:10 & Luke 3:9

Brooklyn – generally composed of those not in membership with us and many not in strict fellowship with any religious society. And we had thankfully to acknowledge that he who opens and none can shut, was graciously near for our help, and opened doctrine suited to the states of those who attended in the several opportunities – to the peace and comfort of my own mind and, I trust, to the instruction and edification of the people.

From thence, we proceeded to New York and attended the meetings in the city on First Day. They were large – many not in profession with us came in (previous information having been given of our being there). And the gospel was freely preached among them in both opportunities – particularly that at Pearl Street, wherein Truth was raised into dominion over all.

Second Day: We attended a meeting by appointment at Westchester, which was also a precious, edifying opportunity. After which, we proceeded to Purchase in order to attend the quarterly meeting at that place, which opened the next day at the 11th hour and continued three days. The meeting for discipline was well conducted, in which I was led to call upon Friends to rally to our standard, the Light Within, which is a principle of perfect rectitude and justice, and if rightly attended to, will lead us to withdraw from all kind of conduct and commerce that is in the least degree tinged with injustice and oppression. And in a particular manner, from a commerce in and the use of articles that are the product of the labor of slaves – the injustice of which was clearly opened and set home on Friends' minds, showing that nothing short of a principle of immutable justice, that may so pervade the minds of mankind as not to have any intercourse with the oppressor in the produce of the labor of the oppressed, will ever be sufficient fully to suppress that monstrous evil and put a final end thereto. It was a very solemn season.

The meeting for worship was likewise a favored season, in which the Divine Presence was witnessed for our help and comfort.

The four following days, we attended meetings at North Castle, Salem, Oblong and the Branch – all large for the places and favored with the overshadowing of heavenly regard, in which ability was received to preach the gospel in the demonstration of the Spirit, and wisdom afforded to divide the word to the different states of those present – each meeting being composed of a variety of professions and conditions. And such was the gracious condescension of the Shepherd of Israel as not to send any away empty if they were willing to receive the portion justly allotted them. And if they refuse because it is not agreeable to their own inclinations, the Lord will be clear and his faithful servants will be clear. And if they are not saved, their blood will be upon their own heads.

These several seasons were comfortable and encouraging to the honest-hearted and strengthening to my exercised mind – a sense of which filled my heart with gratitude and thanksgiving to the Blessed Author of all our mercies. After these meetings, we proceeded to Nine Partners.

On Third Day, the 3rd of 11th month, their quarterly meeting came on. The Meeting of Ministers and Elders opened at the tenth hour and the meeting for discipline the next day. These were both profitable, instructive meetings to many present, and in which way opened fully to relieve my own mind – and felt sweet peace in my labors of love among them.

The three following days, we attended the Quarterly Meeting at Stanford. I had but little active service in the Meeting of Ministers and Elders, yet I found it my place to remind Friends of the danger and bad effects of covering or hiding, and of the advantage of laying ourselves open to the Just Witness, and of entering into an individual investigation when answering the queries – lest we overlook some things, even in ourselves, and so make our answers more clear than truth and equity will warrant. And when the answers to the queries came to be read, I thought there was occasion for the caution, as their answers were generally full and clear.

In the meeting for discipline, I was led to call Friends' attention to the fundamental principle of our profession and to show the drift[1] and design of those precious testimonies – that as good fruit from a good tree naturally emanated from it – especially those two, the most noble and dignified (to wit), against war and slavery. And whether, while we were actively paying taxes to civil government for the purpose of promoting war or warlike purposes in any degree, we were not balking our testimony in that respect. And are pulling down with one hand what we are pretending to build with the other.

And in like manner in regard to slavery, that although we had freed our own hands from holding by active force any of this oppressed people, the Africans and their descendants, in unconditional slavery, yet so long as we voluntarily and of choice are engaged in a commerce in and the free use of the fruits of their labor – wrested from them by the iron hand of oppression through the medium of their cruel and unjust masters – are we not accessory thereto and are partakers in the unrighteous traffic of dealing in our fellow creatures, and in a great measure lay waste our testimony against slavery and oppression.

These subjects were largely opened and the inconsistency of such conduct set home on the minds of Friends, accompanied with strong

---

[1] Drift: natural course

desires that they might have their proper effect in convincing of the unrighteousness of such conduct.

The meeting for worship, or closing meeting, was mostly made up of such as were not members. It was a favored, solemn meeting, and I trust instructive and comfortable to many present, as it was to the satisfaction and peace of my own mind.

First Day, 8th of 11th month: We returned and attended the meeting at Nine Partners. And notice being given of our intention of being there, it was very large – the house being filled with a mixed company of various professions besides Friends – among whom I was largely led forth to declare of the things concerning the kingdom of God. Truth was raised into dominion and a precious solemnity was spread over the assembly. May all the praise be ascribed to the Shepherd of Israel for the unmerited favor.

In the course of this week, after resting on Second and Third Days (in which time I visited some of my relatives), we attended meetings at Chestnut Ridge, Poughquaig, Beekman, and Oswego. These meetings were generally well attended and were, I trust, profitable and instructive to many who attended them.

First Day, 15th: I attended West Branch Meeting in the morning and that at Pleasant Valley in the evening. They were both very crowded gatherings. At the latter, there were many more than the house could contain – composed principally of such as were not in membership with Friends, being of the varied religious professions common among us, and many who were not in strict fellowship with any. At such seasons, where of course, there must be a great variety of states and conditions, I have found it necessary to dwell deep[1] and wait patiently for the arising of the pure spring of gospel ministry, which alone can enable and qualify to divide the word aright, so that each may have their due portion and be spoken to in their own language[2] – a language that sets home the Truth on every mind, as was the case on the day of Pentecost.

On Second Day evening, we had a very large meeting in Poughkeepsie, held in their courthouse – a very commodious room for the purpose, being well-seated, and was thought sufficient to hold near a thousand people. It was much crowded and proved a very solemn, quiet opportunity, in which Truth had the dominion.

The five succeeding days, we attended a large meeting by appointment at Crum Elbow, the monthly meetings of Oswego, Nine Partners, Creek, and Stanford. In all of which meetings, I had good service

---

[1] Jeremiah 49:8&30
[2] Acts 2:6-11

– the several opportunities being favored with the overshadowings of heavenly regard.

First Day, 22nd: We had a very crowded meeting at the Little Nine Partners and the next day we were at an appointed meeting in Friends Meetinghouse near Charles Hoag's in North East town, which was likewise a very full meeting – in both of which, the gospel was freely preached, and its doctrines largely opened and set home on the minds of the people, and the fallacy and emptiness of all formal and ceremonial religion exposed, and the people pressingly invited to gather inward to the immutable principle of Light and Truth in their own souls, as the sure rock of ages,[1] and the only means whereby we can be enabled to work out our salvation. The Lord's power was felt eminently to preside in those solemn assemblies, to the praise of his great and excellent name, who is over all worthy forever. And I parted with them in true peace of mind – the sure result of faithfulness.

Connecticut

Third Day: We rode to Canaan, a town in Connecticut, and the next day had an appointed meeting there with the few Friends at that place and some of their neighbors. It was a comfortable, instructive season.

The following day, we had another meeting by appointment in an adjacent neighborhood – held in a schoolhouse. This was also a favored, powerful meeting. Divers present were much broken and contrited, and Truth reigned over all.

On Sixth Day, we proceeded to Hartford, and on Seventh Day evening, we had an appointed meeting in the city. It was held in a meetinghouse belonging to the Presbyterians – there being only two or three members of our society in the place. The meeting was small, occasioned as I supposed by the inclemency of the weather and the want of proper notice. Nevertheless, the Divine Presence was felt to preside and Truth was declared among them in the demonstration of the Spirit. And I parted with them, under a thankful sense of the Lord's mercy.

The next day being the first of the week, we attended Friends Meeting at West Hartford, which was likewise very small – Friends being but few in number in that place and those mostly appeared in a lukewarm state. And I apprehended they had taken but little care to inform their neighbors of our being there, although we had seasonably requested them so to do – which manifests great insensibility and want of regard for their Friends who have left all their outward enjoyments for the promotion of the gospel and the religious improvement of their Friends and the people, and are

---

[1] "Rock of ages" does not appear in scripture, but the hymn of that name was written in 1775.

going up and down in travail and labor, as with their lives in their hands, as Truth leads the way. And yet, their Friends whom they visit, in some places either think it too much trouble or are so unconcerned as to take little or no care to give their neighbors notice – a sense of which caused me to take leave of my Friends at this place with a heavy heart.

From thence, on Second Day, we proceeded to Woodbury and put up at the house of a friendly man of the Methodist society, where we had a large meeting the next evening with the neighboring inhabitants – composed of Methodists, Episcopalians, Presbyterians, and some others not in strict fellowship with any religious society. It was a very solemn, favored meeting, in which the Lord's presence and power were felt eminently to preside. And many hearts were broken and contrited, and manifested much satisfaction with the opportunity – especially the man of the house, who, in much brokenness of spirit and with gratitude and thankfulness of heart, acknowledged the favor.

And the next morning, after a tendering opportunity in the family, we took leave of them in mutual affection and rode to Middlesex (upwards of forty miles) and lodged with our kind Friend, Samuel Whiting, who, with his affectionate wife and children, received us with marks of true friendship, which is a brook by the way to the weary traveler – and which was our case at this time. And what added further to our comfort was the readiness of mind and concern they manifested in giving their neighbors information of our intention of being at their meeting the next day, and which we accordingly attended. And the Lord graciously condescended to open my mouth among them in a living, powerful testimony to the truths of the gospel. It was a season of great favor. "May the word preached not return void, but accomplish that to which it was sent," is the fervent desire of my spirit.

Back in New York

After this solemn meeting, we proceeded on our journey and rode that afternoon to our Friend, Charles Field, at a place called the Saw Pits. Here, we had a meeting the next day at the 11th hour. There is but one family of Friends in this village – the Friend and his family above named – and one other member. The inhabitants consist of the various professions common among us and some others not in communion with any religious society. A considerable number assembled, with whom we had a very solemn, instructive opportunity, to the comfort and peace of my own mind.

The evening of the next day, we had a precious, favored meeting at Manhattanville on New York Island with Friends of that place, and which was attended by a considerable number of the neighboring inhabitants, who conducted themselves very soberly, suiting the occasion. Many hearts were broken and contrited. And we parted with them under a humbling sense of the Lord's goodness, and with grateful hearts for the unmerited favor.

First Day, 6th of 12th month: We rode to the city. And as Friends of the monthly meeting there had recently opened a new meeting in the eastern part of the town, we attended it – both fore and after noon. And notice being given at the close of the forenoon meeting of our intention of attending in the afternoon, it was a full meeting – more than the house could well contain. These were both memorable meetings, in which the Lord's presence and power were manifested in an eminent degree, breaking and contriting many hearts. And Truth reigned triumphantly over all. It was the Lord's doing, and marvelous in our eyes that he should thus condescend in matchless mercy to notice us poor, unworthy creatures.

At evening, we had a very large meeting by appointment in Friends Meetinghouse in Pearl Street, in which (although much worn down by arduous labor in the three foregoing meetings), I was strengthened to communicate in a full, plain testimony – opening to the people the danger and disadvantage of resting in the forms and empty shadows of the law state, and continuing in the traditions and ceremonies introduced into the professed Christian Churches in the time of the apostasy from primitive simplicity, and the hurtful tendency of observing days and times, like the carnally-minded in the Galatian Church, and for which they were sharply reprehended by the apostle Paul in his epistle to that Church.[1] The people were very quiet and attentive, and a precious solemnity was spread over the meeting, which closed in a solemn manner. Thanks be given to Israel's Unslumbering Shepherd for the unmerited favor.

We tarried in town until Third Day in order to attend the Meeting for Sufferings which came in the course at that time. We also had an appointed meeting in Liberty Street on Second Day evening – it was pretty well attended – in which I was led to open to the people the way of redemption by Christ, the only mediator between God and man, and the way of his working in man in the accomplishment of his salvation – opening in a full and clear manner the emptiness of all shadows and outward ordinances under the Christian dispensation, such as water baptism and the ordinance called the supper or communion, also the hurtful tendency of observing days and times (such as a Seventh Day Sabbath, days of thanksgiving, and fast days of man's appointing) – showing that they all were of Jewish or heathenish original,[2] being a part of the law dispensation and, of course, ended with it. And therefore, the continuance of them under the gospel dispensation was irrational,

---

[1] Galatians 4:10
[2] Original: origin

nonessential, and contrary to Truth – tending to keep the minds of Christian professors under the veil of carnal ordinances, and greatly retarded the progress of reformation and the advancement of real Christianity.

I was led to use great plainness of speech, and the people sat very solid and attentive, and the word preached appeared to have free course.[1] It was a highly favored season, and the honest-hearted were made to rejoice under a humbling sense of the Lord's mercy. And I parted with them in true peace of mind.

And the next day, after attending the Meeting for Sufferings, we rode home and found our families well, which I considered as an additional favor from my Heavenly Father, whose mercy is over all his works.

I was from home at this time about forty-nine days, and attended forty-nine meetings, and traveled about four hundred and fifty miles.

The Requisites to the Being and Well-Being of a Christian

I continued at and about home until the commencement of the year 1819, attending our meetings as they came in course when at home. I also attended two funerals, in which I had good service, and the meeting at Westbury on a First Day, in which I was led to open to Friends the three principal requisites to the being and well-being of a Christian.

The first being a real belief in God and Christ as one undivided essence – known and believed in, inwardly and spiritually.

By secondly, a complete, passive obedience and submission to the divine will and power – inwardly and spiritually manifested – which when known, brings to the Christian state through a crucifixion of the old man with all his ungodly deeds.

And thirdly, in order for the preservation and well-being of a Christian, it is necessary that they often meet and assemble together for the promotion of love and good works, and as good stewards of the manifold grace of God – for which purpose, the Lord's people and children in all ages have been led by his Spirit to appoint times and seasons in which to present themselves before him. Of which times, all being apprised[2] and living within a reasonable distance of the place so appointed, it becomes their bounden[3] duty to attend in order to wait upon and thereby become qualified to worship God in spirit and in truth. And no temporal concern of the greatest magnitude ought to be considered as a sufficient excuse for omitting this great and necessary duty, for the experience of many ages has shown that those who suffer their temporal

---

[1] Free course: spread rapidly (see 2 Thessalonians 3:1)
[2] Apprise: inform
[3] Bounden: under legal or moral obligation

business to divert them from a steady attendance on their religious meetings never make any real proficiency in religion or the true spiritual life.

The communication was impressive, and reached the witness in many minds. And Truth was exalted and the honest-hearted comforted. And I was made glad in believing that my labor had not been in vain. Such seasons are truly worthy of grateful remembrance.

1819

Continuing the Visits in the Yearly Meeting of New York

As on my return home, I did not feel myself released from a further prosecution of my concern and visit to Friends of our yearly meeting, I (with the concurrence of my Friends) retained the minute I had received for that purpose. And on the 2nd day of 1st month 1819, I again left home and proceeded in the engagement. My son-in-law, Valentine Hicks, joined me as companion in the journey.

We proceeded to New York, and the next day being first of the week, we attended Friends Meeting in Pearl Street in the morning. After which in the afternoon, we proceeded on our journey as far as our Friend, Thomas Walker's, at West Farms near Westchester, where we had an appointed meeting at the 6th hour in the evening.

On Second Day, we had an appointed meeting at Mamaroneck. These meetings were in a good degree favored, in which the presence and love of our Heavenly Father were felt to preside.

Third Day: We had another opportunity by appointment at the White Plains in the courthouse. It was rather a season of hard labor, as the truths communicated did not appear to have free course in any general way. But I trust some were instructed and edified.

Fourth and Fifth Days: We attended Friends Meetings at Purchase and Chappaqua. And notice being given of our intention of attending, they were large. And through divine condescension, they proved seasons of favor, in which the truths of the gospel were largely declared in the demonstration of the Spirit, to the edification of the assemblies, and peace of my own mind.

The two following days, we attended meetings at Croton Valley and Amawalk. They were well attended by Friends and some others, among whom I was led to open many essential doctrines of the Christian religion and to show to the people, in the openings of Truth, the way and means by which – and by which only – our redemption and salvation can be effected. The testimonies had a very reaching effect upon the auditories, many of whom were much broken and contrited. And Truth was raised into victory. And a precious solemnity was spread over the meetings to the comfort and edification of the honest-hearted, which was cause of thankfulness and gratitude to the Beneficent Author of all our mercies.

First Day, 10th: We attended Friends Meeting at Croton in the morning and at Peekskill in the evening – both full meetings, in which the power of the gospel was felt to preside, furnishing with wisdom and strength to divide the word to the several states present in a way that seemed to give each their due portion and none sent empty away, but those who refused to take their own part. Many hearts were broken and contrited, and the honest-hearted comforted, and the Lord's name and power praised and exalted over all, who is worthy forever.

On Second Day, we rode to Nine Partners, and on Third Day evening, had an appointed meeting at Dover. It was held in a pretty large schoolhouse – there being no other place so convenient in the neighborhood – but it was too small to contain the people that assembled, some being obliged to stand without for want of room. It was a very solemn, instructive meeting in which Truth reigned triumphant.

Fourth Day: We attended Pleasant Valley Meeting. And notice being given of our intention of being there, it was large – a considerable number of other societies attending, who behaved soberly, consistent with the occasion.[1] My mouth was opened in a large, effective testimony to the truths of the gospel – setting forth in a plain, simple manner, by conclusive arguments, the origin and essence of all good, and the way in which all intelligent beings must come to the experimental knowledge of it. And from which experience, all the wise and good in the varied ages of the world have agreed to call it by the name of God in their conversation one with another. And to which divine essence, they attribute perfect and infinite justice, wisdom, mercy, power, and love. And that through the extension and offer of these to the children of men – as they are willing to receive and unite therewith, and walk in the way to which they lead – man's whole nature becomes so perfected as to be prepared in this state of being to be reunited to this divine essence and commence a never-ending, happy communion with him in the blissful abodes of an endless fruition of joy unspeakable and full of glory.

I was also led in the same conclusive way to show the origin and essence of all evil, and the way in which the children of man come to a certain knowledge of it. And both are only to be known by an inward and spiritual experience, through the openings and revelation of the Spirit of Truth, which is Christ or a Savior within, the Key of David, who opens to man the mysteries of godliness and the mysteries of iniquity – as far as is needful to instruct and enable how to choose the one and refuse the other. The latter of which, all the wise and good have agreed to define in conversation by the term, devil, as comprehending everything that (by its temptations) hurts or wounds the happiness of man. It was a season of great favor, under a sense of which the honest-hearted were made to rejoice.

After which, we proceeded to Poughkeepsie and attended an appointed meeting in the evening at the sixth hour. It was held in their

---

[1] The rest of the paragraph and the next one were deleted from the printed *Journal*.

courthouse – a large convenient room, but not sufficient to contain the people that assembled. Many were obliged to withdraw for want of room – although it was supposed that the room would contain near a thousand. It proved, through the condescending gooding[1] of our Heavenly Father, a blessed meeting to myself and, we had cause to believe, to the assembly in general. Thanks be to God for his unspeakable gifts.

Yet we have reason to suppose there might have been some few present watching for evil – as carpers[2] and opposers, if we judge from the conduct of the hireling priests since I was there a few weeks before – as I was informed this time that they had joined together to calumniate[3] me and lay waste the testimony of Truth I communicated to the people at that time[4] by lies and slander, which the sermons of those priests were principally composed of in the intermediate time of my being there (as I was informed). But all slunk[5] away and dared not appear at this time, for all was now subjected by the Power of Truth, which was felt to prevail in this highly favored season, insomuch that no dog dare open his mouth[6] nor peep against us while present.

Blessed, yea thrice blessed, be the name and power of Israel's God, who is still with his people, and who will ever remain to be a wall of defense to all his faithful children.

We tarried here most of the next day, visiting some of our Friends.

On Sixth Day, we proceeded to Hudson, where we arrived at evening.

And the following evening, we had an appointed meeting in the town of Claverack, about four miles distant from this place. The inhabitants were mostly Dutch. A considerable number attended and conducted pretty soberly. And way opened to communicate divers truths of the gospel in a clear and impressive manner among them, to which they paid good attention and appeared to be generally well satisfied.

The next day being first of the week, we attended Friends Meeting in Hudson and an appointed meeting in the evening. The latter was very large – more than the house could contain. These were favored meetings, in which I was largely led forth in testimony to the truths of the Christian religion – setting forth in a clear manner the ground and source from whence all true religion and true worship have their spring and origin. A general solemnity prevailed, and Truth was raised into dominion over all.

---

[1] Gooding: the action of doing good
[2] Carper: a fault-finder
[3] Calumniate: falsely and maliciously accuse of criminal or disreputable behavior
[4] The rest of the paragraph and the next one were deleted from the printed *Journal*.
[5] Slunk: a past tense of slink, meaning to move in a sneaky way
[6] Exodus 11:7

On Second Day, we proceeded to Kinderhook, where we had a meeting in the evening in their schoolhouse.

And on Third Day afternoon, we had an appointed meeting in Spencertown. These were both crowded meetings – mostly made up of the different societies common among us. Many of them were the descendants of the old Dutch inhabitants – not much acquainted with our customs and order – yet they generally behaved soberly and gave good attention to the testimonies borne. Many gospel truths were opened to their consideration and the Lord's presence and power were felt to preside and crown these solemn assemblies. And I parted from them in true peace and thankfulness of heart.

On Fourth and Fifth Days, we attended Friends Meetings at Klinakill and New Britain, in both of which I had good service for Truth and its blessed cause, and the folly and hurtful tendency of all forms and outward ordinances and ceremonies in religion and worship were laid open and exposed.

On Sixth Day, we proceeded to Troy, where we rested on Seventh Day and wrote to our families.

First Day: Attended Friends Meetings at Troy, both fore and after noon. And information being given of our being there, they were large. At the forenoon meeting, more assembled than the house could contain, and that Gracious Being, who never leaves nor forsakes his dependant children whose trust is fixed on him, was near for our help, and opened my heart and mouth in both meetings to declare largely of the things concerning the kingdom of God, and to open many gospel truths to the people, and to show the fallacy and hurtful tendency of all ceremonial religion that consists in the observance of days and times, and outward ordinances. The people were generally attentive and I found solid peace in my labors of love among them.

On Second Day, we proceeded to Pittstown, and the next day had a meeting appointed there at the 11th hour. It was a large, favored meeting. After which, we proceeded to White Creek and attended Friends Meeting as it came in course the next day. And notice being spread of our being there, it was largely attended. And the Lord's presence was felt to preside and Truth was raised into victory over all.

O my soul! What wilt thou or canst thou render unto the Lord for all his benefits? For his mercies are new every morning and his faithfulness every night.

Vermont

On Fifth Day, we attended an appointed meeting in the town of Shaftsbury on our way to Danby, in which place none of our society reside except one female member, the wife of a friendly-disposed man, at whose house we put up and were very hospitably entertained. The meeting, although small, was attended by the governor of the state and divers of the judges and magistrates. It was a season of favor – many essential doctrines of the Christian religion were opened to them in the demonstration of truth. And I parted with them in thankfulness of heart and with a peaceful mind.

And the next day rode to Danby.

On Seventh Day, we attended an appointed meeting near a village called the Borough in the east part of the town, and on First Day, attended Friends Meeting on the hill. Both were fully attended by Friends and the neighboring inhabitants not in membership with us. These were both solemn, instructive seasons, in which the power of Truth was felt to preside, enabling [me] to preach the gospel in the demonstration of the Spirit, to the comfort and encouragement of the living, faithful few, and to the instruction and edification of the honest-inquirers, whose faces were turned Zionward – likewise spreading caution and reproof to the indolent and careless transgressors.

On Second Day, we proceeded towards Ferrisburg in the lake country, where we arrived on Third Day afternoon, and the next day attended the monthly meeting at that place.

And the four following days, we attended meetings in the following order. On Fifth Day, had an appointed meeting at Monkton. It was large, and proved a very solemn, favored meeting, in which the power of Truth prevailed to the silencing of all opposition and ran as oil – to the comfort, encouragement, and instruction of the honest-hearted.

Bless the Lord, O my soul, and forget not any of his benefits!

On Sixth Day, attended Friends Monthly Meeting at Starksboro.

On Seventh Day, had an appointed meeting in a schoolhouse in the southeast part of the town, where Friends hold a small meeting.

And on First Day, was at Friends Meeting at Lincoln. These were all favored meetings, in which I had good service for Truth and its cause.

On Second Day, we returned into the south part of Monkton and had an evening meeting in a kinsman's house by the name of Stephen Haight. He was convinced of the principles of Friends, but failed in the practical part. This proved a pretty exercising season by reason of the rawness and ignorance of some who attended – especially in the silent part of the meeting – being brought up and educated in the belief and habit that without[1] they are engaged in some bodily exercise, such as outward and vocal singing, praying, preaching, or the like, there is no meeting – being so instructed by their blind teachers that it is very difficult to get them into

---

[1] Without: unless

stillness or into any right condition to hear. This makes hard work for the true gospel minister, whose labor and travail is to get into, and bring others into, a state of true solemn silence, that he may thereby become baptized into the state of the people, and be thereby qualified to administer to their real conditions – for otherwise preaching is vain. But as I continued patient in travail, my mouth was opened in a large, searching testimony, showing the fallacy and emptiness of all outward, ceremonial worship, and how it must inevitably land all those who trust therein in a state of sad disappointment in the end. I was led also to open in a clear manner to the people, the most essential doctrines of the Christian religion – to the information and satisfaction of the honest-inquiring minds.

The next day, we returned to Ferrisburg in order to attend the quarterly meeting, which opened on Fourth Day with the Meeting of Ministers and Elders, which I attended and had good service among them, being led to open in the life the order of true gospel ministry, and the necessity all are under, who are called to that solemn and important office, of keeping their vessels clean – not only from sin and every pollution of flesh and spirit, but also in their ministry from all the dregs or remains of former offerings. For if through the strength of memory, any act upon former offerings, such communications tend to produce death, rather than life. And we find, under the law, that the vessels in the Lord's house were not only at first made pure and holy, but when they were made use of in the Lord's offerings and had been filled with the Lord's holy things, when that season of offering was over, they were then cleansed from all the remains and dregs of such offering and put up in their places clean and empty. And this agrees with the doctrine of Christ to his apostles, "Every branch in me," he says, "that bringeth forth fruit, my Heavenly Father purgeth it, that it may bring forth more fruit."[1] It was, I trust, an instructive season – there being a number present that were young in the ministry.

After this meeting, we rode to Vergennes and attended an appointed meeting at six in the evening. It was pretty well attended by the townspeople, who generally behaved soberly. I was led to open divers, important doctrines of the gospel to their consideration and to caution them against having any fellowship or affording any support to the dark – and what I esteem diabolical – system of Free Masonry. They were generally attentive, and withdrew quietly without making any objection.

The two following days, we attended the quarterly meeting of discipline and the parting meeting for worship. These, I trust, were profitable opportunities – the latter, a highly favored meeting, in which

---

[1] John 15:2

Easton (New York) Meetinghouse

Truth reigned triumphantly over all. And I took leave of my Friends in the sensible feeling of true gospel fellowship.

And we rode that afternoon and evening to Shoreham, and lodged with our kind Friends, Zebulon and Elizabeth Frost. And the next day at evening, had an appointed meeting there, at which many of the neighboring inhabitants attended. It was a solemn time in which many doctrines of the Christian religion were opened for their instruction and consideration. And I parted with them with a peaceful mind.

Back in New York

And the next day, we rode to Granville, and the following day had an appointed meeting there at the 1st hour after noon. This was a greatly favored opportunity – that power that smote Rahab and wounded the dragon was manifest for our help – breaking down and dispelling every opposite spirit, humbling and contriting many hearts, and comforting and strengthening the honest-hearted. Surely it was the Lord's doing – a sense of which inspires gratitude and thankfulness of heart for the unmerited favor.

On Third Day, we rode to Easton.

On Fourth and Fifth Days we attended their quarterly meeting for discipline and public meeting for worship – their Meeting of Ministers and Elders was held on Third Day, previous to our arrival.

On Sixth Day, we had an appointed meeting at Cambridge. These meetings were all comfortable, instructive seasons, in which the doctrines of Truth were largely opened for the information and edification of the people. And Truth was raised into dominion over all.

We rested on Seventh Day, I feeling myself pretty much worn with such continual and almost incessant labor in traveling and in meetings.

On First Day, I again attended Easton Meeting, which was also a large, favored meeting, in which Truth's testimony was exalted over untruth and error.

On Second Day, we proceeded on our way to Queensbury. Took a meeting in our way that I had previously appointed at a large village called Whipple City. It was largely attended by the neighboring inhabitants consisting of the varied professions common among us and some friendly people not joined in profession with any – there were no members of our society in the place. It was, I think, a favored opportunity, in which I was opened to declare the Truth among them, in a large, effective testimony – to the humbling and contriting many minds. And I parted with them in true peace of mind. After which, we proceeded to Queensbury, where we arrived in the edge of the evening.

The three following days, we attended the quarterly meeting held here at this time for Saratoga and Queensbury. I also attended two evening meetings, in the course of the quarter, in two neighboring villages – which I had appointed for the benefit of those of other societies, who pretty generally attended. I think the quarter, in general, was an instructive, favored time, and the two others were laborous seasons. The minds of the people appeared to be very much veiled and in a state of much ignorance – being generally swallowed up too much in worldly pursuits and self-gratifications. This makes hard work for the devoted traveler, who is engaged for the advancement of the cause of Truth and Righteousness in the earth. But as I waited and patiently endured the baptisms necessary for the dead, until I was brought into a feeling of their real conditions, way opened to communicate doctrine suitable for their instruction and help. And although there did not appear much visible effect wrought for the present, yet I had reason to hope that the labor would not be all lost nor the word return void, but would in the end accomplish the thing whereunto it was sent, and be as bread cast upon the waters to return after many days. And my hope in this respect was strengthened from the satisfaction and true peace I felt in the arduous labor I passed through in these seasons of exercise.

The quarterly meeting being over, we proceeded to Saratoga, and on Sixth Day had an appointed meeting there at the 2nd hour after noon. This was a large, favored meeting, in which Truth was raised into victory over all, and under its precious influence, the gospel was preached in the clear demonstration of the Spirit. Thanks be to God for his unspeakable gifts.

From thence, we proceeded to Milton, and on First Day, 28th of 2nd month, we attended Friends Meeting there. It was largely attended by Friends and others. And through the condescending goodness of Israel's Unslumbering Shepherd, it proved an instructive, edifying season.

The five following days, we attended the five following meetings at Greenfield, Galway, Providence, Mayfield, and Northampton. And although things in most places (as it regards the life of religion) appeared rather low, and considerable rawness was apparent in many in that respect, yet such is the unmerited kindness of the Heavenly Father, that he graciously condescended to break the bread and caused it to be distributed to the people in these several opportunities – that none were sent empty away, except those who either neglected or refused to take the portion allotted them. And my spirit was comforted under an evident sense that I had faithfully discharged my duty among them.

From Northampton, we proceeded to New Town, and on First Day, 7th of 3rd month, we attended Friends Meeting at that place. And notice being spread of our coming, it was large – a very considerable more assembled than the house could contain, who were obliged to stand without. For these, I felt much sympathy and concern, as the weather was very cold, and those without, not willing to lose the opportunity, continued until the meeting ended – which held nearly three hours. But I had cause to hope they did not go away unrewarded, as the season proved a very favored one, in which the Divine Presence was felt to preside, enabling [me] to preach the gospel of the grace of God to the people in the demonstration of the truth, and to the comfort and peace of my own mind.

On the evenings of the two following days, I attended meetings by appointment at Waterford and Troy – both largely attended by those not in membership with us.

And on Fourth Day, attended Friends Monthly Meeting at Troy.

And on Fifth Day evening, had a very large meeting in Albany, held in the statehouse, a large, commodious room for the purpose. In these several meetings, Truth was felt to arise in dominion, and ability afforded to discharge myself faithfully in communication to the people who assembled, and I trust to their general satisfaction and edification. May it instructively fasten on their minds, as a nail in a sure place, driven by the Master of Assemblies, that so the word preached may tend to real profit and not return void, but accomplish the end to which it is sent.

From thence we proceeded to Bern, within the compass of Duanesburg Quarterly Meeting, where we arrived on Sixth Day evening and lodged with our kind Friend, Samuel Cary, who with his affectionate wife and children, treated us with great hospitality.

The next evening, we had an appointed meeting at a village about four miles distant, where no member of our society resided – intending to return and attend Friends Meeting here on First Day. But a storm of snow coming on Seventh Day and increasing towards evening with such violence all next day that, although we got to the evening meeting (which was small by reason of the storm), we were not able to return until the following Second Day – and then it was with great difficulty that we got along, the snow was so deep and highways drifted full with the wind.

Nevertheless, we made the attempt to return on First Day morning, and got on our way about half a mile, and could proceed no farther. We then turned in to a house on the way – a good looking mansion belonging to a professor among the Presbyterians. Here, we tarried over First Day, not being able to proceed. We held a little meeting here with this man's family and three of his friends, who were with him on a visit, in which my mind was opened to communicate to them the grounds of our profession and the doctrines of the Christian religion as held by us – which had a very considerable reaching effect on the man's wife, insomuch that she openly acknowledged to the truths delivered and assured all present that she should vindicate them as certain, undeniable truths, which she felt to be so in her own experience.

On the following Fifth Day, we attended Friends Meeting at Bern. And the weather being again stormy and inclement, it was small, by reason that the highways were so blocked up as to prevent many from attending.

The next day we proceeded to Duanesburg. Had a meeting there on Seventh Day, which was a large, favored season.

The next day being the first of the week, we attended meetings at Charleston in the morning and at Carlisle in the evening.

On Second Day, we proceeded to Middleburgh, and the next day had a meeting there.

And the following day, had meetings at Oakhill in the morning and at Rensselaerville in the afternoon. After which, we returned with our Friend, Samuel Cary, who had kindly accompanied us in this little tour, to his house – accompanied with true peace of mind from a consciousness that I had faithfully discharged myself in the service allotted me in those several meetings, void of any influence from the fear or favor of man.

On Fifth Day, we attended Friends Monthly Meeting at Bern. The meeting for worship was attended by a very considerable number of the neighboring inhabitants not in membership with us, who behaved themselves soberly and were very attentive to what was communicated. And many were broken and contrited by the prevalence of Truth, which was raised into dominion in this favored meeting – not only in time of worship, but likewise the meeting for discipline was a comfortable, instructive season.

The two following days, we had meetings at New Baltimore and a village where dwell several families of Friends by the name of Dickenson – from which they call the meeting by that name, *viz*, Dickenson's Meeting, and at Coeymans (alias Stanton Hill). I had good service in those several meetings, in which Friends appeared to be brought near together in the feeling influence of the Truth and in the oneness of the Spirit – in a sense whereof, we had gratefully to acknowledge that the Lord is still mindful of his people, fulfilling all his promises to those who seek him with sincerity of heart. And they that seek him early[1] will find him to be near at hand, a Present Helper in every needful time.

After the latter meeting, we proceeded to Athens, and the next day being first of the week and 28th of 3rd month, we attended Friends Meeting in the morning and had another meeting by appointment in the afternoon. These were laborous meetings, particularly so in the forepart. A great power of darkness seemed so to prevail, as entirely for a considerable time to close up and block the way to any public service. But as I patiently submitted to the baptism and willingly became baptized with and for the dead – as it is only through death that the resurrection from death can be witnessed – a little glimmering of light appeared, in which I felt the necessity of standing up,[2] but with the utmost caution to mind the stepping stones. For my way (for a time) was like passing through a miry bog, enclosed with mist and darkness, with but just light enough to see the way – and that composed of stepping stones, and but one visible at a time. And when I had taken one step and found it to be solid and sure, I had then to look carefully for the next. And as I thus proceeded, keeping my eye single to the light that led the way, the light more and more arose out of obscurity and the darkness vanished. And he that opens and none can shut, and shuts and none but himself can open, made way for the promotion of his own righteous cause and the exaltation of Truth's testimonies. It was the Lord's doing and marvelous in mine eyes.

From hence on Second Day morning, we proceeded to Alexander Young's* at the east part of Esopus – about or near forty miles. This was a day of very hard travel, both for man and horse – the ways being bad by reason that the winter was just breaking up. But we arrived safe in the edge of the evening and were kindly received by our Friends, which made up in part for the toil of the day.

---

[1] Seek him early: seek God diligently or earnestly (from Proverbs 8:17)
[2] The rest of the sentence and the next one were deleted from the printed *Journal*.

At this place, we had an appointed meeting the next day. And the five following days, we had meetings at Rosendale Plains, the Paltz, Plattekill, Newburgh, and Marlborough – which, with the exercise of traveling on the heavy, rough roads, produced a large portion of exercise, both to body and mind. But the Lord's strengthening and consoling presence, vouchsafed from season to season for our help, carried us through and over all – to the praise of his Grace, and to the comfort and peace of our own minds.

On Second Day, 5th of 4th month, we proceeded to Cornwall and attended a meeting by previous appointment at the 11th hour.

And the next day, had an appointed meeting at Smith's Clove. And the day following, [we] were at a place called the Upper Clove (alias Blooming Grove). In these several meetings, I was led largely to open to the people the law state, or dispensation of figure, as comprehensively set forth in the Old Testament, and to show the difference between that and the gospel, and to show how the first ends where the latter begins, and are as distinct from each other as the natural body is from the soul – the first comprehending the salvation of bodies from outward servitude, the latter the salvation of the soul from sin and the death consequent on it – setting forth the use and necessity of all the rituals or shadows of that dispensation during its continuance. Also, how they were all abolished[1] by the outward coming of Christ, and entirely done away by the crucifixion of his body on the cross, by which they were rendered entirely useless under the gospel, and have no part nor lot[2] under that dispensation. I had much service in these meetings, and great cause of gratitude and thankfulness to the Bountiful Author of all our multiplied favors.

The next day, attended Friends Meeting at Kakiat (alias Hampstead). We had a tedious time in getting there – the road, part of the way, being deep with mud and wet and much cut up. But the Lord richly rewarded us for all our toil in giving us a precious meeting with our Friends and a considerable number of the neighboring inhabitants not in membership with us. It was truly a season of grateful remembrance, both by us and our Friends – being made to rejoice together for the unmerited favor. After which, we proceeded to Tappan, to the house of our Friend, John Lawrence. Here is not any meeting, but feeling the way open, we appointed a meeting there at the 2nd hour next day. And although not large, yet I trust it was a comfortable, instructive season to some present.

---

[1] This sentence was edited to remove the words, "by the outward coming of Christ, and entirely done away by the crucifixion of his body on the cross, by which they were rendered entirely useless."

[2] Lot: place or share (from Acts 8:21)

This closed our visit and the next morning we proceeded to New York, where we received tidings of the decease of my kinsman, Benjamin Hicks, with information that he was to be interred the next day. This induced us to proceed home that afternoon, where we arrived between eight and nine at night – much wearied, having traveled in the course of the day upwards of fifty miles, and some of the way but indifferent traveling. But finding our dear families well, accompanied with sweet peace of mind, made rich amends for all our toil – a sense of which inspired my mind with gratitude and thankfulness of heart to the Great and Gracious Author of all our blessings.

I was from home in this journey fourteen weeks, attended seventy-three meetings, three quarterly meetings, four monthly meetings, and traveled one thousand and eighty-four miles.

In & About Home

The next day I attended the funeral of the aforesaid Friend (which was on First Day, 11th of 4th month 1819), which was largely attended by Friends and others – he being a man much esteemed by his friends and neighbors and a useful member of society, both in a religious and moral relation. And his memorial[1] will be blessed. It was a very solemn time, in which my heart and mouth were largely opened to declare to the people of the things concerning the kingdom of God, and to point out to them, in a full and clear manner, the only way and means by which an entrance thereinto is attainable by the children of men. It was a season of favor, and many hearts were made to rejoice under a humbling sense of the gracious extending of heavenly regard to the workmanship of his holy hand.

After this, my lot seemed similar to Mordecai's of old when sitting at the king's gate. I had but little public service when in and about home. This brought to my remembrance the saying of our Lord to his disciples on their return from the service he had sent them out to perform in the land of Israel. When they had given him an account, how well they had succeeded, he invited them to retire awhile and rest.

I was mostly silent in our meetings at home, and was not out, except to attend a funeral in a neighboring town and our quarterly meeting at New York, until our yearly meeting came on – which opened on Seventh Day, 22nd of 5th month 1819 with a Meeting of Ministers and Elders. The Yearly Meeting of Discipline opened on the following Second Day and closed near evening on the Fifth Day following. It was, I think in the general, a favored meeting, although the weaknesses and deficiencies still among us – as manifested by the accounts from our quarterly meetings – were cause of exercise and travail to the honest-hearted who are engaged

---

[1] Memorial: the memory of someone or something

for the promotion of the cause of righteousness and peace in the earth. Yet the condescending goodness of the Shepherd of Israel, in manifesting his life-giving presence for our encouragement and support, inspired the hearts of the living with thanksgiving and gratitude for his unmerited mercies.

We returned home the next day.

I now found it my duty to pay some attention to my temporal concerns – to see that all accounts between myself and others were truly adjusted and settled, as is my general rule from year to year – a rule that every honest man will be led to pursue to prevent trouble and preserve harmony – as a contrary course often leads to vexation and litigation, by which both parties are often hurt and wounded.

First Day, 30th of 5th month: I attended our meeting, as usual when at home. Had a short communication, tending to excite Friends to faithfulness and an inward labor – that the true end of our meeting together might be answered.

I was busily employed in the course of this week in my temporal concerns.

Attended our Fifth Day Meeting and closed the week in quiet.

First Day, 6th of 6th month: I was led in our meeting to show Friends the fallacy of trusting in the outside appearance of things without coming to possess the real substance, as the day is hastening when every foundation will be tried, and all will receive according as their work has been.[1] I was considerably enlarged and Truth's testimony was exalted over all.

I found it my place at this time to keep close at home – both in an inward and outward sense – to arrange my temporal concerns and set things in order at home, not knowing how soon I may be called to leave them all and surrender them, with myself, to the guardian care and disposal of a Gracious Providence, who doth not suffer a sparrow to fall to the ground without his heavenly notice.

I attended our preparative meeting on Fifth Day and the meeting of the Charity Society for schooling the children of the poor black people on Seventh Day – in both of which I felt satisfaction and peace of mind.

First Day, 13th of 6th month 1819: Towards the close of our meeting today, I had to open to Friends the necessity of our individually coming to know what life we are living – whether it be a life after the flesh, which worketh death to the immortal soul, or a life of the Spirit, by which we become spiritually-minded.[2,3] For that life that is and continues to be

---

[1] 1 Corinthians 3:8-14
[2] Romans 8:6
[3] The next sentence was deleted from the printed *Journal*.

predominant in us in this world will likewise be predominant in us in the world to come. And if it be a life in the flesh and in the enjoyment of the things of this world, it will prove, in the world to come, an eternal death to the soul. But if it be a life in the Spirit and in the things of heaven, it will prove an everlasting life to the soul in the world to come, and will crown it with joy unspeakable and full of glory, at God's right hand forevermore.[1]

From this time to our monthly meeting in 7th month, I was pretty steadily at home. Attended our meetings as they came in course, and was very busily and necessarily engaged in my temporal concerns – having a prospect before me of attending the ensuing Yearly Meeting of Ohio and attending some other meetings in that, and in the compass of Baltimore and Philadelphia Yearly Meetings. This concern, I spread before my Friends at our monthly meeting the 15th of 7th month, and obtained their unity and concurrence.

First Day, 18th of 7th month: Attended our meeting. We had the company of our ancient, honest Friend, Thomas Titus. He communicated, for our consideration, some plain truths in order for the stirring up and encouraging Friends to industry and faithfulness in those things that belong to their everlasting peace and welfare. I felt unity with him in his exercise, and found it my place and duty to make some addition – to place the matter close home on the minds of Friends. It was a favored, solemn meeting and most minds seemed well affected with the savoring[2] power which was felt to preside.

In the course of this week was our quarterly meeting, held at this time at Westbury. It was well attended by Friends and the public meeting was very large. It was in the main a favored meeting, especially the public, closing meeting, in which Truth reigned triumphant over error and untruth, and the doctrines of the gospel flowed freely – suited to the varied states of this large, mixed assembly. And a precious solemnity was felt to preside over the whole. And Friends parted from each other in much unity, and apparently with grateful hearts for the unmerited favor.

I likewise opened to this meeting my prospect of attending the Yearly Meeting of Ohio, together with the minute of unity and concurrence from our monthly meeting, which was fully united with by the quarter, and an endorsement thereof made on my certificate – signed by the clerks of both the men's and women's meetings.

First Day, 25th: A silent meeting today. And when such meetings are attended with full acquiescence and entire peace of mind, how precious they are. Thus are the Lord's dedicated children led and instructed, and taught how to suffer want and how to abound – being content in every

---

[1] Psalm 16:11
[2] Savoring: pleasing

dispensation of his divine will and pleasure, and in which condition, all things work together for good to these. Hence we are led to, "Rejoice evermore. Pray without ceasing. In everything, give thanks."

The rest of this week, I was diligently employed in preparing for my intended journey and in arranging my temporal concerns, that no occasion might be given to the adversaries of Truth to reproach the Truth[1] or its cause by any neglect or omission on my part. And that all things might be left sweet and quiet at home, that so I might leave it with peace of mind, freed from every burden and care on that account – that I might be fully at liberty to devote myself wholly to the service of my great and good Master until the allotted portion is accomplished, for which, he hath called me forth to fulfill his will – to whom belongs obedience and worship, and who is over all, God blessed forever. Amen.

> *The original manuscript breaks off at the ellipses in the middle of the following paragraph. From there to the beginning of Hicks' trip to Pennsylvania in 1822, the editorial committee manuscript has been followed.*

First Day, 1st of 8th month: At our meeting today, my mind was led into a view of the excellence and necessity of right faith in God and Christ – it being that by which the just live – as nothing else can qualify to live a life of true righteousness and justice, but a true and living faith in God and Christ. And ... without this faith, it is impossible to please God. The subject spread and led to communication in a large testimony, by which many minds were reached and comforted, and a precious solemnity spread over the meeting. And we parted from each other with grateful hearts for the unmerited favor.

On Fifth Day, I was led to call the attention of my Friends to first principles, and to recur[2] to the uprightness, simplicity, and faithfulness of our worthy predecessors, and to recount the great and sorrowful deviations therefrom by those, who are making the same profession in the present day, in departing from a full reliance and dependence on the power and Spirit that actuated and governed them. Hence, weakness and darkness pervade their minds, by which great reproach is brought upon the society, and occasion given for many to speak evil of the Truth and the principle we hold out to the world as the only sure guide to blessedness – to the wounding of the faithful few, who are yet preserved in a good degree of gospel simplicity, and who live under a daily exercise for the

---

[1] 1 Timothy 5:14
[2] Recur: move back or return to

promotion and advancement of the Messiah's kingdom here on earth, and that it may arise and become the peace and glory of all nations.

A Visit to the Yearly Meeting of Friends in Ohio

Having, as before noted, had it on my mind to attend the next yearly meeting of Friends in the state of Ohio and some other meetings in going to and returning home, and having obtained a minute of unity and concurrence from our monthly and quarterly meeting, I left home in order to accomplish the service, the 17th of 8th month 1819, and proceeded to New York.

The next day being First Day, I attended Friends Meeting in Pearl Street in the morning, which proved a favored season in which I witnessed a renewal of strength and a satisfactory evidence that my procedure was under right direction, for which my mind was reduced into a state of humble gratitude for the unmerited mercy – having left my home in weakness and poverty of spirit, and nothing to lean on in crossing this Jordan, but my slender staff of faith. I attended the meeting at Liberty Street in the afternoon, which, although small, was in a good degree comfortable and encouraging to my much exercised mind.

As our Meeting for Sufferings was the succeeding Third Day, I stayed in town and attended that meeting.

Through New Jersey to Pennsylvania

After this I proceeded on my journey, accompanied by my kind Friend and neighbor, Willet Robbins, who had joined me as a companion in this journey. We attended the Quarterly Meeting at Rahway on our way, which opened the next day with the Meeting of Ministers and Elders. The meeting for discipline was held the day after, and a meeting for public worship, as a parting meeting, the succeeding day. In these several opportunities, way opened to discharge myself faithfully in the exercise of gospel communication to my Friends and others who attended – fully to the relief of my own mind and, I trust, to the instruction and encouragement of many who attended, the Lord having been graciously pleased to manifest his presence and power for our help – to the glory and praise of his own excellent name, who is over all, God blessed forever.

After these solemn opportunities were closed, we took leave of our Friends and proceeded on our journey and arrived at Easton on Seventh Day evening. This is a town on the west side of the River Delaware in the state of Pennsylvania. Having felt my mind led to pass through this town, attended with a concern to have a religious opportunity with the inhabitants, we tarried with them the next day and had a meeting appointed, which was held in their schoolhouse at the 4th hour after noon. It proved, through heavenly help, a favored and, I trust, an instructive season to many. Several of their ministers and most of the principal people attended, and appeared all to go away satisfied, and many apparently with thankful hearts for the present favor. And I parted with them in true peace of mind.

The next morning we proceeded on our journey, and rode to Maidencreek, and lodged with our kind Friend, Isaac Penrose.

The day following being Third Day, we had an appointed meeting at Reading, about eight miles farther on our way. It was held in their courthouse. Many of the inhabitants of the town attended and behaved soberly. And the gospel was preached among them in the plain demonstration of Truth and, I trust, was as a sword or hammer to some present, who were not prepared to meet sound doctrine, but was comfortable and instructive to others – such as were tender in spirit and were honestly seeking the way to peace. It was a solemn and, I trust, profitable opportunity.

After the meeting I made a short visit to a sick woman, who appeared to be drawing fast toward her close. She was comforted in the visit, and when I parted with her, appeared in a quiet resigned state of mind. Her bodily affliction, which had attended her for a considerable time, had, I believe, wrought a good work in her. After this opportunity, we proceeded immediately on our journey, which we continued the four following days through a number of towns and villages where no Friends live.

We arrived on Seventh Day evening at Dunnings Creek, where there is a monthly meeting of Friends. They lie very much detached from the body of society – the nearest meeting to them is about sixty miles distant. We attended their meeting on First Day, which proved through heavenly help, a comfortable, strengthening opportunity. We lodged with our kind Friend, Thomas Penrose.

The next morning, we proceeded on our journey – having the Alleghany and several other mountains and high and rough ridges of land to pass over in our way to the settlements of Friends in the Redstone country. The roads were excessively bad and, in some places, almost impassable, but with two days hard traveling we got safe to Connellsville on the west side of the mountains on Third Day evening.

We put up with a man by the name of John Gibson, who had once a right of membership in our society, but by some means had lost it. Yet he appeared to retain his love to Friends, and was very kind and benevolent, and appeared very glad of the opportunity of entertaining Friends. His family likewise appeared very kind and friendly, and signified it as a matter of considerable regret that they were so far distant from Friends, as not to have the privilege of attending their meetings.

There was one family of Friends in the town and one of their children, an infant of about eight months old, had died a little before our arrival. And the funeral being the next day, we attended it. It was a very solemn opportunity, in which many hearts were contrited by the tendering power of Truth, which was felt to cover the assembly in a very general manner. Such seasons are as a brook by the way to the poor exercised travelers, who often go mourning on their way from a sense of the prevalence of sin and iniquity in the land.

After this solemn opportunity, we proceeded on our journey and the next day attended Friends Monthly Meeting at Westland in Redstone Quarterly Meeting. I had some service – both in the meeting for worship and that for discipline – but things appeared rather low as to the right order of the gospel in both meetings, it being a day of ease and outward tranquility. And this hath a tendency to produce lukewarmness, if not watchfully and diligently guarded against.

Ohio

From this place we proceeded directly to Mount Pleasant in Ohio (where the yearly meeting is held), where we arrived on Seventh Day, 28th of 8th month.

On First Day, 29th, attended Friends Meeting at Short Creek in the morning and had an appointed meeting at Mount Pleasant in the afternoon. They were both largely attended and proved very instructive, satisfactory meetings, in which I had good service and found sweet peace as the result of my labors of love amongst them.

The five following days, meetings were appointed for us at Concord, Saint Clairsville, Plainfield, Flushing, and Harrisville. These were all full meetings – generally more collected than the houses could contain – but Friends were industrious and provided seats outdoors about the house, by which the people were generally accommodated.

On Seventh Day, the Yearly Meeting of Ministers and Elders opened and continued by adjournments until Fifth Day. I think they were generally favored opportunities, the Head of the Church graciously condescending to manifest his presence for the help of his devoted, dedicated children. And this is the crown and diadem of all our religious assemblies.

On First Day, public meetings for worship were held, both fore and after noon, in both Friends Meetinghouses in the neighborhood. That in the town of Mount Pleasant – held in their new meetinghouse, which is one of the largest I ever saw belonging to Friends – was very large. I attended that meeting both fore and after noon, in which I had much service by way of testimony, which appeared to be much to the comfort and general edification of the assemblies, and resulted in the solid peace of my own mind.

On Second Day, the Yearly Meeting for Discipline opened and continued by adjournments until Seventh Day toward evening. It was a season of much travail and exercise to the rightly-concerned, active members – having before them (in addition to their usual business) the revisal of their discipline.[1] I was led under close exercise on the account, and a very considerable portion of active service fell to my lot, with other Friends. It was thought, I believe by Friends generally, to have been the most favored yearly meeting they had had since its institution, and was worthy of grateful remembrance.

I tarried here over First Day and attended their meeting at the old meetinghouse. It was a season of deep travail in the forepart of the meeting, in which my spirit was led into deep baptism with and for the dead. And I was brought into sympathy and fellowship with the Suffering Seed, which appeared to me to be pressed down in the hearts of the formal professors as a cart under sheaves. This, I believed, was too much the situation of a considerable number in that assembly. But as I continued patiently to endure the exercise and kept up the inward travail, light sprang up and dispelled the darkness, accompanied with a motion of life to stand up. And my mouth was opened in a large, searching, and effective testimony, whereby the dead were raised, the lukewarm stirred up, the honest seekers encouraged, and the rightly exercised minds comforted and edified. It was the Lord's doing, and marvelous in mine eyes.

The six succeeding days, meetings were appointed at the following places, which we attended.

On Second Day, at a little village called York, where a few Friends were privileged with an indulged meeting – a meeting not established.

On Third Day, at Smithfield.

On Fourth Day, at Cross Creek.

On Fifth Day, at Franklin, where was also only a small indulged meeting.

On Sixth Day, at Augusta at the 10th hour in the morning, and at Sandy Spring at the 3rd hour in the afternoon.

On Seventh Day, at New Garden.

These were all seasons of favor, wherein I was strengthened to labor in the work of the gospel and to declare largely to these several assemblies of the things concerning the kingdom of God – endeavoring by persuasive arguments founded in the clear demonstration of the Spirit, accompanied

---

[1] Discipline: short for the "Book of Discipline," essentially a handbook for the yearly meeting

Fairfield (Ohio) Meetinghouse

with a lively evidence of divine power, to gather the minds of the people to the Light of Christ, or Christ the Light in their own hearts, as the only sure guide to blessedness and foundation rock on which to build all our hopes of redemption and salvation. A precious solemnity was felt to prevail in those several meetings – most of which were crowded gatherings, many more often collecting than their meetinghouses could contain. And Truth was exalted over all, to the praise of him who is over all, God blessed forever.

After the latter meeting we proceeded to Salem, intending to be at Friends Meeting there the next day, which was First Day, 19th of 9th month. We attended the meeting in the forenoon, but not feeling myself clear, I was led to appoint an afternoon meeting, which was accordingly held at the 3rd hour and was largely attended by Friends and others – among whom way opened fully to discharge and clear myself. And I found peace in my labor of love among them.

On Second and Third Days, I attended meetings by appointment at Springfield and Goshen, two neighboring villages. These were likewise very solemn, instructive seasons, wherein I was largely led forth in ministerial labor – apparently to the comfort and edification of most present. From Goshen we returned back to Salem, intending to be at their monthly meeting to be held the next day, which we accordingly attended. I had good service among my Friends, both in the meeting for worship and that for discipline.

After this we took a final leave of them, in the fresh feelings of mutual love and Christian fellowship, and proceeded on our journey that afternoon to Fairfield, where we had a meeting the next day.

On Sixth Day, was at Columbiana.
On Seventh Day, at Middleton.

And on First Day, 26th, had two meetings – one in the morning at Elkrun and the other at the 3rd hour after noon at Carmel. These meetings were all well attended, wherein I was led forth largely in testimony, apparently to the general satisfaction and edification of the people, and to the comfort and peace of my own mind.

On Second Day, we proceeded to New Lisbon and attended a meeting in their courthouse at the 11th hour. It was a large collection, mostly made up of other societies – there being but few Friends residing in that place. I was led to open several doctrinal points of our profession and to show the great difference between profession and possession, and that no profession of religion was worth esteeming as anything unless it was the effect of the real possession of the thing professed – as, no profession of a thing could of itself give any a possession thereof, but a real possession will manifest itself by its fruits. It was a day of great favor, in which Truth reigned over all.

Back in Pennsylvania

On Third Day, we proceeded to Beaver Falls. Had a meeting there the next day to good satisfaction. After this, we traveled on our way to Pittsburgh, where we arrived the next day about noon and had an appointed meeting there in the evening in their courthouse. It was a large spacious building, but more collected than the house could contain. I had much service among them and the Lord's power was felt to preside – quieting and solemnizing the assembly – and many hearts were humbled and contrited, and Truth raised into dominion over all.

On Sixth Day afternoon, we left Pittsburgh on our way to Brownsville, where we arrived in the afternoon of the next day.

On First Day, we attended Friends Meeting there. And notice being spread among the people at large that we were there, it was a very crowded assembly – more than the house could well contain. And through the condescending goodness of the Shepherd of Israel, I was helped to discharge myself faithfully among them in an effective testimony to the truths of the gospel – proving from clear scripture testimony, accompanied with the demonstration of the Spirit in harmony with right reason, that nothing short of a full belief in and obedience to the revelation of the Spirit of Truth (a manifestation of which is given to every man and woman to profit withal as the only rule of faith and practice) can make a real Christian, and produce redemption and salvation to an immortal soul. It was a very solemn, instructive season, worthy of grateful remembrance.

On Second Day, we had an appointed meeting at Sandy Hill at the 10th hour and another in the evening at Uniontown – held in their courthouse. These were both seasons of favor, producing solid peace to my own mind and, I trust, instructive and edifying to the people in

Hopewell Meetinghouse in Clear Brook, Virginia

general who attended. These meetings closed my labors among Friends and others in the compass of the Yearly Meeting of Ohio.

Through Virginia to Maryland

On Third Day, we set out on our journey over the mountains towards Winchester in Virginia, in order to attend the meetings of Friends in that neighborhood on our way to Baltimore – the distance was about one hundred and sixteen miles. It took three days to accomplish the journey with hard traveling – a considerable part of the way being very rocky, as well as mountainous. We arrived among Friends at Pughtown on Fifth Day evening and had a meeting appointed there the next day at two o'clock in the afternoon, which we attended accordingly.

On Seventh Day, had a meeting at the Ridge.

On First Day at Centre (near Winchester) and the two following days had meetings at Hopewell and Berkeley. I was largely led forth in these meetings to show to the people the inconsistency and unrighteousness of holding our fellow creatures in bondage, and the evil tendency of bringing up our children and families on the fruits of their labor – wrested from them by violence, without paying them an adequate reward for the same. I likewise opened to them the folly and deception of all their profession of worshipping that Being who is perfect in justice, purity, and holiness, while their hands are full of violence and oppression, and living in luxury and idleness on their unrighteous gain. The Lord's power was exalted in these meetings and Truth reigned.

After the latter meeting, we proceeded on our way towards Baltimore, where we arrived on Seventh Day evening – attending meetings at Fredericktown and New Market on our way thither.

On First Day, 17th of 10th month, I attended Friends Meetings in that city – the Western District in the morning and the Eastern District in the afternoon. I was silent in the former, but in the latter, I was largely led forth in gospel communication. As notice had been spread among the citizens of other professions, the meeting was large. And the divine power was felt to preside, which brought a precious solemnity over the meeting and Truth was raised into dominion.

Here, we met with our Friend, Elizabeth Coggeshall from New York, with her companion, Judith Coffin from Nantucket, also our ancient Friend, William Rickman from England. We were mutually glad in seeing each other. Elizabeth felt a concern to see the members of our society – select from those of other societies – in each meeting. Accordingly a Friend (at her request) in the morning meeting, when the service of the first meeting was over, proposed the same to the assembly – when those who were not members quietly withdrew and our dear Friend had good service among them. This also opened an opportunity for me to throw in my mite[1] and set a seal to the service. A similar opportunity was likewise had with Friends at the close of the afternoon meeting in the Eastern District, which was also a favored time.

And as I had felt my mind somewhat similarly engaged in coming into the city, it opened the way to spread my exercise before Friends – which was that of the more select service – of seeing the active members and heads of families of both sexes together. I had an opportunity with those of this description in the Western District and afterwards with those of the Eastern, and was glad in believing that divine love was near – favoring with his enlivening, reconciling presence – which raised a hope, that through the divine blessing, the opportunities would not prove altogether unfruitful, for some disunity and jealousies had prevailed among the members of society in this city.[2]

The next day being Friends' Meeting Day, I felt most easy to stay and attend it. I also found my mind led to some further service among the citizens at large. For although I had had a public opportunity on First Day evening (which seemed for the present to ease my mind), yet a renewed

---

[1] Mite: something small and insignificant

[2] A dispute over control of the Friends graveyard arose when Baltimore Monthly Meeting was split into two separate meetings in 1807. This festered for over a decade without settlement. As a result, in 1819 (about a week following this entry), the separate monthly meetings were laid down and the meetings recombined into a single monthly meeting by the quarterly meeting.

exercise on that account induced a belief it would be right to give the citizens generally another invitation – which Friends readily agreed to and spread the notice accordingly. It was a very large meeting and, through gracious condescension, a highly favored season. The Lord's power was felt to preside, and a precious solemnity spread over the assembly. And I took my leave of them in much peace of mind.

This closed my service among them.

Through Delaware to Pennsylvania

The two following days we rode to Wilmington, where we arrived on Sixth Day evening.

On Seventh Day evening, we had a large meeting by appointment with Friends and the inhabitants of the town. This was a solemn, instructive season, worthy of grateful remembrance.

We also attended the morning meeting of Friends the next day, and then proceeded to Chester, parting with my Friends in much sweet peace and unity. There we had a large solemn meeting in the evening among the few Friends of that place and the inhabitants of the town. I trust, through heavenly goodness, it proved an instructive, edifying season to many.

The two following days, I attended the monthly meetings of Providence and Darby.

On Fourth Day morning, we proceeded to Philadelphia. We stayed in the city until the following Third Day and attended all the meetings of Friends there – some by appointment and the others as they came in course. We were at two of their monthly meetings and their quarterly meeting. The meetings were generally crowded and at several many of the people were obliged to stand outside of the doors for want of room. Through unmerited mercy, the Lord's power was felt to preside, producing a precious solemnity over those large, promiscuous gatherings, and by which Truth was raised into dominion. Surely it was the Lord's doing and marvelous in mine eyes. It was, I trust, a time of renewed visitation to many, especially to the beloved youth.

We left the city on Third Day morning and proceeded to Germantown, where by previous appointment we had a large meeting at the 11th hour.

The two following days, we attended Friends Quarterly Meeting at Horsham. And on Sixth Day, had a large public meeting at Byberry. These were all favored instructive seasons, in which the Lord's presence was manifested for our help, and were worthy of grateful remembrance.

Through New Jersey to Home

On Seventh Day, we attended a meeting at Bristol, and at evening crossed the River Delaware to Burlington and attended Friends fore and after noon meetings on First Day. These were large, favored meetings, in which Truth reigned.

On Second Day, 8th of 11th month, we proceeded to Trenton and had a large meeting there in the evening with the few Friends of that place and the inhabitants of the town, in which divers essential doctrines of the gospel were opened to the consideration of the assembly. It was a solemn meeting. And I parted with them in true peace of mind – which is the certain and consolatory result of disinterested obedience and faithfulness to manifested duty.

We proceeded on Third Day on our way to New York, where we arrived the next day in season to attend Friends Meeting in Pearl Street – it being their usual meeting day. The meeting was generally gathered when I got in, having had some distance to travel to reach there, which occasioned my being a few minutes after the time. My mind, soon after taking my seat, was brought under a renewed exercise on account of the members of our society mixing in with the associations of other people – in their governments and politics, their Bible and missionary societies, and pretended charity associations – which had a very hurtful tendency by leavening[1] the minds of Friends, and leading them to assimilate with the spirit of the world, and turning them away from the simplicity of our profession – thereby neglecting to support our Christian testimonies as it regards plainness of speech, deportment, and apparel. Such conduct is particularly wounding to some of the beloved youth, for they seeing their elder brethren – and especially some who were sometimes active in our meetings for discipline – join with such associations. It leads them into a free familiarity and friendship with such as are light and vain in their conversation and deportment, by which their tender minds are greatly wounded, and they led off from the cross and a strict regard to that sobriety of conduct, which Truth requires of all its professors. I was led to communicate largely on those subjects in a close, searching testimony. And the Lord's power was felt to prevail and the meeting generally brought under a solemn covering. It proved a season of favor, and the right-minded were made to rejoice.

Feeling my mind impressed with a concern to appoint a meeting for the citizens at large, the appointment was accordingly made at seven o'clock the ensuing evening. It was a very large collection – more than the house could contain – and was a highly favored season. A very precious solemnity was spread over the assembly in general. And when I sat down, after standing nearly two hours,[2] I turned my eyes over the congregation, and all was quiet and still, and every countenance seemed expressive of

---

[1] Leavening: debase a pure material by mixing in corrupt matter

[2] In other words, Hicks spoke for nearly two hours.

the solemnity felt, and clothed us together – as with a mantle of love. Surely it was the Lord's doing, and marvelous in our eyes.

The next day I attended Friends Meeting near the Bowery as it came in course. And some notice being given of my intending to be there, we had the company of a number of their neighbors of other societies. This was also a very instructive, favored season.

The ensuing evening, I had another appointed meeting for the citizens at large in Friends Meetinghouse at Liberty Street. This was rather a trying meeting, as many who attended were such as had settled down in a form[1] and were difficult to reach, which makes hard labor for the truly-exercised ministers. However, I had a hope the season would prove profitable to some. And I left them with peace of mind.

This meeting closed my labors in this journey, and the next morning we rode home, 12th of 11th month 1819. I found my family and Friends in usual health and glad to see me, which rendered it a cause of mutual joy, and filled my heart with gratitude and thanksgiving to the God and Father of all our sure mercies, who had led about, instructed and preserved me through all – to the praise of his great and excellent name.

I was from home in this journey about three months, and traveled nearly twelve hundred miles, and attended eighty-seven meetings.

At Home

First Day, 14th: I sat with my Friends in our own meeting, in which I was largely led forth in ministry – setting forth, as it opened on my mind, the cause why so little progress was made in reformation and the true spiritual or real Christian life – and showing that it was principally owing (as it then appeared in the openings of Truth) to be occasioned by the visited children of our Heavenly Father not keeping close to that which first visited them and opened their understanding, but letting their minds out to worldly things. And that by opening the way to a free and familiar converse with the people of the world, many were led and induced thereby to join with them in their manners, maxims, interests, and worldly policies. By which means, they were so yoked together in a free and open friendship, as thereby to become weakened and brought into bondage to them, so as to be ashamed and afraid to stand upright and bear a faithful testimony against this worldly spirit and its fruits. By which, the testimonies of Truth were in a great measure let fall for fear of offending these, their worldly-minded associates, by which the promotion of the cause of Truth was greatly obstructed, and its faithful testimony-bearers grieved and made to go mourning on their way.

---

[1] Settle down in a form: take on only the appearance of worship

Fifth Day: Attended our monthly meeting, in which I also had some close, searching labor to stir up Friends to more diligence and faithfulness in the support of our Christian testimonies, and cautioning them against a worldly spirit, which would lead to extortion and grinding the faces of the poor. For this is very reproachful for any Christian professor – and more so for us, who are making a more exalted profession than any others who go under the Christian name.

First Day, 21st: My mind today was led into a near feeling sympathy with such as had been visited with the day-spring from on high,[1] but who had not so fully given up to the pointing of Truth in what are generally termed little things, as they ought – the natural tendency of which is to lead the mind into a doubting state. For when the creature, in his own will, takes the liberty of judging for himself of what is little or what is great, he departs from the true standard and has no certain evidence to walk by. For if he has a right to judge for himself in one case, why not in every other? Here, doubting will arise in his mind of what is or is not agreeable to the Divine Will, as nothing can give the mind certain evidence, but faithfully complying with the evident sensations which the Light of Truth opens upon it – let them be what the creature may judge to be small or great. For we have no more reason or right to refuse complying with a small requisition than we have a great one, if the requisition proceeds from the same cause. The subject was so opened as to affect many minds with tenderness and contrition, and had a humbling, solemnizing effect on the meeting in general, and was, I believe, gladdening to many minds.

Fifth Day: Attended our meeting in silence – which was very acceptable to me.

First Day, 28th: Mostly silent in meeting today.

A Visit to the Neighboring Inhabitants in 1819 & 1820

On my return home from my late journey, I felt my mind drawn in sympathy – attended with a concern to pay a religious visit to the neighboring inhabitants in the compass of our quarterly meeting. This concern I opened to my Friends, the first monthly meeting after my return, and received their full unity therein. But taking a severe cold soon after I came home, I continued indisposed for some weeks, which with some other necessary concerns, prevented my entering on the visit until after our succeeding monthly meeting.

The Fourth Day following, 22nd of 12th month, I proceeded therein, accompanied by my wife and my kinsman, Isaac Hicks of Westbury. We were from home five days and attended six meetings, mostly among those of other societies. It was a time of deep exercise to me – being led in the

---

[1] Luke 1:78

line of searching labor, pointing to a reform in manners and conduct, and showing the fallacy of all ceremonial religion in the observation of days, and complying with outward ordinances which do not in the least tend to make the comers thereunto a whit the better as it respects the conscience, but lead the observers thereof into a form without the power.[1]

We returned home the following Second Day.

---

[1] 2 Timothy 3:5

1820-1821

I tarried at home until the beginning of the next week, when feeling my mind drawn to attend the Monthly Meeting of Friends in New York, I again left home, accompanied by the aforesaid Friend.

We were at the monthly meeting on Fourth Day, in which I had some close exercise – the meeting having much business before it. And one case in particular was very trying, in which Friends were divided and two or three unqualified individuals seemed determined, for a considerable time, to compel the meeting to comply with their unsanctified wills. But as Friends who were rightly exercised patiently kept up the travail and withstood them, Truth was raised into dominion, and by its power silenced all their caviling,[1] and united the meeting in a right conclusion. The meeting for worship and that for discipline continued upwards of six hours.

We left the city soon after the close of this long meeting, and passed over the river to Brooklyn, where by previous appointment we had a meeting that evening composed of the different professions of the inhabitants of that place – very few Friends residing there. The meeting was pretty large and, in the main, satisfactory.

The next day, we proceeded to Flushing and attended their monthly meeting. I was silent in the meeting for worship, but had some good service in that for discipline. We also had an appointed meeting in the evening for the inhabitants of the town, which was large and solemn.

The next day we returned to Newtown, and had a meeting at Friends Meetinghouse at the Kills in that place at the eleventh hour and another in the evening at the sixth hour in the village. They were both favored meetings. We returned to Flushing after the latter meeting and lodged with our kind Friend, Walter Farrington. And the next day rode home and found my family well.

Labors near & about Home

First Day, 9th of 1st month 1820: I sat with my Friends at home in our own meeting today, which I considered as no small privilege.

On Second Day morning, I was early informed that my kinsman and kind fellow traveler, Isaac Hicks, was taken with a severe illness about ten o'clock the preceding evening and lay at the point of death. I hastened to see him and found him nearly breathing his last – being past noticing anything by his external senses. It was a sudden and unexpected trial to me to be thus almost instantaneously separated from such a kind and valued Friend, who had for a number of years devoted himself in divers

---

[1] Caviling: a frivolous objection

ways to promote the cause of Truth and Righteousness in the earth – and in particular, by encouraging and accompanying Friends in the ministry, when traveling in Truth's service, especially myself, having been with me in several long journeys, as well as divers short ones. I parted with him at the close of one of the latter on the Seventh Day afternoon before his death at his own house and apparently in usual health – although he had been for a considerable time previous thereto much afflicted, at times, with severe pain in his breast and shortness of breath, which created great suffering during their continuance. He had a return thereof the evening before I last parted with him, which occasioned him to observe to me that he thought he should ere long be taken off in one of those attacks – although I then thought quite otherwise, as in other respects he appeared like one in very good health, manifesting by his outward appearance a very healthy countenance.

Such sudden attacks prove with indubitable evidence that mortality is so closely interwoven in the very constitution of these animal bodies that the present moment is the only time we can call our own, and which continually announce the impressive language, "Be ye therefore ready."

Such sudden and unexpected separations from our endeared friends make the loss seem greater – not only to their families and near connections, but to their friends in general, and particularly so to those who know their real worth. But it ever affords a soothing consolation, and induces to acquiesce in the divine will, when we have evident cause to hope that our loss – which is but for a short time – is their eternal gain.

I attended the funeral of my beloved Friend, which was large and solemn. And I was led forth in an impressive testimony to the truths of the gospel, inviting the people to inquire and see and taste for themselves that the Lord is good.[1]

I continued at home until the following Seventh Day, when I again proceeded on my visit to the neighboring towns and villages. I was from home in the course of the four following weeks about thirteen days and attended fifteen meetings, returning home on Sixth Day, 11th of 2nd month 1820. My service in many of those opportunities was very arduous. The lukewarmness and insensibility of the people, as to any right religious concern, make hard work for the honest laborers in this day of ease and carnal security. But true peace of mind, the sure result of faithfulness, crowns the attempts at doing good, as it makes hard things easy and bitter things sweet.[2]

---

[1] Psalm 34:8
[2] This phrase, "makes hard things easy and bitter things sweet" is not scriptural, but occurs in the writings of John Newton, the composer of *Amazing Grace*.

I tarried at home until the latter end of the next week, in the course of which I had a very severe attack of bodily indisposition occasioned by the gravel, with which I have been afflicted at times for near twenty years. These warnings are designed to spur us on to our duty, as they continually announce to the enlightened mind this very useful memento, "Remember to die."

In the latter end of the week, there came to my house my much esteemed Friend and kinsman, Edward Hicks* from Newtown in Bucks County, Pennsylvania, on a religious visit to our parts with his companion, James Walton, an elder. I accompanied them the next day to a meeting they had appointed at Westbury. It was very large, in which Edward had very good service – being largely led forth to open to the people many important doctrines of the Christian religion. I accompanied him to all the meetings he had among us except one, and in some of them had a portion of the service laid upon me, particularly in the meeting at Bethpage.

I accompanied my Friend to four meetings after this, in which he was generally favored to open things suitable to the states of the people – his gift being searching and lively.

After his service was over in the meeting at Cow Neck on First Day, I was led forth in a short testimony and the meeting closed under an evident sense that Truth reigned.

Our next meeting was the day following at Rockaway on Second Day, 28th of 2nd month. It was in the main a favored opportunity – my part was to sit in silence. After this meeting, I parted with my beloved Friend and his companion in the fellowship of the gospel. They proceeded towards New York, and I returned home that evening, and found my family well.

First Day, 5th of 3rd month: I attended our own meeting, which through heavenly help proved a very precious, instructive season. It was larger than usual – many coming in who did not often attend – to whom the gospel was preached in the demonstration of the Spirit, through which Truth was raised into dominion, causing the hearts of many to be warmed within them by the influence of its power, and manifesting itself by much brokenness and contrition of spirit.

Second Day, 13th: Attended the funeral of our Friend, Charles Frost, at which there was a large collection of Friends and neighbors. A meeting was held on the occasion, which was a favored one, and I trust a profitable opportunity to some present and worthy of grateful remembrance.

In the fall of 1820, being, with several other Friends, on an appointment from the yearly meeting requiring our care and attention in the northern quarters, and having for some time previously felt my mind drawn to visit some of the meetings of Friends within the compass of Farmington and Duanesburg Quarterly Meetings, I obtained the unity and concurrence of my Friends at home to attend thereto, after accomplishing the service of the yearly meeting.

I accordingly set out in 9th month, and was favored to go through the visit with peace to my own mind. For he, who is the alone sure helper of all his dependant children, graciously manifested himself to be near for my help and encouragement in the travail and exercise that I was engaged in for the promotion of his noble cause of Truth and Righteousness in the earth – and in a way that was often marvelous in mine eyes, tending to inspire my soul with deep and humble gratitude and thanksgiving for the unmerited favor.

1822

In the summer of 1822, I opened to my Friends a prospect, which for a considerable time had been impressive on my mind – to make a visit in the love of the gospel to Friends and others in some parts of the Yearly Meeting of Philadelphia, and if way should open for it, to visit some of the families of Friends in that city, and also to attend the Yearly Meeting at Baltimore. They united with me in the concern, and left me at liberty to proceed therein.

> *The following section on Hicks' trip to Pennsylvania and Baltimore is based primarily on Hicks' travel journal for this trip with additions from the editorial committee manuscript. Where details from the two manuscripts do not agree (for example, the editorial committee manuscript states that Hicks began the trip in 7th month, not 10th month), I considered the travel journal more reliable.*

A Visit to some parts of Pennsylvania & Baltimore

Left home on Fourth Day, the 2nd of 10th month 1822 in order to perform a visit to Friends and others as way should open in some parts of the Yearly Meetings of Philadelphia and to attend Baltimore Yearly Meeting – having the unity of my Friends therein. My neighbor, David Seaman, an approved elder, joined me as companion in the journey. We rode to Flushing and the next day attended their monthly meeting. We had a large favored meeting at Flushing, which was strengthening and comforting to my mind in first setting out in this arduous engagement, and excited gratitude for the unmerited mercy.

The next day afternoon, we rode to New York and tarried there the following day. My prospect of a meeting at Hester Street (which I had a view of several weeks before I left home) revived with renewed weight. And although from the consternation and interrupted state of the citizens – owing to the prevalence of fever in the city – I had given up the prospect on leaving home, yet I now saw that I could not depart from the city with a quiet mind unless I had a meeting agreeable to my former view. Accordingly, when I got into town I opened my concern to some of my Friends there, who readily united therewith and notice was given. And one of the Friends (who attended about the door at the gathering of the meeting) said there were more people collected than had ever been at any former time in that place. Several hundreds, he said, went away, who could not get into the house for want of room. I had a full opportunity to clear my mind among the people – most of whom were very solid and attentive. Thus we have great cause of gratitude to the gracious Caretaker of his faithfully devoted children – who opens a way for them, when some are ready to conclude there is no way. But he opens the way for those, which none but himself can shut, to the praise of his own great and adorable name, who is over all, blessed forever.

Through New Jersey to Pennsylvania

The next day and 5th of the month, we passed on to Newark in Jersey and had a meeting in the courthouse in the afternoon. There was a pretty large collection of the inhabitants, among whom I had strength and utterance given to open many important doctrines of the Christian religion in a clear and impressive manner, which appeared sensibly to affect and impress the minds of the sober and well-inclined, but many appeared very ignorant and inexperienced as to the real truths of the gospel. But having fully cleared my mind among them, I left them with the answer of peace, and proceeded to Plainfield and lodged with our Friend, Nathan Vail. We attended First Day Meeting there – which was large for the place – and it was favored in an eminent manner to our mutual comfort.

On Second Day, rode to Kingwood and lodged at Henry Clifton's. Had a full and comfortable meeting there the next day, after which rode to Solebury in Pennsylvania and attended a meeting there at the sixth hour in the evening. It was a large meeting, in which I was led to discharge myself faithfully in a close searching testimony. It was a very solemn, quiet opportunity. And I parted with them in peace of mind. We lodged at Aaron Paxson's.

The next day, we rode to Buckingham and attended a meeting there at the 11th hour, after which we rode to Plumstead and lodged at Josiah Brown's.

And the next day, 10th of the month, we attended a meeting there at the 11th hour, after which we rode to Wrightstown and attended their meeting the next day – lodged at Isaac Chapman's. After which, we rode to Newtown and lodged with my kind Friend and kinsman, Edward Hicks.

And the next day, rode to Makefield and attended a meeting at the usual time. It was said to be the largest that had ever been in that place. Rode back to Newtown after dining at W. Taylor's and took tea at Buley Twining's and returned to Edward's and lodged.

And we have abundant cause to bless the name of Israel's Unslumbering Shepherd, who hath graciously condescended to manifest his presence and power for our help and support – opening my way in a marvelous manner in all the meetings I have attended since I left home, uniting my Friends in a joint travail for the promotion of his blessed cause – Truth prevailing in every meeting and running as precious ointment over the assemblies – bearing down all opposition, and spreading, by its power, a sweet and precious solemnity over all. Surely it is the Lord's doing, and marvelous in our eyes. And what is the greatest cause of gratitude and thanksgiving to the Benevolent Author of all our richest blessings is that he causes all these favors to bow my spirit in deep humiliation and fear before him, as unworthy of the least of his mercies. To the sufficiency of his grace may all the praise and glory be ascribed, nothing due to man.

The next day being second of the week and 13th of 10th month, we rode to Horsham and lodged with our Friend, Isaac Parry. Attended their meeting the 14th, after which we rode to Upper Dublin and lodged with our Friend, Daniel Shoemaker. Attended a meeting there the next day. It was a large, favored meeting – the Lord's power and presence was eminently manifested and Truth was raised into dominion over all. After which, we rode to North Wales and lodged with our Friend, Hugh Foulke.

Attended their meeting the next day, after which we proceeded on our way to Plymouth – lodged with our Friend, Jacob Albertson. Was at their meeting the next day and then rode to Providence and lodged with Benjamin Cock. Had a meeting there the day following, after which we rode to Pikeland and lodged with my kind Friend, Emmor Kimber.*

The next day being the first of the week, we had a favored meeting with the few Friends there and a pretty large collection of their neighbors of different professions, and rode that afternoon to Robert Massey's and lodged – he was son-in-law to Emmor Kimber.

The next day, we rode to West Chester and attended a meeting. It was large and I trust, an instructive, edifying season to many. And after dining with our Friend, Cheney Jeffrey, we rode to London Grove and lodged with our kind Friend, William Swayne. We attended an appointed meeting there the next day. It was very large and eminently favored. We rode that afternoon to William Jackson's, accompanied by him and his wife, to West Grove – took dinner on the way at our Friend, Thomas Hicks'.

Maryland

The next day, we rode to Deer Creek on the west side of the River Susquehanna. Dined at George Churchman's* at East Nottingham on our way. We attended Friends Meeting there the next day. And some notice being given of our being there, many of the neighboring inhabitants came in and we had a solid, edifying meeting with them. We lodged here two nights with our Friends, John and Susanna Jewett.

My spirit is humbled in a deep feeling sense of the Lord's goodness vouchsafed for our help, opening a way in the minds of my Friends generally to receive the testimonies given me to bear for the promotion of

West Grove Friends Meeting
West Grove, Pennsylvania
Founded 1786
DRAWN BY JOHN W. WREN, JR.

his righteous cause, with marks of apparent joy and satisfaction, and to our mutual comfort.

We reached Baltimore on Sixth Day, 25th of the month, and put up with our Friend, Gerard T. Hopkins. And the Meeting of Ministers and Elders was opened on the next day at the 10th hour. The yearly meeting continued till Sixth Day evening and was acknowledged to be the largest and the most favored meeting they had known for several years past. The unity of Friends with my exercises – in the public meetings and in those for discipline – was truly grateful, and tended to humble and inspire my mind with gratitude and thanksgiving to my Heavenly Father.

I did not feel myself at liberty to leave the city at the close of the yearly meeting, believing that some more public service among the people was required of me. I had accordingly a public meeting in the Eastern District on Seventh Day evening. It was very large, and among the various subjects that opened for communication to those assembled, I was led to expose the iniquity and deformity of the cruel practice of holding our fellow creatures in bondage. And the injustice and inconsistency of Friends doing any act where the right of slavery was acknowledged and supported. And I think I was enabled to do it in a more full and impressive manner than ever before. We had a very interesting and solemn meeting. Truth appeared to gain the victory and reigned over all.

On First Day, I attended Friends Meetings for the Western District, both the fore and after noon. They were very large, and I had a full opportunity in the morning of clearing myself among them. We had a precious, powerful meeting. And among the divers states addressed, the slaveholders were peculiarly the objects of my exercise and concern. The afternoon meeting, I sat in silence – except the expression of a few words just at the close in taking leave of them and bidding all farewell.

In the evening, I had a precious, interesting opportunity with the colored people in Friends Meetinghouse in the Western District. It was said by Friends to be much the largest known in that place. It was a very quiet, solemn meeting, and the minds of all – both white and colored – seemed animated with gladness and joy for the favor dispensed, and gave manifestations of their thankfulness and gratitude for the opportunity.

> *Much of the remainder of this journey is described only in the travel journal. The editorial committee manuscript depicts Hicks as traveling from Baltimore directly to Philadelphia and contains only a brief summary of his subsequent activities before returning home.*

We tarried at Baltimore until the 5th of 11th month, when we took our leave of our Friends in much unity and feelings of Christian affection and rode to Bush, and attended a meeting at the 3rd hour after noon by previous appointment, and lodged with our Friend, David Malsby.

The next day, we proceeded on our journey towards the Eastern Shore of Maryland in order to visit the meetings of Friends in that Quarter. We rode about twenty-one miles, crossed the River Susquehanna at a place called Havre de Grace near the mouth of said river, and lodged with our kind Friend, John Chew Thomas,* at the head of a small river called North East.

The next day, we pursued our journey to Head of Chester and lodged with our Friend, John Turner. Attended a meeting there the next day, after which we rode to Cecil and lodged with our Friend, Joseph Turner, brother to our aforesaid Friend.

And the following day, had an appointed meeting there, after which in the afternoon, we rode to Chester Neck and lodged at the house of some youngerly Friends by the name of True. They had none of them been married, but were bachelors and maidens, and appeared to live together in harmony and concord.

The next day being the first of the week, we attended their meeting. And toward evening, rode to Chestertown and attended a meeting there at the 6th hour in the evening – having made the appointment the day before as we passed through town. It was held in a house belonging to the Methodist Society. It was a very large collection, made up of the different sects residing in the town. It was a favored opportunity – many truths of the gospel were clearly opened to the people in the demonstration of the Spirit, to the silencing and solemnizing the assembly.

And we left them with peace of mind, and rode the next day to Tuckahoe Neck and lodged with our Friend, Isaac Wilson.

Attended a meeting there the next day, after which we rode to Tuckahoe and lodged with our Friend, Susannah Needles.

Was at their meeting the next day, and in the afternoon rode to Easton and lodged with our Friends, Robert and William Moore.

Attended their monthly meeting the next day.

And the day following, rode to Choptank and attended their meeting, after which we rode back to a Friend's house about three miles below Easton.

The next day, rode to Bayside. Attended their meeting and returned that afternoon to Easton and lodged again at William Moore's.

And the next day being first of the week and 17th of 11th month, we attended Friends Meeting there in the forenoon. And at four o'clock, attended a meeting by appointment among the colored people. And at seven in the evening, had an appointed meeting in the courthouse for the townspeople. It was a very large meeting, some Friends observing that it was larger than any known there before, as also was that in the morning. And through heavenly help, they were highly favored meetings, not soon to be forgotten. And indeed with humble gratitude, we are bound to acknowledge it has generally been the case in all those meetings we have attended in the course of our journey. Surely it is the Lord's doing, and marvelous in our eyes.

On Second Day, we proceeded on our journey to Marshy Creek, having previously appointed a meeting there, after which we rode to Centre – lodged on the way with our Friend, Elisha Dawson.

And the next day, was at Centre Meeting, after which we lodged with our Friend, Willis Charles, and the following day, rode to Northwest Fork and attended a meeting.

This closed our visit to Friends on the Eastern Shore of Maryland and we then set forward towards the state of Delaware. Rode that afternoon to William Melony's and lodged.

Delaware

The next day, rode to Camden and lodged with our Friend, Joseph Rowland, and rested the next day.

On Seventh Day, rode to Motherkiln and attended an appointed meeting at the 11th hour, and returned to Camden and lodged with our aforesaid Friend.

The next day being the first of the week, we attended Friends Meeting there in the morning. And at three in the afternoon, rode to Dover – a pretty large country town, the capital of the state and where their legislature meets – and had a meeting in the statehouse, no Friends living in the town. It was a large meeting and a solemn opportunity, after which we rode back to Camden, and attended a meeting there at seven in the evening appointed by Priscilla Hunt,* a Friend from the state of Indiana.

On Second Day, rode to Little Creek and attended a meeting by appointment. Rode back to Camden and attended a meeting for the colored people in the evening.

The next day, rode to Little Creek in order to attend the Quarterly Meeting for Friends of the Eastern Shore of Maryland and the State of Delaware, which began there today with a Meeting of Ministers and Elders.

And Fourth Day of the week was held their Quarterly Meeting of Discipline.

And the day following, a general meeting was held under the title of a Youths' Meeting. I had much service among them – greatly to my own satisfaction and (from what appeared) to the general satisfaction of Friends and others who attended. After which, we proceeded on towards Smyrna and lodged at night at John Cogel's.

And the next day, attended a meeting there, after which we rode to Appoquinimink and lodged with our Friend, David Wilson.

Attended a meeting there the next day, after which we rode to Wilmington and lodged with our kind Friend, William Poole.

And the next day being first of the week and 1st of 12th month, we attended their fore and after noon meetings. They were large, favored meetings, in which I was favored in the openings of Divine Light to declare unto these large assemblies the things concerning the kingdom of God – pointing them to the way by which all those who were faithful to the ministration of the Spirit of Truth in their own mind would come to be the everlasting inheritors thereof. It was a day to be remembered with gratitude, in which the Lord Almighty magnified his power among the people – a sense of which caused the sincere-hearted to rejoice in the prevalence thereof.

Magnified forever be his right worthy name!

On Second Day, we rested. Spent part of the forenoon writing to our Friends and the afternoon in visiting some of our Friends – two of whom were under considerable bodily indisposition. They appeared to be much comforted with the visits.

On Third Day, we rode back about six miles to a place called Stanton, and had an appointed meeting at the 11th hour, and returned to Wilmington, and had an appointed meeting for the colored people at six o'clock in the evening, and returned to William Poole's and lodged.

Pennsylvania

And next morning, proceeded on our journey to Chester and attended a meeting at the 11th hour, and lodged in the town with our Friend, Samuel Smith.

On Fifth Day, we rode to Providence – attended their meeting at the usual time. Rode after meeting to John Hunt's at Darby and lodged.

The next day, attended Darby Meeting, after which we rode to Edward Garrigues' and lodged.

And the next day, rode to Philadelphia, being the seventh of the week and 7th of 12th month, and I immediately entered on the arduous concern[1] which I had had in prospect, and which I was favored soon comfortably to accomplish.

We stayed in Philadelphia until the 25th, in which time we attended eleven public meetings, and two monthly meetings, and visited the families of Friends composing Green Street Monthly Meeting, being in number one hundred and thirty-six. And we also attended that monthly meeting, and the Monthly Meeting for the Northern District. This closed my visit there and set me at liberty to turn my face homeward.

We left the city on the 25th of 12th month and fourth of the week, and rode to Frankford, and attended their meeting at the 10th hour. The next day, attended Germantown Meeting – lodged the previous night at William Fisher's. We rode from Germantown to Abington and lodged with Jean Shoemaker, the widow of John.

---

[1] The "arduous concern" may refer to events unfolding in late 1822. Hicks was accused of denying the divinity of Jesus in ministry he offered during the Southern Quarterly Meeting in November. There were conflicting accounts of what was he said – Hicks consistently and firmly rejected the accusation – but it resulted in a series of formal and informal meetings in Philadelphia that further opened the cracks between the contending sides in the society. A particularly contentious and unfruitful confrontation occurred at Green Street Meeting on December 12 between seven Orthodox Philadelphia Elders and Hicks (supported by a large group of supporters). This meeting may mark the point of no return on the path leading to separation five years later.

The next day, attended their meeting, after which we rode to Byberry and lodged with our Friend, John Comly.

Rested on Seventh Day.

On First Day, the 29th, attended a meeting at Byberry, after which we lodged at James Walton's.

And on Second Day, rode to Middletown and attended a meeting, after which we rode to Michael Trump's and lodged.

And the next day, 31st, attended a meeting at Bristol, after which we dined at Abraham Warner's, and rode that evening to the Falls and lodged with our Friend, James Simpson, son of John.

Trenton (New Jersey) Meetinghouse

1823

Next day, 1st of 1st month, attended a meeting at the Falls and lodged with David Brown.

New Jersey

And the next day, 2nd, rode to Pennsbury – attended a meeting, after which we rode to Trenton and attended a meeting in the evening. Lodged with Richard Birdsall.

And the next day, 3rd, rode to Crosswicks – attended a meeting at the 11th hour. Thence, rode to Bordentown and had a meeting in the evening, and lodged with Charles Burton.

And the next day, rode to Mansfield. Attended a meeting at the usual hour, after which we rode to Burlington.

And the next day being the first of the week and 5th of the 1st month 1823, we attended their fore and after noon meetings. They were large and favored meetings.

On the next day, being the 6th of the month, we attended their monthly meeting.

On Third Day and 7th of the month, we rode to Mount Holly and attended a meeting there. It was said to be the largest ever held in that place. It was a very solemn opportunity and left them with peace of mind. And rode home with our kind Friend, Joseph Lundy, and lodged – who with his wife and children received and entertained us gladly.

On the next day, we rode to Westfield, and attended a meeting there, and lodged that night with Joseph Justice.

And the next day, rode to Moorestown and attended a meeting – lodged with our kind Friend, William Roberts.

And the next day, rode to Haddonfield and attended a meeting, after which we rode to Woodbury and lodged with our kind Friend, John Tatum.

The next day being the seventh of the week and 11th of 1st month, we rode to Salem (twenty-seven miles) and lodged with our Friend, William Miller.

And the next day being first of the week and 12th of 1st month, we attended their meeting, which was very large and a favored meeting, after which we rode to Woodstown and lodged with our Friend, Thomas Davis, and the next day attended their meeting, after which we rode to Mullica Hill and lodged with our Friend, Chalkley Moore.

And the next day, attended their meeting, after which we rode to Woodbury and lodged with our Friend, James Saunders. And the next day, attended their meeting. These three latter meetings were large and closed our visit to West Jersey, after which we rode home with our kind Friend, Joseph Lundy, who had accompanied us to these nine last meetings. We lodged with him and the next day, set out homeward.

Rode to Stony Brook and lodged with Elisha Clark.

The next day, rode to Rahway and lodged with our Friend, Henry Shotwell. Had a meeting there in the evening.

And the next day, being the seventh of the week and 18th of 1st month, we rode to New York – lodged with my kind hostess, Elizabeth Haydock, and the next day, attended their fore and after noon meetings.

And the next day, rode home. The whole distance was one thousand and thirty-nine miles.

> This marks the end of the travel journal. From here to the beginning of 1828, the text is taken from the editorial committee's copy.

We were favored to reach our homes with feelings of thanksgiving to our gracious Preserver and with the enjoyment of that precious peace, which is experienced by those whose minds are stayed on God. As the prophet declared in his appeal to Jehovah, "Thou wilt keep him in perfect peace, whose mind is stayed on thee, because he trusteth in thee." And he subjoins[1] for our encouragement, "Trust in the Lord forever. For in the Lord Jehovah is everlasting strength."[2]

---

[1] Subjoin: add a related element
[2] Isaiah 26:3-4

May we all dwell here – then nothing can hurt or harm us. For the Lord our Preserver will turn all the designs and cunning devices of those that rise up against us upon their own heads and cause them to fall into their own pit.

A Visit to Some of the Lower Quarterly Meetings

In the latter part of 1823, I felt myself engaged to make a religious visit to Friends and others in several of the lower quarterly meetings. And having obtained the unity of my Friends, I set out in 10th month with Samuel Willis as my companion. After having meetings at Westchester and Mamaroneck, we attended the select quarterly meeting at Purchase – which was small, many of the members being absent. They appeared to be clothed with much weakness. I was led into a feeling sympathy with them, and way was opened to communicate to their states in a way that was comforting and encouraging to the honest-hearted.

The next day was the Quarterly Meeting of Discipline. It was large and, I think in the main, it was a favored, instructive season – although considerably hurt by a long, tedious communication from a Friend not sufficiently clothed with life to make it useful. But the society is in such a mixed and unstable state, and many who presume to be teachers in it are so far from keeping on the original foundation – the Light and Spirit of Truth – and are so built up in mere tradition, that I fear a great portion of the ministry amongst us is doing more harm than good, and is leading back to the weak and beggarly elements to which they seem desirous to be again in bondage.[1]

After leaving Purchase, we had a pretty large and favored meeting at North Castle.

And next day, we went to Oblong, and attended their meeting on First Day. It was large and I had an open time among them through the prevalence of that power which opens and none can shut, and when he shuts none can open. Truth reigned, and the people generally, I believe, were instructed, comforted, and edified. I parted with them in true peace of mind, which leads my heart into deep humility and inspires it with gratitude and thanksgiving to the Great and Blessed Author of all our mercies.

We had a meeting at the Branch, and then proceeded to Nine Partners and attended the Select Quarterly Meeting. It was much like some other meetings of this kind – hard and not very fruitful. The members of those meetings are too generally falling more short of coming up faithfully (according to their stations) than most of the other departments of our society.

---

[1] Galatians 4:9

We attended the Quarterly Meeting for Discipline, also that at Stanford, and soon after turned our faces homeward, where we arrived, accompanied with the fresh feelings of that love that many waters cannot quench – even that powerful love that is stronger than death,[1] and binds together in an indissoluble bond all the newborn children of the Heavenly Father. May we all seek for it and dwell in it. It will cast out all fear, and clothe with that innocent boldness which will enable us to withstand all the dark powers of antichrist and his agents, and all their deceivableness of unrighteousness, and will raise above the fear of death, with all his misshapen and ugly forms, and clothe with the joys of God's salvation here and forever, as we continue steadfast in the faith that overcomes the world.[2]

---

[1] Song of Solomon 8:7
[2] 1 John 5:4

1824-1827

A Visit to the Quarterly Meetings of Cornwall & Stanford

In the summer of 1824, I had the concurrence of my Friends to attend the Quarterly Meetings of Cornwall and Stanford, which I accomplished to my own peace and comfort.

A Visit to Baltimore to Attend the Yearly Meeting

And in the fall of 1824, my Friends also united with a concern which had impressed my mind to attend the ensuing Yearly Meeting in Baltimore. This engagement, through the mercy of him who has hitherto helped me, I was favored to accomplish to the peace and satisfaction of my own mind.

The Yearly Meeting for Discipline opened on Second Day and continued by adjournments until the following Fifth Day – in the afternoon of which it closed under a comfortable evidence of Divine Favor attending. I think it was, in its several sittings, one of the most satisfactory yearly meetings I ever attended. And the business was conducted in much harmony and brotherly love.

In Philadelphia, on my return, I had a severe attack of bodily indisposition, so that, for some time, there seemed but little prospect of my recovery.[1] I lodged at the house of my very kind Friend, Samuel R. Fisher, who, with his worthy children, extended to me the most affectionate care and attention. And I had also the kind sympathy of a large portion of Friends in that city.

A Visit to the Inhabitants of the Eastern Part of Long Island

In the summer of 1825, I obtained the concurrence of my Friends to make a visit in gospel love to the inhabitants of the eastern part of Long Island and I proceeded therein with Samuel Willis as my companion. The people appeared open to receive us and the meetings at the several places we visited were pretty fully attended. Many minds were humbled and contrited, and Truth's testimonies exalted, and the people generally comforted and, I trust, edified.

A Visit to Scipio Quarterly Meeting

In the fall of 1825, being on an appointment of the yearly meeting to attend the opening of Scipio Quarterly Meeting, I obtained the unity of my

---

[1] Hicks seems to have suffered a heart attack. Jemima had accompanied him on this journey, but his condition was so serious that two of their daughters, Abigail and Elisabeth, came to Philadelphia.

Friends to attend some meetings among Friends and others on my way going and returning.

The quarterly meeting, in its several sittings, was conducted in much apparent harmony and condescension. The Truth was so effectually raised into dominion over all, that if there were any discordant spirits present, they were all kept down and subdued by the prevalence of its power. And Friends were united in the bond of brotherly affection and the faithful were made to rejoice for the unmerited favor. The meeting closed on 30th of 9th month with a very large, solemn, public meeting – the public service therein fell to the lot of Thankful Merritt and myself, and Thankful closed the meeting in sweet solemn supplication.

In returning home, I attended several meetings which were large and, through the condescending goodness of the Shepherd of Israel, were favored, satisfactory seasons, in which Truth was raised into dominion and a precious solemnity prevailed.

A Visit to the Southern & Concord Quarterly Meetings

In the latter part of 1826, my Friends united with a concern, which had been for a considerable time impressive on my mind, to make a visit in the love of the gospel to the Southern and Concord Quarterly Meetings in the Yearly Meeting of Philadelphia. I accordingly set out in the 11th month, with Jesse Merritt as my companion.

In passing through Philadelphia, we attended Arch Street Meeting in the forenoon and Green Street in the afternoon. They were both very large meetings, many more coming together than the houses could contain. Truth was powerfully raised into dominion, and at the close of each meeting, Friends manifested in an affectionate manner their unity and satisfaction with my labors amongst them.

We then proceeded on the further service on which we had set out, taking several meetings on the way, which were large and solemn opportunities and favored with the overshadowing wing of divine kindness. And having accomplished the prospects in view, we turned our faces homewards, having thankfully to acknowledge that best help had been near, enabling me to discharge myself faithfully in the various meetings – to the comfort and peace of my own mind.

Visits to Friends in Jericho & Westbury Monthly Meetings

In the early part of 1827, with the unity of my Friends, I entered into the engagement of making a religious visit to the families of Friends within our own and Westbury Monthly Meetings. And I was favored to go through this arduous service to the satisfaction and peace of my own mind.

1828

> *The text of the journey to Richmond, Indiana and back to Long Island comes from the original manuscript.*

Having felt an exercise and travail of spirit in the course of the last year, to pay a religious visit in the love of the gospel to Friends and others in some parts of our own yearly meeting and in the compass of the yearly meetings of Philadelphia, Baltimore, Ohio, Indiana, and a few meetings in Virginia – and apprehending the time had come to move therein – I spread the concern before my Friends at Jericho Monthly Meeting held the 20th of 3rd month 1828, and obtained their unity and concurrence, certified in their certificate, and signed by the clerks of the men's and women's meetings. Which concern, with the certificate from our monthly meeting, I laid before our quarterly meeting held at Westbury, the 24th of 4th month following, and obtained their unity and concurrence, with an endorsement thereof on my certificate signed by the clerk.[1]

Visits to Friends in the Yearly Meetings of New York, Philadelphia, Baltimore, Ohio, Indiana, & Virginia in 1828 & 1829

And in order to the accomplishment of the service above alluded to, I left home the week after our quarterly meeting, the 28th of 4th month, and attended the three quarterly meetings of Purchase, Nine Partners, and Stanford, and the monthly meeting of Oblong, and four particular meetings – three of which were appointed at my request. In all these meetings the Lord, our Gracious Helper, manifested himself to be near for our support – making way for us at times where there seemed to be no way – to our humbling admiration.

I was from home in the prosecution of this little tour of duty two weeks and two days, after which I tarried in and about home until after our yearly meeting.

Soon after which, I again left home (on the 14th of 6th month) and rode to New York, and the day following being the first of the week, we attended their fore and after noon meetings which, through the gracious extendings of heavenly help, proved to be comfortable edifying seasons.

---

[1] Hicks is being very careful to spell out the approvals he obtained before leaving. One of the charges that will be brought against him in the course of this journey is that he is traveling without the approval of his home meeting. The basis of this charge is that the Orthodox meeting of Westbury and Jericho will withdraw approval and call him home – an action he considers illegitimate.

Path of the 1828-29 Journey

New Jersey

And the next day, after taking a sympathetic farewell of our Friends in the city, we proceeded on our journey to Rahway in Jersey and lodged with our kind Friend, William Shotwell, and the next day attended an appointed meeting in that village. It was truly a comfortable and edifying opportunity – many truths of the gospel were clearly opened to the

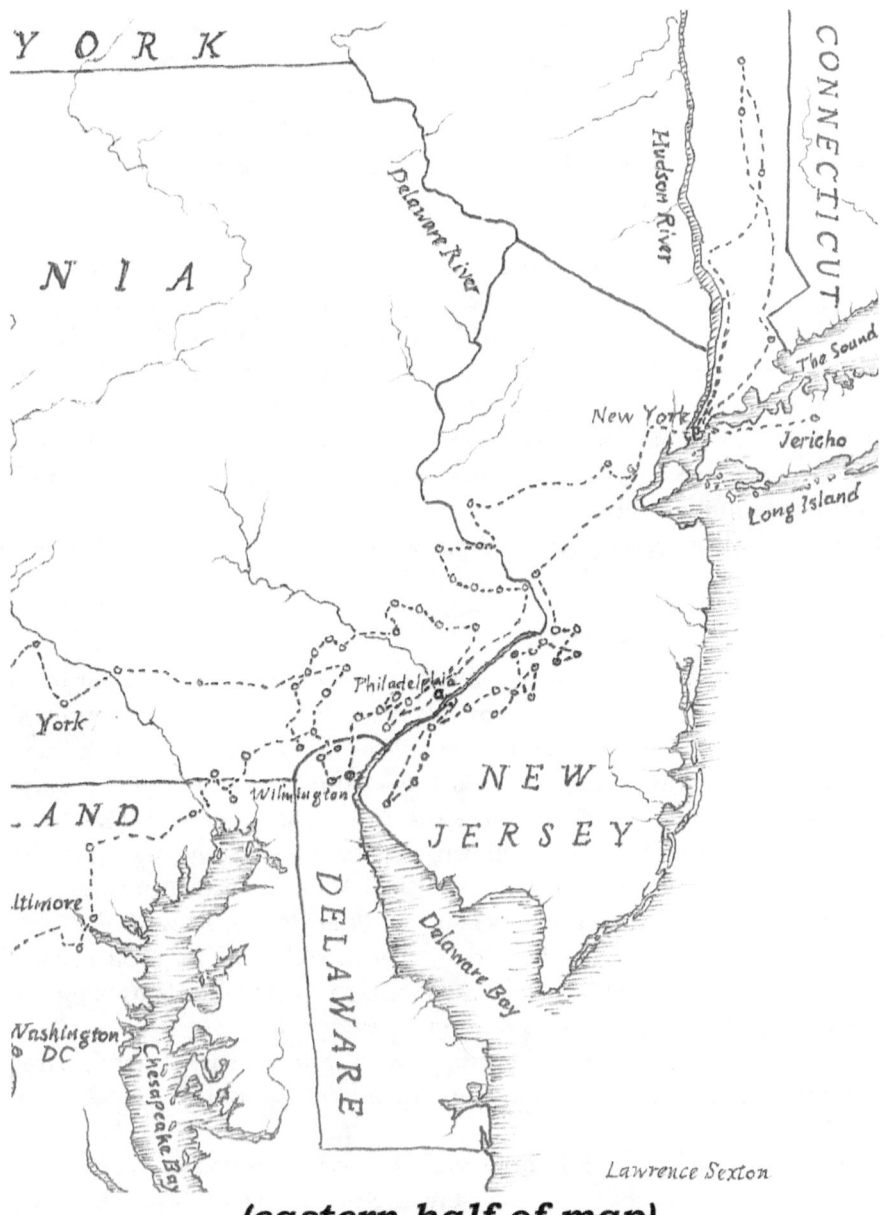

(eastern half of map)

audience, to the humbling and contriting of many present, which inspired our minds with gratitude and thanksgiving to the Blessed Author of all our rich mercies.

The next day being the fourth of the week, we attended Friends Monthly Meeting held at Plainfield for Rahway and Plainfield. The meeting for worship was large by the coming in of many of the neighboring people of other societies to whom, through heavenly help, the gospel was preached in the demonstration of the Spirit, to the solemnizing of the assembly, and Truth raised into victory over all, to the glory of his own excellent name, who is over all, God blessed forever. My mind was also comforted in the meeting for discipline in observing the harmony and brotherly condescension of Friends in the orderly conducting of the affairs of the Church.[1]

The next day, we proceeded on our journey to Kingwood and lodged with our kind Friend, Henry Clifton. We had an appointed meeting here the next day at the 10th hour. And although the number of Friends was small that constituted this meeting, yet as Friends were careful to give their neighbors of other societies information thereof, we had a very full meeting – the house being crowded in every part. And it proved a very solemn, impressive opportunity in which Truth reigned over all, to the comforting and contriting of many minds. After which, we passed on to Solebury in Pennsylvania and lodged with our Friend, Watson Fell, who met us at Kingwood and kindly escorted us home to his house.

In & About Philadelphia

The next day, we had an appointed meeting here at the 4th hour in the afternoon. It was a favored, solemn opportunity, in which many truths of the gospel were opened to the people – apparently to the general satisfaction and edification of the assembly. And I parted with them under a thankful sense of the unmerited favor. After which, we then rode home with our kind Friend, Moses Eastburn, and lodged. And the next being the first of the week, we attended Buckingham Meeting in the morning, and that at Plumstead at four o'clock in the afternoon.[2] These were large crowded meetings. At the last, more assembled than the house could contain, and the Lord's power was felt to preside, solemnizing the assemblies, and Truth was raised into victory over all.

After the latter, we rode home with our worthy Friend, Israel Lancaster, and the next day attended an appointed meeting at Wrightstown.

On Third Day in the forenoon, we attended a meeting in the forenoon at Newtown, and at four o'clock in the afternoon, one at Makefield. These were all large, favored meetings, in which the gospel was preached and many hearts humbled and contrited, and a precious solemnity spread over the meetings, to the comfort and rejoicing the honest-hearted, and to the praise of his Grace, who is calling us to glory and virtue.

---

[1] This harmony contrasts with the raucous meetings that had taken place recently in which Hicksite-Orthodox separations had taken place.

[2] The next sentence was deleted from the printed *Journal*.

Wrightstown (Pennsylvania) Meetinghouse

On Fourth Day, we attended a meeting at the Falls.

On Fifth Day, at Middletown, it being their midweek meeting. And as notice was given of our attendance, the meetings were large and very solemn, and the canopy of love in a very comforting manner was felt to spread of the assemblies. And much kindness and brotherly affection was manifested towards us, not only by our Friends, but by the people in general of other societies that attended.

On Sixth Day, we attended a meeting at Byberry.

On Seventh Day, at Abington.

On First Day, 29th of 6th month, we attended Horsham Meeting in the morning and at four o'clock in the afternoon, one at Upper Dublin. These meetings were all very large – particularly the two latter – at which many more attended than the houses could contain. As the last was assembling, there came on a heavy shower of rain accompanied with an uncommon time of lightning and very heavy peals of thunder – many flashes of which appeared to strike down to the earth within a very small distance from the meetinghouse, which brought a great solemnity over the meeting. And I was thankful in observing the stillness and quiet that prevailed generally among the people. All those meetings were very solemn seasons in which Truth reigned. And I parted with them with peace of mind, and in the fresh feelings of gospel love.

Our kind Friend, Joseph Foulke, met us at Horsham and after the latter meeting, escorted us to his own house, where we met a very cordial welcome and were favored with the company and very entertaining conversation of his ancient and very worthy father, Hugh Foulke.

And the two following days, attended meetings at North Wales and Plymouth. These were large, favored meetings, in which many truths of the gospel were largely opened to the edification, comfort, and apparent satisfaction of those large assemblies and to the peace of my own mind. It was the Lord's doing and to him belongs all the praise – nothing due to man.

West through Pennsylvania

From thence, we proceeded to Charlestown and lodged with our kind Friend, James Wood, and the next day being the fourth of the week, we attended their meeting, after which we rode to Pikeland and were very kindly entertained by our Friends, Emmor Kimber and wife and their children, and had an appointed meeting there the next day. We tarried here until the next morning and then proceeded on to Uwchlan, where we had a meeting by previous appointment at the 11th hour. And although it was in the midst of their harvest and the necessary care for its ingathering very urgent – as many of their fields of grain appeared to be overripe – yet to our own and our Friends admiration, the meetings were unusually large. Frequently, many more assembled than the houses could contain. The people were generally very solid and quiet, and very attentive to hear what was communicated, and many minds were humbled and contrited, and Truth's testimonies exalted, to the mutual comfort and encouragement of the honest-hearted, and to the general satisfaction of the assembled multitudes. And my mind was deeply humbled and made thankful for the continuance of those unmerited favors.

On Seventh Day, 5th of 7th month, we attended a meeting at Downingtown – held in an orchard under the shade of the apple trees. The separatists or self-styled Orthodox having in their possession Friends Meetinghouse in that town, they refused to open the house for the accommodation of the meeting. Which was a favorable circumstance as many more assembled than the meetinghouse could contain, but they were well accommodated in the orchard, where we had a large, solemn, satisfactory meeting.

The next day, we attended Friends Meeting at East Caln and, notice being spread of our being there, the house (although very large) did not contain more than three-quarters of the assembled multitude. It was a season to be remembered with gratitude. The Lord's presence was felt to preside – humbling and contriting many hearts, and Truth raised into victory over all.

On Second Day, we attended a meeting at our appointment at Sadsbury.[1] This was likewise very large – many more attended than the house could contain. A precious solemnity was felt to preside. I was largely exercised among them in the line[2] of the ministry. And we parted with them with thankful hearts – with a lively hope that our labor among them was not in vain.

On Third Day, we attended Friends monthly meeting at this place, and a large number of the neighboring inhabitants of other societies attended the first sitting[3] of the meeting. And way opened for communication and I had good service among them in both sittings, and parted with my Friends in near unity of spirit and the sweet fellowship of the gospel – a number of whom accompanied us from meeting to meeting.

On Fourth Day, we had an appointed meeting at Lampeter, in which the Lord's power and his Truth were raised into victory over all – to the rejoicing and encouragement of the honest-hearted, and to the settlement[4] and confirmation of the wavering, who were halting[5] between two opinions, but were now satisfied and openly declared themselves on the side of Friends – some of whom had previously gone with the Orthodox, but were now convinced of the impropriety of their conduct and cheerfully united with Friends.[6] We returned from this favored meeting – under a grateful sense of the favor vouchsafed and with thankful hearts – to the house of our kind Friend, Thomas Peart, where we lodged the night before. And after dinner, took leave of our Friends in near unity – many of whom accompanied us to this place to bid farewell – and we proceeded on our journey to Columbia and lodged with our kind Friend, William Wright, who, with his worthy and affectionate wife, entertained us with great hospitality.

---

[1] The rest of this paragraph and the next one were deleted from the printed *Journal*.

[2] Line: work

[3] First sitting: a meeting for worship preceding a business meeting. Those who were not members were welcome for this meeting, but were asked to leave when business was conducted.

[4] Settlement: becoming settled in beliefs

[5] Halt: vacillate

[6] Notice that Hicks refers to those on his side of the separation as Friends and those on the other as Orthodox. Those in the other camp likewise called themselves Friends and their opponents as Hicksites.

York Meetinghouse

We had an appointed meeting here the next day, and the two following days, we attended meetings at Little York and Newberry – all of which were favored opportunities in which Truth was raised into dominion. And many hearts were humbled and contrited, and the honest-hearted comforted and made to rejoice together in the unity of the one Spirit – the only sure foundation, on which the true Church has been built in all the varied ages of mankind, from the beginning down to the present day, and on which all future generations must build or their building must and will fall into utter ruin.

On First Day, 7th month 13th, we attended Friends Meeting at Warrington. This was a large solemn opportunity – many hearts were humbled and contrited. And we took leave of them with thankful hearts and rode that afternoon to Huntington and lodged with our ancient Friend, Joseph Griest.

On Second Day, we attended a meeting at this place, and on Third Day, at Menallen. These were also favored seasons, in which strength and ability was vouchsafed by the Blessed Author of all our sure mercies, to preach the gospel to the people in its genuine simplicity and plainness and demonstration of the Spirit – which brought a precious solemnity over the assembly. And I parted with them with the satisfactory evidence of having faithfully discharged myself among them, feeling that true peace of mind that the world with all its fading enjoyments cannot give, neither can it take away. After which, we rode about five miles and lodged with our Friend, Isaac Wierman.

And the next day, being the 16th of 7th month 1828, we proceeded on our journey through the mountains towards Redstone Quarterly Meeting and arrived there on First Day, 20th, at the house of our Friend, Jesse Townsend, at eight o'clock in the morning, and attended their meeting at the 11th hour. It was large, favored meeting. We lodged with our said Friend.[1]

On Second Day, we rested, being much wearied and our horses much worn down – having ridden one hundred and sixty-one miles over a continued course of large mountains and hills – and the roads very rough and stony.

On Third Day, we attended Providence Meeting. It was held in a barn – occasioned by some of the leading Elders in that meeting having, in their blind zeal, risen up in opposition to Friends and shut Friends out of their meetinghouse. But we had a large, comfortable meeting in the barn.

On Fourth Day, we attended Center Meeting, in which Truth reigned triumphant over all opposition. After which, we returned to Brownsville and lodged again with our kind Friend, Jesse Townsend.

Encounters with Thomas Shillitoe

On Fifth Day, we attended Friends Monthly Meeting at Westland and, the people being informed of our coming, there were more assembled than the house could contain.[2] And although (as we afterwards understood), the Orthodox had taken every precaution to prevent our having a public opportunity with the people – as by a previous conclusion, they had agreed that as soon as the meeting was gathered, to close the partition and enter upon the business of the monthly meeting. But such a multitude collected at an early hour that [it] defeated all their purposes, and I had a full opportunity to discharge myself among them in a large, effective testimony, which brought a precious solemnity over the meeting, and many hearts were humbled and contrited. But our old Friend, Thomas Shillitoe,* being present, he (in his blind zeal) must needs rise up and oppose – which greatly disturbed the meeting. I was truly sorry for the old Friend for (if he goes on in the way he is now in) he will not only expose himself to the ridicule of the people, but will become a reproach to the society.

On Sixth Day, we attended an appointed meeting at Pike Run. It was held in the side of a wood under the shadows of the trees – the meetinghouse having previously been burnt down and Friends there met in a small private room, there being but few Friends in that place. This

---

[1] The next three paragraphs were reduced to one line in the printed *Journal*.
[2] The rest of this paragraph was severely edited, removing Thomas Shillitoe's name and making the tone considerably more temperate.

induced Friends to make seats outdoors as the house would not have held half the people that met. It was an unusual, favored season, in the silent part of which the Divine Presence was felt to spread over the assembly, producing such a sweet and precious solemnity that I scarcely ever before witnessed in the same fullness, and which continued through the course of my communication to the people. Surely it was the Lord's doing, and it was marvelous in our eyes.

After this meeting, we dined with our kind Friend, John Grave, after which we rode about three miles on our way back to Brownsville – intending to be at that meeting again on the First Day – and lodged with our Friend, Isaac Walker.

On Seventh Day night, we lodged at the house of our Friend, Solomon Philips, about a mile from Brownsville, and the next morning crossed the River Monongahela into the town and put up again with our kind Friends, Jesse and Edith Townsend, where we had the company of many Friends. And many of the townspeople also came in to see us – as the foolish and false reports of those who style themselves Orthodox having been generally spread over the country. It created a very great excitement in the minds of the people at large, and multitudes flocked to the meetings where we were to hear for themselves. And all (who were not enlisted in the Orthodox party) generally went away satisfied, and many came to see us and acknowledge their satisfaction.

Here, we again fell in with our Friend, Thomas Shillitoe,[1] who attended the meeting with us. And as information was spread that we proposed to be there, many more assembled than the house could contain. And Thomas took the floor pretty early in the meeting and continued his communication so long that a number left the meeting – by which it became very much unsettled. However, when he sat down, I felt an opening to stand up, and the people all returned and crowded into the house. And those that could not get in stood about the doors and windows. And a precious solemnity soon spread over the meeting – and which has been the case in every meeting where they have not been disturbed by others – and the meeting closed in a quiet and orderly manner, and I was very thankful for the favor.

On Second Day, we rested and wrote to our Friends.

On Third Day, we attended their Preparative Meeting of Ministers and Elders[2] – so called, but it was only a meeting of elders as there was no minister belonging thereto.

---

[1] Thomas Shillitoe's name was again deleted from the printed *Journal*.
[2] The rest of the paragraphs was deleted from the printed *Journal*.

On Fourth Day, we attended their monthly meeting.[1] Here, our old Friend, Thomas Shillitoe, behaved very disorderly. [He] was not willing the meeting should acknowledge me as a member, opposed me personally in the meeting for worship – by which he offended the people generally, Friends and others. He blamed Friends very much for appointing meetings for me, but I nevertheless had a favored opportunity with the people in the meeting for worship – to the general satisfaction of the meeting and the peace of my own mind.

On Fifth Day, we attended Westland Meeting again as it came in course and, some notice being spread of our being there, it was pretty large. And we had a very favored meeting, and Friends were comforted together, and the people generally went away satisfied. And my mind was fully relieved and inspired with thankfulness and gratitude to God, who giveth us victory.

On Sixth Day, we attended the Quarterly Meeting of Ministers and Elders held at Westland. Here, we met but little opposition and the next day, we attended the Quarterly Meeting of Discipline. I had good service in the meeting for worship, which was very large – a very great number of the neighboring inhabitants came in of other societies.

Here, we met with some opposition – more particularly in the meeting for discipline in which[2] Thomas came out and charged me with unsoundness in principle and told Friends he would rather his certificate should not be noticed on minute than that it should be the means of minuting mine. The meeting manifested their willingness to leave his off, but insisted that the clerk should minute mine. This caused some stir in the meeting, and some few who were Orthodox contended the matter with so much warmth that although there was a large portion of the meeting who were for minuting of it, I told Friends I thought it better to leave it, which they then submitted to. But Friends were so disturbed with the disorderly conduct of Thomas Shillitoe and his companion, James Emlen, that they insisted that the elders and overseers should take care and see if they could not stop such disorderly conduct. Accordingly, they had the Friends brought up for examination and, after a little time together, agreed to meet again at the close of the meeting next day.

And as information was spread of my being there, the people began to collect at ten o'clock and continued coming until eleven – a great number more than the house could contain assembled. And although Thomas had

---

[1] The rest of the paragraph was re-written in the printed *Journal* to remove the reference to Thomas Shillitoe and his blaming Friends.

[2] The rest of this sentence and the next two were edited in the printed *Journal* to remove the reference to Thomas Shillitoe, the specific charges he made, and the outcome.

so fully discovered that not only Friends, but the people without also had no unity with him, yet soon after the meeting had got settled, he arose with his old story and stood a considerable time. But after he sat down, I felt an opening to stand up and I was favored to clear myself among them in a large, impressive testimony that soon brought a precious solemnity over the meeting, and many hearts were broken and contrited, and I took an affectionate farewell of the assembly in the fresh feelings of gospel love. And as I was about to close the meeting, Thomas Shillitoe rose and began to oppose what had been said by me. This so offended the people (Friends and others) that they rose up and went out by hundreds – and the old man begging them to stay, but they refused and continued going out until he was discouraged calling upon them and sat down. And I closed the meeting, feeling very sorry for the people to see them so imposed on.[1]

After this meeting, we proceeded that afternoon about seven miles on our way to Pittsburgh and lodged with a friendly man by the name of Sheshbazzar Bently, and on Second Day, we rode to Pittsburgh and lodged with our kind Friend, Robert Townsend.

The day following, at evening we had a large, satisfactory meeting in their courthouse. And on Fourth Day, we proceeded on our journey, crossing the Alleghany River at Pittsburgh, and arrived that evening at a village at the Great Beaver Falls. And the next day, had an appointed meeting there – held in a field under the trees, which made a comfortable shade, the weather being very warm and Friends Meetinghouse being much too small to contain the people that assembled. It was a very solemn opportunity, in which Truth was raised into victory over all. And the people appeared thankful for the favor and went away satisfied. And I witnessed the consoling evidence of true peace in faithfully fulfilling my duty.

Into Ohio

After this favored meeting, we went forward that afternoon towards Salem in order to attend the quarterly meeting at that place, which opened on Sixth Day at the 11th hour with a Meeting of Ministers and Elders.[2] But

---

[1] There are a number of violations of the informal, but generally accepted, Quaker protocol for worship in this description. Rising to speak soon after another person finishes, speaking at length to prevent others from speaking, and speaking more than once in a meeting are all considered "unQuakerly." Although Hicks notes Shillitoe's abuses, it is clear that neither man is acting in "the good order of Friends."

[2] The next two sentences and the first part of the third one were deleted from the printed *Journal*.

those who style themselves Orthodox shut the house against us and forcibly kept us out.

The next day was the meeting of discipline in which a separation had taken place. As the Orthodox had shut Friends out of the meetinghouse and would not suffer any of them to come in, Friends met in a schoolhouse that one of them had built and with a temporary shed that Friends put up adjoining to it, in which the men's meeting sat. They were pretty well accommodated, and conducted their business in much unity and concord, and the Lord's presence was eminently felt to cover the assembly.

The next day being first of the week, and notice being spread of our being there, the meeting was very large – it was judged by Friends that upward of two thousand people attended. It was a highly favored season, in which I was favored largely to declare the Truth to the people in the demonstration of the Spirit, and with a power attending that brought a precious solemnity over the meeting, and many hearts were humbled and contrited.

The next day, we had a meeting by appointment at Fairfield.[1] It was held in a meetinghouse occupied by a people who styled themselves Christians. This was also a very large meeting – a great number more collected than the house contained – and I had a favored time among them, and was made thankful for the opportunity, and I had cause to believe my labor was not in vain.

The next day, we attended New Garden Quarterly Meeting. Here Friends had a pretty sharp conflict, as the Orthodox had previously disowned a great number of their members – in their presumption. They being the negative part[2] of that meeting, therefore, Friends did not acknowledge the authenticity of their proceeding, and they all came together as usual in the quarterly meeting. And the Orthodox strove hard to get Friends to withdraw and leave the meeting, but Friends refused and having the clerk on their side, they proceeded in the business, which the Orthodox interrupted for a time. But finding Friends would not give way, they finally left the meeting and retired to the schoolhouse.

And Friends had a comfortable season together, and conducted their business in much harmony and condescension, and were evidently owned by the Head of the Church.[3] At this meeting, I fell in again with Thomas Shillitoe who, as heretofore, made great opposition to my communication in the meeting for worship, which greatly disgusted the general part of the assembly – Friends and others.

---

[1] The next sentence was deleted from the printed *Journal*.
[2] Negative part: the dissenting or destructive part
[3] The next sentence was deleted from the printed *Journal*.

Path of the 1828-29 Journey

The next day, being the fourth of the week, I appointed a meeting for the public at large (Friends and others) and a multitude assembled – many more than the house could contain – and we had a precious meeting. The Lord's power prevailed in an eminent manner. It was a season thankfully to be remembered – a humbling time among the people – after which we

(western half of map)

rode to New Lisbon in order to attend a meeting there the next day, which we had previously appointed.

It was held outdoors, there being no house in the town sufficient to hold the people that assembled. And Friends being aware of this, they erected a booth or shed by setting posts and crotches on which they laid long poles and covered them with limbs of trees, full of leaves to make a shade, as the weather was hot. Under which, we had a very large, favored meeting – to the general satisfaction of the assembly, and peace of my own mind.

The two following days, we attended meetings by our appointment at Springfield and Goshen.[1] At the first, the Orthodox shut Friends out of their meetinghouse and we held our meeting nearby under the shade of some trees – a guard of the Orthodox keeping sentry at the doors of the meetinghouse like soldiers in a time of war. At Goshen, the Orthodox pursued the same course by locking up the house and placing sentries at the doors, but there was an old log meetinghouse, which Friends occupied, and it accommodated the meeting very well. And although these opposers of Truth could shut us out of their meetinghouses, yet they could not shut the Divine Presence from us, for this was felt eminently to preside in both these highly favored meetings.[2] And this was witnessed (in every meeting where the Orthodox made opposition) in a remarkable manner, which afforded great encouragement and strength to Friends – evidencing that they were approved of the Lord.

The next day, being the first of the week and 17th of 8th month, we attended Marlborough Meeting.[3] Here, the Orthodox having possession of the house, they kept Friends out until the time of meeting. And when they opened it, they rushed in and filled the gallery[4] seats in order to oblige us to take the lower seats, but we got room in the upper seat near the middle. The meeting was very large, notice having been previously given of our intention to be there, that hundreds assembled that could not get into the house, and I had an open opportunity among them to proclaim the everlasting gospel in the demonstration of the Spirit, to the satisfaction of this large assembly. Except the Orthodox, who when I sat down, made great opposition, declaring their disunity with me and my ministry, which greatly disgusted the people.[5] They then attempted to break up the meeting, and all the Orthodox arose and went out, but I requested the people to keep their seats, which they did. And there was such a crowd that they had difficulty in getting out, and those not of our society hissed at them and made ridicule of them as they passed by. And when they were all gone out, the meeting again resumed the solemnity, and we had a

---

[1] The next two sentences were deleted from the printed *Journal*.
[2] The next sentence was deleted from the printed *Journal*.
[3] The next two sentences were deleted from the printed *Journal*.
[4] Gallery: usually, this refers to the balcony that was found in many Quaker meetinghouses. In this case, Hicks is clearly referring to the raised benches at the front of the meeting room, facing the congregation, on which the ministers and elders sat during meetings
[5] The rest of the paragraph was deleted from the printed *Journal*.

short season of renewed favor, and parted with each other with thankful hearts. After which, we rode home with our kind Friend, Mahlon Wileman and lodged.

The next day, we rode to Canton and attended a meeting at the 4th hour after noon, previous notice having been publicly given of our intention to be there. It was held in their courthouse – there being no members of our society in that town – most of the respectable inhabitants attended. And Friends of Kendal (a small meeting about seven miles distant) being informed, most of them attended and many other inhabitants of that place came also to the meeting. And we had a favorable opportunity with them, and left them with peace of mind.

After which, we returned to New Garden, and put up again with our kind Friend, Nathan Galbreath, where we lodged when here before.

And the next day, being the fourth of the week, we rode to Salem and attended Friends monthly meeting for that place, in which I was led to stir up Friends to faithfulness in the support of our religious testimonies, as the eyes of the people were upon us – watching our movements in this time of trial and breaking in the society, Friends separating from each other and setting up separate meetings, which caused a great breach of unity, and confusion in most of our meetings in society, which a few years previous thereto had been united together in the bonds of Christian fellowship. But a few envious individuals, letting in the spirit of jealousy, began to accuse their Friends of holding unsound doctrines without any just cause for so doing. [This] greatly disturbed the peace and quiet of society, and being encouraged therein by several Friends who, as ministers in the society from old England (having obtained liberty from their Friends at home) came over on a visit to Friends in this country. And joining with those of our own members who had made a breach in society, they blew up the fire of discord until they brought about an entire division in our once peaceable society – a small minority of which separated themselves from the body and took upon them the government of the whole – styling themselves the weightier part, and set up separate meetings, assuming to themselves as being the legitimate yearly, quarterly, and monthly meetings, although they were but a small, negative part of the body of Friends who previous thereto constituted those meetings, and who in their presumption and pride of their hearts,[1] undertook to deal with, and disown from membership, the great body of the society,[2] among whom was comprehended the most worthy, reputable, and useful members in the society.

---

[1] Jeremiah 49:16 & Obadiah 1:3
[2] The rest of the paragraph was deleted from the printed *Journal*.

The next day, we returned to New Garden and attended Friends monthly meeting there. And the neighboring inhabitants being apprised of our return, a great number came in and greatly enlarged the meeting. And he that openeth and none can shut, and when he shutteth, none can open, graciously condescended to open my mind among them in a large, effective testimony to the truths of the gospel. And many hearts were humbled and contrited, and it appeared as a renewed visitation of the Heavenly Father's love to Friends and others. It was a season gratefully to be remembered by all present. Surely it was the Lord's doing, and it was marvelous in our eyes.[1]

After this favored meeting, we retired to the house of our kind Friend, Jacob Paxson, and dined. And towards evening we returned to our Friend, Nathan Galbreath's, and lodged. And the next day, had an appointed meeting at Sandy Spring at the 4th hour after noon.

This meeting was held in a barn belonging to our kind Friend, John Batten – the Orthodox having shut Friends out of their meetinghouse at that place. The meeting was very large and favored with the overshadowing wing of divine kindness, and a precious solemnity pervaded the assembly. And my mind was opened in a large, effective testimony to the truths of the gospel – to the apparent satisfaction and comfort of the people. And I took leave of them with thankfulness and peace of mind.

We tarried here and lodged with our said Friend and the next day, proceeded on our journey to Richmond (about thirty-five miles) and lodged at an inn.

And the next day being first of the week and 24th of 8th month, we had an appointed meeting in the town. The inhabitants were mostly Presbyterians and Methodists. It was held in their schoolhouse – a large convenient place. The people came in freely and conducted with great propriety and order, and appeared to go away fully satisfied without making any opposition. And I felt true peace in having faithfully in gospel love discharged myself among them. After which, we proceeded about five miles on our way to Smithfield, and the next morning rode to that place. But being considerably out of health, we rested there through the day, and the next day, we had an appointed meeting there at the 4th hour after noon.

Here, the Orthodox shut the meetinghouse against us,[2] but Friends would have broken in – having a right so to do – but I advised against it and it proved a favor that it so happened, for the collection of people was

---

[1] The next two paragraphs were edited in the printed *Journal* to eliminate all names and that the meetinghouse was shut.

[2] The rest of the sentence was deleted from the printed *Journal*.

Mount Pleasant Meetinghouse

so great that the meetinghouse would not have contained more than half the number that assembled. But Friends provided seats under the shade of trees in an adjacent wood, where we had a very solemn, favored meeting, in which the Lord's power prevailed over all in an eminent degree and broke down all opposition. And many hearts were broken and contrited. And we parted with them under a grateful sense of the Lord's mercy for the unmerited favor.

Encounters with Elisha Bates

And the next morning, we proceeded to Mount Pleasant and attended their Fourth Day's Meeting – and the people observing us as we came into town, many of the neighboring inhabitants assembled with Friends. It was a solemn, quiet meeting in the forepart and while I was speaking.[1] But soon after I sat down, Elisha Bates,* an acknowledged minister of that meeting, arose and made opposition to what I had communicated in a long, tedious, repetition of scripture passages, and with a tone of voice that manifested so much irritation, that some of the hearers (not members in society) said he did nothing but scold and were much disgusted with

---

[1] The rest of the paragraph was edited to remove Elisha Bates' name and shorten the description.

his communication. This greatly disturbed the meeting and greatly marred its service.

The next day being the fifth of the week and 28th of 8th month, we attended Short Creek Meeting as it came in course. Here also, the meeting in the forepart was truly a solemn season, in which I had opportunity of declaring many important truths of the gospel to the people, which brought a precious solemnity over the assembly (which was large), and many minds were contrited.[1] But some of the same uneasy, turbulent spirits that disturbed the meeting the day before (although not members of this particular meeting) came to this with no other motive (it was believed) but to make a disturbance in this and with a view, as far as it was in their power, to lay waste my service among the people. But their envy turned back on their own heads, for as soon as I had finished my communication to the people, Elisha Bates arose to make opposition, and went on with a long harangue, in repeating over again and again the same scripture passages and quotations from the writings of our primitive Friends, and extended his communication to so great a length that the people appeared worn out and many of them much disgusted in being thus imposed upon. And as soon as Bates sat down, another minister of the same description (likewise a member of another meeting) arose and went on in the same strain, until we were all tired and our patience exhausted. And when he sat down, I thought it right (as Elisha had endeavored to make the people believe that I was not a regular member of society and that I was an intruder – with several other falsehoods) to stand up and rectify his errors in a few words and then sat down. And as we then thought it was entirely out of order to detain the people any longer, we concluded the meeting, at which time, Elisha again arose and desired the people to sit a little longer. But as the meeting was concluded and the people going out, we considered the request unreasonable. Friends and most of the people of other societies withdrew and left the Orthodox to themselves.

The next day being the sixth of the week, we attended an appointed meeting at Harrisville. Here, we were relieved from any interruption from the Orthodox,[2] as they would not attend any meeting of our appointment – except some of the more moderate, and many of these were brought over to join with Friends by attending our meetings. This was a large, crowded meeting, and very solemn and quiet,[3] which has been the case in all places in the course of our journey where the Orthodox have not disturbed our meetings. Here, I had an open time among the people to declare many

---

[1] The rest of the paragraph was shortened to a single sentence in the printed *Journal*.

[2] The rest of the sentence was deleted from the printed *Journal*.

[3] The rest of the sentence was deleted from the printed *Journal*.

things, both old and new – setting forth the great declension of the professed Christian Churches from the simplicity and integrity of the primitive disciples, and how it was all brought about by a departure from the only sure foundation of true and real Christianity – the Light Within or Spirit of Truth, the immediate revelation of the Spirit of God, the only true teacher of the things of God under the gospel. And as a departure from this only sure guide, and turning back to the letter and external evidence, and building up from these outward materials many diverse systems in their own creaturely wisdom, which brought confusion and anarchy into the Church, which enveloped it into a state of midnight darkness and total death – as to the life and spirit of real Christianity – by which the worst of persecution and the most cruel and sanguinary[1] wars were introduced among Christians, by which every right trait and fruit of real Christianity was banished from among them. And as a departure from and an unbelief in the all-sufficiency of this Inward Guide and Spirit of Truth had introduced into the professed Christian Church all the aforesaid devastation and misery and enveloped her into a state of darkness and death, so nothing short of a full and entire return to first principles – and a full belief in the sufficiency, and placing an entire dependence on the Inward Light and Spirit of Truth, for our salvation – can ever produce a restoration from the apostasy.

I was also led to lay before the people the inconsistency and very hurtful tendency of Bible and Missionary Societies, as believing them all to be set up and associated in the will and wisdom of man, which never did nor never can produce the righteousness of God, but tend to lead the mind down to a state of darkness and death, as a dependence on the letter and external evidence ever has and ever will kill. Therefore according to Paul's doctrine, the Spirit only can give life.

The next day, we had an appointed meeting at West Grove and the day following being the first of the week and 31st of 8th month, we attended Concord Meeting.[2] Both those meetings were seasons of favor in which I had full opportunity to open to the people divers doctrines of the Christian religion suited to the states of the people – to the apparent satisfaction and comfort of those assembled, and to the peace of my own mind.

And the three following days, we attended meetings at Saint Clairsville, Plainfield, and Wrightstown. These were all large, satisfactory meetings in which the gospel was freely preached to the people, and by the power attending, many hearts were broken and contrited, and a precious solemnity was felt to preside, to the comfort and encouragement

---

[1] Sanguinary: bloody
[2] The rest of the paragraph was deleted from the printed *Journal*.

Concord Meetinghouse in Colerain, Ohio

of the honest-hearted – a sense of which inspired my mind with thanksgiving and gratitude to the Blessed Author of all our sure mercies.

On Fifth Day, 4th of 9th month, we had an appointed meeting at a place called Stillwater.[1] Here, the Orthodox barred and locked the meetinghouse doors against us and set a guard of four or five men to keep Friends out. But when the time for meeting came, and a large collection of Friends and others had gathered about the house, a young man got in at one of the windows and opened the house, and it was soon filled. And we had a very large, quiet, and comfortable meeting, and I had a full opportunity in an effective testimony to ease my exercised mind among them – to the comfort and satisfaction of the people, both Friends and others.

And the next day, we rode back to Mount Pleasant. And the day following being the Seventh Day of the week and 6th of 9th month, the yearly meeting opened with a Meeting of Ministers and Elders. When the time came for meeting, Friends gathered to the gate that led into the yard on which the meetinghouse stood and found it guarded by a number of men of the opposing party, who refused to let us in, and Friends had to hold their meeting in the open air on the outside of the yard, and after the first sitting, adjourned to a schoolhouse near by, and after that held their sittings in a private room in Israel French's house.

The next day and first of the week, we attended Mount Pleasant Meeting in the morning and at Short Creek in the afternoon. At the first,

---

[1] The next two sentences were deleted from the printed *Journal*.

Elisha Bates and Anna Braithwaite* made great opposition, endeavoring by long and tedious communications (in which they asserted divers falsehoods, in order to lay waste what I had previously communicated), which very much disturbed and disgusted many of the people. But the afternoon meeting was not interrupted as none of these opposers attended.

The Separation in Ohio Yearly Meeting

On Second Day morning, the yearly meeting opened at the 10th hour.[1] Here, great confusion and disorder took place, as a Friend in the opening of the meeting observed that as the clerk – who served the meeting the year before and whose business it was to open the present meeting and serve as clerk the first sitting until another should be appointed – had disqualified himself to serve in that office by publicly opposing ministering Friends in meetings of worship, contrary to discipline, and had likewise attended a separate meeting, set up in a disorderly manner contrary to discipline, in New York. He thereupon proposed another Friend to sit at the table and open the business of the meeting – which was united with by a considerable number of Friends. And he desired to go to the table, which he attempted to do, but was prevented by Orthodox opposers, and who called upon the former clerk (who sat at the table, having in possession the books and papers belonging to the yearly meeting). This made a great rupture in the meeting, and a number of young men took up the new appointed clerk in their arms and carried him over all that stood in their way to the table.

And the old clerk took the books and papers and moved from the table, and some of the Orthodox laid hold of the table to remove it also, and some of the young men at the same time taking hold of it to keep it in its place – they broke it to pieces and rendered it unfit for use.

And at this juncture, whether from the cracking or some other noise, a loud cry was heard that the galleries above (or some part of the house) were breaking down, which so alarmed the people that the greatest part of the meeting arose *en masse* and pressed towards the doors, and some were

---

[1] Some sources claim that Hicks was not present at the opening business session of Ohio Yearly Meeting. In the printed Journal, the rest of this paragraph, the next two full paragraphs and the first line an one-half of the third one are replaced by "Not being present at this sitting, I was informed that great confusion and disorder took place." All indications are that Hicks was present. Two days later, he wrote a letter to his son-in-law, Valentine Hicks. In it, he gives a more detailed (and somewhat harsher) account of the events of that day and says nothing to indicate that he was not present.

Mount Pleasant (Ohio) Meetinghouse Interior

trodden under foot, and some jumped out of the windows, and many were hurt, but none seriously wounded.

And when the alarm subsided and no sign of the house falling, they pretty soon resumed their seats, and both parties went on with their business (with their separate clerks) for some little time – when those called Orthodox adjourned their meeting to ten o'clock the next day, and left the house in the possession of Friends, who then proceeded quietly on until some time in the afternoon, and then adjourned to nine o'clock the next morning, when they again met.

And near the 10th hour, a deputation from the opposing party came and demanded the use of the house in the name of the Yearly Meeting of Ohio. And Friends informed them that the doors were open and they might come in at their pleasure. And after some further requisition for Friends to withdraw and give them the use of the house, they then went away and did not interrupt Friends any more in that way, but had recourse to the law, and prosecuted a number of Friends – some in an action of trespass and some as rioters – and took them to Steubenville the next day, twenty miles distant. And about forty of their ministers and elders and leading members went on likewise to carry on the suit as the court was then sitting, and were two days absent from the sittings of their yearly meeting. After which, they interrupted Friends no further, and Friends quietly proceeded with their business, and closed with one sitting on the sixth of the week.

And the next day, we proceeded on our journey to Flushing and the next day attended Friends Meeting there. And notice being given of my attendance, the meeting was very large – more than the house could contain. Here at this meeting, those called Orthodox made great opposition, for as soon as I came near the meetinghouse, several of them met me and desired I would not interrupt the meeting. And soon after the meeting was gathered – before it became fully settled – Charles Osborn, an Orthodox minister, kneeled in supplication,[1] and such a prayer I don't think I ever before heard from the lips of any man. He continued on his knees, I believe, for more than an hour[2] and repeated the great name, I apprehend, forty or fifty times. It was truly a distressing scene and it greatly disturbed the meeting and disgusted a great portion of the assembly. And very soon after he took his seat, he again rose on his feet and began to preach and continued his preach for more than an hour – and it was judged by Friends generally that it was previously concluded that he should take up the meeting in that way in order to prevent my having any opportunity with the people.

And although when he sat down, the meeting was much wearied with his lengthy and tedious communications, yet I felt the necessity of standing up and addressing the people, which brought a precious solemnity over the meeting. But as soon as I sat down, he arose again to contradict and tried to lay waste my communication by asserting that I had not the unity of my Friends at home. Which being false, I then informed the meeting that I had certificates with me to prove the falsity of his assertions, which I then produced. But he and his party would not stay to hear them, but in a tumultuous manner arose and left the meeting. But the people generally stayed back and heard them read, to their general satisfaction.

The next day, we proceeded on our journey to Cambridge (about thirty-seven miles) and the day following rode to Zanesville (twenty-four miles) and had an appointed meeting there in the evening, held their courthouse – a large room, but not sufficient to contain all the people that assembled. It was a very solemn, instructive opportunity. And I parted with them under a thankful sense of the Lord's favor, and with peace of mind.

And the two following days, we rode to Wilmington and put up with our Friend, Warren Sabin. Here, we lodged the two following nights.

And the day after our arrival here being the seventh of the week and 20th of 9th month, we rode to Center and attended Friends monthly meeting composed of the preparative meetings of Center and Wilmington.

---

[1] The rest of the sentence was deleted from the printed *Journal*.

[2] The rest of the paragraph was deleted from the printed *Journal*.

It was the first monthly meeting they had held since their separation from their Orthodox brethren and, notice being given of our attendance, the meeting for worship was very large – more than the house could contain. And the Lord, our Never-Failing Helper, manifested his presence over all, to the solemnizing of the assembly and opening the minds of the people to receive the word preached, breaking down all opposition, humbling and contriting the assembly in a very general manner. And we parted from each other with grateful hearts from a humbling sense of the unmerited favor.

We returned that evening to Wilmington and the next day attended Friends Meeting in that town. And as their meetinghouse was small, Friends procured the courthouse in that place to hold the meeting in. The meeting was very large[1] – that although the courthouse was forty feet square, yet it did not hold more than half the people that assembled and Friends, from an apprehension that the house would not contain the people, provided seats around the house at the doors and windows, which being large, they were pretty well accommodated. And we had a very favored opportunity to declare the Truth among them, to their general satisfaction. And the honest-hearted were comforted and edified, and Friends were made to rejoice for the unmerited favor.

At the 4th hour in the afternoon, we had an appointed meeting at a place called Lytle Creek, a short distance from Wilmington.[2] Here, the Orthodox forbade Friends to go into the meetinghouse and, when we came to the place, the people were all standing without and were afraid to go in, although the doors were open. And when we came, the elders and overseers forbade me to go in – declaring that they had no unity with me. And as I had a meeting appointed for us the next day at a place called Springfield (a neighboring meeting), some of the elders at that place came over to this meeting and joined the elders here – forbidding me to have any meeting there. But I told them, I should have a meeting there, and if they shut the house against me, I should use no force to obtain it, but we would hold our meeting in the open air where none had a right to forbid us. I then turned my attention to those present, and asked if there were none present that had a right in the house, and that were willing we should go in, and hold the meeting. And several present signified they had. I then encouraged them to go in, assuring them that we would go in with them – which they agreed to – and the house was soon filled, and the Orthodox gave us no further interruption, and we had a favored opportunity with the people – greatly to their satisfaction.

---

[1] The rest of the sentence was deleted from the printed *Journal*.

[2] The rest of the paragraph, except for the last phrase, was deleted from the printed *Journal*.

And the next day being the second of the week and 22nd of the month, we proceeded on to Springfield. Here, the Orthodox shut the meetinghouse and set guards at the doors to keep us out, and we held our meeting under some trees near by. And a precious season it was, wherein the Lord's power and love were exalted over all opposition, and many minds were humbled and contrited, and thanksgiving and praise were ascribed to his great and adorable name, who is over all, blessed forever.

The next day, we had a favored meeting at a place called the Grove, and Friends Meetinghouse there being very small, we had to hold the meeting outdoors to accommodate the people. It was a very satisfactory opportunity.

The next day, we had an appointed meeting at Lebanon, a pretty large, country town, where there were no members of our society, but many sober, friendly people. It was held in the courthouse, but it was not sufficient to contain the people – about one-third of those that assembled had to stand outdoors. It was an instructive opportunity – many gospel truths were opened to the people and they appeared to go away well satisfied. And I parted from them with true peace of mind.

At Indiana Yearly Meeting[1]

And the next day, we attended the opening of the Yearly Meeting of Indiana with the first sitting of the Meeting of Ministers and Elders of that yearly meeting. And although small, it was a favored, encouraging opportunity to the few that assembled.

The next day, being first of the week and 28th of the month, a multitude assembled together with Friends – a great number had to stand without, although the house was very large. And he that openeth and none can shut, and when he shutteth none can open, opened my mouth among them in a large, effective testimony to the truths of the gospel, in which, through adorable condescension, I was enabled to bring forth out of the Lord's treasury things new and old. And Truth was raised into dominion over all opposition, to the comfort and rejoicing of the honest-hearted, and to the apparent satisfaction and edification of the people in general. Surely it was the Lord's doing, and it was marvelous in our eyes.

The next day the meeting for discipline opened and continued by adjournments until Sixth Day evening – Friends having been favored through the several sittings to conduct the business in much harmony and brotherly condescension.

---

[1] Indiana Yearly Meeting has already split into Hicksite and Orthodox meetings. This is the Hicksite yearly meeting (now known as Ohio Valley Yearly Meeting).

The next day, we proceeded on our journey toward Richmond in Indiana, taking meetings on our way at Springboro, Elk, Westfield, and Eaton. All these meetings were seasons of favor – the Lord graciously manifesting his presence for our help. Blessed be his great and excellent name, for his mercy endureth forever.

From Eaton, we rode home with our kind Friends, John and Elizabeth Barnes, and lodged.[1] We received great kindness from these Friends – Elizabeth was an excellent, sympathizing, motherly woman, and very useful in society.

Indiana

The next day being fourth of the week and 8th of 10th month, we rode to Richmond, where the Orthodox were holding their yearly meeting, and this day was given up for holding a meeting for worship. And notice being given of our intention to be there[2] – that although the Orthodox and Friends held their meetings apart, yet it was judged by those present that there were three thousand people attended Friends Meeting – and proved through adorable condescension a solemn, heart-tendering season, in which Truth reigned over all.

The three following days, we attended meetings at our appointment at Centerville, West Union, and Milford, after which, we returned again to Richmond in order, agreeable to appointment, to attend their First Day Meeting. It was large, like the former – a multitude of people assembled. It was a glorious meeting, in which Truth was triumphant and ran as oil over the assembly, breaking down all opposition – melting a great portion of the assembly into tears of contrition. Surely it was the Lord's doing and marvelous in our eyes, and to him belongeth all the praise, who is over all, blessed forever. And I parted from them with solid satisfaction and peace of mind, and after dinner, took a solemn and very affectionate leave of our Friends and rode on our journey about four miles, and spent the evening at the house of our esteemed Friend, Benjamin Stokes, and returned and lodged at the house of our kind Friend, John Barnes.

The following day, we attended a meeting, at our appointment, at a place called the Ridge – it was a comfortable opportunity.

The next day, we attended a meeting at Orange. Here, the Orthodox made great disturbance and hurt the meeting very considerably.

The next day, we had a meeting at a place called Silver Creek. This was a precious meeting, in which Truth reigned over all.

---

[1] The rest of the paragraph was deleted from the printed *Journal*.
[2] The following material between the dashes was deleted from the printed *Journal*.

Newberry Meetinghouse in Martinsville, Ohio

Back in Ohio

We then proceeded on our journey towards Cincinnati and arrived there on the 18th of 10th month and seventh of the week.

The next day and first of the week, we attended Friends Meeting at that place at the usual time, which was very large – many more attending than the house could contain. And at three o'clock in the afternoon, we appointed a meeting to be held in the courthouse in the city. Both these meetings were highly favored seasons, in which Truth was raised into dominion over all opposition, to the praise of his Grace, who is calling us to glory and to virtue.

On Second Day morning, we proceeded on our journey – turning homeward, taking meetings in our way in the course of the week at Salt Creek, Salem (alias Roachester), Newberry, and Clear Creek. All these meetings were composed of people of the varied professions – to whom the gospel was preached in the demonstration of the Spirit, attended with a power that silenced all opposition, humbling and contriting many hearts, without respect of persons nor sects[1] – as some of the gay and fashionable females (as well as some of the men) appeared bathed in tears at the close of these solemn meetings. And Friends were comforted

---

[1] The rest of the sentence was deleted from the printed *Journal*.

together and made to rejoice for the unmerited favor. And we parted from them under a thankful sense of the Lord's mercy, and with peace of mind.

The next day being first of the week and 26th of 10th month, we attended Fairfield Meeting. And notice being given of our coming, it was very large. Here, the Orthodox made public opposition in the first sitting down of the meeting – one of them informing the assembly that I was traveling without having the unity of my Friends and other incorrect declarations, which I passed over without notice. And the meeting was soon gathered into a solemn quiet, and I had a favored opportunity to declare the Truth among them. And Truth was raised into dominion, and many hearts were humbled and contrited, but before I had concluded my communication, the Orthodox (to manifest further disunity) arose and left the meeting. But at my request,[1] the people all kept their seats, and we had a very solemn close, and great brokenness and contrition were manifest among the people. And to do away the false reports spread by the Orthodox, I had my certificates read, which gave full satisfaction to the assembly,[2] and many of them manifested great offense and disgust at the conduct of the Orthodox for the disturbance they had made. And we took an affectionate farewell of our Friends and others present, and proceeded on our journey to Wheeling in Virginia,[3] which town is situated on the east side of River Ohio.

Virginia & Southwestern Pennsylvania

We arrived here on Sixth Day, 31st, a little before noon and had an appointed meeting in the evening. And as Friends have no meetinghouse in that place, it was held in the Methodists' house, which they kindly offered of their own accord. It was a pretty large collection of people – mostly made up of other societies – the number of Friends there being very small, insomuch that they have no steady meeting in the place. It was a comfortable, favored opportunity and we left them with peace of mind, and proceeded on our journey to Westland in Redstone Quarter, where we arrived on First Day, 2nd of 11th month, timely to attend their meeting.

It was a very solemn, edifying opportunity, in which Truth's testimony was exalted over all apparent opposition. After which, we proceeded on to Redstone (about seven miles), crossing the Monongahela River in the way.

And the next day, had an appointed meeting in that town at the 2nd hour after noon.

---

[1] This phrase was deleted from the printed *Journal*.
[2] The rest of the sentence was deleted from the printed *Journal*.
[3] Prior to the Civil War, West Virginia was part of Virginia.

Goose Creek (Virginia) Meetinghouse

And the next day, we proceeded on our journey towards Waterford (alias Fairfax) in Virginia (two hundred and thirty-six miles), where we arrived on First Day, 9th of 11th month, and attended their meeting at the usual hour. And at two o'clock in the afternoon, had an appointed meeting for the townspeople in general.

And the two following days, attended meetings by appointment at Goose Creek and South Fork. These were all large, favored meetings – particularly the two last, wherein I was led to expose the great evil of oppression, especially that enormous sin of holding our fellow creatures in slavery. And although in my communication I was led to lay judgment to the line and justice to the plumb-line,[1] yet the slaveholders (divers of whom were present) were so brought down and humbled with the force and correctness of the testimony, that they frankly acknowledged the truth and propriety of it. And we parted from them with true peace of mind. And the honest-hearted were made to rejoice for the favor dispensed from the hand of our gracious Benefactor of every blessing.

And the next day, we proceeded on our journey to Alexandria (forty-three miles) and lodged with our kind Friend, Phineas Janney. And the next day, attended their meeting as it came in course. And in the evening, had another meeting for the townspeople in general. These were opportunities of favor – many truths of the gospel were set forth before the

---

[1] Isaiah 28:17

people in the demonstration of the Spirit, which brought a solemnity over the assembly, to the comfort and edification of the upright in heart.

Washington & Maryland

And the next day, we rode to Washington and attended a meeting there in the evening. This was rather a trying season in the forepart, but I trust it ended well.

The next day, we proceeded to Sandy Spring in Maryland and the following day, being the first of the week and 16th of 11th month, we attended Friends Meeting there. And notice being given of our being there, it was large. And through condescending goodness, it proved to be a very favored, instructive season. And I parted with them with a thankful heart and true peace of mind.

The next day, we proceeded on our journey to Elkridge and lodged with our kind Friend, George Ellicott.

And the day following being third of the week, we had by appointment a very comfortable, favored meeting with Friends. Many of the neighboring inhabitants likewise attended and appeared well satisfied with the opportunity. Many minds were humbled and contrited, and a precious solemnity prevailed over the meeting. At the close of which, we dined at our lodgings, and that afternoon, proceeded in company with our kind Friend, John Marsh (who met us at this meeting) six miles on our way to Baltimore and lodged at his house.

And in the morning, rode into the city and on that and the following day, attended Friends midweek meetings at the upper and lower houses. And not feeling fully clear, on Sixth Day evening, had an appointed meeting for the townspeople in general at the upper house. This was a very large meeting, made up of almost every class of the people – high and low, rich and poor – among whom, as to religious profession, were Romanists, Episcopalians, Presbyterians, Baptists, Methodists, Unitarians, and others of divers descriptions – and some slaveholders. These meetings were seasons of favor, particularly the latter, in which Truth in a very extraordinary manner was raised into victory over all, bowing and breaking down all under its baptizing influence,[1] causing all to unite with one voice to bear testimony thereto (both in word and gesture), as there was not an opposing voice heard from any individual. Such a solemnity covered every individual that it appeared as though the whole assembly was baptized into one body. And when the meeting closed, all seemed desirous to take me by the hand,[2] and hundreds appeared unwilling to

---

[1] The rest of the sentence and the first phrase of the next one were deleted from the printed *Journal*.

[2] The rest of the sentence and the next one were deleted from the printed *Journal*.

leave the house until they found opportunity to be gratified therein. And both young and old of every description pressed forward to obtain the privilege. Surely it was the Lord's doing and marvelous in mine eyes. And I parted with them with gratitude and thankfulness of heart.

And the day following, we proceeded to Gunpowder Falls and the next day being first of the week and 23rd of the 11th month, we attended Friends Meeting there. And notice being spread of our being there, the meeting was large and, through the condescending goodness of Israel's Unslumbering Shepherd, whose mercy is over all his works, it proved a precious favored opportunity, in which many hearts were humbled and contrited, and Truth was raised into dominion over all.

The next day, we rode to the Little Falls, and on Third Day, 25th, we attended Friends Meeting in that place, and the day following, we attended Deer Creek Meeting. These were very large, favored opportunities, after which, we proceeded on our journey, crossing the River Susquehanna on our way to Little Britain.

Back in Pennsylvania & Delaware

And on the three following days, we attended meetings at Little Britain, West, and East Nottingham. These were seasons to be remembered, in which the Lord's power was eminently manifested[1] – breaking down all opposition and silencing every opposing spirit by its solemnizing influence. Surely it was the Lord's doing and marvelous in our eyes.

On Second Day, 1st of the 12th month, we proceeded to West Grove in Chester County. Here, our opposing brethren shut the meetinghouse against us and the caretaker of it refused to open it. However, when the people assembled – which they did in great numbers, many more than the house could contain – the house was opened and we had a very favored, solemn opportunity with them, in which Truth reigned victoriously over all.

The three following days, we attended the Monthly Meetings of London Grove, New Garden, and Fallowfield, as they came in their usual course, and notice being given of our attending to the neighboring inhabitants (not in membership with Friends),[2] great numbers of the varied classes of the people assembled with Friends – insomuch, that none of the houses were large enough to contain the multitude that, in some instances, there were near as many standing without as the houses contained. These were all highly favored seasons – the Lord's power evidently presiding over these large assemblies, solemnizing and

---

[1] The rest of the sentence was deleted from the printed *Journal*.
[2] The parenthetical phrase was deleted from the printed *Journal*.

humbling with its overshadowing influence, causing a profound silence to prevail over the assemblies, to the praise of his Grace who is over all, God blessed forever.

On the two following days, we attended meetings at Marlborough and West Chester. The first was by our appointment, the latter on First Day. These were like the former – great numbers attended, more than the houses could contain.[1] And even in the houses, many crowded in and filled every avenue where an individual between the seats could stand on his feet – all such places were filled with men and women standing on their feet. Nevertheless, due order and stillness prevailed over all in a remarkable manner – in and without the houses in every place – to the comfort and rejoicing of Friends, and to the instruction and edification, I trust, of the assembled multitudes. And we took leave of them under a humbling sense of the unmerited favor, and with true peace of mind.

On Second Day, 8th of the month, we attended Kennett Meeting and Third and Fourth Days, we had meetings at Kennett Square and Centre – all crowded assemblies – in all of which the Divine Presence was felt to preside, solemnizing the assemblies to the comfort and rejoicing the honest-hearted.

On Fifth and Sixth Days, we attended meetings at Hockessin and Stanton – both crowded, solemn meetings – and I trust, instructive and profitable to many who were present. After the latter, we rode that afternoon to Wilmington and rested on Seventh Day with our Friend, William Poole, who was in a weak state having had a shock of palsy,[2] but was so far recovered as to walk about.

On First Day, 14th, we attended Friends Meetings in Wilmington – both fore and after noon – they were both very large. In the first, I had good service, but in the afternoon was mostly silent as the people appeared to be too much hungering for words and too indifferent and careless in regard to putting in practice what they had already heard and knew to be their duty. Hence, I was led to learn them in silence.

We left Wilmington on Second Day morning, and proceeded to Concord, and attended a meeting there by previous appointment.

And the four following days, we attended meetings at Middletown, Providence, Chester, and Darby. These were all very large, favored opportunities, in which the Lord's power was felt to preside, causing a precious solemnity to spread over the assemblies, to the humbling and contriting many minds. To the Lord be the praise and glory of his own work, nothing due to man. Leaving Darby, we proceeded on to Philadelphia.

---

[1] The next sentence was deleted from the printed *Journal*.
[2] Shock of palsy: stroke

Concord (Pennsylvania) Meetinghouse

On First Day, 21st of 12th month, we attended Friends Meetings in the city, *viz*, Cherry Street in the morning and Green Street in the afternoon. At both meetings, hundreds more assembled than the houses could contain.

On Second Day, we left the city and attended meetings in the course of the week at Haverford, Radnor, Newtown, Willistown, and the Valley after which we returned to the city again. All these meetings were unusually large – the houses were generally too small to contain the people and many had to stand outdoors for want of room. Nevertheless, the people conducted orderly and the Lord's presence was felt to preside – solemnizing all those crowded assemblies – in all of which, my mind was opened and ability afforded by him who opens and none can shut, and when he shuts, none can open, to preach the gospel to the people in the demonstration of the Spirit and with a power attending that broke down and subjected by its influence every opposing spirit. And many hearts were broken and contrited and went away rejoicing under a thankful sense of the unmerited favor.

On First Day, 28th of the month, we again attended Friends Meetings in the City in the same order as before and on Second Day, we attended Frankford Meeting by appointment. These were all large, favored meetings – hundreds had to leave those in the City for want of room. My opposing brethren had, by their public opposition and false reports, created such excitement in the minds of the people generally of every profession that it induced multitudes to assemble to hear for themselves. And all generally went away satisfied and comforted.

Back in New Jersey

On Third Day, we took leave of our Friends in the city and passed over into the Jerseys, and the four following days, we attended meetings at Mullica Hill, Pilesgrove, Salem, and Woodbury. These were very large, favored meetings, and I felt true peace of mind as a rich reward for my faithful labor and exercise among them.

1829

On First Day, 4th of 1st month 1829, we attended Haddonfield Meeting. Here, Friends and those who styled themselves Orthodox met together in the same house[1] and, the Orthodox taking the lead, two of the elders took the uppermost seat next to the women's apartment,[2] and when I came, I stepped up to them. And knowing, according to the common usage and comely order of society, it was my right and privilege to take the first seat – as I had the full unity of the Monthly and Quarterly Meetings of which I was a member,[3] and a minister and more ancient than those who had taken the first seat, I very respectfully proposed to them to give me the seat next to the women as I was an old man and a stranger. But they refused to grant the request, but had not confidence to look me in the face.

And as notice was given of my attendance, the people assembled in great numbers,[4] and as some came in very late, this disturbed the two Friends so much that one of them, in a tone of voice that manifested much irritation, arose and gave the assembly a pretty sharp rebuke for disturbing and unsettling the meeting – when there was not the least cause for it as there was no other disturbance than the orderly coming in of the people. For as soon as the people were fully assembled, a precious solemnity was felt to spread over the assembly, and the Lord, our Gracious Helper, was near for our support and strength, and Truth was raised triumphantly over all opposition.

And the four following days, we attended meetings at Moorestown, Evesham, Cropwell, Mount Holly, and Upper Evesham. These were very large meetings in which the Lord, our Gracious Helper, made bare his arm for our support – enabling us to hand forth out of the treasury things new and old, to the comfort and edification of the honest-hearted, and solid peace of my own mind. To him be all the praise, nothing due to man.

---

[1] The rest of the paragraph was deleted from the printed *Journal*.

[2] Apartment: an area within a building that is allocated to a particular group. Men and women sat separately during meetings for worship – although with the partitions raised so that people heard ministry offered by ministers of either gender. The ministers and elders sat on raised benches that faced the rest of the congregation with the elders sitting above the ministers. The seats on the central aisle of these facing benches were reserved for the most senior members.

[3] Again, Hicks is emphasizing that he is traveling with the support of his home meetings.

[4] The rest of the sentence was deleted from the printed *Journal*.

Crosswicks (New Jersey) Meetinghouse

On First Day, 11th, we attended Friends Meeting at Rancocas. This was said to be the largest meeting ever known in that place before, in which the Lord's presence was felt to preside, breaking down all opposition,[1] humbling and contriting many minds, and baptizing the whole assembly into a very precious solemnity, and causing the upright in heart to rejoice under a thankful sense of the unmerited favor.

In the course of this week, we attended meetings at Old Springfield on Second Day, Mansfield on Third Day, Upper Springfield on Fourth Day, Arney's Mount on Fifth Day, Crosswicks (alias Chesterfield) on Sixth Day, Bordentown on Seventh Day, and Trenton on First Day. These were all favored opportunities, in all of which (although under considerable indisposition of body) I was favored with strength and way opened to labor faithfully in the Lord's cause, in which I was engaged. That produced that true peace of mind that the world, with all its perishing enjoyments, cannot give nor can all its frowns and opposition take away.

On Second Day, we proceeded on our journey towards New York, being desirous of reaching our quarterly meeting to be held there on the following Fifth Day. We arrived in the city on Third Day in the afternoon. Here, I met my beloved wife and daughter, Elisabeth, and several other branches of my family, and a number more of my near and intimate Friends. And it was truly a season of mutual rejoicing, and my spirit was deeply humbled under a thankful sense of the Lord's preserving power

---

[1] This phrase was deleted from the printed *Journal*.

and adorable mercy in carrying me through and over all opposition – both within and without, and from all the combined force of false brethren[1] – and caused all to work together for good,[2] and the promotion of his own glorious cause of Truth and Righteousness in earth, and landed me safe in the bosom of my dear family and Friends at home, and clothed my spirit with the reward of sweet peace for all my labor and travail.

Praises! Everlasting high praises be ascribed unto our God, for his mercy endureth forever!

On Seventh Day after the quarterly meeting, we returned home, having been out in this journey seven months and ten days and traveled two thousand, three hundred, and ninety-three miles. Took with me in this journey one hundred and thirty dollars to defray my traveling expenses.

> *I have been unable to find the remaining text in Hicks' own handwriting. The next section is taken from a letter to Jesse Townsend dated 5th month 25th 1829.*

The Death of Jemima Hicks

On my return from the Jerseys, by riding in the first snow storm about fourteen miles after a meeting, I took cold. And the weather continuing unfavorable when I got home, I was unwell for three or four weeks. And soon after I recovered my health, my much beloved wife and endeared bosom companion, who likewise had been favored with unusual health during my absence, was taken down with a cold. And although for about five days from the time she was taken, we anticipated her restoration to her usual state of health in a few days, but in this we were disappointed. For about this time, her disorder put on a more serious aspect as it settled on her lungs and brought on an inflammation, which terminated in a dissolution of her precious life on the ninth day from the time she was first taken ill – which being so sudden and unexpected, it was the greatest trial and the greatest loss I ever met with.

Nor could I meet with another as great as it respects my temporal blessings, for she was to me the fullness of comfort and joy that the best of wives could be to a husband. And we have nothing left behind to console us for so great a loss, but a confident belief and an assured hope that it is to her a still greater gain, and that her precious spirit is safely landed on the angelic shore, where the wicked and all opposing spirits cease from troubling, and the weary are at rest. She underwent but little pain in her

---

[1] This phrase was deleted from the printed *Journal*.
[2] Romans 8:28

illness – made but little complaint. Her chief suffering was a difficulty in breathing by the accumulation of phlegm in her lungs, which subsided. And she became entirely easy some time before her close, and passed away as going into a sweet sleep – without sigh or groan or the least bodily emotion.

We enjoyed sweet communion, both as to body and mind, for fifty-eight years and upwards, in which the declaration of our gracious Creator was verified in us, where he says, "It is not good for man to dwell alone, I will make him a helpmeet"[1] – such she was to me indeed. "And the man shall leave father and mother and cleave unto his wife, and they shall no longer be twain, but shall be one flesh."[2] This precious and unbroken union was verified in our experience, which makes the trial greater. Yet I have cause for thankfulness and gratitude to the Blessed Author of all our sure mercies that he brought us together in his counsel, and united our hearts together by his love, and sustained us in the precious enjoyment thereof to old age – a period much longer than is generally experienced by the children of men. Which unmerited favor, I trust and hope, will preserve me from indulging one murmuring thought, but contrariwise, to thank God and take courage, still to press forward in the way everlasting,[3] in full assurance that his mercy endureth forever.[4]

> The description of the final journey in New York and Vermont is from the editorial committee manuscript.

Finishing the Journey

On the 24th of 6th month 1829, I again left home with Cornell Willis for my companion to complete the visit to Friends and others in the compass of our yearly meeting – agreeable to a certificate I received from our monthly and quarterly meetings, expressive of their unity with me therein. This certificate I received in the spring of the year 1828, expressive of my concern to pay a religious visit to Friends and others in parts of the Yearly Meetings of Philadelphia, Baltimore, Virginia, Ohio, Indiana, and New York. I accomplished my visit to the four first, last season – that is, I visited parts of four of them, but found my mind released without going into the Yearly Meeting of Virginia.

Since I left home, we have attended meetings at Flushing, Newtown, Brooklyn, and two at New York last First Day. These were favored,

---

[1] Genesis 2:18
[2] Genesis 2:24, Matthew 19:5-6, & Mark 10:7-8
[3] Psalm 139:24
[4] Psalm 136

comforting opportunities, affording encouragement to persevere in the path of duty.

We left New York on Second Day, 29th, after taking an affectionate farewell of our Friends there, and proceeded to Westchester, and attended a meeting at that place at the 11th hour.

And on the two following days, attended meetings at Mamaroneck and Purchase.

On Fifth Day, we attended Friends Meeting at Middlesex.

And on Sixth and Seventh Days, had meetings appointed for us at a place called the Saw Pits, and at Friends Meetinghouse at North Castle. All these meetings were seasons of favor in which the Divine Presence was felt to preside, solemnizing the assemblies, and affording ability to minister to the people in gospel authority, and tendering and contriting many hearts. To the Lord be all the praise, nothing due to man.

On First Day, 5th of 7th month, we attended Chappaqua Meeting in the morning and had an appointed meeting at Croton Valley at the 4th hour after noon.

The three following days, we attended meetings by our appointment at Amawalk, Salem, and at the Valley called Haviland's Hollow. These were all unusually large meetings, in which Truth reigned over all, to the praise of his great name, who giveth us the victory.

From the latter meeting, we proceeded to Oblong and put up with our kind Friend, Daniel Merritt, and the next day attended their meeting.

The two following days, we had meetings by our appointment at the Branch and Poughquaig, and on First Day attended Nine Partners meeting. Those four meetings were unusually large and very solemn opportunities in which the power of Truth went forth freely, tendering and contriting many hearts, and rejoicing the faithful travelers Zionward.

The two following days, we had meetings at Chestnut Ridge and Oswego. These were likewise large satisfactory meetings. We then proceeded by the way of Poughkeepsie to Marlborough, in order to attend Cornwall Quarterly Meeting, held at Marlborough at this time. It opened on Fourth Day, 15th of 7th month, with a Meeting of Ministers and Elders. The next day the meeting for discipline was held. Both were very favored seasons.

As I did not feel easy to leave the place without having a public opportunity with the people at large in that neighborhood, a meeting was accordingly appointed the next day. This was likewise a large, favored opportunity.

The following day being Seventh Day, we returned to Poughkeepsie in order to attend Friends Meeting on First Day and having also appointed a meeting to be held there at the 5th hour in the afternoon for the inhabitants of the town at large. These meetings were largely attended, in which the power of Truth was exalted over all.

The four following days, we attended meetings at West Branch, Pleasant Valley, Creek, and Crum Elbow. Although it was in the midst of harvest, yet the excitement produced amongst the people by the opposition made by those of our members who had gone off from us and set up separate meetings was such that the people at large of other societies flocked to those meetings in such numbers that our meetinghouses were seldom large enough to contain the assembled multitude. And we had abundant cause for thanksgiving and gratitude to the Blessed Author of all our mercies in condescending to manifest his holy presence and causing it so to preside as to produce a general solemnity – to the tendering and contriting many minds, and comforting and rejoicing the upright in heart.

After the last mentioned meeting, we proceeded on our journey, attending meetings at Stanford, Milan, and on First Day, 26th of 7th month, the fore and after noon meetings at Hudson.

On Second Day, we rested.

On Third Day, attended a meeting at Athens.

On Fourth Day, at Ghent.

On Fifth Day, at Chatham.

On Sixth Day, at Nassau.

And on Seventh Day evening, we had a large meeting in Albany, held in their statehouse and generally composed of people of other professions and inhabitants of the town, who behaved themselves very soberly – becoming the occasion. It was a solemn and, I trust, a profitable opportunity, in which Truth was raised into dominion, and which in like manner was witnessed in all the foregoing meetings – the people coming together very freely and in great numbers. And a general solemnity prevailed over the assemblies from meeting to meeting. Surely it was the Lord's doing, and it was marvelous in our eyes – witnessing that he had not left himself without an evidence of the Truth in each mind, by which their understandings were opened to receive, and many of them to bear testimony to the doctrines delivered in those large, solemn meetings.

From Albany, we proceeded on First Day morning, 2nd of 8th month, to Troy, and attended their fore and after noon meetings – these were very large meetings. The first was held in Friends Meetinghouse, but great numbers collected – more than the house could contain. This induced Friends to accept the offer of a house belonging to the Episcopalians (which was not occupied) for the accommodation of the afternoon meeting. They gave the citizens an invitation to attend and, although it was a very large building, yet it did not contain the people who assembled

– many had to go away for want of room. This was likewise a highly favored opportunity, in which Truth reigned to the comfort and edification of the upright in heart, and to the general satisfaction of the assembled multitude. It was, in the estimation of Friends, the largest meeting that had ever been assembled on any occasion before in that city.

On Second Day, we had an appointed meeting at Greenbush, a village on the east side of the river opposite Albany. After this, we proceeded on our journey about eleven miles to the town of Bethlehem, southwesterly from Albany. Here, we lodged with our kind Friend, Thomas Rushmore, and attended a meeting in his house by appointment on Third Day – the few Friends of that place were privileged with holding a meeting for worship in this Friend's house.[1]

On Fourth Day, we attended Friends Meeting at Stanton Hill, and the three following days, attended meetings at New Baltimore, Rensselaerville, and Oakhill. These were all large satisfactory meetings.

On First Day, we were at Bern Meeting in the morning, and at the 4th hour after noon, had an appointed meeting at a village called Rensselaerville, which was held in a large meetinghouse belonging to the Methodist society. These were very large, favored meetings, in which the truths of the gospel went forth freely to the people and appeared to be gladly and satisfactorily received by them. And I took leave of them with true peace of mind.

On Second Day, we had an appointed meeting at Middleburgh – much to our satisfaction. It was a very solemn, instructive opportunity and the people appeared to receive the word preached with much readiness of mind. And we left them with thankful hearts.

We proceeded on Third Day to Duanesburg, in order to attend their quarterly meeting that opened there the next day with a Meeting of Ministers and Elders and was a favored opportunity. The meeting for discipline was large, and the business conducted in much harmony and condescension. And the public meeting the next day was very large – hundreds had to stand out of doors for want of room – and it was a highly favored season, worthy of grateful remembrance.

From thence, we proceeded to Charleston and attended Friends Meeting there on First Day, 16th of 8th month. This was likewise a very large meeting – the largest, Friends said, that had ever been known there before. It was judged that as many stood without – for want of room – as the house contained. And it was a very solemn time, both within and without the doors. The divine canopy was felt to spread over the whole

---

[1] That is to say that this was an indulged meeting.

assembly, and we took leave of them with true peace of mind and thankfulness of heart, under a grateful sense of the unmerited favor.

On Second Day, we rode to Utica, and the next day had an appointed meeting there at the 11th hour.

After this, we proceeded to Bridgewater and attended their Fourth Day Meeting. These were not so large as in some other places. Neither was there as much openness to receive our testimony as had generally been the case elsewhere. Our opposing Friends had filled their heads with so many strange reports – to which they had given credit without any examination – by which their minds were so strongly prejudiced against me that many in the compass of these two last meetings were not willing to see me nor hear any reasons given to show them their mistakes and that the reports they had heard were altogether unfounded. However, I was favored to communicate the Truth to those who attended, so that they generally went away fully satisfied. And I left them with peace of mind.

From this place, we proceeded to Deruyter, having a meeting at Smyrna on Sixth Day, in our way.

On First Day, we attended Friends Meeting at Deruyter in the morning, and at the 5th hour after noon, had an appointed meeting in Deruyter village for the inhabitants generally, which was held in the Baptist Meetinghouse. These two meetings were very large, and they were highly favored opportunities, in which Truth was raised into dominion over all opposition. And we parted from them with true peace of mind – a rich reward for a faithful discharge of duty.

The next day, 24th of 8th month, we proceeded to Sempronius, having a meeting by previous appointment on our way in the town of Homer at the 11th hour. It was held in a large meetinghouse belonging to the Methodist society, which they freely offered for the accommodation of the people – there being no Friends in the place. A very considerable number of the inhabitants attended and behaved soberly – giving good attention to what was communicated – and went away apparently satisfied. And we parted with them under a humbling sense that the appointment, and our labor and service in this meeting, were owned by the Head of the Church.

We arrived at Sempronius about sunset, and had an appointed meeting there the next day – held in Friends Meetinghouse at the 3rd hour after noon. This was likewise a favored opportunity, in which the power of Truth went forth freely, humbling and contriting many minds.

After this we proceeded to Skaneateles and put up with our kind Friend, William Willets, and rested here the next day.

On Fifth Day, we attended Friends Meeting at this place as it came in course. And notice being given of our intention of attending it, the meeting was large. This was a very comforting, satisfactory opportunity –

apparently so to all present, although composed of many of the members of the varied societies of professed Christians common in our land and divers of their ministers.

On Sixth Day, we had an appointed meeting in the town of Auburn at the 3rd hour after noon, and on Seventh Day, an appointed meeting at North Street in Scipio. These meetings were largely attended, and I trust instructive, profitable opportunities to many who were there. After the latter meeting, we visited several families of Friends and took lodgings with our kind Friend, John Merritt.

The next day being the first of the week, and 30th of 8th month, we attended the meeting at South Street.

The three following days, we had meetings, by appointment, at Salmon Creek, Aurora, and Union Springs. These were all very large, favored meetings, in which the power of Truth went forth freely and appeared to have a ready entrance into the minds of the people in a very general manner – bringing a very comfortable solemnity over these large assemblies. And we took leave of them with thankful hearts and in true peace of mind.

We then proceeded on our journey to Junius, crossing Cayuga Lake on the way. Here, we had a meeting the next day, the fifth of the week and 3rd of 9th month. And the day following had an appointed meeting at Galen. These were highly favored opportunities, in which the Lord's presence was felt to preside, reducing the assemblies into a very solemn state. And Truth was raised into dominion over all, to the comfort and establishment of Friends on the ancient foundation – the Light Within – by the power and efficacy of which our primitive worthies had gathered us to be a people from among the varied societies of professed Christians. For they were settled on that unshaken rock, which Jesus told his disciples he would build his Church upon, *viz*, the revelation of his Heavenly Father, against which the gates of hell should never be able to prevail.[1] And although all the powers of the earth rose up against them, and used all their power and policy – both priests and people – to overthrow them, yet they were never permitted to prevail. For the Lord Jehovah, on whose almighty arm they had placed their entire trust and confidence for support and defense, delivered them from all their tribulations, and set them above their persecutors, and caused them to rejoice on the banks of deliverance. And he is the same God of power that he ever was, and a Present Helper in every needful time.

And although many in the present day – who have left their first love – are rising up and charging their fellow-professors with holding unsound

---

[1] Matthew 16:15-18

doctrines, and are endeavoring by unfounded and reproachful epithets to destroy and undermine their religious and moral character among men, and have separated from their brethren and set up separate meetings – giving them the names of the meetings of Friends – and in their usurped authority undertake to disown all their fellow-members who could not submit to their usurpation, yet all their formal disownments being altogether out of the order of the gospel, our meetings consider them of no effect.

From Galen, we proceeded to South Farmington and attended a meeting there on Seventh Day at the 3rd hour after noon.

And the next day being First Day, we attended North Farmington Meeting.

The three following days, we had meetings at Macedon, Palmyra, and Williamson. These were likewise large, favored meetings in which Truth was exalted over all. And we parted with them in true peace of mind, and proceeded on our journey to Rochester, and had a meeting on Sixth Day by appointment. We also stayed and attended their meeting on First Day.

After this, we proceeded to Wheatland and had an appointed meeting there on Second Day, 14th of 9th month.

On Third Day we were at Henrietta, and on Fourth Day at Mendon. These were all favored opportunities – the people's minds seemed to be open to receive us and our testimony with gladness.

From this place we turned back through Farmington and Scipio to Skaneateles, and attended a meeting by our appointment at a village about five miles from the village of Skaneateles on the east side of the lake.

On First Day, we attended Friends Meeting at Skaneateles.

On Second Day, we proceeded to Verona, and the next day had a meeting there – held in a meetinghouse occupied by the Baptists, Friends Meetinghouse being too small to contain the people who assembled.

The next day being Fourth Day, we proceeded to Utica and had an appointed meeting in the evening. Here, we remained over the next day and attended Friends Meeting as it came in course.

From this place we proceeded to Charleston, and attended their meeting on First Day. These meetings, in like manner, were all solemn seasons and, I trust, profitable and comfortable to many. And I left them with peace of mind.

After the last meeting, we rode about thirteen miles and lodged with our kind Friend, Zacheus Mead.

The following day, we proceeded on our journey to Newtown, and the next day, attended Friends Meeting there.

After this we proceeded to Saratoga and attended Friends Preparative Meeting at that place. And not feeling clear to leave it, we had an appointed meeting there the day after, of which public notice was given. It was very large and it proved a highly favored season. The Lord's presence was manifested for our help, and Truth was raised into dominion and ran like oil over the assembly. Many hearts were broken and contrited, and the upright in heart were made to rejoice for the unmerited favor.

The following day we had an appointed meeting at Milton. After this we proceeded to Galway, and lodged with our ancient Friend, Philip Macomber, who was in the ninety-first year of his age. Here, we had a meeting on Seventh Day.

The next day, 4th of 10th month, we attended Providence Meeting, which was very large.

On Second Day, we had an appointed meeting at Mayfield. These were all seasons of favor – particularly that at Providence, in which Truth was exalted over all opposition and many hearts were contrited. From a sense of which, our minds were bowed in reverence and humiliation before him who is the Author of all our sure mercies.

We proceeded from Mayfield to Greenfield, and on Fourth Day attended Friends monthly meeting at that place, which was composed of that and Milton Preparative Meetings. We had good satisfaction in sitting with our Friends, and in observing their commendable order, and the harmony and condescension manifest in conducting the affairs of the Church.

From thence, we proceeded to Easton and had an appointed meeting there on Sixth Day.

On Seventh Day we were at Cambridge.

On First Day at White Creek.

Vermont

And on Second Day, we rode to Danby, and the next day had a meeting there. These were all large and very solemn seasons, in which the great Head of the Church manifested his gracious presence – convicting and contriting many minds. And the upright in heart were edified.

From Danby we proceeded to Granville and had an appointed meeting there the next day, which was a large, solemn opportunity.

The day after, we proceeded on our journey to Shoreham, a town on the eastern shore of Lake Champlain. Here, we had a meeting the next day with the few Friends of that place and some of the neighboring inhabitants. It was a comfortable opportunity, and we left them with peace of mind.

We then rode to Ferrisburg, and on First Day, 18th of 10th month, had a very large, favored meeting at that place.

On Second Day, we had an appointed meeting at Monkton. This was likewise a large, favored opportunity, in which Truth reigned over all opposition, to the praise of his own excellent name, who is over all, God blessed forever.

As I was somewhat unwell, we rested on Third Day with our kind Friends, Thomas and Rowland T. Robinson.* And feeling my mind now clear from any further service in these parts, on Fourth Day we turned our faces homewards and proceeded back to Shoreham.

On Fifth Day, we had an appointed meeting in that village, principally for those not members of our society. And although the people came together in a negligent manner – as respected the appointed time – yet they generally behaved orderly and appeared to give good attention to what they heard. And my mouth was opened by him who opens and none can shut, in a large, effective testimony to the truths of the gospel – which brought a precious solemnity over the assembly. And they appeared to go away satisfied, and we left them with the answer of peace in our own minds.

Back in New York

The next day we proceeded on our journey to Granville, and from thence the following day to Queensbury.

On First Day, 25th of 10th month, we attended Friends Meeting there. And notice being given to the neighboring inhabitants of our attendance, they came in until the house was filled – and a number had to stand without for want of room. And a blessed meeting we had, in which the power of Truth ran as oil over the assembly – to the tendering and contriting many minds, and to the comfort and rejoicing of the upright in heart.

We had an appointed meeting on the following day at Moreau, which was a large favored meeting. From thence, we proceeded to Saratoga and lodged with our kind Friend, Thomas Wilbur.

And the next day, Thomas accompanied us to Pittstown, where we had an appointed meeting on Fourth Day. This was truly a humbling season, in which Truth was exalted over all. Great brokenness and contrition of spirit were manifested among the people, and we were edified together in love, which inspired our minds with thanksgiving and gratitude for the unmerited favor.

From this place, we proceeded to Troy and, as I was somewhat unwell, we rested the following day with our kind Friend, Isaac Merritt.

On Sixth Day, we proceeded on our journey to the neighborhood of Hudson and put up with our kind Friend, Thomas Wright.

And Seventh Day being very rainy and inclement, we continued here and attended Hudson Meeting on First Day, which was a large satisfactory meeting.

On Second Day, we proceeded on our journey to Stanford and lodged with our kind Friend, John Hull.

The two following days, we attended the Quarterly Meeting at Nine Partners. At this place, there is a very large body of Friends united together in gospel fellowship, and they were favored to conduct the business of the quarterly meeting in harmony and condescension. The public meeting was very large – it was attended by a great number who were not in membership with us and who behaved orderly. And it was indeed a very solemn, edifying season.

After the close of this meeting, we returned that evening to Stanford in order to attend the quarterly meeting at that place, which opened the next day with a Meeting of Ministers and Elders. I attended this and, the following day, the meeting for discipline. A large number of the neighboring inhabitants attended this meeting and sat with Friends until the partition between the men and women was closed.[1] They behaved very orderly, and a precious solemnity spread over the assembly, and many essential doctrines of the gospel were opened to the people in the demonstration of the Spirit. And Truth raised into victory over all, and the upright in heart were edified and comforted. The Meeting of Ministers and Elders was likewise a precious opportunity, in which comfort and encouragement were freely administered to them.

From Stanford, we proceeded on our journey to Cornwall, crossing the Hudson River on our way. We arrived here on Seventh Day evening and attended their meeting on First Day, 8th of 11th month. This meeting was large, and a truly baptizing season, in which many hearts were humbled and contrited, and Truth reigned over all. Thanks be to God, who giveth us the victory, nothing due to man.

The two following days, we had meetings appointed at the Lower and Upper Clove. These were well attended and, I trust, profitable, edifying seasons to many present. They were composed of people of various professions, conditions, and states, yet all appeared to be brought down and subjected by the solemnizing influence and power of Truth that reigned victoriously over all. Surely it was the Lord's doing, and it was marvelous in our eyes.

---

[1] Meetinghouses had separate men's and women's sides, with a movable partition between them. For worship, the partition was raised to allow Friends on both sides to hear ministry offered on either side. The partition remained open for a period of worship before business meetings, but was lowered when business commenced, to allow men and women to conduct their business separately. Only members were allowed to attend business meetings.

> *In a letter to Thomas Wilbur's son, Elias Wilbur, Hicks relates a much fuller account of his visit to Upper Clove. It seems likely that this would have been included in his original manuscript:*
>
> "On Second and Third Days, we had appointed meetings at the Lower and Upper Clove. At the Upper Clove, Friends and the Orthodox continued to meet together on First Days, and word was sent forward to Friends of that meeting to spread the notice at the close of their First Day Meeting of our appointment on Third Day – which was accordingly done by our Friend, Wait Pearsall – which raised the resentment of the Orthodox. And one of their principal leaders, as soon as the meeting was closed, fell upon the Friend who gave the notice and asked him how he dare give out notice for me, who was a deist, etc., and had been regularly disowned. And two or three of the Orthodox got about him and assured him that we should not have the privilege of going into the house, but the Friend assured them that he would have the house opened. However, they appeared determined that we should not have the house. And to prevent Friends getting in, they sent the key away – two miles off – and secreted it. But before the time of our meeting came, they took wit in their anger and their chief man went and got the key and opened the house without giving Friends any more trouble. And we had a large, favored meeting without any interruption."

These meetings closed my labor and exercise in the gospel to Friends and others in the Yearly Meetings of Philadelphia, Baltimore, Ohio, Indiana, and New York, as expressed in a certificate of unity and concurrence, given me by the Monthly Meeting of Jericho, and Quarterly Meeting of Westbury.

From the latter meeting, we proceeded the next day directly to New York, where we arrived on Fourth Day evening.

The day after we attended Friends Meeting at Hester Street, it being their usual meeting day. And a marriage being consummated at the close of it, it was larger than usual, as many of the neighboring inhabitants attended. Way opened for me to declare the Truth among them – to the peace of my own mind, and to the mutual comfort and encouragement of the upright in heart.

I rested here until First Day and attended Friends Meeting at Rose Street in the morning and that held at Hester Street in the afternoon. They were both very large, solemn meetings.

On Second Day evening, I had an appointed meeting at Brooklyn – likewise a large and very favored season. In all of these meetings, I had free course in the openings of Truth to declare to these large, mixed

Smith's Clove (New York) Meetinghouse

assemblages many things concerning the kingdom of God and the only sure way by which an admittance into his kingdom of peace and joy may be obtained by the children of men.

The foregoing meetings were times of favor and as a seal from the hand of our Gracious and Never-failing Helper to the labor and travail which he has led me into and enabled me to perform for the promotion of his great and noble cause of Truth and Righteousness in the earth as set forth in the foregoing account, and not suffering any weapon formed against me to prosper. "This is the heritage of the servants of the Lord, and their righteousness is of me, saith the Lord."[1]

For all these unmerited favors and mercies, in deep humiliation my soul doth magnify the Lord,[2] and return thanksgiving and glory to his great and excellent name, for his mercy endureth forever.

On Third Day, we proceeded homeward and attended Westbury Monthly Meeting on Fourth Day on our way. After this I rode home and found my family well, to our mutual rejoicing. And we greeted each other with thankful hearts for the unmerited favor.

We traveled in this journey nearly fifteen hundred miles.

---

[1] Isaiah 54:17
[2] Luke 1:46

1830

> Elias Hicks returned home on November 18, 1829. Two months later, on Sunday, February 14, 1830, he suffered a stroke just after finishing a letter to his old Friend, Hugh Judge. He died in the evening of February 27. As in the printed edition of the Journal, the text of his final letter is included below.

Dear Hugh,

Thy very acceptable letter of the 22nd ultimo was duly received and was read with interest – tending to excite renewed sympathetic and mutual fellow-feeling, and brought to my remembrance the cheering salutation of the blessed Jesus, our holy and perfect pattern and example, whom we are bound to follow if we are his disciples by walking in the same path of self-denial and the cross which he trod to blessedness, "Be of good cheer, I have overcome the world." By which he assured his disciples that they – by walking in the same pathway of self-denial that he walked in – they would also overcome the world, as nothing has ever enabled any rational being in any age of the world to overcome the spirit of the world, which lieth in wickedness, but the cross of Christ.

Some may query, what is the cross of Christ? To these, I answer, it is the perfect law of God that was written on the tablet of his heart and on the heart of every rational creature in such indelible characters that all the power of mortals cannot erase nor obliterate. Neither is there any other power or means given or dispensed to the children of men, but this Inward Law and Light, by which the true and saving knowledge of God can be obtained. And by this Inward Law and Light, all will be either justified or condemned. And all will be made to know God for themselves and be left without excuse, agreeable to the prophecy of Jeremiah and the corroborating testimony of Jesus in his last counsel and commands to his disciples – to tarry at Jerusalem until they should receive power from on high[1] – assuring them that they should receive power when they had received the pouring forth of the Spirit upon them,[2] which would qualify them to bear witness of him in Judah, Jerusalem, Samaria, and to the uttermost parts of the earth.[3] That is, it would empower them to preach the gospel with the Holy Ghost sent down from heaven, which was verified in a marvelous manner on the day of Pentecost, when thousands

---

[1] Luke 24:49
[2] Joel 2:28-29 & Acts 2:17-18
[3] Acts 1:8

were converted to the Christian faith in one day.[1] By which, it is evident that nothing but this Inward Light and Law, as it is heeded and obeyed, ever did or ever can make a true and real Christian and child of God. And until the professors of Christianity agree to lay aside all their nonessentials in religion and rally to this unchangeable foundation and standard of truth, wars and fightings, confusion and error will prevail, and the angelic song cannot be heard in our land – that of, "Glory to God in the highest, and on earth peace and goodwill to men." But when all nations are made willing to make this Inward Law and Light the rule and standard of all their faith and works, then we shall be brought to know and believe alike – that there is but one Lord, one faith, and but one baptism – one God and Father that is above all, through all, and in all.[2] And then will those glorious and consoling prophecies recorded in the scriptures of truth be fulfilled. Isaiah the 2nd and 4th verse, "And he shall judge among the nations, and rebuke many people, and they shall beat their swords into ploughshares and their spears into pruning-hooks. Nation shall not lift up sword against nation, neither shall they learn war any more." Isaiah, chapter 11th, "The wolf also shall dwell with the lamb, and the leopard shall lie down with the kid, and the calf and the young lion and the fatling together, and a little child shall lead them. And the cow and the bear shall feed, their young ones shall lie down together. And the lion shall eat straw like the ox. And the suckling child shall play on the hole of the asp, and the weaned child shall put his hand on the cockatrice's den. They shall not hurt nor destroy in all my holy mountain, for the earth (that is our earthly tabernacles) shall be full of the knowledge of the Lord, as the waters cover the sea."[3]

These scripture testimonies give a true and correct description of the gospel state, and no rational being can be a real Christian and true disciple of Christ until he comes to know all these things verified in his own experience – as every man and woman has more or less of all those different animal propensities and passions in their animal nature. And these predominate and bear rule and are the source and fountain from whence all wars and every evil work proceed and will continue, so long as man remains in his first nature and is governed by his animal spirit and propensities – which constitutes the natural man, which Paul tells us receiveth not the things of the Spirit of God, for they are foolishness unto him, neither can he know them, because they are spiritually discerned.[4] This corroborates the declaration of Jesus to Nicodemus that except a man

---

[1] Acts 2:41
[2] Ephesians 4:5-6
[3] Isaiah 11:6-9
[4] 1 Corinthians 2:14

be born again, he cannot see the kingdom of God. For that which is born of the flesh is flesh, and that which is born of Spirit is spirit.[1] Here, Jesus assures us beyond all doubt that nothing but spirit can either see or enter into the kingdom of God. And this confirms Paul's doctrine that as many as are led by the Spirit of God are sons of God and joint heirs with Christ.[2]

And Jesus assures us by his declaration to his disciples (John, chapter the 14th, 16th and 17th verses), "If you love me, keep my commandments. And I will pray the Father and he shall give you another comforter that he may abide with you forever, even the Spirit of Truth whom the world cannot receive (that is, men and women in their natural state, who have not given up to be led by this Spirit of Truth that leads and guides into all truth), because they see him not, neither do they know him, but ye know him, for he dwelleth with you, and shall be in you."[3] And as thou gives up to be wholly led and guided by him, the new birth is brought forth in them. And they witness the truth of another testimony of Paul's, even that of being created anew in Christ Jesus unto good works, which God foreordained, that all his newborn children should walk in them and thereby show forth by their fruits[4] and good works that they were truly the children of God – born of his Spirit and taught of him, agreeable to the testimony of the prophet, that the children of the Lord are all taught of the Lord, and in righteousness established, and great is the peace of his children, and nothing can make them afraid that man can do unto them.[5]

As saith the prophet in his appeal to Jehovah, "Thou wilt keep them in perfect peace whose mind is stayed on thee, because he trusteth in thee." Therefore, let everyone that loves the Truth (for God is Truth), "Trust in the Lord forever, for in the Lord Jehovah is everlasting strength."

I write these things to thee not as though thou didst not know them, but as a witness to thy experience, as "Two is better than one … and a three-fold cord is not quickly broken."[6]

I will now draw to a close with just adding for thy encouragement, be of good cheer. For no new thing has happened to us,[7] for it has ever been the lot of the righteous to pass through many trials and tribulations in their passage to that glorious and everlasting, peaceful and happy abode, where all sorrow and sighing end[8] – the value of which is above all price.

---

[1] John 3:6
[2] Romans 8:14&17
[3] John 14:15-17
[4] Matthew 7:20
[5] Matthew 10:28
[6] Ecclesiastes 4:9&12
[7] Ecclesiastes 1:9
[8] Isaiah 35:10

For when we have given all we can give and suffered all we can suffer, yet it is below its true value, for thou knows that that which costs us nothing is scarcely worth having.

I will now conclude. And in the fullness of brotherly love and Christian fellowship, in which my family unites, to thee and thine, I subscribe, thy affectionate friend, as ever,

Elias Hicks

Please to present my love to all Friends.

Quaker Structure & Terminology

Structure

Indulged Meeting: a meeting, subordinate to a monthly meeting, that differs from a preparative meeting in that it meets only for worship and does not prepare agenda items for the monthly business meeting.

Meeting for Discipline (also referred to as a "business meeting," "meeting of discipline," or "monthly meeting"): a meeting to conduct business. Only members were allowed to attend business meetings. Note that there were separate meetings for men and women.

Meeting for Sufferings: originally, a committee of London Yearly Meeting established to address the costs of persecution (monetary or otherwise), that is, to assist Friends who suffered on account of their faith. Over time, it evolved into an executive committee for the yearly meeting. The name was adopted by other yearly meetings for their executive committees.

Meeting for Worship (also, "meeting of worship"): A worship service performed in the manner of Friends. At this time, all Friends meetings were unprogrammed. The congregation gathered at the designated time in silence. If one or more members felt called by God to offer ministry, he or she would do so. There were normally three meetings for worship in a week, two on Sunday – a forenoon meeting in the morning and an afternoon meeting in the late afternoon or early evening – and a midweek meeting on Wednesday or Thursday evening.

Men and women sat separately during meetings for worship – although with the meetinghouse partitions raised so that people could hear ministry offered by either gender. The ministers and elders sat on raised benches that faced the rest of the congregation with the elders sitting above the ministers. The seats on the central aisle of these facing benches were reserved for the most senior members.

Meeting of Ministers and Elders (also, "Select Meeting"): all ministers and elders from a quarterly or yearly meeting met together just before the corresponding meeting for discipline. These meetings were not open to all, but ministers and elders traveling with a minute from their home meeting were welcome. The Quarterly Meeting was also referred to as the Preparative Meeting of Ministers and Elders, since it prepared business for consideration by the corresponding meeting at the yearly meeting level.

Quaker Structure & Terminology 455

Monthly Meeting: A regional collection of preparative and indulged meetings that came together once a month (hence the name) for worship, business, and mutual support. Note that although a monthly meeting may have the same name as one of its particular meetings, this conferred no special status on that meeting. It remained just one of the constituent particular meetings. The site of the monthly gathering might rotate among some of its particular meetings. Monthly Meetings were subordinate to Quarterly Meetings. The term was used interchangeably to refer to the collection of particular meetings and the monthly gatherings to conduct business. Sometimes it was referred to simply as a "monthly."

Particular Meeting: a local congregation, whether an indulged meeting or a preparative meeting.

Preparative Meeting: A local congregation, subordinate to a Monthly Meeting, that met weekly for worship and once a month to prepare business (hence the name) to be placed before the monthly meeting. Sometimes referred to simply as a "preparative."

Quarterly Meeting: A regional grouping of monthly meetings that met together once each three months or quarter of the year (hence, the name) for worship, business, and mutual support. Although a quarter may have the same name as one of its monthly meetings, the site of the quarterly meeting might rotate among some its particular meetings. Quarterly Meetings were subordinate to Yearly Meetings. The name was used interchangeably to refer to the collection of monthly meetings and the quarterly gatherings to conduct business. Sometimes referred to simply as a "quarter" or a "quarterly."

Select Meeting: A meeting that is not open to all. Most often, this term is used to refer to Meetings of Ministers and Elders, but it could also be used to describe a business meeting, since these were open only to members, or to a meeting for worship that was specially called for members only.

Yearly Meeting: A regional group of quarterly meetings that met together annually (hence the name) for worship, business, and mutual support. The name was used interchangeably to refer to the collection of subordinate meetings and the annual business sessions. Each yearly meeting was independent of the others, although London and Philadelphia enjoyed an extra degree of prestige.

Selected Terms

Appear in the line of the ministry: speak in meeting for worship

Appointed meeting: not a regularly scheduled meeting, often scheduled for a traveling minister. These may be held at a Friends Meetinghouse, a private house, or in a public building. (Also, a "meeting by appointment")

Birthright member: a person whose parents were members of the Religious Society of Friends when he or she was born and who is therefore automatically also a member

Book of Discipline: originally, these were collections of extracts from the minutes of a yearly meeting's annual business sessions. Following the close of the meeting, an extract of the minutes was prepared and copies were sent to each meeting. Locally, these were copied into a "Book of Extracts." Extracts from the minutes of the quarterly meeting or the monthly meeting might also be included. Over time, these books became unwieldy and errors likely crept in. By the early nineteenth century, they had been replaced in each yearly meeting by a printed book, organized by topics. This evolved from a compilation of extracted minutes to a collection of statements on each topic that were periodically reviewed and revised by the yearly meeting. (Also referred to simply as the "discipline.")

Clerk: There were no paid staff in Friends meetings. The clerk was a member appointed for a term to preside at business meetings. In principle, this conferred no special status on the person asked to serve, but in practice, clerks exercised a great deal of influence in most meetings. Particularly skilled individuals would often continue in the position for many years.

Day of Visitation: According to early Friends, each person faced a choice between spiritual life and death at a single, particular point in his or her life. The outcome was either to choose God and salvation or eternal damnation. Later Friends (including Hicks) believed that God offered this opportunity repeatedly throughout each person's life.

Discipline: the accepted manner of conduct among Friends; a synonym for "discipleship;" also sometimes used as a short form of the "Book of Discipline."

Elder: a man or woman appointed by a monthly meeting with the concurrence of the quarterly meeting to take responsibility for the spiritual condition of the meeting. This included overseeing the ministry offered during meeting for worship, nurturing the spiritual growth of members (especially the youth), and caring for the ministers. As a general practice, elders did not speak in meetings for worship. (Note: A person could not serve as both a minister and an elder.)

Epistle: usually a letter sent by a yearly meeting. Annually, each yearly meeting sent general greetings to the other yearly meetings and to its subordinate meetings. Sometimes, it also sent a separate letter to subordinate meetings containing queries or giving direction.

Extracts or Book of Extracts: prior to the publication of books of discipline or of annual minutes, the formal minutes adopted by superior meetings were copied and these extracts were sent to each subordinate meeting. These were copied into a book which was used for guidance by local congregations.

First sitting: a meeting for worship preceding a business meeting

Go out in marriage: marry someone who was not a Quaker and, consequently, lose membership among Friends.

Indiscrete appearance: offer inappropriate vocal ministry

Lose one's right: disowned; lose membership in the Society of Friends

Meetinghouse: Friends considered "church" to properly refer only to the people of God, not to any physical structure, so their buildings were called by this name. Other denominations buildings also might be called meetinghouses.

Meetinghouses had separate men's and women's sides, with a movable partition between them. For worship, the partition was raised to allow Friends on both sides to hear ministry offered on either side. The partition remained open for a period of worship before business meetings, but was lowered when business commenced, to allow men and women to conduct their business separately.

Member by Convincement or Convinced Friend: a person who becomes a member of the Religious Society of Friends by their own application

Minister: This was an unpaid position among Friends, but one that required formal acknowledgment. When a local meeting recognized that a man or woman had a gift in vocal ministry and the quarterly meeting concurred, this was formally acknowledged by a monthly meeting.

Ministering Friend: A man or woman traveling in the ministry.

Minute: A formal decision made by a business meeting. These were written during the business meeting in a bound, handwritten minute book.

Names for Days and Months: Friends traditionally did not use the common names for the days of the week and months of the year, since some of these names originally honored pagan deities. These were, instead, referred to by only by number (e.g., Thursday or Thor's Day was called Fifth Day and March, which was named for Mars, the Roman god of war, was called Third Month.).

Open the way (also, "way opening" or "way opened"): something becomes possible (e.g., offering ministry in a meeting for worship or undertaking travel in the ministry) by God's removal of a spiritual impediment or "stop."

Opportunity: a chance to worship God in the manner of Friends. These frequently occurred in a home when Quaker ministers or elders visited.

Overseer: a person appointed by the monthly meeting to "exercise a vigilant and tender care over their fellow members; that if anything repugnant to the harmony and good order of the society appears among them, it may be timely attended to and not neglected" (from the 1806 *Rules of Discipline of the Yearly Meeting of Friends held in Philadelphia*). While the Elders were responsible for the spiritual condition of the meeting, the overseers were concerned with ordinary behavior.

People without: people not within the Society of Friends

Plainness: the traditional Quaker set of clothes, also called plain clothes

Public Meeting: A meeting for worship that is open to all.

Queries: Each yearly meeting had a set of questions that were answered by its subordinate meetings annually. Each preparative meeting sent its answers to the monthly meeting. The monthly meeting, in turn wrote summary answers that were forwarded to the quarterly meeting. The answers from each quarter were read at the annual sessions of the yearly meeting. Originally, these were used to collect practical information (births, deaths, etc.), but over time began to inquire into the spiritual state of the meeting as well. The wording of the queries changed rarely and the answers in many cases were repeated word-for-word.

Right reason: this is a term that figures prominently in the writings of some early Friends. In the seventeenth century, the mind was understood to be a property of the soul and right reason referred to thinking under divine guidance, as opposed to ordinary reasoning. Although Hicks seems to use the term in the same way, it is not clear that he recognizes the distinction. He may mean only "correct or accurate reasoning" rather than "divinely guided reasoning."

Select Quarterly Meeting: the Meeting of Ministers and Elders from all monthly meetings in a quarterly meeting.

Select: when applied to an individual, a minister or elder. When applied to a meeting, one that is open only to members of the Religious Society of Friends.

Stop: a spiritual obstacle to undertaking an action.

Travel in the ministry: when a recognized minister felt called to travel for religious purposes.

Travel minute: If a minister wished to travel in the ministry outside the territory of his or her home quarterly meeting, he or she would ask for permission from the monthly meeting and, if traveling outside the home yearly meeting, from the quarterly meeting before proceeding. Meeting approval would be in the form of a minute, signed by the meeting clerks indicating the meeting's approval of the undertaking. During the journey, those visited endorsed the minute, often in a note on the back of the page, expressing their approval or disapproval. On completion of the journey, the minute was returned to the minister's home meeting and retained in the meeting records.

Annotated Word & Phrase List

Abase: lower in rank or honor
Abasedness: being in a low, humble or downcast state
Abide: wait patiently
Abode: past tense of abide
Abortive: doomed to fail
Abound: to have to overflowing
Abrogate: formally abolish
Acquit: surrender any claim on
Actuate: inspire or enliven; spur to action
Actuated: active
Admiration: astonishment
Admire: surprise or amaze
Admit: assume for the sake of argument
Advent: Jesus' coming into the world
Allow: believe
Ardent liquor: distilled liquor
Apartment: an area within a building that is allocated to a particular group
Apoplectic fit: probably a cerebral hemorrhage
Apostasy: falling away from true religion
Appear largely: speak at length
Appearance: presentation of vocal ministry
Apprise: inform
Armor: weapons
Arrest: remain fixed in consideration of a subject
Ascription: giving credit
Assay: attempt
Auditory: audience
Avenue: aisle; route for access
Aver: declare to be true
Avidity: eagerness and greed
Awakening: arousing
Balk: shirk or evade
Baptism: a spiritual trial
Baptize: severely tested or tried
Beck: the slightest indication of a command, e.g., a nod
Becoming: admirable; suitable or fitting
Beds of ease: complacence and self-indulgence
Besure: surely

Bid fair: seem likely
Blood on their heads: hold accountable for
Bore: past tense of bear, in this case meaning the British army controlled Long Island
Borrowed: not our own, i.e., belonging to God
Bounden: under legal or moral obligation
Brave: praiseworthy
Bring down: humbled
By dint of: through persistence
Calumniate: falsely and maliciously accuse of criminal or disreputable behavior
Carnal: worldly
Carper: a fault-finder
Caviling: a frivolous objection
Center down: turn inward and focus spiritually
Chaise: a light, horse-drawn carriage
Chargeable: for a charge, i.e., for pay
Church militant: the Church on earth considered as warring against the powers of evil
Circumstanced: in the condition of
Clear: free of a spiritual obligation
Commissary: An officer in charge of the supply of food, stores, and transport, for a body of soldiers
Compassionate: regard or treat with compassion
Condescension: graciousness and consideration
Conduct: behave
Confession: a public affirmation of a statement of faith or a creed
Confusion of face: shame
Confusion: ruin or perdition
Connections: family and close friends
Consanguinity: descended from a common ancestor
Consolatory: bringing consolation
Constrain: compel
Contrariwise: on the contrary
Conversation: manner of conducting oneself in the world
Converse: conversation
Conviction: guilt
Convince: convict or prove guilty
Countenance: favor or patronage

Crook: a shepherd's staff
Cross: opposed or contrary to
Crowning: concluding
Cumber: distress or encumber
Declension: decline or degeneration
Deism: a belief in the existence of God combined with a rejection of revealed religion
Delightsome: delightful
Department: a part of a whole
Dependent being: one that is subordinate to and dependent on God
Derive: come; communicate
Derogatory to: takes away from
Design: purpose or intention
Diadem: crown or symbol of honor
Diffusion: outpouring or spreading widely
Dignified: stately, noble, majestic
Dilatory: procrastinating
Disannul: cancel or make null and void
Discharge faithfully: to offer appropriate vocal ministry
Disinterested: unbiased by self-interest, free of self-seeking
Distrain: the seizure of goods or money by the state in recompense for unpaid taxes
Divers: various
Doctor of physic: physician
Draft: a sense of duty
Drift: natural course
Drone: a male honeybee, which does not work, but only serves to impregnate the queen
Dry shod: with dry shoes
Dwarfishness: stunted development
Earnest: a foretaste or promise of something to be received in abundance in the future
Ebenezer: a memorial stone set up by the prophet Samuel
Ecstasy: anxiety and fear
Effective: powerful in its effect on people
Ejaculation: a short prayer
Elect: selected for its excellence
Election: salvation
Elementary: composed of elements or matter

Embalm: preserve in sweet and honored memory
Embassy: the mission of a person sent to represent a sovereign
End: purpose
Endue: endow with qualities
Ensample: example
Entrance: permission or allowance to enter one's mind; positive influence
Essay: first draft
Essential: existing, real, or actual
Establish: found or base; sustain and support
Example to silence: remain silent in meeting for worship
Excite: stir up or set in motion
Exculpate: clear from guilt or blame
Exercised: active or involved; troubled
Experimental: based on direct, personal experience rather than mere testimony or conjecture
Expostulate: to plainly demonstrate in a friendly manner
Express exercise: offer ministry
Felicity: state of happiness
Figure: an imperfect prefiguration of a corresponding perfect thing that is still to come. To Hicks, it is an act, ceremony, or person in the Old Testament that prefigures an event, object, or person revealed in the New Testament. (See also, Type and Shadow)
Fit: make suitable or proper
Foreordination: predestination
Forward: mature
Forwardness: presumptuousness
Free course: spread rapidly
Fresh: unaffected by the passage of time
Friendly: as used by Hicks, "friendly" refers to people who were not members of the Society of Friends, but were, in his opinion, sympathetic to its beliefs
Froward: perverse, difficult, hard to please
Galled: sore from chaffing
Gallery: usually, this refers to the balcony that was found in many Quaker meetinghouses. In the one use in this work, Hicks is clearly referring to the raised benches at the front of the meeting room, facing the congregation, on which the ministers and elders sat during meetings
Gender: engender, produce
Generality: people in general

Germ: that from which a thing will emerge
Gloss: An interpretation or explanation of a text
Gooding: the action of doing good
Gravel: kidney stones
Great chain of nature: an ordered sequence of all beings, starting with God and extending to the "lowest creature." It was a way of understanding and explaining the order of the natural world that dates back at least to the classical Greek philosophers.
Guard: keep safe from
Guarded education: education in Friends Schools
Halt: vacillate
Hand: a hired laborer
Hank: hanker or desire
Hardiness: audacity
Hardy: bold or audacious
Helpmeet: a suitable helper, usually applied to a spouse
High day: a day of special solemnity
Humiliated: humble
Humor: whim
Ideal: arising from one's own ideas
Imbrue: stain or defile
Import: communicate
Importunity: inappropriate suggestion
Impotent: physically weak or disabled
Impress: impression
Impression: attack or assault
Impressive: inspiring deep feelings
Imputed righteousness: the doctrine (rejected by Friends) that people are considered to be righteous (i.e., righteousness is imputed to them) due to Christ's atoning death, while remaining sinners
Inadmissible: not to be considered
Income: coming in of a divine influence
Incumbency: duty or necessity
Indifferent: not good or having no particular value
Indubitable: impossible to doubt
Ineffable: indescribable and inexpressible
Infelicity: a state of unhappiness and misfortune
Intelligencer: one who conveys information
Intervene: hinder

Inutility: uselessness
Invention: something contrived by the human mind
Jostle: disturb or upset
Keep down: humbly attend to
Large: lengthy and comprehensive
Largely: at length and in detail
Lay: place in a grave or bury
Leading (also, a "motion"): a prompting from God
Leavening: debase a pure material by mixing in corrupt matter
Lengthen out: extended, i.e., not over
Let up: give up
Liable: subject to the possibility of doing or undergoing something undesirable
Light, lightness: lack of seriousness
Line: work
Lists: a place of combat
Lively: convincing
Lopped: pruned
Lot: place or share
Low and little: humble
Low: vulgar, weak, or degenerate
Main: mainland
Make way with self: commit suicide
Malignity: wicked hatred
Maxim: a guiding principle for personal conduct
Medium: course of action; intermediary
Meet: appropriate, suitable, or proper
Melioration: amelioration or improvement
Memento: a reminder, warning, or hint as to future events
Memorial: an aid to memory; the memory of someone or something
Mite: something small and insignificant
Mixture: mixing in incompatible elements
Moment: importance
Moral: based on natural religion or social principles
Mortification: gangrene
Motion (also, a "leading"): a prompting from God
Murmuring: inarticulate, muttered complaints
Negative part: the dissenting or destructive part

Nicholites: a sect founded in the 1760s by Joseph Nichols (ca. 1730-ca. 1775) in Delaware and Maryland. He appears to have been influenced to some extent by John Woolman. Many Nicholites affiliated with Friends in the early 19th century and the sect disappeared as an independent body.

No respecter of persons: shows no partiality between people – from Acts 10:34

Original: origin

Outside: outward

Overshadow: shelter and protect

Pale-faced Messenger: Death's messenger

Partial: biased or favoring one over another, i.e., not impartial – in this case, favoring humans over other creatures

Pathetic: pitiable or causing deep sadness

Pompous: characterized by pomp or a stately show

Prescience: foreknowledge

Pretend: claim or assert

Profession: to claim membership

Professor: one who claims membership in a religious body

Promiscuous: mixed, usually it means containing both men and women, but it can also mean people of various religious denominations

Proneness: tendency

Pronery: disposition

Provender: feed or fodder

Proving: test

Quicken: to give or restore life

Rack: pull out of shape

Ran out and got scattered: a flock is not following its shepherd's lead – an allusion to Christ as our shepherd

Reaching: mentally or spiritually stretching

Rebound: be thrown back or rejected

Recruit: regain one's health

Recur: move back or return to

Redound: to cast honor or blame

Reduce: subjugate to the will of God

Rehearse: reiterate

Remain quiet: be left alone

Repine: to feel discontented or dissatisfied

Reprehension: rebuke

Reprobation: shame or censure; the opposite of election; rejected by God and condemned to eternal damnation
Reproof: disgrace or reproach
Requester: a person who makes a request
Requisition: A demand, usually made by a creditor that a debt be paid, or an obligation fulfilled
Reward: what one deserves, either good or bad
Rod: 16.5 feet
Rotation: recurring succession of duties
Rubbage: rubbish
Rumor: talk of a distinguished person or of a laudatory nature
Run before one's gift: get ahead of the leading of the Holy Spirit
Sanguinary: bloody
Savoring: pleasing
Scythe and cradle: a tool used to cut hay by hand
Season: this term can be used to refer to a variety of periods of time
Second: support and encourage
Secret: private, unseen
Seek him early: seek God diligently or earnestly
Selah: A Hebrew word of uncertain meaning that occurs at the end of a line in some psalms
Sensible: aware; obvious or recognizable; palpable, something that can be felt
Separate: set apart for a particular purpose; disown
Set home: made clear and irrefutable
Settle down in a form: take on only the appearance of worship
Settlement: becoming settled in beliefs
Several: separate and distinct
Shadow: an imperfect or insubstantial thing that foreshadows a corresponding reality or "substance." (See also, Figure and Type)
Shake off: give up the use of
Shed: scatter
Shock of palsy: stroke
Shrewd: severe, harsh, or stern
Sign: an outward representation that symbolizes an inward, spiritual reality
Signal: remarkable, significant
Sittings: sessions
Slide along: let slide or give insufficient attention to
Slunk: a past tense of slink, meaning to move in a sneaky way

Small: insignificant
Solid: sober-minded
Soliloquy: talking to oneself
Sophistical: using intentionally deceptive arguments
Specious: pleasing or beautiful
Standing out: continued resistance
Stay: focus; reliance
Stock: farm animals
Stop: a spiritual obstacle to undertaking an action
Store: storage space
Straitened: constrained
Strip: expose one's true character or condition
Subjoin: add a related element
Substance: a spiritual reality. The opposite of a shadow
Suffer: allow
Suit: prosecution
Superadd: add on top of what has already been added
Surfeiting: indulged to excess
Temporals: temporal matters
Tenant at will: one who holds or possesses property solely at the pleasure of the lessor
Tender: become gentle, contrite, and compassionate
Tenement: building
Thereaway: in those parts
Thronged: crowded
Thrust: collision
Tidings: news
Travail: toil, hardship, suffering
Try: test
Turpitude: wickedness
Type out: prefigure or foreshadow as a type, i.e., an imperfect symbol of a perfect anti-type. (See also, Figure and Shadow)
Typical: characteristic of a type which will be fulfilled in an antitype
Uncountable: unaccountable or inexplicable
Unfold: explain
Use of: being used to
Visitation: a visit by God
Viz: that is
Vouch: testify to

Vouchsafe: bestow
Waste: melt away
Way-mark: a guide to travelers
Weight, weighty: seriousness
Will-less: giving up one's own desires and surrendering one's will to God
Will-worship: Will-worship: putting one's own will or desires ahead of God's. In this instance, adopting forms of worship that are determined by one's own preferences, rather than worshiping according to the divine will
Without a helm: lacking any means to steer or control, rudderless
Without: outside, i.e., the opposite of "within;" unless
Woe: distress or misfortune
Wonderful: something that caused wonder or astonishment
Wreck: act of destruction
Wrest: take by force
Wrought: formed or fashioned
Yield: surrender

Selected People Mentioned

Elisha Bates (1781-1861) was a seventh-generation Friend. Born in Virginia, he married Sarah Harrison in 1803 and moved with his in-laws to Mount Pleasant, Ohio in 1816, where he was a printer and abolitionist newspaper publisher. He was clerk of Virginia Yearly Meeting from 1813 to 1816, and of Ohio Yearly Meeting several times between 1818 and 1831 (but not at the time of the separations). Strongly evangelical, he sided with the Orthodox branch of the society, contributing to the acrimony prior to the separations by the publication in 1825 of *The Doctrines of Friends*, which stressed theological similarities between Friends and other Christians. He traveled in the ministry, notably to England in 1832-34 and again two years later. In 1836, he left Friends, was baptized, and joined the Methodists, but late in life attended Friends meetings. He is interred in the Quaker burial ground at Mount Pleasant, Ohio.

Samuel Bownas (1676–1753) was an English travelling minister and a writer. He is best known for writing *A Description of the Qualifications Necessary to a Gospel Minister*, first printed in 1750. In 1696, his life was changed when Anne Wilson challenged him in a meeting for worship, saying, "A traditional Quaker, thou comest to meeting as thou went from it and goes from it as thou came to it, but art no better for thy coming. What wilt thou do in the end?" In response, he felt called to change his life. At twenty-two, he undertook his first travels in the ministry. In 1702, he left England and journeyed to the American colonies. Wherever he went he was followed by George Keith, a former Friend who had been sent by the Church of England to convert Quakers in the colonies. At Hempstead, on November 21, 1702, Bownas preached in the home of Thomas Pearsall in violation of New York law. Keith, finding he could silence Bownas no other way, informed the authorities. As a result, Bownas was arrested on November 29. He was ordered to post an exorbitant bail, but replied that he would give no bail, not even were it reduced to three half-pence. Justice Whitehead expressed his willingness to provide the bail, but Bownas rejected the offer and was sent to prison for three months. In February 1703, a grand jury was empanelled, which refused to indict him. Thomas Hicks, a Justice of the Common Pleas Court, visited Bownas in prison and comforted him to the best of his ability. Despite his many friends, however, Bownas remained in close confinement until October when he was finally discharged from custody.

Anna Braithwaite (1788-1859) was an English Evangelical Friend. She was clerk of the London Yearly Meeting Women's Meeting in 1819 and 1821-23. She traveled widely in the ministry in England, Ireland, and the United States, coming to America in 1823-24, 1825, and 1827, twice accompanied by her husband, Isaac. The Braithwaites visited with Hicks in January and March 1824. An account of Anna's conversation with Hicks was published in 1825 as evidence of Hicks' theological unsoundness, setting off a lengthy pamphlet war. Becoming increasingly evangelistic and fundamentalist, eventually she became a leader among the Beaconites, a group of about four hundred who withdrew from London Yearly Meeting, rejecting the Inward Light as a delusion. Her descendants played prominent roles in London Yearly Meeting over the next century.

George Churchman (1730-1814) was the son of John Churchman, an important leaders in the mid-eighteenth century Quaker reform movement. He was among the founders of the Westtown School.

Elizabeth Coggeshall (1770-1851) was born in Newport, Rhode Island. and married Caleb Coggeshall in 1793. She was acknowledged as a minister in 1796 and a year later felt a calling to travel in the ministry to England, Ireland, and on the Continent. She left in 1798 as companion to Hannah Barnard, whose views on scripture led to disownment. Barnard was sent home in 1800, but Coggeshall continued her mission for another year. She traveled extensively in the ministry and is said to have visited every meeting in North America. She returned to Europe in 1814-15. Lucretia Mott reported that Coggeshall's ministry deeply affected her spiritual development. In the separations, Coggeshall allied with the Orthodox branch.

John Comly (1773-1850) was a leader among Hicksite Friends. A teacher and schoolmaster at Friends schools in the Philadelphia area, he resigned in 1815 to devote himself to farming and extensive travel in the ministry in the United States. Like Hicks, Comly was a quietist – distrusting banks, the development of canals, and the growth of reform societies. He served as assistant clerk of Philadelphia Yearly Meeting in 1827 and was the Hicksite candidate to become clerk. When this effort failed, he advocated a temporary separation to allow tempers to cool. He then served as clerk of the Hicksite men's meeting, while his wife clerked the women's meeting. From 1831 to 1839, he published

Friends Miscellany with his brother, Isaac, and produced a new edition of the *Journal of John Woolman* in 1837.

Pliny Earle (December 17, 1762 – November 19, 1832) was a Quaker inventor who made wool and cotton carding machines. After retiring, he devoted his time principally to literary work, publishing *An Essay on Penal Law*, *An Essay on the Rights of States to Alter and to Annul their Charters*, *A Treatise on Railroads and Internal Communications*, and *A Life of Benjamin Lundy*.

Edward Garrigues (1756-1845) was a carpenter and clerk of a yearly meeting committee appointed to visit the poor. He kept a diary during the 1798 Philadelphia Yellow Fever Epidemic which provides a description of Quaker activities, meetings, social, and domestic events.

Stephen Haight (1782-1841) of Monkton, Vermont was not a Quaker. He served for many years in the state legislature, was a sheriff, and a judge of the county court. He died on the January 12, 1841 in Washington, DC, while holding the office of sergeant-at-arms in the Senate of the United States.

Edward Hicks (1780-1849), a second cousin of Elias Hicks, is best known as the painter of "The Peaceable Kingdom" series. When his father was exiled during the Revolutionary War, Hicks was taken in by Elizabeth and David Twining, a Quaker family in Bucks County. He joined Friends in 1803, was recognized as a minister in 1810, and began to travel in the ministry in 1813. Edward Hicks earned his living as a coach and sign painter, not as an artist (an occupation that, as a quietist, he would have seen as a distraction from a spiritual life). He aligned with the Hicksites in the separations, but later was critical of their Unitarian, anti-scriptural, and liberal tendencies.

Isaac Hicks (1767-1820) was Valentine Hick's brother and a native of Westbury. He moved to New York City at 22 and became a very wealthy merchant, eventually dealing principally in cotton, a slave product. This may have troubled his conscience – in 1805, he retired and devoted the rest of his life to service in the Society of Friends. He was a frequent traveling companion of Elias Hicks (who made use of his extensive library) and others. His death is described in the entry (above) for 10th of 1st month 1820.

Valentine Hicks (1784-1850) was a cousin of Elias Hicks and husband of Elias' daughter, Abigail. As a young man, he moved to New York City and accumulated a fortune of $50,000. After ten years, he retired to Jericho. While in the city, he was among the leaders of the Society for

Establishing a Free School, a movement that later became the public school system. He is reported to have been active in assisting runaway slaves and their house may have been a station on the Underground Railroad. In 1837, he was elected president of the Long Island Railroad – an activity that would have distressed his father-in-law.

Whitehead Hicks (1772-1843) was a cousin of Elias Hicks and a successful merchant, who moved to New York City in 1796, where he made a fortune in the lumber business and as a builder. (Note: this is not the Whitehead Hicks who served as the last royal mayor of New York City during the Revolutionary War).

Gerard T. Hopkins served as secretary of Baltimore Yearly Meeting of Friends and as a member of its Committee on Indian Affairs. In 1804, he was part of a yearly meeting delegation that traveled to Fort Wayne in the Indian country to instruct the natives in "agriculture and other useful knowledge." He frequently hosted Elias Hicks in Baltimore, but aligned with the Orthodox in the separations.

Priscilla Hunt (1786-1859) was born Priscilla Coffin in North Carolina. She married into the prominent Quaker Hunt family, but her husband died after two years in 1813. The next year, she and her daughter moved to Indiana, where she developed into a mesmerizing preacher. She traveled in the ministry, but was not welcomed by the Orthodox leadership of Philadelphia, where in 1823, she told of a vision of the society being undermined by the work of some within it and only a remnant remaining faithful. She sided with the Hicksites in the separations. In her travels, she visited every existing meeting.

William Jackson (1746-1834) was a Quaker preacher, born in London Grove, Pennsylvania. He first appeared in the ministry in 1775. After his marriage to Hannah in 1778, he moved to Westbury, his wife's home, but returned with her to Pennsylvania in 1790. In 1802, he visited Great Britain and Ireland on a religious mission. Latter in life, he attended the yearly meetings of Maryland, Virginia, Philadelphia, New York, and New England. He was an impressive, though not a frequent, preacher, and a strong advocate of frugal living and primitive simplicity in attire and furniture. He sided with the Orthodox in the separations, but advocated an amicable relationship in his monthly meeting after it split.

George Keith (1638-1716) was raised a Presbyterian, but joined Friends in 1663. A friend of the early Quaker theologian, Robert Barclay, he quickly became a leader among Friends, first in Scotland, then in

England and the American colonies. He was disowned in 1692 and started a new body called the Christian Quakers. In 1700, he joined the Church of England and in 1702 was ordained a priest. He returned to the colonies to convert dissenters and Quakers, but without much success. While in America, he prosecuted Samuel Bownas for making statements critical of the Church of England, resulting in Bownas' lengthy imprisonment.

Emmor Kimber (1775-1850) was a Quaker teacher who left Westtown School in 1818 to establish the French Creek Boarding School for Girls in Kimberton, Pennsylvania. He and his 4 daughters taught at and ran the school until 1848. It became known as a model for progressive education which drew students from great distances. Kimber was an entrepreneur, once owning all the buildings and businesses at the Kimberton crossroads. He was involved in many broader enterprises, including the development of the Reading Railroad. He was also an abolitionist, operating a stop on the Underground Railroad under the school. In 1820, facing bankruptcy, Kimber asked Philadelphia Yearly Meeting to form a committee to meet with him and his creditors. The meeting refused and he was disowned for extending his trade beyond his ability to manage. Hicks stayed in his house two years later and Kimber was accepted as a member by the Hicksites following the separations.

Isaac Martin (1791-1823) was an itinerant Quaker preacher from Rahway. Martin visited Friends meetings in New Jersey and the surrounding states and described these visits in *A Journal of the Life, Travels, Labours, and Religious Exercises of Isaac Martin, Late of Rahway, in East Jersey, Deceased.*

Mary Naftel (1756-1820) was born in Cornwall, England and joyfully traveled in the ministry in England, Scotland, Ireland, the Isle of Man, and the United States. Contrary to his opinion of many of the traveling English Friends, Hicks seems to have admired her.

Thomas Paine (1737-1809) is counted among the heroes of the American Revolution as the author of *Common Sense*, but he was loathed by Friends. Born into an English Quaker family and educated in Quaker schools, Paine abandoned the society and frequently attacked it in print. A critic who is an outsider can be dismissed as misinformed or benighted, but a turncoat is one who learned the Truth and threw it away. Paine's later work, *The Age of Reason*, advocated deism and broadly attacked Christian doctrines.

Selected People Mentioned 475

William Poole (1764-1829) was Elias Hicks' closes confidant and most frequent correspondent. Poole was very active in Wilmington, Delaware business, civic, and political affairs. He was an organizer of the Library Company of Wilmington, an officer and trustee of Wilmington Academy, a member of the Wilmington Turnpike Company, and the first President of the Bank of Wilmington and Brandywine. In marked contrast to Hicks, he was a longtime Abolition Society member. Even more remarkable is his political service as an Assistant Burgess of Wilmington in 1794-1796, 1802, and 1804, and as a member of the Delaware General Assembly in 1822. He was a member of the Meeting for Ministers and Elders and served on the Meeting for Sufferings of Philadelphia Yearly Meeting. He sided with the Hicksites in the separations.

William Rickman (1745-1839) was born in England, but lived in New York from 1749 to 1785. He traveled among Friends in Britain, Ireland, and France. In 1818, he accompanied Hannah Field (who was returning to the United States from travels in the ministry in England) and visited Quaker meetings in the United States.

Rowland Thomas Robinson (1796-1879) was the son of Thomas and Jemima Robinson. As a young man, Rowland T. Robinson was sent to the Quaker boarding school at Nine Partners, New York, where he met his future wife, Rachel Gilpin. They married in 1820. Although he helped his father operate the family mills and sheep farm, Rowland's true calling was as a Garrisonian abolitionist and radical reformer. He was active in anti-slavery societies on the local and national levels, and harbored many fugitive slaves. In addition, he was a temperance activist, campaigned against capital punishment, and investigated the best methods of pauper relief.

Thomas Richardson Robinson (1761-1851) and **Jemima Fish Robinson** (1761-1846) were raised in wealthy and well-established Newport, Rhode Island Quaker families. They moved their young family to the wilds of Ferrisburg, Vermont, in 1793 and purchased Rokeby, home to their descendents into the twentieth century. Thomas opened saw and grist mills on the Lewis Creek and in 1810 purchased some of the first Merino sheep to be imported into the United States. This set Rokeby on the path to distinction as one of the largest sheep farms in the region.

Samuel Rodman (1753-1835) was a whaling merchant. Remarkably, he served his apprenticeship with Abraham Riveira, a successful Jewish merchant in Newport, Rhode Island. In the 1780s and 1790s, his business interests diversified. He was one of the first investors in cotton mills in Massachusetts and was active in banking. In 1808-10 and 1814, he served as clerk of New England Yearly Meeting and as clerk of the yearly meeting's Meeting for Sufferings in 1802-22. He became involved with the "New Lights," a liberal movement within the Society of Friends. In 1823, much of this group resigned, joining the Unitarians. He was Thomas Rotch's brother-in-law.

Thomas Rotch (1767-1823) was active in whaling and shipping in Nantucket and New Bedford, Massachusetts from 1790 to 1801; in farming, sheep-raising and woolen manufacture in Hartford, Connecticut from 1801 to 1811; and laying out and settling of the town of Kendal (now Massillon), Ohio in 1811 – establishing farming, sheep-raising, and manufacturing there. He was Samuel Rodman's brother-in-law.

Henry Scudder (1742-1822) was not a Quaker. He served as spy and an irregular soldier (guerilla) for the American army in the Revolutionary War, staging raids on Long Island from a base in Connecticut. He served in the New York Assembly from 1788 to 1792 and was a member of the convention that framed the New York State Constitution.

Gideon Seaman (c. 1744-1837) was an elder of Westbury Monthly Meeting. He accompanied Elias Hicks on his visit to Purchase Quarterly Meeting in 1813, but frequently labored with Hicks over doctrinal issues before the separations. Joining the Orthodox in 1827, he was the clerk of the Orthodox meeting that ordered Hicks to return from his journey to Ohio in 1828 and disowned Hicks the following year. His daughter, Rachel, married Elias Hicks' nephew, Abraham Hicks, and became a prominent Hicksite minister.

Thomas Shillitoe (1754-1836) was born into an Anglican family in London, England. By 1778, he had become a member of the Society of Friends and given up his job in a bank because it required that he deal in lottery tickets. In 1806, he retired and devoted himself to traveling widely among Friends, coming to the United States from 1826 to 1829. Humble, sincere, and mystical, he was also very much an evangelical Protestant – perhaps a remnant of his Anglican upbringing. Initially, he planned to travel by foot (as he had in England), but found the distances in the west too great. He and Elias Hicks took parallel journeys to Ohio in 1828, frequently speaking in the same meeting for worship, to Hicks' evident displeasure.

John Chew Thomas (1764-1836), a Quaker, was a member of the Maryland state House of Delegates, 1796-97, and the U.S. House of Representatives, 1799-1801.

Thomas Willis (1771-1864) began to travel in the ministry when he was 21, accompanying Peter Yarnell of Philadelphia in visiting Friends in New England. He also traveled with Elias Hicks on his 1806 visits to Purchase, Nine Partners, and Stanford Quarterly Meetings, but labored with Hicks over his beliefs. His wife, Phebe Willis, caused a stir by publishing a private letter from Elias Hicks that seemed to outline unorthodox theological views. In 1826, he, his wife, and mother sent a letter to the Westbury Ministers and Elders stating that their beliefs differed from those of other Friends in the meeting. They all sided with the Orthodox in the separations.

Alexander Young (1769-?) was a prominent Orthodox Friends minister, well known throughout the country. He owned and operated an extensive mill at Esopus, Ulster County, New York on the Hudson. In 1827, Young helped Sojourner Truth recover her son, Peter, who had been illegally sold and sent to Alabama to avoid emancipation under New York state law.

Places Mentioned

> *Not all cities, towns, or Meetings that were mentioned are included below. A town or city that can be found with standard mapping programs (e.g., Google Maps) will not be listed. Likewise, a Meeting that has the same name as an easily located city or town will not be listed.*

Connecticut

Horse Neck: Name of the peninsula on which Greenwich is located
Middlesex: Meeting in Darien, part of Purchase (New York) Monthly Meeting
New Cambridge: Former name of Bristol
New Milford: Meeting in New Milford, part of Oblong (New York) Monthly Meeting
Plainfield: Meeting in Windham city, part of Greenwich (Rhode Island) Monthly Meeting

Delaware

Appoquinimink: Meeting in Odessa, part of Duck Creek Monthly Meeting
Centre: Meeting in Hockessin near Centreville
Cool Spring: Meeting, possibly in Sussex, part of Camden Monthly Meeting
Duck Creek: Former name of Camden Meeting
Milford: Meeting in Milford, part of Camden Monthly Meeting
Motherkiln: Perhaps Murderkill Meeting near Magnolia

Indiana

Milford: Meeting in Milton
Orange: Meeting in Elkhorn, part of Whitewater Monthly Meeting
Ridge: Meeting, part of Whitewater Monthly Meeting
Silver Creek: Former name of Salem Meeting in Liberty

Maine

Berwick: Meeting in North Berwick
Falmouth: Meeting in Portland and the name of a town seven miles north of Portland
Vassalboro: Meeting in East Vassalboro

Winthrop: almost certainly not the town in Kennebec County. From Hicks' description, it should be in the vicinity of Lisbon Falls. Perhaps coincidentally, there is a Quaker Meeting House Road just a little south of Lisbon Falls.

Maryland

Bayside: Meeting, part of Third Haven Monthly Meeting
Bush Creek: Meeting, possibly in Frederick, part of Pipe Creek Monthly Meeting
Bush River: Meeting, in Harford County, part of Deer Creek Monthly Meeting
Cecil: Meeting in Lynch
Centre: Meeting in Burrsville, part of Third Haven Monthly Meeting
Chester Neck: Meeting in Pomona, part of Cecil Monthly Meeting
Chester River: Meeting in Chestertown
Choptank: Meeting, part of Third Haven Monthly Meeting
Deer Creek: Meeting in Darlington
Eastern District: Former name of Homewood Meeting in Baltimore
Easton: site of Third Haven Meeting
Fredericktown: Former name of Frederick
Greensboro: site of Queen Anne's Meeting, part of Third Haven Monthly Meeting
Gunpowder: Meeting in Sparks
Head of Chester: Meeting in Sassafras, part of Cecil Monthly Meeting
Indian Spring: Meeting near Laurel, part of Sandy Spring Meeting
Little Falls: Meeting in Fallston
Marshy Creek: Preston Meeting in Preston, part of Third Haven Monthly Meeting
Northwest Fork: Meeting in Denton
Nottingham: East Nottingham Meeting in Calvert
Pipe Creek: Meeting near Union Bridge Station
Third Haven: Meeting in Easton
Tuckahoe: Area along the Tuckahoe River in Talbot County
Tuckahoe Neck: Meeting, part of Third Haven Monthly Meeting
Western District: Former name of Stony Run Meeting in Baltimore

Massachusetts

Acoaxet: Former name of Westport Meeting
Apponagansett: alternate name of Dartmouth (Smith's Neck) Meeting
Centre: Alternate name of Westport Meeting

East Hoosac: Meeting in Adams, part of Easton (New York) Monthly Meeting
Leicester: former name of Meeting in Worcester, part of Uxbridge Monthly Meeting
Long Plain: Meeting in Mattapoisett, part of New Bedford Monthly Meeting
Newtown: Meeting between Westport and Dartmouth, part of Dartmouth (Smith's Neck) Monthly Meeting
Seabrook: Former name of Amesbury Meeting in Amesbury
South Mendon: Meeting in Blackstone

New Hampshire

Weare: Meeting in Henniker, part of Amesbury Monthly Meeting

New Jersey

Alloways Creek: Meeting in Hancock's Bridge, part of Greenwich Monthly Meeting
Arney's Mount: Meeting in Pemberton
Chester: former name of Moorestown Meeting
Chesterfield: also known as Crosswicks Meeting
Cropwell: Meeting in Marlton
Drowned Lands: Area in Northern New Jersey
Easton: Meeting in Masonville
Elizabethtown: Former name of Elizabeth
English Neighborhood: Former name of Fairview
Evesham: Meeting in Mount Laurel
Great Egg Harbor: Meeting in Somers Point
Hardwick: Hardwick and Randolph Meeting in Blairstown
Kingwood: Former name of Quakertown Meeting
Little Egg Harbor: Meeting in Tuckerton
Lower Evesham: probably Evesham Meeting
Lower Greenwich: probably Greenwich Meeting
Lower Mansfield: Meeting in Bustleton
Maurice River: Meeting in Elizabeth
Newton: Meeting in Camden
Old Springfield: Meeting in Jacksonville
Pilesgrove: another name for Woodstown Meeting
Randolph: Meeting in Mendon, part of Hardwick & Randolph Monthly Meeting
Squan: Former name of Manasquan Meeting

Places Mentioned 481

Squancome: Meeting, possibly in Farmingdale, part of Manasquan Monthly Meeting
Stony Brook: another name for Princeton Meeting, part of Chesterfield Monthly Meeting
Upper Evesham: Former name of Medford Meeting
Upper Greenwich: Former name of Mickleton Meeting
Upper Penn's Neck: Meeting in Pedrickstown, part of Pilesgrove Monthly Meeting
Upper Springfield: Meeting in Columbus
Westfield: Meeting in Cinnaminson

New York

Beekman: Meeting in Arthursburg, part of Poughkeepsie Monthly Meeting
Bern: Meeting in Berne, part of Rensselaerville Monthly Meeting
Blooming Grove: Meeting in Blooming Grove, part of Cornwall Monthly Meeting
Branch: Meeting in Dover, part of Oblong Monthly Meeting. Also, Village of the Branch on Long Island
Bushwick: Neighborhood in Brooklyn
Cedar Swamp: Former name of Glen Head
Chatham: Meeting in Rayville, part of Hudson Monthly Meeting
Chestnut Ridge: site of Ridge Meeting, part of Nine Partners Monthly Meeting
Claverack Landing: Former name of Hudson
Coeyman's Patent: Former name of the town of Coeymans
Coeymans: Meeting in New Baltimore
Cow Neck: Former name of Manhasset Meeting
Creek: Meeting in Clinton Corners, Dutchess County
Croton: Meeting, possibly in Croton-on-Hudson, part of Amawalk Monthly Meeting
Croton Valley: Meeting, old meetinghouse is under the lake backed up by Croton Dam, part of Chappaqua Monthly Meeting
Crum Elbow: Meeting in Clinton, part of Creek Monthly Meeting
Danby: Former name of Meeting in Granville and the name of a nearby town in Vermont
East Hoosac: Meeting in Adams, Massachusetts
Eastern District: Meeting, also known as Pearl Street, part of New York Monthly Meeting (name changed to Southern District in 1824)
Easton: Meeting in North Easton
Fire Place: Former name of Brookhaven

Flatbush: Neighborhood in Brooklyn

Flatlands: Neighborhood in Brooklyn

Flushing: Neighborhood in Queens in which there have been two Meetings. The first was renamed New York Meeting in 1795. The second was established in 1805.

Fresh Meadows: Neighborhood in Queens

Frog's Neck: Former name of Throgs Neck, a neighborhood in the Bronx

Galen: site of Junius Meeting

Ghent: Meeting, part of Hudson Monthly Meeting (Klinakill Meeting until 1819)

Gravesend: Neighborhood in Brooklyn

Great Cow Harbor: Former name of Northport

Greenbush: Former name for Rensselaer

Half Way Hollow Hills: Former name of Wyandanch

Hampstead: Former name of the town of Ramapo

Harrison's Purchase: Former name of Purchase

Haviland's Hollow: Alternate name for Valley Meeting in Patterson

Hempstead Harbor: Former name of Roslyn

Henrietta: Meeting in West Henrietta, part of Farmington Monthly Meeting

Hester Street: Alternate name for Northern District Meeting

Huntington South: Former name of Babylon

Huntington West Neck: possibly Amityville

Hurlgate: (Also called Hellgate) now part of the Elmhurst neighborhood in Queens

Jamaica: Neighborhood in Queens

Jerusalem: Area in Levitown

Juniper Swamp: Former name of Middle Village, a neighborhood in Queens

Junius: Meeting in Galen

Kakiat: Meeting in Haverstraw, part of Cornwall Monthly Meeting

Kills: probably Dutch Kills, former name of Long Island City, a neighborhood in Queens

Kingsbridge: Neighborhood in the Bronx

Klinakill: Name of Ghent Meeting until 1819

Liberty Street: Alternate name for the Western District Meeting

Little Esopus: Meeting, probably in Esopus, part of Plains Monthly Meeting

Little Nine Partners: Meeting in Milan, part of Stanford Monthly Meeting

Places Mentioned 483

Lower Clove: Alternate name for Smith's Clove
Marlborough: Meeting in Milton
Matinecock: Meeting in Locust Valley, part of Westbury Monthly Meeting
Middlesex: Meeting in Darien, Connecticut, part of Purchase Monthly Meeting
Milton: Meeting in Ballston Spa
Moscheto Cove: also called Mosquito Cove, former name of Glen Cove on Long Island
New Britain: Alternate name for Chatham Meeting in New Lebanon, part of Hudson Monthly Meeting
New Marlborough: Former name of Marlborough
New Town: Unknown town probably in Schenectady or Saratoga Counties
New Utrecht: Neighborhood in Brooklyn
New Woodstock: a small town in Madison County, not to be confused with Woodstock in Ulster County
Newburgh Valley: Although there was a town of Newburgh Valley in Walden, given the direction of his travels, Hicks might mean Pleasant Valley Meeting, part of Oswego Monthly Meeting
Newtown: Meeting in the Elmhurst neighborhood of Queens, part of Flushing Monthly Meeting
Newtown Kills: Neighborhood in Queens
Nine Partners: Meeting and school in Millbrook
North Farmington: Farmington Meeting (the meeting on the north side of Farmington)
North Street: Meeting in Ledyard, part of Scipio Monthly Meeting
North East: Meeting in Bethel
Northern District: Meeting, part of New York Monthly Meeting
Oakhill: Meeting in Durham, part of Rensselaerville Monthly Meeting
Oblong: Meeting in Pawling
Oswego: Meeting in central Dutchess County
Oyster Pond Point: Former name of Orient Point
Paltz: Meeting in Butterville, part of Plains Monthly Meeting
Peach Pond: Meeting, probably in or near North Salem, part of Oblong Monthly Meeting
Pearl Street: Alternate name for the Eastern District Meeting
Peleg Woods: Unknown location west of Huntington on Long Island (possibly misspelled)
Plains: Meeting in Tillson
Plattekill: Former name of Clintondale Meeting

Poughquaig: Meeting in Gardner Hollow, near Poughquag, part of Oblong Monthly Meeting
Queensbury: Meeting near Glens Falls
Rose Street: Meeting in New York City
Ridge: Meeting in Chestnut Ridge
Rockaway: East Rockaway
Rosendale Plains: Former name of Tillson Meeting
Saint George's Manor: Large area in central Suffolk County, the manor itself is in Mastic. Manorville derives its name from the area
Salem: Meeting in Goldens Bridge, part of Amawalk Monthly Meeting
Salmon Creek: Meeting in Venice, part of Scipio Monthly Meeting
Saratoga: There have been two meetings called Saratoga. The name of the first was changed to Easton in 1795. At that time, the second Saratoga Meeting was established as part of Easton Monthly Meeting
Saw Pits: Former name of Port Chester
Smith's Clove: Meeting in Highland Mills, part of Cornwall Monthly Meeting
South Farmington: Farmington South Meeting, part of Farmington Monthly Meeting (the Meeting on the south side of Farmington)
South Street: Alternate name for Scipio Meeting (to distinguish it from the North Street Meeting in nearby Ledyard)
Southern District: Meeting, also known as Pearl Street, part of New York Monthly Meeting (name changed from Eastern District in 1824)
Springfield: Unknown location on Long Island
Stanton Hill: Historic name for an area near Coeymans
Success: Former name of Lake Success
Upper Clove: Former name of Blooming Grove Meeting
Valley: Meeting in the Patterson area, part of Oblong Monthly Meeting
West Branch: Meeting in Oswego, part of Oswego Monthly Meeting
West Farms: Formerly a town in Westchester County, now part of the Bronx
Western District: Meeting, also know as Liberty Street, part of New York Monthly Meeting (laid down in 1822)
Whipple City: Former name of Greenwich, a village about 5 miles north of Easton
White Creek: Meeting, probably in White Creek, part of Easton Monthly Meeting
Williamstown: Town in western Massachusetts
Wolver Hollow: Former name of Brookville

Ohio

Carmel: Meeting in Rogers in Columbiana County
Center: Meeting in Wilmington
Clear Creek: Meeting in Leesburg
Concord: Meeting in Colerain
Cross Creek: Meeting in Harrisville
Deer Creek: Meeting in Limaville
Elk: Meeting in West Elkton
Elkrun: township in Columbiana County. Also, site of a meeting, part of Middleton Monthly Meeting
Fairfield: Meeting in Leesburg, and township in Columbiana County, and site of a meeting, part of Middleton Monthly Meeting
Franklin: township in Harrison County
Goshen: township in Mahoning County, northwest of Salem, and Meeting in Zanesville
Kendal: Meeting, part of Marlborough Monthly Meeting
Marlborough: Meeting in Alliance
Middleton: Meeting in Columbiana
New Garden: Meeting in Winona
New Lisbon: Former name of Lisbon. Also, meeting, part of Middleton Monthly Meeting
Newberry: Former name of Martinsville Meeting
Plainfield: Meeting in Saint Clairsville
Salem (Roachester): Most likely, this is Hopewell Preparative Meeting in Roachester
Salt Creek: Indulged Meeting, part of Fairfield Monthly Meeting
Sandy Spring: Former name of Augusta Meeting
Short Creek: Meeting in Harrisville
Springfield: township in Columbiana County west of Salem, site of Upper Springfield Meeting in Damascus. Also, a city in southwest Ohio
Stillwater: Meeting in Barnesville
Westfield: Meeting in College Corner
York: township in Belmont County

Pennsylvania

Abington: Meeting in Jenkintown
Bradford: Meeting in Marshallton
Buckingham: Meeting in Lahaska
Byberry: Meeting in Philadelphia

Caln: Meeting in Coatesville
Centre: Meeting, part of Providence Monthly Meeting. Also a meeting in Hockessin, Delaware that is part of Kennett (Newark) Monthly Meeting
Charlestown: Meeting in Phoenixville
Chichester: Meeting in Boothwyn, part of Concord Monthly Meeting
Concord: Meeting in Concordville
Doe Run: Meeting in Londonderry, part of Fallowfield Monthly Meeting
Dunnings Creek: Meeting in Fishertown, Bedford County
Fallowfield: Meeting in Ercildoun
Falls: Meeting in Fallsington
Fishing Creek: Alternate name for Greenwood Meeting in Milville, part of Pennsdale Monthly Meeting
Frankford: Meeting in Philadelphia
Germantown: Meeting in Philadelphia
Goshen: Meeting in Goshenville
Great Swamp: Name of Richland Meeting until 1742
Green Street: Meeting in Philadelphia
Huntington: Town about 25 miles west of York
Kennett: Meeting in Kennett Square
Little Britain: Meeting in Peach Bottom
Little York: May be a former name for York or a small community very near to York
Makefield: Meeting in Dolington
Marlborough: Meeting in Unionville
Menallen: Meeting in Biglerville
Middletown: Meeting in Langhorne, Bucks County, and Meeting in Lima, Delaware County
Muncy: Meeting in Pennsdale
Nantmeal: Meeting, part of Uwchlan Monthly Meeting
New Garden: Meeting in Toughkenamon
Newbury: Meeting, part of York Monthly Meeting
North Wales: Borough in Montgomery County
Northern District: Meeting in Philadelphia
Pennsbury: Meeting in Morrisville, part of Falls Monthly Meeting
Pennsdale: Meeting in Muncy
Pike Run: Meeting, part of Westland Monthly Meeting
Pikeland: Meeting in Kimberton, part of Uwchlan Monthly Meeting
Pine Grove: Meeting, part of Pennsdale Monthly Meeting

Places Mentioned 487

Plumstead: Meeting in Gardenville
Plymouth: Meeting in Plymouth Meeting
Providence: Meeting in Media
Providence: Meeting in Perryopolis
Radnor: Meeting in Ithan
Redstone: Meeting in Brownsville
Richland: Meeting in Quakertown
Roaring Creek: Meeting in Slabtown
Robeson: Meeting in Birdsboro
Sadsbury: Meeting in Christiana
Sandy Creek: Meeting, probably in Preston County, West Virginia, part of Redstone Monthly Meeting
Sandy Hill: Meeting, probably in Uniontown, part of Redstone Monthly Meeting
Sewickley: Meeting in Herminie
Southern District: Meeting in Philadelphia
Upper Dublin: Meeting in Fort Washington
Uwchlan: Meeting in Downingtown
Valley: Meeting in Strafford
Warrington: Meeting in Wellsville
West Nottingham: Meeting, part of Nottingham Monthly Meeting
Western District: Meeting in Philadelphia
Westland: Meeting in Brownsville
Willistown: Meeting in Newtown Square, part of Concord Monthly Meeting
Wrightstown: Meeting in Newtown

Rhode Island

Conanicut: Meeting in Jamestown, part of Rhode Island Monthly Meeting
Douglas: Meeting, part of Smithfield Monthly Meeting
Greenwich: Meeting in East Greenwich
Newport: Meeting in Middletown
Plainfield: Meeting in Windham, Connecticut, part of Greenwich Monthly Meeting
Smithfield: Meeting in Woonsocket
South Kingston: Meeting in Wakefield
South Mendon: site of Blackstone Meeting, part of Smithfield (may be just across the border in Massachusetts)
Wankeg: Unknown location, possibly Woonsocket

Vermont

Borough: Area near Danby
Creek: Meeting in Bristol
Danby: Both the name of a town in Vermont and the former name of the meeting in Granville, New York, which is nearby
Ferrisburgh: Meeting in Ferrisburg
Hollow: name of an area near North Ferrisburg
Lincoln: Meeting, became part of Starksborough Meeting in 1813
Windsor: Town opposite Cornish Mills, New Hampshire

Virginia

Back Creek: Meeting, part of Hopewell Monthly Meeting
Bear Garden: Meeting near Bear Garden Mountain in what is now West Virginia
Berkeley: Meeting, near Charles Town, part of Hopewell Monthly Meeting
Centre: Meeting in Winchester, part of Hopewell Monthly Meeting
Crooked Run: Meeting in Front Royal, part of Hopewell Monthly Meeting
Fairfax: Meeting in Waterford
Gap: unknown location, possibly Pott's Meeting
Goose Creek: Meeting in Lincoln
Hopewell: Meeting in Clear Brook
Lower Ridge: Meeting north of Winchester, part of Hopewell Monthly Meeting
Middle Creek: Meeting, part of Hopewell Monthly Meeting
Mount Pleasant: Meeting, part of Crooked Run Monthly Meeting
Penn's Town: Location of Back Creek Meeting
Pughtown: Unknown location
Ridge: also know as Lower Ridge Meeting, part of Hopewell Monthly Meeting
Sandy Creek: Meeting, probably in Preston County, West Virginia (then Virginia), part of Redstone Monthly Meeting in Pennsylvania
South Fork: Meeting, part of Goose Creek Monthly Meeting

Bibliography

Dictionary of Quaker Biography. An unpublished typescript with short biographical sketches of approximately twenty thousand Quakers in England and the United States. In the Quaker and Special Collections, Magill Library, Haverford College.

The Old Discipline: Nineteenth-Century Friends' Disciplines in America. Glenside, Pennsylvania: Quaker Heritage Press, 1999.

Barbour, Hugh and J. Wilson Frost. *The Quakers*. Richmond, Indiana: Friends United Press, 1988.

Braithwaite, William C. *The Second Period of Quakerism*. (Second Edition, Henry J. Cadbury, editor). New York: Cambridge University Press, 1961.

Brown, Lesley (editor). *The New Shorter Oxford English Dictionary, Thumb Index Edition*. Oxford: Clarendon Press, 1973, 1993.

Buckley, Paul. *Thy Affectionate Friend: The Letters of Elias Hicks and William Poole*. Unpublished Masters Thesis, Earlham School of Religion, 2001.

Forbush, Bliss. *Elias Hicks, Quaker Liberal*. New York: Columbia University Press, 1956.

Hamm, Thomas. *The Transformation of American Quakerism: Orthodox Friends, 1800-1907*. Bloomington and Indianapolis: Indiana University Press, 1988.

Hicks, Elias. *Journal of the Life and Religious Labours of Elias Hicks*. New York: Isaac T. Hopper, 1832.

Ingle, H. Larry. *Quakers in Conflict: The Hicksite Reformation*. Knoxville: The University of Tennessee Press, 1986.

Russell, Elbert. *The History of Quakerism*. Richmond, Indiana: Friends United Press, 1979.

Trueblood, D. Elton. "The Career of Elias Hicks," in *Byways in Quaker History*, Howard H. Brinton (editor). Wallingford, PA: Pendle Hill, 1944, 77-93.

Wilbur, Henry W. *Life and Labors of Elias Hicks*. Philadelphia: Philadelphia: Walter H. Jenkins, 1910.

On-line Resources

A number of websites were particularly valuable in writing this book:

Baltimore Yearly Meeting: http://www.bym-rsf.org/

Earlham School of Religion Digital Quaker Collection:
    http://dqc.esr.earlham.edu:8080/xmlmm/login.html

ePodunk: http://www.epodunk.com/

Google Maps: http://maps.google.com/

Google: http://www.google.com/

Monthly Meetings in North America: A Quaker Index:
    http://www.quakermeetings.com/

New England Yearly Meeting: http://www.neym.org/

New York Yearly Meeting: http://www.nyym.org/

Philadelphia Yearly Meeting: http://www.pym.org/

Swarthmore Friends Historical Library:
    http://www.swarthmore.edu/fhl.xml

Index of People Mentioned

Albertson, Jacob 386
Albertson, Sarah 331
Bailey, John 271
Barker, Joseph 263
Barnes, Elizabeth 426
Barnes, John 426
Bassett, Jared 41
Bates, Elisha 417, 418, 421, 470
Batten, John 416
Bently, Sheshbazzar 410
Berry, Mary 68
Betts, Jane 250
Birdsall, Richard 393
Bishop, Phebe 244
Bishop, Samuel 244
Blake, Timothy 34
Blount, Cornelius 113
Boorman, Thomas 112
Bownas, Samuel 2, 470
Bowne, Joseph 283
Braithwaite, Anna 421, 471
Breed, Ebenezer 51
Brewer, Widow 114
Brown, David 393
Brown, Josiah 385
Brown, Nathaniel 132
Brown, Samuel 115
Burton, Charles 393
Button, Joseph 42
Buzby, Isaac 64
Byrd, Joseph 132, 247
Carman, Samuel 279
Cary, Samuel 360
Caustin, Joseph 24
Chapman, Isaac 385
Charles, Willis 389
Cheshire, Amos 204, 331
Churchman, George 386, 471
Clark, Elisha 394
Clifton, Henry 385, 402
Cobb, William 257
Cock, Benjamin 386
Coffin, Judith 374
Coffin, William 58
Cogel, John 390
Coggeshall, Elizabeth 302, 374, 471
Collins, Amos 45
Comfort, Stephen 230
Comly, John 230, 392, 471
Cook, John 40
Cooper, Joseph 63
Cornell, Daniel 26
Cornell, Widow 30
Cronk, Jacob 113
Crosby, Abigail 90
Crosby, Ebenezer 90
Davis, Thomas 394
Dawson, Elisha 389
Dorland, Enoch 123, 130, 247
Dorland, John 113, 114
Dorland, Samuel 130
Doughty, Benjamin 30
Doughty, Samuel 29, 31, 34
Earle, Pliny 254, 472
Eastburn, Moses 402
Ellicott, George 430
Ellis, William 104
Ellwood, Thomas 171
Emlen, James 409
Evans, Joshua 65
Everitt, John 114
Farrington, Walter 380
Fell, Watson 402
Field, Charles 347
Field, Phebe 332

Fisher, Samuel R. 397
Fisher, William 391
Flanner, William 186
Foulke, Hugh 386, 404
Foulke, Joseph 404
Franklin, Matthew 208
French, Israel 420
Frost, Charles 382
Frost, Elizabeth 357
Frost, George 146
Frost, Thomas 38
Frost, Zebulon 357
Fry, John 255
Fulsome, Joshua 52
Galbreath, Nathan 415, 416
Gardner, Widow 54
Garnrick, Zachariah 118
Garrigues, Edward 317, 391, 472
Gibson, John 368
Gilbert, Charles 245
Gilbert, Ruth 245
Grave, John 408
Griest, Joseph 406
Haight, Daniel 114
Haight, Stephen 58, 355, 472
Halbert, Cornelius 58
Harnad, Jacob 334
Haydock, Elizabeth 394
Hewlett, Divine 204, 281
Hicks, Abigail 130
Hicks, Benjamin 363
Hicks, Edward 382, 385, 472
Hicks, Elisabeth 207, 244, 295, 322, 332, 436
Hicks, Isaac 146, 249, 254, 325, 378, 380, 472

Hicks, Jemima 15, 16, 17, 44, 59, 89, 92, 130, 131, 132, 144, 183, 185, 186, 207, 239, 244, 246, 247, 254, 272, 274, 295, 296, 320, 322, 332, 338, 378, 436, 437
Hicks, John 2
Hicks, Martha 2
Hicks, Samuel 303
Hicks, Samuel 324
Hicks, Stephen 289
Hicks, Thomas 2, 386
Hicks, Valentine 308, 322, 351, 421, 472
Hicks, Whitehead 247, 473
Hoag, Charles 346
Holden, Stephen 127
Holmes, Nicholas 58
Hopkins, Gerard T. 336, 387, 473
Howland, Azariah 245
Hubbs, Robert 112
Hull, Henry 162, 166
Hull, John 447
Hull, Tideman 43
Hunt, John 391
Hunt, Priscilla 390, 473
Huntington, Zebulon 57
Jackson, William 334, 386, 473
Janney, Phineas 429
Jeffrey, Cheney 386
Jewett, John 386
Jewett, Susanna 386
Johnson, Jervis 91
Jones, Elizabeth 290
Jones, Ezekiel 51
Jones, Samuel 290
Jones, Thomas 111
Jordan, James 247
Judge, Hugh 60, 450

Index of People Mentioned

Justice, Joseph 394
Keese, Richard 58
Keith, George 2, 473
Kimber, Emmor 386, 404, 474
Lake, Richard 49
Lapham, Abraham 115
Lapham, David 119
Lawrence, Daniel 39
Lawrence, John 362
Lundy, Joseph 394
Macomber, Philip 118, 445
Malsby, David 388
Marsh, John 430
Martin, Isaac 282, 474
Massey, Robert 386
Mead, Zacheus 444
Melony, William 389
Merritt, Daniel 439
Merritt, Isaac 446
Merritt, Jesse 398
Merritt, John 443
Merritt, Phebe 208
Merritt, Thankful 398
Miller, Mark 64
Miller, William 394
Mixer, Phineas 40
Moore, Chalkley 394
Moore, Robert 389
Moore, William 389
Mott, Jacob 45
Mott, James 44
Mott, Keziah 31
Mott, Richard 123
Naftel, Mary 332, 474
Needles, Susannah 389
Nichols, Joseph 67
Oakley, James 32
Osborn, Charles 423
Packer, Job 105

Paine, Thomas 77, 474
Parry, Isaac 386
Parsons, James 34
Parsons, Samuel 215
Paxson, Aaron 385
Paxson, Jacob 416
Paxton, Oliver 311
Pearsall, Edmund 279
Pearsall, Walt 448
Peart, Thomas 405
Penrose, Isaac 368
Penrose, Thomas 368
Philbrick, Joseph 258
Philips, Solomon 408
Poole, William 315, 390, 391, 432, 475
Post, Mary 274
Pound, Elijah 38
Powell, Joshua 300
Prague, Simeon 39
Prawl, Peter 33
Ramsdale, George 54
Raynor, John 279
Richards, Charles 39, 93
Richardson, Richard 79
Rickman, William 340, 374, 475
Ridgway, Mary 37
Ridgway, Thomas 33
Ridgway, Widow 37
Robbins, Daniel 282
Robbins, Willet 367
Roberts, William 394
Robinson, Jemima 475
Robinson, John 55
Robinson, Rowland T. 446, 475
Robinson, Thomas 58, 446, 475
Rodman, Hannah 45
Rodman, Mary 45, 46
Rodman, Samuel 48, 475

Rodman, Sarah 45
Rotch, Thomas 48, 476
Rowland, Joseph 390
Rulon, Henry 64
Rushmore, James 290, 329
Rushmore, Thomas 441
Sabin, Warren 423
Sands, Thomas 32
Saunders, James 394
Scudder, Henry 334, 476
Seaman, David 384
Seaman, Elisabeth 16
Seaman, Gideon 138, 476
Seaman, Jemima 15
Seaman, Jonathan 15
Seaman, Robert 199, 248
Seaman, Sarah 248
Seaman, Thomas 32
Seaman, Widow 39
Sherman, Elijah 245
Shillitoe, Thomas 407, 408, 409, 410, 411, 476
Shipley, Ann 302
Shoemaker, Daniel 386
Shoemaker, Jean 391
Shoemaker, John 23
Shoemaker, John 391
Shotwell, Henry 282, 309, 394
Shotwell, Joseph 38
Shotwell, William 400
Simpson, James 392
Simpson, John 392
Smith, Elias 334
Smith, Jacob 334
Smith, John 31
Smith, Joshua 32
Smith, Samuel 391
Smith, Widow 33
Stackhouse, Joseph 38

Stackpole, Thomas 258
Stokes, Benjamin 426
Swayne, William 386
Talbot, John 152
Tatum, John 394
Taylor W., 385
Thomas, John Chew 388, 477
Thorne, Anne 245
Thorne, Charles 330
Thorne, Isaac 245
Thorne, James 39
Thorne, William 39
Thornton, James 23
Titus, Daniel 44, 111
Titus, Samuel 44
Titus, Thomas 365
Titus, William 39
Townsend, Edith 408
Townsend, Jesse 407, 408, 437
Townsend, Richard 166
Townsend, Robert 410
Trump, Michael 392
Turner, John 388
Turner, Joseph 388
Twining, Buley 385
Underhill, Abraham 130
Underhill, Andrew 37
Underhill, Elizabeth 244
Underhill, Isaac 31, 301
Underhill, Jacob 331
Underhill, Thomas 244
Vail, Nathan 385
Vail, Stephen 32
Valentine, Charles 211
Valentine, David 211
Valentine, Hannah 282
Valentine, William 24
Walker, Enoch 313
Walker, Isaac 408

Index of People Mentioned

Walker, Thomas 351
Walton, James 382, 392
Warner, Abraham 392
Watson, John 23
Way, Daniel 112
Webb, Richard 72
Weeks, Joseph 43
Whiting, Samuel 347
Whitson, Amos 93
Whitson, Thomas 290, 330
Wierman, Isaac 406
Wilbur, Elias 448
Wilbur, Thomas 119, 446, 448
Wileman, Mahlon 415
Willard, James 40
Willets, Charles 133
Willets, William 442
Williams, John 57
Willis, Cornell 438
Willis, Edmund 95
Willis, Fry 33
Willis, John 21, 23
Willis, Samuel 342, 395, 397
Willis, Thomas 123, 477
Willits, Jacob 290
Willits, Joshua 290, 330
Wilson, David 390
Wilson, Isaac 389
Wine, John 177
Winslow, John 203, 204, 257
Wood, James 404
Wood, Jonah 32, 334
Woodward, Thomas 254
Wright, Thomas 446
Wright, William 405
Young, Alexander 361, 477

Index of Places

Abington 86, 99, 156, 391, 403
Acoaxet 47, 262
Acushnet 48, 261
Adolphustown 112, 113, 114, 134
Albany 25, 59, 124, 359, 440, 441
Alexandria 74, 154, 314, 429
Alloways Creek 319
Amagansett 32
Amawalk 24, 43, 92, 123, 132, 267, 351, 439
Amesbury 51, 258
Apponagansett 48, 262
Appoquinimink 66, 390
Arch Street 150, 317, 398
Athens 361, 440
Auburn 443
Augusta 370
Aurora 443
Babylon 77, 91, 290, 329
Back Creek 107
Ballston 59, 118
Baltimore 73, 142, 145, 154, 155, 302, 304, 308, 314, 315, 336, 361, 365, 373, 374, 384, 387, 388, 397, 399, 430, 438, 441, 448
Barnegat 64, 319
Bayside 68, 389
Bear Garden 107
Beaver Falls 372, 410
Bedford 48, 261
Beekman 345
Berkeley 107, 373
Bern 127, 359, 360, 441
Berwick 53, 102, 256, 257
Bethesda 335
Bethlehem 441

Bethpage 144, 164, 182, 186, 200, 204, 213, 224, 228, 238, 271, 274, 287, 296, 298, 302, 308, 327, 338, 382
Birmingham 84, 153
Black River 112, 115
Blooming Grove 362
Blue Point 32
Bolton 57, 255
Bordentown 88, 148, 393, 436
Boston 50, 56
Bowdoinham 54
Bowery 209, 377
Bradford 84, 153
Brandywine 315
Bridgeport 245, 254
Bridgewater 126, 442
Bristol 110, 115, 156, 375, 392
Brookfield 126
Brooklyn 34, 37, 123, 216, 285, 326, 343, 380, 438, 448
Brooklyn Ferry 31
Brownsville 372, 407, 408
Brunswick 38, 146
Buckingham 23, 108, 311, 385, 402
Bucks 108, 382
Burlington 88, 126, 127, 148, 375, 393
Bush 388
Bush Creek 78, 79, 314
Bush River 73, 315
Bushwick 31
Byberry 23, 99, 156, 375, 392, 403
Caln 81, 100, 101
Cambridge 92, 358, 423, 445
Camden 66, 390
Canaan 346
Canada 111, 112, 114, 134, 136

Index of Places 497

Canton 415
Cape Elizabeth 257
Cape May 64
Carlisle 360
Carmel 372
Casco 53, 256
Catawissa 101
Cayuga 116, 443
Cazenovia 126
Cecil 70, 388
Cedar Swamp 331
Center 318, 407, 423
Centerville 426
Centre 47, 67, 82, 105, 107, 152, 262, 373, 389, 432
Chappaqua 26, 35, 92, 123, 132, 268, 351, 439
Charleston 125, 360, 441, 444
Charlestown 313, 404
Chatham 440
Cherry Street 433
Cheshire 204, 331
Chester 66, 85, 100, 150, 151, 375, 391, 431
Chester Neck 388
Chester River 70
Chesterfield 148, 436
Chestertown 70, 389
Chestnut Ridge 43, 120, 345, 439
Chichester 83, 151
Choptank 68, 389
Cincinnati 427
Claremont 40
Claverack 25, 353
Clear Creek 427
Coeymans 361
Cold Spring 281
Cold Spring Harbor 187, 204, 334
Columbia 108, 155, 313, 405

Columbiana 371
Commack 334
Conanicut Island 45
Concord 84, 152, 317, 369, 398, 419, 432
Connecticut 34, 39, 40, 41, 44, 45, 57, 89, 93, 131, 138, 244, 254, 265, 346
Connellsville 107, 368
Cool Spring 67
Coram 32
Cornwall 34, 39, 89, 93, 110, 246, 362, 397, 439, 447
Cow Neck 163, 205, 272, 282, 286, 326, 335, 382
Crab Meadow 32
Cranston 56
Creek 43, 60, 62, 119, 120, 123, 345, 440
Crompond 132
Crooked Run 107
Cropwell 86, 150, 435
Cross Creek 370
Crosswicks 95, 148, 393, 436
Croton 92, 247, 267, 351
Croton River 120, 130
Croton Valley 268, 351, 439
Crum Elbow 43, 119, 345, 440
Danby 26, 35, 42, 354, 355, 445
Darby 66, 151, 317, 375, 391, 432
Dartmouth 41, 48, 262
Deer Creek 72, 154, 315, 386, 431
Delaware 63, 65, 66, 67, 86, 110, 150, 315, 318, 367, 375, 389, 390, 431
Deruyter 126, 127, 442
Dickenson 361
Dix Hills 334
Doe Run 155

Douglas 57
Dover 53, 55, 256, 257, 258, 352, 390
Downingtown 156, 404
Drowned Lands 23
Duanesburg 125, 127, 359, 360, 383, 441
Dublin 312, 386, 403
Duck Creek 66
Dunnings Creek 105, 368
Durham 53, 54, 257
East Branch 146, 147
East Caln 84, 156, 404
East Greenwich 56
East Hampton 32
East Hoosac 26, 42, 61, 118
East Jersey 38, 309
East Nottingham 71, 154, 315, 386, 431
Eastchester 92
Eastern District 154, 155, 374, 387
Eastern Shore 388, 389, 390
Eastland 154
Easton 26, 35, 42, 58, 61, 69, 118, 134, 149, 357, 358, 367, 389, 445
Eaton 426
Elizabethtown 38, 95, 146, 309
Elk 74, 154, 155, 314, 426, 430
Elkridge 74, 154, 155, 314, 430
Elkrun 372
Epping 52, 255
Ernest 114
Esopus 361
Evesham 435
Exeter 101
Fairfax 75, 78, 107, 314, 429
Fairfield 54, 371, 411, 428
Fallowfield 81, 105, 156, 431

Falmouth 49, 53, 54, 256, 257
Farmington 116, 134, 383, 444
Fawn 72
Ferrisburg 58, 355, 356, 445
Fishing Creek 102
Fishkill 39
Flatbush 31, 218
Flatlands 29, 31
Flushing 24, 31, 37, 132, 162, 177, 186, 198, 215, 218, 249, 251, 279, 280, 284, 285, 301, 308, 323, 326, 342, 369, 380, 384, 423, 438
Foster 31, 56, 265
Frankford 98, 150, 391, 433
Franklin 208, 370
Fredericktown 374
Freehold 95, 146, 147
Freetown 56
Fresh Meadows 31
Galen 443, 444
Galway 117, 359, 445
Gap 76
Genesee 115, 134
Georgetown 54, 155
Germantown 98, 150, 375, 391
Ghent 440
Gilmanton 55
Glocester 57
Goose Creek 75, 76, 314, 429
Gorham 55, 257
Goshen 39, 84, 89, 93, 111, 153, 371, 414
Grand Isle 58
Granville 357, 445, 446
Gravesend 29, 31
Great Cow Harbor 32, 334
Great Egg Harbor 64
Great Swamp 108

Index of Places 499

Green Point 112
Green Street 391, 398, 433
Greenbush 441
Greene 54
Greenfield 59, 359, 445
Greensboro 67
Greenwich 56
Gunpowder 73, 154, 431
Gunpowder Falls 431
Hackensack 38
Haddonfield 65, 86, 150, 394, 435
Hadley 40
Halestown 51
Half Way Hollow Hills 188, 290, 329
Half Year Meeting 136
Halfmoon 105
Hallowell 112
Hamilton 126
Hampstead 362
Hampton 56
Hancock 119
Hanover 34, 41, 57
Hardwick 22, 23, 110, 310
Harlem 132, 326
Harrison's Purchase 21
Harrisville 369, 418
Hartford 89, 90, 91, 92, 131, 132, 244, 245, 254, 265, 346
Hartland 40
Hartwick 127
Hauppauge 334
Haverford 85, 151, 433
Havre de Grace 388
Haydock 394
Head of Chester 71, 388
Hempstead 2, 30, 31, 32, 202, 206, 279, 282, 287, 326, 329

Hempstead Harbor 30, 206, 282, 326
Henrietta 444
Herricks 30, 326
Hester Street 384, 448
Hockessin 82, 152, 432
Homer 442
Hopewell 107, 373
Hopkinton 45
Horeb 174
Horse Neck 44
Horsham 99, 312, 375, 386, 403, 404
Hudson 25, 35, 39, 42, 43, 59, 61, 112, 118, 119, 123, 128, 353, 440, 446, 447
Huntington 32, 80, 187, 188, 204, 313, 334, 406
Huntington South 32
Huntington West Neck 204
Hurlgate 33, 132
Indian Spring 74, 154, 314
Indiana 390, 399, 425, 426, 438, 448
Islip 32, 207, 290, 330
Jamaica 2, 28, 31, 34, 223, 284
Jamaica South 34
Jeffrey 386
Jericho 16, 165, 175, 204, 398, 399, 448
Jerusalem 32, 78, 83, 97, 159, 200, 204, 213, 240, 271, 322, 329, 450
Juniper Swamp 33
Junius 443
Kakiat 39, 111, 362
Kendal 415
Kennebec 54
Kennett 82, 152, 432

Kent 93
Kinderhook 354
Kingsbridge 21
Kingston 114, 115
Kingwood 22, 110, 385, 402
Kittery 56
Klinakill 42, 61, 119, 124, 354
Lampeter 81, 155, 405
Lancaster 81, 402
Lansingburgh 124
Lebanon 425
Lee 55, 256
Leicester 57, 254
Lewiston 54
Liberty Street 131, 138, 146, 209, 215, 216, 217, 228, 250, 309, 326, 348, 367, 377
Limington 55
Lincoln 355
Litchfield 89
Little Britain 72, 154, 431
Little Compton 47, 262
Little Creek 66, 390
Little Egg Harbor 64, 319
Little Esopus 43
Little Falls 73, 154, 431
Little Nine Partners 24, 43, 119, 123, 346
Little Plains 30
Little York 108, 155, 313, 406
London Grove 81, 153, 315, 386, 431
Long Island 2, 19, 20, 24, 28, 30, 34, 36, 93, 122, 137, 210, 218, 397
Long Island Sound 24, 26, 44, 60
Long Plain 48, 261
Looneburg 128
Lower Clove 447, 448

Lower Evesham 86, 150
Lower Greenwich 319
Lower Mansfield 148
Lower Ridge 107
Lynn 50, 56, 255, 261
Lytle Creek 424
Macedon 444
Madbury 56
Maidencreek 101, 368
Maine 53, 56, 203, 256
Makefield 109, 312, 385, 402
Mamaroneck 19, 26, 43, 44, 123, 268, 351, 395, 439
Manhattanville 209, 217, 247, 326, 347
Mansfield 88, 148, 393, 436
Mansfield Neck 88
Market Street 96, 97
Marlborough 22, 43, 62, 110, 153, 246, 362, 414, 432, 439
Marshy Creek 67, 389
Maryland 63, 67, 68, 71, 78, 154, 314, 373, 386, 388, 389, 390, 430
Matinecock 164, 201, 230, 282, 287, 322, 330, 331
Maurice River 64, 319
Mayfield 359, 445
Menallen 80, 313, 314, 406
Mendham 110, 310
Mendon 444
Merion 86, 151
Middle Creek 107
Middleburgh 360, 441
Middlesex 92, 244, 347, 439
Middleton 371
Middletown 23, 85, 110, 151, 156, 392, 403, 432
Milan 440

Index of Places

Milesburg 105
Milford 66, 266, 426
Milton 359, 445
Monkton 58, 355, 445
Montague 40
Montauk 32
Moorestown 87, 394, 435
Moreau 446
Moscheto Cove 211, 282, 330
Motherkiln 66, 390
Mount Holly 149, 393, 435
Mount Pleasant 107, 369, 417, 420
Mullica Hill 65, 319, 394, 434
Muncy 104
Nantmeal 84, 313
Nantucket 48, 374
Nassau 440
New Britain 26, 42, 61, 119, 124, 354
New England 44, 57, 59, 137, 203, 249, 254, 270, 271
New Garden 82, 153, 370, 411, 415, 416, 431
New Hampshire 34, 40, 51, 55, 57, 255, 258
New Haven 254
New Jersey 22, 23, 38, 63, 86, 95, 110, 146, 309, 318, 367, 375, 385, 393, 400, 434
New Lisbon 372, 413
New Market 374
New Rochelle 60
New Windsor 39
Newark 38, 88, 146, 309, 385
Newberry 80, 313, 406, 427
Newburgh 362
Newburgh Valley 43, 110
Newbury 51, 258, 259
Newport 45, 46, 263

Newton 51, 65, 150, 233, 318, 381
Newtown 31, 33, 37, 48, 85, 109, 118, 151, 218, 249, 262, 285, 308, 312, 326, 342, 380, 382, 385, 402, 433, 439, 445
Newtown Kills 218
Nicholites 67
Nine Partners 21, 23, 26, 30, 35, 39, 43, 60, 61, 62, 89, 90, 93, 120, 122, 123, 126, 128, 131, 133, 134, 135, 162, 244, 245, 246, 247, 344, 345, 352, 395, 399, 439, 447
Norristown 312
North Babylon 188
North Castle 92, 268, 343, 395, 439
North East 123, 346, 388
North Farmington 444
North Greenfield 118
North Salem 266
North Sandwich 55
North Sea 32
North Street 443
North Wales 99, 312, 386, 404
Northampton 34, 40, 359
Northbridge 57
Northern District 97, 150, 391
Northern Quarter 19
Northfield 40
Northwest Fork 67, 389
Norwich 40, 57
Oakhill 127, 360, 441
Oblong 21, 24, 26, 43, 59, 89, 93, 245, 266, 343, 395, 399, 439
Ohio 186, 365, 367, 369, 373, 399, 410, 421, 422, 425, 427, 428, 438, 448
Old Springfield 148, 436
Ontario 23, 112

Ophir 231
Orange 426
Oswego 23, 30, 43, 120, 123, 132, 246, 247, 345, 439
Otego 125, 127
Oyster Bay 16, 204, 281
Oyster Pond Point 32
Palmyra 115, 444
Paltz 110, 362
Patchogue 32
Patterson 266
Paulingskiln 110
Peach Pond 24
Pearl Street 131, 138, 146, 209, 210, 216, 217, 228, 250, 288, 309, 325, 343, 348, 351, 367, 376
Pearsall 279
Peekskill 123, 132, 267, 351
Peleg Woods 204
Pembroke 50, 271
Pennsbury 393
Pennsylvania 21, 22, 63, 65, 71, 80, 95, 96, 108, 142, 150, 155, 273, 311, 315, 334, 367, 372, 375, 382, 384, 385, 391, 402, 404, 428, 431
Philadelphia 20, 21, 22, 65, 81, 86, 96, 145, 150, 273, 302, 304, 308, 317, 365, 375, 384, 391, 397, 398, 399, 402, 432, 438, 448
Philipstown 124
Pike Run 105, 407
Pikeland 84, 313, 386, 404
Pilesgrove 64, 319, 434
Pine Grove 104
Pine Plains 119
Pipe Creek 79, 314

Pittsburgh 372, 410
Pittsfield 55, 127
Pittstown 42, 118, 354, 446
Plainfield 38, 88, 146, 265, 309, 369, 385, 401, 419
Plattekill 362
Pleasant Valley 43, 120, 128, 345, 352, 440
Plumstead 23, 108, 311, 385, 402
Plymouth 100, 156, 313, 386, 404
Poquonock 90
Port Elizabeth 319
Portland 53, 54, 256, 257
Portsmouth 45, 46, 263
Pottstown 108
Poughkeepsie 128, 345, 352, 439, 440
Poughquaig 23, 30, 43, 120, 132, 345, 439
Providence 56, 85, 100, 105, 118, 151, 263, 313, 359, 375, 386, 391, 432, 445
Providence Meeting 100, 407, 445
Pughtown 373
Purchase 24, 26, 34, 43, 60, 93, 122, 123, 131, 133, 135, 137, 138, 193, 268, 343, 351, 395, 399, 439
Queens 2
Queensbury 42, 58, 358, 446
Quogue 32
Radnor 86, 151, 433
Rahway 38, 88, 146, 309, 310, 367, 394, 400, 401
Rancocas 87, 149, 436
Randolph 310
Raynor 279
Reading 101, 368

Index of Places

Westerly 45
Western District 374, 388
Westfield 40, 150, 394, 426
Westland 105, 369, 407, 409, 428
Westport 47, 262
Wheatland 444
Wheeling 428
Whipple City 358
White Clay Creek 66
White Creek 26, 118, 354, 445
White Plains 92, 351
Williamson 444
Williamsport 104
Williamstown 42
Williston 58
Willistown 84, 153, 433
Wilmington 66, 152, 315, 375, 390, 391, 423, 424, 432

Winchester 373
Windham 55, 257
Windsor 40, 91
Winthrop 54
Wolver Hollow 214, 283
Woodbridge 38, 95
Woodbury 65, 92, 245, 266, 318, 347, 394, 434
Woodstock 126
Woodstown 64, 394
Wrightstown 23, 108, 312, 385, 402, 419
Yarmouth 50
York 81, 370
Zanesville 423
Zion 30, 62, 78, 80, 85, 96, 119, 128, 153, 246, 327

Key Word Index

Africans 177, 264, 283, 336, 344
Apostasy 73, 149, 348, 419
Atonement 171, 175, 313
Baptism 41, 42, 51, 52, 57, 66, 67, 70, 76, 80, 97, 128, 176, 211, 218, 224, 274, 294, 313, 348, 361, 370, 451
Bible 2, 32, 94, 194, 376, 419
Black Man 28, 29
Black People 31, 69, 74, 86, 165, 204, 247, 283, 289, 308, 364
Bundling 7
Butchering a Steer 169
Carnal 10, 80, 91, 99, 109, 110, 150, 153, 173, 176, 220, 265, 288, 293, 313, 349, 381
Ceremonial 206, 211, 307, 346, 354, 356, 379
Ceremonials 122
Ceremonies 348, 354
Colored People 388, 389, 390, 391
Commandment 297
Commandments 176, 181, 452
Convinced 8, 34, 36, 37, 41, 57, 74, 102, 122, 128, 161, 173, 188, 189, 214, 224, 227, 279, 307, 335, 355, 405
Convincement 37, 128, 173, 177, 214
Convinces 260
Creaturely 84, 87, 109, 159, 173, 174, 191, 227, 236, 249, 251, 265, 267, 298, 419
Day of Visitation 9
Devil 109, 195, 297
Doctrine 11, 27, 32, 35, 42, 43, 65, 66, 68, 81, 90, 101, 104, 114, 122, 129, 139, 151, 152, 161, 163, 182, 197, 204, 218, 219, 241, 254, 255, 260, 264, 268, 279, 282, 289, 295, 303, 313, 322, 328, 329, 331, 335, 343, 356, 358, 368, 419, 452
Doctrines 11, 54, 90, 91, 99, 130, 171, 182, 183, 205, 206, 210, 213, 214, 218, 244, 247, 249, 256, 265, 267, 287, 292, 309, 314, 315, 318, 319, 323, 325, 326, 329, 330, 346, 351, 355, 356, 357, 358, 360, 365, 376, 382, 385, 415, 419, 440, 444, 447
Dream 28
Election 8, 11, 32, 41, 42, 49, 57, 163, 254, 333
External 90, 158, 188, 380, 419
Foreordination 11, 167

Key Word Index

Free-Agency 261
Governments 73, 85, 98, 199, 376
Grace 2, 3, 12, 17, 35, 41, 42, 57, 64, 80, 89, 124, 127, 129, 132, 153, 158, 162, 167, 187, 190, 205, 216, 219, 220, 227, 233, 238, 240, 241, 244, 245, 250, 252, 271, 280, 305, 306, 307, 311, 324, 327, 339, 342, 349, 359, 362, 381, 386, 388, 402, 427, 432
Horseracing 5, 6, 180, 207, 241, 242
Imputative Righteousness 90, 175, 218, 219
Ordinances 142, 168, 176, 210, 265, 313, 348, 354, 379
Orthodox Friends 391, 399, 402, 404, 405, 407, 408, 409, 411, 414, 416, 418, 420, 421, 422, 423, 424, 425, 426, 428, 435, 448
People of Color 209, 264, 283, 307, 315
Plainness 62, 82, 85, 101, 102, 167, 180, 230, 239, 349, 376, 406
Predestination 11, 54, 163, 167
Revelation 36, 45, 77, 91, 98, 99, 133, 139, 154, 162, 174, 195, 212, 229, 244, 279, 305, 311, 322, 323, 328, 337, 352, 372, 419, 443
Rite 176
Rituals 168, 210, 219, 266, 294, 362
Sabbath 176, 265, 266, 348
Salvation 11, 44, 51, 52, 55, 67, 81, 83, 85, 86, 92, 99, 101, 103, 107, 129, 137, 146, 149, 151, 156, 160, 166, 167, 175, 177, 179, 195, 199, 202, 204, 206, 214, 219, 227, 232, 234, 236, 241, 253, 254, 256, 260, 261, 267, 271, 272, 282, 297, 302, 303, 304, 306, 309, 313, 314, 320, 324, 325, 332, 335, 339, 346, 348, 351, 362, 371, 372, 396, 419
Sanctification 90, 122, 192, 235
Save 137, 148, 185, 220
Saved 57, 220, 223, 230, 232, 240, 242, 244, 278, 340, 343
Saveth 161
Savior 67, 90, 130, 164, 179, 189, 197, 221, 269, 303, 304, 328, 333, 352
Scripture 8, 41, 54, 75, 84, 98, 130, 156, 164, 168, 189, 205, 211, 219, 220, 221, 231, 254, 272, 275, 277, 282, 293, 313, 314, 328, 329, 346, 372, 417, 418, 451
Self-Abasement 340
Self-Denial 67, 110, 195, 450
Self-Denying 11, 68, 82, 269
Self-Government 261
Self-Gratification 4, 5, 8, 242, 358
Selfish 159, 227, 228, 251, 252
Selfishness 104, 305, 338

Self-Love 111, 305
Self-Righteous 84, 141, 233, 323
Self-Sufficiency 99, 233
Self-Will 84, 111, 242, 293
Shadows 149, 168, 210, 211, 219, 330, 341, 348, 362, 407
Shooting Little Birds 12
Simplicity 59, 62, 68, 73, 82, 97, 134, 167, 230, 280, 288, 295, 311, 348, 366, 376, 406, 419
Sin 3, 5, 7, 8, 10, 12, 14, 17, 54, 72, 74, 75, 78, 90, 99, 106, 109, 110, 118, 122, 129, 148, 163, 165, 167, 168, 175, 183, 189, 190, 194, 201, 214, 220, 223, 232, 239, 242, 250, 258, 260, 261, 264, 266, 285, 292, 295, 320, 325, 328, 337, 338, 339, 356, 362, 369, 429
Slaveholders 388, 429, 430
Slavery 74, 177, 264, 344, 387, 429
Slaves 67, 74, 177, 337, 343
Temptation 2, 8, 127, 186, 234, 239, 303
Temptations 3, 5, 7, 8, 17, 158, 200, 269, 275, 292, 352
The Cross 11, 57, 140, 163, 167, 175, 176, 192, 222, 223, 227, 251, 261, 266, 269, 328, 338, 339, 362, 376, 450
The Flesh 86, 165, 195, 211, 265, 364, 452
The World 2, 17, 41, 52, 64, 71, 73, 74, 75, 77, 78, 85, 97, 98, 99, 106, 108, 110, 128, 139, 140, 142, 143, 144, 151, 153, 161, 164, 165, 167, 179, 181, 186, 189, 191, 195, 199, 200, 234, 236, 248, 264, 269, 279, 282, 284, 289, 292, 299, 300, 315, 328, 330, 337, 352, 365, 366, 376, 377, 396, 406, 436, 450, 452
Transgressing 328, 339
Transgression 168, 176, 210, 220, 223, 266, 327, 328
Transgressors 53, 355
Undisciplined 72, 106, 327
Unfaithful 40, 148, 177, 316
Unfaithfulness 229, 249, 267
Unsanctified 53, 324, 380
Vanity 2, 5, 8, 142, 164, 180, 181, 295, 303
Vision 3, 27, 28, 77
Visitation 3, 95, 99, 100, 105, 109, 124, 135, 152, 164, 215, 240, 278, 306, 317, 375, 416
War 2, 19, 20, 22, 84, 98, 99, 137, 144, 165, 175, 196, 197, 199, 202, 203, 208, 211, 225, 228, 264, 344, 414, 428, 451
Wicked 10, 20, 109, 163, 209, 212, 241, 242, 292, 296, 437

Wickedness 12, 140, 164, 180, 193, 333, 337, 450
Willful 277
Will-Less 322
Worldly Concerns 56, 139, 165
Worldly Spirit 60, 78, 80, 83, 102, 284, 377, 378
Worldly-Minded 25, 87, 97, 120, 165, 311, 316, 377
Yoke 167, 211, 300

www.ingramcontent.com/pod-product-compliance
Lightning Source LLC
Chambersburg PA
CBHW021824220426
43663CB00005B/120